Self-Determination, Dignity and End-of-Life Care

Queen Mary Studies in International Law

Edited by

Malgosia Fitzmaurice
Panos Merkouris
Phoebe Okowa

VOLUME 7

The titles published in this series are listed at brill.nl/qmil

Self-Determination, Dignity and End-of-Life Care

Regulating Advance Directives in International and Comparative Perspective

Edited by

Stefania Negri

MARTINUS
NIJHOFF
PUBLISHERS

LEIDEN · BOSTON
2011

Library of Congress Cataloging-in-Publication Data

Negri, Stefania.
  Self-determination, dignity and end-of-life care : regulating advance directives in international and comparative perspective / edited by Stefania Negri.
    p. cm. -- (Queen Mary Studies in International Law ; 7)
  Includes bibliographical references and index.
  ISBN 978-90-04-22357-8 (hardback : alk. paper) 1. Advance directives (Medical care)--Law and legislation 2. Informed consent (Medical law) 3. Right to die--Law and legislation 4. Terminal care--Law and legislation. 5. Life and death, Power over. I. Title.

  K3611.I5N44 2012
  344.04'197--dc23

                                                                    2011049232

This publication has been typeset in the multilingual "Brill" typeface. With over 5,100 characters covering Latin, IPA, Greek, and Cyrillic, this typeface is especially suitable for use in the humanities. For more information, please see www.brill.nl/brill-typeface.

ISSN 1877-4822
ISBN 978 90 04 22357 8 (hardback)
ISBN 978 90 04 22358 5 (e-book)

Copyright 2011 by Koninklijke Brill NV, Leiden, The Netherlands.
Koninklijke Brill NV incorporates the imprints Brill, Global Oriental, Hotei Publishing, IDC Publishers, Martinus Nijhoff Publishers and VSP.

This book is printed on acid-free paper.

PRINTED BY DRUKKERIJ WILCO B.V. - AMERSFOORT, THE NETHERLANDS

CONTENTS

PART III

THE ONGOING DEBATE ON ADVANCE DIRECTIVES
REGULATION IN ITALY

FOREWORD

Today, advances in medical care offer more options than ever for the treatment of diseases and the prolongation of life. Many people are now surviving with conditions that were fatal in previous generations. This represents, of course, a very significant progress. After all, the scope of medicine is the fight against disease and death. Yet there are circumstances in which patients themselves do not see advancements in clinical treatment and in life-sustaining technologies as a blessing but rather as a curse. This especially happens when patients are placed in situations of very poor prognosis and are, at the same time, confronted with aggressive medical treatments that appear to be more harmful than helpful.

In modern medical ethics and law it is widely accepted that patients have the right to refuse any kind of medical treatments. Patients' self-determination, which is the foundation of the requirement of informed consent, also includes this possibility, even if such a refusal might shorten patients' life. But what when patients have lost their decision-making capacity due to a condition that is not likely to be reversible (e.g. persistent vegetative state, coma, severe head injury, dementia, etc.)?

At present, an increasing number of people wish to make provisions for such situations by drafting a document that includes their preferences regarding the provision or the withholding of specified treatments (living will), or by empowering a trusted individual to make such decisions on their behalf (lasting power of attorney), or by combining both options. This trend is relatively recent in Europe. Only in the last few years a number of countries are realizing the value in promoting patients' self-determination and enacting specific legislation on advance directives, while others are still reluctant to regulate this issue.

Also the Council of Europe is seriously involved in the establishment of common standards relating to this matter: first, through the adoption of the Biomedicine Convention in 1997, and second, by the development of the Recommendation (2009)11 on "continuing powers of attorney and advance directives for incapacity" in December 2009.

This volume, edited by Professor Stefania Negri (University of Salerno, Italy) has succeeded in bringing together contributors from all around the world to provide a valuable comparative examination of advance directives and of the policy documents relating to them. Part I presents the issue from the international and common European law perspectives. Part II focuses on the role and validity of advance directives in a number of specific countries. Part III addresses the current debate on advance directives and end-of-life issues that is taking place in the Italian context.

It may be hoped that this book will become a valuable resource to policy-makers and to all those seeking effective strategies for dealing with this new and challenging issue.

Roberto Andorno

EDITOR'S PREFACE

This book originates from the results of an international research project on *Bioethics and international law at the intersection of life, death and dignity*, which was carried out in the framework of the research activities of the *Observatory on Human Rights: Bioethics, Health, Environment*, a network of academic experts promoting international cooperation in teaching and research between the Faculty of Law of the University of Salerno and foreign academic institutions.

The volume gathers the contributions of leading academics and lawyers engaged in the fields of bioethics and biolaw, health and medical law, and human rights law. By providing an interdisciplinary reading of advance directives against the background of European and International Law and jurisprudence, this book aims to offer new insights into the most hotly debated legal issues surrounding the theme of dignity and autonomy at the end of life, including euthanasia and assisted suicide, advance refusal of life-saving and life-sustaining treatments, the rights of the terminally ill and dying patients, the right to die with dignity.

Focus on the relevant international legal framework represents the distinguishing feature of this work as compared to much of the existing literature on the subject, while cross-cultural perspectives from Europe, the Americas, Australia and China offer a comprehensive, comparative analysis of legal approaches to end-of-life decision-making and care in a considerable number of selected countries, also giving an up-to-date account of recent developments in domestic legislation and case-law. Special attention is devoted to the Italian legal system and the ongoing scholarly and political discussion on the Italian Draft Bill entitled "Dispositions in matter of therapeutic alliance, informed consent and advance treatment directives", which was first passed by the Senate of the Italian Republic on 29 March 2009, later approved with amendments by the Chamber of Deputies on 12 July 2011, and currently awaiting final adoption.

Of course, this endeavour would not have been possible without the important contribution of all the Authors who have kindly agreed to put their expertise at the disposal of this initiative. I owe a debt of gratitude to all of them.

I am particularly indebted to Professor Roberto Andorno for his invaluable and continued support and advice and to my colleague Professor

Vitulia Ivone for her friendly and unconditional support offered throughout the whole implementation of this project. I also wish to appreciatively
acknowledge the kind supervision of Professor Penney Lewis over the
English translation of the Italian Draft Bill which is reproduced as an
Annex to the book.

Last but not least, I would like to thank very warmly Professor Malgosia
Fitzmaurice and Brill for the inclusion of this volume in the prestigious
series *Queen Mary Studies in International Law*.

Finally, I personally dedicate this book to the memory of my beloved
father and to all the victims of incurable diseases.

Stefania Negri

PART I

PERSPECTIVES OF INTERNATIONAL AND EUROPEAN LAW ON
DIGNITY AND SELF-DETERMINATION AT THE END OF LIFE

HUMAN DIGNITY:
FROM CORNERSTONE IN INTERNATIONAL HUMAN RIGHTS LAW
TO CORNERSTONE IN INTERNATIONAL BIOLAW?

*Angela Di Stasi**

I. The "End-of-Life" Choices and Human Dignity

It is indubitable that the new frontiers of (Bioethics and) Biolaw are characterized by a strong need for normativization[1] implying a difficult definition of the limits to be imposed on the so-called sovereignty of the individual over his body.[2] The scientific and technological process, showing the extraordinary potentials that the new sciences have provided to man, has caused a sort of "eagerness of lawfulness" in relation to several needs of the human beings, which are halfway between life and death[3] and may influence the process of enlargement of the international "catalogues" of human rights.[4]

---

* Professor of European Union Law and of International Relations at the Faculty of Law of the University of Salerno, Italy; email: angeladistasi@tiscali.it.

[1] At least according to the prevailing approach of the European doctrine which includes those rights pertaining to Bioethics and Life Sciences among the so called "rights of third generation".

[2] In the Italian legal literature see, among others, Andrea Bompiani, Adriana Loreti Beghé and Luca Marini, *Bioetica e diritti dell'uomo nella prospettiva del diritto internazionale e comunitario* (Torino, 2001); Nerina Boschiero (ed.), *Bioetica e biotecnologie nel diritto internazionale e comunitario* (Torino, 2006); Francesco Francioni (ed.), *Biotechnologies and International Human Rights* (Oxford, 2007). See, particularly Maria Rita Saulle, *Bioetica (diritto internazionale)*, in *Enciclopedia del diritto (Aggiornamento)* (Milano, 1997), pp. 252–264. For an interdisciplinary approach, see the huge treatise directed by Stefano Rodotà and Paolo Zatti, *Trattato di biodiritto*, and with regard to the subject of this chapter see especially volume V, edited by Rosario Ferrara, *Salute e Sanità* (Milano, 2010).

[3] It is our translation of that "insistent eagerness of lawfulness" referred to by Salvatore Amato, "Diritto e corpo: il soggetto incarnato", 29 *Democrazia e diritto* (1988), pp. 63–92, at 69. It is then one of the aspects of the wider problem about "what is the role of law in the age of technique". See on this point a well known passage taken from the interview to M. Heidegger published in *Spiegel* on September 23rd, 1966 which is referred to by Caterina Resta, *Stato mondiale e nomos della terra* (Roma, 1999). For an investigation of this subject from the constitutional point of view, see, with special reference to euthanasia, Chiara Tripodina, *Il diritto nell'età della tecnica. Il caso dell'eutanasia* (Napoli, 2004), especially the Introduction. With specific reference to the living will and the proxy consent see the same text at p. 103 ff.

[4] As it is well known, the borders of the category of human rights have undergone significant reconsiderations in the context of a marked relativization in a space-time sense.

S. Negri (ed.), *Self-Determination, Dignity and End-of-Life Care*
2011 Koninklijke Brill NV. Printed in The Netherlands. ISBN 978 90 04 22357 8. pp. 3–22

With specific reference to the "End-of-life" choices and with specific regard to the debate on Advance Directives Regulations, such call for normativization could not but have to do with a search for a more ore less "shared" social consensus. Lack of such consensus delays or hinders the legislator's activity,[5] as it is shown—just like it happens in other legal systems—by the difficult course followed by the Italian Draft Bill concerning "Disposizioni in materia di alleanza terapeutica, di consenso informato e di dichiarazioni anticipate di trattamento", which has been approved by the Senate and recently amended by the Chamber of Deputies.[6]

As it is well known, European States share a substantially uniform position as to the exact definition of the notion of death, which is considered as brain death.[7] However, the aspiration of individuals (and of their relatives) to orient "End-of-life" choices by extending the decision-making autonomy even to a such really delicate moment of a man's existence, does not find any unified solution either in national or in international and European legal systems.[8] This lack of unicity is the consequence of the

Once the rights of the individualistic tradition of the so called first generation (i.e. civil and political rights) have been recognized, those of the "socialist" tradition of the so called second generation (i.e. economic, social and cultural rights) have been added, as well as further sub-categories, among which there is first of all the one concerning the rights of the so called third (and fourth) generation. See, in particular, Norberto Bobbio, *L'età dei diritti* (Bologna, 1992), p. 27 ff., and Paolo Barile, "Nuovi diritti e libertà fondamentali", in AA.VV., *Nuovi diritti dell'età tecnologica (Atti del Convegno di Roma 5–6 maggio 1991)* (Milano, 1991), p. 36. On "human rights between universalism, regionalisms and multiplicity of constitutions" we refer to Angela Di Stasi, *Diritti umani e sicurezza regionale. Il «sistema» europeo* (Napoli, 2011), particularly at p. 125 and the following, as well as by the same author, *Il sistema americano dei diritti umani. Circolazione e mutamento di una international legal tradition* (Torino, 2004), particularly the introduction.

[5] On shared or "by intersection" consent see Raffaele Prodromo, "Etica di fine vita: é possibile un consenso condiviso sulle direttive anticipate?", in Francesco Lucrezi and Francesco Mancuso (eds.), *Diritto e vita* (Catanzaro, 2010), pp. 179–195 referring to Rawls (at 180). On the necessity that the questions raised by the developments of biology and medicine can be the subject of a public debate, see Article 28 of the Convention for the Protection of Human Rights and Dignity of the Human Being with regard to the application of Biology and Medicine (see *below*). It provides that: "Parties to this Convention shall see to it that the fundamental questions raised by the developments of biology and medicine are the subject of appropriate public discussion in the light, in particular, of relevant medical, social, economic, ethical and legal implications, and that their possible application is made the subject of appropriate consultation".

[6] The Bill, which has been approved by the Chamber of Deputies on 13 July 2011, outlines a discipline which is more restrictive than the one adopted by other European countries, leaving vital treatments out of the range of those wishes that the individual concerned may express in the so called leaving will.

[7] See art. 1 of the law No. 578 dated 29 December 1993, concerning "Norme per l'accertamento e la certificazione di morte".

[8] It is shown by some debated judgements. See, recently, the judgement dated 25 June 2010 issued by the German Supreme Court (Bundesgerichtshof), and the comments by

necessary collocation of such question within the wider context of the respect of the "sacred nature" of life, both in the light of the moral Hebrew-Christian tradition and of the laic idea of the "sacred character" of biological life.

It is undoubted that Advance Directives at the "End of life" affect those fundamental rights and values of the individual which can potentially be even opposed to each other. Among others there are: the prohibition of degrading treatment, the right to life, the right to privacy and the right to make individual choices (self-determination). In particular they state a suitable consideration of free and informed consent, a fundamental principle concerning health protection whose sources have by now overcome the borders of the national legal system as also witnessed by the Italian Constitutional Court.[9]

How is it possible to strike a fair balance within the context of a right which is defined as "hard"?[10]

The purpose of this work is to examine the role that human dignity, in its bio-ethical and bio-juridical implications, can play between

---

Cristina Campiglio, "Decisioni di fine vita: la sentenza del *Bundesgerichtshof* nel contesto della prassi europea", 4 *Diritti umani e Diritto internazionale* (2010), pp. 543–553 and Giorgio Resta, "Dignità e autodeterminazione nelle scelte di fine vita: il *Bundesgerichtshof* espande la tutela dei diritti fondamentali", 4 *Diritti umani e Diritto internazionale* (2010), pp. 566–574. See, as regards the normative solutions experimented in other Countries, the dossier no. 104/2009 drawn up by the Servizio studi del Senato della Repubblica (available online at http://www.senato.it) and entitled "La disciplina sul testamento biologico in alcuni Paesi (Francia, Germania, Regno Unito, Spagna e Stati Uniti)". See Roberto Andorno, Nikola Biller-Andorno, and Susanne Brauer, "Advance Health Care Directives: Towards a Coordinated European Policy", 16 *European Journal of Human Rights* (2009), pp. 207–227. As it is well known, among the European countries, The Netherlands were the first country to legalize assisted suicide and euthanasia (law dated April 12th 2001, in force from April 1st 2002).

[9] See Constitutional Court, Judgement No. 438 of 15 December 2008, available online at http://www.cortecostituzionale.it. In this judgement (drawn up by Judge Saulle) the need for the patient's informed consent to medical treatments is traced not only by referring to domestic sources, but also according to Article 24 of the Convention on the Rights of the Child, of Article 5 of the Convention for the Protection of Human Rights and Dignity of the Human Being with regard to the Application of Biology and Medicine, of Article 3 of the Charter of Fundamental Rights of the European Union. On free and informed consent see a wide account in the chapter by Stefania Negri, "The Right to Informed Consent at the Convergence of International Biolaw and International Human Rights Law", in this book.

[10] This unusual term is used by Stefano Rodotà, "Dal soggetto alla persona. Trasformazioni di una categoria giuridica", *Filosofia politica* (2007), pp. 365–378, where (at 375) the term "hard" right stands for a right which "does not send life off from itself, but tries to penetrate it, a right which does not fix an unchangeable rule but outlines a procedure for the continuous and joint involvement of different individuals" (our translation from the original into English).

self-determination and end-of-life care.[11] The Human Rights approach—which is here adopted—is based on the conviction of the necessary interface between Bioethics and Human Rights, considering that bio-medical issues, when they deal with fundamental values and rights, not only concern the bio-medical field but also require the conceptual support of International Biolaw. It states the overcoming of oppositions between the progress of science and knowledge and the protection of human rights; it also identifies, in the existing and coming instruments of International Biolaw, the attitude to generate a dynamic process giving an increasing role to individuals in the international society.[12]

In the by now recurring debate on Advance Directives—which starting from the Natural Death Act[13] has found in international instruments a variety of reference sources, even if sometimes only indirectly—does the defence of human dignity represent a starting point or a point of arrival?

From being an ethical and pre-juridical value, a principle informing catalogues and deontological codes,[14] it aims more and more at assuming,

---

[11] Any attempts for a historical-philosophical reconstruction of the concept of human dignity clearly lie beyond the purpose of this chapter. On the relationship between dignity and freedom we limit ourselves to mention the perspectives outlined by Immanuel Kant (see in *Fondazione della metafisica dei costumi*, Italian translation by Vittorio Mathieu, Milano, 1944, pp. 144–145), according to whom human dignity resides in personal autonomy and in its promotion and respect for the individual's dignity is respect for the individual's autonomy.

[12] We refer to an international society as universal society where "a continuous relationship of material and spiritual exchanges exists, through which the whole mankind shows itself to be a society that civil development tends to make more intense" or a society that identifies itself "in order to find its own *raison d'être* or to portrait its *way of being* according to the existence of independent or sovereign entities" and therefore international society or community *in its own sense* (our translation from the original into English). Then the classical realistic approach of Rolando Quadri, *Diritto Internazionale Pubblico* (Napoli, 1968), V ed., p. 19. See the enlightened reflections by Piero Ziccardi, (heading) *Diritto internazionale*, in *Enciclopedia del Diritto* (Milano, 1964), vol. XII, p. 1004 where, with reference to a pluralistic conception, the distinguished Author defines a legal system as "any environment of social coexistence, both among individuals, and groups of already associated individuals, admitting their unlimited multiplicity", and also by the same author, in *Diritto internazionale* (Milano, 1962), p. 79 where the existence of "a universal, naturally juridical community, the norms of which are meant both for single individuals and States" (our translation from the original into English) is emphasized. About the mixed international community, as society of States and individuals, see particularly Umberto Leanza and Ida Caracciolo, *Il diritto internazionale: diritto per gli Stati e diritto per gli individui*, Parte generale (Torino, 2008), II ed., with specific reference to chapter 4: "Oltre la soggettività internazionale: i beneficiari delle norme internazionali".

[13] Adopted in the State of California by Law 3060 of 1976.

[14] See, inter alia, art. 39 of the Deontological Code of Medical Profession of 2006, that consecrates the absolute respect for the person's "dignity, freedom and autonomy".

in International and European Law,[15] a juridical value, as basis and source of the respect of all (or almost all) human rights.

Within the international community, the emergence of new values linked to the respect of human dignity and their submission to States' compliance, in terms not only of *facere* but also of *non facere* obligations, has helped the more general evolution of the principle of non-intervention and the progressive erosion of the State's reserved domain[16] in the field of human rights protection.[17] Moreover, if it is indubitable that the categories of human rights, both of internal and international source, represent an *evolving list*[18] continuously subject to modifications according to

---

[15] There is an extensive legal literature on this subject. See the publications existing since the '80s, by Oscar Schachter, "Human Dignity as Normative Concept", 77 *The American Journal of International Law* (1983), pp.103–110 and David Feldman, "Human Dignity as a Legal Value", *Public Law* (1999), pp. 682–702. See the wide references included, among others, in Deryck Beyleveld and Roger Brownsword, *Human Dignity in Bioethics and Biolaw* (Oxford, 2001); David Kretzmer and Eckart Klein (eds.), *The Concept of Human Dignity in Human Rights Discourse* (The Hague, 2002); Matthias Kettner (ed.), *Biomedizin und Menschenwürde* (Frankfurt am Main, 2004); Mariana Blengio Valdés, *El derecho al reconocimiento de la dignidad umana* (Montevideo, 2007). This process concerns, of course, several sectors of the legal system. See above all, Luigi Manconi and Roberta Dameno (eds.), *Dignità nel morire* (Milano, 2003) as well as Pier Paolo Portinaro, "La dignità dell'uomo messa a dura prova", in A. Argiroffi, P. Becchi and D. Anselmo (eds.), *Colloqui sulla dignità umana. Atti del Convegno internazionale*, Palermo, ottobre 2007 (Roma, 2008), p. 221 when, by drawing on Häberle, he affirms that "human dignity is the anthropological-cultural basis for a constitutional State" (our translation from the original into English). The idea of the equal dignity of all human beings can be found, among others, in the French Constitution dating back to 1789. In the Italian Constitution the reference to human dignity appears in the first paragraph of art. 3 as "equal social dignity" of citizens and in the second paragraph of art. 41 as limit to the freedom of private economic enterprise which "cannot be carried out ... in a way that may cause damage ... to human dignity". But the reference to human dignity as the fundamental value of the whole legal system appears in several other Constitutions (see e.g. the Canadian, Danish, Portuguese, Swedish, Swiss, and the American Constitutions). Remember the provision of the German Constitution which in art. 1 states: "Human dignity is inviolable. To respect and protect it is a duty of each power of the State".

[16] See art. 2, para. 7, of the United Nations Charter.

[17] Fallen within the province of International Law, human rights have "overcome national borders and have become a problem of the international community". See in this sense Claudio Zanghì, *Diritti dell'uomo (protezione internazionale dei)*, in *Enciclopedia giuridica Treccani*, vol. XI, pp. 1–9, particularly p. 1, followed by Jacques Mourgeon (in *Les droits de l'Homme*, Paris, 1996, p. 75) who affirms: "l'affirmation internationale des droits a cessé d'être balbutiante pour être abondante et nette".

[18] It does not close the "catalogue" of human rights, as the very new rights consecrated in a variety of international instruments issued over the last year (from the right to inhabiting, to the right of protection of the young as regards compulsory education in the social Charter revised by the Council of Europe, from the prohibition of eugenic practices to the right to the protection of personal data in the Charter of Fundamental Rights of the European Union, joining the rights already codified some decennia before). It is not

the new needs of human beings, respect for human dignity has become a
unifying element in the slow affirmation, within the universal and regional
contexts, of the indivisibility of human rights, which together with universalism represents one of the most significant achievements of the World
Conference on Human Rights.[19]

In the inter-individual community, dignity is a central value, as well as
the sum and presumption of new values—in an international sense of
protection of the *homo*, not only the *homo œconomicus*. Can it also become
a limit among limits, and a criterion suitable to identify the legitimacy of
interventions aiming at protecting the individual against himself?

Dignity is the informing principle, as we will see below, of old and new
catalogues of rights and of international instruments of different kind,
which find a common element within the respect of a value not deprived

---

meaningless that the "lists" of rights themselves, included in some international conventions on human rights, are usually enlarged by the States parties through the execution of
additional protocols which enrich the original catalogue of rights. Let us remember, with
reference to an extra-European agreement, that the American Convention on Human
Rights was integrated by the Protocol of San Salvador concerning economic, social and
cultural rights, as a meaningful proof of the overcoming of the old dichotomy between
these rights and the civil and political rights already consecrated in the conventional text.
Art. 26 of the Convention of San José occupied the whole chapter III with a discipline
merely programmatic as regards economic, social and cultural rights. But within a
European context too, we refer to a large number of protocols which have enlarged the
catalogue of rights included in the European Convention for the Protection of Human
Rights and Fundamental Freedoms (ECHR) dating back to 1950.

[19] World Conference on Human Rights, Vienna, 14–25 June 1993. See United Nations,
Doc. A/CONF.157/PC57, Doc. A/CONF. 157/PC58, Doc. A/CONF. 157/PC59. In the Universal
Declaration of Human Rights (1948)—on which see below—the search for a common
vision of human rights, that can be accepted by all the States of the international commu-
nity had led to the adoption of the western catalogue of rights. Based on the relationship
State-individual, it was linked only to the respect of civil and political rights, with the inclu-
sion of the right to ownership and the exclusion of peoples' rights. The International
Covenants—the drafting of which had started, as it is known, together with that of the
Universal Declaration—on specifying the categories of rights included in it overcame the
opposition of a hierarchical kind between the category of civil and political rights and that
of economic, social and cultural rights, hoped for by an intense normative activity of the
General Assembly. The conception of human rights as "indivisible, interdependent and
intrinsically connected with each other" (as it is underlined in the Word Conference on
Human Rights of 1993) is also assumed within the normative activity of the institutions of
the European Union. This is witnessed, in particular, by the catalogue of human rights
included in the Charter of Fundamental Rights of the European Union (Nice 2000 –
Strasbourg 2007)—to which we refer below—that, in completely overcoming the biparti-
tion between the two macro-categories of rights that characterized the original Project,
classifies them as fundamental "values" corresponding to the headings of dignity, freedom,
equality, solidarity, citizenship and justice. The statement of the indivisibility of human
rights within the European Convention for the Protection of Human Rights and
Fundamental Freedoms (ECHR) appears to be harder, since it privileged only civil and
political rights in the original text.

of semantic ambiguities that often invalidate its normative contents. On the other hand, the persisting lack, in international instruments, of a juridical definition of human dignity represents the logic consequence of the failed (and perhaps impossible) solution of questions of meta-juridical character. They seem to have important implications in the bioethical debate and, indeed, in international instruments concerned with biotechnology and biomedicine, above all with reference to the definition of the importance of the obligation to protect dignity itself (through positive and negative action). In this context, the indeterminate semantic character of this idea of dignity applied to such sciences, and the impossibility of establishing its contents *ex ante*, causes a consequential "relational" use of it, thus giving primary importance to jurisprudential interpretation.[20]

The above mentioned and well known criticism of semantic ambiguity—in the sense that dignity is referred to as a vague notion which might be used to support even opposed opinions—is indeed paralleled by the difficulty of providing a full, and above all, shared justification of this idea.[21] Therefore, those who criticize the notion of dignity consequently

---

[20] Recognition of human dignity as a value is recurrent in the case-law of the Court of Justice of the European Community. See (on free circulation of workers) the Judgment dated July 3rd 1974, Case 9/74, *Casagrande* [1974] ECR 773. See, the more recent Judgement dated October 14th 2004, Case C-36/02 *Omega* [2004] ECR I-9609. In it (see paras. 34–35, 39–41) it is stated that the "Community law does not preclude an economic activity consisting of the commercial exploitation of games simulating acts of homicide from being made subject to a national prohibition measure adopted on grounds of protecting public policy by reason of the fact that that activity is an affront to *human dignity*"... And moreover: "the protection of fundamental rights, it being stated that the Community legal order undeniably strives to ensure respect for *human dignity* as a general principle of law, constitutes a legitimate interest capable in principle of justifying a restriction on the obligations imposed by Community law, even by virtue of a fundamental freedom guaranteed by the Treaty such as the freedom to provide services. Secondly, the measure in question corresponds to the level of protection of *human dignity* which the national constitution intended to ensure in the territory of the Member State concerned and does not go beyond what is necessary to achieve the objective pursued" (underscore added). See the undeniable contribution of the European Court of Human Rights (and before it of the Commission) in reconstructing, from a jurisprudential point of view, the principle of dignity, not expressly provided by the European Convention for the Protection of Human Rights and Fundamental Freedoms, as well as of a right to self-determination of the individual (not without limits) by the interpretation of art. 8 of the ECHR, concerning the respect for private and family life. See Guido Alpa, "Dignità. Usi giurisprudenziali e confini concettuali", *Nuova giurisprudenza civile commentata* (2000), part. II. The recognition of a right to live with dignity is also recurrent in the case-law of the Interamerican Court of Human Rights: see Luisa Cassetti, "Il diritto di 'vivere con dignità' nella giurisprudenza della Corte interamericana dei diritti umani", in *Scritti in onore di Franco Modugno* (Napoli, 2011), vol. I, pp. 645–666.

[21] Among the critics of such a notion, see above all, Ruth Macklin, "Dignity Is a Useless Concept", 327 *British Medical Journal* (2003), pp. 1419–1420. In this article the American bioethician carries out a reassessment of references to dignity included in international

emphasize its inevitable normative weakness, which would invalidate the concrete possibility of having recourse to it. However, the use of the notion of human dignity, at the stage of the "End of life", that is in moments in which rationality, autonomy and moral conscience are evidently compromised, causes a new challenge both to traditional ethics (based on the protection of life), and modern ethics (based on the defence of autonomy).[22]

The possible refutation of the first two objections does not fall within the subject of this work. Viceversa, we will try to make some observations on the third objection (normative fragility of the notion of dignity) in the following analysis.

II. Normative References to Dignity in International Human Rights Law and in International Biolaw

In human rights instruments there is no human right to die with dignity. There are several rights of a more general nature and potentially the most important one is the right of each person to human dignity. If the "right"[23] to human dignity and the right to life[24] include a right to live with dignity, do they also include a right to end one's life in dignity?[25]

The answer to this question—that lies outside the subject of this chapter—implies the solution of a preliminary question: is it possible to assign to human dignity a normative value?

The recognition of such a character to human dignity or to dignity *tout court* implies a short review of a set of international instruments of

---

instruments either because they cannot be referred to bioethics or because they are considered (as in the case of the Convention on Human Rights and Biomedicine, about which see below) widely reproducing the classical topics of medical ethics. In the opposite direction see Roberto Andorno, "La notion de dignité humaine est-elle superflue en bioétique?", 16 *Revue Générale de Droit Medical* (2005), pp. 95–102. In his introduction he starts just from the qualification by Macklin of dignity as useless concept for reasoning, to say, on the contrary, that "la notion de dignité n'est ni inutile, ni superflue".

[22] There are also studies aiming at enhancing the idea of a (prebirth) or after death dignity of the person, within the "autonomistic" vision of Kant. See Paolo Becchi, "L'idea kantiana di dignità umana e le sue attuali implicazioni in ambito bioetico", in P. Becchi, G. Cunico and O. Meo (eds.), *Kant e l'idea di Europa* (Genova, 2005), pp. 15–37.

[23] See below about the characters of human dignity.

[24] See William A. Schabas, "Right to life", in D.P. Forsythe (ed.), *Encyclopedia of Human Rights* (Oxford, 2009), pp. 440–447.

[25] Among those who "recommend greater recognition of a general human right to die with dignity" see Jordan J. Paust, "The Human Right to Die with Dignity: A Policy-Oriented Essay", 17 *Human Rights Quarterly* (1995), pp. 463–487. See also Yale Kamisar, "The 'Right to Die': On Drawing (and Erasing) Lines", 35 *Duquesne Law Review* (1996), pp. 481–522.

different kind, both as regards their importance (universal, regional or sub-regional), and as regards their juridical *vis* (*hard law* instruments and instruments that, to a large extent, can be considered as being included in *soft law*), and their more or less recent adoption.

The identification of the relevant norms does not always appear to be easy, not only for the large number of instruments containing references to dignity, but also because they find their basis in a "source" or pseudo-source of production of *human rights*, such as *soft law*, which has an integrative and/or substitutive relationship with the sources of *hard law*.[26] The research of sources seems to be more complex than an usual review operation, since it is meant to identify a specific meaning in comparison with instruments (such as declarations, resolutions of the UN General Assembly or of UNESCO, etc.) which, although deprived of any binding force, are nevertheless productive of ultra-political effects of legitimation of individual or collective State behaviours. They often represent the starting point of a *legal process* which may become an international agreement or may help, if accompanied by a univocal international practice, the definition of general international norms as manifestation of the *opinio iuris* of States. At the same time, the failed transformation of these normative statements into International Law norms (as it happened, on the contrary, for the recognition of some of the provisions of the Universal Declaration of Human Rights within binding instruments such as the International Covenants of 1966) causes the risk of elevating *general social values* or mere *desiderata*, awaiting recognition in different international contexts, to the rank of rights.

It is worth specifying here that the reference to human dignity is not typical of normative instruments concerning bioethical issues, while it represents, instead, a constant element of inspiration—implicitly or explicitly—of most instruments concerning the international protection

---

[26] *Ex multis* see Edmondo Mostacci, *La soft law nel sistema delle fonti* (Padova, 2008); Salem H. Nasser, *Sources and Norms of International Law. A study on soft law* (Glienicke-Berlin, 2008); Rüdiger Wolfrum (ed.), *Legitimacy in International Law* (Berlin, 2008). See also Mauricio I. del Toro Huerta, "El fenómeno del *soft law* y las nuevas perspectivas del derecho internacional", 6 *Anuario Mexicano de Derecho Internacional* (2006), pp. 513–549; Francesco Sindico, "Soft Law and the Elusive Quest for Sustainable Global Governance", 19 *Leiden Journal of International Law* (2006), pp. 829–846. On the relationship between *soft law* and *hard law* see, among others, Christine M. Chinkin, "The Challenge of Soft Law: Development and Change in International Law", 38 *International and Comparative Law Quarterly* (1989), pp. 850–866; Karl Zemanek, *Is the Term "Soft Law" Convenient?*, in G. Hafner, G. Loibl, A. Rest and L. Sucharipa-Behrmann, *Liber Amicorum Professor Seidl-Hohenveldern in honour of his 80th birthday* (The Hague-London-Boston, 1998), pp. 843–861.

of human rights. But, within the branch of International Biolaw, has human dignity become an "overarching principle"?[27]

Without pretending to be exhaustive, we shall try here to briefly review the references to dignity included in some international instruments.

The reference to dignity characterizes the Charter of the United Nations (the Preamble affirms the "faith in fundamental human rights, in the *dignity* and worth of the human person, in the equal rights of men and women and of large and small nations") and represents the basic inspiration of the International Covenant on Civil and Political Rights (ICCPR) and of the International Covenant on Economic Social and Cultural Rights (ICESCR).[28] In the preamble of both of them, it is stated "that, in accordance with the principles proclaimed in the Charter of the United Nations, the recognition of the *inherent dignity* and of the equal and inalienable rights of all members of the human family is the foundation of freedom, justice and peace in the world", and it is recognized "that these rights derive from the *inherent dignity* of the human person".

It is worth remembering that reference to dignity is also to be found in the *Universal Declaration of Human Rights*.[29] There are several mentions in this instrument and dignity was referred to (like in the Charter of the United Nations or in the International Covenants) as inherent dignity. In the Preamble (an obvious introduction to this document) the first Considerandum was expressed as follows: "Whereas recognition of the *inherent dignity* and of the equal and inalienable rights of all members of the human family is the foundation of freedom, justice and peace in the

---

[27] So Roberto Andorno, "Human Dignity and Human Rights as a Common Ground for a Global Bioethics", 34 *Journal of Medicine and Philosophy* (2009), pp. 223–240.

[28] The International Covenant on Civil and Political Rights was adopted and opened for signature, ratification and accession by General Assembly resolution 2200A (XXI) of December 16th 1966 and entered in force on March 23rd 1976, in accordance with Article 49. The International Covenant on Economic Social and Cultural Rights was adopted and opened for signature, ratification and accession by General Assembly resolution 2200A (XXI) of December 16th 1966 and entered in force on January 3rd 1976, in accordance with article 27.

[29] The Universal Declaration of Human Rights was adopted by the United Nations General Assembly on December 10th, 1948 with the Resolution 217 A (Doc.A/810), p. 71. On this subject, being much debated in the doctrine, see above all, SIOI (ed.), *Dichiarazione Universale dei diritti dell'uomo* (Padova, 1950); Alfred Verdoodt, *Naissance et signification de la Déclaration Universelle des Droits de l'Homme* (Louvain, 1964); Francesco Durante and Maria Felicita Gennarelli, *I diritti dell'uomo in Italia. L'applicazione della Dichiarazione universale nell'ordinamento italiano* (Milano, 1998), vols. 1 and 2. See Vinodh Jaichand and Markku Suksi (eds.), *60 Years of the Universal Declaration of Human Rights in Europe* (Antwerp-Oxford-Portland, 2009). See also Hilary Charlesworth, "Universal Declaration of Human Rights (1948)", in *Max Planck Encyclopedia of Public International Law* (Heidelberg-Oxford, 2009), available at http://www.mpepil.com.

world" while the fifth Considerandum used the above mentioned formula: "Whereas the peoples of the United Nations have in the Charter reaffirmed their faith in fundamental human rights, in *the dignity and worth of the human person* and in the equal rights of men and women and have determined to promote social progress and better standards of life in larger freedom". Article 1 provided, then, the classical formula according to which "All human beings are born free and equal in *dignity* and rights".[30]

It would be impossible to fully investigate the references to dignity within international conventions of universal application. We only refer, among all of them, to the Convention on the Rights of the Child and the provisions of its Preamble ("Considering that … recognition of the *inherent dignity* and of the equal and inalienable rights of all members of the human family is the foundation of freedom, justice and peace in the world, … reaffirmed their faith in fundamental human rights and in the *dignity* and worth of the human person, and have determined to promote social progress and better standards of life in larger freedom").[31]

Subsequent regional instruments also invoke dignity.[32] In the American continent, for example, the American Convention on Human Rights provides in Article 11, para. 1, that: "Everyone has the right to have his honor respected and his *dignity* recognized" while Article 5 of the African Charter on Human and Peoples Rights (1981) states that: "Every individual shall have the right to respect of the *dignity inherent* in a human being". In the Astana Commemorative Declaration *Towards a Security Community* "the inherent dignity of the individual is at the core of comprehensive security".[33]

If then the consolidation of human dignity represents the "juridical good" protected by Public International Law and particularly by Human Rights Law,[34] we must remember, with specific regard to the instruments

---

[30] The article continues providing that: "They are endowed with reason and conscience and should act towards one another in a spirit of brotherhood".

[31] Adopted and opened for signature, ratification and accession by General Assembly resolution 44/25 issued on November 20th 1989 and in force from September 2nd 1990, in accordance with article 49.

[32] See the large number of references to dignity included in the Preamble of the American Declaration of the Rights and Duties of Man (OAS Res. XXX), adopted by the Ninth International Conference of American States (April 1948).

[33] OSCE Summit Meeting of 3 December 2010, para. 6.

[34] So Heber Arbuet-Vignali, *Naturaleza y extensión de la protección internacional de los Derechos Humanos y sus vinculaciones con la soberanía*, in *Héctor Gros Espiell Amicorum Liber* (Bruxelles, 1997), pp. 30 ff., in particular p. 34. See Hersch Lauterpacht, *International Law and Human Rights* (London, 1950), p. 69 where he affirms "… in relation to both rights and duties the individual is the final subject of all law".

of International Human Rights Law in the field of Bioethics, that in the *Universal Declaration on Bioethics and Human Rights* the General Conference of the United Nations Educational, Scientific and Cultural Organization (UNESCO) recognizes "that ethical issues raised by the rapid advances in science and their technological applications should be examined with due respect to the *dignity* of the human person and universal respect for, and observance of, human rights and fundamental freedoms".[35] Moreover, in Article 2, para. c), among the objectives of the

---

[35] Adopted by acclamation on 19 October 2005. The Preamble of UNESCO's Constitution refers to "the democratic principles of the *dignity*, equality and mutual respect of men", and ... stipulates "that the wide diffusion of culture, and the education of humanity for justice and liberty and peace are indispensable to the *dignity* of men". In the Universal Declaration on the Human Genome and Human Rights (UNESCO), adopted on 11 November 1997, references to human dignity are very many and dignity seems to be linked to the uniqueness and identity of human beings. In its preamble it appears where it is stated that "Recognizing that research on the human genome and the resulting applications open up vast prospects for progress in improving the health of individuals and of humankind as a whole, but emphasizing that such research should fully respect *human dignity*, freedom and human rights, as well as the prohibition of all forms of discrimination based on genetic characteristics". In para. A of the Declaration, specifically entitled "Human Dignity and the Human Genome", we above all point out Article 2 where it is specified that: "a) Everyone has a right to respect for their *dignity* and for their rights regardless of their genetic characteristics. b) That *dignity* makes it imperative not to reduce individuals to their genetic characteristics and to respect their uniqueness and diversity. In para. B of the same Declaration, devoted to "Rights of the Persons Concerned" Article 6 provides that "No one shall be subjected to discrimination based on genetic characteristics that is intended to infringe or has the effect of infringing human rights, fundamental freedoms and *human dignity*". Finally in para. C devoted to "Research on the Human Genome" Article 10 establishes that "No research or research applications concerning the human genome, in particular in the fields of biology, genetics and medicine, should prevail over respect for the human rights, fundamental freedoms and *human dignity* of individuals or, where applicable, of groups of people" and Article 11 states "Practices which are contrary to *human dignity*, such as reproductive cloning of human beings, shall not be permitted ...". Article 12 provides that "a) Benefits from advances in biology, genetics and medicine, concerning the human genome, shall be made available to all, with due regard for the *dignity* and human rights of each individual." (our underlingning). In para. D devoted to "Conditions for the Exercise of Scientific Activity" Article 15 establishes that "States should take appropriate steps to provide the framework for the free exercise of research on the human genome with due regard for the principles set out in this Declaration, in order to safeguard respect for human rights, fundamental freedoms and *human dignity* and to protect public health ...". In para. F devoted to "Promotion of the Principles Set Out in the Declaration" Article 21 establishes that "States should take appropriate measures to encourage other forms of research, training and information dissemination conducive to raising the awareness of society and all of its members of their responsibilities regarding the fundamental issues relating to the defence of *human dignity* which may be raised by research in biology, in genetics and in medicine, and its applications". In para. G devoted to "Implementation of the Declaration" Article 24 provides that "The International Bioethics Committee of UNESCO ... should make recommendations, in accordance with UNESCO's statutory procedures, addressed to the General Conference and give advice

Declaration there is that "to promote respect for *human dignity* and protect human rights, by ensuring respect for the life of human beings, and fundamental freedoms, consistent with international human rights law". Article 3, specifically entitled *Human dignity* and human rights, provides at no. 1 that "Human dignity, human rights and fundamental freedoms are to be fully respected".[36] In the *Universal Declaration on Bioethics and Human Rights*, even if a specific definition of it still continues to be lacking, human dignity plays, together with the respect for human rights, the role of "the best, if not the only available grounds for the development of international legal standard for biomedicine".[37] The Declaration, to be intended as a set of guiding norms in the field of biomedicine,[38] not only recommends specific conducts of States, integrating the content of obligations in force, but also pursues the aim of regulating sectors which are not yet regulated.[39]

Then moving from the universal to the regional field (which is here intended in a broad sense)[40] the protection of human dignity represents the basic value of the *Convention for the Protection of Human Rights and Dignity of the Human Being with regard to the Application of Biology and Medicine*, as confirmed by para. 9 of the Explanatory Report.[41]

---

concerning the follow-up of this Declaration, in particular regarding the identification of practices that could be contrary to *human dignity*, such as germ-line interventions". A similar number of references can be found in the International Declaration on Human Genetic Data adopted on 16 October 2003.

[36] In no. 2 of the same article it is provided that: "The interests and welfare of the individual should have priority over the sole interest of science or society". In this connection, see the considerations by Thomas A. Faunce, "Will International Human Rights Subsume Medical Ethics? Intersections in Unesco Universal Bioethics Declaration", 31 *Global Medical Ethics* (2005), pp. 173–178 where he affirms: "Creation of such a Unesco Universal Bioethics Declaration represents a pivotal stage in the process whereby the moral, political and international law aspects of human rights begin to subsume medical ethics" (at 177).

[37] So Roberto Andorno, "Human Dignity", *supra* note 27, in particular at p. 224.

[38] On the attitude of the Universal Declaration on Bioethics and Human Rights to exert a normative power (standard setting) see Fabrizio Turoldo (ed.), *La globalizzazione della bioetica. Un commento alla Dichiarazione universale sulla Bioetica e i diritti umani dell'UNESCO* (Padova, 2007).

[39] The Declaration confirms the recourse by UNESCO, since 1966, to an instrument not provided either in the Constitution of the organization or in its Rules of Procedure.

[40] Open to be joined by other extra-European States, such as the United States and Canada. Let us remember as well, that in the jurisprudence of the Court of Strasbourg it is stated that dignity is "foundation and leit motiv of the Convention" (Judgement of 29 April 2002, *Pretty v. United Kingdom*, case no. 2346/02).

[41] Oviedo, 4 April 1997, hereinafter Convention on Human Rights and Biomedicine. Para. 9 of the Explanatory Report (Council of Europe, Directorate of Legal Affairs, DIR/JUR (97) 5) provides that "The concept of human dignity, which is also highlighted, constitutes the essential value to be upheld. It is at the basis of most of the values emphasised in the

Besides the reference included in the title of the Convention, dignity is mentioned three times in its Preamble: the first one when "the need to respect the human being both as an individual and as a member of the human species and recognising the importance of ensuring the *dignity* of the human being" is stated; the second one when it seems to be based on the cosciousness that "the misuse of biology and medicine may lead to acts endangering *human dignity*"; the third one when the will "to take such measures as are necessary to safeguard *human dignity* and the fundamental rights and freedoms of the individual with regard to the application of biology and medicine" is emphasized.

The Convention on Human Rights and Biomedicine, a multilateral treaty of universal significance, in establishing in Article 1 (Purpose and object) that the "Parties ... shall protect the *dignity* and identity of all human beings and guarantee everyone, without discrimination, respect for their integrity and other rights and fundamental freedoms with regard to the application of biology and medicine", carries out the synthesis between bioethical expectations and those of respect of human rights, in the light of a deontologically correct use both of biology and medicine.

In the Convention on Human Rights and Biomedicine the respect of dignity (and identity of the human being) is specified with reference to the ways of manifesting consent. In Chapter II, devoted to Consent, Article 5 defines as a "General rule" the "free and informed consent" (no. 1) while in no. 3 it provides for the revocability of a given consent.[42] As far as the "End of life" is concerned, Articles 6 and 9 are to be mentioned. The first one (para. 3) regulates the protection of subjects incapable of giving their own consent to medical treatments in these terms: "Where, according to law, an adult does not have the capacity to consent to an intervention

---

Convention". See the text of the Convention in the web site http://conventions.coe.int/. The Convention, as of 1 December 2010, was ratified by 26 States; signature of the Convention was not followed by the filing of the ratification instrument by 8 States (among them there is Italy, which signed it on 4 April 1997). On the Convention see Ilja R. Pavone, *La Convenzione europea sulla biomedicina* (Milano, 2009). On the preliminary stage see Claudio Zanghì and Lina Panella (eds.), *Recenti sviluppi in materia di bioetica. In margine al progetto di Convenzione sulla bioetica del Consiglio d'Europa* (Torino, 1996) and Maria Rita Saulle (ed.), *Minori, bioetica e norme standard nel diritto internazionale* (Napoli, 1995), p. 115 ff. In the Additional Protocol to Convention for the Protection of Human Rights and Dignity of the Human Being with regard to the application of Biology and Medicine on the prohibition of cloning human rights (see the text in the web site http://conventions.coe.int/) dignity plays a central role as well. The Additional Protocol (Paris, 12 January 1998) was ratified by 20 States, it was signed but not followed by the filing of the ratification instrument by 12 States (among which there is Italy, which signed it on 12 January 1998).

    [42] "The person concerned may freely withdraw consent at any time".

because of a mental disability, a disease or for similar reasons, the intervention may only be carried out with the authorisation of his or her representative or an authority or a person or body provided for by law". As the Explanatory Report clarifies "The term 'similar reasons' refers to such situations or accidents or states of coma, for example, where the patient is unable to formulate his or her wishes ot to communicate them". In addition, Article 9 on "Previously expressed wishes"[43] takes under due consideration the expression of will of the person who, at the moment of the intervention, is no longer able to express it.[44] It is indeed the exercise of what was already defined in the '80s as "precedent autonomy"[45] that gets important only when the individual is no longer able to manifest his or her consent.

In the *Charter of Fundamental Rights of the European Union* dignity becomes part of Title I, while human dignity becomes the heading of Article 1, which states "*Human dignity* is inviolable. It must be respected and protected".[46] It is not consecrated as a right to dignity, but it is set up as a general clause, implying the recognition of the character of an inviolable, juridically protected, good. In the same Title 1 dignity is specified,

---

[43] Article 9 establishes that "The previously expressed wishes relating to a medical intervention by a patient who is not, at the time of the intervention, in a state to express his or her wishes shall be taken into account".

[44] The Explanatory Report explains at para. 62 the application range of art. 9 and the merely advisory value of the expressed will. It is formulated as follows: "The article lays down that when persons have previously expressed their wishes, these shall be taken into account. Nevertheless, taking previously expressed wishes into account does not mean that they should necessarily be followed. For example, when the wishes were expressed a long time before the intervention and science has since progressed, there may be grounds for not heeding the patient's opinion. The practitioner should thus, as far as possible, be satisfied that the wishes of the patient apply to the present situation and are still valid, taking account in particular of technical progress in medicine". In the Explanatory Report consent is intended as "either assent or refusal" while the provided situation is both that of emergency and of incapacity "for example in the event of progressive disease such as senile dementia".

[45] See Gerald Dworkin, *The Theory and Practice of Autonomy* (Cambridge, 1988).

[46] See *Official Journal of the European Union*, C 83/389 of 30 March 2010. See, as regards a selection of jurisprudential decisions on the subject Massimo Panebianco (directed by), *Repertorio alla Carta dei diritti fondamentali dell'Unione europea*, (Napoli, 2001), pp. 50–60; Massimo Panebianco and Francesco Buonomenna (eds.), *Repertorio della Costituzione europea* (Napoli, 2005), pp. 249 ff. See the vibrant criticism expressed by Pierfrancesco Grossi, "Dignità umana e libertà nella Carta dei diritti fondamentali dell'UE", in M. Siclari (ed.) *Contributi allo studio della Carta dei diritti fondamentali dell'Unione europea* (Torino, 2003) on the editing technique adopted which would make some provisions of the Charter merely rhetorical. See also Nino Palermo, "Dignità umana e uguaglianza nella Carta dei diritti fondamentali dell'Unione europea", in A. Galasso (ed.), *Diritti fondamentali e multi-etnicità. Una ricerca per la Costituzione dell'Unione europea* (Palermo, 2003), p. 98 ff.

with reference to the specific subject of this work, as the "Right to the integrity of the person" (Article 3) which, at no. 2 (para. *a*), provides "the free and informed consent of the person concerned, according to the procedures laid down by law". It also appears in the Preamble, where human dignity is mentioned as the first value among the "indivisible (and) universal values" on which the European Union is founded.

It is evident that in devoting the heading of Title 1 to dignity (before the Title II "Freedoms" and the Title III "Equality"),[47] and adding to it, as *incipit*, Article 1 in its wide conception, the Charter of Fundamental Rights of the European Union confers on it an almost "holy character": it makes it become a sort of "sanctuary" implying that the human person, since it is a unique and unrepeatable being, able of self-determination, is the holder of a value transcending any condition in which he could find himself.[48] But the Charter does not limit itself to assigning to dignity the rank of *character indelebilis*,[49] that is to recognize it, as the Explanations to Article 1 of the Charter of Fundamental Rights state, "not only [as] a fundamental right in itself but [as] ... the real basis of fundamental rights".[50] Besides its peculiar systematic choice of assigning to it "the axiological presumption of fundamental rights"[51] (thus anticipating its provision, compared with the same "right to life" provided in Article 2), besides using the category of inviolability only for itself, adds a specification of such value through the following norms and, with reference to the subject of this writing, to the already mentioned "right to the integrity of the person".

---

[47] On the so called "triangle of Constitutionalism" see Susanne Baer, "Dignity, Liberty, Equality: A Fundamental Rights Triangle of Constitutionalism", 59 *University of Toronto Law Journal* (2009), pp. 417–468.

[48] See Marco Olivetti, "Art. 1. Dignità umana", in R. Bifulco, M. Cartabia and A. Celotto (eds.), *L'Europa dei diritti. Commento alla Carta dei diritti fondamentali dell'Unione europea* (Bologna, 2001), p. 38 ff. The term "sanctuary" is used in this work. It is not to be forgotten that in the Charter there are further references to dignity concerning its disciplined applications, with reference to specific categories of individuals: see Article 25 devoted to "the rights of the elderly" which also provides ... "to lead a life of dignity". For the symbolic value of dignity in the Charter see Guido Alpa, "Dignità personale e diritti fondamentali", in *Scritti Modugno, supra* note 20, pp. 43–57.

[49] For this definition see Giovanna Pistorio, "Art. 1. Dignità umana", in G. Bisogni, G. Bronzini and V. Piccone, *La Carta dei diritti. Casi e materiali* (Taranto, 2009), p. 39 ff., in particular at 39.

[50] See *Official Journal of the European Union*, C 83/02 of 30 March 2010. On the Explanations we dare refer to Angela Di Stasi, "Brevi osservazioni intorno alle «spiegazioni» alla Carta dei diritti fondamentali dell'Unione europea", in Claudio Zanghì and Lina Panella (eds.), *Il Trattato di Lisbona tra conferme e novità* (Torino, 2010), pp. 425–454.

[51] So Gaetano Silvestri, *Considerazioni sul valore costituzionale della dignità della persona*, Intervention at the trilateral Meeting of the Italian, Portuguese, and Spanish Constitutions (Rome, 1 October 2007), available at http://www.associazionedeicostituzionalisti.it, p. 2.

Indeed, in consecrating "the right to respect for his or her physical and mental integrity" (para. 1) in the fields of medicine and biology (para. 2), Article 3 of the Charter provides "the free and informed consent of the person concerned, according to the procedures laid down by law" (first alinéa).[52] The innovative character of this norm cannot go unnoticed, since its difficult aim is that of making controversial subjects fall within the range of the fundamental rights of the European Union, even if they are the subject of a recommendation or of special conventions binding more or less large groups of States (as the above mentioned Convention on Human Rights and Biomedicine which is expressly referred to in the Explanations on Article 3). If its content does not greatly wanders off the provision of the already mentioned Convention, the inclusion of such norm in the Title devoted to dignity, is very meaningful. The right to respect for physical and mental integrity (Article 3, para. 1) becomes (in para. 2 of the same norm) the guarantee of a number of corollaries of human dignity, among which there is "the free and informed consent of the person concerned"; however, as regards the ways of manifestation of it, we refer "to the procedures laid down by law".

Such references get, as it is well known, a full normative relevance because of (Article 6, para. 1) the equalization of the legal value of the Charter of Fundamental Rights of the European Union with that of the Treaty on the European Union (TUE) and the Treaty on the Functioning of the European Union (TFUE). In this regard we must not forget that the respect for human dignity assumes, in the same treaties, the role of a founding value of the European Union (Article 2 TUE), and also a principle of the Union's external action (Article 21, para. 1).

III. Final Observations

Although the concept of human dignity is increasingly invoked in the bioethical debate and, indeed, in international instruments concerning biotechnology and biomedicine, some commentators consider appeals to human dignity to be little more than rhetoric. The brief analysis we have carried out has shown that the notion of dignity used—implicitly or explicitly—in international instruments corresponds to the universally

---

[52] See Raffaele Bifulco, "Commento all'art. 3", in *L'Europa dei diritti, supra* note 48, p. 53 ff., and Ignazio Juan Patrone, "Art. 3. Diritto all'integrità della persona", in *La Carta dei diritti, supra* note 49, p. 65 ff.

based concept of inherent dignity. It concerns the intrinsic value of humans that, as such, is to be considered independently of age, sex, religion or other factors. According to this meaning any human being represents a *unicum*, with the consequence that human dignity cannot be graduated or eliminated because of state actions. Since it is an inherent dignity, it also becomes an element of equality between human beings, joining them all together according to the formula already used in the above mentioned Article 1 of the Universal Declaration of Human Rights. If human dignity is the same for all human beings, they have equal basic rights even, with reference to the subject of this work, in relation to the "End of life". Moreover, because it is pre-positive, it is the basis of human rights and the foundation of them all.

In International Biolaw the recurrent mention of the term dignity is that of inherent dignity. It also sometimes assumes the meaning of dignity as "psychological" dignity, consisting on the perception of one's own value and strictly connected with one's own identity and physical integrity.

The reference to dignity, in the International and European instruments of International Biolaw, as inherent dignity does not allow us to eschew considering it as subject to each human being's changeable conditions of living (as regards, for example, the persistence of an autonomous will manifested in a period of life preceding the "End of life") thus making the contrast between human rights and individual freedom always possible.

In this perspective, human dignity (and its respect), considered as the founding value of the normative system still under construction as regards the "End of life", will help to direct the activity not only of the internal, but also of the "international" legislator, towards the production of norms categorised as both medical ethics and international human rights law. It will also play an important role to help all law operators (above all internal and international judges) to apply norms in a field characterized by a sensible instability and changeability like that of the "End of life".

On the other hand, we cannot deny in this regard that the new instruments of International Biolaw (as the Convention on Human Rights and Biomedicine) do not institute judicial enforcement mechanisms and that the European Court of Human Rights and the Court of Justice of the European Union have already ruled biomedical and biotechnology cases on the basis of the existing instruments. Then, without confuting the right motivation of criticisms (which can be partly shared) on the use of the idea of dignity in International and European Biolaw, if it is rightly mentioned, without misinterpretations, it can become a lighting beacon even in the new or renewed normative and judicial choices concerning Life Sciences and specially future Directives. We affirm this not only as corollary of the limit found by International Biolaw with regard to some human fundamental rights, but also as barrier against any alterations that the biotechnological progress or an "overevaluation" of the individual's autonomy, could cause just of the dignity of human beings, at the very delicate moment of the "End of life".

Objective reason or justification basis for the recognition of human rights, dignity demands concretization through reference to a basket of rights and values being in a relationship of mutual dependence: the right to life, the right to privacy, the right to free and informed consent, the right to physical and mental integrity, the right to access to basic health care, the right to non discrimination, etc.

Human dignity: from cornerstone in International Human Rights Law to cornerstone in International Biolaw?

THE RIGHT TO INFORMED CONSENT AT THE CONVERGENCE OF INTERNATIONAL BIOLAW AND INTERNATIONAL HUMAN RIGHTS LAW

*Stefania Negri**

I. Exploring Informed Consent in International Legal Perspective

Informed consent is a fundamental tenet of medical ethics conjugating ethical imperatives and respect for human rights in biomedical research as well as in the exercise of the medical profession. It is considered the foundation of the "new ethos of patient autonomy",[1] since recognition of autonomy in health care decision-making has enabled and empowered competent patients to retain control of their lives and has come to govern the doctor-patient relationship consistently with respect for the right to self-determination.

From the legal viewpoint, informed consent represents a well-established rule of both biolaw and of human rights law. In fact, the bioethical and human rights-based approaches to the life sciences share common foundations and values, converging over the common objective of protecting human dignity and the integrity of every human being from the risks posed by the progress of technology and its applications to the natural processes governing the beginning and the end of life.[2] Hence, in the relative paucity of universally agreed principles providing a frame-work for ethical conduct in the biomedical field, informed consent—just like the basic principle of respect for human dignity—stands as the cornerstone of biomedical law and human rights law alike.[3]

---

* Associate Professor of International Law and of International Human Rights Law at the Faculty of Law of the University of Salerno, Italy; email: snegri@unisa.it.
[1] See Stephen Wear, *Informed Consent. Patient Autonomy and Physician Beneficence within Clinical Medicine* (Dordrecht, 1992), Chapter two.
[2] On the idea that bioethics and human rights converge to a certain extent in consideration of their commonalities, see the critical analysis of Richard E. Ashcroft, "Could Human Rights Supersede Bioethics?", 10 *Human Rights Law Review* (2010), pp. 639–660.
[3] On the fundamental role of dignity in the fields of bioethics and biolaw, see especially the introductory chapter to this book: Angela Di Stasi, *Human Dignity: From Cornerstone in International Human Rights Law to Cornerstone in International Biolaw?*.

S. Negri (ed.), *Self-Determination, Dignity and End-of-Life Care*
2011 Koninklijke Brill NV. Printed in The Netherlands. ISBN 978 90 04 22357 8. pp. 23–72.

Exploring the nature and scope of informed consent is definitely not sailing into uncharted waters, especially in consideration of the fact that an impressive wealth of important contributions has been devoted to the subject in both philosophical and legal literature.[4] However, since informed consent has mainly been studied within the framework of domestic law and jurisprudence, it is worth making the point on its present status from the viewpoint of international law and case law. This perspective reveals some interesting insights inasmuch as informed consent has gained remarkable importance in the international legal framework too, and it is by now widely recognised that also "from the standpoint of international law, the only accepted position is that no medical act may be performed without the patients' freely given and informed consent".[5] Moreover, it is particularly telling that some relevant steps were recently taken within the United Nations human rights system—namely, the issuance of a specific report in November 2009 by the Special Rapporteur on the right to health and the adoption in September 2010 of the Human Rights Council's resolution on the right to health—inviting all States to "safeguard informed consent within the health counselling, testing and treatment continuum, including in clinical practice, public health and medical research, as a critical element of the right of everyone to the enjoyment of the highest attainable standard of physical and mental health".[6]

---

[4] The body of literature on informed consent is really vast. See, *ex plurimis*, Ruth R. Faden, Tom L. Beauchamp and Nancy M.P. King, *A History and Theory of Informed Consent* (New York, 1986); Ferdinand van Oosten, *The Doctrine of Informed Consent in Medical Law* (Frankfurt am Main, 1991); Peter H. Schuck, "Rethinking Informed Consent", 103 *The Yale Law Journal* (1994), pp. 899–959; Amedeo Santosuosso (ed.), *Il consenso informato: tra giustificazione per il medico e diritto del paziente* (Milano, 1996); Irene S. Switankowsky, *A New Paradigm for Informed Consent* (Lanham, 1998); Emmanuel Roucounas, "Le droit au consentement et ses restrictions dans la Convention sur les droits de l'homme et la biomédicine (1997)", in R.-J. Dupuy (ed.), *Mélanges en l'honneur de Nicolas Valticos* (Paris, 1999), pp. 479–495; Jessica W. Berg, Paul S. Appelbaum, Lisa S. Parker and Charles W. Lidz, *Informed Consent: Legal Theory and Clinical Practice* (Oxford, 2nd ed., 2001); Annick Dorsner-Dolivet, "Le consentement au traitement médical: une liberté fondamentale en démi-teinte", 19 *Revue française de droit administrative* (2003), pp. 528–535; Giovanni G. Pasinelli, *Il consenso informato: una svolta nell'etica medica* (Milano, 2004); Steve Clarke and Justin Oakley (eds.), *Informed Consent and Clinician Accountability* (Cambridge, 2007); Neil C. Manson and Onora O'Neill, *Rethinking Informed Consent in Bioethics* (New York, 2007); Carlo Casonato, "Il consenso informato: profili di diritto comparato", 11 *Diritto pubblico comparato ed europeo* (2009), pp. 1052–1073; Alasdair R. Maclean, *Autonomy, Informed Consent and Medical Law: A Relational Challenge* (Cambridge, 2009).

[5] Council of Europe, Parliamentary Assembly, *Human stem cell research*, Report of 10 June 2003, Doc. 9816, para. 8.

[6] *Report of the Special Rapporteur on the right of everyone to the enjoyment of the highest attainable standard of physical and mental health*, Anand Grover, U.N. Doc. A/64/272, 10

Therefore, attempting to systematise the origin, nature and scope of informed consent in an international law perspective, this chapter will first expand on its evolution in international biolaw from the Nuremberg Code to the Unesco Universal Declaration on Bioethics and Human Rights, illustrating the normative process through which informed consent has come to acquire the status of a generally accepted legal principle. Then, the 'filiation' of informed consent from some fundamental human rights such as the prohibition of inhuman and degrading treatment, the right to physical integrity and the right to health will be examined as a starting point to support the argument that an autonomous 'right to informed consent' has emerged from the convergence of international biolaw and international human rights law. Further this chapter will deal with the reverse side of the coin of informed consent, that is the right to refuse treatment and its relevance for treatment options at the end of life and for the debate on the controversial existence of a 'right to die in dignity', to suggest that the non-derogable nature of the right to informed consent for competent patients should be given paramount consideration in determining the legal value of advance treatments directives.

II. Informed Consent in International Biolaw

A. *Historical Origins and Legal Sources of Informed Consent in International Biolaw*

Over the last century, following the famous and mostly cited opinion delivered by Justice Benjamin Cardozo in the landmark *Schloendorff* case—"every human being of adult years and sound mind has a right to determine what shall be done with his own body"[7]—informed consent has been developed as a legal doctrine mainly by Western domestic courts. Today, this doctrine is globally recognized as dictating the *conditio sine qua non* for clinical practice and biomedical research. Its significance in international biolaw is reflected by the fact that virtually all international agreements and declarations on ethical and legal standards in medicine and biomedical research endorse the basic rule of informed consent.[8]

August 2009 (hereinafter '*Report 2009*'); Human Rights Council, Resolution 15/22, 30 September 2010, para. 4 (*o*) (adopted by consensus).

[7] Opinion of Justice Benjamin Cardozo, *Schloendorff v. The Society of New York Hospitals* (105 N.E. 92), Court of Appeals of New York, 14 April 1914, available at http://biotech.law.lsu.edu/cases/consent/Schoendorff.htm.

[8] See Regine Kollek, "Article 6: Consent", in H.A.M.J. ten Have and M.S. Jean (eds.), *The UNESCO Universal Declaration on Bioethics and Human Rights. Background, principles and application* (Paris, 2009), pp. 123–138, at 124.

Although it is argued that truly universal acceptance of informed consent as a key bioethical principle is probably linked to the adoption of the Unesco Universal Declaration on Bioethics and Human Rights of 2005, the acknowledgement of its importance at the international level is not such recent phenomenon. From a historical point of view, in fact, the start of a rising tide in favour of the recognition of the right to bodily integrity in the medical field, accompanied by the shaping of corresponding duties and responsibilities of healthcare providers and researchers, can be traced back to the aftermath of World War II and the Nuremberg Trials.[9] In that regard, the international community's revulsion at the disclosure of the medical atrocities committed by Nazi physicians, especially the 'scientific experiments' performed by the infamous Josef Mengele, led to the harsh condemnation of non-voluntary human experimentation and prompted the drafting of the Nuremberg Code. Being the first internationally recognized set of ethical standards in non-therapeutic research, the Code was meant to avert that similar crimes be committed in the future in the name of science. To this end it articulated a universal standard of physician responsibility and set forth those fundamental principles that still today lie at the heart of research ethics (including voluntary and informed consent, absence of coercion, opt-out possibility, protection against grievous bodily harm, and proportionality of risk).[10] This is the reason why the Code is considered a 'pioneer' text in international bioethics or even "le véritable acte de naissance du droit de la bioéthique".[11]

[9] See in particular the famous *Doctors' Trial*: Military Tribunal I, *United States of America v. Karl Brandt, et al.*, Judgment of 21 August 1947. Among the several relevant contributions, see Georges J. Annas and Michael A. Grodin, "Medical Ethics and Human Rights: Legacies of Nuremberg", in F. Ohne, S. Kolb and H. Sithe (eds.), *Medicine and Conscience* (Berlin, 1998); Paul J. Weindling, "The Origins of Informed Consent: The International Scientific Commission on Medical War Crimes, and the Nuremberg Code", 75 *Bulletin of the History of Medicine* (2001), pp. 37–71; Id., *Nazi Medicine and the Nuremberg Trials. From Medical War Crimes to Informed Consent* (Basingstoke, 2006). From a different perspective, compare Panagiota Dalla-Vorgia, John Lascaratos, Panagiotis Skiadas and Tina Garanis-Papadatos, "Is Consent in Medicine a Concept only of Modern Times?", 27 *Journal of Medical Ethics* (2001), pp. 59–61.

[10] The Nuremberg Code (1947) was printed in *Trials of War Criminals before the Nuremberg Military Tribunals under Control Council Law No. 10*, vol. 2, pp. 181–182, Washington D.C., U.S. Government Printing Office, 1949; it is also available at http://ohsr.od.nih.gov/guidelines/nuremberg.html.

[11] Noëlle Lenoir, "Le droit international pénal de la bioéthique", in H. Ascensio, E. Decaux and A. Pellet (eds.), *Droit international pénal* (Paris, 2000), pp. 405–415, at 406; see also Bertrand Mathieu, "Du Code de Nuremberg à la Bioéthique: les prolongements d'un texte fondateur", 49 *Recueil international de legislation sanitaire* (1998), p. 571 ff.;

The first and best known provision of the Nuremberg Code stated:

> The voluntary consent of the human subject is absolutely essential. This means that the person involved should have legal capacity to give consent; should be so situated as to be able to exercise free power of choice, without the intervention of any element of force, fraud, deceit, duress, overreaching, or other ulterior form of constraint or coercion; and should have sufficient knowledge and comprehension of the elements of the subject matter involved as to enable him to make an understanding and enlightened decision. ...

Since then, informed consent has enjoyed growing widespread consensus and gained over time broader scope. Well before professional associations worldwide endorsed it within their deontological guidelines and codes of ethics, their most representative international institution, the World Medical Association, had proclaimed the right of competent patients to accept or refuse treatment in its 1949 International Code of Medical Ethics.[12] The WMA later upheld the rule of informed consent both in the Helsinki Declaration on Ethical Principles for Medical Research[13] and in the Lisbon Declaration on the Rights of the Patient.[14] Although not binding, these acts predated domestic laws regulating biomedical issues and served as reference codes of conduct for biomedical practice and research worldwide.

The same objective was also achieved by the several legal instruments— of both 'hard' and 'soft' law—adopted by the major international organisations engaged at different levels in the field of health care and ethics,

---

Nerina Boschiero, "Le biotecnologie tra etica e principi generali del diritto internazionale", in N. Boschiero (ed.), *Bioetica e biotecnologie nel diritto internazionale e comunitario* (Torino, 2006), pp. 3–126, at 11.

[12] WMA, *International Code of Medical Ethics*, adopted by the 3rd General Assembly of the World Medical Association, London, October 1949, as amended in 1968, 1983 and 2006; available at http://www.wma.net/en/30publications/10policies/c8/index.html.

[13] WMA, *Declaration of Helsinki: Ethical Principles for Medical Research Involving Human Subjects*, adopted by the 18th World Medical Assembly, Helsinki, June 1964, as subsequently amended and revised up to October 2008, available at http://www.wma.net/en/30publications/10policies/b3/index.html. According to Annas and Grodin, the Declaration "focused more on physicians' rights than patients' rights" and in requiring consent only for non-therapeutic research it "thereby undermined the primacy of subject consent as it appeared in the Nuremberg Code and replaced it with the paternalistic values of the traditional doctor-patient relationship" (George J. Annas and Michael A. Grodin, "Medicine and Human Rights: Reflections on the Fiftieth Anniversary of the Doctors' Trial", 2 *Health and Human Rights* (1996), pp. 6–21, at 11–12).

[14] WMA, *Declaration on the Rights of the Patient*, adopted by the 34th World Medical Assembly, Lisbon, September/October 1981, and amended by the 47th WMA General Assembly Bali, Indonesia, September 1995, available at http://www.wma.net/en/30publications/10policies/l4/index.html.

which have later substantially contributed to the legal recognition of
informed consent as a basic principle of the emerging international biomedical law.[15] In this respect, it is necessary to recall, first and foremost,
the WHO Declaration on the Promotion of Patients' Rights in Europe of
1994,[16] the Council of Europe's Convention on Human Rights and
Biomedicine of 1997 and its Additional Protocols,[17] as well as the Unesco
Universal Declarations on the Human Genome and Human Rights of 1997
and on Bioethics and Human Rights of 2005.[18] To these it is worth also adding the WHO Guidelines for Good Clinical Practice,[19] the International
Ethical Guidelines for Biomedical Research Involving Human Subjects
prepared by the WHO in collaboration with the Council for International
Organizations of Medical Sciences,[20] and at regional level, the European
Union Clinical Trials Directive of 2001.[21]

Through these and other relevant documents, international organisations have codified the basic legal and regulatory standards of biomedical

---

[15] See especially Roberto Andorno and Allyn Taylor (eds.), *International Biomedical
Law: Theory and Practice* (Ardsley N.Y., 2004).

[16] WHO/EURO, European Consultation on the Rights of Patients, Amsterdam 28–30
March 1994, *A Declaration on the Promotion of Patients' Rights in Europe*, ICP/HLE 121,
28 June 1994 (hereinafter '*Amsterdam Declaration*').

[17] See Chapter II of the *Convention for the Protection of Human Rights and Dignity of the
Human Being with regard to the Application of Biology and Medicine: Convention on Human
Rights and Biomedicine*, Oviedo, 4 April 1997, ETS No. 164, entered into force on 1 December
1999 (hereinafter 'Oviedo Convention'). See also Articles 13, 14 and 17 of the *Additional
Protocol to the Convention on Human Rights and Biomedicine concerning Transplantation of
Organs and Tissues of Human Origin*, Strasbourg, 24 January 2002, ETS No. 186, entered into
force on 1 May 2006; Chapters IV and V of the *Additional Protocol to the Convention on
Human Rights and Biomedicine, concerning Biomedical Research*, Strasbourg, 25 January
2005, ETS No. 195, entered into force on 1 September 2007; Articles 9 to 15 of the *Additional
Protocol to the Convention on Human Rights and Biomedicine, concerning Genetic Testing for
Health Purposes*, Strasbourg, 27 November 2008, ETS No. 203, not yet in force.

[18] See Article 5 of the *Universal Declaration on the Human Genome and Human Rights*,
11 November 1997, and Articles 6 and 7 of the *Universal Declaration on Bioethics and Human
Rights*, 19 October 2005. As far as the collection, use and storage of biological samples are
concerned, see the Unesco *International Declaration on Human Genetic Data*, 16 October
2003, in particular Articles 8, 9 and 16.

[19] WHO, *Guidelines for Good Clinical Practice for Trials on Pharmaceutical Products*
(Geneva, 1995). See also the UN Special Rapporteur's recommendations as formulated in
his Report containing the *Human Rights Guidelines for Pharmaceutical Companies in relation to Access to Medicines* (U.N. Doc. A/63/263, 11 August 2008, paras. 21–22).

[20] CIOMS-WHO, *International Ethical Guidelines for Biomedical Research Involving Human Subjects* (Geneva, 2002), Guideline 4, p. 32, available at http://www.cioms.ch/
publications/layout_guide2002.pdf.

[21] Directive 2001/20/EC of the European Parliament and of the Council of 4 April 2001 on
the approximation of the laws, regulations and administrative provisions of the Member
States relating to the implementation of good clinical practice in the conduct of clinical

ethics—which have by now gained the status of internationally accepted principles—thus contributing to international biomedical law-making.[22]

B. *The Scope of Informed Consent:* Voluntas aegroti suprema lex

It is indisputable that the doctrine of informed consent is today widely acknowledged as the expression of one of the basic principles in international biolaw, serving as the cornerstone for the protection of the fundamental rights to physical integrity and self-determination in every field of medical intervention.

According to a commonly used formula, informed consent provides in its essence that any preventive, diagnostic and therapeutic medical intervention as well as any scientific research involving human subjects may only be performed after the person concerned has given prior, free, and informed consent, based on adequate information. This approach has definitely superseded all paternalistic—and even 'imperialistic'[23]—medical attitudes and enhanced the 'rooting' of the key concepts of patients' self-determination and autonomy in health care decision-making.[24] Therefore, from a legal viewpoint, informed consent is not merely a 'prerequisite' to treatment, as it is often labelled:[25] it is the very foundation of legitimacy for any medical treatment, so much so that, even if administered in the patient's interest, interventions and cares provided without prior consent could be qualified as illegal 'bodily assaults', potentially triggering the liability, both civil and criminal, of health care providers.[26]

---

trials on medicinal products for human use, *Official Journal of the European Communities*, L 121/34, 1 May 2001.

[22] See a collection of the relevant texts in André den Exter, *International Health Law & Ethics. Basic Documents* (Apeldoorn, 2009).

[23] René Savatier, *Impérialism medical sur le terrain du droit* (Paris, 1952).

[24] In 1979, along with the Belmont Report (The National Commission for the Protection of Human Subjects of Biomedical and Behavioral Research, *Ethical Principles and Guidelines for the protection of human subjects of research*, April 18, 1979), the first edition of the seminal work by Beauchamp and Childress proposed the influential approach of the four moral principles (namely, respect for autonomy, beneficence, non-maleficence, and justice) to biomedical ethics (see their 6th edition, Tom L. Beauchamp and James F. Childress, *Principles of Biomedical Ethics*, Oxford, 2008). Respect for autonomy represented the core of their 'principlism theory' and appeared to be the predominant moral principle; informed consent was the result of its application to biomedical research.

[25] *Amsterdam Declaration, supra* note 16, paras. 3.1, 3.10. See also, in legal scholarship, Kollek, "Article 6", *supra* note 8, at 124.

[26] See Justice Cardozo in *Schloendorff v. Society of New York Hospital, supra* note 7: "a surgeon who performs an operation without his patient's consent commits an assault, for which he is liable in damages".

In the same vein, biomedical research performed without the informed consent of the research subjects is considered unethical and illegal.

However, simply consenting to treatment is not enough. In his report on informed consent, the UN Special Rapporteur on the right to health stressed that consent is "not mere acceptance of a medical intervention, but a voluntary and sufficiently informed decision, protecting the right of the patient to be involved in medical decision-making, and assigning associated duties and obligations to health-care providers."[27] Indeed, there are several preconditions that have to be fulfilled to make consent to treatment valid. In essence, to deploy its legal effects prior consent must be 'free and informed', which means that the patient's autonomous decision to accept or refuse to undergo a medical treatment or to take part in scientific research has to meet some specific requirements. It should be noted in this respect that the formulas consistently adopted by the aforementioned international legal instruments evidence that such requirements are definitely acknowledged as well-established rules at the international level.

First of all, such documents provide that in order to validly consent to treatment the person involved must be conscious and fully competent; he/she must have legal capacity to give consent. Consent must be voluntary, i.e. the outcome of a decision-making process devoid of any element of force, fraud, deceit, duress, threat or any other form of constraint or coercion. It must be based on the appropriate disclosure to the patient, by the responsible healthcare professional, of adequate and understandable information concerning the diagnostic assessment, the purpose, method, likely duration, expected benefit and chances of success of the proposed treatment; of the alternative modes of treatment, including those less intrusive; of possible pain or discomfort, risks and side-effects of the proposed treatment; of the chances and risks associated with lack of treatment. Moreover, consent must be clearly given and recorded (in some cases in written form) and can be withdrawn at any time, even if withdrawal appears to be contrary to the person's best interest.

In light of the foregoing factual and legal requirements, it is 'genuine consent'[28] that represents the core element of the doctor-patient relationship, which has to be understood as a fiduciary relationship in which enhanced dialogue and mutual trust and confidence are essential. In this

---

[27] *Report 2009, supra* note 6, para. 9.
[28] On the concepts of 'genuine consent' or 'understood consent', see Zulfiqar A. Bhutta, "Beyond informed consent", 82 *Bulletin of the World Health Organization* (2004), pp. 771–777, at 773–774.

perspective, the quality of the communication between health care providers and patients becomes of dramatic importance for the exercise of
the latters' right to self-determination and autonomy. This means that relevant information should be provided in plain language and readily
understandable terms, and in sufficient amount so as to ensure that the
patient's ultimate decision is based on an appreciable knowledge of their
condition. According to the aforementioned UN Report, "[t]his requires
States to ensure that information is fully available, acceptable, accessible
and of good quality, and imparted and comprehended by means of supportive and protective measures such as counselling and involvement of
community networks".[29] Nonetheless, while it is self-evident that the role
of health professionals is central in the process of informed consent, other
important concurring elements demand special attention. In this connection it is interesting to note that, with regard to scientific research involving human participants, the manual prepared for the World Health
Organization by Professor Carl Coleman and other international experts—
which outlines ethical guidelines aimed to support the work of national
research ethics committees—highlights the following factors that might
undermine the process of informed consent: "the social and economic
context: illiteracy, inadequate access to care; the cultural environment:
the role of the community and family and of different sets of values; the
asymmetrical nature of the knowledge of the investigators and that of the
participants, which puts the latter in a subordinate relationship; the tendency of individuals to confuse being a participant in research with receiving individualized medical care (the 'therapeutic misconception')."[30] Here
again, it is confirmed that only 'genuine consent' lies at the basis of the
researcher-subject relationship.

Once the contours of consent have been shaped, it is necessary to consider any legitimate exception and limitation that will help to better
define its scope. On this point, it is agreed that the general rule of informed
consent is not absolute. Special regimes and derogations have progressively been accepted in particular situations, or in respect of groups of
vulnerable patients that call for increased protection and appropriate
legal regulation.[31] There has resulted a set of derogatory rules applicable in
specific conditions.

---

[29] *Report 2009, supra* note 6, para. 93.

[30] WHO, *Research ethics committees. Basic concepts for capacity-building* (Geneva,
2009), p. 46, and more generally pp. 43–47.

[31] See Christian P. Selinger, "The right to consent: Is it absolute?", 2 *British
Journal of Medical Practitioners* (2009), pp. 50–54. The Author argues that on the basis of

First of all, in case of medical emergency and whenever the patient is unconscious or otherwise unable to express their will and their life is at risk, urgent interventions and life-saving treatments are in any case legitimate and lawful; in these circumstances the patient's consent may be presumed, unless it is obvious from a previous declared expression of will that consent would have been refused in a similar situation.[32] In different conditions, interventions on persons who find themselves in a *de facto* incapacity (e.g. the consequences of an accident or a state of coma) can be performed only if of direct benefit to them and under conditions approved by law; normally, the previously expressed wishes of a patient who is not able to give their consent at the time of the intervention should be taken into account.[33]

For patients with a reduced capacity of understanding or whose legal capacity is limited by law for reasons of age or because of mental illness (e.g. minors,[34] incapacitated adults and adults with mental disorders[35]) the consent is provided by a legal representative (guardian or proxy) or

---

philosophical, ethical, legal and practical considerations there is no absolute right to consent. The situations of incompetent minors, adults lacking capacity, some mentally ill patients and patients suffering from some infectious diseases would be cases in point. It should also be noted that, consistently with the exceptions stated in Articles 6 to 8, the Oviedo Convention does not include Article 5 among those non-derogable dispositions mentioned in Article 26, para. 2, while it only provides that no restrictions be placed on its protective provisions contained in Article 17, concerning persons not able to consent to research.

[32] See Article 8 of the Oviedo Convention: "When because of an emergency situation the appropriate consent cannot be obtained, any medically necessary intervention may be carried out immediately for the benefit of the health of the individual concerned", and paras. 56–58 of the Explanatory report: "In emergencies, doctors may be faced with a conflict of duties between their obligations to provide care and seek the patient's consent. This article allows the practitioner to act immediately in such situations without waiting until the consent of the patient or the authorisation of the legal representative where appropriate can be given. ... First, this possibility is restricted to emergencies which prevent the practitioner from obtaining the appropriate consent. The article applies both to persons who are capable and to persons who are unable either *de jure* or *de facto* to give consent. An example that might be put forward is that of a patient in a coma who is thus unable to give his consent ..., or that of a doctor who is unable to contact an incapacitated person's legal representative who would normally have to authorise an urgent intervention. ... Next, the possibility is limited solely to medically necessary interventions which cannot be delayed. ..."

[33] See Article 9 of the Oviedo Convention and the observations on advance directives, *infra* para. V and most of all in the chapter authored by Professor Roberto Andorno, "Regulating Advance Directives at the Council of Europe", in this book.

[34] See Loes Stultiëns, Tom Goffin, Pascal Borry, Kris Dierickx, Herman Nys, "Minors and Informed Consent: A Comparative Approach", 14 *European Journal of Health Law* (2007), pp. 21–46.

[35] See also: Article 7 of the Oviedo Convention; Principle 11 of the United Nations *Principles for the Protection of Persons with Mental Illness and the Improvement of Mental*

independent body provided for by law; however, the participation of adults unable to consent must not be totally ruled out: in principle, the appointment of a representative does not relieve from the obligation to involve the subject in the decision-making process to the fullest extent which his capacity allows.[36] When a legal representative is appointed as substitute decision-maker, an intervention in case of urgent need can be performed whenever there is no possibility to obtain the representative's consent[37] and if the legal representative refuses consent to an intervention that the physician deems appropriate and useful in the best interest of the patient, it is necessary to resort to a court or some form of arbitration of an independent body for *super partes* decision.[38] Moreover, legal representatives have no right to withdraw consent unless withdrawal is clearly justified in light of the patient's best interest.

According to well-established standards, in all other situations where the patient is unable to give consent and where there is no legal representative or proxy, appropriate measures should be taken to provide for a substitute decision-making process, taking into account what is known and, to the greatest extent possible, what may be presumed about the wishes of the patient.[39] Even in emergency situations, where no previous expression of will exists, health care professionals must make every reasonable effort to determine what the patient would want.[40]

Last but not least, medical research should not in principle involve subjects who are physically or mentally unable to express their will,[41] unless

---

Health Care, General Assembly Resolution 46/119 of 17 December 1991; *Progress of efforts to ensure the full recognition and enjoyment of the human rights of persons with disabilities*, Report of the Secretary-General, U.N. Doc. A/58/181, 24 July 2003; Commission on Human Rights, *Report of Paul Hunt, Special Rapporteur on the right of everyone to the enjoyment of the highest attainable standard of physical and mental health*, U.N. Doc. E/CN.4/2005/51, 11 February 2005 (hereinafter 'Report 2005').

[36] See Article 6 of the Oviedo Convention and the *Amsterdam Declaration, supra* note 16, at para. 3.5. This rule is in line with Article 12 of the United Nations Convention on the Rights of the Child, which stipulates that "States Parties shall assure the child, who is capable of forming his or her own views the right to express those views freely in all matters affecting the child, the views of the child being given due weight in accordance with the age and maturity of the child".

[37] *Amsterdam Declaration, supra* note 16, para. 3.4.

[38] Ibid., para. 3.6.

[39] Ibid., para. 3.7. This brings to the question of the difficult task of reconstructing, sometimes within judicial proceedings, the patient's wishes in crucial situations such as those concerning end-of-life care and substitute decision-making. On the reconstruction of the patient's wishes according to his ideas, beliefs and life style, see, e.g., the much debated Englaro case occurred in Italy and examined in Part III of this book.

[40] See the Explanatory report to the Oviedo Convention, at para. 57.

[41] According to the *Helsinki Declaration, supra* note 13, research "may be done only if the physical or mental condition that prevents giving informed consent is a necessary

the consent of a legally authorized representative has been sought and obtained, and the research would likely be in the direct interest of the person.[42] Incompetent persons may be involved in observational research of significant value which is not of direct benefit to their health, provided that there is a negligible risk and minimal burden for them;[43] lacking any potential direct benefit to incompetent research subjects, the research "should only be undertaken by way of exception, with the utmost restraint".[44]

All this said, it is remarkable that according to international (hard and soft) biolaw exceptions to the basic rule of informed consent are allowed solely when provided by law in accordance with ethical and legal standards adopted by States, strictly for "compelling reasons within the bounds of public international law" and subject to compliance with international human rights law.[45] This important *caveat*, included in the Oviedo

---

characteristic of the research population. In such circumstances the physician should seek informed consent from the legally authorized representative. If no such representative is available and if the research cannot be delayed, the study may proceed without informed consent provided that the specific reasons for involving subjects with a condition that renders them unable to give informed consent have been stated in the research protocol and the study has been approved by a research ethics committee" (para. 29).

[42] See Article 17 of the Oviedo Convention and Article 15 of the Additional Protocol on Biomedical Research.

[43] *Amsterdam Declaration, supra* note 16, para. 3.10; *Helsinki Declaration, supra* note 13, para. 27. *Adde* WHO, *Handbook for good clinical research practice (GCP): guidance for implementation* (Geneva, 2005) and, on best practices suggested for informed consent in research concerning HIV-AIDS, see WHO, *Principles and practices: The implementation of ethical guidelines for research on HIV*, available at www.who.int/hiv/strategic/mt020603/en/.

[44] See Article 5 of the Universal Declaration on the Human Genome and Article. 7, para. (b) of the Universal Declaration on Bioethics and Human Rights.

[45] See Article 9 of the Universal Declaration on the Human Genome and Article 6 of the Universal Declaration on Bioethics and Human Rights. According to Article 27 of the latter, such compelling reasons may include the need to protect public safety and public health, which finds evidence in Articles 23, para. 3 and 31, para. 2 of the International Health Regulations (2005), legitimising States to apply health measures to travellers, including compulsory examination and vaccination, when there is evidence of an imminent public health risk. Another relevant example would be mandatory screening supported by UNAIDS and WHO for HIV and other blood borne viruses of all blood that is destined for transfusion or for manufacture of blood products, as well as mandatory screening of donors before all procedures involving transfer of bodily fluids or body parts, such as artificial insemination, corneal grafts and organ transplant. However, it is interesting to note that the protection afforded by the International Covenant on Civil and Political Rights under Article 7 is even stricter than the one guaranteed by the norms of international biolaw, since that provision allows no derogations or limitation, not even in times of emergency (Article 4, para. 2).

Convention,[46] in the Unesco Declarations as well as in the resolutions of the United Nations Commission on Human Rights and of the Committee of Ministers of the Council of Europe,[47] recalls very closely the pattern of lawful limitations adopted within conventional human rights regimes[48] and lends support to the argument that informed consent is by now a rule grounded in international law, including human rights law, just as much as it is in bioethics.

C. *Informed Consent as a General Principle of International Biolaw*

Strictly connected to other key ethical and legal principles such as respect for human dignity and autonomy, informed consent has come to enjoy the status of a general principle of international biomedical law due to its widespread recognition and application.[49] It represents one of those principles which, "ethical in nature, ... have been incorporated into the rule of law by means of legal instruments, either laws within national legal systems or conventions and/or declarations or recommendations at the international level".[50] In effect, it is upheld and proclaimed by the most authoritative international instruments issued from those normative processes aimed at providing an international regulation of biomedical issues.

In this last perspective, informed consent can be considered one of those founding principles upon which a body of international biolaw is

---

[46] See Article 26 of the Oviedo Convention, which however does not allow restrictions on the rules governing protection of persons not able to consent to research or to organ removal. These are considered '*unconditional* norms' (see Roberto Andorno, "The Oviedo Convention: A European Legal Framework at the Intersection of Human Rights and Health Law", 2 *Journal of International Biotechnology Law* (2005), pp. 133–143, at 136).

[47] Commission on Human Rights, Resolution 2003/69, *Human rights and bioethics*, adopted by consensus on 25 April 2003; Committee of Ministers, *Recommendation R(99)4 to Member States on Principles Governing the Legal Protection of Incapable Adults*, 23 February 1999, principle 28.

[48] Compare the proviso formulated in Articles 8 to 11 of the European Convention on Human Rights; Articles 12, 18–19, 21–22 of the International Covenant on Civil and Political Rights; Articles 12–13, 15–16 and 22 of the American Convention on Human Rights; Articles 11–12 of the African Charter on Human and Peoples' Rights. The conditions of legitimacy of the restrictions placed on human rights are by now considered the object of a customary rule: see David P. Fidler, *International Law and Public Health* (New York, 2000), pp. 293–294.

[49] According to Professors Lenoir and Mathieu the bioethical principles enunciated in the Nuremberg Code are now part of customary law: see Noëlle Lenoir and Bertrand Mathieu, *Les normes internationales de la bioéthique* (Paris, 1998), p. 19.

[50] See Pierre-Marie Dupuy, "State Responsibility for Violations of Basic Principles of Bioethics", in F. Francioni (ed.), *Biotechnologies and International Human Rights* (Oxford, 2007), pp. 33–42, at 33.

being progressively built, notwithstanding the objective difficulties in the setting of common standards and in their transformation into positive law. It is in fact generally acknowledged that cultural and religious diversity, and the ensuing pluralistic approach to moral and legal values, play a crucial role in preventing easy consensus on bioethical issues (and their possible legal regulation). Nevertheless, despite the diversities inherent in human societies and also characterising the international community, a quest for universal standards is the distinctive feature of international bioethics. This aspiration has posed the greatest challenge to the emerging international biolaw: to succeed in translating shared values into a globally accepted codification of ethical and normative rules applicable to biomedical research and practice.[51]

Such generalised strive to overcome the contrast between pluralism and universalism has led to the entrustment of the task to frame general principles of biomedical law to widely representative international *fora*, where all the relevant actors and stakeholders can make their voice heard. The negotiation of the emerging norms of international biolaw has thus moved from traditional interstate agreement to multi-level institutionalised norm-making processes, carried out within international organisations and mainly based on the work of international bioethics committees.[52] With this shift in paradigm, States and non-State actors have made sensitive efforts to surmount the differences in traditions and ideologies with the aim to achieve a progressive development of international biomedical law. In this perspective, achieving a global consensus on rules and principles of universal significance has come to be considered the proper instrument to legitimise international legal regulation of life sciences and biomedicine.[53]

---

[51] On the issue whether 'universal bioethical standards' can possibly be translated into legal norms, see Ryuichi Ida, "Bioethics and International Law", in N. Boschiero (ed.), *Ordine internazionale e valori etici* (Naples, 2004), pp. 366–380, at 376–377. According to this Author, "Although bioethics legislation exists at the national level … and at the regional level …, there are no international or universal legal rules. The diversity of values within each community is the main reason for this absence of universal legal instruments" (at 377–378).

[52] See also Hélène Boussard, "The 'Normative Spectrum' of an Ethically-inspired Legal Instrument: The 2005 Universal Declaration on Bioethics and Human Rights", in *Biotechnologies*, *supra* note 50, pp. 97–127. With special reference to the Unesco Declarations, the Author states that they started a new norm-making process characterized by the convergence of legal and ethical norm-making processes (at 100).

[53] This idea has been expressed several times by Professor Bertrand Mathieu in his writings on international bioethics. However this Author also contends that universal consensus is reached on rules that represent an 'empty shell', since bioethical rules cannot

The most telling example of this change in paradigm is the normative activity performed at both universal and regional levels by international organisations such as Unesco and the Council of Europe, which—to say it with Professor Sandrine Maljean-Dubois—have "largement soutenu la dynamique du droit international de la bioéthique".[54]

This new process of norm-making, where a plurality of stakeholders have made efforts to reach consensus over general principles of international biomedical law, has been the subject of diverging views. On the one hand the critique was put forward by Professor David Benatar that:

> When a number of people with a range of different ethical views seek to formulate a declaration that enjoys the support of all (or even most) of them, the resultant declaration will suffer from one or both of two possible short-comings—minimalism and vagueness. By 'minimalism' I mean the phenomenon of agreeing on the lowest common denominator. In other words one includes items that everybody agrees upon, and one ignores items about which there is no consensus. The other way to gloss over disagreement is to choose formulations that are sufficiently vague that each person can interpret them consistently with his or her own view.[55]

By contrast—while conceding that a certain generality in the formulation of principles is needed to aptly balance universalism and cultural diversity—the same process has been considered by Professor Roberto Andorno as an important step to achieve the goal of agreeing on global minimum standards and promoting responsible biomedical research and clinical practice consistently with human rights and fundamental freedoms:[56]

---

successfully reproduce in the field of biomedical practice and research the same truly universal scope of the fundamental principles concerning human rights protection to which they are linked (see Bertrand Mathieu, "La bioéthique, ou comment déroger au droit commun des droits de l'homme", in S. Maljean-Dubois (ed.), *La société internationale et les enjeux bioéthiques* (Paris, 2006), pp. 85–94, at 85–87). See also Roberto Andorno, "Biomedicine and international human rights law: in search of a global consensus", 80 *Bulletin of the World Health Organization* (2002), pp. 959–963.

[54] Sandrine Maljean-Dubois, "Bioéthique et droit international", 46 *Annuaire Français de Droit International* (2000), pp. 82–110, at 89.

[55] David Benatar, "The Trouble with Universal Declarations", 5 *Developing World Bioethics* (2005), pp. 220–224, at 221.

[56] Roberto Andorno, "Global Bioethics at UNESCO: in defence of the Universal Declaration on Bioethics and Human Rights", 33 *Journal of Medical Ethics* (2007), pp. 150–154, at 150–151. See also Michel Revel, "Article 12: Respect for Cultural Diversity and Pluralism", in *The UNESCO Universal Declaration, supra* note 8, pp. 199–209. The same considerations on 'flexibility in form' and 'minimalism of content', as characteristics of international bioethical instruments, are applicable also to the Oviedo Convention (Andorno, "The Oviedo Convention", *supra* note 46, at 135; see also by the same Author: "Towards an international bioethics law", 15 *Journal International de Bioéthique* (2004), pp. 129–149). Compare also Maljean-Dubois, "Bioéthique", *supra* note 54, at 97 ff.

Certainly, the search for common responses to the new bioethical dilemmas is an arduous task. One may even get the impression that it is impossible to reach substantive agreement on such sensitive issues between countries with different socio-cultural and religious backgrounds. Fortunately, however, the situation is not as desperate as it might seem. The enterprise of setting common standards in the biomedical field, although difficult, is possible because international human rights law presupposes that some basic principles transcend cultural diversity. Of course, the major challenge is to identify those universal principles with regard to biomedical issues, but it is possible through promotion of an open and constructive dialogue between cultures. This would explain why international organizations, in which different cultural traditions and values are represented, seem to provide the ideal arena for the discovery of such common criteria.[57]

In effect, while it is a commonly shared objective consideration that international law-making in this field is not a straightforward endeavour, it is indubitable that the Council of Europe and Unesco have provided so far the most authoritative sources of legal principles and biorights of universal significance. However, to some extent, scholarship disagrees also on this last point.

The real scope of the Oviedo Convention—which is the first international binding instrument devoting a specific chapter to consent—is not yet univocally gauged in legal literature.[58] On the one hand, it is contended

---

[57] Andorno, "Biomedicine and international human rights", *supra* note 53, at 959.

[58] See, in general, Adriano Bompiani, "Una valutazione della 'Convenzione sui diritti dell'uomo e la biomedicina' del Consiglio d'Europa", 47 *Medicina e morale* (1997), pp. 37–54; Id., *Consiglio d'Europa, diritti umani e biomedicina. Genesi della Convenzione di Oviedo e dei Protocolli* (Roma, 2009); Elio Sgreccia, "La Convenzione sui diritti dell'uomo e la biomedicina", ibid., pp. 9–13; Aart Hendriks, "Convention on Human Rights and Biomedicine", 15 *Netherlands Quarterly of Human Rights* (1997), pp. 119–130; Henriette Roscam Abbing, "The Convention on Human Rights and Biomedicine An Appraisal of the Council of Europe Convention", 5 *European Journal of Health Law* (1998), pp. 377–387; Rosario Sapienza, "La Convenzione europea sui diritti dell'uomo e la biomedicina", 81 *Rivista di diritto internazionale* (1998), pp. 457–470; Adriana Loreti Beghè, "La Convenzione sui diritti dell'uomo e la biomedicina", 46 *Jus* (1999), pp. 131–144; Giuseppe Cataldi, "La Convenzione del Consiglio d'Europa sui diritti dell'uomo e la biomedicina", in L. Chieffi (ed.), *Bioetica e diritti dell'uomo* (Torino, 2000), pp. 267 ff.; Id., "La Convenzione del Consiglio d'Europa sui diritti dell'uomo e la biomedicina", in L. Pineschi (ed.), *La tutela internazionale dei diritti umani. Norme, garanzie, prassi* (Milano, 2006), pp. 589–606; Herman Nys, "La Convencion Europea de Bioética. Objetivos, principios rectores y posibles limitaciones", 12 *Revista de Derecho y Genoma Humana* (2000), pp. 67–87; Id., "The Biomedicine Convention as an Object and a Stimulus for Comparative Research in the European Journal of Health Law", 15 *European Journal of Health Law* (2008) pp. 273–283; Id., *The European Convention on human rights and biomedicine: a European patient rights instrument* (available at http://www.coe.int/t/dg3/healthbioethic/Activities/10th_Anniversary/Herman Nys.pdf); Chrystian Byk, "La Convention européenne sur la biomédicine et les droits de l'homme et l'ordre juridique International", 128 *Journal du Droit International* (2001), pp. 47–70; Cinzia Piciocchi, "La Convenzione di Oviedo sui

that the Convention seeks to promote the universal dimension of the bio-rights it enunciates;[59] on the other hand, it is denied any 'universal aspira-tion', although it is conceded that the participation to its negotiation of Canada, the USA, Japan, Australia, the European Union and the Holy See undoubtedly confers an added value to the quality and representativeness of its rules.[60] In any case, the major criticism addressed to the Convention is its very low rate of ratification, which diminishes its strength and pre-vents it from invoking any truly universal 'vocation'.

Quite different is the case of the relevant declarations adopted by Unesco and of their legal value.[61] They are considered as the expression of an international *opinio juris* that can foster the later creation of legal norms, thus contributing to the progressive development and advance-ment of international law. In this perspective, the Unesco declarations prepare the difficult transition from ethical values to legal rights through a gradual crystallisation of general standards into written rules. Providing "a universal framework of principles and procedures to guide States in the formulation of their legislations, policies or other instruments in the field of bioethics",[62] such *soft law* rules may in their turn influence the

---

diritti dell'uomo e la biomedicina: verso una bioetica europea?", 3 *Diritto pubblico com-parato ed europeo* (2001), pp. 1301–1311; Jochen Taupitz (ed.), *Das Menschenrechtsübereinkommen zur Biomedizin des Europarates – taugliches Vorbild für eine weltweit geltende Regelung? / The Convention on Human Rights and Biomedicine of the Council of Europe – a Suitable Model for World-Wide Regulation?* (Berlin-Heidelberg, 2002); Andorno, "The Oviedo Convention", *supra* note 46; Sjef J.K.M. Gevers, Ewoud H. Hondius and Joep H. Hubben (eds.), *Health Law, Human Rights and the Biomedicine Convention* (Leiden, 2005); Héctor Gros Espiell, Jean Michaud, Gérard Teboul (eds.), *La Convention sur les Droits de l'Homme et la Biomédecine. Analyses et commentaires* (Paris, 2009); Ilja R. Pavone, *La Convenzione europea sulla biomedicina* (Milano, 2009).

[59] Susan Millns, "Consolidating Bio-rights in Europe", in *Biotechnologies, supra* note 50, pp. 71–84, at 78; see also Elaine Gadd, "The Global Significance of the Convention on Human Rights and Biomedicine", in *Health Law, Human Rights and the Biomedicine Convention, supra* note 58, pp. 35–46; Boschiero, "Le biotecnologie", *supra* note 11, at 51.

[60] Maljean-Dubois, "Bioéthique", *supra* note 54, at 91–92.

[61] See Herman Nys, "Towards an International Treaty on Human Rights and Biomedicine? Some Reflections Inspired by UNESCO's Universal Declaration on Bioethics and Human Rights", 13 *European Journal of Health Law* (2006), pp. 5–8; Christian Byk, *Bioéthique et droit international. Autour de la Déclaration universelle sur la bioéthique et les droits de l'hommes* (Paris, 2007); Id., "The Universal Declaration on Bioethics and Human Rights: Bioethics, a Civilizing Utopia in the Age of Globalization?", in B.A. Hocking (ed.), *The Nexus of Law and Biology. New Ethical Challenges* (Farnham, 2009), pp. 175–190; Fabrizio Turoldo (ed.), *La globalizzazione della bioetica* (Padova, 2007). According to Ida, the Unesco Declaration on the Human Genome and Human Rights, though devoid of offi-cial legal force, "has a quasi-legal value" since it was approved by the Organisation's General Conference and later endorsed by the UN General Assembly (*supra* note 51, at 378).

[62] Article 2.*a* of the Universal Declaration on Bioethics and Human Rights.

production of legal norms at the national level. Therefore, although they do not immediately create justiciable rights, their influence on the conduct of States is not negligible.[63]

Notwithstanding some harsh criticism on the effectiveness of the results achieved,[64] the Unesco declarations represent the normative expression of those values that are considered common to humankind and hence worth of universal protection. They

> proclaim some basic principles and standards in the field of bioethics that have provided, and continue to provide, inspiration and guidance to States in decisions in this area. ... The norms they articulate appear to enjoy a broad consensus at the international level. They also seem to have become a standard of reference and a source of inspiration for legal or ethical rules to be established by States or by professional bodies throughout the world.[65]

According to Professor Maljean-Dubois it is necessary to assess the legal effects of these documents with a less formalistic approach, which may allow to appraise their normative value as extending beyond the mere role of pre-legal texts.[66] Her opinion is in line with the one expressed by the late Professor Héctor Gros Espiell, former Chairman of the Unesco Legal Committee, who stated that

> les déclarations proclamées par l'organe suprême d'une organisation intergouvernementale, plus particulièrement de la famille des Nations Unies – si elles sont adoptées dans certaines conditions ... – produisent

---

[63] See the observations of Professor Maljean-Dubois on the concept of 'infra-droit', a sort of 'pre-law' which fosters the difficult passage from ethics to law ("Bioéthique", *supra* note 54, at 86; see also Sandrine Maljean-Dubois, "Les timides développements d'un bio-droit mondial face aux rapides avancées des sciences de la vie", in *La société internationale*, *supra* note 53, pp. 13–32). Add also Christian Byk, "Le droit international de la « bioéthique » : « *jus gentium* » ou « *lex mercatoria* »?", 124 *Journal du Droit International* (1997), pp. 913–944, at 917. Compare also Roberto Andorno, "The Invaluable Role of Soft Law in the Development of Universal Norms in Bioethics", July 2007, available at http://www.unesco.de/1507.html; Id., "Human Dignity and Human Rights as a Common Ground for a Global Bioethics", 34 *Journal of Medicine and Philosophy* (2009), pp. 223–240, at 225–226.

[64] See e.g. Udo Schuklenk, "Defending the Indefensible. The UNESCO Declaration on Bioethics and Human Rights: A Reply to Levitt and Zwart", 7 *Bioethical Inquiry* (2010), pp. 83–88.

[65] Abdulqawi A. Yusuf, "The UNESCO Declarations on bioethics: emerging principles and standards of an 'international biolaw'?", in *Bioetica e biotecnologie*, *supra* note 11, pp. 129–139, at 131 ff., quotations from pp. 132 and 139.

[66] See Maljean-Dubois, "Bioéthique", *supra* note 54, at 89: "en rejetant une approche trop formaliste, force est de convenir que ces résolutions et déclarations ... n'ont pas seulement un rôle préparatoire à l'adoption de textes contraignants. Bien souvent, elles tiennent lieu de droit et s'auto-suffisent".

un effet juridique et deviennent sources de droits et d'obligations internationales.[67]

Thus, just like the Universal Declaration of Human Rights,[68] the Universal Declarations adopted by Unesco—first and foremost the Declaration on the Human Genome, which was also endorsed by the General Assembly of the United Nations[69]—set universally recognised standards and translate shared values into positive law.

This means that informed consent is by now a global bioethical standard translated into positive law. It enjoys robust consensus since there is a substantial convergence and complementarity of norms disseminated through formal and informal instruments that proclaim, uphold, repeat and detail the contents of this principle. The stratification of these norms has "gradually shaped social consciousness in the international community"[70] around this basic rule, which epitomizes the current generally accepted decision-making model in health care and embodies the essence of key concepts such as self-determination and autonomy, as well as integrity and inviolability of the human being.

In consideration of the above, not only can informed consent be considered a universally recognised imperative of bioethics, but also, legally speaking, it can be viewed as one of those principles imposed by the will of the international society[71] as expressed by its various actors and

---

[67] Héctor Gros Espiell, *Projet d'un instrument international pour la protection du genome humain*, quotation reported in Maljean-Dubois, "Bioéthique", *supra* note 54, at 90.

[68] *Universal Declaration of Human Rights*, adopted by General Assembly Resolution 217 (III), 10 December 1948. "The 50 years since the adoption of the Universal Declaration have seen the adoption of many international human rights instruments developing the principles and norms contained in the Declaration, and these have gained universal acceptance. Thus, the rights and freedoms proclaimed in the Universal Declaration are now recognized by those taking part in international relations as legally binding customary or treaty norms. Today, the Universal Declaration is one of the main sources of law and serves as a model that is widely employed by many countries for the elaboration of individual provisions of their constitutions and various laws and instruments relating to human rights." (Sub-Commission on Prevention of Discrimination and Protection of Minorities, *Working Paper on the Observance of human rights by States which are not parties to United Nations human rights conventions*, U.N. Doc. E/CN.4/Sub.2/1999/29, 15 June 1999, paras. 4–5).

[69] See Resolution 53/152 of 9 December 1998.

[70] See Pierre-Marie Dupuy, "The Impact of Legal Instruments Adopted by UNESCO on General International Law", in A. Yusuf (ed.), *Standard-Setting in UNESCO* (Paris, 2007), pp. 351–363, at 356.

[71] The doctrine of 'realism', according to which the general principles of international law are the product of the 'prevailing will' of the social body to which dominant States and less powerful ones contribute alike, was conceptualised in Italian scholarship by Rolando Quadri: *Lezioni di Diritto Internazionale* (Padova-Bologna, 1945–46) and *Diritto internazionale pubblico* (Napoli, V ed., 1968), especially pp. 25–33, and before him, to some extent, by Alberico Gentili and his conception of custom: see on this point Giorgio Badiali, *Il*

stakeholders in those institutionalised fora where international biolaw
has been emerging out of an interdisciplinary debate interfacing scientific
legitimacy and political legitimacy.[72] Moreover, contrary to what is usually
stated with regard to many biolaw rules, this principle is couched in clear
and plain terms, and since its content and scope have so far achieved an
appreciable degree of specification, it seems not to suffer from the aforementioned 'vagueness and minimalism' shortcomings.[73]

III. Informed Consent in International Human Rights Law

A. The "Filiation" of Informed Consent from Human Rights

Although we are used to consider informed consent as one of the core
principles of medical ethics transposed into national and international
biolaw, its filiation from international human rights law is quite evident.
Actually, there is a clear relationship of derivation between biomedical
law and human rights law: the most influential literature on the subject
insists on the concept of international biolaw texts being the 'natural
extension' of human rights instruments as applied to the life sciences and
biomedicine.[74] Moreover, according to a commonly shared scholarly view,

---

diritto di pace di Alberico Gentili (Fagnano Alto, 2010), pp. 29–30. This theory is similar to
that of the 'common consent of Nations' as expressed in Anglo-American scholarship: see
mainly Wilfred Jenks, *Law, Freedom and Welfare* (1963), Chapter 5: "The Will of the World
Community as the Basis of Obligation in International Law", pp. 83–100.

[72] See Bertrand Mathieu, *Génome humain et droits fondamentaux* (Paris, 2000), p. 15,
who speaks of ethics committees "dans lesquels le droit se prépare", such as those instituted by Unesco and the Council of Europe, as an "interface entre la légitimité scientifique
et la légitimité politique". Compare also Andorno, who defines the Universal Declaration
of 2005 as "a kind of compromise between a theoretical conceptualisation made by experts
and what is practically achievable given the political choices of governments" ("Global bioethics at UNESCO", *supra* note 56, at 151).

[73] It is not one of those principles formulated in a general and vague wording due to lack
of consensus, nor is it subject to different interpretations linked to multicultural
approaches; it is neither a pre-legal rule aimed solely at inspiring bioethical codes of best
practice nor a softly enunciated principle which has never been translated into hard law.
See, by contrast, the considerations made by Pierre-Marie Dupuy with regard to some principles governing biotechnologies ("State Responsibility", *supra* note 50, at 38–41).

[74] According to Professor Andorno, the Oviedo Convention can be regarded as the
"extension of human rights law in the biomedical field" ("Regulating Advance Directives at
the Council of Europe", in this book); see also Maljean-Dubois, "Bioéthique", *supra* note 54,
at 93; Boschiero, "Le biotecnologie", *supra* note 11, at 13, 15; Mathieu, "La bioéthique, ou
comment déroger", *supra* note 53, at 85. According to these Authors the Oviedo Convention
develops and concretizes in the field of biomedicine the principles of the European
Convention on Human Rights and other human rights instruments, while 'updating' the

it is most opportune and correct that biolaw be conveyed within the framework of human rights law in order that human rights and fundamental freedoms may find appropriate tools of legal protection from the challenges of progress.[75]

It is also interesting to note that, in the context of a more general discussion on the emergence of international biolaw, Professor Michelle Lenoir observed that well before becoming a new field of academic endeavour "la bioéthique apparaissait déjà en filigrane dans les grands instruments internationaux relatifs aux droits de l'homme".[76] In this respect, it is often pointed out that all major human rights treaties contain some guarantees relating to the protection of fundamental rights in patient care. Although only some of these conventions have been almost universally ratified, however they all set minimum standards that can be considered morally binding also on non-Party States. Moreover, the link between international human rights law and biomedical law is ever more apparent in the wording of the major biolaw instruments, which regularly refer to the key human rights acts and endorse them as foundational framework and cornerstones for 'supplements' of protection urged by the 'potential implications of scientific actions' and the need to shield the individual from any threat resulting from the developments in biology and medicine.[77]

---

catalogue of fundamental rights and freedoms with the guarantee of new basic rights which cannot be derogated from; the same is to be said with regard to the Unesco Universal Declaration on Bioethics and Human Rights, which recalls the principles of the United Nations Universal Declaration of Human Rights. See also Christian Byk, "Bioéthique et Convention européenne des droits de l'homme", in C.E. Pettiti, E. Décaux and P.H. Imbert (eds.), *La Convention européenne des droits de l'homme. Commentaire article par article* (Paris, 1995), pp. 101 ff.

[75] Adriana Loreti Beghè and Luca Marini, "Il riconoscimento e la tutela dei diritti fondamentali dell'uomo rilevanti in ambito biomedico", in A. Bompiani, A. Loreti Beghè, and L. Marini, *Bioetica e diritti dell'uomo nella prospettiva del diritto internazionale e comunitario* (Torino, 2001), Chapter II, p. 44; Andorno, "Biomedicine and international human rights", *supra* note 53, at 960; Boschiero, "Le biotecnologie", *supra* note 11, at 14.

[76] Lenoir, "Le droit international pénal de la bioéthique", *supra* note 11, at 407. In the same sense, see also Andorno, "The Oviedo Convention", *supra* note 46, at 133, where the Author acknowledges the fact that the essence of some principles enunciated by the Oviedo Convention were already framed in more general terms in previous human rights treaties.

[77] See the Explanatory Report to the Oviedo Convention, paras. 11–13. See also the Preambles to the Oviedo Convention and to the Unesco Universal Declarations, all 'solemnly recalling the attachment to the universal principles of human rights'.

1. *The Link with the Right to Physical Integrity: The Evolutive Interpretation of the Rights to Freedom from Torture, Inhuman or Degrading Treatment and to Respect for Private Life*

Informed consent is generally interpreted as part of the right to physical integrity. Although not specifically recognised in most human rights conventions, the right to bodily integrity is a well-established fundamental right protecting the universal values of the dignity and inviolability of the human being. It has been considered as a derivation of the rights to security of the person and to privacy, and above all of the right to be free from torture, and from cruel, inhuman and degrading treatment. In this sense, its first indirect sources in international human rights law are usually traced back to Article 5 of the Universal Declaration of Human Rights and Article 3 of the European Convention on Human Rights, both stating the prohibition of torture and of cruel, inhuman or degrading treatment.[78]

A specific reference to informed consent is to be found in Article 7 of the International Covenant on Civil and Political Rights, which, according to the Human Rights Committee, is aimed at protecting both the dignity and the physical and mental integrity of the individual.[79] This provision adds to the aforementioned proscription of torture the express ban on medical and scientific experimentations carried out without the free consent of the person concerned.[80] The importance of this specification lies in

---

[78] According to Annas and Grodin most physicians would never consider their actions as amounting to torture, however they point out that "it is when a doctor disregards a person's bodily integrity that torture and involuntary human experimentation become virtually indistinguishable" ("Medicine and Human Rights", *supra* note 13, at 9).

[79] *International Covenant on Civil and Political Rights*, adopted and opened for signature, ratification and accession by General Assembly Resolution 2200A (XXI), 16 December 1966, entered into force on 23 March 1976; CCPR, *General Comment No. 20: Replaces general comment 7 concerning prohibition of torture and cruel treatment or punishment (Art. 7)*, 10 March 1992.

[80] According to the Committee's interpretation, Article 7 allows no limitations or derogations and implies that the Parties to the Covenant have a legal duty to guarantee protection through legislative and other measures against the acts prohibited by this provision, "whether inflicted by people acting in their official capacity, outside their official capacity or in a private capacity". Moreover, as for the specific prohibition of non-consensual experimentations, the Committee argues that special protection is necessary with regard to persons not capable of giving valid consent, and in fact it recommends that "When there is doubt as to the ability of a person or a category of persons to give such consent, e.g. prisoners, the only experimental treatment compatible with article 7 would be treatment chosen as the most appropriate to meet the medical needs of the individual". See *General Comment No. 20*, paras. 2 and 7; Consideration of Reports Submitted by States Parties under Article 40 of the Covenant: Concluding Observations of the Human Rights Committee: United States of America, U.N. Doc. CCPR/C/USA/CO/3, 15 September 2006, para. 31.

the fact that not only does it explicit the link between physical integrity and informed consent, but it also confirms the fact that, although it is usually discussed in the context of protecting individuals from torture, the right to physical integrity extends well beyond that.[81]

The same formula used in Article 7 of the Covenant was reiterated in Article 15 of the Convention on the Rights of Persons with Disabilities, which however clearly spelt out the right to integrity of the person in Article 17 and also made express reference to informed consent in Article 25, para. *d*, in the context of the recognition of the right to non-discriminatory enjoyment of the right to health.[82]

Other relevant provisions, as contained in regional instruments, include Article 5, para. 1, of the American Convention on Human Rights, protecting the right to physical, mental and moral integrity,[83] as well as Article 4 of the African Charter on Human and Peoples' Rights, affirming the inviolability of human beings and their entitlement to respect for their life and integrity of the person.[84] It is also worth mentioning the Protocol to the African Charter on Human and Peoples' Rights on the Rights of Women in Africa,[85] which states at Article 4, para. 1, that every woman is entitled to respect for life and integrity of her person, while at para. 2.*h* it mandates States Parties to take appropriate and effective measures to "prohibit all medical or scientific experiments on women without their informed consent".[86]

At the European level, the most salient expression of the intertwining between the right to physical integrity and informed consent is provided

---

[81] Unfortunately, there is actually no significant case law by the Human Rights Committee concerning violations of Article 7 for imposition of compulsory medication or experiments. Consult for example the SIM database provided by The Netherlands Institute of Human Rights (Utrecht School of Law), available at http://sim.law.uu.nl/SIM/Dochome.nsf?Open.

[82] Convention on the Rights of Persons with Disabilities, New York, 13 December 2006, entered into force on 3 May 2008.

[83] American Convention on Human Rights, San José, 22 November 1969, entered into force on 18 July 1978.

[84] African (Banjul) Charter on Human and Peoples' Rights, Nairobi, 27 June 1981, entered into force on 21 October 1986.

[85] Protocol to the African Charter on Human and Peoples' Rights on the Rights of Women in Africa, Maputo, 11 July 2003, entered into force on 25 November 2005.

[86] It should be added that this protection had been earlier invoked by the Committee on the Elimination of Discrimination against Women in its General Recommendation No. 24 of 1999 concerning action by the States parties to the Convention on the Elimination of All Forms of Discrimination against Women, where the Committee stated that States Parties had to "Require all health services to be consistent with the human rights of women, including the rights to autonomy, privacy, confidentiality, informed consent and choice" (para. 31, al. *e*).

by Article 3 of the Charter of Fundamental Rights of the European Union, where informed consent is listed on top of the core principles of biomedical law, including the prohibitions of selective eugenetic practices, of making the human body a source of financial gain, and of reproductive cloning of the human being (and it should be noted that this time the filiation relationship is inverse, since the EU Charter draws on international biolaw, especially on the Oviedo Convention).[87] In this respect, it will be interesting to appraise to what extent the new binding value of the Charter will enable the Court of Justice of the European Union to develop a new bioethically-oriented, or bioethics-sensitive jurisprudence. For the moment, it is worth recalling that, so long, where needed respect for informed consent was guaranteed at European Union level by means of reference to the right to physical integrity and with respect to the relevant provisions of the European Convention on Human Rights, especially Article 8. For example, in the judgment delivered by the then Court of First Instance (today General Court) in the case *X. v. Commission of the European Communities*, which concerned pre-recruitment medical examination, the Court stated in principle that "the taking of blood in order to investigate the possible presence of HIV antibodies constitutes interference with the physical integrity of the person concerned and can be carried out on a candidate only with his informed consent". On appeal the Court of Justice justified the refusal to undergo an AIDS screening test in light of the right to respect for private life as protected by Article 8 of the European Convention and the common constitutional traditions of Member States. Declaring that "a person's refusal must be respected in its entirety", the Court concluded that medical officers are precluded from carrying out any test liable to point to the existence of the illness in respect of which the person has refused disclosure.[88]

The approach endorsed by the EU Courts was perfectly in line with the most relevant Strasbourg case law,[89] which has been construing the imposition of non-consensual medical treatment or testing as a violation of

---

[87] See Luca Marini, *Il diritto internazionale e comunitario della bioetica* (Torino, 2006), pp. 65, 70.

[88] Judgment of the Court of First Instance of 18 September 1992, Joined Case T-121/89 and T-13/90, *X. v. Commission of the European Communities*, ECR 1992, p. II-2195, para. 58; Judgment of the Court of Justice of 5 October 1994, Case C-404/92P, *X. v. Commission of the European Communities*, ECR 1994, p. I-4737, para. 23.

[89] See the survey carried out by the Research Division of the European Court of Human Rights in its working document on *Bioethics and the case-law of the ECHR*, available at http://www.coe.int/t/dg3/healthbioethic/texts_and_documents/Bioethics_and_the_case -law_of_the_Court.pdf.

both Article 3 and Article 8 of the Convention, as both encompassing the right to physical and mental integrity[90] by way of their extensive and dynamic interpretation.[91] Of course, the most significant consequence of these two different constructions lies in the admissibility of limitations, provided that Article 3 is absolutely non-derogable while Article 8 allows limitations and interferences "in accordance with the law and ... necessary in a democratic society in the interests of national security, public safety or the economic well-being of the country, for the prevention of disorder or crime, for the protection of health or morals, or for the protection of the rights and freedoms of others".[92]

Turning to Strasbourg jurisprudence, the first ruling linking informed consent to the prohibition of inhuman and degrading treatment was made by the European Commission in the case of *X v. Denmark*, when it stated that in principle "medical treatment of an experimental character and without the consent of the person involved may under certain circumstances be regarded as prohibited by Article 3 of the Convention".[93] The test is however very strict, since compulsory experimentation or treatment must amount to an ill-treatment attaining a minimum level of severity, consisting in premeditated action causing either actual bodily injury or intense physical and mental suffering or being capable of

---

[90] See, for example, *X and Y v. the Netherlands*, Judgment of 26 March 1985, Series A no. 91, para. 22.

[91] On the issue of evolutive interpretation, see especially Malgosia Fitzmaurice, "Dynamic (Evolutive) Interpretation of Treaties, Part I", 21 *Hague Yearbook of International Law* (2008), pp. 101–153; Id., "Dynamic (Evolutive) Interpretation of Treaties, Part II", 22 *Hague Yearbook of International Law* (2009), pp. 3–31.

[92] In *Juhke v. Turkey* (no. 52515/99, 13 May 2008, para. 72), the Court noted that "Even where it is not motivated by reasons of medical necessity, Articles 3 and 8 of the Convention do not as such prohibit recourse to a medical procedure in defiance of the will of a suspect in order to obtain from him or her evidence of his or her involvement in the commission of a criminal offence. However, any recourse to a forcible medical intervention in order to obtain evidence of a crime must be convincingly justified on the facts of a particular case and the manner in which a person is subjected to a forcible medical procedure must not exceed the minimum level of severity prescribed by the Court's case-law under Article 3 of the Convention (see *Jalloh v. Germany* [GC], no. 54810/00, §§ 70–71, ECHR 2006-...)."

[93] ECHR, *X. v. Denmark*, no. 9974/82, Commission decision of 2 March 1983, DR 32, p. 282. Also the European Committee for the Prevention of Torture and Inhuman or Degrading Treatment or Punishment has repeatedly stressed that "patients should, in principle, be placed in a position to give their free and informed written consent to treatment. Every competent patient, whether voluntary or involuntary, should be given the opportunity to refuse treatment or any other medical intervention. Any derogation from this fundamental principle should be based upon law and only relate to clearly and strictly defined exceptional circumstances" (see at http://www.cpt.coe.int/en/hudoc-cpt.htm).

humiliating and debasing the person concerned and possibly breaking their physical or moral resistance.

In a different perspective, both the Commission and the Court have also developed a consistent case law on Article 8 as embracing the right to be free from non-consensual medical treatment or examination, holding that "a compulsory medical intervention, even if it is of minor importance",[94] as well as the imposition of a medical examination, constitute an interference with the right to private life.[95]

The Court has also had occasion to distinguish between situations concerning competent adults and minors (be they mentally disabled or not), always highlighting the importance of respect for informed consent consistently with internationally agreed standards (the reference texts being the Oviedo Convention and the Universal Declaration on Bioethics and Human Rights). For example, in *Pretty v. UK*, a case concerning assisted suicide, the Court said that "the imposition of medical treatment, without the consent of a mentally competent adult patient, would interfere with a person's physical integrity in a manner capable of engaging the rights protected under article 8 § 1of the Convention".[96] In *Glass v. UK*, a case dealing with the issue of withdrawal of consent and possible derogations in situations of emergency, the Court considered that the decision to impose treatment on a severely handicapped child in defiance of his mother's (acting as legal proxy) objections gave rise to an interference with the child's right to respect for his private life, and in particular his right to physical integrity.[97] Recently, in the case of *M.A.K. and R.K. v. UK*, the Court found the same kind of violation of a minor's rights due to the taking of blood samples and photographs without parental consent.[98]

One last consideration is that the Court has also further expanded on the 'informed consent limb' of the right to privacy, including in it the duty of States "to adopt the necessary regulatory measures to ensure that doctors consider the foreseeable consequences of the planned medical

---

[94] See, for example, ECHR, *X v. Austria*, no. 8278/78, Commission decision of 13 December 1979, DR 18, p. 155; *Acmanne and Others v. Belgium*, no. 10435/83, Commission decision of 10 December 1984, DR 40, p. 254.

[95] ECtHR, *Y.F. v. Turkey*, no. 24209/94, Judgment of 22 July 2003, ECHR 2003-IX, para. 33; *Juhnke v. Turkey*, *supra* note 92, para. 71.

[96] ECtHR, *Pretty v. The United Kingdom*, no. 2346/02, Judgment of 29 April 2002, ECHR 2002-III, para. 63.

[97] ECtHR, *Glass v. The United Kingdom*, no. 61827/00, Judgment of 9 March 2004, ECHR 2004-II, para. 70.

[98] ECtHR, *M.A.K. e RK v. The United Kingdom*, nos. 45901/05 and 40146/06, Judgment of 23 March 2010, para. 75.

procedure on their patients' physical integrity and to inform patients of these beforehand in such a way that they are able to give informed consent." The Court inferred this duty from a consideration of the importance of having access to information concerning health-related risks, hence concluding that "if a foreseeable risk ... materialises without the patient having been duly informed in advance by doctors, and if ... those doctors work in a public hospital, the State Party concerned may be directly liable under Article 8 for this lack of information".[99]

2. The Link with the Right to Health: Respect for Informed Consent as Being Instrumental to the Fulfilment of Right to Health Obligations

Informed consent is also considered an integral part of the right to health as protected by several human rights treaties.[100]

According to the Committee's General Comment on Article 12 of the Covenant on Economic Social and Cultural Rights, the right to health "contains both freedoms and entitlements. The freedoms include the right to control one's health and body ... and the right to be free from interference, such as the right to be free from torture, non-consensual medical treatment and experimentation".[101]

Building on the Committee's interpretation of Article 12, the former UN Special Rapporteur on the right to health, Paul Hunt, observed in his Report of 2005 that although the issue of informed consent

---

[99] ECtHR, *Trocellier v. France*, no. 75725/01, Decision on admissibility of 5 October 2006, ECHR 2006-XIV, para. 4.

[100] Réné-Jean Dupuy (ed.), *The Right to Health as a Human Right* (Alphen aan den Rijn, 1979); Virginia A. Leary, "The Right to Health in International Human Rights Law", 1 *Health and Human Rights* (1994), pp. 24–56; Aart Hendriks, "The Right to Health in National and International Jurisprudence", 5 *European Journal of Health Law* (1998), pp. 389–408; Brigit C.A. Toebes, *The Right to Health as a Human Right in International Law* (Antwerpen, 1999); Stefania Negri, "Emergenze sanitarie e diritto internazionale: il paradigma salute-diritti umani e la strategia globale di lotta alle pandemie ed al bioterrorismo", in *Scritti in onore di Vincenzo Starace* (Napoli, 2008), pp. 571–605; Id., "Saúde e direito internacional: algumas reflexões sobre a afirmação tardia de um direito fundamental", 24 *Boletim da Saúde* (2010), pp. 63–74; Eibe Riedel, "The International Protection of the Right to Health", in R. Wolfrum et al. (eds.), *Encyclopedia of Public International Law* (Heidelberg, 2008); OHCHR-WHO, *The Right to Health*, Human Rights Fact Sheet No. 31 (Geneva, 2008); Mary Robinson and Andrew Clapham (eds.), *Realizing the Right to Health* (Zurich, 2009).

[101] International Covenant on Economic, Social and Cultural Rights, adopted by General Assembly Resolution 2200A (XXI) of 16 December 1966, entered into force on 3 January 1976; CESCR, *General Comment No. 14 (2000) on the right to the highest attainable standard of health (article 12 of the International Covenant on Economic, Social and Cultural Rights)*, U.N. Doc. E/C.12/2000/4, 11 August 2000, para. 8. Another important element is access to

is often considered in relation to the right to liberty and security of the person, as well as the prohibition against inhuman and degrading treatment, it is less frequently considered in the context of the right to health. However, consent to treatment is intimately connected with a vital element of the right to health: the freedom to control one's health and body.[102]

Professor Hunt's call for an "urgent reconsideration [of that issue] with a view to better protecting, at the international and national levels, the right to informed consent" and for strict respect for "procedural safeguards protecting the right to informed consent",[103] prompted his successor, Anand Grover, to carry out an in-depth analysis of the evolution and the main components of informed consent, which he discussed in a report specifically dedicated to it.

The 2009 Report is particularly interesting because it represents an important attempt to systematise informed consent from an international viewpoint. In this perspective, the Special Rapporteur first provided his definition of informed consent, balancing an individual's right to participate in decision-making with the relevant obligations stemming from it, and stating that it "is not mere acceptance of a medical intervention, but a voluntary and sufficiently informed decision, protecting the right of the patient to be involved in medical decision-making, and assigning associated duties and obligations to health-care providers."[104] He then totally embraced the view that informed consent to treatment is a cornerstone of the right to health, stating that

> Guaranteeing informed consent *is fundamental to achieving the enjoyment of the right to health* through practices, policies and research that are respectful of autonomy, self-determination and human dignity. An enabling environment that prioritizes informed consent links counselling, testing and treatment, creating an effective voluntary health-care continuum. *Safeguarding informed consent along the health-care continuum is an obligation placed on States and third parties engaged in respecting, promoting and fulfilling the right to health.*[105]

As in the passage above and throughout the whole Report, the Special Rapporteur mainly focused on the obligatory aspects linked to informed consent, addressing the relevant duties incumbent on States in the

---

health-related information for health decision-making (paras. 21–23) since information accessibility is a specific aspect of one of the four cornerstone elements of the right to health, namely availability, accessibility, acceptability, quality (para. 12).

[102] *Report 2005, supra* note 35, para. 87.
[103] Ibid., para. 90.
[104] *Report 2009, supra* note 6, para. 9.
[105] Ibid., summary, p. 2 (emphasis added).

perspective of fulfilling the obligation to protect the right to health.[106] This approach is consistent with the existence of indirect references to the rule of informed consent in the definition of State obligations stemming from Article 12 of the Covenant, according to the traditional tripartite typology (to respect, protect, fulfil) employed in the language of the Committee as well as in the relevant scholarship.[107] In this respect, it is interesting to note that in General Comment No. 14 the Committee explained that the

> obligations to respect include a State's obligation to refrain ... from applying coercive medical treatments, unless on an exceptional basis for the treatment of mental illness or the prevention and control of communicable diseases. Such exceptional cases should be subject to specific and restrictive conditions, respecting best practices and applicable international standards ... In addition, States should refrain from ... censoring, withholding or intentionally misrepresenting health-related information ... as well as from preventing people's participation in health-related matters. ...
>
> Obligations to *protect* include, *inter alia*, the duties of States ... to prevent third parties from coercing women to undergo traditional practices, e.g. female genital mutilation ... States should also ensure that third parties do not limit people's access to health-related information and services.
>
> ...
>
> The obligation to *fulfil* (*promote*) the right to health requires States to undertake actions that create, maintain and restore the health of the population. Such obligations include: ...(iv) supporting people in making informed choices about their health.[108]

This approach was recently upheld in a resolution adopted by the Human Rights Council, where all States were for the first time invited to

---

[106] Ibid., paras. 5, 18.

[107] The tripartite typology of State obligations was originally introduced by Henry Shue (see *Basic Rights: Subsistence, Affluence and U.S. Foreign Policy*, 2nd ed., Princeton, 1996) and later proposed in its present formulation by Asbjorn Eide acting as Special Rapporteur to the UN Sub-Commission on Human Rights: *The Right to Food as a Human Right*, 7 July 1987, E/CN.4/Sub.2/1987/23. A detailed report of this evolution is made by María Magdalena Sepulveda, *The Nature of the Obligations under the International Covenant on Economic, Social and Cultural Rights* (Antwerp, 2003), Chapter V. Despite its being questioned as the most appropriate tool for advancing the conceptual clarification of economic, social and cultural rights (see Ida Elisabeth Koch, "Dichotomies, Trichotomies or Waves of Duties?", 5 *Human Rights Law Review* n. 1 (2005), 81–103), the 'respect, protect and fulfil' paradigm is considered by the former Special Rapporteur on the right to health, Paul Hunt, especially useful as a way of sharpening legal analysis of this right (*The right of everyone to the enjoyment of the highest attainable standard of physical and mental health*, Report of the Special Rapporteur, Paul Hunt, U.N. Doc. E/CN.4/2004/49, 16 February 2004, para. 43; *Report 2005, supra* note 35, para. 47).

[108] *General Comment No. 14, supra* note 101, paras. 34, 35 and 37.

"safeguard informed consent within the health counselling, testing and treatment continuum, including in clinical practice, public health and medical research, as a critical element of the right of everyone to the enjoyment of the highest attainable standard of physical and mental health".[109]

Since no further guidance can be drawn on this subject from international jurisprudence—given the paucity of case law concerning the interpretation and application of conventional norms protecting the right to health at both the universal and the regional level[110]—it is remarkable that the stance taken within the United Nations, as emerged from the documents examined so far, tends to emphasise the nature of informed consent as an ancillary element of the fundamental right to health, and clearly suggests that respect for informed consent is not an obligation *per se*, but only part of a more general duty to guarantee the enjoyment of that right.

B. *Is There an International Human Right to Informed Consent?*

1. *The Legal Qualification of Informed Consent*

It is interesting to note that there is apparently no unequivocal consensus in international instruments and scholarship on the legal qualification of informed consent.

On the one hand, in legal literature it is quite frequent to read that informed consent is a 'requirement' that protects the patients' fundamental rights to integrity and self-determination—of which it is also defined as a 'corollary'[111]—and that such 'requirement' is based on the principles of 'respect for persons' and 'respect for human dignity'.[112] It is also very often defined as a general and basic principle of biomedical law,[113] while

---

[109] See *supra* note 6.

[110] This is mainly due, as it is well-known, to the still current lack of jurisdiction of the ESCR Committee and to the lack of competence *ratione materiae* of both the Interamerican Commission of Human Rights and of the Strasbourg Court.

[111] Boschiero, "Le biotecnologie", *supra* note 11, at 14.

[112] Kollek, "Article 6", *supra* note 8, at 126. Similarly, see Millns, who argues that "fundamental bio-rights and freedoms are to be respected *through the provisions governing the requirement to obtain an individual's free and informed consent* to medical interventions" ("Consolidating Bio-rights", *supra* note 59, at 79) and again she speaks of "the general consent requirements imposed by articles 5 and 6" (at 79–80), however, when dealing with the Charter of Fundamental Rights of the European Union she recognises free and informed consent as one of the four basic principles provided by Article 3 adding that the "remit of these is striking in its overlap with that of the principles enshrined in the Biomedicine Convention" (at 80–81).

[113] See for instance Maljean-Dubois, "Bioéthique", *supra* note 54, at 94–95; Marini, *Il diritto internazionale, supra* note 87, at 69, 328; Boschiero, "Le biotecnologie", *supra* note 11,

sometimes it is referred to as a principle and a right at a time.[114] But it also happens that it is not qualified at all.[115]

On the other hand, the textual analysis of international biolaw instruments does not shed any clearer light on this.

The Oviedo Convention, the first binding instrument to address the issue of consent in a detailed fashion, does not provide any specific legal qualification of informed consent. This vague approach is consistently adopted also in its Explanatory Report, save in one single case, where consent is defined as the "general principle in Article 5". Throughout the Explanatory Report, consent is instead referred to as a "general rule" that affirms at the international level an "already well-established rule", a "rule [that] makes clear patients' autonomy". By contrast, some specific elements of it are clearly defined as individual rights, such as 'the patient's right to information' and 'the right to withdraw consent'.[116]

The Universal Declarations issued by Unesco do not seem to be of much more help either, since they regulate consent under the rubric of both 'rights of the persons concerned' and 'principles'.[117] However, some guidance is offered by the Explanatory Memorandum on the Preliminary Draft Declaration on Bioethics and Human Rights, which makes it clear that informed consent is one of those ethical guiding principles that are directly related to human dignity, together with respect for human rights and fundamental freedoms, benefit and harm, autonomy and confidentiality.[118]

---

at 51. Professor Andorno stresses the fact that in the Oviedo Convention informed consent is "required for the first time as a general principle for any biomedical intervention" ("The Oviedo Convention", *supra* note 46, at 136, 138).

[114] Compare Antonello Tancredi, "Genetica umana ed altre biotecnologie nel diritto comunitario ed europeo", in *Ordine internazionale e valori etici*, *supra* note 51, pp. 381–411, who observes that the 'principle' is considered the basis of the doctor-patient relationship while, illustrating the relevant European case-law, he refers to it as the 'right in question' (at 397).

[115] See e.g. Bompiani, Loreti Beghé and Marini, who define informed consent (as well as dissent), as the "expression" of the principles of autonomy and self-determination, while refusal of futile therapies is instead construed as a "right" (*Bioetica e diritti dell'uomo*, *supra* note 75, at 13).

[116] See the Explanatory Report to the Oviedo Convention, especially paras. 34, 40, 48, 101 and 136.

[117] See, respectively, Article 5 of the Declaration on the Human Genome and Human Rights and Article 6 of the Declaration on Bioethics and Human Rights. However, Article 9 of the former defined consent as a principle.

[118] Unesco, Explanatory Memorandum on the Elaboration of the Preliminary Draft Declaration on Universal Norms on Bioethics, SHS/EST/05/CONF.203/4, 24 February 2005, para. 37.

Also moving to other relevant soft law acts, it is worthy of note that the WMA Lisbon Declaration proclaims, within the right to self-determination, "the right to give or withhold consent to any diagnostic procedure or therapy", while the WMA Declaration of Helsinki, though expanding on consent in medical research, only provides that "the potential subject must be informed of the right to refuse to participate in the study or to withdraw consent to participate".[119] On the contrary, the European Charter on Patients' Rights, inspired by the EU Charter of Fundamental Rights, proclaims a 'right to consent'.[120]

Even the views of the UN Special Rapporteurs on the right to health are not perfectly coincident. In fact, while Professor Hunt straightly referred to a 'right to informed consent' and urged the devising of measures for a better protection of this right,[121] the 2009 Report seems to embrace a less clear-cut position, setting as its objective the analysis of "the fundamental role that informed consent plays in respecting, protecting and fulfilling the right to health, discussing specifically the areas of clinical practice, public health and medical research".[122] As a matter of fact, the Rapporteur mentions a right to consent a few times: referring to legal capacity, which confers on adults "the right to consent to, refuse or choose an alternative medical intervention"; in respect to "the need for special protections guaranteeing a woman's right to informed consent" especially in the field of sexual and reproductive health; concerning the fact that "the right to consent to treatment also includes the right to refuse treatment"; and with reference to those regional instruments that he considers to be the legal sources of such a right (i.e. the Oviedo Convention and its Additional Protocol on Biomedical Research, the EU Charter and the EU Directive on Clinical Trials).[123] This notwithstanding, the whole Report, as anticipated above, is much more inspired by the idea that informed consent is only an integral part of the right to health and an element instrumental to the successful protection of a number of other relevant fundamental rights. This conclusion seems corroborated by the several passages of the Report where emphasis is laid on the fact that informed consent "promotes" patients autonomy, bodily integrity and well-being and that safeguarding an individual's "ability" to exercise informed consent in health is

---

[119] See, respectively, para. 3*b* and para. 24.
[120] Active Citizenship Network, *Europe Charter on Patients' Rights*, Rome, November 2002, Article 4.
[121] See *supra* note 103 and corresponding text.
[122] See *Report 2009*, *supra* note 6, para. 5.
[123] Ibid., paras. 10, 20, 28, and 57.

fundamental to ensuring full enjoyment of those health-related basic rights such as the rights to self-determination, freedom from discrimination, freedom from non-consensual experimentation, security and dignity of the human person, recognition before the law, freedom of thought and expression and reproductive self-determination.[124] These statements convey the idea that informed consent should be respected as a 'feature' of other fundamental rights and inasmuch as it guarantees a better protection of the right to health, without itself enjoying almost any independent status. Even the conclusions drawn by the Rapporteur do not hint to the need to enhance and reinforce protection of an individual 'right to consent'; rather, emphasis is placed on the considerations that "guaranteeing informed consent is a fundamental dimension of the right to health" and that "safeguarding informed consent along the health-care continuum is an obligation placed on States and third parties engaged in respecting, promoting and fulfilling the right to health", so that it is recommended that national and international bodies "emphasize the importance of informed consent as a fundamental aspect of the right to health in relevant policy and practice" and "that States consider whether they are meeting their obligations to safeguard informed consent as a critical element of the right to health".[125]

All this considered, a contribution to the ongoing debate on the nature and scope of informed consent would require that a crucial point be discussed: is there an internationally protected autonomous right to informed consent?

While a 'right to informed consent' is by now well-established in both domestic law and jurisprudence, a positive and clear-cut answer is rarely to be found in the literature devoted to international biolaw. One such influential assertion is made by Professor Nerina Boschiero, who states that the 'right to express an informed consent' is codified in the Universal Declaration on Bioethics and Human Rights.[126] In the same vein, Article 5 of the Oviedo Convention has been interpreted as an enunciation of the 'right of the patient to give his free and informed consent' by the researchers of the Leuven Centre for Biomedical Ethics and Law working at the EuroGentest Project under the direction of Professor Herman Nys.[127]

---

[124] Ibid., paras. 9, 19, 43.

[125] Ibid., paras. 7, 93–94.

[126] Boschiero, "Le biotecnologie", *supra* note 11, at 53.

[127] See   at   http://europatientrights.eu/biomedicine_convention/biomedicine _convention_patient_rights.html.

However, such clear positions are not at all common and scholars tend to use more vaguely worded expressions.

This said, the argument is here made that under the present status of international law there is evidence to support the view that a human right to informed consent has definitely emerged from the convergence of international human rights law and international biolaw over the same key objective: the protection of dignity and of the inviolability of the human being. In this perspective it is one of those new biorights—or human rights of fourth generation—that are progressively borne out of the intersection of bioethics and law, in order to protect, to say it with the philosopher Norberto Bobbio, the freedom of the individual from the attacks deriving from technological progress and the enhanced power of men to dominate over the nature and other men.[128]

To make the point on its content and scope as illustrated in the paragraphs above, it is clear that the right to informed consent is pivotal in regulating the patient-doctor relationship. In essence, the substantive limb of the right entitles all competent adults to express their free and informed consent or refusal to any medical or scientific intervention, be it performed for preventive care, diagnosis, treatment, rehabilitation, research, etc., and prohibits that any such intervention be carried out in the absence of assent by the person concerned or, where applicable, by a substitute decision-maker provided by law (e.g. legal representative or proxy). The procedural limb of the right prescribes that all health professionals and workers provide the necessary information and seek consent before acting, and that consent be validly expressed according to the forms required by law and medical practice.

Moreover, despite its robust rooting in other basic human rights, the right to informed consent has come to live of its own life and can be considered sufficiently independent of them, of which it constitutes an associate right. In effect, the scope of informed consent is broader and is neither completely linked to the right to health (not only is there a right to assent to or refuse medical treatment, but also a right to consent to organs and tissue removal and donation or to participation in non-therapeutic experimentations, both being independent of any healing activity of direct benefit to the person concerned) nor to the right to bodily integrity (since not all interventions impinge on mental and physical integrity). As it is suggested below, the close link to other human rights has been

---

[128] Norberto Bobbio, *L'età dei diritti* (3rd ed., Torino, 1997), p. xv.

emphasised and elucidated in international case law—especially by the Strasbourg Court who has addressed the issue of informed consent through the lens of physical integrity and privacy—to provide this right with judicial protection in the absence of any specific international protective machinery devised by the relevant instruments of international biomedical law.

2. *Enforceability, Accountability and Redress*

The effectiveness of the asserted right to informed consent depends first and foremost on its enforceability, on the possibility to punish relevant violations amounting to a crime and on appropriate guarantees of redress.

While it is indubitable that at national level this right is justiciable before both civil and criminal courts—inasmuch as unlawful derogations from it entitle the patient, their personal representative, or any interested person to appeal to a judicial or other independent authority in order that it scrutinise the legitimacy of any involuntary treatment performed[129]—the situation at the international level is rather different.

Scholars have often commented negatively on the lack of appropriate jurisdictional guarantees associated to the rights of fourth generation. Many share the view that it is the national judge who is best entitled to satisfy the need for justiciability of bioethical rights, especially through the application of those general guiding principles and minimum standards set at the international level, which may also lend help in the evolutive or extensive interpretation of domestic rules with a view to adapting them to new and previously unforeseen bioethical problems.[130]

But are biorights effectively devoid of international judicial protection?

Chapter VIII of the Oviedo Convention articulates the obligations incumbent on States Parties to guarantee a right to justice through the provision of an appropriate judicial protection for unlawful infringements and threats of infringement of the rights and principles set therein (Article 23), the adoption of sanctioning measures (Article 25) and the

---

[129] It has also been contended that Articles 5 to 9 of the Oviedo Convention have direct effect in domestic legal orders, so that they can be the object of proceedings before national courts: compare Andorno, "The Oviedo Convention", *supra* note 46, at 136; Nys, "The European Convention", *supra* note 58; Boschiero, "Le biotecnologie", *supra* note 11, at 15.

[130] See on this point especially Marini, *Il diritto internazionale*, *supra* note 87, at 29, and 56–57; Tancredi, "Genetica umana", *supra* note 114, at 408–409; Maljean-Dubois, "Bioéthique", *supra* note 54, at 92.

effective guarantee of redress (Article 24). While the Convention establishes a monitoring system based on State reports, no international protective machinery is devised and no litigation before the Strasbourg Court
is allowed, unless the jurisdiction of this Court is triggered because the
violation of the Oviedo Convention also amounts to a breach of one of the
rights protected under the European Convention on Human Rights.[131]

Actually, as illustrated above, the wealth of European case law concerning infringements of the right to informed consent under the rubric of
Articles 3 and 8 violations shows that, albeit indirectly, biorights such as
the one in question can indeed enjoy judicial protection before international human rights courts. Moreover, it has been observed that the
Strasbourg Court is increasingly making reference to the Oviedo
Convention even in cases where the respondent State is not a Party to it,[132]
so that the Biomedicine Convention has become an important reference
text[133] offering authoritative guidance on those internationally-shared
standards, principles and rights that can help interpreting the European
Convention on Human Rights in harmony with international biolaw and
in line with the new challenges posed by the scientific progress.[134]

The same paradigm may apply at the universal level, but it is not easy to
appraise the real chances of quasi-jurisdictional protection offered by
treaty-based bodies given the current lack of competence of the Economic,
Social and Cultural Rights Committee to receive and consider individual
communications concerning Article 12 of the Covenant (due to the fact

---

[131] Article 29 of the Oviedo Convention only confers on the European Court of Human
Rights the competence to deliver advisory opinions on general legal questions concerning
the interpretation of the Convention independently of any judicial proceedings pending
before national courts (see also the Explanatory Report, paras. 164–165). This advisory
competence has raised criticism and perplexities as to its scope and 'side effects': see
Tancredi, "Genetica umana", *supra* note 114, at 408.

[132] This happened for example in the following cases brought against the United
Kingdom: *Glass*, *supra* note 97, para. 58, *M.A.K. and R.K.*, *supra* note 98, para. 31. On the
reference to the Oviedo Convention and the Unesco Universal Declaration in the limited
context of informed consent, see the survey of Strasbourg case law carried out by Thérèse
Murphy and Gearóid Cuinn, "Works in Progress: New Technologies and the European
Court of Human Rights", 10 *Human Rights Law Review* (2010), pp. 601–638, at 612.

[133] See the long-sighted reflections made by Professor Roscam Abbing on the prospective value of the Convention in Strasbourg case law in "The Convention on Human Rights",
supra note 58, at 380.

[134] The issue of the evolutive interpretation of the European Convention in light of the
developments of international law and case-law, as registered even beyond the European
system, was discussed to some extent in Stefania Negri, "Interpreting the European
Convention on Human Rights in Harmony with International Law and Jurisprudence:
What Lessons from *Öcalan v. Turkey*?", in 4 *The Global Community. Yearbook of International
Law and Jurisprudence 2004* (2005), pp. 243–291.

that its Optional Protocol is not yet in force), and the scarcity of relevant case law developed so far by the Human Rights Committee with regard to Article 7 of the Covenant on Civil and Political Rights. In this regard, it should be noted that the potential role of the Human Rights Committee is yet unexpressed, since it could ascertain violations of the right to informed consent (amounting to a violation of the right to physical integrity and of the prohibition of non-consensual experimentation) as committed by any health-care provider, be it an agent of the State or a private individual or entity, which is particularly important in the perspective of guaranteeing effective respect for this right also in case of private health service delivery and in case of privatisation of the public health sector.[135]

In conclusion, it is evident that much has still to be done to achieve an appropriate protection of biorights at the international level in order to enhance their effectiveness as human rights. The need for such improvement was also urged by the UN Special Rapporteur on the right to health:

> Monitoring mechanisms to identify situations compromising informed consent within the health-care continuum need to be established. Mechanisms for redress should be made available at the local, regional and international levels to ensure that those whose actions threaten human dignity and autonomy in the health-care setting are held accountable for their actions and further violations are prevented.[136]

Such recommendations add new impetus to the views of those scholars who have already addressed criticism over the shortcomings of the

---

[135] In General Comment No. 31, the Human Rights Committee stated that "The article 2, paragraph 1, obligations are binding on States [Parties] and do not, as such, have direct horizontal effect as a matter of international law. The Covenant cannot be viewed as a substitute for domestic criminal or civil law. However the positive obligations on States Parties to ensure Covenant rights will only be fully discharged if individuals are protected by the State, *not just against violations of Covenant rights by its agents, but also against acts committed by private persons or entities that would impair the enjoyment of Covenant rights in so far as they are amenable to application between private persons or entities*. There may be circumstances in which a failure to ensure Covenant rights as required by article 2 would give rise to violations by States Parties of those rights, as a result of States Parties' permitting or failing to take appropriate measures or to exercise due diligence to prevent, punish, investigate or redress the harm caused by such acts by private persons or entities. ... The Covenant itself envisages in some articles certain areas where there are positive obligations on States Parties to address the activities of private persons or entities. ... *It is also implicit in article 7 that States Parties have to take positive measures to ensure that private persons or entities do not inflict torture or cruel, inhuman or degrading treatment or punishment on others within their power*." (CCPR, *General Comment No. 31* [80] *Nature of the General Legal Obligation Imposed on States Parties to the Covenant*, 29 March 2004, para. 8, emphasis added).

[136] *Report 2009, supra* note 6, para. 101.

accountability measures available at present and called for the development of a specific international criminal law of bioethics,[137] or even for the
institution of an international medical tribunal for criminal prosecution
of bioethical crimes and physicians' abuses of human rights.[138]

IV. Informed Consent in End-of-Life Care: Informed Refusal and the Boundaries of Patients' Autonomy

The relevance of informed consent for treatment options at the end of life
is particularly replete with ethical conflicts and dilemmas which still
prompt attentive discussion and penetrating understanding. In fact, one
of the most intensely debated and problematic issues is to define the
boundaries of patients' autonomy in end-of-life decision-making.

The scope of self-determination in end-of-life care is deeply intertwined
with the universal recognition of the value and protection of human life.
Around this theme, two approaches based on different moral and philosophical rationale contrast each other in medical ethics: the 'sanctity of
life' approach, according to which life is valuable *per se* and is worth
protecting independently of any physical disability or psychological

---

[137] From the perspective of international criminal law, there is yet no specific regulation
concerning liability for violation of human rights linked to biomedical practices. However,
it is worth mentioning that the Rome Statute includes in the crimes over which the
International Criminal Court has jurisdiction—as patent violations of the right to self-
determination and informed consent—enforced sterilization in both the categories of
crimes against humanity and war crimes (art. 5, para. 1g; art. 8, para. 2b.xxii; art. 8, para.
2e.vi), and biological experiments (art. 8, para. 2a.ii) as well as "medical or scientific experiments of any kind which are neither justified by the medical, dental or hospital treatment
of the person concerned nor carried out in his or her interest" (art. 8, para. 2b.x; art. 8, para.
2e.xi) among war crimes (see Rome Statute of the International Criminal Court, U.N. Doc.
A/CONF.183/9, 17 July 1998, entered into force on 1 July 2002). In consideration of the fact
that these crimes trigger international criminal liability of individuals only in case of
armed conflict or of widespread and systematic violations, several scholars have highlighted the need for a specific regulation at the international level of at least the most hei-
nous biomedical practices contrary to human rights and ethics (i.e. human cloning, illegal
traffic of organs, non-consensual experiments). The best means to guarantee such result
would be the drafting of specific conventions also concerning transnational crimes, or in
the alternative, those international organizations which are more actively engaged in the
field of international bioethics should adopt recommendations or general guidelines
prompting member States to pass criminal legislation and allowing universal jurisdiction
for the most serious bioethical crimes. See Lenoir, "Le droit international pénal de la bioéthique", *supra* note 11, at 410–414.
[138] Annas and Grodin, "Medicine and Human Rights", *supra* note 13, at 16. On this issue
see the opposite view of Benjamin Mason Meier, "International Criminal Prosecution of
Physicians: A Critique of Professors Annas and Grodin's Proposed International Medical
Tribunal", 30 *American Journal of Law & Medicine* (2004), pp. 419–452.

deficiency; the 'quality of life' approach, which posits that life can be renounced when physical existence is not supported by mental and social qualities that make living meaningful.[139] In connection with ethical and legal dilemmas in end-of-life care, the foundational contrast and almost irreconcilable conflict between Christian bioethics and secular bioethics has been the object of in-depth scholarly reflections.[140]

In the context of international biolaw the principle of autonomy posits that no authority is entitled to deprive the individual of his right to choose what he deems to be best for him, especially in the field of health, life and death.[141] Hence, autonomy endows individuals with the exclusive right to make independent life choices on the basis of their conscience and beliefs (right to self-determination), and the most significant expression of this principle in health care is the right to informed consent, with its associate right to refuse or halt medical treatments.[142]

As far as 'informed refusal' is concerned, there is substantially no disagreement on the fact that it is to be considered an integral part of autonomy and the reverse side of informed consent. Its scope is narrower than that of the right to self-determination, since the latter shifts the focus from mere refusal of treatment to freedom of choice in one's own best interest. However, the most controversial aspect of informed refusal is whether respect for the right to refuse or stop treatment should be disregarded when it leads to the patient's death. In other words, the critical point is whether the freedom element inherent in the right to self-determination may encompass 'self-termination'.

In this connection, a lively discussion has developed on the legal limits of patients' autonomy, especially when referred to the practice of end-of-life care. The debate has focused on two major issues: whether there is a recognised right to die, or to die with dignity, and whether respect for individual autonomy may legitimise euthanasia and assistance to suicide at the request of a terminally ill or a dying patient.

---

[139] Albin Eser, "«Sanctity» and «Quality» of Life: An Historical Review from a German Perspective", 29 *Israel Yearbook on Human Rights* (1999), pp. 11–22, at 11–12.
[140] See, for example, among the most recent contributions, H. Tristram Engelhardt, "Christian Bioethics after Christendom: Living in a Secular Fundamentalist Polity and Culture", 17 *Christian Bioethics* (2011), pp. 64–95; Christopher Tollefsen, "Mind the Gap: Charting the Distance between Christian and Secular Bioethics", ibid., pp. 47–53.
[141] See Boschiero, "Le biotecnologie", *supra* note 11, at 52.
[142] See Europe Charter on Patients' Rights, *supra* note 120, Article 4; *Amsterdam Declaration, supra* note 16, para. 3.2; *Report 2009, supra* note 6, para. 28; UN Mental Illness Principles, *supra* note 35, para. 4.

As a preliminary observation, it is necessary to point out that for these patients a clear distinction is to be made between refusal or withdrawal of life-sustaining, life-prolonging, disproportionate or futile treatments upon request or by will of the interested person (including passive euthanasia or 'letting die'), and the taking of action lacking medical, therapeutic or palliative justification, but intended solely to terminate life (active euthanasia or to some extent assistance to suicide, which are considered as amounting to an arbitrary taking of life contrary to international human rights law).

In the second place, it is remarkable that international law, as it stands today, cannot yet provide any exhaustive and clear-cut answer to such challenging issues. As far as international biolaw is concerned, a *lacuna* exists on almost all issues related to the end of life, given the absence of any generally accepted standard in this domain – and this is particularly telling of the asserted impossibility to reach universal consensus on the most critical bioethical dilemmas. As for international human rights law, no relevant instrument protects any right to die or to die with dignity, so the debate has mainly developed in the framework of the protection of the right to life.

In this respect, it is noteworthy that human rights treaties are couched in terms that every human being has the inherent right to life which is protected by law, and "no one shall be arbitrarily deprived of his life". They envisage only limited circumstances in which a person can be deprived of this right and none of these relate to suicide or euthanasia.[143]

Once again it is the activity of human rights bodies that offers some guidance on the subject, although, in this case too, there is a substantial difference between the contribution given at the universal level by the Human Rights Committee and the one provided at regional level by the European Court of Human Rights.

The Human Rights Committee interpreted the right to life as "the supreme right from which no derogation is permitted",[144] that is to say a right which enjoys the status of *jus cogens*.[145] This notwithstanding, when

---

[143] Article 6 of the Covenant on Civil and Political Rights, Article 4 of the American Convention on Human Rights, Article 4 of the African Charter on Human and Peoples' Rights, and Article 2 of the European Convention on Human Rights.

[144] CCPR, *General Comment No. 06: The right to life (art. 6)*, 30 April 1982, para. 1. See, in this respect, Article 15 of the European Convention on Human Rights, Article 4 of the International Covenant on Civil and Political Rights, and Article 27 of the American Convention on Human Rights.

[145] Claudio Zanghì, *La protezione internazionale dei diritti dell'uomo* (Torino, 2006), p. 62.

it had the occasion to scrutinise the compatibility of the Dutch law on euthanasia of 2001 with Article 6 of the Covenant—which in essence proscribes the arbitrary taking of someone else's life—it did not find that such law was contrary to the treaty, but merely recommended that it be revised in light of that provision with a view to strengthening some of its guarantees.[146] Even recently, in considering the Swiss legislation on assisted suicide, the Committee limited itself to recommending that Switzerland ought to "consider amending its legislation in order to ensure independent or judicial oversight to determine that a person who is seeking assistance for suicide is acting with full free and informed consent."[147]

Turning to the regional framework, it is not necessary to examine in detail the issue of euthanasia and assisted suicide as approached by the organs of the Council of Europe or the European Court of Human Rights, since this subject is extensively treated in other chapters of this book.[148] However, it is important to recall at least the core of the Parliamentary Assembly's statements and Strasbourg case law on the subject.

In its resolution of 1976 on the rights of the sick and the dying, the Assembly focused on the best interest of these persons viewed through the lens of the effective benefits of aggressive and futile treatments, which is one of the still more controversial issues in end-of-life care, together with the problematic qualification of artificial nutrition and hydration and the possibility to forego life-sustaining treatments.[149] Starting from the assumption that "no other interests may be considered in establishing the moment of death than those of the dying person", it observed that "the true interests of the sick are not always best served by a zealous application of the most modern techniques for prolonging life" and thus invited "the responsible bodies in the medical profession in the member states to

---

[146] CCPR, *Consideration of Reports Submitted by States Parties under Article 40 of the Covenant: Concluding Observations of the Human Rights Committee: Netherlands*, CCPR/CO/72/NET, 27 August 2001 and *Concluding Observations of the Human Rights Committee*, CCPR/C/NLD/CO/4, 11 August 2009, para. 7.

[147] CCPR, *Consideration of Reports Submitted by States Parties under Article 40 of the Covenant : Concluding Observations of the Human Rights Committee: Switzerland*, CCPR/C/CHE/CO/3, 3 November 2009.

[148] See Estelle Brosset, "Le droit européen et la fin de la vie"; Panos Merkouris, "Assisted Suicide in the Jurisprudence of the European Court of Human Rights: A Matter of Life and Death".

[149] See for example Laurie Barclay, "Aggressive Treatments at End of Life Linked to Worse Quality of Death for Cancer Patients", *Medscape Medical News*, 3 May 2007; Ralf J. Jox, Mirjam Krebs, Martin Fegg, Stella Reiter-Theil, Lorenz Frey, Wolfgang Eisenmenger, and Gian Domenico Borasio, "Limiting life-sustaining treatment in German intensive care units: A multiprofessional survey", 25 *Journal of Critical Care* (2010), pp. 413–419.

examine critically the criteria upon which decisions are currently based with respect to the initiation of reanimation procedures and the placing of patients into long-term care requiring artificial means of sustaining life".[150] These questions were again addressed in recommendation 1418 (1999) on the protection of the human rights and dignity of the terminally ill and the dying, where the right of these vulnerable patients to 'die in dignity' was balanced with the need to keep faithful to a strict protection of the right to life. According to the Assembly, in fact, while terminally ill and dying patients should be shielded from the risk of being subject to an "artificial prolongation of the dying process by ... disproportionate medical measures or the ... [continuance of] treatment without ... consent", having regard to the obligation of States Parties under Article 2 of the Convention "a terminally ill or dying person's wish to die never constitutes any legal claim to die at the hand of another person" or "a legal justification to carry out actions intended to bring about death".[151] These issues raised by the recommendation should be read through the lens of the critical observations made by Professor Douwe Korff in relation to the questions posed by the formulation of Article 2:

> First of all: when does life—and therefore the right to protection of life by law—end? Secondly: is it acceptable to provide palliative care to a terminally ill or dying person, even if the treatment may, as a side-effect, contribute to the shortening of the patient's life? And should the patient be consulted on this? Third, may, or must, the State "protect" the right to life even of a person who does not want to live any longer, against that person's own wishes? Or do people have, under the Convention, not just a right to life, and to live—but also a right to die as and when they choose: to commit suicide? And if so, can they seek assistance from others to end their lives? And fourth: can the State allow the ending of life in order to end suffering, even if the person concerned cannot express his or her wishes in this respect?[152]

As pointed out by the Committee of Ministers, "as yet, there is no case law of the Court which could provide precise answers to all the questions raised in the Recommendation [1418]".[153] In fact, the so far limited case law

---

[150] Parliamentary Assembly, Resolution 613 (1976), *On the rights of the sick and dying*, 29 January 1976.

[151] Parliamentary Assembly, Recommendation 1418 (1999), *Protection of the human rights and dignity of the terminally ill and the dying*, 25 June 1999, paras. 7.iii and 9.c.

[152] Douwe Korff, *The right to life. A guide to the implementation of Article 2 of the European Convention on Human Rights* (Strasbourg, 2006), p. 15.

[153] Parliamentary Assembly, Doc. 9404, 8 April 2002, *Protection of the human rights and dignity of the terminally ill and the dying*, Recommendation 1418 (1999), Reply from the

of the European Court has not dealt in any exhaustive manner with such crucial problems, nor has it ever ruled in straight and clear-cut wording that euthanasia is contrary to Article 2.[154]

In principle, the Court stated that Article 2 allows no further derogations than those enunciated therein and that the "circumstances when the deprivation of life may be justified" must be "strictly construed".[155] However, in consideration of the fact that the cases of *Sanles Sanles* and *Ada Rossi et al.* were declared inadmissible *ratione personae*,[156] the only two relevant proceedings dealing with euthanasia and assisted suicide are the already famous *Pretty* case[157] and the more recent *Haas* case.[158]

In *Pretty* the Court addressed the question whether the right to life and the right to privacy include a right to die. In the first place, it considered that Article 2 could not be construed in terms implying recognition of a negative aspect of the right to life, that is a right to choose not to live; in the second place, it observed that such provision is phrased in terms that are "unconcerned with issues to do with the quality of living or what a person chooses to do with his or her life", so that it concluded that

> Article 2 cannot, without a distortion of language, be interpreted as conferring the diametrically opposite right, namely a right to die; nor can it create

---

Committee of Ministers adopted at the 790th meeting of the Ministers' Deputies (26 March 2002), par. 3.

[154] In the *Widmer case* the European Commission found that failure to criminalise passive euthanasia by the Swiss legislator was not incompatible with either Article 2 or Article 8 of the Convention (ECHR, *Widmer v. Switzerland*, no. 20527/92, Commission decision of 10 February 1993).

[155] In principle the Court found that no further derogations from the proviso of Article 2 could be admitted: see ECtHR, *McCann and others v. the United Kingdom*, no. 18984/91, Judgment of 27 September 1995, A 324, para. 147.

[156] ECtHR, *Sanles Sanles v. Spain*, no. 48335/99, Decision of 26 October 2000; *Ada Rossi and Others v. Italy*, nos. 55185/08, 55483/08, 55516/08, 55519/08, 56010/08, 56278/08, 58420/08 and 58424/08, Decision of 16 December 2008.

[157] ECtHR, *Pretty v. the United Kingdom*, no. 2346/02, Judgment of 29 April 2002. See commentaries of the case in M.A. Sanderson, *Pretty v. United Kingdom*, 96 *American Journal of International Law* (2002), pp. 943–949; Olivier De Schutter, "L'aide au suicide devant la Cour européenne des droits de l'homme (à propos de l'arrêt *Pretty c. le Royaume-Uni* du 29 avril 2002)", 52 *Revue trimestrielle des droits de l'homme* (2003), pp. 71–112; Brenda Hale, "A *Pretty* Pass: When is There a Right to Die?", 32 *Common Law World Review* (2003), pp. 1–14; John Keown, "European Court of Human Rights: Death in Strasbourg – Assisted Suicide, the *Pretty Case*, and the European Convention on Human Rights", 1 *International Journal of Constitutional Law* (2003), pp. 722–730; Antje Pedain, "The Human Rights Dimension of the *Diane Pretty Case*", 62 *Cambridge Law Journal* (2003), pp. 181–206; Janna Satz Nugent, "'Walking into the Sea' of Legal Fiction: An Examination of the European Court of Human Rights, *Pretty v. United Kingdom* and the Universal Right to Die", 13 *Journal of Transnational Law and Policy* (2003–2004), pp. 183–212.

[158] ECtHR, *Haas v. Switzerland*, no. 31322/07, Judgment of 20 January 2011.

a right to self-determination in the sense of conferring on an individual the entitlement to choose death rather than life. ... The Court accordingly finds that no right to die, whether at the hands of a third person or with the assistance of a public authority, can be derived from Article 2 of the Convention.[159]

In this regard, it also recalled Recommendation 1418 (1999) as a relevant document confirming this view. Moreover, concerning Article 8, the Court acknowledged the importance of the principle of personal autonomy in the interpretation of the guarantees provided by the European Convention and hence asserted the right to self-determination as included in the right to private life.[160] It observed that

> the ability to conduct one's life in a manner of one's own choosing may also include the opportunity to pursue activities perceived to be of a physically or morally harmful or dangerous nature for the individual concerned. The extent to which a State can use compulsory powers or the criminal law to protect people from the consequences of their chosen lifestyle has long been a topic of moral and jurisprudential discussion, the fact that the interference is often viewed as trespassing on the private and personal sphere adding to the vigour of the debate. However, even where the conduct poses a danger to health or, arguably, where it is of a life-threatening nature, the case-law of the Convention institutions has regarded the State's imposition of compulsory or criminal measures as impinging on the private life of the applicant within the meaning of Article 8 § 1 and requiring justification in terms of the second paragraph.[161]

In this connection, the Court made some important statements of principle on the intensely debated and controversial right to die transposing the considerations reported above in the sphere of medical treatment. It therefore stated that

> the refusal to accept a particular treatment might, inevitably, lead to a fatal outcome, yet the imposition of medical treatment, without the consent of a mentally competent adult patient, would interfere with a person's physical integrity in a manner capable of engaging the rights protected under Article 8 § 1 of the Convention.[162]

Most interestingly, it put into close relationship the right to informed refusal with the right to die, and in referring also to domestic case-law, it recognised that "a person may claim to exercise a choice to die by declining to consent to treatment which might have the effect of prolonging his

---

[159] *Pretty, supra* note 157, para. 39
[160] Ibid., para. 61.
[161] Ibid., para. 62.
[162] Ibid., para. 63.

life".[163] Furthermore, the Court tried to take an equidistant position between the traditional opposite approaches of Christian and secular bioethics, to admit that personal autonomy may lead to choices which are not necessarily respectful of the concept of the inviolability of life:

> Without in any way negating the principle of sanctity of life protected under the Convention, the Court considers that it is under Article 8 that notions of the quality of life take on significance. In an era of growing medical sophistication combined with longer life expectancies, many people are concerned that they should not be forced to linger on in old age or in states of advanced physical or mental decrepitude which conflict with strongly held ideas of self and personal identity.[164]

This important reflection led the Court to conclude that it was "not prepared to exclude" that the existence of a law preventing individuals from exercising their personal choice to avoid what they consider as an undignified and distressing end to their life would constitute an interference with their right to respect for private life.[165]

Mutatis mutandis, such cautious approach was later developed in *Haas v. Switzerland*, where the Court for the first time almost recognised an individual 'right to suicide', finding that one limb of the right to privacy is the right to decide the time and modalities of the end of one's own life, provided that such decision be taken freely and knowingly and that suicide be carried out autonomously and without the help of third persons.[166] The bolder stance taken by the Court was however 'mitigated' by its placing special emphasis on two elements: the need to interpret Article 8 in light of Article 2—which in the Court's views compels national authorities to avoid that suicidal acts be performed as a result of a decision that is not completely freely and knowingly taken—and the absence of a general consensus among the Members of the Council of Europe as to the existence of a right to choose how and when to put an end to one's life—which shifts again the attention to the States' margin of appreciation and explains why the Court implicitly admits that the Swiss legislation is not incompatible with the Convention. Although these considerations finally led the

---

[163] Id.

[164] Ibid., para. 65.

[165] Ibid., para. 67.

[166] *Haas, supra* note 158, para. 51: "la Cour estime que le droit d'un individu de décider de quelle manière et à quel moment sa vie doit prendre fin, à condition qu'il soit en mesure de forger librement sa propre volonté à ce propos et d'agir en conséquence, est l'un des aspects du droit au respect de sa vie privée au sens de l'article 8 de la Convention". See also the similar case of *Koch v. Germany*, no. 497/09, still pending.

Court to conclude that no positive obligations existed for the State to adopt measures aimed at guaranteeing a 'right to a dignified suicide', and hence a 'right to die in dignity', it is nonetheless noteworthy that some steps taken by the Court in this case—especially when, in balancing the opposing interests at stake, it takes note and "admet la volonté du requérant de se suicider de manière sûre, digne et sans douleur et souffrances superflues"—may be considered promising of a further evolution of its case-law in this particularly delicate field.

V. Concluding Remarks: Informed Consent, Advance Treatment Directives and the Right to Die in Dignity

As it has been suggested so far, a right to informed consent, along with its associate right to refuse treatment, have emerged and gained prominence in the international legal order.

It is also widely accepted that the right to give or withhold consent includes the patient's right to express in advance their preferences as to the treatment options to be performed in case they lose temporarily or permanently their capacity to take part in medical decision-making.[167] The legal instruments designed to enable patients to retain decisional authority even in cases of incompetence are the so-called advance directives, which provide a viable alternative to contemporaneous decisions and serve the scope of protecting precedent autonomy.

Advance decision-making can take the form of either instructional directives, also known as living wills (providing specific instructions or setting out general principles to be followed for health care to be delivered when decision-making capacity has been lost) or proxy directives, also known as durable powers of attorney for health care (naming surrogate decision-makers such as proxies).[168]

---

[167] The Directives can apply not only to end-of-life situations but also to situations of a transitory or short term nature where the patient is unable to express himself.

[168] On advance directives see especially Roberto Andorno, Nikolas Biller-Andorno and Susanne Brauer, "Advance Health Care Directives: Towards a Coordinated European Policy?", 16 *European Journal of Health Law* (2009), pp. 207–227; Roberto Andorno, "An Important Step in the Promotion of Patients' Self-Determination", 17 *European Journal of Health Law* (2010), pp. 119–124; Id., "Regulating Advance Directives at the Council of Europe", in this book. See also the monographic studies by Norman L. Cantor, *Advance Directives and the Pursuit of Death with Dignity* (Bloomington, 1993); Nancy M.P. King, *Making Sense of Advance Directives* (Washington, 1996); Robert S. Olick, *Taking Advance Directives Seriously. Prospective autonomy and decisions near the end of life* (Washington, 2001); Carol Krohm and Scott K. Summers, *Advance Health Care Directives: A Handbook for*

Advance directives have long been in the spotlight of the bioethical and biolegal discourse at both national and the international level. Depending on the jurisdiction, domestic laws may grant specific legal status to either kind of directive and require a specific format and specific procedural rules. However, while there is a general trend in European countries towards regulation of advance directives, the legal effect to be given to these documents is still controversial and debated[169] and their binding authority has been the object of both moral and practical attacks.[170]

From the standpoint of international law, advance directives lack any specific regulation and even in international instruments of 'soft biolaw' express reference to them is really scant.[171] The only relevant normative provision is to be found in Article 9 of the Oviedo Convention, which refers to the patient's "previously expressed wishes". As explained by Professor Andorno in this book, this proviso is not devoid of ambiguities and shortcomings that the Council of Europe has tried to put right with the Committee of Ministers recent recommendation (2009)11 of 9 December 2009 on principles concerning continuing powers of attorney and advance directives for incapacity.

This notwithstanding, it is quite clear that Article 9 of the Convention is considered an important reference point to enhance the status of advance directives both at the global[172] and regional level. In fact, although the

---

Professionals (Chicago, 2002); Yvon Englert and Alfons van Orshoven (eds.), « *Testaments de vie* » *et autres directives anticipées* (Bruxelles, 2003); Fabrizio Turoldo, *Le dichiarazioni anticipate di trattamento. Un testamento per la vita* (Padova, 2006); Jacqueline M. Atkinson, *Advance Directives in Mental Health. Theory, Practice and Ethics* (London, 2007); Federico G. Pizzetti, *Alle frontiere della vita: il testamento biologico tra valori costituzionali e promozione della persona* (Milano, 2008) and the very useful practical guide *Planificación anticipada de la asistencia médica. Historia de valores; Instrucciones previas; Decisiones de representación* (Madrid, 2011), also containing an extensive bibliography.

[169] Andorno, "An Important Step", *supra* note 168, at 119, 123.

[170] See Alasdair MacLean, "Advance Directives and the Rocky Waters of Anticipatory Decision-Making", 16 *Medical Law Review* (2008), pp. 1–22; Carlo Casonato, *Le direttive anticipate di trattamento: un fenomeno paradigmatico dei problemi del biodiritto*, in Francesco Lucrezi and Francesco Mancuso (eds.), *Diritto e vita. Biodiritto, bioetica, biopolitica* (Soveria Mannelli, 2010), pp. 323–337, at 328.

[171] For example, the *Amsterdam Declaration, supra* note 16, took into account "a previous declared expression of will" to the effect of preventing, even in situations of urgent need, the performance of a medical intervention based on a presumed informed consent when, according to such previous will, it is clear that the patient would have refused consent (para. 3.3).

[172] See for example Violeta Beširević, "End-of-Life Care in the 21st Century: Advance Directives in Universal Rights Discourse", 24 *Bioethics* (2010), pp. 105–112, at 107: "the standards concerning the role of precedent autonomy in treating incompetent patients, guaranteed in Article 9 of the Oviedo Convention could, at least potentially, be implemented on a territory much wider than the territory of the Council of Europe Member States".

Convention has not yet been ratified by many of the European Union Member States, it is noteworthy that in a recent resolution on the situation of fundamental rights in the Union, the European Parliament invited *all Member States* lacking a specific legislation on living wills to adopt such laws as necessary

> to ensure that, according to Article 9 of the Oviedo Convention on Human Rights and Biomedicine, 'The previously expressed wishes relating to a medical intervention by a patient who is not, at the time of the intervention, in a state to express his or her wishes shall be taken into account' and *to ensure the right to dignity at the end of life.*[173]

This recommendation is remarkable for two main reasons. First, because it calls for implementation of a principle whose legal source is a provision that is not binding on all EU Member States, which amounts to recognising that the standard set by Article 9 has general scope and effect extending also to States not Parties to the Oviedo Convention. Second, because it associates respect, or at least due consideration, of advance directives to the right to dignity at the end of life.

The latter aspect is particularly interesting since it lends support to the argument that advance directives favour death with dignity inasmuch as they translate into medical instructions the patient's personal views, values and beliefs as to their idea of a dignified death. This element deserves special consideration and respect because it represents the expression and exercise of two fundamental and non-derogable rights: the right to dignity and the right to informed consent.[174]

Actually, advance directives originated as a way to avoid the excesses of life-prolonging measures as provided by advanced medical technology, and a means of protecting patients from unnecessary prolonging of the dying process in conditions that they would not want to endure. This is the reason why instructional directives very often consist in the advance refusal of futile, disproportionate or aggressive treatment and life-sustaining measures (such as mechanical ventilation or artificial nutrition and hydration) or in DNR orders (i.e. 'do not resuscitate' orders amounting to a refusal of life-saving measures, such as cardiopulmonary

---

[173] European Parliament, Resolution of 14 January 2009 on the situation of fundamental rights in the European Union 2004–2008, *Official Journal of the European Union*, C 46E/08, 24 February 2010, pp. 48–69, para. 167 (emphasis added).

[174] At least for adult competent patients, and where derogations due to emergency situations and public health interests do not apply, the non-derogable nature of informed consent is no longer controversial: see Wear, *Informed Consent, supra* note 1, p. 1.

resuscitation). Their rationale obviously resides in the patient's will to escape the risk of being subject either to prolonged unbearable suffering or to a condition of mere physical survival devoid of any cognitive functions, which may be considered contrary to one's own concept of dignity. In situations like these, it has been contended that there should be no automatic protection of the sanctity of life at the expense of human dignity, least of all in violation of the patient's expressed will and specific requests.[175]

Therefore, since international law as it stands today recognises that compulsory treatments or interventions, even if life-saving, are inconsistent and irreconcilable with the right to self-determination and the right to informed consent, but however it does not recognise and protect any right to die or to die in dignity, the relevance of the right to refuse treatment and the fundamental right to human dignity should be the starting point for determining the legal value of advance directives from an international law perspective, as well as for assessing the consistency of relevant domestic regulation with international law.

---

[175] Leon Sheleff, "Active euthanasia, denial of dignity, and medical responsibility for bystander inaction", 29 *Israel Yearbook on Human Rights* (1999), pp. 91–103; at 97.

REGULATING ADVANCE DIRECTIVES AT THE COUNCIL OF EUROPE

*Roberto Andorno**

I. INTRODUCTION

It is now widely accepted that patients' right to informed consent presupposes the possibility for them to refuse treatments, especially when these are perceived by them as excessive, futile or psychologically harmful. Both consent and refusal of consent are indeed envisaged today as two different expressions of the same patients' right to self-determination. Thus, refusals of medical treatments are also to be respected, even if they might adversely affect patients' health or shorten their life.

But a problem emerges when patients have lost their decision-making capacity due to a condition that is not likely to be reversible (e.g. persistent vegetative state, severe head injury, dementia, etc.). Who shall decide for them in such cases? Which criteria should be used in the decision-making process? What if family members disagree about treatments to be provided or withheld? What if doctors and patient's relatives have different views on what is best for the patient? Here is where the potential utility of advance directives comes into play. Advance health care planning can take two different forms, which are not necessarily exclusive of each other, since they both can be combined in the same document:

a) The *living wills*, which are (usually written) instructions that specify ahead of time personal preferences regarding the provision—or the withholding—of particular treatments in the event that the individual becomes unable to make decisions in the future;

b) The *lasting (or durable) powers of attorney for health care*, which allow individuals to appoint someone as a "health care proxy" (for example a trusted relative or friend) to make health care decisions on their behalf once they lose the ability to do so.

* Senior Research Fellow at the School of Law of the University of Zurich, Switzerland; email: roberto.andorno@rwi.uzh.ch.

S. Negri (ed.), *Self-Determination, Dignity and End-of-Life Care*
2011 Koninklijke Brill NV. Printed in The Netherlands. ISBN 978 90 04 22357 8. pp. 73–86

At present, European countries have very different or no legal standards at all on this matter. The current situation may create problems with the increasing cross-border movement of EU citizens. In addition, the growing of the aging population of European societies is likely to create an increased demand for advance directives in the next years. What seems to be clear is that a reliable solution has to be found to solve the practical problem posed by advance directives made in one European country and implemented in another.

Since the end of the 1990s, especially with the adoption of the Convention on Human Rights and Biomedicine (thereafter "Biomedicine Convention" or "Oviedo Convention"), the Council of Europe has made significant efforts to set up common standards in this field. This paper will first outline the strengths and shortcomings of Article 9 of the Biomedicine Convention, which specifically deals with living wills. It will then analyze the Council of Europe's Recommendation (2009)11 on continuing powers of attorney and advance directives for incapacity.

II. Advance Directives in the Biomedicine Convention

A. *The Biomedicine Convention as a Framework Instrument*

The Council of Europe is indisputably the leading intergovernmental organization in the development of common European norms relating to bioethics. It is worth remembering that this body, which gathers at present 47 Member States (that is, virtually all European countries), was established a few years after the end of the Second World War to promote respect for democracy and human rights across Europe. To achieve this purpose, it adopted in 1950 the European Convention on Human Rights and subsequently various mechanisms aimed at ensuring respect for human rights in the Old Continent such as the European Court of Human Rights.

It was the same foundational goal of promoting human rights that led the Council to address various bioethical issues since the early 1980s. From that time, the Parliamentary Assembly (the deliberative body of the Council of Europe) as well as the Committee of Ministers (composed by all Foreign Ministers of Member States) issued a number of recommendations on topics such as genetic engineering, embryo research, patients' rights, health databases, etc.

The most significant step in this process was undoubtedly the adoption of the Biomedicine Convention. After four years of discussion and consultations, the Convention was approved by the Committee of Ministers on 19 November 1996 and opened for signature in Oviedo on 4 April 1997. The Convention entered into force in December 1999, following the fifth ratification, that of Spain.[1]

The importance of the Biomedicine Convention lies in the fact that it is the only binding intergovernmental instrument that comprehensively addresses the link between human rights and biomedicine. The Convention's purpose, as indicated by its Preamble, is to specifically safeguard respect for human dignity and human rights with regard to the applications of biology and medicine. In other words, this instrument can be regarded as an *extension of human rights law into the biomedical field.*[2]

For a correct analysis of the Convention it is necessary to keep in mind that it has been conceived as a *framework* instrument. This means that it only includes general guiding principles and does not intend to offer a detailed regulation of biomedical issues. The Convention only attempts to identify the most basic legal standards that are accepted by all European countries in order, first, to create a solid basis for further developments by means of additional protocols, and second, to urge states to enact consistent legislation.[3] This minimalist approach was chosen for both substantive and practical reasons, that is, for the need to respect the cultural specificities of each country, and for the impossibility of a deeper consensus, respectively.

B. *Article 9 of the Biomedicine Convention*

There is a striking contrast between the decades-long attention paid to advance health care planning in the United States and the only recent interest given to it in Europe. In the U.S., the public debate about the scope and legal efficacy of advance directives started around thirty years ago. The American lawyer Luis Kutner seems to have been the first to suggest the concept of living wills in 1967.[4] The Congress passed in 1990 the

---

[1] At the time of this article (November 2010), the Biomedicine Convention was signed by 34 countries and ratified by 23 of them. See the updated list of signatures and ratifications at: http://www.coe.int/bioethics (accessed on 25 November 2010).

[2] See Roberto Andorno, "The Oviedo Convention: A European Legal Framework at the Intersection of Human Rights and Health Law", 2 *Journal of International Biotechnology Law* (2005), n. 4, pp. 133–143.

[3] Four additional protocols have already been adopted: on human cloning (1998), on organ transplantation (2002), on biomedical research (2005), and on genetic testing for health purposes (2008).

[4] See Alasdair MacLean, "Advance Directives and the Rocky Waters of Anticipatory Decision-Making", 16 *Medical Law Review* (2008), n. 1, pp. 1–22.

Patient Self-Determination Act, which requires hospitals to ask every patient on admission whether they have completed an advance directive (either a living will or a durable power of attorney, or both) and, if so, to bring a copy to the hospital. If the patient does not have an advance directive but would like more information about these documents, hospitals must also provide the information. At present, all U.S. states have specific laws recognizing the use of advance directives and often provide a model document that may (or in some states *must*) be followed.[5]

In contrast, the attention given to advance directives in most European countries is very recent. Only in the last few years some of states have enacted specific laws to regulate this matter, while others are still reluctant to do so.[6] The fact is that it is still unusual in Europe to base clinical decisions regarding incompetent patients on their previously expressed wishes.

The Biomedicine Convention only covers this issue in Article 9, which provides that:

> The previously expressed wishes relating to a medical intervention by a patient who is not, at the time of the intervention, in a state to express his or her wishes shall be taken into account.

This provision is certainly important as it marks the first recognition of the value of advance directives in a common European binding instrument. Although European countries are not obliged under Article 9 to give legally binding force to advance directives, they must *at least* recognize their advisory effect. Professor Adriano Bompiani, who was directly involved in the drafting of the Convention as Italian representative, points out that the expression "taken into account" used in Article 9 was adopted as a way to find a balance between, on the one hand, due consideration of the patient's wishes expressed in advance, and on the other, a technical, objective assessment of the current clinical situation of the patient and of the elementary duties of the doctor to choose the more adequate treatment according to the current circumstances.[7]

---

[5] See the complete list of model documents state by state at: http://www.uslegalforms .com/livingwills/ (accessed on 25 November 2010). In the US operates a privately held organization (U.S. Living Will Registry) that electronically stores advance directives and makes them available to health care providers across the country. See http://www .uslivingwillregistry.com/ (accessed on 25 November 2010).

[6] See Roberto Andorno, Nikola Biller-Andorno and Susanne Brauer, "Advance Health Care Directives: Towards a Coordinated European Policy?", 16 *European Journal of Health Law* (2009), n° 3, pp. 207–227.

[7] Adriano Bompiani, *Consiglio d'Europa, diritti umani e biomedicina. Genesi della Convenzione di Oviedo e dei Protocolli* (Rome, 2009), p. 86.

While this compromise formula is understandable in the light of the conflicting views of European countries on this matter, and of the framework nature of the Biomedicine Convention, the fact is that the wording of Article 9 is problematic in the sense that the expression "to take into account", without any additional clarification, is too ambiguous and can be interpreted in very different ways.[8] It would have been preferable to have clearer guidance for doctors as to what extent, or under what conditions, patients wishes expressed in advance must be implemented. It is obvious that if health care professionals could arbitrarily decide, without giving any serious reason, not to comply with patients' preferences, the patient's effort of making an advance directive becomes useless. This is the key point of the current controversy, which becomes also visible in the use of the wording "previously expressed wishes" instead of "advance directives" in the title of Article 9. This latter expression, which does appear neither in the Convention nor in its Explanatory Report, was not included on the ground that it presupposes the *binding* nature of such documents.

Another shortcoming of Article 9 is that it is exclusively focused on living wills, but totally ignores the other form that advance directives may take (the continuing power of attorney). This becomes especially clear when one reads the Explanatory Report to the Convention, which never refers to the possibility of appointing a health care proxy.[9] The Council of Europe's Recommendation (2009)11, as will be mentioned hereafter, attempts to fill this lacuna.

It should also be mentioned that the Explanatory Report to the Convention does not resolve the ambiguity of Article 9. It only states that the expression "taken into account" "does not mean that previously expressed wishes should necessarily be followed" and provides two examples to illustrate why in some circumstances the practitioner may have good reasons not to comply with the patient's wishes on the grounds that they do not apply anymore to the situation at hand: a) when they have been expressed a long time before the intervention; b) when medical technology has made significant progress since the time when the advance

---

[8] See, for instance, Dominique Manaï, "Images du droit du patient au miroir de la Convention européenne pour les droits de l'homme et la biomédecine", in F. Werro (ed.), *L'européanisation du droit privé? Vers un code civil européen?* (Fribourg, 1998), pp. 113–127, p. 120; Hans-Ludwig Schreiber, "The European Ethical Convention: Legal Aspects", in A. Schauer, H. L. Schreiber and Z. Ryn (eds.), *Ethics in Medicine* (Göttingen, 2001), pp. 241–248, p. 247; Gilbert Hottois, "A Philosophical and Critical Analysis of the European Convention of Bioethics", 25 *Journal of Medicine and Philosophy* (2000), n° 2, pp. 133–146, p. 139.

[9] See paragraphs 60 to 62.

directive was signed and it can be reasonably assumed that, in the present circumstances, the will of the patient would have been different.[10] In light of these examples it would seem that the spirit of Article 9 is that doctors cannot act arbitrarily, i.e., they need to have *good reasons* to disregard the patient's legitimate wishes expressed in an advance directive. The problem is that this basic principle has not been explicitly included in the Convention itself, nor there is any indication as to what reasons can be validly given by health care professionals for not complying with the patient's explicit will.

Therefore, the central point is whether it would be possible (and desirable) to reach at least a minimum consensus among European countries on the two following issues:

- *The minimal formal requirements for the validity of advance directives* such as for instance the individual's legal capacity and freedom of choice at the time of its drafting; his/her incompetence at the time of its implementation; absence of revocation in the meantime; the need of a previous consultation with a health care professional, etc.
- *The legal effect of advance directives*, which directly relates to extent to which doctors are obliged to comply with patients' preferences and the *reasons* they can legitimately give for not doing so. Among the possible reasons the following can be mentioned: that the patient's will is contrary to law; that the document was written too many years before its implementation; that there have been significant advances in medical sciences that are relevant to the advance directive in question; that there are some serious evidence suggesting that the patient would have a different view had he/she had adequate knowledge of the current circumstances.

III. The Recommendation (2009)11

A. *General Features of the Recommendation*

The Council of Europe's Committee of Ministers adopted on 9 December 2009 the Recommendation (2009)11 on "continuing powers of attorney and advance directives for incapacity". This document is of great relevance regarding advance directives as it seeks to fill the two above mentioned gaps of the Biomedicine Convention (the vagueness of Article 9 regarding

---

[10] Explanatory Report to the Convention on Human Rights and Biomedicine, paragraph 62.

the legal efficacy of living wills, and the lack of regulation of continuing powers of attorney).

Before focusing on the analysis of the recommendation, two preliminary remarks ought to be made. The first is that the scope of the recommendation is actually much broader than health care, since it also covers decisions regarding welfare, and economic and financial matters. The second is that the recommendation uses the expression "advance directives" in a narrow sense, as a synonym for "living wills". Continuing powers of attorney are treated as a separate category. In order to avoid misunderstandings, this paper will use below the expression "advance directive" in this narrow meaning.

The recommendation consists of a preamble and seventeen principles. It makes it clear from the very beginning that its overarching scope is "to promote self-determination of capable adults in the event of their future incapacity, by means of continuing powers of attorney and advance directives" (Principle 1.1). "Self-determination", which is mentioned five times in the whole recommendation, clearly embodies the key value of this document.

The preamble draws attention to previous international and regional instruments relating to this matter, in particular, to the Recommendation (99)4 of 23 February 1999 on principles concerning the legal protection of incapable adults. This latter document is recognized as a "valuable and up-to-date international instrument" in this field. However, it is also recognized that there is a need to build upon the principles of subsidiarity and necessity already contained in the Recommendation (99)4, and to "supplement" it by giving prominence to the principle of self-determination. There is indeed a substantive difference between both documents: the 1999 recommendation deals with measures of protection provided by *competent authorities* (i.e., courts), while the 2009 one covers decisions made privately by the *individuals concerned themselves*, either by appointing a proxy or by making an advance directive. According to the recommendation, this new strategy for protecting the interests of incapacitated adults should be given priority over other measures of protection (Principle 1.1), not only more because it is more in line with the principle of self-determination, but also because it avoids time-consuming and sometimes costly, sensitive and burdensome judicial and administrative proceedings.[11]

---

[11] The Preamble notes that "that in some member states continuing powers of attorney are a preferred alternative to court decisions on representation".

Nevertheless, the two means of self-determination covered by the 2009 recommendation do not seem to be put on an equal level: the document appears to give preference to the use of surrogate decision-making over living wills: while most of its provisions (Principles 3 to 13) concern continuing powers of attorney, living wills receive little attention: only the last four principles (14 to 17) deal with them, and in a very succinct way. It is true that continuing powers of attorney cover a broad spectrum of possible uses (financial, economic, welfare and medical ones) and therefore need to be regulated in more detail, while living wills are particularly (though not exclusively) conceived to serve health care purposes.[12] But there are more substantive reasons explaining this disparity. First of all, European states are well familiarized with the use of powers of attorney, which have a very long tradition in the continent (beginning with the contract of *mandatum* in Roman law), even if only recently they began to be used for making decisions about medical treatment. In contrast, living wills are an entirely new and more controversial way of stating health care preferences ahead of time. Secondly, the implementation of living wills raises difficult (and sometimes unsolvable) problems of interpretation, which do not exist, or are less serious, with surrogate decision-making. Thirdly, some states are concerned with the possibility that living wills could be misused, leading to the neglect of vulnerable or elderly patients, even maybe for purely economic reasons. In addition, it must be noted that over the last years, doubts have been raised about the real utility of living wills, especially when they are drafted in general terms (as it is often the case). Looking back at the long, and according to them, unsuccessful experience with living wills in the United States, some experts suggest that it is time to change the strategy and give priority to continuing powers on attorney, or at least to a combination of living wills and continuing powers of attorney.[13]

B. *Continuing Powers of Attorney*

As it was just mentioned, one of the well-known problems with living wills is the difficulty of drafting a sufficiently specific document without knowing the particular condition in which one will be placed. When there is

---

[12] The Explanatory Memorandum to the Recommendation is explicit in this regard: "The most important type of legally regulated advance directives concerns health issues" (n° 65).

[13] Angela Fagerlin and Carl E. Schneider, "Enough. The Failure of the Living Will", 34 *Hastings Center Report* (2004), n° 2, pp. 30–41.

already a diagnosis that makes a serious condition predictable, the spectrum of decisions regarding alternative treatments is relatively limited and easy to handle. But how can healthy individuals decide in advance in specific terms the kind of treatments they would like to have or not, if they do not know in which situation they will be placed? In contrast, continuing powers of attorney have the great advantage of allowing the doctor to enter into a dialogue with a person (the attorney, or proxy), rather than being merely confronted with a piece of paper, which necessarily has to be interpreted. The proxy can directly discuss with the health care professional about the various available options, about the benefits and risks of each one, and this taking into account the concrete circumstances in which the patient is placed.

The proper role of the proxy in the decision-making process can differ depending upon which modality of surrogate decision is adopted. There are basically two different models:

a. *Substituted judgement*, where proxies, based on their knowledge of the patients' preferences, make a judgement intended to reflect, as closely as possible, the judgement the patients would make if they were competent. This approach attempts to simulate an incompetent patient's autonomous decision by considering the personal values and preferences held by the patient and is therefore justified by the *principle of respect for autonomy*.

b. *Best interests*, where the proxy makes an assessment of the patient's best interests and decides based on that assessment. In this approach, the proxy must consider, from an objective point of view, what course of action would result in the greatest benefit and least harm to the patient. Here the proxy does not need to imagine the situation from the incompetent patient's perspective, but rather makes a decision *on behalf* of the patient. This approach is justified by the *principles of beneficence and non-maleficence*.[14]

These two models of surrogate decision-making can be combined, but in such cases it is advisable to make it clear which approach has the priority and which one is only subsidiary to the first one. For instance, when proxies have no basis on which to make a reasonable judgment about the patient's preferences, it is reasonable to encourage them to

---

[14] John E. Snyder and Candace Gauthier, *Evidence-Based Medical Ethics. Cases for Practice-Based Learning* (Charlotte, 2008), p. 19.

consider the best interests of the patient. On the contrary, the attempt to simultaneously combine both approaches risks creating confusion about the proper role of the proxies and about the criteria they should use in making a decision.[15] It may happen that both criteria appear to be in conflict. What if the proxy considers that a particular treatment is in the best interest of the patient, but it seems to be contrary to the patient's wishes?

In this regard, the Recommendation (2009)11 is not sufficiently clear. On the one hand, proxies are required to make their decisions in accordance with the continuing power of attorney and in the (best) interests of the patient (Principle 10.1). On the other hand, they must also take into account, "as far as possible", "the wishes and feelings" of the patient and give them "due respect" (Principle 10.2). How can both requirements be harmonized? A possible way out of this dilemma is to consider that the best interest of the patient, which is mentioned in the first paragraph and without any particular condition, is a general principle that should always guide the proxy's decision. This standard embodies the basic guiding value for surrogate decision-making, and offers the conceptual framework for the proxy's decisions. On the contrary, the "wishes and feelings" of the patient are an element among others that the proxy must take into account, "as far as possible", to determine what is in the best interest of the patient.

It should be acknowledged, however, that the concept of "best interest of the patient" is highly abstract and can be interpreted in different ways when confronted with the need to make a concrete decision. For instance, can decisions leading to the withholding or withdrawal of a treatment because it regarded as futile or unduly burdensome be in the best interests of the patient? The most common answer to this question seems to be yes, even if it is foreseen that such a decision may also hasten that person's death.[16] However, in practice things are not always that clear-cut. In this regard, the UK Mental Capacity Act, passed in 2005, offers a very detailed and helpful guidance for identifying what might be, or not, in the best interests of the patient (Section 4). Especially important is Section 4.5, which provides, in relation to life-sustaining treatments, that the

---

[15] See Anthony Wrigley, "Proxy consent: moral authority misconceived", 33 *Journal of Medical Ethics* (2007), n° 9, pp. 527–531.

[16] I do not include in this statement the withdrawal of artificial nutrition and hydration of patients in persistent vegetative state, which remains controversial, as was shown by the cases of Terri Schiavo in the US and of Eluana Englaro in Italy.

individual making the decision "must not, in considering whether the treatment is in the best interests of the person concerned, be motivated by a desire to bring about his death". This means that the notion of "best interests" relates to the benefits and burdens of the treatment itself (and may eventually justify the withholding or withdrawal of life-sustaining measures), but such decisions should not reflect a judgement that the patient's life is not worth living. Thus, in the effort to determine what is in the best interests of the patient, a very delicate balance is needed to prevent, on the one hand, futile or too burdensome treatments and, on the other hand, a slippery slope towards intentional killing of incapacitated patients by omission.

The definition of "continuing power of attorney" given by the Recommendation (2009)11 is somehow confusing, and needs a clarification. According to Principle 2.1, it is "a mandate given by a capable adult with the purpose that it shall remain in force, or enter into force, in the event of the granter's incapacity". The use of two different expressions ("remain in force" and "enter into force") obeys to the fact that the definition includes the point of time in which the power of attorney will become operative, and this varies depending on the purpose of the document: those for economic and financial matters may become effective immediately, and remain valid after the granter's incapacity; those for health, welfare and personal matters only will be in effect in the event of the granter's incapacity.

Under the recommendation, any competent individual, and not necessarily a family member, can be appointed as attorney (Principle 4.1). Granters can appoint more than one person, but in such cases they should indicate how the attorneys are to act (jointly, separately, jointly in relation to some matters and separately in relation to others, as substitutes, etc.) (Principle 4.2).

Regarding the formalities to be complied with, the recommendation requires that the power of attorney "shall be in writing" (Principle 5.1), and that the document shall explicitly state that it will become effective in the event of the granter's incapacity (Principle 5.2). Although the recommendation does not mention that the document must be signed, this seems to be an obvious requirement, especially considering that the attorney will have the power to make decisions on matters of life and death pertaining to the granter. The recommendation leaves to the states to determine other formal requirements for the validity of the power of attorney (for instance, notarization, presence of witnesses, registration with a public office, etc.) (Principles 5.3 and 8).

C. *Advance Directives*

Principle 2.3 defines advance directives (living wills) as "instructions given or wishes made by a capable adult concerning issues that may arise in the event of his or her incapacity". The use of two terms ("instructions" and "wishes") does not serve a merely rhetorical function: the word "instructions" is employed to refer to advance directives that are legally binding, while "wishes" is used to indicate that such documents have a merely advisory value.[17] This double terminology, which also appears in Principle 15, shows well the deep disagreement between European countries concerning the legal effect to be given to advance directives.

The new recommendation does not bring to an end this lack of consensus. States are still left to decide whether advances directives should be legally binding or not. This does not mean that no progress has been made in this field since the Biomedicine Convention. Today there is a growing awareness of the importance of enhancing patients' self-determination and avoiding futile or disproportionate treatments. Precisely in an attempt to promote patients' autonomous decisions, a number of European countries have in recent years passed specific laws on advance directives, or are on the way of enacting legislation in this area. The Biomedicine Convention has played a role in this process, and there is no doubt that it has even had an impact on those countries that did not ratify it yet. But the fact is that disagreements still persist about the norms that should govern advance directives.

Interestingly, the terminology used in Principle 15 to refer to previously expressed wishes is slightly different from the one found in Article 9 of the Biomedicine Convention. While this latter provides that such wishes "shall be taken into account", the recommendation stipulates that they should be given "due respect". This latter wording sounds stronger than the one of the Biomedicine Convention. In this regard, it is interesting to note that some countries employ the verb 'to respect' in their domestic laws precisely in order to make advance directives binding.[18] Was this

---

[17] Explanatory Memorandum to the Recommendation, n° 178.

[18] For instance, the new Article 372.2 of the Swiss Civil Code, adopted in 2008 and which will enter into effect in January 2013 provides that advance directives must be "respected" by the doctor and this is commonly interpreted as a recognition that they are *prima facie* binding. Such binding effect is not absolute as the doctors is not obliged to follow the patient's preferences if he or she considers that there are serious reasons to believe that they do not reflect anymore the patient's wishes in the current circumstances. The French version of Article 372.2 reads: "Le médecin respecte les directives anticipées du patient, sauf si elles violent des dispositions légales, ou si des doutes sérieux laissent supposer

difference in the wording deliberate or simply an oversight? The latter is more likely since it only appears in the English version of the recommendation, while the French text employs the same verb that is used in Article 9 of the Biomedicine Convention ("prendre en compte", that is, "take into account").

Regarding the formalities to be observed, in general, advance directives do not necessarily have to be in writing. A person can communicate orally his or her preferences to family members, friends, medical staff, etc. However it is clear that a written decision is to be preferred over a verbal one. In any case, if the advance directive is intended to have binding effect, it should be in writing, or at least recorded in some way (Principle 16). States are also asked to address the issue of substantial changes in circumstances in order to determine how that will affect the validity of advance directives (Principle 15.2).

IV. Conclusion

The Council of Europe has achieved two important milestones in the promotion of patients' self-determination regarding medical care to be implemented in the event of future decisional incapacity: the Biomedicine Convention and the Recommendation (2009)11. The former represents the first European binding instrument recognizing that living wills should have, at least, an advisory value and that therefore they must be "taken into account" by health care professionals. The latter is an attempt to further develop that recognition by means of a soft law instrument, and especially, to draw the attention of European states to an alternative and less controversial tool for planning health care in advance: the continuing power of attorney.

Further studies and discussion are needed to determine whether the Council of Europe could do more to promote health care decisions ahead of time, given the different and even opposed views among European countries, or whether it is desirable (and possible) to seek for greater substantive consensus on this matter.

---

qu'elles ne sont pas l'expression de sa libre volonté ou qu'elles ne correspondent pas à sa volonté présumée dans la situation donnée."

LA FIN DE LA VIE ET LE DROIT EUROPÉEN

Estelle Brosset*

> « La vie c'est ça, un bout de lumière qui finit dans la nuit »
> (Louis-Ferdinand Céline)[1]

Lumière qui devient nuit, la vie prend inexorablement fin, suivant ici un phénomène ancestral, universel et naturel, mais néanmoins tragique[2] ...

... Dans cette nuit, trouve-t-on la figure du droit européen ? La réponse n'est pas aisée, mais nécessaire si l'on veut avoir une vue exacte, ce qui est l'ambitieux objectif de cet ouvrage, du droit positif en la matière.

Elle n'est pas aisée parce l'existence d'un droit européen sur des questions aussi intimes et complexes que celle de la fin de vie pose tout à la fois des questions relatives à la légitimité et la faisabilité d'un droit européen. L'universalisation, plus particulièrement l'européanisation est-elle possible, surtout au regard des conflits profonds, d'ordre spirituel, culturel ou idéologique, qui divisent les États sur la question de la vie ? La renationalisation[3] c'est-à-dire le maintien d'une diversité juridique n'est-elle pas inévitable ? Le consensus, même exclusivement européen, est-il possible sur ces questions ? Il faut d'emblée dire que le consensus n'est pas facilité par la profusion des concepts – euthanasie active ou passive, suicide assisté, soins palliatifs, stade terminal, non acharnement thérapeutique ... – et la variabilité des définitions. À l'échelle parfois d'un seul pays,

---

* Maître de conférences habilité à diriger les recherches en droit public, Université Paul Cézanne, France ; membre du Centre de droit de la santé, membre associé au Centre d'Etudes et de Recherches Internationales et Communautaires ; email : estelle.brosset@ univ-cezanne.fr.

[1] Louis-Ferdinand Céline, *Voyage au bout de la nuit*, Editions Denoël et Steele, Paris, 1932.

[2] « *D'un côté la mort reste bien un phénomène naturel, qui est dans l'ordre des choses, qui permet que les vivants meurent pour que d'autres renaissent ; d'un autre côté, la mort est une épreuve qui fait disparaître un être unique insubstituable, ce qui reste un scandale pour la conscience et un mystère pour l'esprit* » : CDBI, 35ième réunion, 2–5 décembre 2008, *Les décisions médicales dans les situations de fin de vie et les implications éthiques des choix possibles*, rapport préparé par le Dr. Lucie Hacpille, http://www.coe.int/t/dg3/healthbioethic/ Activities/09_Euthanasia/default_fr.asp, p. 13.

[3] Voir Catherine Girard, « Le droit international de la bioéthique, l'universalisation à visage humain ? » in Stephanie Hennette-Vauchez (dir.), *Bioéthique, biodroit, biopolitique, réflexions à l'occasion de la loi du 4 août 2004*, LGDJ, Paris, 2006, pp. 51–69.

S. Negri (ed.), *Self-Determination, Dignity and End-of-Life Care*
2011 Koninklijke Brill NV. Printed in The Netherlands. ISBN 978 90 04 22357 8. pp. 87–106

la question du vocabulaire employé pour décrire la fin de vie ou encore à ce qu'on appelle la phase terminale suscite débat.[4] Déjà en 1976, l'Assemblée Parlementaire du Conseil de l'Europe dans une Résolution 613 « *craignant que l'incertitude quant aux critères les plus valables de définition de la mort ne soit un tourment inutile* » (...) et invitait « *à examiner, à la lumière des connaissances et techniques médicales actuelles, les critères en vigueur dans les différents pays européens pour constater le décès, et à formuler des propositions d'harmonisation de ces critères qui permettent d'en généraliser l'application non seulement dans les hôpitaux, mais dans toute la pratique médicale* ». Surtout s'il est un domaine où l' « *indécidabilité* »[5] est forte, c'est celui de la mort, indécision personnelle quant aux choix à opérer pour soi, pour ses proches, indécision encore plus grande au plan collectif quand aux normes à consacrer. « *Même si, à certains égards, on assiste à un certain rapprochement entre pays européens concernant l'éthos démocratique, les valeurs communes, on constate aussi des différences sensibles quant à l'approche de certains problèmes de société tels que l' euthanasie, l'aide aux mourants ou les soins palliatifs. Sur ces sujets comme dans d'autres domaines, l'Europe institutionnelle est une chose, celle des pratiques culturelles, des choix de valeurs en est une autre. Et d'un pays à l'autre, l'écart entre le discours et la réalité peut s'avérer considérable* ».[6]

Il n'en demeure pas moins que l'on peut repérer, ici ou là, une « *intrusion* »[7] du droit européen. Il faut dire que plusieurs facteurs y ont participé, principalement, les changements radicaux qu'a connu la fin de vie. La technologie médicale a en effet, ces dernières décennies, non seulement permis l'allongement de l'espérance de vie mais aussi prolongé le temps d'incertitude entre la vie et la mort, parfois aux prix d'interminables agonies. La fin de vie est désormais de plus en plus médicalisée et hospitalière et la mort perçue comme un échec — « *la mort c'est quand la médecine décide d'arrêter* »[8] —, échec que l'on s'efforce nécessairement de refouler dans une sorte de syndrome de « *déni de la mort* ».[9] Logiquement,

---

[4] Voir l'effort de clarification en France réalisé par le Rapport de l'Assemblée nationale sur l'accompagnement de la fin de vie, M. Jean Léonetti, n° 1708, 30 juin 2004, pt 1–1.

[5] Jean-Luc Baudoin et Catherine Labrusse-Riou, *Produire l'homme : de quel droit ?*, PUF, Paris, 1987, p. 260.

[6] Philippe Pedrot, « Existe-t-il un droit de mourir dans la dignité ? L'affaire *Pretty c. Royaume-Uni* de la Cour européenne des droits de l'Homme du 29 avril 2002 », *Revue de droit sanitaire et social*, 2002, pp. 475–480, p. 477.

[7] Louis Dubouis, « La fin de vie et le droit européen », in Antoine Leca et Sophie De Cacqueray (dir.), *La fin de vie et l'euthanasie*, Les études hospitalières, Bordeaux, 2008, p. 77.

[8] *Les décisions médicales dans les situations de fin de vie*, supra note 2, p. 3.

[9] Rapport de l'Assemblée nationale sur l'accompagnement de la fin de vie, *supra* note 4.

cette transformation a suscité de nouvelles interrogations, en particulier relatives aux droits fondamentaux de la personne et a débouché sur des adaptations législatives parfois très variables en fonction des Etats. Or, le droit européen, en ce qu'il consacre un corpus de droits fondamentaux (le droit à a vie ou la protection de la vie privée) et en ce qu'il permet l'harmonisation des législations,[10] ne pouvait manquer d'interférer avec ce débat.

Il n'est dès lors pas surprenant de recenser quelques recommandations de l'Assemblée Parlementaire du Conseil de l'Europe,[11] quelques rapports du Comité Directeur pour la bioéthique (CDBI),[12] quelques articles épars dans la Convention d'Oviedo[13] ou dans la Charte des droits fondamentaux de l'Union européenne.[14] Constatons toutefois que, malgré quelques exceptions, comme la Convention de biomédecine, qui cependant comporte le plus souvent des formulations extrêmement prudentes, la portion la plus importante du droit européen en la matière est constituée de rapports et études de comités d'éthique, de déclarations des États ou encore de résolutions des organisations compétentes, en bref, d'un ensemble

---

[10] L'harmonisation est souvent « demandée » par l'opinion publique qui comprend mal les disparités entre législations. « *Que l'euthanasie soit interdite à Lyon et Lille mais qu'on puisse y recourir si l'on se rend à Zurich ou Bruxelles provoque un réel malaise* » : Dubouis, *supra* note 7, p. 78.

[11] Recommandation 1418 (1999), *Protection des droits de l'homme et de la dignité des malades incurables et des mourants* ; Recommandation 779 (1976) *relative aux droits des malades et des mourants*.

[12] Rapport sur les lois en vigueur ou pratiques appliquées dans les Etats membres relatives aux questions soulevées par la Recommandation 1418 (1999) de l'Assemblée parlementaire relative à la protection des droits de l'homme et de la dignité des malades incurables et des mourants [831 Réunion] : Réponses au questionnaire pour les Etats membres relatif à l'euthanasie, 20 janvier 2003, CDBI/INF (2003) 8.

[13] Convention signée sous l'égide du Conseil de l'Europe à Oviedo le 4 avril 1997. Voir notamment l'article 1 : « *Les Parties à la présente Convention protègent l'être humain dans sa dignité et son identité et garantissent à toute personne, sans discrimination, le respect de son intégrité et de ses autres droits et libertés fondamentales à l'égard des applications de la biologie et de la médecine. Chaque Partie prend dans son droit interne les mesures nécessaires pour donner effet aux dispositions de la présente Convention* ». Voir également l'article 5 ou l'article 9 voir plus bas.

[14] Article 3 :
« *1. Toute personne a droit à son intégrité physique et morale.*
   2. Dans le cadre de la médecine et de la biologie, doivent notamment être respectés :
      - *le consentement libre et éclairé de la personne concernée, selon les modalités définies par la loi,*
      - *l'interdiction des pratiques eugéniques, notamment celles qui ont pour but la sélection des personnes,*
      - *l'interdiction de faire du corps humain et de ses parties, en tant que tels, une source de profit,*
      - *l'interdiction du clonage reproductif des êtres humains* ».

juridique non contraignant parfois qualifié d' « *infra droit* ».[15] La redon-
dance est d'ailleurs telle qu'il faut nécessairement y voir « *plus qu'une
maladie de jeunesse* »,[16] les questions de bioéthique comme celles de la fin
de vie s'inscrivant plus facilement « *dans l'argile des résolutions dont la
force juridique est faible que dans l'airain de conventions contraignantes* ».[17]
À ces textes s'ajoute toutefois la jurisprudence, en particulier la jurisprudence de la Cour européenne des droits de l'homme, qui a le mérite de
dégager, à la charge des Etats, de véritables obligations, limitées toutefois
aux cas d'espèce. Concernant la fin de vie, la jurisprudence est maigre,
mais formée d'un arrêt resté « *dans les annales* »,[18] l'arrêt *Pretty*.[19] On se
souvient que Mme Pretty, la requérante, âgée de 43 ans, atteinte d'une
maladie neurodégénérative, irréversible et incurable,[20] mais qui gardait
toutes ses facultés intellectuelles, souhaitait que son mari soit autorisé à
l'assister dans son suicide sans encourir de poursuites. Elle affirmait
devant la Cour que le refus par le *Director of Public Prosecutions* d'accorder
une indemnité de poursuites à son mari à la suite d'une aide au suicide et
la prohibition de cette aide édictée par le droit anglais[21] enfreignaient les
droits garantis par la Convention européenne, en particulier les articles 2,
3, 8, 9 et 14. Rejetant la demande de Mme Pretty et estimant que la Grande-
Bretagne n'avait violé aucun des articles de la Convention, les juges ont,
dans cette affaire, fixé plusieurs jalons importants s'agissant de la confrontation entre les droit garantis par la Convention et la décision de mettre
fin à sa vie.

Ce corpus de droit européen peut être appréhendé au travers d'un
double mouvement : si d'une part l'on assiste à la protection par le droit
européen de l'autonomie des individus désireux de « bien » finir leur vie

---

[15] L'expression est tirée de l'article particulièrement éclairant de Sandrine Maljean-
Dubois, « Bioéthique et droit international », *Annuaire français de droit international*, 2000,
pp. 83–110, p. 86.
[16] Ibid., p. 110.
[17] Noëlle Lenoir et Bertrand Mathieu, *Les normes internationales de bioéthique*, PUF,
Paris, 1998, p. 43.
[18] Jean-Pierre Marguénaud, « Hymnes à la vie et à l'autonomie personnelle », *Revue
trimestrielle de droit civil*, 2002, p. 858 ss.
[19] CEDH, 29 avril 2002, *Pretty c/Royaume-Uni*, n° 2346/98; *Revue de science criminelle*,
2002, p. 645, note Florence Massias; *Recueil Dalloz*, 2002, p. 1596; *Revue juridique personnes
et famille*, 2002, p. 11, obs. Eric Garaud; *JCP* (*La semaine juridique*), 2002, I.157, n° 1 et 13, obs.
Frédéric Sudre; *Defrénois*, 2002, p. 1131, obs. Philippe Malaurie.
[20] Une sclérose latérale amyotrophyque qui l'a paralysait du cou jusqu'aux pieds.
[21] Le suicide en droit anglais, n'est pas considéré comme une infraction mais Mme
Pretty était dans l'impossibilité d'accomplir un tel acte sans assistance. Or, aider quelqu'un
à mettre fin à ses jours est en revanche, sanctionné par l'article 2 § 1er de la loi de 1961 sur
le suicide.

(I), d'autre part, le droit européen reste relativement en retrait, discret lorsque l'individu décide de mourir, ne se prononçant pas ou très peu dans le débat sur l'euthanasie (II).

I. Bien finir sa vie

La fin de la vie a été profondément modifiée non seulement par les avancées importantes des technologies de maintien de la vie et d'amélioration de la qualité de la fin de vie mais encore par la place accordée à l'autonomie du patient dans l'adoption des décisions médicales le concernant. Le droit européen a incontestablement participé à la consolidation de cette autonomie, affirmant d'abord, d'une manière peu contraignante, le droit de refuser un traitement médical non désiré, y compris si une telle décision le mène à la mort (A), consacrant ensuite une véritable obligation pour les Etats de respecter le droit de chaque personne de choisir sa mort (B).

A. *L'affirmation d'un droit de refuser un traitement médical non désiré*

Le consentement au traitement médical et le droit subséquent d'un individu de refuser un traitement médical non désiré, même si ce traitement est vital pour lui, ont été reconnus de longue date en droit européen. L'accumulation d'affirmations est cependant tempérée par la faible portée contraignante de celles-ci.

1. *L'accumulation de références*

L'accumulation est nette. La *Recommandation 779* du 29 janvier 1976, de l'Assemblée parlementaire du Conseil de l'Europe, relative aux droits des malades et des mourants précisait déjà que les médecins doivent avant tout respecter la volonté de l'intéressé en ce qui concerne le traitement.[22] La *Déclaration sur la promotion des droits des patients en Europe* de 1994 consacre également le consentement en disposant qu'aucun acte médical ne peut être pratiqué sans le consentement éclairé et préalable du patient, et ajoute que ce dernier a le droit de refuser un acte médical ou de l'interrompre en exigeant du médecin une claire explication de la portée d'un tel choix.[23] La *Convention sur les droits de l'homme et la biomédecine*

---

[22] § 4 de ladite Recommandation.
[23] § 3.1 de ladite Déclaration.

dispose dans son article 5 qu'une intervention dans le domaine de la santé ne peut être effectuée qu'après avoir obtenu le consentement libre et éclairé de la personne concernée et que, ce qui est une première en droit international, « *la personne concernée peut, à tout moment librement retirer son consentement* ». Enfin, l'on peut citer également la *Charte des droits fondamentaux de l'Union européenne* du 18 décembre 2000, qui consacre de manière identique le droit des citoyens à décider librement sur les questions médicales après en avoir été informés. Naturellement, ce droit ne vaut que si le patient est conscient et capable d'exprimer sa volonté ou s'il ne l'est plus, s'il a exprimé sa volonté à un moment où il était pleinement capable de le faire à travers une directive anticipée. Plusieurs instruments évoquent d'ailleurs cette hypothèse. La Convention de biomédecine précise, dans son article 9, que les souhaits manifestés avant l'intervention médicale par un patient qui ne se trouve pas en situation d'exprimer sa volonté au moment de cette intervention, doivent être entendus car ils font partie du consentement nécessaire. Dans le prolongement, la *Recommandation 1418* du 25 juin 1999 de l'Assemblée parlementaire enjoint expressément les Etats membres de tout mettre en oeuvre pour faire « *respecter les instructions ou la déclaration formelle (living will) rejetant certains traitements médicaux données ou faites par avance par des malades incurables ou des mourants désormais incapables d'exprimer leur volonté* ».[24]

2. *De faibles contraintes pour les Etats*

Précoces et continues, ces affirmations n'en demeurent pas moins faiblement contraignantes. D'abord, la majorité des textes n'est pas dotée d'une force obligatoire et n'oblige en rien juridiquement les Etats qui sont plutôt « invités à ». Certes, il y a bien la Charte des droits fondamentaux, mais sa portée contraignante est relativement récente.[25] Il y a bien également la Convention biomédecine. Toutefois, cet instrument contraignant souffre de plusieurs défauts. D'abord, elle n'a recueilli qu'un faible nombre de ratifications ;[26] ensuite, elle a établi un mécanisme de contrôle du respect de ses dispositions « *particulièrement timide* » ;[27] enfin, ses formulations

---

[24] § 9, b, IV de ladite Recommandation.

[25] Elle a été acquise dans le traité de Lisbonne entré en vigueur le 1er décembre 2009.

[26] La Convention, entrée en vigueur le 1er décembre 1999, n'a obtenu, pour l'heure, que 26 ratifications.

[27] Christian Byk, « La Convention européenne sur la biomédecine et les droits de l'homme et l'ordre juridique international », *Journal du droit international*, 2001, n° 1,

restent le plus souvent très prudentes. Il en est ainsi de l'article 9 de la Convention relative aux directives anticipées.[28] Ladite disposition n'oblige pas en effet les Etats à conférer à ces documents un caractère contraignant : « *les souhaits précédemment exprimés (...) seront pris en compte* ». D'ailleurs le rapport explicatif dit les choses sans détour : « *la prise en compte (...) ne signifie pas que ceux-ci devront être nécessairement suivis. Ainsi, par exemple, lorsque ces souhaits ont été exprimés très longtemps avant l'intervention et que les conditions scientifiques ont évolué, il peut être justifié de ne pas suivre l'opinion du patient. Le praticien doit donc, dans la mesure du possible, s'assurer que les souhaits du patient s'appliquent à la situation présente et sont toujours valables, compte tenu notamment de l'évolution des techniques médicales* ».[29] Autre prudence, l'article ne prévoit pas les conditions, notamment formelles, d'élaboration et donc de validité de ces documents, laissant en l'espèce une marge d'appréciation aux Etats. Le rapport du CDBI sur les souhaits précédemment exprimés au sujet des soins de santé[30] évoque l'hypothèse de l'adoption de dispositions européennes plus précises qui pourraient être incluses dans un protocole additionnel, réglant non seulement les exigences formelles mais aussi l'effet juridique de ces directives anticipées. Cependant, au vu de la forte disparité des statuts juridiques des directives anticipées dans les pays européens, recensés dans le même rapport, le consensus paraît hypothétique.

D'ailleurs, la réalité des pratiques médicales est bien souvent en décalage avec ce principe d'autonomie ainsi qu'en attestent plusieurs études visant à récolter des données européennes. Une étude, étude Ethicus, s'est déroulée entre 1999 et 2000 dans 37 services de réanimation de 17 pays européens. Ayant pour objet d'examiner les décisions de fin de vie en réanimation, cette étude a mis en évidence, par-delà même les différences

---

pp. 47–70, p. 57. Voir notamment l'article 29 de la Convention : la Cour européenne des droits de l'homme ne se voit pas conférer de compétence similaire à celle qu'elle exerce dans le cadre de la Convention européenne des droits de l'homme, son intervention demeurant simplement consultative et limitée puisqu'elle devra être dégagée de tout lien avec un litige concret soumis à une juridiction nationale.

[28] À noter toutefois que les directives anticipées incluent non seulement les testaments de vie qui expriment les préférences des personnes concernant les recours à des traitements précis et la procuration pour soins de santé qui permet à une personne de désigner quelqu'un pour prendre des décisions en matière de santé en leur nom.

[29] § 62 du rapport explicatif à la Convention.

[30] CDBI, 35 ième réunion, 2–5 décembre 2008, *Les souhaits précédemment exprimés au sujets de soins de santé. Principes communs et différentes règles applicables dans les systèmes juridiques nationaux*, rapport préparé par le Professeur Roberto Andorno, http://www.coe.int/t/dg3/healthbioethic/Activities/09_Euthanasia/default_fr.asp.

entre les processus décisionnels, que le concept d'autonomie, pourtant valorisé au plan législatif, joue un rôle peu important en Europe, les médecins gardant une culture « paternaliste » dans leurs pratiques de réanimation. On peut aussi citer l'enquête Eurled qui a fait le point sur le pratiques médicales en fin de vie dans 6 pays européens (Italie, Suède, Belgique, Danemark, Pays-Bas, Suisse) à partir des certificats de décès[31] avec pour objectif de mesurer et comparer la fréquence des décisions médicales susceptibles d'abréger la vie. D'après l'enquête, un quart à la moitié des décès font l'objet d'une décision médicale relative à la décision de fin de vie, la plus grosse partie étant formée par des décisions de mise en œuvre de traitements de la douleur (avec pour effet d'abréger la vie). Ensuite, viennent les décisions de ne pas mettre en œuvre ou d'interrompre un traitement. Au total, le décès assisté est assez peu fréquent. L'étude démontre également que « *même lorsque l'intention de mettre un terme à la vie du patient est explicite, celui-ci ou les membres de sa famille ne sont pas toujours impliqués dans le processus de décision* »[32]...

B. *La consécration d'un véritable droit de choisir sa fin de vie*

La Cour européenne des droits de l'homme a joué, au travers de sa jurisprudence, un rôle important dans la consolidation de l'autonomie de l'individu en fin de vie. S'arrimant à l'un des articles de la Convention, l'article 8 relatif au droit au respect de la vie privée et familiale, le juge européen a en effet dégagé un véritable droit à l'autodétermination qui emporte, à la charge des Etats, de véritables obligations, néanmoins susceptibles, dans certaines conditions, de connaître des limites.

1. *L'apparition d'un droit à l'autodétermination*

L'on sait combien la notion de vie privée est une notion dont la Cour, loin de donner une définition exhaustive, a, au contraire, eu une acceptation très large afin d'assurer une protection forte de l'article 8. La Cour y a ainsi inclus, au-delà de la protection de la sphère intime de la personne, le droit au développement personnel mais encore le droit d'établir et d'entretenir des rapports avec d'autres êtres humains et le monde extérieur.[33] Dans son aspect « intime », la vie privée a également reçu une compréhension très

---

[31] Johan Bilsen, Joachim Cohen et Luc Deliens, « La fin de vie en Europe : le point sur les pratiques médicales », *Population et Sociétés*, janvier 2007, n° 430, pp. 1–4.
[32] Ibid., p. 3.
[33] CEDH, 16 décembre 1992, *Niemetz c/ Allemagne*, Série A n° 251-B, § 29.

étendue, recouvrant, on le sait, l'intégrité morale ou physique de la personne,[34] sa vie sexuelle[35] ou encore son image ou ses données personnelles.[36] D'ailleurs, la Commission européenne des droits de l'homme, puis la Cour elle-même avaient déjà eu, à plusieurs reprises, l'occasion de laisser entendre que l'administration non consenti d'un traitement médical portait atteinte à l'article 8 et déclenchait la responsabilité de l'Etat partie pour violation de son obligation d'assurer une protection appropriée de l'intégrité physique de la personne. La Commission avait ainsi déjà affirmé qu'une « *intervention médicale sous la contrainte, même si elle est d'importance minime, doit être considérée comme une atteinte à ce droit* ».[37] La Cour avait emboîté le pas estimant que l'administration de la diamorphine à un enfant de 12 ans que les médecins estimaient être entré en phase terminale, contre la volonté de la mère, « *s'analyse en une atteinte au droit du premier au respect de sa vie privée et plus particulièrement à son droit à l'intégrité physique* »[38] ou encore que l'administration forcée d'un traitement médical à une jeune femme majeure internée à la demande de son père dans un service de clinique psychiatrique porte atteinte au respect de la vie privée de l'intéressé.[39]

Il a toutefois fallu attendre l'arrêt *Pretty* du 29 avril 2002 pour avoir une confirmation de l'applicabilité de cette jurisprudence en situation de fin de vie. Faisant le constat qu'« *à une époque où l'on assiste à une sophistication médicale croissante et à une augmentation de l'espérance de vie, de nombreuses personnes redoutent qu'on ne les force à se maintenir en vie jusqu'à un âge très avancé ou dans un état de grave délabrement physique ou mental aux antipodes de la perception aiguë qu'elles ont d'elles-mêmes et de leur identité personnelle* », la Cour admet, sans difficulté, que la protection de l'intégrité de la personne âgée est garantie par l'article 8 et rappelle le principe précédent : « *l'imposition d'un traitement médical sans le consentement du patient, s'il est adulte et sain d'esprit, s'analyserait en une*

---

[34] CEDH, 26 mars 1985, *X. et Y. c/ Pays-Bas*, Série A n° 91, § 21 et s.

[35] Ibid., § 22.

[36] CEDH, 21 février 2002, *Schüssel c/ Autriche*, n° 42409/98, non publiée.

[37] Com EDH, *X. c/ Autriche*, 13 décembre 1979, DR 18, p. 154. Voir également, Com EDH, *X. c/ Pays-Bas*, 4 décembre 1978, DR 16, p. 86. Pour un autre exemple, dans une affaire *Acmanne c/ Belgique* du 10 décembre 1984, D.10435.83, la Commission avait admis le droit d'exercer un choix relatif à des traitements médicaux et avait analysé l'obligation de vaccination et d'examen radiologique comme des ingérences dans l'exercice du droit au respect de la vie privée.

[38] CEDH, 9 mars 2004, *Glass c/ Royaume Uni*, Rec. 2004-II, § 70.

[39] CEDH, 16 juin 2005, *Storck c/ Allemagne*, req n° 61603/00, *JCP G.*, 2005, I, 159, n° 15, chron. Frédéric Sudre.

atteinte à l'intégrité physique de l'intéressé pouvant mettre en cause les droits protégés par l'article 8 §b1 de la Convention ».[40] Ici la différence est que Mme Pretty ne demandait pas à ne pas en bénéficier d'un traitement médical, mais souhaitait être assistée dans son suicide. La question était autrement plus délicate : il s'agissait de savoir si l'interdiction du suicide assistée tel que prévu par le droit anglais[41] devait être considérée comme constituant une ingérence non autorisée dans le droit au respect de sa vie privée. Pour répondre à cette question, la Cour développe un raisonnement pour le moins audacieux qui débouche sur une innovation assez « *considérable* ».[42] Bien qu'il n'ait été établi dans aucune affaire antérieure que l'article 8 de la Convention comporte un droit à l'autodétermination en tant que tel, la Cour considère ici que « *la notion d'autonomie personnelle reflète un principe important qui sous-tend l'interprétation des garanties de l'article 8* »[43] et peut s'entendre « *au sens du droit d'opérer des choix concernant son propre corps* ».[44] La Cour affirme que, sur ce fondement, « *la façon dont elle choisit de passer les derniers instants de son existence fait partie de l'acte de vivre et elle a le droit de demander que cela soit aussi respecté* » et de conclure que « *la requérante en l'espèce est empêchée par la loi d'exercer son choix d'éviter ce qui, à ses yeux, constituera une fin de vie indigne et pénible. La Cour ne peut exclure que cela représente une atteinte au droit de l'intéressé au respect de sa vie privée, au sens de l'article 8-1 de la Convention* ».[45] La Cour confère au final à ce nouveau droit à l'autodétermination, depuis lors largement repris,[46] une portée très large puisque cela inclut le droit de choisir sa fin de vie, c'est-à-dire le droit de refuser de consentir à un traitement qui pourrait avoir pour effet de prolonger sa vie et plus généralement le droit de choisir le moment de sa mort et ses conditions.

---

[40] § 63 de l'arrêt *Pretty*.
[41] Cf. note 18.
[42] Olivier De Schutter, « L'aide au suicide devant la Cour européenne des droits de l'homme », *Revue trimestrielle des droits de l'homme*, 2003, pp. 71–111, p. 84.
[43] § 61 de l'arrêt.
[44] § 66 de l'arrêt.
[45] § 67 de l'arrêt.
[46] Confirmation en est donnée par exemple par l'arrêt *K.A et A. D. c/ Belgique* du 17 février 2005 où la Cour consacre le droit de disposer de son corps et affirme que la notion d'autonomie personnelle peut s'entendre au sens d'opérer des choix concernant son propre corps (§ 83). Le développement a d'ailleurs été tel qu'il a provoqué les réaction d'une partie de la doctrine qui souligne le paradoxe qu'il y aurait à déduire de l'autonomie personne la renonciation par une personne à son intégrité corporelle : voir parmi d'autres Muriel Fabre-Magnan, « Le domaine de l'autonomie personne (indisponibilité du corps humain et justice sociale) », *Recueil Dalloz*, 2008, pp. 31–39.

2. *Les limites possibles au droit à l'autodétermination*

Toutefois, ce droit à l'autodétermination peut connaître des limites. Aux termes de l'article 8 § 2, les Etats ont en effet le droit de contrôler, au travers de l'application du droit pénal, les activités préjudiciables à la vie et à la sécurité d'autrui à condition que l'ingérence soit prévue par la loi et soit nécessaire, dans une société démocratique, à la poursuite d'un but légitime.[47] En l'espèce, ayant admis que l'interdiction faite à la requérante d'être assistée dans son suicide constituait une ingérence dans son droit au respect de sa vie privée, la Cour devait donc examiner l'éventuelle justification de cette ingérence au regard de l'article 8 § 2. Comme l'interdiction du suicide assisté était prévue par la loi et qu'elle poursuivait le but légitime de préserver la vie et donc les droits d'autrui, les difficultés se concentraient sur le point de savoir si l'ingérence était nécessaire, c'est-à-dire proportionnée au but légitime poursuivi. La Cour conclut que l'ingérence peut être considérée comme proportionnée étant donné « *le risque d'abus et les conséquences probables des abus éventuellement commis qu'impliquerait un assouplissement de l'interdiction générale du suicide assisté ou la création d'exceptions au principe* »,[48] notamment pour les personnes les plus vulnérables. Elle construit son raisonnement, principalement,[49] autour de l'idée — peu rigoureuse juridiquement, mais plutôt convaincante empiriquement — de « *pente glissante* »:[50] « *en dépénalisant l'assistance au suicide dans certains cas déterminés d'où tout risque d'abus serait absent (...) l'on glisserait immanquablement vers une dépénalisation plus large, au détriment de la protection à laquelle ont droit de la part de l'Etat les personnes les plus vulnérables* ».[51] C'est le risque de créer un

---

[47] Selon la disposition, il s'agit des mesures nécessaires à « *la sécurité nationale, à la sûreté publique, au bien-être économique du pays, à la défense de l'ordre et à la prévention des infractions pénales, à la protection de la santé ou de la morale, ou à la protection des droits et libertés d'autrui* ».

[48] § 74 de l'arrêt.

[49] Plus étonnants sont les propos additionnels de la Cour qui, pour conclure à la proportionnalité de la loi anglaise, rappelle que les poursuites pénales qu'elles prévoient pour les proches qui assistent un malade à se suicider ne sont pas toujours mises à exécution ! L'absence de violation d'un droit fondamental de la Convention dépend ici des possibilités de non application de la loi... : voir le § 76 où la Cour explique qu'il ne lui paraît pas arbitraire que « *le droit reflète l'importance du droit à la vie en interdisant le suicide assisté tout en prévoyant un régime d'application et d'appréciation par la justice qui permet de prendre en compte dans chaque cas concret tant l'intérêt public à entamer des poursuites que les exigences justes et adéquates de la rétribution et de la dissuasion* ».

[50] De Schutter, *supra* note 42, p. 92.

[51] Surtout si l'on se souvient que, médicalement, toute personne en phase terminale d'une maladie est le plus souvent gravement déprimée et donc de ce fait vulnérable.

précédent qui a fondé l'argumentation du juge européen. « *Concrètement, elle révèle le souci légitime de la Cour de ne pas jouer aux apprentis sorciers en ouvrant trop facilement les portes de l'euthanasie aux personnes vulnérables à partir du cas exemplaire d'une requérante dont la lucidité et la saine détermination forçaient l'admiration* ».[52] Au total, si le droit de choisir le moment de sa mort et ses conditions afin d'éviter une fin de vie indigne semble incluse dans le droit au respect de la vie privée, en l'espèce la Cour juge que l'interdiction légale du suicide assisté s'avère nécessaire dans une société démocratique à la protection de la santé et de la sécurité publique. Ainsi semble s'esquisser une différence entre le droit de choisir sa fin de vie et les conditions de sa mort et le droit de mettre fin à ses jours.

II. Décider de mourir

La décision de mourir qui renvoie au point le plus extrême de la fin de la vie est au centre de débats passionnés entre les partisans d'une autonomie complète étendue jusqu'à la possibilité de choisir la mort et les défenseurs de l'interdit de la mort « donnée », quelque soit les raisons. Logiquement et heureusement pourrait-on dire, dans ce contexte, le droit européen a emprunté nettement la voie de la discrétion. Précisant que le droit à la vie n'implique en aucun cas un droit de mourir (A), le droit européen est en effet resté très prudent dans le débat sur l'euthanasie (B).

A. *Le refus du juge européen de consacrer un droit de mourir*

Le refus du juge européen est tout à la fois net et logique.

1. *La netteté de la position du juge européen*

L'arrêt *Pretty* présentait un second intérêt en ce que la requérante invoquait l'article 2 qui dispose que « *le droit de toute personne à la vie est protégé par la loi* ». La requérante soutenait que l'autoriser à se faire aider pour mettre un terme à son existence ne serait pas contraire à cet article au motif que ce dernier garantirait non seulement le droit à la vie, mais également, de façon corollaire, le droit de mourir. Il faut dire que certains droits garantis par la Convention ont été interprétés comme conférant des droits à ne pas faire, c'est-à-dire des droits constituant l'antithèse de ce

---

[52] Marguénaud, *supra* note 18, p. 859.

que le droit explicitement reconnu autorise à faire. L'article 11 par exemple relatif à la liberté d'association confère, selon la Cour, un droit à ne pas adhérer à une association ;[53] l'article 9 sur la liberté de conscience et de religion comporte un droit à ne pas être soumis à aucune obligation d'exprimer ses pensées, de changer d'avis ou de divulguer ses convictions.[54] La réponse de la Cour est, à propos de l'article 2, nette. Explicitant bien la spécificité du droit à la vie, qui à la différence des libertés « *n'implique aucune dimension de « choix » dans le chef des individus* »,[55] elle en conclu que l'article 2 « *ne saurait, sans distorsion de langage, être interprété comme conférant un droit diamétralement opposé, à savoir un droit à mourir ; il ne saurait davantage créer un droit à l'autodétermination au sens où il donnerait à l'individu le droit de choisir la mort plutôt que la vie (...) La Cour estime donc qu'il n'est pas possible de déduire de l'article 2 de la Convention un droit à mourir, que ce soit de la main d'un tiers ou avec l'assistance d'une autorité publique* ».[56] Ce refus de reconnaître au droit à la vie un aspect négatif peut être « *critiqué, discuté, regretté, force est néanmoins de reconnaître qu'il tranche une question de principe avec courage et netteté sans ensevelir la réponse, comme il arrive trop souvent, sous un fatras méthodologique dérivant du concept particulièrement flou de « marge nationale d'appréciation ». »*[57]

2. *La logique de la position du juge européen*

Cette affirmation très forte est parfaitement cohérente avec l'obligation positive que le juge européen met, depuis longtemps, à la charge des Etats au titre de l'article 2, celle non seulement de s'abstenir de donner la mort de manière intentionnelle, mais aussi de prendre les mesures nécessaires à la protection de vie.[58] Elle l'est également avec la valeur reconnue par la Cour à l'article 2. Le droit à la vie est, de jurisprudence constante, considéré comme « *l'une des valeurs fondamentales des sociétés démocratiques qui forment le Conseil de l'Europe* ».[59] D'ailleurs, l'arrêt accentue encore la « valorisation » de ce droit puisqu'elle va jusqu'à lui accorder ici « *la prééminence* » au motif que, sans lui, « *la jouissance de l'un quelconque des*

---

[53] Voir par exemple CEDH, 29 avril 1999, *Chassagnou et al. c/ France*, n° 25088/94, 28331/95 et 28443/95, §§ 91–92, CEDH 1999-III, § 103.
[54] CEDH, 23 octobre 1990, *Darby*, A. 187.
[55] De Schutter, *supra* note 42, p. 79.
[56] § 39–40 de l'arrêt.
[57] Marguénaud, *supra* note 18, p. 858.
[58] CEDH, 9 juin 1998, *L.C.B. c/ Royaume-Uni*, Rec. 1998-III, p. 1403, § 36.
[59] CEDH, 27 septembre 1995, *Mac Cann c/ Royaume Uni*, série A, n° 324, § 147.

autres droits et libertés garantis par la Convention serait illusoire ».[60]
*« La Cour a ici réalisé une avancée significative dans l'établissement de
la hiérarchie des droits de l'homme en désignant clairement « le Roi des
Droits ». »*[61]

B. *L'abstention du droit européen dans le débat sur l'euthanasie*

Il est classique de distinguer entre l'euthanasie passive où la mort n'est pas
l'effet directement recherché, mais ce qui l'est c'est l'administration ou le
refus de soins qui auront pour effet secondaire d'entraîner la mort et l'euthanasie active où la mort est l'effet recherché. C'est cette seconde forme
d'euthanasie, qui recouvre le suicide assistée, mais également toutes décisions, notamment médicales ayant pour but directement de mettre un
terme à une vie, qui fait débat. Naturellement, ce débat se retrouve au
plan européen où la tension est perceptible entre les instances qui prônent
l'autonomie des malades au stade terminal[62] et celles qui réaffirment l'interdit de tuer.[63] Faute de consensus, pour l'heure, la situation est pour le
moins paradoxale : l'euthanasie est en effet, dans la majorité des pays
européens, un délit, mais se pratique tous les jours. Seules les lois belges[64]
et néerlandaises[65] entrées en vigueur en 2002 permettent aux médecins

---

[60] § 37 de l'arrêt.

[61] Marguénaud, *supra* note 18, p. 858.

[62] Proposition de résolution sur l'assistance aux mourants, adoptée par le Parlement
européen le 25 avril 1991, article 8.43.

[63] Recommandation n° 1418 du Conseil de l'Europe du 25 juin 1999 sur la protection
des droits de l'homme et la dignité des malades mourants ou en phase terminale, approu-
vée le 26 mars 2002, § 9.

[64] On entend par « la loi belge » la loi du 28 mai 2002 relative à l'euthanasie (*Moniteur
belge*, 22 juin 2002, http://www.just.fgov.be/cgi/welcome.pl). Le médecin qui pratique une
euthanasie ne commet pas d'infraction s'il respecte les conditions et procédures prescrites
et il s'est assuré que :
- le patient est majeur ou mineur émancipé, capable et conscient au moment de sa
   demande (qui doit être faite par écrit) ;
- la demande est formulée de manière volontaire, réfléchie et répétée, et qu'elle ne
   résulte pas d'une pression extérieure ;
- le patient se trouve dans une situation médicale sans issue et fait état d'une souffrance physique ou psychique constante et insupportable qui ne peut être apaisée
   et qui résulte d'une affection accidentelle ou pathologique grave et incurable.

[65] La loi relative au « contrôle des interruptions de vie pratiquées à la demande du
patient et des aides au suicide », entrée en vigueur aux Pays-Bas le 1ᵉʳ avril 2002. En substance, la nouvelle loi contient un amendement à l'article 293 du Code pénal stipulant que,
bien que quiconque mettant fin à la vie d'une personne sur demande expresse et ardente
de ladite personne soit passible d'une peine d'emprisonnement ne dépassant pas douze
ans ou d'une amende de cinquième catégorie, un tel acte ne sera pas un délit s'il est perpé-
tré par un médecin qui en notifie l'expert médico-légal de la commune conformément à la

qui accèdent à des demandes d'euthanasie volontaire active ou de suicide assisté formulée par un patient d'échapper aux poursuites, dans certaines conditions rigoureuses.[66]

Or, à son propos, sauf une exception mais d'une valeur uniquement recommandatoire,[67] le droit européen reste particulièrement peu disert :[68] à l'impossible consensus textuel s'ajoute la discrétion du juge européen en ce domaine.

1. *L'absence de consensus textuel*

Dans la Convention d'Oveido, dès le départ, il avait été décidé de ne pas aborder deux problèmes éthiques importants : l'avortement et

---

législation en vigueur et qui remplit les critères de soin stipulés. Selon ces critères, le médecin concerné doit :
    a. avoir la conviction que le malade a fait une demande volontaire et mûrement réfléchie ;
    b. avoir la conviction que la souffrance du malade est intolérable et qu'il n'y a aucune perspective d'amélioration ;
    c. avoir informé le malade sur sa situation et ses perspectives ;
    d. être arrivé à la conclusion, avec le malade, qu'il n'y a pas d'alternative possible compte tenu de sa situation ;
    e. avoir consulté au moins un autre médecin indépendant, lequel doit avoir vu le malade et donné un avis écrit sur les critères de soin énoncés plus haut (voir les paragraphes a. à d.) ;
    f. avoir mis fin à la vie du malade ou aidé à son suicide avec tous les soins médicaux et l'attention qui se doivent.

[66] Yves-Henri Leleu et Gilles Genicot, « L'euthanasie en Belgique et aux Pays-Bas, Variations sur le thème de l'autodétermination », *Revue trimestrielle des droits de l'homme*, 2004, n° 57, pp. 5–50.

[67] La Recommandation 1418 (1999) de l'Assemblée parlementaire du Conseil de l'Europe énonce au paragraphe 9 : « *L'Assemblée recommande par conséquent au Comité des Ministres d'encourager les Etats membres du Conseil de l'Europe à respecter et à protéger la dignité des malades incurables et des mourants à tous égards:*

    c. *en maintenant l'interdiction absolue de mettre intentionnellement fin à la vie des malades incurables et des mourants:*

        i. *vu que le droit à la vie, notamment en ce qui concerne les malades incurables et les mourants, est garanti par les Etats membres, conformément à l'article 2 de la Convention européenne des Droits de l'Homme qui dispose que « la mort ne peut être infligée à quiconque intentionnellement »;*
        ii. *vu que le désir de mourir exprimé par un malade incurable ou un mourant ne peut jamais constituer un fondement juridique à sa mort de la main d'un tiers;*
        iii. *vu que le désir de mourir exprimé par un malade incurable ou un mourant ne peut en soi servir de justification légale à l'exécution d'actions destinées à entraîner la mort ».*

[68] Voir sur ce sujet : Christian Byk, *Euthanasie : la nécessité d'une loi au regard du droit européen des droits de l'homme ?* disponible sur le site : http://www.iales.org/dossiers/dossier-euthanasie/euthanasie-la-necessite-d-une-loi.pdf.

l'euthanasie. Vu les divergences d'opinions dans les Etats membres et entre les Etats membres, aucun accord fructueux sur ces deux questions ne pouvait être escompté. En 2001, une enquête menée par le CDBI à la demande du Comité des Ministres avait d'ailleurs confirmé l'hétérogénéité des lois et pratiques pertinentes en matière d'euthanasie et autres décisions sur la fin de vie.[69] Un peu plus tard, la Commission des questions sociales, de la santé et de la famille de l'Assemblée parlementaire rendait, quatre ans après l'adoption de la Recommandation 1418, un rapport, le Rapport Marty, le 10 septembre 2003 qui préconisait l'adoption d'une Résolution sur ce sujet. Toutefois, faute de majorité, cette résolution n'a jamais été adoptée.

2. *La discrétion du juge européen*

Surtout, le juge européen est resté très discret sur cette question. Certes, dans son arrêt *Pretty*, il a conclu à l'absence d'incompatibilité d'une interdiction générale (et d'une incrimination) du suicide assisté, telle que celle prévue par la loi anglaise, avec les articles 2, 3[70] et 8 de la Convention. Toutefois, s'il y a un risque que l'arrêt *Pretty* soit lu de manière à lui faire dire ce qu'il ne dit pas, c'est-à-dire comme une condamnation implicite de la dépénalisation de l'euthanasie,[71] il faut bien admettre que l'arrêt ne dit rien de tel. La Cour souligne que le refus de toute dépénalisation ne constitue pas une violation de l'article 2 si certaines justifications sont présentes, mais elle ne dit rien sur l'admission d'une dépénalisation du suicide assisté ou plus généralement de l'euthanasie. La Cour aurait eu l'occasion de

---

[69] Le CDBI avait adressé aux Etats membres du Conseil de l'Europe un questionnaire relatif à leurs lois et pratiques en matière d'euthanasie et autres décisions sur la fin de vie. Le document final contient une analyse des réponses des 35 Etats membres ayant répondu. L'expert qui a dirigé l'enquête a également rédigé un rapport concomitant, non publié par le CDBI. Rapport sur les lois en vigueur ou pratiques appliquées dans les Etats membres relatives aux questions soulevées par la Recommandation 1418 (1999) de l'Assemblée parlementaire relative à la protection des droits de l'homme et de la dignité des malades incurables et des mourants [831 Réunion] : Réponses au questionnaire pour les Etats membres relatif à l'euthanasie, 20 janvier 2003, CDBI/INF (2003) 8.

[70] L'incrimination de l'assistance au suicide n'est pas un traitement inhumain ou dégradant selon la Cour : « *en l'espèce, la souffrance de la requérante n'est pas la conséquence d'un comportement actif des autorités. Ce n'est pas plus la conséquence d'un défaut de protection vis-à-vis des agissements d'un tiers. Ce n'est pas non plus l'inaction des autorités, leur défaut de prendre en compte la maladie d'une personne dont elles ont la charge qui sont en cause. La souffrance, aussi grande soit-elle, résultant de la maladie ne peut être considérée comme un traitement* ». Florence Massias, Note sous l'arrêt, *Revue de science criminelle*, 2002, p. 647. En bref, personne ne pouvait sérieusement reprocher à l'Etat d'avoir infligé à la malade le moindre mauvais traitement puisqu'elle avait toujours reçu les soins adéquats de la part des autorités médicales.

[71] De Schutter, *supra* note 42, p. 74.

s'exprimer à nouveau sur la question de l'euthanasie dans l'affaire relative à Eluana Englaro[72] déclenchée par la décision de la Cour d'appel de Milan autorisant le père d'Eluana à faire interrompre l'alimentation et l'hydratation artificielle de sa fille. En effet, dans l'arrêt *Ada Rossi et autres & sept requêtes c. Italie*,[73] plusieurs tuteurs de personnes en état végétatif, quelques associations composées notamment de proches de personnes lourdement handicapées, de médecins, de psychologues et d'avocats assistant ces personnes ainsi qu'une association de défense des droits de l'homme avaient introduit une requête devant la Cour se plaignant des effets négatifs que l'exécution de l'arrêt rendu par la Cour d'appel de Milan pourrait avoir à leur égard, notamment en ce qu'elle engendrerait une discrimination pour les personnes lourdement handicapées et les mettrait à la merci des tiers qui pourraient librement disposer de leur vie. Toutefois, la Cour n'a pas eu à se prononcer sur le fond, déclarant les requêtes irrecevables au motif que les requérants ne pouvaient être considérés comme victimes d'une violation de la Convention aux sens de l'article 34 de la Convention.[74] Pour l'heure, donc cette question n'a jamais été soumise directement au jugement de la Cour.

---

[72] Victime d'un accident de la route survenu en janvier 1992, au cours duquel elle subit un traumatisme crânien et se fractura une vertèbre, une jeune femme âgée de 20 ans prénommée E.E. tomba dans le coma. Par la suite, on diagnostiqua chez elle un état végétatif avec tétraplégie spastique et perte de toute faculté psychique supérieure. En décembre 1996, E.E. fut placée sous la tutelle de son père. En janvier 1999, celui-ci diligenta une procédure en vue d'obtenir l'autorisation de faire interrompre l'alimentation et l'hydratation artificielles de sa fille, soutenant que tel aurait été le vœu de celle-ci compte tenu de sa personnalité et des idées qu'elle avait exprimées sur la vie et la dignité humaine avant son accident. Refusée à deux reprises, l'autorisation est finalement donnée par une décision du 25 juin 2008, de la cour d'appel de Milan, statuant sur renvoi, au double motif que l'état végétatif de celle-ci était irréversible et qu'il existait des preuves claires, concordantes et convaincantes de ce que cette demande reflétait fidèlement la volonté de la personne représentée telle qu'elle pouvait se déduire du style de vie de celle-ci, de ses convictions et des vues qu'elle avait exprimées sur la dignité humaine avant de sombrer dans l'inconscience.

[73] Deuxième Section, 16 décembre 2008, requête n° 55185/08 et autres.

[74] La Cour rappelle que cet article « exige qu'un individu requérant se prétende effectivement lésé par la violation qu'il allègue. Il n'institue pas au profit des particuliers une sorte d'*actio popularis* pour l'interprétation de la Convention ; il ne les autorise pas à se plaindre *in abstracto* d'une loi par cela seul qu'elle leur semble enfreindre la Convention. En principe, il ne suffit pas à un individu requérant de soutenir qu'une loi viole par sa simple existence les droits dont il jouit aux termes de la Convention ; elle doit avoir été appliquée à son détriment. Toutefois, la Cour a déjà admis qu'un requérant peut se prétendre potentiellement victime d'une violation de la Convention lorsqu'il n'est pas en mesure de démontrer que la législation incriminée lui a été effectivement appliquée, pour autant qu'il existe des indices raisonnables et convaincants de la probabilité de réalisation d'une violation en ce qui le concerne personnellement. En l'espèce, la Cour estime les requérants n'ont pas satisfait à cette obligation. D'abord, la juridiction s'est prononcée dans des circonstances bien précises, ensuite, elle a bien rappelé l'indispensable prise en compte de la volonté du malade exprimée par le tuteur.

Il pourrait d'ailleurs tout à fait être soutenu que la dépénalisation de l'euthanasie n'équivaudrait pas à la reconnaissance d'un droit à mettre fin à sa vie et pourrait donc être compatible avec l'article 2, sous certaines conditions précises, en particulier que le malade en ait fait la demande consciente.[75] Le Conseil d'Etat belge, dans son avis sur la loi alors en préparation avait abouti à une telle conclusion.[76] Il avait noté, en particulier, après analyse de la jurisprudence de la Cour européenne des droits de l'homme, que l'obligation positive qu'ont les Parties de protéger le droit à la vie ne doit pas empêcher de tenir compte, notamment, du droit des personnes à l'autodétermination. Cela signifie que l'obligation des autorités de protéger le droit à la vie doit être placée en regard du droit des personnes à être protégées des peines ou traitements inhumains et du droit à l'intégrité physique et morale, qui dérive du droit au respect de la vie privée. Or, la Convention ne donne pas de directive sur la manière de résoudre ce conflit entre les droits fondamentaux. Selon la haute Assemblée, il revient d'abord au législateur d'user de son pouvoir discrétionnaire pour résoudre ce conflit, le juge (et l'interprète) devant « *respecter le pouvoir d'appréciation du législateur et ne pouvant se substituer à lui* ». La Cour a déjà tenu ce genre de propos, affirmant ainsi que « *le législateur étant le mieux à même d'arbitrer entre les divers courants politiques et éthiques, on comprend qu'il faille s'interdire de juger son œuvre d'un point de vue moral, du moins en tant que juriste et respecter son choix de faire prévaloir la liberté individuelle contre l'opinion selon laquelle la vie humaine est rigoureusement et radicalement indisponible* ».[77] Quelque soit l'interprétation, en tous les cas, dans le débat sur la dépénalisation de l'euthanasie, la jurisprudence européenne « *laisse ouverte la voie de l'expérimentation* ».[78]

Au final, le droit européen n'apporte, sur les questions relatives à la fin de vie, que des « morceaux » de réponses, quelques jalons ici et là (absence du droit de mourir, mais existence d'un droit de choisir sa mort)

---

[75] En outre, il est impératif que l'état médical soit sans issue et constaté comme tel. La question est évidemment plus délicate pour les personnes inconscientes ou incapables de manifester leur volonté d'où l'intérêt d'une déclaration anticipée. On comprend dès lors que les lois belge et néerlandaise prévoit que l'élément fondamental qui permet de justifier le mécanisme est la demande du patient, fût-elle anticipée. Les conditions relatives à la qualité de la demande font obstacle à ce que celle-ci émane de personnes inconscientes (coma, état végétatif permanent ...) ou ne disposant plus d'une clarté d'esprit suffisante pour la formuler (maladie d'Alzheimer). Les deux législateurs leur permettent néanmoins de bénéficier d'une euthanasie grâce à la technique de la déclaration anticipée.

[76] Conseil d'Etat, section de législation, avis du 2 juillet 2001, Doc. parl., Sénat, 2000–2001, no 2-244/21, *Revue trimestrielle des droits de l'homme*, 2001, p. 259, note François Rigaux.

[77] CEDH, 19 mai 1982, *H. c. Norvège*.

[78] De Schutter, *supra* note 42, p. 111.

qui encadrent les choix des Etats certes, mais bien à la marge. N'est-ce toutefois par ici « *faire preuve de sagesse face à la diversité des conceptions sur ce qu'implique le respect de la dignité de la personne humaine en fin de vie* » ?[79] En d'autres termes, n'est-ce pas heureux que le droit européen n'éclaire pas trop la nuit qu'est notre mort ... ?

NB : Depuis la rédaction de l'article, un arrêt important a été rendu par la Cour européenne des droits de l'homme sur la question du suicide assisté, le 20 janvier 2011, dans l'affaire *Haas c/ Suisse.*[80] Dans cet arrêt, la Cour suit la même démarche de prudence que dans l'affaire *Pretty* alors même que la situation est bien différente puisque l'objet du litige était ici de savoir si, en vertu de l'article 8, l'Etat devait faire en sorte que le requérant, qui ne pouvait pas « *véritablement être considéré comme une personne infirme, dans la mesure où il ne se trouve pas au stade terminal d'une maladie dégénérative incurable* »,[81] puisse obtenir, pour mourir sans douleur et risque d'échec, une substance nécessaire à son projet de suicide. Soulignant que « *les recherches effectuées par [elle] lui permettent de conclure que l'on est loin d'un consensus au sein des Etats membres du Conseil de l'Europe quant au droit d'un individu de choisir quand et de quelle manière il veut mettre fin à ses jours* » et que « *la grande majorité des Etats membres semblent donner plus de poids à la protection de la vie de l'individu qu'à son droit d'y mettre fin* »,[82] les juges concluent que l'article 8 ne peut être interprété comme imposant aux Etats une obligation positive d'adopter les mesures permettant de faciliter un suicide dans la dignité. La Cour instille toutefois quelques éléments nouveaux sur la question notamment lorsqu'elle constate que, « *même à supposer que les Etats aient une (telle) obligation positive (...) les autorités suisses n'ont pas violé cette obligation dans le cas d'espèce* »[83] puisque la législation suisse permet l'obtention d'une telle substance sous réserve d'obtenir une ordonnance médicale, délivrée sur le fondement d'une expertise psychiatrique complète. La Cour reconnaît ici

---

[79] Dubouis, *supra* note 7, p. 87.
[80] CEDH, 20 janvier 2011, *Haas c/ Suisse*, n° 31322/07.
[81] § 52. Atteint « *d'un grave trouble affectif bipolaire depuis une vingtaine d'années* », un homme de nationalité suisse cherche à mettre fin à ses jours car il estime ne « *plus [pouvoir] vivre d'une manière digne en raison de sa maladie, difficile à traiter* » (§ 7). Adhérent de l'association « *Dignitas* » qui « *propose en particulier une assistance au suicide* », l'intéressé tenta d'obtenir la substance nécessaire à son projet de suicide, « *à savoir 15 grammes de pentobarbital sodique, substance soumise à prescription médicale* ». Puisque tous les psychiatres qu'il consulta refusèrent de lui prescrire une telle substance, il sollicita - en vain - une autorisation en ce sens auprès des autorités médicales suisses. Par un arrêt rendu en 2006, le Tribunal fédéral suisse confirma ces refus.
[82] § 55.
[83] § 61.

la légitimité de ce dispositif car il sert l'intérêt (légitime) de « *protéger notamment toute personne d'une prise de décision précipitée, ainsi que de prévenir des abus, notamment d'éviter qu'un patient incapable de discernement obtienne une dose mortelle de pentobarbital sodique* ».[84] Elle poursuit en vérifiant que l'obtention d'une telle substance n'existe pas seulement « *de manière théorique et illusoire* » notamment eu égard à « *la menace de poursuites pénales qui pèse sur les médecins prêts à fournir une expertise approfondie afin de faciliter un suicide* » concluant que, « *au vu des informations qui lui ont été soumises, la Cour n'est pas convaincue que le requérant se trouvait dans l'impossibilité de trouver un spécialiste prêt à l'assister* ».[85] Or, ce faisant, la Cour pose deux jalons précieux dans le domaine du suicide assisté: d'abord, elle évoque l'hypothèse d'une possible obligation positive qui, pourrait, dans d'autres cas, semble-t-il, être admise. Surtout, elle inaugure un contrôle exigeant des législations et pratiques en matière de suicide assisté qui doivent permettre de respecter « *le droit d'un individu de décider de quelle manière et à quel moment sa vie doit prendre fin, à condition qu'il soit en mesure de forger librement sa propre volonté à ce propos et d'agir en conséquence* ».[86] Une affaire, en cours, l'affaire *Koch c/ Allemagne* devrait permettre de préciser encore le raisonnement du juge européen en la matière.[87]

---

[84] § 56.

[85] § 59 et 60.

[86] § 51.

[87] En l'espèce, le requérant, Ulrich Koch, est un ressortissant allemand qui se plaint du refus des autorités allemandes d'autoriser son épouse à acquérir une dose létale d'un médicament pour lui permettre de se suicider. L'épouse du requérant – qui était presque entièrement paralysée, avait été placée sous assistance respiratoire et nécessitait des soins infirmiers constants depuis une chute qu'elle avait faite devant chez elle – souhaitait mettre fin à ses jours. Elle demanda à l'institut fédéral des médicaments et des produits médicaux de lui accorder l'autorisation d'acquérir une dose létale d'un médicament afin qu'elle pût se suicider à son domicile. L'institut refusa la demande, estimant que le souhait de l'intéressée de mettre fin à ses jours allait à l'encontre du but de la loi allemande sur les stupéfiants, à savoir assurer à la population les soins médicaux nécessaires. M. Koch et son épouse contestèrent cette décision. Le 12 février 2005, Mme Koch se suicida en Suisse, avec l'aide de l'association *Dignitas*. Le 3 mars 2005, l'institut confirma sa décision et en avril M. Koch introduisit une action afin de faire déclarer par les différents tribunaux que les décisions de l'institut étaient illégales et que celui-ci se devait d'accorder l'autorisation sollicitée par son épouse. Les différentes juridictions ont déclaré la demande irrecevable, considérant que M. Koch n'avait pas qualité pour introduire l'action puisqu'il ne pouvait se prétendre victime d'une violation de ses propres droits. Mr Koch a porté sa requête devant la Cour estimant que ce refus a porté atteinte au droit de son épouse au respect de sa vie privée et familiale garanti par l'article 8, en particulier à son droit de mourir dans la dignité, ainsi qu'à son propre droit au respect de sa vie privée et familiale du fait qu'il a été contraint de voyager en Suisse pour permettre à son épouse de se suicider. Sous l'angle de l'article 13, il soutient en outre que les juridictions allemandes ont méconnu son droit à un recours effectif en lui refusant le droit d'attaquer le refus de l'institut d'accorder à son épouse l'autorisation requise.

ASSISTED SUICIDE IN THE JURISPRUDENCE OF THE EUR.
COURT OF HUMAN RIGHTS: A MATTER OF LIFE AND DEATH

*Panos Merkouris**

O ignorant are they of their ills, who do not laud death and look forward to it as the most precious discovery of Nature! Whether it shuts off prosperity, or repels calamity, or terminates the satiety and weariness of the old man, or leads off the youth in the bloom of life while he still hopes for happier things, or calls back the boy before the harsher stages of life are reached, it is to all the end, to many a relief, to some an answer to prayer and to none does it show more favour than to those to whom it comes before it is asked for! ... this it is, I say, that keeps my birth from being a punishment, that keeps me from falling in the face of threatening misfortunes, that makes it possible to keep my soul unharmed and master of itself: I have a last appeal. Yonder I see instruments of torture, not indeed of a single kind, but differently contrived by different peoples; some hang their victims with head toward the ground, some impale their private parts, others stretch out their arms on a fork-shaped gibbet; I see cords, I see scourges, and for each separate limb and each joint there is a separate engine of torture! But I see also Death. There, too, are bloodthirsty enemies and proud fellow-countrymen; but yonder, too, I see Death. Slavery is no hardship when, if a man wearies of the yoke, by a single step he may pass to freedom. O Life, by the favour of Death I hold thee dear! [1]

Seneca, *On Consolation to Marcia*, para. XX

I. Prolegomena

The right to life as a fundamental human right is unquestionable. However, both law and society recognize that there might exist some cases where allowing an individual to die might be the most humane option. In the passage from *De Consolatione ad Marciam* (On Consolation to Marcia) cited above, Seneca approaches death not as a punishment but something that could be even regarded as a gift:

* Queen Mary, University of London & Managing Editor of the *International Community Law Review*; email: p.merkouris@qmul.ac.uk.
[1] Lucius Annaeus Seneca, *De Consolatione ad Marciam*, para. XX; translated in: John W. Basore, *Seneca: Moral Essays with an English Translation by John W. Basore, Ph.D., Vol. II* (London, 1932), pp. 67–69.

S. Negri (ed.), *Self-Determination, Dignity and End-of-Life Care*
2011 Koninklijke Brill NV. Printed in The Netherlands. ISBN 978 90 04 22357 8. pp. 107–126

[death] is to all the end, to many a relief, to some an answer to prayer and to none does it show more favour than to those to whom it comes before it is asked for... O Life, by the favour of Death I hold thee dear.[2]

Although the aim is to offer Marcia some form of consolation[3] it is notable that this consolation work seems to be lacking in empathy towards Marcia and her loss, the death of her son, and is more an exposition on the tenets of Stoic philosophy on life and death.[4] However, this seems to be in line with the general tradition of formulation of such essays, and in any event *De Consolatione ad Marciam* offers a unique insight into the mind and beliefs of one of the greatest philosophers of the Roman era with respect to the value of life and death.[5] In addition to this, the statements made within as to the value of death may be considered as reflective of the greater degree of tolerance, if not acceptance, of suicide in Antiquity. As Lecky points out

> there can be no question that the ancient view of suicide was broadly and strongly opposed to our own. A general approval of it floated down through most of the schools of philosophy, and even to those who condemned it, it never seems to have assumed its present aspect of extreme enormity. This was in the first instance due to the ancient notion of death; and we have also to remember that when a society once learns to tolerate suicide, the deed, in ceasing to be disgraceful, loses much of its actual criminality, for those who are most firmly convinced that the stigma and suffering it now brings upon the family of the deceased do not constitute its entire guilt, will readily acknowledge that they greatly aggravate it. In the conditions of ancient thought, this aggravation did not exist ... [and] it was in the Roman Empire and among the Roman Stoics that suicide assumed its greatest prominence, and its philosophy was most fully elaborated.[6]

However, the focus of the present article is slightly different than what Lecky examined, both temporally and substantively. Whereas Lecky examined the evolution of morals[7] in Europe from Antiquity to early Middle Ages, the present article shall examine the *current legal* situation with respect to the issue of *assisted suicide*, as this is reflected in the

---

[2] Seneca, *supra* note 1.
[3] Or even to gain her favour.
[4] Vasily Rudich, *Dissidence and Literature under Nero: The Price of Rhetoricization* (London, 1997), pp. 27–35.
[5] Interesting is also another moral essay by Seneca, *i.e. De Brevitate Vitae* (On Shortness of Life), where he elaborates on the need of making the most of our allotted time; a translation of this essay can be found in Basore, *supra* note 1.
[6] William Edward Hartpole Lecky, *History of European Morals from Augustus to Charlemagne, Vol. I* (New York, 3rd ed. Revise, 1921), at Chapter II.
[7] Including the stance to suicide.

jurisprudence of the European Court of Human Rights (ECtHR) with respect to the issue of euthanasia and the reasoning behind it. Up until recently, the only case that so far that had raised the issues of suicide and assisted suicide had been *Pretty v. the United Kingdom*.[8] Mrs. Pretty suffered from motor neurone disease (MND), which is a progressive degenerative illness affecting motor neurones. This means that such activities, as walking, moving limbs, speaking, swallowing and breathing are affected with a gradual and irreversible deterioration. MND, however, leaves the intellectual and decision-making capacities unaffected. Mrs. Pretty aware of the situation, and facing the spectrum of death by suffocation, when her respiratory muscles would fail, made an application to compel the Director of Public Prosecutions to provide her husband with assurances of indemnification from prosecution should he assist Mrs. Pretty with the termination of her life when she so expressly conveyed but would be unable to do so herself due to her degenerative illness. At this point it has to be clarified that suicide at the time was not a crime in England, whereas assisted suicide was under Section 2(1) of the 1961 Suicide Act.[9] On 29 November 2001 the House of Lords rejected Diane Pretty's application,[10] which prompted Diane Pretty to lodge an application to ECtHR, claiming that the refusal of the UK authorities to grant her and her husband the assurances she had requested constituted a violation of the European Convention on Human Rights (ECHR); in particular, violation of Article 2 (right to life), Article 3 (prohibition of torture or inhuman or degrading treatment or punishment), Article 8 (right to private and family life), Article 9 (freedom of thought, conscience and religion) and Article 14 (non-discrimination).

---

[8] *Pretty v. the United Kingdom*, Judgment of 29 April 2002, 35 *EHRR* 1; for comments on this case *see* Dame Brenda Hale, "A Pretty Pass: When is There a Right to Die?", 32 *Common Law World Review* (2003), pp. 1–14; J.M.T. Labuschagne, "The European Court of Human Rights and the Right to Assisted Suicide in International Human Rights Law", 17 *South African Journal of Criminal Justice* (2004), pp. 87–98; Janna Satz Nugent, "'Walking into the Sea' of Legal Fiction: An Examination of the European Court of Human Rights, *Pretty v. United Kingdom* and the Universal Right to Die", 13 *Journal of Transnational Law and Policy* (2003–2004), pp. 183–212; "European Court of Human Rights: Case of *Pretty v. the United Kingdom*", 18 *Issues in Law and Medicine* (2002), pp. 67–89; Karen Reid, *A Practitioner's Guide to the European Convention on Human Rights* (London, 3rd ed., 2008), pp. 289–291; John Keown, "European Court of Human Rights: Death in Strasbourg – Assisted Suicide, the *Pretty* Case, and the European Convention on Human Rights", 1 *International Journal of Constitutional Law* (2003), pp. 722–730.

[9] For the circumstances of the case, *see Pretty v. the United Kingdom, supra* note 8, paras. 7 *et seq.*

[10] *R. (Pretty) v. Director of Public Prosecutions (Secretary of State for the Home |Department intervening)*, Judgment of 29 November 2001, [2001] *UKHL* 61; [2002] 1 *A.C.* 800.

In a much awaited judgement the ECtHR, on 29 April 2002, held that no violation of the abovementioned articles existed. It should come, thus, as no surprise that no other similar case had been brought in front of the ECtHR until very recently. Not only was the Court clear in its rejection of the claims made in the *Pretty* case, but one should also consider the toll, financial, sentimental and temporal, that such proceedings take on its applicants.

The second case that dealt with issues of suicide and assisted suicide was *Haas v. Switzerland*.[11] In that cases, the Applicant claimed that his rights, protected under Article 8 of the ECHR, had been violated. Mr. Haas suffered from a bipolar disorder and had attempted twice to commit suicide. On 1 July 2004 he had become a member of *Dignitas*, an association that offers, amongst others, assistance in committing suicide.[12] The Applicant wished to commit suicide by the use of a substance called 'sodium pentobarbital'. However, according to Swiss law, such a substance could be obtained only via a medical prescription. The Applicant failed to obtain any such prescription. The Applicant's requests before the Swiss courts to obtain an exemption from this requirement of prior medical prescription were equally unsuccessful.[13] Having exhausted all local remedies, the Applicant turned to the ECtHR claiming that by not giving him access to sodium pentobarbital, Switzerland infringed upon his 'right to suicide' and was in violation of Article 8. The Court eventually held that no such violation had taken place.

Despite the rejection of all the claims brought before the Court in the *Pretty* and *Haas* cases, it is extremely useful to examine the reasoning of the Court in order to better understand the reasons for the adoption of such a stance and to gage the possibility of any future reversal.

II. RIGHT TO LIFE VS. 'RIGHT TO DIE'

Article 2 of the ECHR guarantees the protection of the right to life. In the *Pretty* case, what was disputed was whether Article 2 also includes the

---

[11] *Haas v. Switzerland*, Judgment of 20 January 2011, available at: http://cmiskp.echr.coe.int/tkp197/view.asp?action=html&documentId=880260&portal=hbkm&source=external bydocnumber&table=F69A27FD8FB86142BF01C1166DEA398649 (last accessed on 1 March 2011). The text of the judgment is currently available only in French. For the purposes of the present Article, any quotes from the *Haas* case are the author's translation.

[12] Ibid., para. 7.

[13] Ibid., paras. 7 *et seq.*

converse aspect as well, i.e. a right to die.[14] The Court held, however, that no such negative aspect was inherent in Article 2. If one accepts that death is the antithesis of life, then the notion of death is not a sub-set or an overlapping set with that of the notion of life. The object and purpose of Article 2 is to protect life, not the quality of living. To explain this different reading of Article 2 compared to Article 11, which does include a negative aspect, the Court felt it necessary to elaborate on the reasons why the interpretation of Article 11 could not apply *mutatis mutandis* to Article 2:

> *Article 2 of the Convention is phrased in different terms.* It is unconcerned with issues to do with the quality of living or what a person chooses to do with his or her life. To the extent that these aspects are recognised as so fundamental to the human condition that they require protection from State interference, they may be reflected in the rights guaranteed by other Articles of the Convention, or in other international human rights instruments. *Article 2 cannot, without a distortion of language, be interpreted as conferring the diametrically opposite right, namely a right to die; nor can it create a right to self-determination in the sense of conferring on an individual the entitlement to choose death rather than life.*[15]

This interpretation was further reinforced by Recommendation 1418 (1999) of the Parliamentary Assembly of the Council of Europe.[16]

In connection to the claim of violation of Article 2, the Applicants also raised the issue, that if the Court rejected the interpretation of Article 2 as permitting the inclusion of a 'right to die' then this would *ipso facto* mean that all States that permit assisted suicide were in clear violation of their

---

[14] Similarly to the understanding of Article 11 of the ECHR, which while providing for the protection of the freedom of association, also encompasses the negative aspect, i.e. the right not to be a member of an association; *see Young, James and Webster v. the United Kingdom*, Judgment of 13 August 1981, 4 *EHRR* 38, para. 52; *Sigurður A. Sigurjónsson v. Iceland*, Judgment of 30 June 1993, 16 *EHRR* 462, para. 35; *see also* Antje Pedain, "The Human Rights Dimension of the *Diane Pretty* Case", 62 *Cambridge Law Journal* (2003), pp. 181–206, at 188.

[15] *Pretty v. the United Kingdom, supra* note 8, para. 39 (emphasis added).

[16] *Recommendation 1418 on protection of the human rights and dignity of the terminally ill and the dying (1999),* available at: http://assembly.coe.int/main.asp?link=/Documents/ AdoptedText/ta99/EREC1418.htm (last accessed on 30 November 2010); an even earlier document is the Hubinek/Voogd Report of 1976, containing the so-called 'euthanasia declaration', held that "the prolongation of life should not in itself constitute the overriding aim of medical practice, which must be concerned equally with the relief of suffering"; *Hubinek/Voogd Report concerning the Rights of the Sick and the Dying,* Parliamentary Assembly of the Council of Europe, 27th Session, *Documents*, Doc. 3699, pp. 2–3; *see also* Pieter van Dijk, Fired van Hoof, Arjen van Rijn and Leo Zwaak (eds.), *Theory and Practice of the European Convention on Human Rights* (Antwerpen-Oxford, 2006), at 391–392.

obligations under Article 2 of the ECHR.[17] Although Article 2 creates positive obligations for the State any measures taken in order to protect an
individual within the context of the protection offered by that Article, will
have to be measured and balanced against the protection offered by other
provisions of the Convention, such as the right to liberty and security and
the right to privacy.[18] This balancing act can not take place based on a pre-
existent formula, but will be the result of an *ad hoc* evaluation of all relevant elements of each particular case. In this manner, the Court avoided
addressing this issue, even more so since that was not the case at hand and
since the United Kingdom had provisions that did not allow assisted
suicide.[19]

   In summation the Court summarily dismissed the claim that Article 2
incorporates a 'right to die', based on a textual interpretation of Article 2
reinforced by its object and purpose and supplemented by relevant documentation, Recommendation 1418, as indicative of the current intention
of the Parties and the correct interpretation of Article 2.

III. Prolongation of Life as Torture

As an additional basis, the Applicant also raised the issue that by not
granting her request the British authorities were in violation of Article 3 of
the ECHR, which prohibits torture or inhuman or degrading treatment.
In order to understand this claim one has to keep in mind the degenerative character of Mrs. Pretty's condition. In late 2001, she was already unable to move any muscles below the neck and as MND would progress she
would eventually lose the capacity to breathe, eventually dying of asphyx-
iation. Consequently, Diane Pretty argued, by refusing her request for

---

   [17] *Pretty v. the United Kingdom*, *supra* note 8, para. 41; it has to be noted here that the
Court has accepted in its jurisprudence that Article 2 is not restricted to a negative obligation by the State to refrain from the intentional and unlawful deprivation of life but
imposes certain positive obligations, as well, on the State to protect the right to life; *see LCB
v. the United Kingdom*, Judgment of 9 June 1998, 27 *EHRR* 212, para. 36; *Osman v. the United
Kingdom*, Judgment of 28 October 1998, 29 *EHRR* 245, para. 115; *Kılıç v. Turkey*, Judgment of
28 March 2000, 33 *EHRR* 1357, paras. 62, 76; *Denizci, v. Cyprus*, Judgment of 23 May 2001,
para. 375; *Öneryildiz v. Turkey*, Judgment of 18 June 2002, 39 *EHRR* 12, para. 63; *Makaratzis
v. Greece*, Judgment of 20 December 2004, para. 57.
   [18] *See Keenan v. the United Kingdom*, Judgment of 3 April 2001, 33 *EHRR* 38, paras. 91–92;
Laskey, Jaggard and Brown v. the United Kingdom, Judgment of 19 February 1997, 24 *EHRR*
39; *Sanles v. Spain*, Judgment of 26 October 2000, [2001] *EHRR* 348.
   [19] *Pretty v. the United Kingdom*, *supra* note 8, para. 41.

indemnification of her husband, should he assist her in terminating her life, the British authorities, essentially, refused her the right to die with dignity[20] and forced her to live out the remainder of her life that entailed a significant degree of pain and suffering. This situation according to the Applicant amounted to an 'ill-treatment' that fell within the scope of Article 3 of the Convention.

In this context, it is noteworthy that the notion of the preservation of life at all costs may be of a degrading character is not completely unknown in jurisprudence. In the *Cruzan* case[21] Justice Brennan of the US Supreme Court wrote that

> [f]or many, the thought of an ignoble end, steeped in decay, is abhorrent. A quiet, proud death, bodily integrity intact, is a matter of extreme consequence. 'In certain, thankfully rare, circumstances the burden of maintaining the corporeal existence *degrades the very humanity it was meant to serve'*.[22]

In the same case, Justice O'Connor had reflected on the fact that "[a] seriously ill or dying patient whose wishes are not honored may feel a captive of the machinery required for life-sustaining measures".[23]

Some authors argue that, in some cases, such a situation could amount to 'torture' or at least 'inhuman or degrading treatment';[24] however the ECtHR was of a different opinion. Although it was

> sympathetic to the applicant's apprehension that without the possibility of ending her life she faces the prospect of a distressing death ...[and that] she is unable to commit suicide herself due to physical incapacity and that the state of law is such that her husband faces the risk of prosecution if he renders her assistance[25]

---

[20] Which was also the basis for her claim of a violation of Article 2 of the ECHR.

[21] Dealing with the issue of whether the State of Missouri had the right to require 'clear and convincing evidence' in order for the Cruzan family to request that their daughter be removed from life support.

[22] *Cruzan v. Director, Missouri Department of Health*, Judgment of 25 June 1990, Dissenting Opinion of Justice Brennan, US Supreme Court, 497 *U.S.* 261, at 311 (emphasis added); citing also *Brophy v. New England Sinai Hospital, Inc.*, (1986), 398 *Mass.* 417, 434, 497 N.E.2d 626, 635–6.

[23] *Cruzan v. Director, Missouri Department of Health, supra* note 22, 288.

[24] Jordan J. Paust, "The Human Right to Die with Dignity: A Policy-Oriented Essay", 17 *Human Rights Quarterly* (1995), pp. 463–487, at 481, citing also George G. Garbesi, "Suicide: An International Human Right", 14 *Israel Yearbook on Human Rights* (1984), pp. 249–273, at 265–6; Jordan J. Paust, "Human Dignity as a Constitutional Right: A Jurisprudentially Based Inquiry into Criteria and Content", 27 *Howard Law Journal* (1984), pp. 145–225, at 179, 182.

[25] *Pretty v. the United Kingdom, supra* note 8, para. 55.

it nevertheless held that the Applicant's request boiled down to arguing that a State had a positive obligation to "sanction actions intended to terminate life".[26]

Similarly to Article 2, Article 3 of the ECHR poses on the States both negative and positive obligations.[27] As the Court clarifies

> It may be described in general terms as imposing a primarily negative obligation on States to refrain from inflicting serious harm on persons within their jurisdiction. However, in light of the fundamental importance of Article 3, the Court has reserved to itself sufficient flexibility to address the application of that Article in other situations that might arise.[28]

However, in order for a particular form of 'ill-treatment' to be considered as falling within the regulatory scope of Article 3 it must attain "a minimum level of severity and [involve] actual bodily injury or intense physical or mental suffering".[29] In the present case, however, the United Kingdom had neither inflicted itself any ill-treatment on the Applicant, nor refused to provide adequate care.[30] As for the existence of a positive obligation of the State to permit assisted suicide, the Court held that this fell outside the object and purpose of Article 3 and could not be interpreted into it.[31]

IV. Self-Determination of the Individual

In *R. (Pretty) v. Director of Public Prosecutions*, the House of Lords seemed to reject the claim that the notion of 'private life' of Article 8(1) of the

---

[26] Id.

[27] *D. v. the United Kingdom*, Judgment of 2 May 1997, 24 *EHRR* 423; *A. v. the United Kingdom*, Judgment of 23 September 1998, 27 *EHRR* 611; *Z and Others v. the United Kingdom*, Judgment of 10 May 2001, 34 *EHRR* 97; *Kudła v. Poland*, Judgment of 26 October 2000, 35 *EHRR* 11, para. 94; *Assenov and Others v. Bulgaria*, Judgment of 28 October 1998, 28 *EHRR* 652, para. 102; *Labita v. Italy*, Judgment of 6 April 2000, 46 *EHRR* 1228, para. 131; *Ahmet Ozkan v. Turkey*, Judgment of 6 April 2004, para. 359; *Costello Roberts v. the United Kingdom*, Judgment of 25 March 1993, 19 *EHRR* 112, para. 28.

[28] *Pretty v. the United Kingdom*, supra note 8, para. 50.

[29] Ibid., para. 52, citing *Ireland v. UK*, Judgment of 18 January 1978, 2 *EHRR* 25, para. 167; *V. v. the United Kingdom*, Judgment of 16 December 1999, 30 *EHRR* 121, para. 71; on other cases clarifying the level of severity required *see*: *Price v. the United Kingdom*, Judgment of 10 July 2001, 34 *EHRR* 1285, paras. 24–30; *Valašinas v. Lithuania*, Judgment of 24 July 2001, para. 117; *Bensaid v. the United Kingdom*, Judgment of 6 February 2001, 33 *EHRR* 10; *Kudla v. Poland*, supra note 27, para. 92; *Tyrer v. the United Kingdom*, Judgment of 25 April 1978, 2 *EHRR* 1, para. 29.

[30] *Pretty v. the United Kingdom*, supra note 8, para. 53. This last element distinguishes the present case from that of *D. v. the United Kingdom*, supra note 27.

[31] *Pretty v. the United Kingdom*, supra note 8, paras. 55–56.

ECHR included the right of an individual to choose the manner in which he/she wishes to die. According to Lord Steyn "the guarantee under Article 8 prohibits interference with the way in which an individual *leads his life and it does not relate to the manner in which he wishes to die*".[32] A similar approach was adopted by Lord Bingham, who opined that Article 8 is "directed to protection of *the personal autonomy while individuals are living their lives*, and there is *nothing to suggest that the article has reference to the choice to live no longer*".[33]

The ECtHR, however, felt that Mrs. Pretty's decision was clearly within the regulatory framework of Article 8. This was due to the fact that the concept of 'private life' is a 'generic term' "not susceptible to exhaustible definition",[34] as it has held in the *Niemietz*[35] and *Peck*[36] cases. Furthermore, although

> no previous case has established as such any right to self-determination as being contained in Article 8 of the Convention, the Court considers that the notion of personal autonomy is an important principle underlying the interpretation of its guarantees.[37]

Furthermore, the end result of Diane Pretty's decision, her death, should not be the decisive factor. What is relevant is that this was a conscious decision on Mrs. Pretty's part, while she was still alive, on how to pass the last moments of her life. As Lord Hope had stated in the House of Lords, and with which the ECtHR concurred:

> The way she chooses to pass the closing moments of her life is part of the act of living, and she has a right to ask that this too must be respected. In that respect Mrs. Pretty has a right to self-determination. In that sense, her private life is engaged even where in the face of a terminal illness she seeks to choose death rather than life.[38]

---

[32] *R. (Pretty) v. Director of Public Prosecutions, supra* note 10, Lord Steyn, at 1 (emphasis added).

[33] Ibid., Lord Bingham, at 23 (emphasis added).

[34] *Pretty v. the United Kingdom, supra* note 8, para. 61; citing in support: *X and Y v. the Netherlands*, Judgment of 26 March 1985, 8 *EHRR* 235, para. 22; *Mikulić v. Croatia*, Judgment of 7 February 2002, para. 53; *Burghartz v. Switzerland*, Judgment of 22 February 1994, 18 *EHRR* 101, para. 24; *Dudgeon v. the United Kingdom*, Judgment of 22 October 1981, 4 *EHRR* 149, para. 41; and *Laskey, Jaggard and Brown v. the United Kingdom*, Judgment of 19 February 1997, 24 *EHRR* 39, para. 36.

[35] *Niemietz v. Germany*, Judgment of 16 December 1992, 16 *EHRR* 97, para. 29.

[36] *Peck v. the United Kingdom*, Judgment of 28 January 2003, 36 *EHRR* 719, para. 57.

[37] *Pretty v. the United Kingdom, supra* note 8, para. 61; with respect to the notion of personal autonomy the Court also makes reference to *Rodriguez v. the Attorney General of Canada* [1994], 2 *Law Reports of Canada* 136, of the Supreme Court of Canada.

[38] *R. (Pretty) v. Director of Public Prosecutions, supra* note 10, Lord Hope, at 100.

The fact, however, that the Applicant's decision falls within Article 8(1) of the Convention does not *ipso facto* mean that a violation of that Article has occurred. Even if interference has taken place with the enjoyment of the right protected under Article 8, said interference would be lawful if it is 'in accordance with the law', has an aim or aims that is or are legitimate under that paragraph and is 'necessary in a democratic society'.[39] The only point of dispute was whether the interference by the national authorities was 'necessary'. In order to determine that, the Court would have to examine if there was a 'pressing social need', if the interference was proportionate, while at the same time taking into consideration the 'margin of appreciation' allowed to States.

It is at this point, that the judgment of the Court becomes extremely mercurial. In analysing the 'margin of appreciation' left to States the Court refers to the *Dudgeon* and *A.D.T.* cases, relating to interferences with respect to an individual's sexual life and recalls that in such instances the margin of appreciation should be narrow.[40] Then making a transposition to the case at hand, it arbitrarily concludes that

> [a]lthough the applicant has argued that there must therefore be particularly compelling reasons for the interference in her case, the Court does not find that the matter under consideration in this case can be regarded as of the same nature, or as attracting the same reasoning.[41]

This amounts to saying that the margin of appreciation for interferences in sexual life is narrower than that for interferences in an individual's right to self-determination. This logically presupposes that an individual's freedom of sexual identity and orientation is of a greater degree of importance than 'self-determination'.

This paradoxical construction is further aggravated by the laconic statement of the Court, which does not further elaborate on this point. So the point remains unclear whether this was what the judges of the ECtHR intended to convey or if it was one unfortunate incident of poor draftsmanship.

The Court then turned its attention on whether the blanket ban on assisted suicide was disproportionate. The national legislation was put in place in order to protect a group of people, that were in a vulnerable

---

[39] *See Dudgeon v. the United Kingdom*, *supra* note 34, para. 43.

[40] *Dudgeon v. the United Kingdom*, *supra* note 34, para. 52; *A.D.T. v. the United Kingdom*, Judgment of 31 July 2000, 31 *EHRR* 33, para. 37.

[41] *Pretty v. the United Kingdom*, *supra* note 8, para. 71.

situation, from their rights being abused. Although Dianne Pretty was not vulnerable, in the sense that the request for assisted suicide was a conscious and rational decision on her part, the Court felt that the pressing need to protect a much larger group of vulnerable individuals allowed for infringements of the 'personal autonomy' of individuals such as Diane Pretty.[42] The reverse, i.e. allowing for a number of exceptions, could be a 'slippery slope', opening the floodgates for abuse of those exceptions and for even more pronounced infringements on fundamental human rights.[43] Based on these considerations the Court held that the infringement on Diane Pretty's right under Article 8, was a lawful one and permitted under Article 8(2).

In *Haas v. Switzerland*, as mentioned above, the issue raised by the Applicant was that Switzerland required by law that a sick person wishing to end his life through the use of a particular substance (sodium pentobarbital) could obtain it only via a medical prescription. Such a restriction according to the Applicant was in violation of Article 8 of the ECHR. The Court, after repeating that "the notion of 'private life' is not susceptible to an exhaustive definition"[44] it, nevertheless, outlines some of its manifestations, one of them being that "the choice of the applicant to avoid that, which to her eyes, would constitute an undignified and painful end to her life", falls within the scope of application of Article 8 as the Court had concluded in the *Pretty* case.[45] Of great importance is the statement made by the Court immediately afterwards. In no unclear terms it acknowledges that the right of an individual to decide at which point in time and in what manner he wishes to put an end to his life is one of the aspects of the right protected under Article 8, under the condition that the individual in question has the capacity to forge his own will freely and act upon it accordingly.[46]

Having reaffirmed its findings under the *Pretty* case, the Court then tries to dispel any misunderstanding by pointing out that the *Haas* case differs significantly from the *Pretty* case. Whereas the *Pretty* case, as will be shown in the present article, argued a violation of numerous provisions, claiming amongst others 'a right to die', the *Haas* case not only

---

[42] Ibid., paras. 73–77.
[43] Id.
[44] *Haas v. Switzerland, supra* note 11, para. 50.
[45] Id.
[46] Ibid., para. 51.

revolved solely around Article 8 but the Applicant, as well, unlike Mrs. Pretty was not a physically disabled person.[47]

The crucial point of the *Haas* case was, in essence, whether the States had a 'positive obligation' to ensure that all necessary measures are taken, which would allow for a dignified suicide.[48] For the Court to decide on this it would have to take into consideration the balance of interests that were in play, the fact that with respect to Article 8 States have a 'margin of appreciation', and that the Convention must be read and interpreted as a whole[49] and under the light of present day conditions.[50]

The Court held that Article 8 had not been violated, because not only the legal approach to assisted suicide, which varied wildly between the individual European States, but also the interests at stake, e.g. protection of vulnerable individuals, protection of health and public safety, indicated that the measures taken by Switzerland[51] were well within its margin of appreciation.

A final interesting point that the Court considered was with respect to the 170 letters that the Applicant had sent to various medical professionals in an attempt to secure the required prescription, all of which had been rejected. According to established jurisprudence of the ECtHR the Convention is designed to "guarantee not rights that are theoretical or illusory but rights that are practical and effective".[52] The question was whether due to the criminal penalties that the Swiss legislation imposed on those professionals that abused the provisions relating to assisted suicide[53] the protection of the right of Article 8 was essentially non-existent.

The Court first of all clarifies that the 170 letters were sent after the Applicant's appeal to the Federal Tribunal had been rejected. Consequently, these letters could not be taken *a priori* into consideration.[54]

---

[47] Ibid., para. 52.

[48] Ibid., para. 53.

[49] Id., citing *Verein gegen Tierfabriken Schweiz (VgT) v. Switzerland*, Judgment of 30 June 2009, para. 83.Thus any alleged violation of Article 8 would have to be examined by taking into consideration the obligations imposed on States by Article 2.

[50] *Haas v. Switzerland, supra* note 11, paras. 53–54.

[51] Requiring prior medical authorization before releasing 'sodium pentobarbital' to individuals.

[52] *Artico v. Italy*, Judgment of 13 May 1980, 3 EHRR 1, para. 33; *Airey v. Ireland*, Judgment of 9 October 1979, 2 *EHRR* 305, para. 24; *Imbrioscia v. Switzerland*, Judgment of 24 November 1993, 17 EHRR 441, para. 38; *Daud v. Portugal*, Judgment of 21 April 1998, 30 *EHRR* 400, para. 38; *Hermi v. Italy*, Judgment of 18 November 2006, 46 *EHRR* 46, para. 95.

[53] By providing prescriptions even to those people, who had not formed freely their decision to commit suicide.

[54] *Haas v. Switzerland, supra* note 11, para. 60.

Nonetheless, the Court felt it necessary to make certain remarks regarding these letters. It considered that it was the content of these letters, and not the legislation itself, that was probably the driving force behind the constant rejection of the Applicant's request "insofar as the applicant specified [in the letters] that he rejected any therapy, thus excluding the thorough study of possible alternatives to suicide".[55]

In the *Haas* case the Court came to similar conclusions as in the *Pretty* case. While it acknowledged that the choice of how one ends his life falls within Article 8, it nevertheless held that the State has a wide 'margin of appreciation' and that the measures taken were within that margin. As to the existence or not of a *positive obligation* on the part of Switzerland the Court refrained from making any pronouncements opting for expressing itself in hypotheticals in the ultimate paragraph of the judgment: "even assuming that the States have a positive obligation to adopt measures allowing the facilitation of committing suicide in dignity, the Swiss authorities have not violated this obligation in the present case".[56]

V. Assisted Suicide as Religion or Belief

A further argument raised by the Applicant was that she believed in and supported the notion of assisted suicide and consequently the present situation violated her right protected under Article 9 of the ECHR. The Court has interpreted the terms 'religion or belief' quite expansively. Pacifism[57] and even veganism[58] may fall within the scope of Article 9; however, as the Court clarified in the *Pretty* case, this does not mean that "all opinions or convictions constitute beliefs".[59] As Ben Vermeulen correctly points out that the latter concept would seem to be "more akin to the concept of 'religious and philosophical convictions' that appears in Article 2 of Protocol No. 1, denoting 'views that attain a certain level of cogency, seriousness, cohesion and importance'."[60] Since the notion of assisted

---

[55] Ibid., para. 60.

[56] Ibid., para. 61.

[57] *Arrowsmith v. the United Kingdom*, Report of 12 October 1978, 19 *D&R* (1980), p. 5; *Le Court Grandmaison and Fritz v. France*, Decision of 6 July 1987, 53 *D&R* (1987), p. 150.

[58] *W v. the United Kingdom*, App. 18187/91 & Decision of 10 February 1993.

[59] *Pretty v. the United Kingdom*, *supra* note 8, para. 82.

[60] Ben Vermeulen, "Chapter 13: Freedom of Thought, Conscience and Religion (Article 9)", in *Theory and Practice of the European Convention on Human Rights*, *supra* note 16, pp. 751–772, at 760, citing *Campbell and Cosans v. the United Kingdom*, Judgment of 25 February 1982, 4 *EHRR* 293, para. 36.

suicide would not seem to meet these criteria of cogency, seriousness, cohesion and importance it is no surprise that the Court summarily rejected the claim that there was a violation of Article 9,[61] adding further that to the extent that the Applicant's views reflected her view on *personal autonomy* they were nothing more than a simple reiteration of her claims under Article 8, which had already been rejected.[62]

VI. NON-DISCRIMINATION

In a similarly concise manner the Court tackled the issue of whether the fact that Diane Pretty was not allowed to commit assisted suicide was a discriminatory measure against, which would be in violation of Article 14 of the ECHR. This argument had also been raised in the House of Lords. The *dicta* of the judges in that case, can create the impression that they understood Article 14 as being invocable, in a supplementary fashion, only when another provision of the ECHR had been found to have been violated.[63] However, this may be a misreading of that judgment, and could have been a couched reminder to the reader that since they had already rejected any claims with respect to a violation of Article 8(1) of the ECHR, any claims with respect to a violation of Article 8(2) were discussed only *ex hypothesi* and the same was the case with any discussion of Article 14.[64]

Regarding the accessory character of Article 14, the ECtHR has consistently held that

> Article 14 complements the other substantive provisions of the Convention and the Protocols. It has no independent existence, since it has effect solely in relation to 'the enjoyment of the rights and freedoms' safeguarded by those provisions. Although the application of Article 14 does not necessarily presuppose a breach of other provisions—and to this extent it is autonomous –, there can be no room for its application unless the facts at issue fall within the ambit of one or more of the latter.[65]

---

[61] An inability of the Applicant to establish that the aforementioned criteria were met, has led to the rejection of the claims of a 'Wiccan' and a 'Lichtanbeter' in *X. v. the United Kingdom*, Decision of 4 October 1977, 11 *D&R* (1978), pp. 55–56 and *X. v. Federal Republic of Germany*, Decision of 1 April 1970, 37 *Collection of Decisions* (1971), pp. 119–123, at 121–122.

[62] *Pretty v. the United Kingdom*, *supra* note 8, para. 82.

[63] *R. (Pretty) v. Director of Public Prosecutions*, *supra* note 10, Lord Bingham, at 34 & Lord Steyn, at 64.

[64] Pedain, *supra* note 14, at 196.

[65] *Abdulasiz, Cabales and Balkandali v. the United Kingdom*, Judgment of 28 May 1985, 7 *EHRR* 471, para. 71; this formula has been reiterated in a variety of other cases, such as:

Consequently, the Court in examining a possible violation of Article 14, shows that it felt that the facts of the case, clearly fell within the ambit of one or more of the provisions of the ECHR, and in this particular case the relevant provision was Article 8.[66]

There are two ways in which the alleged discrimination can be argued. On the one hand, whereas the domestic law of the United Kingdom permits able-bodied persons to commit suicide, it prevents an incapacitated person to do the same (through assisted suicide). On the other hand one could see it under the prism of identical treatment of non-identical cases, i.e. that the Suicide Act does not permit assisted suicide, without making any distinction, whether the individual concerned is incapable of committing suicide on his/her own or not. As has been stated in the *Thlimmenos* case, a violation of Article 14 of the ECHR may arise not only when individuals are treated differently in analogous situations, but also when States "without an objective and reasonable justification fail to treat differently persons whose situations are significantly different".[67]

However, the Court did not focus on the existence or not of a differentiated treatment, but on whether there existed an 'objective and reasonable justification' for it and concluded that its reasoning with respect to Article 8,[68] equally applied in this context as well. The crux seems to be the 'slippery slope' argument and a need to balance conflicting interests. On the one hand, there is a need to allow for individuals to take decisions in exercising their 'personal autonomy'; on the other hand there is the need to protect a whole class of vulnerable people. The concern was that should the laws on assisted suicide be relaxed, and exceptions created, this option would be abused and would lead to a gradual erosion of the rights of the

---

Belgian Linguistics Case, Judgment of 23 July 1968, 1 *EHRR* 252, para. 9; *Thlimmenos v. Greece*, Judgment of 6 April 2000, 31 *EHRR* 411; *Rasmussen v. Denmark*, Judgment of 28 November 1984, 7 *EHRR* 371, para. 29; *Van der Mussele v. Belgium*, Judgment of 23 November 1983, 6 *EHRR* 163, para. 43; *Karlheinz Schmidt v. Germany*, Judgment of 18 July 1994, 18 *EHRR* 513, para. 22; *Van Raalte v. the Netherlands*, Judgment of 21 February 1997, 24 *EHRR* 503, para. 33; *Botta v. Italy*, Judgment of 24 February 1998, 26 *EHRR* 241, para. 39.

[66] In para. 87 of the judgment, the Court unequivocally states that: "The Court has found above that the applicant's rights under Article 8 of the Convention were engaged (see paragraphs 61–67). It must therefore consider the applicant's complaints that she has been discriminated against in the enjoyment of the rights guaranteed under that provision".

[67] *Thlimmenos v. Greece, supra* note 65, para. 11; in addition to this States "enjoy a margin of appreciation in assessing whether and to what extent differences in otherwise similar situations justify a different treatment", *Pretty v. the United Kingdom, supra* note 8, para. 88 and *Camp and Bourimi v. the Netherlands*, Judgment of 3 October 2000, 34 EHRR 59, para. 37.

[68] In particular para. 74 of the judgment.

ECHR and a complete distortion of the *raison d'être* of the inclusion of exceptions permitting assisted suicide. These concerns, the Court held, constituted a 'reasonable and objective justification' for

> not seeking to distinguish between those who are able and those who are unable to commit suicide unaided. The borderline between the two catego-ries will often be a very fine one and to seek to build into the law an exemp-tion for those judged to be incapable of committing suicide would seriously undermine the protection of life which the 1961 Act was intended to safe-guard and greatly increase the risk of abuse.

In essence, in the balancing of the rights and interests concerned, the result was that the rights of the group of people that want to but are una-ble to commit suicide unaided, were taken to have to give way to the superseding need to protect the right to life of a larger group of vulnerable people.[69]

VII. Concluding Remarks

Issues relating to matters of life and death, or to be more exact to issues relating to when life starts and when it ends or when it should be allowed to end have always been extremely difficult from a legal viewpoint,[70] not

---

[69] Also due to the fine borderline between these two groups, this *prima facie* discrimi-nation would seem to fall, based on the ruling of the Court, within the margin of apprecia-tion of a State.

[70] *See* for instance, the other side of the coin i.e. the cases in relation to abortion; *A., B., and C. v. Ireland*, Application No. 25579/5; *Tysiac v. Poland*, Judgment of 20 March 2007, 45 *EHRR* 42; *Vo. v. France*, Judgment of 8 July 2004, 40 *EHRR* 12; Jakob Pichon, "Does the Unborn Child Have a Right to Life? The Insufficient Answer of the European Court of Human Rights in the Judgment *Vo. V. France'*", 7 *German Law Journal* (2006), pp. 433–444; on the interplay between human rights and bioethics *see: Evans v. the United Kingdom*, [GC], Judgment of 10 April 2007; Convention for the Protection of Human Rights and the Dignity of the Human Being with Regard to the Application of Biology and Medicine, adopted by the Council of Europe in Oviedo, on April 4, 1997: Convention on Human Rights and Biomedicine (Oviedo Convention), *CETS* No. 164; Judit Sándor, "Human Rights and Bioethics: Competitors or Allies? The Role of International Law in Shaping the Contours of a New Discipline", 27 *Medicine and Law* (2008), pp. 15–28; on the issue of assisted suicide *see*, in addition to those already cited *supra*, Marie Therese Meulders-Klein, "The Right over One's Own Body: Its Scope and Limits in Comparative Law", 6 *Boston College International & Comparative Law Review* (1983), pp. 29–79; Andrew Grubb, Pat Walsh and Neil Lambe, "Reporting on the Persistent Vegetative State in Europe", 6 *Medical Law Review* (1998), pp. 161–219; George Zdenkowski, "The International Covenant on Civil and Political Rights and Euthanasia", 20 *UNSW Law Journal* (1997), pp. 170–194; Peter de Cruz, "The *Burke* Case: The Terminally Ill Patient and the Right to Life", 70 *Modern Law Review* (2007), pp. 306–317; Suzanne Rode, "End-of-Life Decisionmaking for Patients in Persistent Vegetative States: A Comparative Analysis", 30 *Hastings International and*

only due to the fundamental importance of the rights involved, but also due to the fact that they are inextricably linked with the moral identity of a society at a given time.

In the case of assisted suicide the issue becomes almost a *Gordian Knot* from a legal standpoint. Although on a cursory glance the only right to be affected would be the right to life, as the *Pretty* case demonstrated, a gamut of ECHR provisions come into play; prohibition of torture or inhuman/degrading treatment, right to privacy, freedom of thought, conscience, religion and non-discrimination. Despite the multitude of relevant provisions, however, the ECtHR in the *Pretty* case came to the conclusion that the prohibition of assisted suicide by the British Authorities did not constitute a violation of any of the provisions of the ECHR.

Taking into consideration that the ECtHR is famous for its dynamic (evolutive) interpretation of the ECHR[71] one could wonder why the Court

---

Comparative Law Review (2006–2007), pp. 477–503; Andrzej Redelbach, "Protection of the Right to Life by Law and by Other Means", in B.G. Ramcharan (ed.), *The Right to Life in International Law* (Dordrecht, 1985), pp. 182–220; Xiaobing Xu and George Wilison, "On Conflict of Human Rights", 5 *Pierce Law Review* (2006–2007), pp. 31–58; Estelle Brosset, "La fin de la vie et le droit européen", (in the present volume).

[71] There is extensive bibliography on this topic. *See* indicatively, Malgosia Fitzmaurice, "Dynamic (Evolutive) Interpretation of Treaties: Part I", 21 *Hague Yearbook of International Law* (2008), pp. 101–153; Malgosia Fitzmaurice, "Dynamic (Evolutive) Interpretation of Treaties: Part II", 22 *Hague Yearbook of International Law* (2009), pp. 3–31; Malgosia Fitzmaurice and Jill Marshall, "The Human Right to a Clean Environment-Phantom or Reality? The European Court of Human Rights and English Courts Perspective on Balancing Rights in Environmental Cases", 76 *Nordic Journal of International Law* (2007), pp. 103–151; Alan Boyle, "Human Rights or Environmental Rights: A Reassessment", 18 *Fordham Environmental Law Review* (2007), pp. 471–511; Loukis Loucaides, "Environmental Protection through the Jurisprudence of the European Convention on Human Rights", 75 *British Yearbook of International Law* (2004), pp. 249–267; John Merrills, "Environmental Rights", in D. Bodansky, J. Brunnée and E. Hey (eds.), *Oxford Handbook of Environmental Law* (Oxford, 2007), pp. 663–680; George Letsas, *Theory of Interpretation of the European Convention on Human Rights* (Oxford, 2007); George Letsas, "The Truth in Autonomous Concepts: How to Interpret the ECHR", 15 *European Journal of International Law* (2004), pp. 279–305; George Letsas, "Intentionalism and the Interpretation of the European Convention on Human Rights", in M. Fitzmaurice, O. Elias and P. Merkouris (eds.), *Treaty Interpretation and the Vienna Convention on the Law of Treaties: 30 Years On* (Leiden, 2010), pp. 257–272; Peter McRae, "The Search for Meaning: Continuing Problems with the Interpretation of Treaties", 33 *Victoria University of Wellington Law Review* (2002), pp. 209–260; Rudolf Bernhard, "Evolutive Treaty Interpretation, Especially of the European Convention on Human Rights", 42 *German Yearbook of International Law* (1999), pp. 11–25; Andrew Drzemczewski, "The *Sui Generis* Nature of the European Convention on Human Rights", 29 *International and Comparative Law Quarterly* (1980), pp. 54–63; Alexander Orakhelashvili, "Restrictive Interpretation of Human Rights Treaties in the Recent Jurisprudence of the European Court Human Rights", 14 *European Journal of International*

could not find in favour of an expansive interpretation of at least one of
the apposite provisions, most notably Article 2, and the inclusion of a negative aspect to the right to life, i.e. of a 'right to die'.[72] However, this is based
on the false premise, that dynamic equals expansive. A dynamic interpretation can not and should not be equated in each case with an expansive
one.[73] Dynamic interpretation stems from addressing treaties as 'living
instruments' whose content and generic terms fluctuate to better reflect
not only the intentions of the parties, but also the evolution of law and the
international community as a whole. Such dynamism ensures a greater
degree of adaptability of the treaties, an essential survival trait.

So, the apposite question is whether the current situation in the
Member States of the ECHR reflects an expansive interpretation. The
issues of end of life for the sick and dying, and within it the issue of assisted
suicide, has been raised several times within the Council of Europe. The
1976 *Hubinek/Voogd Report*,[74] *Resolution 613 (1976) on the rights of the sick
and dying*[75] and *Recommendation 1418 (1999) on protection of the human
rights and dignity of the terminally ill and the dying* of the Parliamentary
Assembly of the Council of Europe[76] are but a few of a plethora of relevant
documents. However, despite the fact that the issue of euthanasia and
assisted suicide has been raised several times within the ambit of the
Council of Europe, Member States have been reluctant to adopt any definitive Resolution on the topic. As recently as 2005 the Parliamentary
Assembly rejected a *draft Resolution on Assistance to Patients at End*

Law (2002), pp. 529–568; Paul Mahoney, "Judicial Activism and Judicial Self-Restraint in
the Court: Two Sides of the Same Coin", 11 *Human Rights Law Journal* (1990), pp. 57–88;
Paul Mahoney, "Speculating on the Future of Reformed European Court of Human Rights",
20 *Human Rights Law Journal* (1999), pp. 1–4.

[72] Or at least, a 'right to a dignified death'.

[73] *See* in more detail, Fitzmaurice, "Dynamic (Evolutive) Interpretation of Treaties: Part
I & II", *supra* note 71.

[74] Containing the 'euthanasia declaration'; *Hubinek/Voogd Report, supra* note 16.

[75] Stating amongst others that: "1. Believing, for reasons set out in its Recommendation
779 (1976) on the rights of the sick, and explained in the report of its Committee on Social
and Health Questions (Doc. 3699), that the true interests of the sick are not always best
served by a zealous application of the most modern techniques for prolonging life;

2. Convinced that what dying patients most want is to die in peace and dignity, if
possible with the comfort and support of their family and friends"; *Resolution 613 (1976) on
the rights of the sick and dying*, available at: http://assembly.coe.int/main.asp?Link=/
documents/adoptedtext/ta76/eres613.htm (last accessed on 30 November 2010).

[76] *Recommendation 1418 on protection of the human rights and dignity of the terminally ill
and the dying (1999), supra* note 16.

of Life.[77] The picture in various countries of the Council of Europe is also quite indicative. A Short Report prepared for the Council of Europe in 2003, entitled '*Law and Practice Short Report: Law and Practices Relating to Euthanasia and Assisted Suicide in 34 Countries of the Council of Europe and the USA*', revealed a lack of harmonization with respect to euthanasia and assisted suicide.[78] Due to the lack of a harmonized approach amongst States it is highly unlikely that a top-down approach can be successful within the European framework and in order to avoid alienating States the international courts[79] "will continue allowing national discretion in these types of policy areas".[80]

Bearing in mind the aforementioned, it should, then, come as no surprise that the position adopted by the Court in the *Pretty* and *Haas* cases reflects the fragmented landscape of assisted suicide in Europe. The lack of a harmonized approach was a strong indication that an expansive interpretation of the relevant provisions of the ECHR would not be adopted by the Court, especially in such a highly controversial issue as that of assisted suicide. However, once again reflecting the variety of approaches to assisted suicide within the European context, the Court chose to avoid any general pronouncements as to the legality or not of permitting assisted suicide.[81] Thus, although finding that the prohibition of assisted suicide was permitted under the ECHR, it did not consider it either necessary or appropriate to rule on the reverse situation, i.e. whether the permission of assisted suicide was in violation of the Convention. Finally, considering

---

[77] Parliamentary Assembly, Council of Europe, *Verbatim Records: 2005 Ordinary Session (Second Part)*, *12th Sitting, Wednesday, 27 April 2005*, available at: http://assembly.coe.int/ Main.asp?link=/Documents/Records/2005/E/0504271000E.htm#4t (last accessed on 30 November 2010). This draft Resolution, would have prompted Member States to legalise euthanasia in certain cases; the draft Resolution was based on *Doc.10455 on Assistance to Patients at End of Life*, of 9 February 2005, available at: http://assembly.coe.int/Main .asp?link=/Documents/WorkingDocs/Doc05/EDOC10455.htm (last accessed on 30 November 2010).

[78] Council of Europe, *Law and Practice Short Report: Law and Practices Relating to Euthanasia and Assisted Suicide in 34 Countries of the Council of Europe and the USA*, reproduced in 22 *Medicine and Law* (2003), p. 197 *et seq.*; on the lack of harmonized approach *see also* J. Lucy Pridgeon, "Euthanasia Legislation in the European Union: Is a Universal Law Possible?", 2 *Hanse Law Review* (2006), pp. 45–60; Emily Wada, "A Pretty Picture: The Margin of Appreciation and the Right to Assisted Suicide", 27 *Loyola Los Angeles International and Comparative Law Review* (2005), pp. 275–289.

[79] And the ECtHR in particular.

[80] Pridgeon, *supra* note 78, at 60.

[81] *Pretty v. the United Kingdom*, *supra* note 8, para. 41.

the recent rejection of the *draft Resolution on Assistance to Patients at End of Life*, it would seem that in the near future it would be highly improbable that either the situation in Europe or the jurisprudence of the ECtHR changes dramatically, as has been, even more recently, confirmed by the ruling in the *Haas* case.

A PRIVATE INTERNATIONAL LAW PERSPECTIVE: CONFLICT RULES IN ADVANCE DIRECTIVES AND EUTHANASIA LEGISLATION

Mario J. A. Oyarzábal[*]

I. INTRODUCTION

In an article published in 2006, Italian Professor Tito Ballarino asked himself if a conflict rule for living wills and euthanasia was needed.[1] Short of providing a straightforward answer, he suggests that the problem may not be ripe for a 'traditional' conflict of laws solution and the 'allocation-to-one law' method, but rather that a 'flexible' *critère de rattachement* may be advisable. This approach seems to have prevailed so far in Italy, where the proposed legislation regarding therapeutic alliance, informed consent and advance directives, does not provide for conflict rules on the matters.[2]

Indeed, to my knowledge, no country has enacted special conflict of laws' rules on living wills and/or on euthanasia. Although these problems are not new, modern legislations provide only for 'substantive' rules, e.g. setting the contents, limits and forms of declarations of advance directives or informed consent, leaving the territorial and personal scope of application of the said rules undefined. More likely than not, this is based on the assumption that those rules will be implemented locally to patients who become incapacitated and are nationals and residing in the country where they need medical treatment. Also because the implementation of advance directives and of euthanasic practices, where allowed, are subject to stringent procedures, often involving the intervention of physicians and health care institutions which are bound to apply their *lex artis*. Yet, when the patients are foreign nationals and/or they reside abroad

* Adjunct Professor of International Law, University of La Plata, Argentina; diplomat currently serving at the Permanent Mission of Argentina to the United Nations; email: mario@mariooyarzabal.net.

[1] Tito Ballarino, "Is a Conflict Rule for Living Wills and Euthanasia Needed?", 8 *Yearbook of Private International Law* (2006), pp. 5–26.

[2] "Disposizioni in materia di alleanza terapeutica, di consenso informato e di dichiarazioni anticipate di trattamento", Draft Bill approved by the Senate of the Italian Republic on 26 March 2009, approved with amendments by the Chamber of Deputies on 12 July 2011 and currently under discussion by the Senate, available at http://www.senato.it.

S. Negri (ed.), *Self-Determination, Dignity and End-of-Life Care*
2011 Koninklijke Brill NV. Printed in The Netherlands. ISBN 978 90 04 22357 8. pp. 127–140

(depending on whether the country adheres to the 'national' or to the 'domiciliary' principle), the question remains if the legislators' intent was—or the consequence of the legal *lacunae* is—that the usual conflict rules shall apply, or rather that these institutions are falling outside the realm of conflicts of laws and are only subject to the law of the country where euthanasia and physician-assisted dying occurs.[3]

II. Conflict of Laws and the Problem of Characterization

Cases of conflict of laws arise in situations related to living wills and to euthanasia, like in many other private law cases, from differences between legal systems. As of January 2011, euthanasia is legal only in a handful of jurisdictions, namely the countries of Colombia (since 1997), Albania (since 1999), The Netherlands (since 2002), Belgium (since 2002), Luxemburg (since 2008), and Germany (since 2009) as well as in some regions of Mexico (in Mexico City since 2007, and in the central state of Aguascalientes since 2008). Although some countries are moving towards legalizing or rather towards depenalizing euthanasia or the physician-assisted suicide, such as Japan, Norway and Switzerland, euthanasia remains unlawful in most of the World.[4] Even among jurisdictions which permit euthanasia, what is legal—'active' vis-à-vis 'passive' euthanasia—as well as the conditions to be met in either case vary.[5] Some countries only allow 'passive' euthanasia, like Ireland and some states of the United States. Other differences concern whether or not the death of the patient is inevitable and/or near; the requirement that the patient be suffering from unbearable physical pain; if the patient's consent must be obtained and preserved prior to

---

[3] See Ballarino, *supra* note 1, p. 13.
[4] See http://en.wikipedia.org/wiki/Legality_of_euthanasia.
[5] In 'active' euthanasia, a medical professional or another person take an action that causes the patient to die (e.g. a lethal injection); while in 'passive' euthanasia the doctors lets the patient die, either because they omit to do something that is necessary to keep the patient alive, or they stop doing something that is keeping the patient alive (e.g. switching off life-support machines, disconnecting a feeding tube, not performing life-extending operations, or not giving life-extending drugs). On the alleged moral differences between 'killing' and 'letting die' which may inform differences in legal regimes, see the BBC Ethics Guide: Active and passive euthanasia, available at http://www.bbc.co.uk/ethics/euthanasia/overview/activepassive_1.shtml. For modern literature in Spanish-speaking countries, see Luis Fernando Niño, *Eutanasia. Morir con dignidad. Consecuencias jurídico-penales* (Buenos Aires, 2005); María José Parejo Guzmán, *La eutanasia: ¿Un derecho?* (Navarra, 2005); José Luis Medina Frisancho, *Eutanasia e imputación objetiva en derecho penal. Una interpretación normativa de los ámbitos de responsabilidad en la decisión de la propia muerte* (Lima, 2010), and the literature cited therein.

death and/or if it can/cannot be presumed; regarding the validity of the decision made by a minor or by a person that is mentally ill to terminate their life; the authority of the appointed guardian or the designated person to 'pull the plug' or even who such person should be in case the patient is unable and has not designated someone to make health care decisions; the justification for not seeking medical advise in certain circumstances; and the need to obtain prior court approval or from other competent authority. Because of these differences, when a person becomes incapacitated or terminally-ill in a country different than his or her own, the important and difficult question which arises is what law or laws apply.

Often the terminology used and the euthanasia protocols also vary from place to place. For example, when a doctor hands over the lethal injection to the patient instead of administering the lethal medicine, is this 'active euthanasia' or assisted-suicide? Also, voluntary refusal of food and fluids (VRFF) or patient refusal of nutrition and hydration (PRNH) is sometimes suggested as a legal alternative to euthanasia in jurisdictions disallowing euthanasia. This brings us to the question of what law defines euthanasia and discerns legal from illegal practices regardless of the terms use (the problem of 'characterization' in the jargon of private international law).

The above considerations apply equally to advance health care directives, also known as advance or personal directives, advance decisions and living wills.[6] Again, the legal situation by jurisdiction varies. Most countries where living wills are legal, require that the patient's declaration be in writing and signed (Germany[7]; the Netherlands[8]; Switzerland; and the Italian Draft Bill[9]); some require that the patient's clinical conditions be verified by a medical board (Italian Draft Bill) or by at least two physicians, one of them being totally unrelated to the first physician and with no prior knowledge of the medical case (Germany); some jurisdictions

---

[6] A 'living will' is one form of advance directive, making provisions for health care in the event that in the future the person becomes unable to make decisions. Another type of advance directive is the 'durable power of attorney for health care' (or 'health care proxy' in the American literature) where someone is appointed to make health care decisions on behalf of the patient should the latter become incapacitated to make those decisions on his or her own. In this study 'advance directive' and 'living will' are used synonymously.

[7] "German Law on Advance Directives", applicable since 1 September 2009.

[8] "Termination of Life on Request and Assisted Suicide (Review Procedures) Act", in force as of 1 April 2002, available in English at http://policyprojects.ac.nz/jasonrenwick/files/2010/10/Testo-legge-olandese-eutanasia1-6.pdf

[9] See *supra* note 2.

provide for health care decision-making for incompetent persons (the US state of Pennsylvania[10]); some prohibit to stop providing the patient with the nutrition and hydration necessary for the essential physiologic functions of the body, except in given circumstances (Italian Draft Bill), with an aim not to fall in what could be characterized as euthanasia; and yet, most countries have not enacted a regulatory framework for living wills; these legal differences causing the need for the identification of the applicable law (a choice of law problem).

III. Applicability and Scope of Application of the Patient's
Personal Law

Except for derogations imposed for justified reasons, most notably in some common law countries, capacity and personal status are governed by the personal law of the individual concerned.[11] The *statut personnel* refers to and includes all the problems that a person has over his or her own body: beginning and end of human personhood (if a human individual's existence begins at conception, fetal viability or birth; and if it ends following cessation of cardio-respiratory function or when brain function has irreversibly ceased), name, gender, as well as the so-called 'personality rights' comprising aspects of personality which are legally protected such as a person's reputation and privacy.[12] There is consensus on the need that

---

[10] "Advance Directive for Health Care Act", 16 April 1992, as revised in 2006 to provide greater clarity to individuals and health care providers regarding the use of advance directives.

[11] In Argentina, the general conflict rule on personal status appears in Articles 6, 7 and 948 of the Civil Code, subjecting 'capacity' to the law of domicile, but that jurisprudence and doctrine consider also applicable to other personal status' issues not specifically provided for.

[12] Conflict problems of personal status have raised this author's attention for quite some time. Publications, in Spanish, include: Mario J. A. Oyarzábal, "Aspectos internacionales de la presunción de fallecimiento" [Presumption of Death. Internacional Aspects], *La ley* (2001-F), pp. 1417–1424; *Ausencia y presunción de fallecimiento en el derecho internacional privado* [Absence and Presumption of Death in Private Internacional Law] (Buenos Aires, 2003); "Observaciones generales sobre el estatuto personal en derecho internacional privado" [Some Remarks on the Issue of Personal Status in Private International Law], 14 *Revista de derecho del Tribunal Supremo de Justicia de la República Bolivariana de Venezuela* (2004), pp. 165–181; "La capacidad en el derecho internacional privado argentino" [Capacity in Argentine Private International Law], 17 *Revista mexicana de derecho internacional privado y comparado* (2005), pp. 9–24; "Los actos de estado civil en derecho internacional privado y la competencia específica de los agentes diplomáticos y consulares argentinos" [Acts of Civil Status in Private International Law and the Competence of Argentine Diplomatic and Consular Authorities], 13 *Anuario argentino de derecho internacional*

most of—if not all—these matters should be in principle subjected to the law of the person, whichever the personal law may be in accordance to the conflict rule of the competent court. It is common knowledge that, while most continental European countries adhere to the law of the person's nationality, Latin-American countries as well as most common law jurisdictions adhere to the law of the person's domicile (either the domicile of origin or the domicile of choice). In order to overcome this controversy between nationality and the domicile laws, which lays in the origin of a good share of the uncertainty affecting private international law cases and in the failure of numerous attempts to harmonize conflict rules, a new connecting factor has been gaining ground, thank partly to the work of the Hague Conference on Private International Law: the law of the habitual residence. The concept of 'habitual residence' is close to that of 'domicile' but focuses more on the *factum* or presence of the individual in a given place (where the person actually lives and that may be considered their 'home', to which they routinely return after visiting other places) rather than on an intention to reside there indefinitely (the *animus simper manendi*, which is a requirement for domicile). Yet, despite the progress made, in most legal systems there remain some core issues subjected respectively to the nationality or the domicile law.[13]

(2004), pp. 125–139; "El inicio y el fin de la existencia de las personas humanas en el derecho internacional privado" [Beginning and End of Legal Personality of Natural Persons in Private International Law], 210 *El Derecho* (2005), pp. 1146–1149; "El nombre y la protección de la identidad de las personas. Cuestiones de derecho internacional público y privado" [Name and Protection of Personal Identity. Issues Raised in the Fields of Public and Private International Law], 58 *Prudentia Iuris* (2004), pp. 73–97, reprinted in Fernando Parra-Aranguren (ed.), *Studia iuris civilis–Libro homenaje a Gert F. Kummerow Aigster* (Caracas, 2004), pp. 459–478; "Algunos problemas derivados del hermafroditismo y de la transexualidad en el derecho internacional privado argentino" [Hermaphroditism and Transexualism in Argentine Private International Law], 30 *Revista de derecho de familia* (2005), pp. 97–105; "El derecho a la intimidad y el tratamiento de datos personales en el derecho internacional privado argentino" [The Right to Privacy and Transborder Personal Data Flows in Argentine Private International Law], 83 *Lecciones y ensayos* (2007), pp. 49–78, reprinted in Diego P. Fernández Arroyo y Nuria González Martín (eds.), *Tendencias y relaciones: Derecho internacional privado actual* (Mexico, 2010), pp. 267–294; "El 'domicilio' en el derecho internacional privado" [Domicile in Private International Law], in Diego P. Fernández Arroyo, Gonzalo Parra Aranguren, Didier Opertti Badan, José Antonio Moreno Rodríguez y Jürgen Basedow (eds.), *Derecho internacional privado: Derecho de la libertad y el respeto mutuo. Ensayos a la memoria de Tatiana B. de Maekelt* (Asunción, 2010), pp. 453–476.
[13] Elisa Pérez Vera, "Las personas físicas", in Elisa Pérez Vera (ed.), *Derecho internacional privado* (Madrid, 1998), vol. II, p. 27. In Argentina, 'habitual residence' lacks of legal significance, except as provided by a treaty, or when the person has no fixed domicile in which case they are considered domiciled where they reside (Article 90(5) of the Argentine Civil Code). For an account of the problems originated by the conflict between the nationality

It is this author's view that no good reason exists to subject the 'right to die' to other than the personal law, when all other problems which are *intuitu personae* are subjected to said law.

Generally speaking, the capacity of a man or woman to dispose, i.e. to make decisions regarding health care in case he or she becomes terminally-ill or incapacitated, is governed by the personal law in force at the time he or she made the living will. As Professor Ballarino explains, "[i]n view of the fact that the person may become incapacitated [what] is important is the psychological and juridical capacity at the moment of the act".[14] Indeed, this solution may be regarded as an application of the solution given to most other conflicts of laws regarding capacity, e.g., in matters of testament validity.[15]

The personal law determines which is the age of consent, i.e., the minimum age at which a person is considered to be legally competent of making health care and/or life-termination decisions, the right of minors to be heard and their wishes to be taken into consideration, as well as the possibility that a surrogate (parents or a guardian) may make a request for the death of a child or of an incapacitated adult. The personal law also decides upon the role that personal values may play, notably when religious motives are expressed to refuse a medical treatment that is necessary to keep the patient alive (so-called 'conscientious objection').

Although the formalities of a declaration of advance directives or of a declaration on euthanasia, for their validity, will be normally subjected to the law of the place where a declaration is made (*locus regit actum*), the ways to express the will, notably if it must be in written form, in a 'public instrument' (recorded with and/or authenticated by a court, an administrative authority or a notary public), signed by the interested person, and in the presence of witnesses, also falls within the scope of application of the personal law, those being requirements purported to warrant and record a person's informed consent, freely and consciously given.

Finally, the clinical and other relevant conditions for a valid request for death (e.g., the need for the patient to be suffering intolerable pain, his or her death being imminent and/or irreversible, or that he or she is at a terminal stage), or as to the medical treatments that the person wishes to receive or not to receive in the event of a future loss of mental capacity,

---

and the domiciliary principles in personal status matters, see Benedetta Ubertazzi, *La capacità delle persone fisiche nel diritto internazionale privato* (Padova, 2006), pp. 66–88.

[14] See Ballarino, *supra* note 1, p. 8.

[15] See generally, François Rigaux, *Derecho internacional privado. Parte general* (Madrid, 1985), pp. 404–407.

shall also be sought in the laws (the written provisions and case law) of the country to which the person belongs (i.e., the law of his or her nationality, domicile, or habitual residence, in accordance with the connecting factor in place in the private international law system of the competent court intervening in the given case).

The above conclusions are generally supported by the authority of Professor Ballarino.[16] However, I cannot share his call for a 'flexible' approach,[17] except as *de lege ferenda* or when the possibility to set aside the law of the person's nationality or domicile is mandated or allowed by the conflict rule of the competent court. However strongly one may feel about the application of the law of the person's habitual residence—and the distinguished colleague has certainly made his case regarding the need for the *centre-de-vie* State to provide for the legal grounds for euthanasia and health treatments—in most legal systems the conflict rules concerning personal status are not disposable by the parties or even by the courts. Notwithstanding this, I do agree that the law of habitual residence seems more appropriate than the laws of the State of domicile or of the State of nationality when the individual does not currently live there, particularly if the personal law (nationality or domicile) forbids euthanasia or advance directives and the law of the State where euthanasia or the treatment occur and where the patient actually lives allows them.

IV. Scope of Application of the *Lex Artis Medica* and *Ordre Public*

The countries where euthanasia is legal carefully control its implementation requiring the fulfillment of specific conditions,[18] in defect of which euthanasia remains a criminal offense. In The Netherlands, the patient's suffering must be unbearable with no prospect of improvement; his or her request must be voluntary and persist over time; the patient must be fully aware of his or her condition, prospect and options; the patient's condition must be consulted with an independent doctor; the death must be carried out in a medically appropriate fashion by a doctor or the patient in the presence of a doctor; and the patient must be at least 12 years old, patients between 12 and 16 requiring the consent of

---

[16] See Ballarino, *supra* note 1, pp. 7–8, 13, 23.
[17] See Ballarino, *supra* note 1, p. 12, 16–17, 24, 26.
[18] See Ballarino, *supra* note 1, p. 14.

their parents.[19] In Belgium, the patient must be in a hopeless medical condition and bearing untolerable physical or mental pain; the request must
me done in writing; at least one month must elapse between the request
and the 'mercy killing'; he or she must be informed by a physician of the
state or his or her health as well as the availabilities and consequences of
palliative care; and all mercy killing must be fully documented and presented to a permanent monitoring committee.[20]

It is most likely that if euthanasia is illegal according to the local law, its
implementation will carry penal consequences for the doctor or the surrogate person who performs it, even if euthanasia were considered legal
by—and it fulfilled all the requirements of—the patient's personal law,
because the act will remain a 'homicide' for the laws in place at the country where it occurred in virtue of the 'territoriality' of criminal law and
despite the fact that the permissive foreign law could eventually be considered an attenuating circumstance of the 'crime'.

Conversely, if euthanasia is legal according to the laws where it is to
occur, it should only be performed in the case of foreign residents or
nationals if the patient were allowed to choose to die according to his
or her personal law. Should the patient's personal law forbid euthanasia,
or the legal conditions thereby prescribed for euthanasia were not fulfilled, euthanasia should not be carried out even if all the legal conditions
prescribed by the local law were met. The personal law should prevail for
the reasons stated above.

Finally, if both countries allow euthanasia, which is not so common in
the current state of affairs, a comparison between both laws is necessary.
In the first place, the fulfillment of all the requirements subject to the personal law will have to be observed (capacity to consent; validity of the
form used; suffering of untolerable pain and/or irreversible death; etc.).[21]
This being the case, the mandatory laws of the State where euthanasia
occurs must also be complied with as *lex fori profesional* or otherwise. For
a start, the doctor must follow the procedures and apply the protocols of
the *lex artis medica* as prescribed in the country where the professional is

---

[19] See *supra* note 8.
[20] "The Belgian Act on Euthanasia" of 28 May 2002, available in English at http://
www.kuleuven.ac.be/cbmer/viewpic.php?LAN=E&TABLE=DOCS&ID=23. See also Rafael
Cohen-Almagor, "Euthanasia Policy and Practice in Belgium: Critical Observations and
Suggestions for Improvement", 24-3 *Issues in Law & Medicine* (2009), pp. 187–218, available
at http://hcc.haifa.ac.il/~rca/articles/Belgium%20Euthanasia%20Policy_Practice.pdf.
[21] See *supra* para. III.

licensed to practice medicine, e.g. verify that the patient's request is voluntary; document properly the case; consult with and/or provide the necessary information to the competent local professional, judicial or administrative organs; as well as any other prerequisites embodied in the laws of the respective State. The conditions prescribed for performing euthanasia are normally 'mandatory' as they are intended to circumscribe it to 'justifiable' cases (to relieve extreme pain when a person's quality of life is low, i.e. for his or her alleged benefit, in case the person chooses to die) and avoid non-mercy non-voluntary deaths. The differences among prerequisites and procedures for euthanasia prescribed in the various national legislations reflect the local social values, i.e. what is considered acceptable for a given society at a certain time. Because of the objectives sought and the important personal and social values at stake, the rules concerning euthanasia are normally not disposable, meaning that neither the patient nor the doctor or the person performing euthanasia may choose not to abide by them. They are what the doctrine calls *lois de police*, laws which are applicable on the grounds of public policy (*ordre public*),[22] applicable to both purely domestic cases and to cases with a foreign element alike.

What has just been said about euthanasia, applies equally to living wills whenever national laws differ about the conditions for the validity of advance directives, including the capacity and ways to express the informed consent, its contents and limitations, the appointment of a trustee, the need for judicial or administrative authorization, etc. It would suffice to compare the laws on advance directives of Germany,[23] of the State of Oregon in the United States[24] and the Italian Draft Bill.[25] In Germany, an

---

[22] The literature abounds regarding the characterization and application of mandatory norms (also referred to as 'lois d'application immediate', 'norme con apposita delimitazione della sfera di efficacia', 'spacially conditioned rules', 'peremptory norms', 'normas rígidas', 'Exklusivsätze', 'lois de police', etc.), that because of public policy considerations, exclude the application of otherwise applicable conflict rules. See, generally, Phocion Francescakis, "Quelques précisions sur les lois d'application immédiate et leurs rapports avec les règles de conflit de lois", 55 *Revue critique de droit international privé* (1966), pp. 1–18; Rodolfo De Nova, "I conflitti di legge e le norme con apposita delimitazione della sfera di efficacia", in *Diritto internazionale* (Milano, 1959), pp. 13 et seq.; Hilding Eek, "Peremptory Norms and Private International law", 139 *Recueil des cours de l'Académie de droit international de la Haye* (1973-II), pp. 1–74; Gerhard Kegel, *Internationales Privatrecht* (München, 1977), pp. 87 et seq.
[23] See *supra* note 7.
[24] "The Health Care Decisions Act", 2009, available at http://www.oregon.gov/DCBS/SHIBA/advanced_directives.shtml.
[25] See *supra* note 2.

advance directive must be respected in any decision regarding medical treatment, regardless of the stage of the illness; it is revocable at any time, even if the patient has limited decision-making capacity; it does not need notarization or routine updating after certain time intervals; and provided that a surrogate or health care proxy has been appointed, they must assert the patient's will.[26] Oregon's law permits an individual to preauthorize health care representatives to allow the natural dying process if he or she is medically confirmed to be close to death or permanently unconscious, or suffering from an advanced progressive illness or extraordinary suffering; the advance directive must have been developed while the person is able to clearly and definitely express him or herself verbally, in writing or in sign language; and it does not affect routine care for cleanliness and comfort, which must be given whether or not there is an advance directive. Finally, if the Italian Draft Bill passes, a declaration of advance directives will have to be made in written form and signed with autograph signature; it shall not contain instructions that correspond to the crimes of 'murder', 'murder by consent' or 'aiding and abetting suicide' as typified in the Italian Criminal Code; and artificial nutrition and hydration must be kept until the end of life.

In application of the principles previously stated, declarations of advance directives developed by foreign nationals or domiciliaries must fulfil the conditions prescribed by the applicable foreign personal law of the patient, and ultimately comply with the mandatory rules of the place where the person is hospitalized. Yet, special care must be taken when identifying and applying local mandatory laws, since not any difference with the local law is enough to displace the application of the personal law, but only if a fundamental 'principle' is contradicted to the point of gravely affecting interests and values that the local legislator deemed important to protect.[27]

---

[26] See Urban Wiesing, Ralf J. Jox, Hans-Joachim Heßler, and Gian Domenico Borasio, "A New Law on Advance Directives in Germany", 36 *Journal on Medical Ethics* (2010), pp. 779–783.

[27] In Argentina, a difference is made between domestic or 'internal' public policy (*orden público interno*) and 'international' public policy (*orden público internacional*). *Orden público interno* relates to the rules applicable to purely domestic cases; and *orden público internacional* to the rules applicable to cases with a foreign element and the recognition of foreign legal relationships, in which cases a less demanding threshold is applied, accepting the application of more permissive foreign laws. See, generally, Werner Goldschmidt, *Derecho internacional privado. Derecho de la tolerancia* (Buenos Aires, 2009), pp. 231–247.

V. Human Rights and Patient's Autonomy as Foundations
for Euthanasia and the Living Will

Euthanasia has been the subject of moral, religious, philosophical and legal, as much as of human rights debate.[28] Although this matter is discussed more in depth and length earlier in this book by Professor Negri, it may be useful to place the current argument insofar it can influence the functioning of conflict rules. The question remains whether it may be successfully argued that there is an overriding international human right to 'die with dignity', or to refuse medical treatment for that matter, that should be respected and enforced even in countries where euthanasia is unlawful notably when the conflict rule of the *forum* prescribes as applicable a foreign law—that of the State of the personal law of the patient—which does allow euthanasia; or to allow a person to commit euthanasia in a country where euthanasia is legal, dismissing the application of the personal foreign law of the patient that forbids it, on the grounds that the latter violates the person's human right to die with dignity. Although the response will ultimately depend on the legal reasoning and decision of the competent court in the case at hand, where many factors will play a role in the interpretation and application of international law rules, including the relationship between international law and domestic law in a given country and the model adopted by the constitution to implement or incorporate into municipal law international rules, the core question becomes whether there is an international human right to euthanasia stemming from international human rights instruments and/or from customary international law.

In this author's view, no such right may be derived with a reasonable degree of certainty at the present stage from written international law or the practice of States. Indeed, the 'right to die' or to refuse medical treatment is not explicitly or clearly defined in any of the major international or regional human rights instruments, which in turn do provide explicitly and clearly for a 'right to life' even when it appears qualified in different and sometimes controversial manners.[29] Without going as far as to uphold

---

[28] For the debate in Australia, see "Human Rights and Euthanasia", Australian Human Rights Commission, available at http://www.hreoc.gov.au/human_rights/euthanasia/index.html.

[29] See, *inter alia*, Article 6(1) of the International Covenant on Civil and Political Rights (ICCPR), Article 3 of the Universal Declaration of Human Rights, Article 4 of the American Convention on Human Rights, Article 2 of the European Convention for the Protection of

that voluntary euthanasia violates international law,[30] which is equally unjustifiable if one reads the current international instruments without a preconceived religious, moral or philosophical state of mind in the light of their *travaux préparatoires*,[31] the debate—often heated—that often surrounds this issue due to the difficulty of reconciling competing values at stake, added to the fact that as of 2011 only a limited number of countries allow for advance directives and even less countries allow euthanasia, show the limitations faced by the argument that sees in the 'right to die' an international human right.

Perhaps the existence of an 'international human right' to choose freely one's medical treatment may be more clearly asserted when the treatment chosen is not directed to or will inevitably cause his or her death and is in conformity with the appropriate care protocols, as such right could be derived from the internationally protected rights to 'life' and to 'personal integrity'.

As an unlimited patient's autonomy cannot be assumed from an international legal perspective, any such autonomy permitting people to prospectively express their choice about medical treatment including the choice to die can only be derived from the applicable national law or laws, either the substantive rules of the State where the patient is undergoing treatment or where euthanasia occurs (*lex fori*), the patient's personal law or a combination of both.

In my view, a faculty of the person to designate as applicable the law which favors the 'validity' of the will should not be disregarded *a priori*, as Professor Ballarino sustains.[32] For such faculty to be exercised validly, it is suggested that two conditions must be met. First, the personal law of the patient (national or domicile in accordance to the conflict rule of the *forum*) must unhesitantly allow the patient to choose a more favorable foreign law, not just simply to matters of personal status generally, but in matters of therapeutic alliance preferably. Hypothetically, the chosen law may have no relation with the person or the case, but it must remain one

---

Human Rights and Fundamental Freedoms, and Article 4 of the African Charter on Human and Peoples' Rights.

[30] In the case of legislation providing for involuntary euthanasia, it could more clearly be argued that a violation of Article 6 of the ICCPR, which provides that "[n]o one shall be arbitrarily deprived of his life", may be involved.

[31] The text and the intention of the Parties, as provided for in Articles 31 and 32 of the Vienna Convention on the Law of Treaties, are unanimously seen as the proper basis for interpretation of treaties in International Law.

[32] Ballarino, *supra* note 1, p. 8.

of the laws among which the person was allowed to choose from in conformity with his or her personal law. The limits will come hand in hand
with the mandatory norms of the chosen law and, ultimately, the public
policy of the country where the *forum* (i.e., where the treatment is taking
place). Those laws could reasonably be the laws of the countries of the
person's nationality (or one of his or her nationalities), domicile or habitual residence,[33] or the country where the person is hospitalized. Second,
the persistence of the patient's will must be ascertained, particularly when
a change in legislation has taken place either at the country of the chosen
law or at the country of the personal law between the time of choice was
expressed and the time the person became incapacitated. These conditions shall be applied accumulatively.

V. Conclusions

Euthanasia and living will raise, in the realm of private international law,
issues which are similar to those raised by other new institutions, like
same-sex marriage and artificial insemination, where national legislations
differ greatly in view of the social, moral, religious and philosophical values that prevail at a given society. Also in the area of same-sex marriage, to
use an analogy, at least two laws enter into play when one of the contract-
ing parties is a foreign national or domiciliary: the law of the place of cel-
ebration of marriage and the personal law, which most likely than not, will
differ about the legality of a union between people of the same sex. Here,
the debate has also been placed in terms of international human rights—
whether international human rights mandates States to allow same sex
marriage or forbids it—, and, to a lesser extent, in terms of the faculty to
choose a person of one's same sex to form a legally recognized family
with.[34] Beyond family law matters, the use of electronic communications

---

[33] See, generally, Jean-Yves Carlier, *Autonomie de la volonté et statut personnel. Etude
prospective de droit international privé* (Bruxelles, 1992), pp. 261–263, and the bibliography
cited therein; P. Gannage, "La pénétration de l'autonomie de la volonté dans le droit international privé de la famille", *Revue critique de droit international privé* (1992–3), pp. 425–
454; Mario J. A. Oyarzábal, "Observaciones generales sobre el estatuto personal en derecho
internacional privado", *supra* note 12, pp. 177–178.

[34] For the state of the debate, before the enactment in Argentina on 15 July 2010 of 'equal
rights' (Law No. 26.618, BO 22/7/2010, which gave homosexual couples all the same rights
as heterosexual ones, known as "Egalitarian Marriage Law"), see Mario J. A. Oyarzábal,
"Efectos en la Argentina de matrimonios extranjeros entre personas del mismo sexo"
[Effects in Argentina of Foreign Same-Sex Marriages], 44 *Revista de derecho de
familia* (2009), pp. 123–129. On problems raised by assisted reproductive technology in the

and the Internet has also raised concerns regarding the appropriateness to apply the rules of classic private international law to the new problems, some claiming that a conflict of laws approach should be left aside altogether and some urging for a more 'flexible', open-ended, approach.[35]

Yet, like in the case of other 'modern' problems, one can conclude from the preceding paragraphs that the traditional conflict rules provide effective enough solutions to the problems arising from the issuance of advance health care and life termination decisions. Generally speaking, the legal problems posed by euthanasia and living wills are similar to the ones posed by other personal status matters in a globalized World. Euthanasia and advance directives raise issues of personal capacity, formal validity of declarations and recognition and enforcement of foreign decisions, including the appointment of a trustee or a surrogate, in other countries with a different set of values enshrined in law. These are ordinary problems that private international law has been dealing with for centuries in relation to contracts, torts and family related matters; and there is no evidence that the methods (i.e., conflict, materially oriented and peremptory rules), principles (e.g., the search for a fair, effective solution which is whenever possible the same irrespective of what country's court the case has raised before) and 'devices' (e.g., characterization, *renvoi* or *ordre public*) that the private international law doctrine and the practice developed to solve traditional problems, are unable to cope with new problems such as those posed by living wills and euthanasia.

conflict of laws, see Mario J. A. Oyarzábal, "El reconocimiento en la Argentina de la paternidad de hijos concebidos en el extranjero por inseminación artificial de una pareja de homosexuales hombres" [Recognition in Argentina of the Paternity of Children born Abroad by Artificial Insemination to a Same-Sex Couple], *La ley-Actualidad*, 21/2/2006 (both articles published in Spanish).

[35] For a discussion and references on this issue, see Mario J. A. Oyarzábal, "International Electronic Contracts. A Note on Argentine Choice of Law Rules", 35 *University of Miami Inter-American Law Review* (2004), pp. 520–526.

PART II

ADVANCE DIRECTIVES, END-OF-LIFE DECISION-MAKING
AND EUTHANASIA IN COMPARATIVE LEGAL PERSPECTIVE

EUTHANASIA FACE OF THE LAW IN LATIN AMERICA

*Heloisa Helena Barboza**

Being born and dying, in the common sense, have always been under-stood as natural facts occurring at a given moment, determined by divine will for those who believe in the power of a God over human existence, or by the simple passage of time, which marks the beginning and the end of a vital cycle. However, biologically, death and birth stem from a process, a sequence of events, among which one is chosen to point out the com-mencement for the production, or the ceasing of legal effects, an issue afforded diverse treatment in the legislation of different countries.[1]

Not always, however, and perhaps in the major urban centers with a certain frequency, the moment of birth is determined "by nature". Delivery often occurs through a surgical procedure, on a date chosen by the mother and/or the father. Thus, the beginning of life for a person (the child) derives from the exercising of autonomy by another (the mother), not only by a "work of nature".

It is also ascertained that conception itself may also result from the exercising of a couple's reproductive autonomy,[2] by means of concep-tion control,[3] or only by the woman (or the man), with or without partici-pation of the father (or mother), when one of the assisted reproduction

---

* Head Teacher of the Chair of Civil Law at the Rio de Janeiro State University – UERJ Law School, Brazil; email: h2b@uol.com.br.

[1] In Brazil, it is understood that there has been birth with life, as from the separation of the fetus from the mother's womb, either naturally or by means of medical procedures, within a normal term, or not. For the prevailing doctrine, birth with life is featured by the oxygen-carbon exchange with the environment, that is, there is life as from the first moment in which the fetus breathes with its lungs, even though the umbilical cord has not been cut yet—if it breathes, it is alive.

[2] The Brazilian Republic Constitution (article 226, §6) acknowledges the so-called "reproductive autonomy", ensuring, based on the principles of the dignity of the human person and of responsible fatherhood, the right to family planning, which comprises the constitution, limitation, or increase in the number of children, and is submitted to a free decision by the woman. It is the duty of the State to provide educational and scientific resources for the exercising of this right.

[3] It is important to point out that abortion is not a means for limitation of the number of children, even though there is the likelihood of the mother to decide, also in the exercis-ing of her autonomy, on the interruption of pregnancy, an act which shall be licit or illicit (this is the case of Brazil), according to the standard of law to which it is submitted.

S. Negri (ed.), *Self-Determination, Dignity and End-of-Life Care*
2011 Koninklijke Brill NV. Printed in The Netherlands. ISBN 978 90 04 22357 8. pp. 143–154

techniques is used in fertilization. Conception, thus, is not a work "of nature" or "of chance". Through the aforesaid techniques, women and men who have not reproduced "naturally", can have children, by joining their will to biotechnoscientific resources.[4]

The exercising of autonomy by a person can as may be seen, fully bear influence on the arising (and even in the extinction) of one life from another, when dealing with birth. The same cannot be said, however, when deciding on one's own death, even in case of extreme suffering from an incurable disease. It is possible to induce that the principle of liberty, which purports autonomy as one of its expressions, yields, at first sight, before the right to life, whose inviolability is constitutionally assured in several countries.

The position of different legal stances before this issue has varied. Devoid of any intention of exhausting the issue, this work reviews the standing legislation on the theme, in a number of Latin American countries, with the purpose of contributing to its debate and to the development of the expected solutions.

I. EUTHANASIA

The issue of abbreviating suffering at the end of life has been debated since Antiquity. Growing medicalization of life and of death, started in modern times, coupled to the biotechnoscientific apparatus, has brought new and major challenges to mankind, especially as to ethics and to the law, on account of the power of doctors to abbreviate or extend the process of death. The quantity and quality of life has started to be the object of evaluation and debate, in the terminal phase of human existence. The proportion of the problem is greater when medical practice paradigms are taken into account, with the three paradigms debated in Brazil serving as example: technoscientific, commercial-entrepreneurial, and that of humanitarian and solidary benignity. The choice of priorities and strategies, in face of the terminal patient and its suffering shall be made according to the paradigm adopted, according to Leonard M. Martin.[5]

---

[4] On the term *biotechnoscience*, see Fermin Roland Schramm and Miguel Kotow Lang, "Bioethics and Biotechnology: The Human among Two Paradigms", 2 *Acta Bioethica* (2001), pp. 259–267, www.scielo.org.

[5] Leonard M. Martin C.Ss.R., "Euthanasia and Dysthanasia", in S. Ibiapina Ferreira Costa, V. Garrafa, and G. Oselka (eds.), *Introduction to Bioethics* (Brasília, 1998), pp. 171–172.

Martin's considerations allow for ascertaining that the human "dying issue" comprises different situations, which are assigned different denominations. It is consequently necessary to distinguish *euthanasia*, in its active and passive form, *dysthanasia*, and *orthothanasia*,[6] so that the legal and ethical effects of each one of these "forms of dying" may be determined.

One understands as *dysthanasia*,[7] a situation opposite to euthanasia, in which there occurs the painful and useless prolonging of the process of dying, through medical technology.[8] This comprises the so-called *therapeutic obstinacy*, which entails the keeping of life by means of disproportionate treatments which extend the patient's physical and/or psychological suffering, there occurring "a deepening of the features which render, in fact, death into a kind of *hyperdeath*".[9]

Orthothanasia is "the art of dying well", the death which is faced "with a certain calm" and which is not denied or hidden, as common in Western culture. Instead of searching for the cure, which is not possible, one takes care of the sick patient, to keep life "while this is the right procedure".[10] It is also understood as death in the right time, without disproportionate treatments (dysthanasia) and without abbreviation of the process of dying (euthanasia).[11] One should consider, for the purpose of evaluating the "correct procedure", that which is acceptable under the ethical and legal viewpoint. Regarding the "right time" for death, in the light of the principle of human dignity, one may consider that which is determined by the patient, in exercising his autonomy or by a third party (a physician or a family member[12]) to prevent or terminate dysthanasia. Fermin Roland Schramm and Rodrigo Siqueira Batista, although they admit the patient's autonomy to decide on "the right time to die", deem that the determining of this time is at times impossible in view of the almost-inexhaustible resources which

---

[6] *Mysthanasia* or *social euthanasia* shall not be object of consideration in this work; this term designates miserable, untimely death, pursuant to dearth of minimal living conditions, a theme reviewed by Leonard M. Martin, in the work mentioned.

[7] Fermin Roland Schramm and Rodrigo Siqueira Batista, "Conversations on the 'Good Death': The Bioethical Debate on Euthanasia", 21 *Public Health Newsletters* (2005), n° 1, pp. 111–119, at 114, clarify that etymologically the term *dysthanasia* contains the idea of "double death" (in the Greek origin, that which dies twice, in Latin, the *dis* brings the idea of separation and negation)".

[8] Martin, *supra* note 5, p. 172.

[9] Schramm and Siqueira Batista, *supra* note 7, p. 114.

[10] Martin, *supra* note 5, p. 190.

[11] Schramm and Siqueira Batista, *supra* note 7, p. 114.

[12] The issue of whom the power of decision pertains to, under such hypothesis is tormented, its analysis being outside the narrow limits of this work.

allow for extending life, hindering the distinction between not intervening and letting death occur at "the apparently right moment".[13]

Schramm and Batista[14] state that the word *euthanasia* finds its origins
in Greek and means "good death", as denoted by the prefix *eu*, which indicates *well*, with *kindness*, with *benevolence*. Thus, this comprises "passing
away without pain and suffering". In the 20th century, "good death"
became a public question, "ending up by crystallizing a markedly negative
connotation, for having been associated to Nazi practices, on account of a
program funded by the government, aimed at eliminating "lives which
were not worth living", and which led to the death of more than one hun-
dred thousand persons (Gypsies, Blacks and Jews), in its two years of operation. This "biography" of the word *euthanasia* explains its great polysemy
and the countless mistakes in its linkage to the ideas of homicide, "influenced suicide", or even genocide, which not rarely leads to extreme pas-
sionate positions.[15]

There was great rejection to the theme of euthanasia, especially in the
post-war period. The debates were only resumed in the 1960's and 1970's,
especially in face of the technoscientific advances which have allowed for
the lengthening of human lives, even deprived of any prospect of recovery
and of insurmountable and diversified "clinical situations", which placed
at outright confrontation the quantity of life and the quality of life leading
to questions on the morality of euthanasia and of assisted suicide. The
debates were further heightened, in the opinion of the abovementioned
authors, by the approval of laws authorizing euthanasia in various countries in the world, such as Australia (July 1996), The Netherlands (April
2001), Switzerland and Belgium (May 2002).[16]

Distinct situations are lodged under the generic concept of euthanasia,
which Schramm and Batista examine taking as reference "the act in itself"
and "the ill person's consent". The first referential being considered, one
has: a) *active euthanasia*—the deliberate act of causing the patient's death
without suffering, by humanitarian means (e.g. using a lethal injection);
b) *passive euthanasia*—when death occurs by intentional omission of a

---

[13] Schramm and Siqueira Batista, *supra* note 7, p. 114.

[14] Ibid., p. 112.

[15] Ibid., p. 113.

[16] Ibid., p. 114, the authors refer to the cases of Karen Ann Quinlan (1975–1976), Spring
(1977–1980), Diane-Quill (1996), Ramón San Pedro (1998), Jack Kevorkian, the "Doctor
Death" (the 1990's) and Vincent Humbert (2003), as well as to other causes which extend
the process of death, such as advanced senescence, which subjects people to chronic and
degenerative diseases which increase their suffering.

medical action which would ensure overlife (e.g. failure to deliver medication or by adopting an indispensible procedure to keep the patient's life)[17]; c) *euthanasia by double effect*—in the cases in which death is made faster as a consequence of medical actions aiming at relieving the patient's suffering, but which are lethal (e.g. the use of morphine to control pain, thereby secondarily leading to breathing depression and death).[18]

Taking into account the patient's consent, euthanasia can be as follows: a) *voluntary*—in response to the patient's express *will*—which would be a synonym of *assisted suicide*; b) *involuntary*—when life is abbreviated without the patient's will being known, or else the act is performed *against* the patient's will.[19]

In any case of euthanasia (active, passive, or in the double effect), the manifestation of the patient's express will toward the "good death" (voluntary euthanasia) and the existence of humanitarian reasons does not prevent, in a general manner, and by itself, the application of legal sanctions. However, the characterization of a delict under such conditions will depend on the analysis of other elements, such as culpability (existence of malice or guilt), as well as possible excludents of criminality, according to the stipulations of the law.

Of special interest is that, in *non*-voluntary euthanasia, the ascertaining of existence of a patient's manifestation of will, contrary to euthanasia, is of basic importance to characterize homicide. Nothing legitimizes the action which contradicts the will of the person who wishes to keep his or her life, even under intense suffering. There is, undoubtedly, in such hypothesis, disrespect to its autonomy, which prevails over alleged humanitarian reasons. Thus, the act can typify the crime of homicide, even though committed on account of the patient's deep suffering. Morally, Schramm and Batista consider that there is a justification for *voluntary euthanasia* and, eventually, for *involuntary euthanasia*, in case the

---

[17] Schramm and Siqueira Batista, ibid. p. 112, question whether there would be a true limit between *passive euthanasia*—not intervening and letting in fact die—and the said *orthothanasia*—let die at the apparently right moment. They consider the distinction conceptually untenable, impossible to be established in certain cases: "after all, not using life-support systems in a patient suffering from terminal neoplasia that is, denying him the possibility of keeping himself alive, would it be tantamount to let death arrive at the *right time* or perform in fact passive euthanasia?"

[18] Ibid., p. 113.

[19] Ibid., the authors distinguish *involuntary euthanasia*, when the act is performed *against* the will of the sick person which, in general lines can be equaled to "homicide", from *non-voluntary euthanasia*, when life is abbreviated without the patient's will being known.

patient's will is unknown, but not if the latter is contrary to the abbreviation of death, a case in which the act shall be criminal, to the point to which it represents a violation of the patient's will.[20]

In view of the recognition of the dignity inherent to all members of the human family and of its equal and inalienable rights such as the basis of freedom,[21] respect to humanitarian ends (which every and any care or treatment should observe) and to the patient's autonomy should not be deferred, particularly in face of intolerable and protracted suffering. *Voluntary passive euthanasia*, that is, intentional *omission* of medical action, should be analyzed under this viewpoint on account of the patient's express refusal to a possible treatment, thereby exercising his or her autonomy. The rejection of treatment can operate to avoid dysthanasia or, simply, because the patient does not accept treatment for an irreversible and incurable illness.

These considerations having been made, euthanasia can be understood as "the employment or abstaining of procedures which allow for expediting or cause the death of an incurable patient, in order to free him from the extreme suffering which assail him or her".[22] The patient is not always conscious, in euthanasia, such as the case of a patient in a coma, who breathes with the help of devices which are then turned off, thereby causing death. In *assisted suicides*, the patient is conscious and manifests his or her will, but requests the help of another person to die, as he or she is not in conditions to do so, a situation which can be comprised under voluntary euthanasia. At any rate, the consummation of euthanasia depends on the participation of another person, for example, a health professional, who, for humanitarian reasons, abbreviates the process of death.[23]

II. The Laws of Latin American Countries on Euthanasia

A review of the existing legislation reveals different positions facing the issue as presented in summary below.

---

[20] Ibid., p. 114.

[21] Universal Declaration of Human Rights adopted and proclaimed by resolution 217 A (III) of the General Assembly of the United Nations on December 10th, 1948, preamble, available at http://portal.mj.gov.br/sedh/ct/legis_intern/ddh_bib_inter_universal.htm.

[22] Schramm and Siqueira Batista, *supra* note 7, p. 113.

[23] The films "The Sea Inside" and "Million Dollar Baby" provide examples of the above-mentioned situations, respectively.

There is no general statute on euthanasia in the Argentine law, but rather, only isolated provisions at the national and provincial level.[24] The Argentine Penal Code envisages sanctions for assisting suicide, punishing, with a prison sentence of one to four years, the party who instigates another to suicide or provides help for the latter to commit it, in case suicide is attempted or consummated.[25]

The Medical Ethics Code of the Argentine Medical Confederation establishes that, under no circumstances, a doctor is authorized to abbreviate a patient's life, except to relieve illness with therapeutic resources applicable to the case; a doctor has the obligation of attempting the patient's cure or improvement whenever possible and, when this is not possible any more, his obligation remains for applying appropriate measures to secure the patient's well-being, although this may lead, despite its correct use, to a shortening of life. A doctor shall not start or continue hopeless, useless, or obstinate diagnostic or therapeutic action; he should consider the patient's explicit will to refuse treatment to extend his or her life, and value previous indications put forth by him, or the opinion of the next-of-kin, responsible for the patient. The Argentine Code of Ethics makes it clear, however, that a doctor shall not intentionally cause the death of any patient, not even in the case of an express request by the latter.[26]

As can be observed, the orientation found in Argentina, accepted by Courts, is in the sense of respecting the patient's autonomy, admitting passive voluntary euthanasia, which finds its foundations in the right to self-determination and dignity towards the human being, contemplated in the Human Rights Treaties with a Constitutional hierarchy and under article 19 of the Constitution of the Argentine Nation (22 August 1994),[27] as clarified by Graciela Medina.[28]

Bolivian law does not purport a specific rule on euthanasia, as well, but envisages, in its Penal Code, under article 257, the "pitiful homicide",

---

[24] Graciela Medina, "¿Prolongar la vida o prolongar la agonía? La eutanasia en Derecho argentino" [Extending Life or Extending Agony? Euthanasia in Argentine Law], 3 *Revista Latinoamericana de Derecho* (2006), pp. 263–294; http://www.Juridicas.Unam.Mx/Publica/Librev/Rev/Revlad/Cont/6/Cnt/Cnt11.pdf.

[25] The Argentine Nation Penal Code, Law 11,179 (T.O. 1984 Updated), article 83. Available at http://www.infoleg.gov.ar/infolegInternet/anexos/15000-19999/16546/texact.htm#15.

[26] The Medical Ethical Code of the Argentine Republic Medical Confederation, articles 131, 132, 133 and 135. Available at http://www.comra.org.ar/.

[27] Available at http://www.argentina.gov.ar/argentina/portal/documentos/constitucion_nacional.pdf.

[28] Medina, *supra* note 24, p. 268.

which refers to the possibility of reducing the sentence contemplated for the said delict and, exceptionally, the granting of a court pardon if, for the homicide, pitiful and urgent motives were determining factors, as well as the terminating of serious suffering or probably incurable physical injuries.[29] Euthanasia, understood as the deliberate act of bringing to an end the life of a patient, is expressly considered as contrary to medical ethics, by the Bolivian Medical Ethics and Deontology Code.[30]

In Brazil, euthanasia, in any of its modes (active, passive, or in double effect) is not admitted. Manifestation of the patient's express will in the sense of "good death" (voluntary euthanasia) or the existence of humanitarian reasons does not prevent the application of penal law. However, the characterization of a delict under such situation shall depend on the analysis of other elements, such as culpability (existence of malice or guilt), as well as on eventual exclusions of criminality. Under such assumptions, the act of abbreviating the process of death may typify (in theory) one of the crimes below: homicide, inducement, instigation or help to commit suicide, absconding help.[31]

The Brazilian Medical Ethics Code[32] proscribes doctors from failing to ensure patients the exercising of the right to freely decide on their persons or well-being, as well as exercising their authority to limit it. In the cases of incurable and terminal diseases, a doctor should provide all available palliative care without undertaking useless or obstinate diagnostic or therapeutic actions, always taking into account the patient's express will or, in case such expression is impossible, that of his or her legal representative.

The Federal Council of Medicine (CFM) has allowed doctors to limit or suspend procedures and treatments which may extend a patient's life in the terminal phase of serious and incurable diseases, assuring him or her the necessary care to relieve the symptoms leading to suffering, in the perspective of full assistance, in compliance with the patient's wishes or with those of his or her legal representatives. In its stance, the CFM took into

---

[29] Bolivian Penal Code. Decree-Law 10426, of 23 August 1972. Available at http://www.oas.org/Juridico/mla/sp/bol/sp_bol-int-text-cp.html.

[30] Available at http://www.colegiomedicobolivia.org.bo/codigotem.html.

[31] Decree-law 2,848, dated 12 July 1940, Penal Code, article 121, 122, 135, respectively; https://www.planalto.gov.br/ccivil_03/Decreto-Lei/del2848.htm.

[32] Federal Medical Council, Resolution 1931, dated 17 September 2009, articles 24 and article 41. Available at http://portal.cfm.org.br/index.php?option=com_content&view=category&id=9&Itemid=122.

consideration constitutional provisions, to wit: the principle of the dignity of the human being, and the determination that no one shall be submitted to either torture or to inhuman or degrading treatment. However, the Resolution authorizing such procedure has been suspended on account of an injunction by the Supreme Federal Court and is currently awaiting judgment by the said Court.[33]

In Chile, euthanasia is also not allowed. The Chilean Medical Code of Ethics sets forth that a doctor may not perform actions whose direct objective comprises putting an end to a patient's life, under any consideration whatsoever.[34] Assistance to suicide is considered a crime.[35]

The Colombian Penal Code penalizes the party who kills someone out of mercy, to terminate intense suffering stemming from bodily injury or serious and incurable disease (mercy homicide or mercy killing).[36] However, Colombia's Constitutional Court understands that "in the cases of terminal patients, the doctors performing the act described in penal law with the consent of a passive subject shall not be, therefore, object of sanction and, consequently, the judges should exonerate from liability whoever acts so".

The Colombian Court, by majority, has declared applicable (*exequible*) article 326, from Decree 100, dated 1980 (Penal Code), with the warning that, in the case of terminal patients in which the free will of the passive subject of the act is concurrent, the physician involved in the act shall not be deemed liable, as his conduct is justified. At the end of the decision, it is stated that the Court, in the name of legal security, exhorts Congress to, within the shortest term ever, and pursuant to the constitutional principles and the basic considerations of humanity, regulate the dignified death theme.[37] As the Colombian Congress has not yet pronounced itself to date on the issue, the matter has been placed in a kind of "legal limbo": the conduct, which may be considered as voluntary active euthanasia (consented), is deemed as justified by the Judiciary, but is not legally authorized.

---

[33] This comprises Resolution 1,805/2006, dated 28 November 2006, suspended by injunction from the Hon. Judge of the 14th Federal Court, as per Public Civil Action n. 2007.34.00.014809-3, filed by the Federal Public Ministry.

[34] Code of Ethics 2008, Chilean Medical Collegiate A.G., art. 9; http://www.colegiomedico.cl/Default.aspx?tabid=248.

[35] Penal Code, art. 393. Available at http://www.leychile.cl/Navegar?idNorma=1984.

[36] Penal Code, Law 599, dated 2000, article 106. Available at http://www.oas.org/juridico/MLA/sp/col/sp_col-int-text-cp.pdf.

[37] Constitutional Court of Colombia, Decision C-239/97, 20 May 1997. Available at http://www.corteconstitucional.gov.co/relatoria/1997/C-239-97.htm

The criminalization of mercy homicide, or mercy killing, even with the reduction of the sentence, is found in other countries, which do not bear rules on euthanasia, and also penalize the instigation or help to suicide. Paraguay,[38] Peru,[39] Venezuela,[40] Cuba,[41] El Salvador,[42] Guatemala,[43] Honduras,[44] and Nicaragua[45] are found in this category.

There is express prohibition of euthanasia in Panama, in the law regulating the patients' rights and obligations, in the matter of information and of free and informed[46] decision, in addition to the criminalization of help to suicide.[47]

Ecuador, penalizes, in addition to instigation or assistance to suicide, the party which voluntarily administers substances who gravely alter health, without the intention of causing death but which, in fact, lead to it. Intention to cause death is assumed if the party which administered the noxious substances is a doctor, a pharmacist, or a chemist, or if the party has knowledge in such professions, even though not having diplomas to perform them.[48]

The Dominican Republic approved, on 26 January 2010, by a wide majority, a constitutional rule setting forth "the right to life and its inviolability from conception to death", thereby excluding any possibility for the practice of euthanasia.[49]

---

[38] Penal Code, Law 1,160, dated 1997, art. 106. Available at http://www.oas.org/juridico/ MLA/sp/pry/sp_pry-int-text-cp.pdf.

[39] Penal Code, Legislative Decree 635, dated 1991. Available at http://www.oas.org/ juridico/MLA/sp/per/sp_per-int-text-cp.pdf.

[40] Penal Code, art. 412. Available at http://www.ministeriopublico.gob.ve/web/guest/ codigo-penal1.

[41] Penal Code, Law 62, article 266. Available at http://www.gacetaoficial.cu/html/ codigo_penal.html.

[42] Penal Code, Decree 1,030, article 130. Available at http://www.csj.gob.sv/leyes.nsf/ ed400a03431a688906256a84005aec75/29961fcd8682863406256d02005a3cd4.

[43] Penal Code, article 128. Available at http://www.oas.org/juridico/mla/sp/gtm/ sp_gtm-int-text-cp.pdf.

[44] Penal Code, Decree 144-83, article 125. Available at http://www.oas.org/juridico/ MLA/sp/hnd/sp_hnd-int-text-cp.pdf.

[45] Penal Code, article 151. Available at http://www.oas.org/juridico/mla/sp/nic/ sp_nic-int-text-cp.html.

[46] Law 68, dated 20 November 2003, article 32. Available at http://docs.panama.justia .com/federales/leyes/68-de-2003-nov-25-2003.pdf.

[47] Penal Code, article 135. Available at http://www.oas.org/juridico/mla/sp/pan/ sp_pan-int-text-cp.pdf.

[48] Penal Code, articles 454, 456 and 457. Available at http://www.oas.org/juridico/mla/ sp/ecu/sp_ecu-int-text-cp.pdf.

[49] Constitution of the Dominican Republic, article 37. Available at http://www.suprema .gov.do/Normativas/constitucion.aspx.

Mexico displays a peculiar situation. Assistance to suicide is penalized,[50] and euthanasia bears no specific regulation in general. Active euthanasia can be considered as homicide, but passive euthanasia is allowed in Mexico City, in Aguascalientes, and in Michoacán. There are reports that approximately 45% of the terminal patients in intensive care services are submitted to passive euthanasia.[51]

In January 2008, the Federal District's Early Will Law[52] was promulgated, by means of which changes were made in the Penal Code and in the Health Law of the capital city of Mexico. The law established the standards, requirements and forms for the exercising of the will of the person who does not wish to submit himself or herself to means, treatments or medical procedures which unnecessarily prolong his or her life, when it is not any more possible to keep it in a natural manner. The early will document should be made by any patient in a terminal phase, duly diagnosed by physicians, or by his or her family members, when the person is unable to express his or her wish, or, still, by his or her parents or guardians in case of minors. The "early will" was regulated in Aguascalientes as from April 2009,[53] and in Michoacán in September 2009.[54]

In 2008, the Mexican Senate passed a bill changing the General Health Law as to palliative care, so as to assure terminal patients the right to voluntarily request suspension of treatment to uselessly prolong life, which characterizes therapeutic obstinacy, and opt only for procedures which mitigate pain and bring well-being to a patient, allowing for the disease to evolve naturally.[55]

Uruguay stands out in view of the other countries. Contrary to most of its Latin American counterparts, which criminalize euthanasia under the penal type of mercy homicide, or mercy killing, Uruguay deals with the issue as one of the causes of impunity, by setting forth that the judges are allowed to exonerate from punishment a subject with praiseworthy antecedents (*antecedentes honorables*), and who perpetrates homicide, performed by reason of mercy, on account of repeated pleas by the victim.[56]

[50] Federal Penal Code, revision of 19 August 2010, article 312. Available at http://www.diputados.gob.mx/LeyesBiblio/pdf/9.pdf.

[51] Available at http://www.cronica.com.mx/nota.php?id_nota=315674.

[52] Available at http://cgservicios.df.gob.mx/prontuario/vigente/1712.pdf.

[53] Available at http://www.aguascalientes.gob.mx/gobierno/leyes/leyes_PDF/23042009_115353.pdf.

[54] Available at http://leyes.michoacan.gob.mx/destino/O3153po.pdf.

[55] Available at http://www.senado.gob.mx/gace.php?sesion=2008/11/25/1&documento=67.

[56] Penal Code, Law 9,414, dated 29 June 1934, article 37. Available at http://www.parlamento.gub.uy/codigos/codigopenal/cod_pen.htm.

Uruguay was probably one of the first countries in the world to legislate on the possibility of performance of euthanasia. Its current Penal Code, which provides for the impunity of mercy homicide, or mercy killing, dates as far back as 1934. According to José Roberto Goldim, "the Uruguayan proposal, drafted in 1933, is quite similar to that used in The Netherlands, as from 1993".[57] As the author remarks, there is not, in either case, an authorization for the performing of euthanasia, but the possibility of not punishing the agent which causes death as long as pursuant to the conditions envisaged in the Law. This orientation was based on the doctrine of Spanish penal scholar Jiménez de Asúa.

This understanding does not apply to the case in which there is determination or help to suicide, a behavior characterizing a delict, with the prospect of sentence increase if perpetrated against someone under the age of eighteen, or a person whose intelligence has been reduced on account of disease, alcohol or drugs.[58] There is no prospect in the Law for legal pardon in this case.

III. Final Considerations

This quick overview of the legal treatment ascribed by Latin American countries to euthanasia affords a number of findings. Most countries do not bear specific regulation on the matter, but forbid euthanasia, in its various forms. There are, in certain cases, ethical rules addressed to doctors. As a consequence, the issue is restricted to a penal scope.

Nevertheless, Colombia is inclined toward non-penalizing voluntary passive euthanasia. While Brazil awaits a decision by the Supreme Federal Court on the possibility of the practice of orthothanasia, Mexico has already regulated this possibility in at least two States and in the Federal District. Uruguay is the only country, among those researched, which does not criminalize active euthanasia, as long as there is a plea by the victim and the other legal conditions are complied with.

---

[57] José Roberto Goldim, "Euthanasia – Uruguay", available at http://www.bioetica.ufrgs .br/eutanuru.htm.
[58] Penal Code, Law 9,414, dated 29 June 1934, article 315. Available at http://www .parlamento.gub.uy/codigos/codigopenal/cod_pen.htm.

LEGAL OVERSIGHT OF END-OF-LIFE TREATMENT DECISIONS IN UNITED STATES LAW

*Carl H. Coleman**

The law on end-of-life decision-making in the United States is determined primarily at the state level, within the broad contours identified as constitutionally permissible by the United States Supreme Court. In some areas—most notably, the termination of treatment for incapacitated patients without advanced directives, and the prescription of lethal medications for the purpose of hastening death—there is considerable variation among different states' legal regimes. This chapter will explore the major approaches states have taken with respect to end-of-life legal issues, as well as the relevant federal constitutional principles to which all states are required to conform. It will conclude by identifying a few similarities and differences between American approaches and the pending Italian legislation on end-of-life care.

I. Judicial Recognition of the Right to Refuse Treatment

The foundational principle of all American approaches to end-of-life decision-making is Judge Benjamin Cardozo's famous dictum, in the 1914 case of *Schloendorff v. Society of New York Hospital*,[1] that "every human being of adult years and sound mind has a right to determine what shall be done with his own body."[2] Based on this principle, Cardozo ruled, "a surgeon who performs an operation without his patient's consent" can be held liable for damages. The requirement of obtaining consent to medical treatment was grounded in the common-law doctrine of battery, under which any intentional and unauthorized "harmful or offensive touching" is considered a legally compensable wrong.[3] By the 1970s, American courts also began to recognize a cause of action in situations in which consent,

---

* J.D., Professor of Law, Seton Hall University School of Law, Newark, NJ, USA; email: carl.coleman@shu.edu.
[1] 211 N.Y. 125; 105 N.E. 92 (1914).
[2] 211 N.Y. at 129, 105 N.E. at 93.
[3] See, e.g., *Love v. Port Clinton*, 37 Ohio St. 3d 98 (1988).

S. Negri (ed.), *Self-Determination, Dignity and End-of-Life Care*
2011 Koninklijke Brill NV. Printed in The Netherlands. ISBN 978 90 04 22357 8. pp. 155–172

although formally obtained, was not preceded by an adequate disclosure of the risks, benefits, and alternatives to treatment.[4] These cases, which were based in negligence principles, established the modern legal doctrine of "informed consent."

Initially, informed consent cases were brought after treatment had already been provided, in order to obtain compensation for injuries resulting from the treatment. The theory of these cases was that, if adequate information about the risks, benefits, and alternatives of treatment had been disclosed, the patient would have refused to undergo the procedure and thereby avoided the harm.[5] Soon, however, courts were confronted with a different sort of informed consent scenario: patients, or their representatives, seeking to refuse or stop treatment prospectively, rather than seeking damages for treatment that had occurred in the past.

The most prominent of these cases was the 1976 case of *In re Karen Ann Quinlan*.[6] Quinlan was a 22-year-old woman who fell into a persistent vegetative state after an overdose of drugs and alcohol. Her father sough to be appointed her guardian and given permission to discontinue her respirator, without which doctors believed she would not be able to survive.[7]

Although *Quinlan* was a natural outgrowth of prior informed consent jurisprudence, it was different from previous informed consent cases in two important respects. First, because Quinlan was permanently unconscious, she was obviously not in a position to make her own medical decisions. Instead, the claim was brought by her father, acting as her next of kin. Second, unlike previous informed consent cases, the problem was not that there were unintended side effects or complications associated with the treatment. Rather, the objection was to the use of "extraordinary" medical technology to keep a permanently unconscious patient alive.

In a landmark opinion, the New Jersey Supreme Court held that Quinlan's father was entitled to act as her guardian and to insist on the removal of the respirator. The court found that, if the patient "were herself miraculously lucid for an interval (not altering the existing prognosis of

---

[4] *Canterbury v. Spence*, 464 F.2d 772 (1972), *Cobbs v. Grant*, 8 Cal.3d 229, 502 P.2d 1 (1972).

[5] See *Canterbury*, 464 F.2d at 790 (noting that "the very purpose of the disclosure rule is to protect the patient against consequences which, if known, he would have avoided by foregoing the treatment").

[6] 70 N.J. 10, 355 A.2d 647 (1976).

[7] In fact, after the court authorized the removal of the ventilator, Karen survived an additional nine years. See Annette E. Clark, "The Right to Die: The Broken Road from Quinlan to Schiavo," 37 *Loyola University of Chicago Law Journal* (2006), pp. 385–405, at 393.

the condition to which she would soon return)," she would be entitled to order the termination of her life-sustaining treatment based on her fundamental right to privacy.[8] It saw "no external compelling interest of the State that could compel Karen to endure the unendurable, only to vegetate a few measurable months with no realistic possibility of returning to any semblance of cognitive or sapient life."[9] Although it recognized that the State had a legitimate interest in "the preservation and sanctity of human life and defense of the right of the physician to administer medical treatment according to his best judgment," it concluded that "the State's interest ... weakens and the individual's right to privacy grows as the degree of bodily invasion increases and the prognosis dims."[10] The court also found that "the only practical way to prevent destruction of the right" to refuse treatment for incapacitated patients was to authorize the exercise of that right by the patient's next of kin.[11]

Courts in other states embraced the *Quinlan* opinion. For example, in *In re Fiori*,[12] the Supreme Court of Pennsylvania relied on *Quilan* in approving a mother's request to refuse life-sustaining treatment on behalf of her permanently unconscious adult son, commenting that "the right to self-determination does not cease on the incapacitation of the individual."[13] In *Superintendent of Belchertown State School v. Saikewicz*,[14] the Supreme Judicial Court of Massachusetts authorized the refusal of chemotherapy by the guardian of a profoundly mentally retarded patient with terminal cancer, affirming that the right recognized in *Quinlan* was not limited to patients who were permanently unconscious. According to the court, the critical question was determining what the patient would choose for himself if able to do so, taking into account all evidence relevant to a determination of the patient's "actual interests and preferences."[15]

Courts also cited *Quinlan* in affirming the decision-making rights of mentally competent patients, with some opinions implying that there were virtually no limits on a competent patient's right to refuse medical treatment. For example, in *Bartling v. Superior Court*,[16] the Court of

[8]   70 N.J. at 39, 355 A.2d at 663.
[9]   70 N.J. at 40, 355 A.2d at 663.
[10]   70 N.J. at 43, 355 A.2d at 664.
[11]   70 N.J. at 44, 355 A.2d at 664.
[12]   543 Pa. 592, 673 A.2d 905 (1996).
[13]   543 Pa. at 601, 673 A.2d at 910.
[14]   373 Mass. 728, 370 N.E.2d 417 (1977).
[15]   373 Mass. at 755, 370 N.E.2d at 432.
[16]   163 Cal. App.3d 186; 209 Cal. Rptr. 220 (1984).

Appeal of California held that a mentally competent patient whose lung had collapsed should have been granted the right to insist on the removal of his ventilator, finding that the trial court "was incorrect when it held that the right to have life-support equipment disconnected was limited to comatose, terminally ill patients, or representatives acting on their behalf."[17] In *Fosmire v. Nicoleau*,[18] the New York Court of Appeals upheld the right of a "young, otherwise healthy" pregnant woman to refuse blood transfusions that doctors thought necessary to preserve the woman's life. The court found that no state interest existed that could outweigh a competent adult's "right to make her own medical choices," even when those choices would likely be fatal.[19]

II. Judicial Retrenchment and the "Clear and Convincing Evidence" Rule

While no state supreme court disputed the right of a competent adult to refuse life-sustaining medical treatment, a few states adopted more restrictive approaches in cases involving the withholding or withdrawal of life-sustaining treatment for patients without decision-making capacity. The New York Court of Appeals' decisions in the 1981 cases of *In re Eichner* and *In re Storar*[20] exemplified this approach. *Eichner* involved an 83-year-old member of the Society of Mary, who, like Karen Ann Quinlan, was being maintained on a respirator in a persistent vegetative state. *Storar*, similar to the *Saikewicz* case in Massachusetts, concerned a profoundly mentally retarded 52-year-old man with terminal cancer of the bladder, whose mother had refused to authorize blood transfusions.

Ruling on both cases together, the New York Court of Appeals approved the removal of the respirator in *Eichner*, but not the withholding of the blood transfusions in *Storar*. The determinative fact in *Eichner* was that the patient, prior to losing capacity, had expressly indicated that he would not want to be kept on a respirator in a state of permanent unconsciousness. Evidence of the patient's prior decision included statements he made in response to news reports about the Karen Ann Quinlan case, in which he said "that he would not want any of this 'extraordinary business'

---

[17] 163 Cal. App.3d at 193, 209 Cal. Rptr. at 220.
[18] 75 N.Y.2d 218, 551 N.E.2d 77 (1990).
[19] 75 N.Y.2d at 231 n.3, 551 N.E.2d at 84 n.3.
[20] 52 N.Y.2d 363, 420 N.E.2d 64 (1981).

done for him under those circumstances."[21] In *Storar*, by contrast, it was impossible to know what the patient would have decided, because he had always lacked the mental capacity to make medical decisions.[22] Implicitly rejecting the approach adopted in *Quinlan*, the court held that the right to refuse life-sustaining treatment is a personal right that cannot be exercised by a relative on a behalf of a loved one. Before withholding or withdrawing life-sustaining treatment from a patient without capacity, the court concluded, there must be "clear and convincing evidence" of the patient's prior competent choice.[23]

In a subsequent case, *In re Westchester County Medical Center (O'Connor)*,[24] the New York Court of Appeals underscored the strictness of the "clear and convincing evidence" standard. That case involved an elderly nursing home resident whose daughters had refused the insertion of a nasogastric feeding tube on the grounds that doing so would be incompatible with their mother's statements that she "would never want any sort of ... life support systems to maintain or prolong her life."[25] The court held that the statements, although repeated frequently over a number of years, did not establish sufficient proof "that the patient held a firm and settled commitment to the termination of life supports under the circumstances like those presented."[26] The court emphasized that the patient's statements were "generally prompted by her experience with persons suffering terminal illness," and that they therefore did not apply to her present situation, in which she was "aged and infirm" but not imminently dying.[27] The court expressed concern that, if general statements about avoiding "life-sustaining machinery" and retaining one's dignity "were routinely held to be clear and convincing proof of a general intent to decline all medical treatment once incompetency sets in, few nursing home patients would ever receive life-sustaining medical treatment in the future."[28]

New York was not the only state to adopt a restrictive approach to the refusal of life-sustaining treatment for incapacitated patients. In the case of *Cruzan v. Harmon*,[29] the Missouri Supreme Court relied on a similar

---

[21] 52 N.Y.2d at 372, 420 N.E.2d at 68.
[22] 52 N.Y.2d at 380, 420 N.E.2d at 72.
[23] 52 N.Y.2d at 378–79, 420 N.E.2d at 72.
[24] 72 N.Y.2d 517, 531 N.E.2d 607 (1988).
[25] 72 N.Y.2d at 527, 531 N.E.2d at 611.
[26] 72 N.Y.2d at 531, 531 N.E.2d at 613.
[27] 72 N.Y.2d at 533, 531 N.E.2d at 615.
[28] 72 N.Y.2d at 531, 531 N.E.2d at 613.
[29] 760 S.W.2d 408 (Mo. 1988).

analysis to reject a family's request to terminate artificial nutrition and hydration for a young woman who had entered into a persistent vegetative state following a car accident. *Cruzan* was ultimately appealed to the United States Supreme Court, which was asked to decide whether requiring clear and convincing evidence of the patient's prior decision to refuse life-sustaining treatment was permissible under the United States Constitution. In a 5-4 opinion, the Supreme Court ruled that it was.[30]

The majority opinion for the Supreme Court, written by Chief Justice William J. Rehnquist, started by "assuming" that the Constitution would protect a competent adult's "right to refuse lifesaving hydration and nutrition."[31] It found, however, that it did not make sense to speak of a right to refuse treatment for an incapacitated patient, as such individuals are "not able to make an informed and voluntary choice to exercise a hypothetical right to refuse treatment or any other right."[32] Noting that states have a legitimate interest in protecting and preserving human life, the court found no constitutional impediment to Missouri's requirement of clear and convincing evidence of an incapacitated patient's prior choice to refuse life-sustaining treatment. The court suggested that such a requirement respected the "personal element" of the decision to refuse life-sustaining treatment, while also guarding against "potential abuses" by family members.[33] The court recognized that Missouri's standard might result in the provision of life-sustaining treatment to someone who did not want it, but it found that the risk of this error was less serious than the risk of stopping treatment prematurely, as "an erroneous decision to withdraw life-sustaining treatment ... is not susceptible of correction."[34]

The dissenting justices in *Cruzan* took a very different view of the constitutional issues. Unlike the majority, which held that states can legitimately assert an "unqualified interest in the preservation of human life,"[35] the dissent found that states have "no legitimate general interest in someone's life, completely abstracted from the interest of the person living that life."[36] Thus, for the dissent, the only valid justification for regulating decisions about life-sustaining treatment for incapacitated patients

---

[30]   *Cruzan v. Director, Missouri Dept. of Health*, 497 U.S. 261, 110 S. Ct. 2841 (1990).
[31]   497 U.S. at 279, 110 S. Ct. at 2852.
[32]   497 U.S. at 280, 110 S. Ct. at 2852.
[33]   497 U.S. at 281, 110 S. Ct. at 2853.
[34]   497 U.S. at 283, 110 S. Ct. at 2854.
[35]   497 U.S. at 282, 110 S. Ct. at 2853.
[36]   497 U.S. at 313, 110 S. Ct. at 2870 (Brennan, J., dissenting).

was to ensure "as accurate as possible a determination" of how the patient would have decided if able to do so.[37] Yet, instead of facilitating an accurate determination of what the patient would have decided, the clear and convincing evidence created a "markedly asymmetrical evidentiary burden,"[38] as it required "specific statements of treatment choice" only for individuals who wanted to limit the use of life-sustaining treatment, while authorizing the unlimited provision of treatment without any evidence whatsoever of what the patient would want.

Importantly, the Supreme Court's decision in *Cruzan* did not *require* states to condition the withholding or withdrawal of life-sustaining treatment for incapacitated patients on clear and convincing evidence of the patient's prior competent decision. Rather, *Cruzan* said only that states *may* impose such limits without running afoul of the United States Constitution. In fact, most states, perhaps persuaded by the dissent's arguments in *Cruzan*, have rejected the stringent clear and convincing evidence rule in favor of approaches more similar to the decision in *Quinlan*. In some states, including Maryland[39] and New York,[40] court decisions adopting the clear and convincing evidence standard were subsequently overruled by the adoption of "family consent" statutes, as discussed further below.

III. THE CURRENT STATE OF THE LAW: ADVANCE DIRECTIVES, FAMILY
CONSENT STATUTES, AND JUDICIALLY-CREATED STANDARDS

Court decisions involving disputes about life-sustaining treatment for incapacitated patients led to greater recognition of the value of planning for medical care before losing decision-making capacity. Today, all states recognize two ways in which competent adults can control their future medical treatment: the "living will," which provides substantive instructions about future medical treatment, and the "health care proxy" (also sometimes called the "durable power of attorney for health care"), in which individuals appoint another person to make treatment decisions if they can no longer make decisions for themselves. This section examines

---

[37] 497 U.S. at 315, 110 S. Ct. at 2871 (Brennan, J., dissenting).

[38] 497 U.S. at 316, 110 S. Ct. at 2871 (Brennan, J., dissenting).

[39] Md. HEALTH-GENERAL Code Ann. § 5–601 (2010) (replacing approach adopted by the Maryland Supreme Court in Mack v. Mack, 329 Md. 188, 618 A.2d 744 (1993).

[40] N.Y. Pub. Health Law Article 29-CC (2010) (replacing approach adopted by the New York Court of Appeals in the *Storar* and *O'Connor* cases, discussed above).

the current state of the law with respect to living wills and health care proxies, both of which are considered types of "advance directives." It also explores the more challenging question of how decisions are made for incapacitated patients for whom no advance directive exists.

A. *Living Wills*

In a living will, competent individuals can describe the kind of treatment they do or do not want to receive in the event of a future loss of decision-making capacity. There are two essential elements to a valid living will: a description of the circumstances under which the instructions in the document are to become effective, and a specific statement of the treatments the patient does or does want to receive under those circumstances. For example, a living will might state, "If I am in a persistent vegetative state, I do not want to be put on a respirator or receive artificial nutrition and hydration." The New York Court of Appeals has described living wills as the "ideal" way to establish evidence of a patient's wishes about medical treatment. The existence of a written document, the court observed, "suggests the author's seriousness of purpose" and prevents the need for attempting to divine a person's intentions based on "casual remarks."[41]

Many states have statutes that specify the format of living wills and the circumstances under which they are intended to apply.[42] For example, New Jersey's living will statute authorizes individuals to direct the withholding or withdrawal of life-sustaining treatment under the following circumstances:

1. When the life-sustaining treatment is experimental and not a proven therapy, or is likely to be ineffective or futile in prolonging life, or is likely to merely prolong an imminent dying process;
2. When the patient is permanently unconscious, as determined by the attending physician and confirmed by a second qualified physician;
3. When the patient is in a terminal condition, as determined by the attending physician and confirmed by a second physician; or
4. In the event none of the above circumstances applies, when the patient has a serious irreversible illness or condition, and the likely risks and burdens associated with the medical intervention to be

---

[41] 72 N.Y.2d at 531, 531 N.E.2d at 613.

[42] For a frequently-updated summary of state advance directive legislation, see the chart produced by the American Bar Association Commission on Law and Aging, *available at* http://new.abanet.org/aging/PublicDocuments/HCPA-CHT%2009%20corrrected.pdf.

withheld or withdrawn may reasonably be judged to outweigh the likely benefits to the patient from such intervention, or the imposition of the medical intervention on an unwilling patient would be inhumane.[43]

New Jersey requires living wills to be signed and dated in the presence of two adult witnesses, who must attest that the individual creating the living will is "of sound mind and free of duress and undue influence."[44]

Some states' living will statutes contain significant restrictions. For example, some statutes specify that a living will is not effective if the patient is pregnant.[45] Others appear to limit the patient's right to refuse life-sustaining treatment to specific medical situations, such as terminal illness.[46]

The legal significance of limitations in living will statutes remains an unresolved question. On the one hand, a living will that complies with statutory requirements will be presumed to be valid, and health care providers who rely on it in good faith will be protected from liability. On the other hand, a living will that is created in a state without a living will statute, or that is not written in conformity with statutory requirements—for example, a living will that expresses a desire to refuse life-sustaining treatment in broader circumstances than the living will statute specifically authorizes—would still demonstrate the patient's wishes about medical treatment. As long as the living will is sufficiently specific, it is difficult to see how a state could constitutionally refuse to enforce it. While the United States Supreme Court has never directly addressed this question, its decision in *Cruzan* strongly suggests that an individual who has left clear and convincing evidence of a decision to refuse treatment has a constitutional right to have that decision respected, regardless of the format in which that evidence is documented.[47] Thus, as long as the living will constitutes clear and convincing evidence of the patient's prior

---

[43] N.J. Stat. § 26:2H-67 (2010).

[44] N.J. Stat. § 26:2H-56 (2010).

[45] See, e.g., the Georgia living will law, O.C.G.A. § 31-32-9 (2010).

[46] See, e.g., the Montana statute, Mont. Code Anno., § 50-9-105 (2010).

[47] *Cruzan* itself addressed the opposite situation: whether states may *refuse* to allow the withholding or withdrawal of life-sustaining treatment from incapacitated patients who have *not* left clear and convincing evidence of their wishes. In answering this question in the affirmative, the Court strongly implied that if clear and convincing evidence of the patient's decision were present, a state could not constitutionally interfere with implementation of the patient's prior competent choice.

competent decision, it may well be enforceable even without any statutory authorization.[48]

The problem with living wills has less to do with their legal status than
with practical considerations. As many commentators have observed, it is
difficult to predict the kind of medical circumstances that one might face
years in the future, let alone how one might feel about the kind of treatment decisions that might eventually arise.[49] Moreover, individuals' opinions about the kind of circumstances under which they are willing to live,
and the kind of medical interventions they are willing to endure, often
change over time. What once seemed unthinkable from the perspective of
youth and good health may become acceptable later in life, particularly
after the experience of living with a chronic or terminal disease. Moreover,
even when living wills accurately reflect what the patient would have
decided if able to do so, they are ultimately just pieces of paper that are
not self enforcing. Unless the patient has family or friends who are willing
to insist that the instructions in the living will are respected, a living will
can all too easily be ignored.[50]

B. *Health Care Proxies*

Health care proxies, unlike living wills, are primarily procedural documents. Rather than attempting to specify all possible treatment scenarios
that might arise in the future, a health care proxy designates a trusted
individual (known as the "health care agent") to make decisions for the
patient as they arise in real time. Unless the health care proxy contains
express limitations, health care agents generally have the right to make
any and all health care decisions for an incapacitated patient that the
patient could have made directly if capable of doing so—regardless of the
patient's medical condition, and regardless of the type of treatment at
stake. Agents must make decisions based on the patient's wishes, if known,
or if the patient's wishes are not known, based on a good-faith assessment
of the patient's best interests.[51] If health care providers or others close to

---

[48] For further analysis of this question, see Emma Murphy Sisti, "Die Free or Live: The
Constitutionality of New Hampshire's Living Will Pregnancy Exception", 30 *Vermont Law
Review* (2005), pp. 143–177.

[49] Angela Fagerlin and Carl E. Schneider, "Enough: The Failure of the Living Will," 34
Hastings Center Report (2004), n. 2, pp. 30–42.

[50] See id. at 35 (noting that "the living will may be signed years before it is used, and its
existence and location may vanish in the mists of time").

[51] See, e.g., Md. Health-General Code Ann. § 5–605 (c)(1).

the patient believe that the agent has improperly assessed the patient's wishes or best interests, they have the burden of going to court to challenge the agent's decision.[52]

It is possible to have just a living will, just a health care proxy, or both documents together. If a patient has both a living will and a health care proxy, the health care agent will generally be required to adhere to the instructions in the living will, unless it can be shown that the patient changed his or her mind after the living will was created. However, when the living will is ambiguous, or when it does not apply to a particular situation, decisions would be made by the health care agent based on the wishes/best interests standard, just as they would if the living will did not exist.

C. Decisions for Patients without Advance Directives

Despite decades of efforts to encourage individuals to create advance directives—including enactment of the federal Patient Self-Determination Act, which requires hospitals and other health care facilities to inform patients upon admission of their right to create advance directives[53]— most Americans have not created either a living will or a health care proxy.[54] As a result, most decisions about withholding or withdrawing life-sustaining treatment for incapacitated patients must be made without the benefit of prior written instructions. States vary in their approaches to how these decisions must be made.

1. Family Consent Statutes

In response to highly-publicized court decisions like *Quinlan* and *Cruzan*, most states have enacted legislation governing decisions about the withholding or withdrawal of life-sustaining treatment from incapacitated patients without advance directives. These laws designate surrogate decision-makers to make treatment decisions on the patient's behalf, based on an assessment of the patients' wishes or, if the patient's wishes cannot be determined, the patient's best interests. Most states with family

---

[52] See, e.g., NY Pub. Health L. § 2992 (2010) (authorizing special proceeding to override an agent's decision on the grounds that it was made in bad faith or in violation of the wishes/best interests standard).

[53] 42 U.S.C. § 1395cc(f) (2010).

[54] See Nina A. Kohn and Jeremy A. Blumenthal, "Designating Healthcare Decisionmakers for Patients without Advance Directives: A Psychological Critique," 42 *Georgia Law Review* (2008), pp. 979–1018, at 980.

consent laws establish a hierarchy of surrogate decision-makers, typically beginning with the spouse (and, in some states, non-marital "domestic partners"), and then going through a list that includes siblings, adult children, and sometimes close friends.[55] A few states use other approaches, such as requiring the patient's family and close friends to agree on a surrogate decision-maker.[56]

Although a surrogate's role is similar to that of a health care agent appointed via a health care proxy, it is not identical. Unlike health care proxy laws, which give agents the authority to make any and all health care decisions the patient could have made if competent to do so, family consent statutes generally limit the surrogate's authority to refuse life-sustaining treatment to particular medical circumstances—typically, terminal illness, permanent unconsciousness, and in some states, a more open-ended category such as "incurable and irreversible illness."[57] Moreover, some family consent statutes require external approval of the surrogate's decision in certain situations. For example, under New York's recently-enacted Family Health Care Decisions Act, a surrogate's decision to withhold or withdraw artificial nutrition or hydration from an incapacitated hospital patient who is neither terminally ill nor permanently unconscious must be approved by the hospital's ethics committee.[58]

2. *Judicially-Created Balancing Tests*

Some states that do not have family consent statutes have court decisions that authorize family members to refuse life-sustaining treatment from incapacitated patients under particular circumstances. An important example of this approach is the New Jersey Supreme Court's decision in *In re: Conroy*.[59] The facts of that case were similar to those of the *O'Connor*

---

[55] See, e.g., N.Y. Public Health Law § 2994-d(1) (2010).

[56] See, e.g., Colorado's statute, C.R.S. 15-18.5-103(4)(a) (2010) (requiring "interested persons ... to make reasonable efforts to reach a consensus as to whom among them shall make medical treatment decisions on behalf of the patient").

[57] See, e.g., the Illinois statute, which specifies that a "qualified condition" includes terminal condition, permanent unconsciousness, or "incurable or irreversible illness," defined as "an illness or injury (i) for which there is no reasonable prospect of cure or recovery, (ii) that ultimately will cause the patient's death even if life-sustaining treatment is initiated or continued, (iii) that imposes severe pain or otherwise imposes an inhumane burden on the patient, and (iv) for which initiating or continuing life-sustaining treatment, in light of the patient's medical condition, provides only minimal medical benefit." 755 ILCS 40/10 (2010).

[58] N.Y. Pub. Health Law § 2994-d(5)(c).

[59] 98 N.J. 321, 486 A.2d 1209 (1985).

case in New York: an elderly nursing home resident who was conscious and not suffering from a terminal illness, but who was severely debilitated and unable to make her own medical decisions. As in *O'Connor*, the patient's daughter in *Conroy* sought to refuse the provision of artificial nutrition and hydration on the patient's behalf.

In the absence of a statute governing life-sustaining treatment decisions for incapacitated patients without advance directives, the New Jersey Supreme Court recognized three circumstances under which life-sustaining treatment could be withheld or withdrawn. First, under the "subjective" test, it found that life-sustaining treatment can be withheld or withdrawn from an incapacitated patient "when it is clear that the particular patient would have refused the treatment under the circumstances involved."[60] This test, similar to the clear and convincing evidence standard used by the Missouri Supreme Court in *Cruzan*, requires specific written or oral evidence of a "carefully considered" decision made by the patient before losing capacity. Second, under the "limited objective test," a family member can refuse life-sustaining treatment for an incapacitated patient "when there is some trustworthy evidence that the patient would have refused the treatment, and the decision-maker is satisfied that it is clear that the burdens of the patient's continued life with the treatment outweigh the benefits of that life for him."[61] This test permits the refusal of life-sustaining treatment even when the patient "had not unequivocally expressed his desires before becoming incompetent," but only "when it is clear and that treatment in question would merely prolong the patient's suffering."[62] Finally, the court held that, even in the absence of any evidence of the patient's wishes, life-sustaining treatment could be withheld from an incapacitated patient based on a "pure objective" standard if, in light of "the recurring, unavoidable and severe pain of the patient's life with the treatment" the continuation of treatment "would be inhumane."[63]

The *Conroy* court emphasized that, in the absence of specific evidence of the patient's prior competent decision, the focus must be on the "pain, suffering, and possible enjoyment" the patient is experiencing, not on the patient's "personal worth or social utility."[64] It cautioned decision-makers

---

[60] 98 N.J. at 360, 486 A.2d at 1229.
[61] 98 N.J. at 365, 486 A.2d at 1232.
[62] Id.
[63] 98 N.J. at 366, 486 A.2d at 1232.
[64] 98 N.J. at 367, 486 A.2d at 1232–1233.

to "exercise extreme caution in determining the patient's intent and in evaluating medical evidence of the patient's pain and possible enjoyment."[65] Observing that nursing home residents are a particularly vulnerable population, the court required the state office of the ombudsman to be notified of all decisions to withholding or withdraw life-sustaining treatment from an institutionalized elderly patient.[66] In addition, two physicians unaffiliated with the facility must confirm the patient's medical condition and prognosis.[67] The court further required that, if either of the two "objective" tests is used, all of the patient's close relatives—"that is, the patient's spouse, parents, and children, or, in their absence, the patient's next of kin, if any"—must concur in the decision.[68]

3. *Minority Approaches*

A few states continue to condition the withholding or withdrawal of life-sustaining treatment for incapacitated patients without advance directives on clear and convincing evidence of the patient's prior competent decision. For example, in Missouri, the decision in *Cruzan* has never been overruled, although one lower court has concluded that the decision should be limited to the refusal of artificial nutrition and hydration.[69] In Michigan and California, courts have required clear and convincing evidence of the patient's prior decision when the patient is incapacitated, lacks an advance directive, and is not terminally ill or permanently unconscious.[70]

IV. USE OF LETHAL MEDICATIONS

As discussed above, all states recognize that competent adults have the right to refuse life-sustaining medical treatment and to create advance directives. In addition, all states permit life-sustaining treatment to be withheld or withdrawn from incapacitated patients without advance directives in at least some circumstances. However, the law draws a sharp

---

[65] 98 N.J. at 368, 486 A.2d at 1233.
[66] 98 N.J. at 383, 486 A.2d at 1241.
[67] 98 N.J. at 384, 486 A.2d at 1242.
[68] 98 N.J. at 384–385, 486 A.2d at 1242.
[69] *In re Warren*, 858 S.W.2d 263 (Mo. Ct. App. 1993).
[70] *In re Martin*, 450 Mich. 204, 538 N.W.2d 399 (1995), *Conservatorship of Wendland*, 26 Cal. 4th 519, 28 P.3d 151 (2001).

distinction between the refusal of life-sustaining treatment and the use of lethal medications intended to bring about the patient's death.

Only two states, Oregon and Washington, permit physicians to prescribe lethal medications for the purpose of hastening death. In both these states, the laws are limited to mentally competent patients who are terminally ill. The physician's authority is limited to prescribing the medications, which the patient must self-administer.[71]

In the 1990s, a group of terminally ill patients and their providers challenged the constitutionality of state prohibitions of assisted suicide as applied to mentally competent terminally ill patients who sought to obtain lethal medications.[72] The plaintiffs argued that the laws interfered with the liberty of mentally competent, terminally ill patients to determine the manner and timing of their death. They also argued that, under the Equal Protection Clause, because terminally ill patients on life-sustaining treatment were permitted to "hasten their death" by directing the removal of their treatment, states could not constitutionally deny a comparable right to terminally ill patients who wanted to die but had no life-sustaining treatment to remove.

The Supreme Court rejected both of these arguments. First, it concluded that the Constitution did not protect a "fundamental right" to determine the timing and manner of death, observing that even though "many of the rights and liberties protected by the Due Process Clause sound in personal autonomy," that does not mean that "any and all important, intimate, and personal decisions are so protected."[73] It also found that laws prohibiting assistance in suicide served legitimate state interests, including preserving human life, protecting the integrity of the medical profession, protecting the vulnerable, and resisting "the path to voluntary and perhaps even involuntary euthanasia."[74] As to the plaintiffs' Equal Protection argument, the Court concluded that "the distinction between assisting suicide and withdrawing life-sustaining treatment, a distinction widely recognized and endorsed in the medical profession and in our legal traditions, is both important and logical; it is certainly rational."[75]

---

[71] Oregon Death with Dignity Act, ORS 127.800 to 127.897 (2010); Washington Death with Dignity Act, RCW 70.245 (2010).

[72] *Washington v. Glucksberg*, 521 U.S. 702, 117 S. Ct. 2258 (1997); *Vacco v. Quill*, 521 U.S. 793, 117 S. Ct. 2293 (1997).

[73] *Glucksberg*, 521 U.S. at 727, 117 S. Ct. at 2271.

[74] *Glucksberg*, 521 U.S. at 728–733, 117 S. Ct. at 2272–2274.

[75] *Vacco*, 521 U.S. at 800–801, 117 S. Ct. at 2298.

Although the Supreme Court did not recognize a constitutional right to physician-assisted suicide, a majority of the Justices suggested that terminally ill patients may have a constitutional right to obtain medications necessary for palliative care. For example, in her concurring opinion in the physician-assisted suicide cases, Justice Sandra Day O'Connor emphasized that the state laws being challenged did not prevent physicians from providing medications to alleviate a terminally ill patient's pain, "even to the point of causing unconsciousness and hastening death."[76] Some commentators have interpreted this statement as implying that laws prohibiting the use of medications for legitimate pain management would be constitutionally problematic, even if those medications create a foreseeable risk of death.[77] Thus, while the administration of lethal medications *for the purpose of* causing death is currently permissible only in two United States jurisdictions, it appears that, in all states, physicians cannot be prevented from prescribing medications that create a *risk* of death, provided that doing so is medically necessary to relieve the patient's pain.

V. CONCLUDING OBSERVATIONS ON THE PENDING ITALIAN LEGISLATION

The pending Italian legislation on end-of-life medical treatment is similar to American approaches in several important respects, including its emphasis on the importance of informed consent to medical treatment, its distinction between the refusal of treatment and "euthanasia or assistance to suicide," and its recognition of the patient's right to receive palliative care. In addition, like American laws, the Italian legislation also affirms that patients' right to appropriate medical treatment does not end with a loss of decision-making capacity. It therefore recognizes the possibility of advance directives and surrogate decision-making on behalf of patients unable to decide for themselves.

The chief difference between the Italian legislation and laws on end-of-life care in American jurisdictions is that, under the Italian approach, advance directives appear to be the primary—perhaps even the exclusive—basis for decisions to withhold or withdraw life-sustaining medical treatment. For example, the draft bill states that treatment instructions that do not adhere to the statute's "forms and modalities" cannot be considered as evidence of an incapacitated patient's prior competent decision (Article 4, para. 2). This implies that, even if a patient

---

[76] *Vacco, Glucksberg*, 521 U.S. at 809, 117 S. Ct. at 2303 (O'Connor, J., concurring).
[77] Robert A. Burt, "The Supreme Court Speaks—Not Assisted Suicide but a Constitutional Right to Palliative Care", 337 *New England Journal of Medicine* (1997), pp. 1234–1236.

has made clear and repeated statements about his preferences about treatment, those statements can be disregarded if they do not comply with the statutorily-recognized format. The draft legislation also provides that, if no advance directive exists, health care providers have "a duty to act with the sole aim of safeguarding the patient's health" (Article 2, para. 8), a standard that could be interpreted to preclude the withholding or withdrawal of life-sustaining treatment from incapacitated patients without advance directives under any circumstances at all.

The Italian legislation also differs from American approaches in its standard for decisions about artificial nutrition and hydration. Specifically, Article 3 of the draft bill states that "artificial nutrition and hydration, in the various forms that science and technology can provide, must be maintained until the end of life, except in cases where they are no longer efficacious in providing the patient with the nutritional elements necessary for the essential physiological functions of the body. They shall not be the object of an advance treatment directive" (Article 3, para. 4). This approach would appear to preclude the withholding or withdrawal of artificial nutrition and hydration from permanently unconscious patients, except in the relatively rare circumstances where the food and fluids cannot be assimilated. Although the bill suggests that this approach is required by the United Nations Convention on the Rights of Persons with Disabilities, the Convention says nothing about the use of medically-administered nutrition and hydration. Rather, it prohibits only the "discriminatory denial of health care or health services or food and fluids,"[78] a standard that seems inapplicable to situations in which artificial nutrition and hydration is refused based on an individualized assessment of the patient's condition and prognosis. This is particularly true when an advance directive expressing the patient's desire to refuse artificial nutrition and hydration exists.

Overall, adoption of the pending Italian legislation would shift Italy in the direction of the American legal framework governing end-of-life decision-making. However, as is perhaps appropriate given the country's differing legal and cultural traditions, Italy and the United States would continue to have very different approaches to decisions about the refusal of life-sustaining treatment for incapacitated patients, particularly for those who have not created advance directives (which, if American experience is any guide, is likely to be the majority of the population). The extent of these differences would depend in part on how Italian physicians, lawyers, and judges interpret the legislation after it takes effect.

---

[78] United Nations Convention on the Rights of Persons with Disabilities, Article 25(f).

A COMPARATIVE PERSPECTIVE ON AUSTRALIAN END-OF-LIFE LAW

Thomas A. Faunce* and Ruth Townsend**

I. INTRODUCTION

The Italian *Eluana Englaro Case*[1] and the related Italian Bill "Dispositions in matter of therapeutic alliance, informed consent and advance directives" ("the Bill")[2] highlight a number of significant points of divergence with regulation of end-of-life decision-making and advance directives under Australian state and federal law. This chapter aims to provide a comparative overview of Australian case law and statutory provisions in this area. It discusses these differences in the context of a view that regardless of the deontological importance of respecting individual patient rights in end-of-life decision-making, the financial constraints upon governments to care for an ageing population will increasingly provide consequentialist interest not only in facilitating advance directives that allow technically 'futile' treatment to be withdrawn or withheld from incompetent patients, but in permitting physician-assisted suicide when requested by competent, non-depressed patients with a terminal illness who have already received reasonable palliative care.

A. *Initial Comparisons of the* Eluana Englaro *Case and Australian Law*

The *Eluana Englaro Case* concerned an application to the Supreme Court of Italy (after an earlier decision by the Appeal Court of Milan) of a guardian (the father) to obtain an authorization to cease the artificial nutrition of Eluana who had been in vegetative state since 1992 following to a car accident. The application was opposed by the Public Prosecutor of Milan

* Associate Professor College of Law and Medical School (joint appointment), Australian National University; Australian Research Council Future Fellow; email: fauncet@law.anu.edu.au.

** Lecturer College of Law and Medical School (joint appointment), Australian National University; email: townsendr@law.anu.edu.au.

[1] Italian Supreme Court of Cassation, United Civil Sections, Judgment 11–13 November 2008, no. 27145.

[2] "Dispositions in matter of therapeutic alliance, informed consent and advance directives" Bill approved by the Senate of the Italian Republic on 26 March 2009 and discussed by the Chamber of Deputies as Bill No. 2350.

S. Negri (ed.), *Self-Determination, Dignity and End-of-Life Care*
2011 Koninklijke Brill NV. Printed in The Netherlands. ISBN 978 90 04 22357 8. pp. 173–194

who sought to impugn the Milan Court of Appeal's finding (on expert testimony) that the patient was in a persistent vegetative state. The patient had made no advance directive.

As will be shown, this type of case is uncommon in Australia where intensive care physicians are normally able to make decisions to withdraw treatment from patients when treatment is technically futile ("no reasonable prospect of returning to a meaningful quality of life") without having to apply to either a hospital clinical ethics committee or a court. Applications to such a committee or court tend to be reserved for those situations where the treating physicians and the patient's family have become involved in a protracted dispute over whether treatment should be withdrawn or withheld.

Where a patient requiring an end-of-life decision is incompetent in Australia legislation in different states generally requires that doctors approach a hierarchy of next of kin to act as a surrogate decision-maker. The situation is also covered by case law permitting the treating doctors to make a decision in the best interests of the patient, usually in close association with the patient's family.

Australian cases similar to Eluana Englaro's are not common but do exist. In 2004, for example, in the *Messiha Case*[3] a 75 year old man with a history of cardiac surgery and cardiac arrest was admitted to an intensive care unit after an out of hospital heart attack with 25 mins cerebral hypoxia. The treating doctors soon formed the view that there was no reasonable prospect of the patient returning to a meaningful quality of life (treatment was technically 'futile'). This conclusion was opposed by the family despite consultation and the matter was taken before a judge who confirmed the capacity of the doctors to withdraw treatment.[4]

In 2009 the Supreme Court of Western Australia heard the case of *Brightwater v Rossiter*. Mr Rossiter was a mentally competent quadriplegic who required 24 hour care at Brightwater nursing home. He was fed via a percutaneous endoscopic gastrostomy (PEG) tube surgically inserted into his stomach and communicated through a trachostomy. On multiple occasions Mr Rossiter requested that the staff of Brightwater nursing home cease his nutrition and hydration such that he might starve to death as he had no other means by which to commit suicide. The nursing home

---

[3] *Messiha v South East Health* [2004] NSWSC 1061.
[4] Thomas A. Faunce and Cameron Stewart "The *Messiha* and *Schiavo* cases: Third-party Ethical and Legal Interventions in Futile Care Disputes", 183(5) *Medical Journal of Australia* (2005), pp. 261–263.

brought the case to the Supreme Court in order to seek declaratory relief as to whether they were legally obliged to obey Mr Rossiter's request and effectively cause his death or whether as a medical service provider their duty of care refrains them from doing so. In addition to this they sought declaratory relief from criminal prosecution if they were to prescribe analgesics to Mr Rossiter if his starvation were to eventuate. Chief Justice (CJ) Martin ruled that Brightwater had the duty to provide the necessities of life through medical treatment. Mr Rossiter, however, also being of full age and mental capacity was capable of legally refusing medical treatment provided that his refusal was an informed decision and that he could revoke his refusal at a later stage if he so wished. On the second issue the court permitted only the provision of medication such that it would neither cause nor hasten the death of Mr Rossiter.[5]

The cases of *Messiah* and *Brightwater v Rossiter* highlight public debate in Australia over the rights of patients, their family and doctors to make decisions ending the lives of patients whose treatment is deemed 'futile' either on objective clinical criteria determined by doctors (for an incompetent patient) or by a competent but terminally ill patient according to more subjective criteria (a situation more likely to be referred to as euthanasia).

II. EUTHANASIA DEBATE IN AUSTRALIA

Each year in Australia there are 77,000 deaths from chronic terminal disease.[6] Unsurprisingly many of these deaths are brought on prematurely as patients seek to alleviate their pain and suffering through euthanasia, despite having access to excellent palliative care. It is anticipated that the problem of the legality of euthanasia will be given increased attention as the population ages, chronic disease becomes more prolific and the consequent public and private costs increase.

Currently Australian law distinguishes between the following different forms of euthanasia (although some of these categories are not referred to as 'euthanasia' by the medical or legal systems because of the negative connotations of that word):

---

[5] *Brightwater Care Group (Inc) v Rossiter* [2009] WASC 229.
[6] National Health and Medical Research Council (NHMRC) 'New guidelines for communicating end-of-life-issues'. Viewed October 2010 http://www.nhmrc.gov.au/media/media/rel07/180607.htm.

1. Voluntary active euthanasia:
   a. where a person's life is ended through some form of medical intervention at their request;
2. Involuntary active euthanasia:
   a. where a decision to terminate life by medical intervention is made by another because the person concerned lacks the necessary capacity to consent to such termination, OR
   b. where the person concerned may possess the capacity to consent but their life is terminated against their will (both are also recognised as murder/manslaughter, but are distinguished by Australian law from situations where treating physicians withdraw or withhold 'futile' treatment from an incompetent patient, even though such withdrawal can involve actions (for example extubation) highly likely to lead to death);
3. Voluntary passive euthanasia:
   a. Where the patient requests that treatment be withheld and symptomatic pain relief provided such that premature death results (e.g. hospice and palliative care).
4. Involuntary passive euthanasia:
   a. Where a decision is made to terminate life is made by another because the person concerned lacks the necessary capacity to consent to termination (if the person making the decision is a treating physician then this can fall within the category of lawful withdrawal and withholding of 'futile' treatment).

In 1997 Kuhse, Singer et al. undertook a study which revealed that active voluntary euthanasia and physician-assisted suicide play a role in approximately 1.8% of all Australian deaths.[7] The results of this study are still accepted as reasonably accurate and as highlighting the dangers inherent

---

[7] To complicate matters further, the study showed that in 0.5% of the cases confronted by the doctors in the study, the doctors felt that hastening the death of the patient would be in the patient's best interest and that discussing this option with the patient might cause undue distress and was therefore not undertaken. The study also uncovered that the decision not to treat with the objective of quickening death or not extending a patient's life occurred in an estimated 24.7% of all Australian deaths, 14.3% of such deaths were preceded by a medical decision. Of great concern is that only a tenth of these decisions were made at the patient's request and of the remainder, dementia and handicap only accounted for 1.6% of cases where such a request may not be possible and 6.5% of all Australian deaths pain or symptoms were alleviated with opioids with the secondary intention of hastening death. Helga Kuhse, Peter Singer, Peter Baume, Malcolm Clark and Maurice Rickard, "End-of-life decisions in Australian medical practice", 166 *Medical Journal of Australia* (1997), pp. 191–196.

within the relatively unregulated practice of doctors making and acting on end-of-life decisions. They confirm the existing system is more open to abuse than a regulated, transparent voluntary euthanasia scheme which takes appropriate advantage of advance care directives.

Opposition to euthanasia continues, particularly from the Australian Catholic church, Aboriginal groups, the Australian Association for Hospice and Palliative Care and the Australian Medical Association.[8] A poll conducted in 2007 however found that 80 percent of Australians favoured the terminally ill possessing the rights to choose a medically assisted death. In 2010 another poll revealed that three out of four Australians support legalizing euthanasia.[9] Despite this community support for regulated euthanasia many Australian politicians (out of personal religious conviction or respect for religious pressure groups) remain reluctant to openly support it.

A. *The Brief History of Legislated Active Voluntary Euthanasia in Australia*

Euthanasia legislation has been an area of considerable controversy in Australia. Due to the constitutional split of Federal and State power in Australia, the Commonwealth of Australia has limited capacity to legislate nationally on end-of-life matters.[10] Despite the six Australian States possessing legislative power with respect to euthanasia and advance care directives, the Australian Commonwealth retains legislative control over the two territories of Australia (Australian Capital territory and Northern Territory) by means of s122 of the Commonwealth Constitution.[11]

In 1997 in an effort to prevent pro-euthanasia legislation in the Northern Territory and the Australian Capital Territory, the Australian federal government enacted the *Euthanasia Laws Act 1997*.[12] Schedule 1 of the *Euthanasia Laws Act 1997* altered the legislative powers of the Northern Territory government by way of amending s50A of the *Northern Territory (Self Government) Act 1978* such that they lacked the ability to make laws

---

[8] Martin B Van Der Weyden, "Deaths, Dying and the Euthanasia Debate in Australia", 166 *Medical Journal of Australia* (1997), p. 173.

[9] Dying with Dignity, Victoria. 'Australian's back the right to die.' Viewed November 2010 http://www.dwdv.org.au/News/News0621.html.

[10] Matters upon which the Commonwealth may legislate are listed under s51 of the Commonwealth Constitution and all residual legislative power falls upon the State governments *Commonwealth of Australia Constitution Act* s51.

[11] *Commonwealth of Australia Constitution Act* s122.

[12] Nicola Cica, "Euthanasia - the Australian Law in an International Context", Australian Parliamentary Library Research Paper 3 (1996–97) viewed October 2010 http://www.aph.gov.au/library/pubs/rp/1996-97/97rp3.htm.

in "the form of intentional killing of another called euthanasia (which includes mercy killing) or assisting of a person to terminate his or her life."[13] This amendment went further and explicitly withdrew the force of the previous NT advance care directive legislation, *Rights of the Terminally Ill Act 1995*, with the exception of actions taken prior to the commencement of the amendment.[14]

Schedule 2 of the *Euthanasia Laws Act 1997* similarly amended the *Australian Capital Territory (Self Government) Act 1988* by inserting into it subsections s23(1)(1A) to prohibit the Territory's capacity to legislate on the subject.[15] This situation persists despite the ACT having a *Human Rights Act 2004 (ACT)*[16] that recognises the right to protection from torture and cruel, inhuman or degrading treatment.[17]

Within the Northern Territory there had been a great deal of conflict over the introduction of the *Rights of the Terminally Ill Act 1995 (NT)* prior to the interference of the *Euthanasia Laws Act 1997 (Cth)*. During this brief 2 year timeframe there were 5 legally identified voluntary active euthanasia deaths (all certified as terminally ill and not depressed) some of which were performed by Dr Phillip Nitschke who famously said the following of active voluntary euthanasia:

> I would see this as an act of compassion, an act of concern, an act of love, in fact consistent with good medical practice.[18]

Dr Djiniyinni Gondarra, an Aboriginal Minister of the Uniting Church and Dr Chris Wake, the President of the Northern Territory Branch of the AMA, disagreed with Dr Nitschke and appealed a decision by the Northern Territory Supreme Court to the High Court of Australia on the validity of

---

[13] *Euthanasia Laws Act 1997*.

[14] Id.

[15] Id.

[16] *Human Rights Act 2004 (ACT)* s10.

[17] However, there is the potential for conflict within the legislation as the Act also recognizes the right to life and states no life "may be arbitrarily deprived", *Human Rights Act 2004 (ACT)*, s9. In 2004 there was an unsuccessful attempt to repeal the *Euthanasia Laws Act 1997 (Cth)*, restore the *Rights of the Terminally Ill Act 1995* to the NT and reinstate the ability of the ACT and Norfolk island to legislate on euthanasia. The argument for the repeal was largely focused on two grounds being that the Commonwealth was wrongly interfering with the democratic right of the people within the territories self governing jurisdiction and further the Commonwealth was discriminating between the states. Notably the moral or ethical principles of euthanasia and content of the schedules were not considered in great detail or represented as a driver for the repeal.

[18] ABC The 7.30 Report Transcript: "WA case puts focus on voluntary euthanasia legislation" viewed December 2010 http://www.abc.net.au/7.30/stories/s219321.htm.

the *Rights of the Terminally Ill Act 1995 (NT)*.[19] The High Court adjourned the application in anticipation of the *Euthanasia Laws Act 1997 (Cth)* being passed in the Senate.[20]

B. *Present Statutory Law on Euthanasia in the Australian States*

The common law of Australia has transitioned from seeing suicide as indicative of mental illness to accepting it as a situation where possible psychiatric or psychological issues may exist but not necessarily to the extent that testamentary capacity is extinguished.[21] This shift in collective judicial thinking facilitated the move to have suicide decriminalized in all states.[22] Queensland, Tasmania and Western Australia criminal legislation and codes omit suicide as an offence.

However, legislation in Western Australia and Queensland holds that aiding suicide is a crime where "a person procures, aids or counsels to induce another to kill themselves".[23] The Tasmanian Criminal Code is more succinct in finding it a crime to either instigate or aid another to kill himself.[24] South Australia, New South Wales, Victoria and the Australian Capital Territory use near identical language in finding an indictable offence where a person 'aids, abets or counsels the suicide of another, or an attempt by another to commit suicide'.[25] However, South Australia takes the offence one step further in finding that actions of 'fraud, duress or undue influence' that procure suicide or an attempted suicide are crimes of murder or attempted murder depending on the circumstance.[26] The Northern Territory legislation is much like that of NSW and the ACT, however, it omits the language of 'abetting' or 'counselling' and complicates the offence by requiring that accused have intended his or her conduct to assist the other to commit suicide.[27]

---

[19] *Christopher John Wake and Djiniyini Gondarra v Northern Territory of Australia and the Hon. Kieth John Austin ASCHE AC QC The Administrator of the Northern Territory* (1996) 109 NTR 1.

[20] Id.

[21] *Stuart v Kirkland-Veenstra* [2009] HCA 15.

[22] *Crimes Act 1900 (NSW)* s31A, *Criminal Law Consolidation Act 1935* (SA) s13A(1), *Crimes Act 1958* (Vic) s6A, *Criminal Code* (WA) s288, *Criminal Code* (QLD) s311, *Criminal Code* (Tas) s163.

[23] *Criminal Code* (WA) s288, *Criminal Code* (QLD) s311.

[24] *Criminal Code* (Tas) s163.

[25] *Criminal Consolidation Act 1935* (SA) s13A, *Crimes Act 1900* (NSW) s31C, *Crimes Act 1900* (ACT) s17.

[26] *Criminal Code* (SA).

[27] *Criminal Code* (NT) s162(2).

Regardless of the language used all of the legislation can be categorised as applicable to situations of voluntary active euthanasia or a mercy killings and such actions attract a criminal penalty from 5 years to life imprisonment.

In Western Australia s288 of the *Criminal Code* (WA) carries the penalty of imprisonment for life for the crime of aiding suicide. Hence, when Mr Rossiter requested assistance from his doctor in *Brightwater v Rossiter* his doctor sought declaratory relief from criminal prosecution in his compliance with the request.[28] Declarations of this sort against proposed future criminal conduct can be a valid form of protection but such protection cannot be afforded for conduct already performed.[29] The *Criminal Code* (WA) further supplements the protection from euthanasia granted by s288 by stating there is a duty to provide the necessaries of life where a person has the charge of another who is unable to provide themselves with the necessaries of life due to age, sickness, mental impairment, detention, or other cause.[30] There is a corollary to this under another provision of the *Criminal Code* (WA) concerning surgical and medical treatment such that:

> a person is not criminally responsible for administering, in good faith and with reasonable care and skill, surgical or medical treatment (including palliative care) if that course is reasonable, having regard to the patient's state at the time and to all the circumstances of the case.[31]

The usage of the words 'all circumstances' is intentionally broad and might facilitate a defence against any charges of aiding or abetting suicide if informed consensual treatment of a patient using pain medication were given such as in Mr Rossiter's situation.

The law relating to assistance in the form of a suicide pact varies significantly in Australian legislation. For instance the *Crimes Act 1900* (NSW) exempts a suicide pact participant from murder or manslaughter charges if the accused can prove the existence of the pact on the balance of probabilities.[32] However, the *Crimes Act 1958* (VIC) states that the party who survives a suicide pact is guilty of manslaughter.[33]

---

[28] *Brightwater Care Group (Inc) v Rossiter* [2009] WASC 229.
[29] *Commonwealth v Sterling Nicholas Duty Free Pty Ltd* [1972] 126 CLR 297.
[30] S262 Criminal Code (WA).
[31] Id.
[32] *Crimes Act* 1900 (NSW) s31B.
[33] *Crimes Act* 1958 (VIC) s6B(1).

C. *Australian Common Law and Mercy Killing*

Interestingly Australian courts have been inconsistent in relation to ver-
dicts about mercy killing crimes. In *R v Maxwell* [*2003*][34] and *R v Hood*
[*2002*][35] both defendants received suspended sentences. Coldrey J who
presided over both cases commented:

> The law may be seen as life-affirming and not life-denying and directed
> at discouraging suicide as a response to the emotional vicissitudes of life.
> The degree of moral blame attributable to a person who assists or encour-
> ages an act of suicide may vary greatly from case to case. At one end of the
> spectrum may be placed a person who assists or encourages a person to
> commit suicide in order to inherit property or for some other ulterior
> motive; at the other end, there is the individual who supplies potentially
> lethal medication to a terminally ill person, perhaps a loved one who is in
> extreme pain and who wishes to end that suffering at the earliest possible
> opportunity.[36]

He went on to say that there existed such situations where 'justice may be
tempered with mercy' such that minimal punishment might be imposed
where the act is performed out of kindness.[37]

The above decisions contrast sharply with the rulings in cases such as
R v Justins [*2008*].[38] In *R v Justins* [*2008*] Shirley Justins was found guilty by
a jury of assisting the suicide of Graham Wylie (negligent manslaughter)
and sentenced to a non parole period of 22 months with a balance of term
of 8 months.[39] In this trial the judge emphasised the deceased had the
right to making the decision to commit suicide himself and not have it
made by another on his or her behalf despite the fact that the deceased
had undertaken many avenues in which to take his own life previously.[40]
On the facts this case differed from that of *R v Hood*[41] and *R v Maxwell*[42] in
that the defendant was extensively involved in the planning process of the
death and somewhat dishonest in admitting a potential ulterior motive,
the deceased was somewhat compromised mentally.

---

[34] *R v Maxwell* [2003] VSC 278.
[35] *R v Hood* [2002] VSC 123.
[36] Id.
[37] Id.
[38] *R v Justins* [2008] NSWSC 1194.
[39] Id.
[40] Id.
[41] *R v Hood* [2002] VSC 123.
[42] *R v Maxwell* [2003] VSC 278.

It is in such cases that Australian law struggles to clarify its position on voluntary and involuntary active euthanasia and cases are very much decided on a case-by-case basis rather than on a broader policy position. Indeed, if there is a consistent position amongst these cases it is that the court will discourage a secondary person's involvement in the voluntary death of another even for the relief of suffering (under the ethical doctrine of 'double effect'), unless that person is a doctor. There have been no cases of a doctor having been prosecuted for assisting a patient to die in Australia despite numerous studies highlighting the existence of that practice.

III. Difference between Euthanasia and Withdrawing Treatment

The involuntary aspect of involuntary euthanasia derives from the incapacity or refusal of the patient to grant consent to the termination of their life. The refusal to consent to termination of life by a competent person falls neatly into the categories of murder and manslaughter but where a patient lacks the capacity to communicate his/her wishes it is infinitely more complex in Australian law. This incapacity can take many forms including as dementia and mental incapacity (*R v Justins*)[43] and as a persistent vegetative state, which in Australia's leading case in this area was considered in *Re BMV, Ex parte Gardner*.[44] In *Re BMV* the Victorian Supreme Court ruled that artificial nutrition and hydration was a medical procedure, not palliative care or passive in nature, and could therefore be legally withdrawn from a person in persistent vegetative state regardless of its use to sustain life.[45] The case also reaffirmed the rights of patients (or their appointed guardians if the patient is incompetent), to refuse treatment even if to do so would result in their death. This is consistent with the court's position on upholding the rights of the individual to bodily inviolability.

Involuntary active euthanasia attracts criminal liability in all States and Territories of Australia under the offences of manslaughter and murder. Each state and territory of Australia has legislation to the effect of it being 'unlawful to kill any person unless such killing is authorised or justified or

---

[43] *R v Justins* [2008] NSWSC 1194.
[44] *Re BMV, Ex parte Gardner* [2003] VSC 173.
[45] The Australian Capital Territory (ACT) legislation differs from this position. It states that palliative care cannot be refused and the provision of reasonable food and water is a requirement of the *Medical Treatment (Health Directions) Act* 2006.

excused by law.'[46] Murder specifically being where the conduct engaged is intentional or there exists reckless indifference to human life and death of another occurs.[47] Manslaughter, being the residual form of homicide if murder is not satisfied on the facts, is where the requisite intention is lacking or where the death results by way of reckless or negligent conduct.[48]

In the Australian context, doctors and lawyers alike are realising that it is a fine line between active euthanasia, attracting the offence of murder/manslaughter, and that of physicians withdrawing and withholding futile treatment, where liability is non-existent. This is despite the fact that in the latter cases patients are routinely administered respiratory depressive opioids which in reality hastens death not unlike other forms of assisted death.[49] Studies like Kuhse and Singer's demonstrate that doctors administer this form of "pain relief" without discussing it with the patient and/or their guardian first. The crucial distinction seems to be that with withdrawal of futile treatment the doctors involved are never certain that death will result—some patients may rally physiologically and if this occurs treatment is continued.

V. Patient Autonomy at the End of Life

A. *Overview*

Despite legislation facilitating written and oral advance directives, government-funded research projects and a plethora of official policies promoting them, very few elderly or terminally ill patients make advance directives in Australia. Some senior Australian physicians still refuse to make not-for-resuscitation orders despite manifest and accepted futility of treatment for the patient in question, owing to irrational fears of legal liability. Cardiac arrests in such situations can result in the phenomenon of a 'slow-code' where doctors and nurses go through the outward forms of resuscitation to permit documentation required of them as a result of desuetude and/or ignorance of the law by the treating physician.

If an Advance Care Directive (ACD) does exist an Australian medical team will discuss the process of withdrawal or withholding of treatment

---

[46] *Criminal Code Act* 1913 (WA) s268.
[47] *Crimes Act* 1900 (NSW) s18.
[48] *Criminal Code* (NT) s160.
[49] Barry M. Kinzbrunner; Neal J. Weinreb and Joel S. Policzer, *20 Common Problems in End of Life Care* (New York, 2002).

with the patient and/or their family in most settings. If treatment is declared clinical futile and treatment is withdrawn or withheld in accordance with an ACD, the cause of the patient's death is noted on the medical record and death certificate as the disease process or injury that was the underlying causative factor. In states that have legislated on ACDs there are broad protections available for staff who act in good faith (prioritising basic medical ethics principles such as beneficence over autonomy) either to accept or ignore an ACD.

Just as in the Italian case, informed consent is an essential component to recognising the weight of the autonomy of the patient in this setting. The Australian High Court in a series of cases (*Rogers v Whitaker*,[50] *Chappel v Hart*,[51] and *Rosenberg v Percival*[52]) has determined that the doctor's duty of care requires provision of information not just about the broad nature and effect of any treatment (or withholding/withdrawal of treatment), but also of reasonably likely material risks or those of particular concern to this patient.[53] If the patient indicates he or she would go ahead with the decision regardless of what material risk information is presented then failure to provide such information does not create tortuous liability.[54]

In *F v R*[55] with King CJ elaborating the disclosure process stated:

> the nature of that matter to be disclosed; the nature of the treatment, the desire of the patient or information, the temperament and health of the patient; and the general surrounding circumstances.[56]

In *Hunter and New England Area Health Service v A* the court adopted the UK decision in *Re MB (Medical Treatment)*[57] whereby a person of full age is deemed capable of having the capacity to consent to or refuse medical treatment.[58] Provided that the duty of care is satisfied and patients are sufficiently informed the High Court of Australia ruled in *Secretary of Department of Health and Community Services v B [1992]* that patients possess the right to refuse treatment.[59] It was acknowledged that such a rule

---

[50] *Rogers v Whitaker* (1992) 175 CLR 479.
[51] *Chappell v Hart* (1998) 195 CLR 232.
[52] *Rosenberg v Percival* (2001) 205 CLR 434.
[53] *Rogers v Whitaker* (1992) 175 CLR 479.
[54] *Rosenberg v Percival* (2001) 205 CLR 434.
[55] *F v R* (1983) 33 SASR 189.
[56] Id.
[57] *Re MB (Medical Treatment)* [1997] EWCA Civ 1361.
[58] *Hunter and New England Area Health Service v A* [2009] NSWSC 761.
[59] *Secretary of Department of Health and Community Services v B* [1992] HCA 15; (1992) CLR 218.

was to be applied regardless of 'irrational, non-existent or incomplete knowledge of the patient's reasoning in making their decision to refuse treatment'.[60]

B. *The Rights of Children to Refuse Treatment in Australia*

In Australia there is a presumption that all adults are competent to accept or refuse medical treatment unless the alternative is evidenced. At common law however the presumption is that children under the age of 18 lack such competence unless they can demonstrate they have achieved 'a sufficient understanding and intelligence to enable him or her to understand fully what is proposed.'[61] Despite this potential for children to refuse medical treatment, the outcome of cases heard in the Australian courts suggests that where the refusal of treatment of a child will result in the child's death even if the decision is made by a 'competent' child, the courts will override the child's refusal.[62] It is interesting to note that in two of these cases the children were refusing blood transfusions on the basis of their religious beliefs.

South Australian legislation better captures this position. The *Consent to Medical Treatment and Palliative Care Act 1995* (SA) facilitated the informed refusal of medical treatment of children provided they are over 16 years of age including where the treatment might be life sustaining and where it might be anticipatory refusal.[63] The legislation provides, however, that the child's decision may be overridden by a parent or guardian and that two doctors are required to have consensus on the child and ensure there is a full understanding of the implications of such refusal.[64]

In practice in Australia many physicians will prioritise the ethical principle of beneficence over that of autonomy where a child is refusing life sustaining treatment because of religious views. They reason that adults can risk their lives in this way, but the risk of mental manipulation and immaturity of understanding is too great to allow children to risk their lives for an ideology that in their maturity they may or may not reject.

---

[60] *Re T (Adult: Refusal of Treatment)* [1992] 4 All ER 649, *Hunter and New England Area Health Service v A* [2009] NSWSC 761.

[61] Known as *Gillick competence* after *Gillick v West Norfolk AHA* [1986] AC 112.

[62] *H and W* (1995) FLC 92–598; *DOCS v Y* [1999] NSWSC 644; *Minister for Health v AS* [2004] WASC 286; *Royal Alexander Hospital for Children v Joseph* [2005] NSWSC 422.

[63] *Consent to Medical Treatment and Palliative Care Act 1995* (SA).

[64] Id.

C. Legislation on Advance Care Directives in Australia

The primary mechanism by which the recognition of an adult's voluntary anticipatory refusal of medical treatment is achieved in Australia is through living wills and enduring powers of attorney.[65] The most important component of an ACD (rarely included) for a guardian or clinician making an end-of-life decision about an incompetent patient, is a clear statement of the minimum level of a meaningful quality of life that the particular patient is willing to accept.

South Australia and the Northern Territory legislation allows advance directives but limits their use to situations of terminal illness and for consent or refusal of specified treatments.[66] South Australia additionally provides for circumstances of persistent vegetative state and has legislated similarly to Victoria and the Australian Capital Territory in providing that a competent adult can give effect to an enduring power of attorney. The enduring power of attorney allows the principal competent adult to engage an agent to make medical decisions on their behalf in the event that they are rendered incompetent. Thus, through the agent the principal effectively has a legal means of refusing medical treatment with the caveat that the refusal is consistent with the wishes of the principal and does not conflict with any instructions provided by the principal in the power of attorney document whilst they were competent.[67] In effect the power of attorney legislation facilitates the indirect decision making of the principal prospectively. Notably the legislation does not displace the competent principal's capacity to give other forms of binding anticipatory refusal for undesired medical treatment.

South Australia introduced the *Consent to Medical Treatment and Palliative Care Act 1995 (SA)*[68] which renders any health care professional free from both civil and criminal liability if they act in accordance with the directions of the principal; in good faith and without negligence; and in compliance with the professional standards of medical practice.[69]

---

[65] Ben White, Lindy Willmott, Colleen Cartwright, Malcolm Parker and Gail Williams, *Withholding and withdrawing life-sustaining treatment from adults lacking capacity: enhancing medical decision-making through doctors' compliance with the law.* Presented at AABHL conference, Adelaide, July 2010.

[66] *Consent to Medical Treatment and Palliative Care Act* 1995 (SA), *Natural Death Act 1988* (NT).

[67] *Natural Death Act 1983* (SA), *Medical Treatment Act 1988* (VIC), *Medical Treatment (Health Directions) Act 2006* (ACT).

[68] *Consent to Medical Treatment and Palliative Care Act* 1995 (SA).

[69] Id.

The *Consent to Medical Treatment and Palliative Care Act* substitutes the regime founded in the *Guardianship and Administration Act 1993 (SA)* for the appointment of agents to act under the enduring power of attorney. The new regime provides that a person of sound mind who has attained 18 years of age can implement a medical power of attorney to appoint an agent to act on their behalf in regards to medical treatment provided it is written, witnessed by a justice of the peace or similar proclaimed figure.[70] [71] It is also explicit in this legislation that the medical power of attorney does not empower the agent to refuse the supply of food and water, drugs for pain and distress nor refuse treatment which might enable the principal to regain their capacity to consent unless there is no expectation that the principal might recover or have a 'remission of symptoms' in terminal illness.[72] Additionally the doctor cannot treat a patient over 16 years of age if he/she is aware of the patient's anticipatory refusal or existence of an appointed agent where the agent is available.

The current Northern Territory legislation, *Natural Death Act 1988 (NT)* resembles closely that of South Australian Act in allowing competent terminally ill persons to make written directives for the refusal of 'extraordinary measures',[73] however, it omits the process for the appointment of an agent under an enduring power of attorney.

Victoria's *Medical Treatment Act 1988 (VIC)* allows for advance care directives solely by way of a 'refusal of treatment certificate' subsequent to the patient's either oral, written or otherwise communicated request.[74] This legislation restricts the use of such a certificate by requiring the treatment refused be for a current condition, is voluntary and is witness by both a doctor and another person who are satisfied of the patient's adequate understanding of the consequences of such a decision.[75] A doctor who does not comply with the refusal of treatment certificate becomes liable for medical trespass. The *Medical Treatment Act 1988 (VIC)* was

---

[70] These include:
      (a) a commissioner for taking affidavits in the Supreme Court; or
      (b) a member of the clergy; or
      (c) a registered pharmacist.
[71] *Consent to Medical Treatment and Palliative Care Act* 1995 (SA).
[72] Id.
[73] "Extraordinary measures" means medical or surgical measures that prolong life, or are intended to prolong life, by supplanting or maintaining the operation of bodily functions that are temporarily or permanently incapable of independent operation; - *Natural Death Act 1988 (NT)*.
[74] *Medical Treatment Act 1988* (VIC).
[75] Id.

amended in 1990 and 1992 to permit the appointment of agent and alternate agent in the presence of a justice of the peace and other by way of enduring power of attorney provisions.[76] Power is acquired by the alternate agent only upon the unavailability, death or incompetency of the original agent. The agent is refrained from refusing palliative care and confined in his/her power to treatments which the agent considers the principal would deem wanton or result in unreasonable distress.[77] Again a certificate of refusal of treatment is demanded for any decisions of the agent.[78] The advance directive self terminates should the principal's condition change in such a manner that the directive is not applicable to the current condition[79] The advance directive self terminates should the principal's condition change in such a manner that the directive is not applicable to the current condition.[80] In Victoria a guardian under the *Guardianship and Administration Act 1986* (*VIC*) has the same power as that of an agent under the *Medical Treatment Act 1988* (*VIC*).

Advance directives in the ACT, the *Medical Treatment* (*Health Directions*) *Act 2006* (*ACT*)[81] are sculpted upon that of the *Medical Treatment Act 1988* (*VIC*) as is the Queensland legislation *Powers of Attorney Act 1998* (*QLD*), which additionally allows for situations where the patient is dependent upon life-support machinery. Under the *Medical Treatment Act 1994* (*ACT*) an agent may be appointed to make medical decisions under enduring power of attorney but their power is only realised when the doctor declares the principal incapacitated.

Presently New South Wales lacks any formal legislation relating to end-of-life decisions but it does have non-binding guidelines which indicates that an advance care directive should be considered as sufficient authority for a medical treatment decision provided that it is specific to the disease or injury relevant to the decision, current and made by a competent individual.[82] Markedly there is no prescribed form in which the directive must take, it is not necessary a witness be present (although encouraged) and

---

[76] Id.
[77] Id.
[78] Id.
[79] Id.
[80] Id.
[81] *Medical Treatment* (*Health Directions*) *Act 2006* (ACT).
[82] *NSW Health "Guidelines for end-of-life care and decision making"*, http://www.health.nsw.gov.au/pubs/2005/pdf/end_of_life_care.pdf, NSW Health *"Using Advance Care Directives"* viewed December 2010, http://www.health.nsw.gov.au/policies/gl/2005/pdf/GL2005_056.pdf.

no health professional is required to have informed the patient prior to the writing of the directive.[83] It need not even be in writing.

To date Tasmania has not legally attempted to address the topic of advance care directives and so possesses no legislation either allowing directives to be made or followed. Western Australia similarly has not enabled advance care directives by legislating for them, though numerous unsuccessful attempts were made to pass the *Medical Care of the Dying Bill 1995 (WA)* despite the Western Australian law reform commission advocating its introduction into law.[84]

With the exception of Tasmania and Western Australia, Australia has a substantial body of legislation dealing with advance directives. Yet the Australian judicial system is reluctant to engage in a dialogue addressing the uncertainties that still exist within much of the current law on end-of-life decisions.[85]

D. *Guardianship Laws in Australia*

The subjective needs of an individual are difficult to evaluate in situations where a patient is incapable of giving consent to medical procedures. In these circumstances the law in NSW defers to the *Guardianship Act 1987 (NSW)* which applies to incapable persons above the age of 16.[86] It functions by providing for proxy consent by an appointed guardian or where one is not available another 'person responsible'.[87] The person responsible existing in a form of hierarchy whereby it is in the first instance priority is given to a spouse where there is a strong, long relationship, then the carer and where no carer nor spouse is available the person responsible is assigned to a close relative or friend.[88] This statutory scheme only permits the person responsible to make decisions on the principal's behalf where there is a positive action of consent to medical treatment. *Prima facie* it fails to be a device by which refusal or discontinuation of treatment and so

---

[83] Id.

[84] Law Reform Commission of Western Australia – *30th Anniversary Reform Implementation Report* (2002) – *Medical Treatment for the Dying*.

[85] Cameron Stewart, "Qumsieh's Case, Civil Liability and the Right to Refuse Medical Treatment", 8 *Journal of Law and Medicine* (2000), pp. 56–62; Thomas A. Faunce and Cameron Stewart, "The *Messiha* and *Schiavo* Cases: Third-Party Ethical and Legal Interventions in Futile Care Disputes", 183(5) *Medical Journal of Australia* (2005), pp. 261–263.

[86] *Guardianship Act 1987 (NSW)*.

[87] Id.

[88] Cameron Stewart, "Who Decides when I Can Die? Problems with Proxy Decisions to Forego Life-Sustaining Treatment", 4 *Journal of Law and Medicine* (1997), pp. 386–401.

cannot be utilised as a form of advance care directive achieved via previous communication in the course of a relationship. In *WK v Public Guardian ADT 93* it was identified that another means of recourse by which the guardian might be granted the power of refusal or discontinuation of treatment would be through an application to the NSW Supreme Court for an assessment of the patient's best interests under *parens patriae* jurisdiction.[89]

Victorian common law is somewhat more liberal than that of NSW. This can be seen in *Re BWV, Ex parte Gardner*[90] where the court ruled that it was the parliamentary intention of the Victorian *Guardianship and Administration Act 1986* that refusal of treatment for a ward be an option able to be adopted by a guardian. *Re BWV, Ex parte Gardner* also is the common law authority stating that where no guardian had been appointed a family member or physician could legally make the decision to withdraw nutrition and hydration where it is considered to be in the patient's best interests.

With the exception of *Re BWV, Ex parte Gardner* the courts have been reluctant to engage with the subject matter of guardianship and advance care directives. *Qumsieh v Guardianship and Administration Board* was one case which sought to resolve the dilemma of guardians possessing the authority to override patient advance care directives for the refusal of specific treatment. Instead of a definitive ruling the case was dismissed from the Victorian Court of Appeal on the grounds of that the subject matter was moot though there existed some discussion that advance care directives were often of such a specific nature that they are easily made inapplicable and jurisdiction granted to the person responsible.[91]

V. Contrasting Australian and Italian Law on End-of-Life Decisions

The Italian legal order appears to adopt a position closer to that of United States courts under the doctrine there known as "substituted judgment": a legal representative giving voice to the wishes of the patient (insofar as they have been manifested) as to the withdrawal or withholding of 'futile'

---

[89] *WK v Public Guardian* [2006] ADT 93.
[90] *Re BMV, Ex parte Gardner* [2003] VSC 173.
[91] Faunce and Stewart, *supra* note 85.

medical treatment. The Australian legal system, on the other hand, appears to prioritise the interpretation of a guardian and/or the patient's physicians as to the patient's "best interests".

The Italian Supreme Court found that the Milan Public Prosecutor's lacked power to impugn a judicial finding of persistent vegetative state. The Bill (No. 2350), approved by the Senate of the Italian Republic on 26 March 2009 and recently amended by the Chamber of Deputies, prohibits (under articles 575, 579 and 580 of the Italian criminal code) any form of euthanasia and assistance to suicide. This position is similar to most jurisdictions in Australia—although two jurisdictions, the Northern Territory and the Australian Capital Territory (as mentioned) attempted to pass legislation permitting euthanasia in circumstances where the patient is certified independently by two expert doctors to be suffering a terminal illness, to not be suffering mental impairment and to be fully informed about palliative care options.

The disinclination of Australia to legally embrace or bestow legal certainty in relation to voluntary euthanasia and physician-assisted suicide may become a driver for the popularity of overseas euthanasia tourism.[92] The Exit International website created a political storm in Australia and became one of the blacklist targets of proposed mandatory internet censorship legislation.[93] Already Exit International has countered the censorship legislation by offering master classes in computer hacking to evade the filtering technology.[94]

Due to the illegality of physician-assisted suicide, covert euthanasia involving the medical profession is probably widespread in Australia (for example creation of a false clinical pretext enabling the administration of mounting doses of drugs or fabrications as to the official cause of death).[95]

In its judgment in the *Eluana Englaro Case* the Italian Supreme Court confirmed that adult fully informed and competent patients have the

---

[92] Exit International (Assisted suicide/voluntary euthanasia) viewed December 2010 http://www.exitinternational.net/.

[93] *Measures to Improve Safety of the Internet for Families Bill 2010 (Cth).*

[94] Exit International (Assisted suicide/voluntary euthanasia) viewed December 2010 http://www.exitinternational.net/.

[95] In 2004 Roger Magnusson of Sydney Law School reported on interviews he had conducted with doctors who had engaged in voluntary active euthanasia of HIV/AIDS patients. His report details a troubling twenty percent of physician assisted suicide attempts were bungled and occasionally led to suffocation and strangulation. Roger Magnusson, "'Underground Euthanasia' and the Harm Minimization Debate", 32 *Journal of Law, Medicine & Ethics* (2004), pp. 486–495.

right to refuse treatment even if such a course is reasonably likely to lead to his or her death.[96] This is also the law in Australia.

Like Australia, Italy has endeavoured to prohibit euthanasia and advocate for advance care directives through its Bill.[97] The Bill is closely aligned with the current Australian position by criminalising active voluntary and involuntary euthanasia but it achieves this goal in a slightly more explicit manner by identifying murder by consent as a specific crime.[98] The Bill facilitates pain therapies along the lines of palliative care much like the Australian law. It allows health professionals to act with their own initiative for the safeguarding of the patient's health where advance care directives are non-existent. This contrasts with the Australian position of assigning a 'person responsible' as a guardian to make similar decisions.

The two jurisdictions are disagree in relation to the provision of artificial nutrition and hydration. The Australian common law enables withdrawal and withholding of such support in situations of clinical futility, under advance care directives (it holds that food and water are a form of medical treatment for the critically ill) and medical treatment refusal, whilst the Italian bill requires such nutrition be maintained until end of life in all circumstances where it sustains bodily functions. Prior to the Bill the Italian courts had a softer stance on the withdrawal of artificial nutrition. It was only in 2008 that they enunciated that guardian possessed the power to make a legitimate decision of this sort where the vegetative state was irreversible and where such an action was perceivably a "true expression" of the patient's wishes as unequivocally determined by lifestyle, beliefs, personality, declarations and their notion of dignity.

There is a generalised consensus in Australia that advance care directives come into play at any time where a patient is incompetent and has provided a direction of adequate specificity in compliance with the rules of creation. However, the Bill intentionally limits advance care directives to situations of permanent incompetence as declared by a medical board and so are inapplicable where patients might waiver in and out of mental competence throughout their illness.

The Bill also states that advance directives can be only in written and signed form whereas the law in Australia recognises that patients who have certain disabilities or have deteriorated may not be able to sign such a document so oral agreement of advance directives is allowed.

---

[96] Supreme Court, Crim. Sect. I, 11 July 2002.
[97] See *supra* note 2.
[98] Article 579 Criminal Code (Italian).

Notably the Italian law allows doctors to override patient advance directives in cases of urgency whereas the Australian law does not.

The two countries differ in their methodology for the appointment of competent trustees, the Italians presenting a more streamlined process attached to the creation of the advance directive whilst the Australian law appears to segregate the creation of the advance directive from the law on powers of attorney for appointment of an agent. However, both methods serve the same end and see that the principal's wishes are observed by the appointed agent. Even so, in Italy it is proposed that the doctor is given authority to disregard both the advance care directive and the trustee after consideration and with reason, this option is not contemplated by the Australian law and doctors have a duty to comply with patient wishes.

Australia has no national regulation on the use of Advance Directives, instead each of the six states and two territories have their own laws (both common law and legislation) that refer to the construction and use of these instruments.[99]

Despite Australia being a largely secular society, religious groups still influence political decision making and Australia's lack of any constitutional rights or Bill of Rights has meant that the any explicit 'right to die' has largely not been legally considered. It has arguably been dealt with, however, in acknowledging the right to individual bodily inviolability and the recognition of advance care directives as a potential instrument for the expression of this right.[100] The enactment of human rights legislation in Australian jurisdictions (particularly that prohibiting cruel, unusual or degrading medical treatment) will become an increasingly important method for protecting their ageing populations facing the prospect of dying in either a hospital intensive care unit or under palliative care.

---

[99] *Medical Treatment (Health Directions) Act* 2006 (ACT); *Natural Death Act* 1988 (NT); *Powers of Attorney Act* 1998 (Qld); *Consent to Medical Treatment and Palliative Care Act* 1995 (SA); *Medical Treatment Act* 1988 (Vic); *Guardianship and Administration Act 1990* (WA); NSW and Tas common law.

[100] Thomas A Faunce, Kathy Shats, and Susannah Jefferys, "Re Herrington: Aboriginality and the Quality of Human Rights Jurisprudence in End-of-Life Decisions by the Australian Judiciary", 15(2) *Journal of Law and Medicine* (2007), pp. 201–209; Thomas A Faunce, "Emerging Roles for Law and Human Rights in Ethical Conflicts Surrounding Neuro Critical Care", 7(3) *Critical Care and Resuscitation* (2005), pp. 221–226.

LES DIRECTIVES ANTICIPÉES EN FRANCE, UN INDICE DE CONSENTEMENT À EFFETS LIMITÉS

*Brigitte Feuillet**

La loi française du 22 avril 2005[1] a introduit les directives anticipées, offrant ainsi la possibilité pour une personne majeure, au cas où elle serait hors d'état de manifester sa volonté en fin de vie, d'exprimer ses souhaits « sur les conditions de la limitation ou l'arrêt de traitement ».[2] Ces directives semblent donc avoir pour objectif d'énoncer un refus de soin par anticipation. A ce titre, la technique semble intéressante en ce qu'elle pourrait apporter des solutions à la difficile et complexe question de l'expression du consentement du patient en fin de vie. Or, l'examen approfondi de cet outil montre qu'il n'en est rien et que ces directives peuvent même n'avoir aucun impact sur la décision du médecin d'interrompre un traitement. Pour comprendre cette réalité, il est intéressant de replacer l'avènement des directives dans le contexte général de l'évolution des règles en matière de consentement.

Le consentement du patient est l'élément fondamental de la relation médicale. Aucune intervention médicale n'est envisageable sans celui-ci.

---

* Professeur à la Faculté de droit et de science politique de Rennes, Membre de l'Institut Universitaire de France, Directeur du CRJO (Institut de l'Ouest : Droit et Europe, UMR CNRS 6262), Faculté de droit et de science politique de Rennes, France ; email : brigitte. le-mintier@univ-rennes1.fr.

[1] Loi n° 2005–370 relative aux droits des malades et à la fin de vie, dîtes loi *Léonetti*. Rapport fait au nom de la mission d'information sur l'accompagnement de la fin de vie n° 1708, Tomes 1 et 2, Assemblée Nationale 30 juin 2004. Rapport d'information Léonetti fait au nom de la mission d'évaluation de la loi n° 2005–370 du 22 avril 2005 relative aux droits des malades et à la fin de vie n° 1287, Tomes 1 et.2, Assemblée Nationale 28 novembre 2008. Frédérique Dreifuss-Netter, « Les directives anticipées : de l'autonomie de la volonté à l'autonomie de la personne », *Gazette du Palais*, 9 juin 2006, n° 160, p. 23 ; Roger Mislawski, « Directives anticipées et autonomie de la personne en fin de vie », *Médecine et droit*, juillet 2009, n° 97, pp. 103–106 ; Gilles Raoul-Cormeil, « Les "directives anticipées" sur la fin de vie médicalisée », *Revue Lamy Droit Civil*, septembre 2006, n°30, pp. 57–65.

[2] Article 7 de la loi du 22 avril 2005 devenu l'article L 1111-11 CSPub. Décret n° 2006–120 du 6 février 2006 relatif aux directives anticipées prévues par la loi n° 2005–370 du 22 avril 2005 relative aux droits des malades et à la fin de vie et modifiant le code de la santé publique, JORF, n° 32, 7 février 2006, p. 1973. Décret n° 2010–107 du 29 janvier 2010 relatif aux conditions de mise en œuvre des décisions de limitation ou d'arrêt de traitement, JORF n° 0025, 30 janvier 2010, p. 1869.

S. Negri (ed.), *Self-Determination, Dignity and End-of-Life Care*
2011 Koninklijke Brill NV. Printed in The Netherlands. ISBN 978 90 04 22357 8. pp. 195–208

Dès 1942,[3] la cour de cassation imposait cette obligation. Les fondements invoqués de cette exigence sont multiples :[4] le consentement est un élément de formation de tout contrat (donc du contrat médical[5]) mais aussi un droit fondamental de la personne,[6] il relève du principe de la liberté individuelle,[7] il doit être exigé pour concilier le principe d'inviolabilité du corps humain et la liberté de la personne de disposer de son corps ou encore il est le moyen d'assurer le respect de la dignité de la personne.[8] Si ces fondements sont discutés en doctrine, la règle du consentement du malade à la décision médicale est unanimement admise. Le droit français[9] exige que ce consentement soit recueilli préalablement. Ainsi, la volonté du patient (de se soigner ou de ne pas le faire) s'impose au médecin[10] car nul ne peut être contraint de subir une intervention médicale ou chirurgicale.[11]

Pourtant, en pratique, la question du consentement est complexe. En effet, même lorsque les meilleures conditions sont réalisées (la personne est en possession de toutes ses facultés mentales), il peut y avoir

---

³ Cass. Req., 8 janvier 1942, DC 1942, p. 63 (*arrêt Teyssier*).

⁴ Sur la distinction entre consentement et volonté, voir Diane Roman, « Le respect de la volonté du malade : une obligation limitée ? », *Revue de droit sanitaire et social*, 2005, p. 423 et plus généralement Marie-Anne Frison-Roche, « Remarques sur la distinction de la volonté et du consentement en droit des contrats », *Revue trimestrielle de droit civil*, 1995, pp. 573–578 ; Denis Berthiau, « Comprendre le principe d'autonomie en droit de la santé », *Médecine et Droit*, 2006, pp. 53–60.

⁵ Roger Nerson, « Le respect par le médecin de la volonté du malade », in *Mélanges dédiés à Gabriel Marty*, Presses de l'Université Toulouse 1 Capitole, Toulouse, 1978, pp. 853–880, p. 870. Ce qui n'est pas sans poser le problème de la nécessité du consentement dans la relation (non contractuelle) du patient avec le médecin exerçant dans un établissement hospitalier. D'où la tendance de certains auteurs à raisonner en termes de « décision médicale ». Voir Anne Laude, Bertrand Mathieu, Didier Tabuteau, *Droit de la santé*, Thémis droit, PUF, Paris, 2007, p. 351. La nature contractuelle de la relation médicale est d'ailleurs de plus en plus discutée.

⁶ Certains considèrent qu'en consacrant le consentement non plus comme une obligation mais comme un droit fondamental de la personne du malade, la loi du 4 mars 2002 devrait conduire à analyser le consentement comme un élément de formation de la relation médecin–patient. Voir Pascal Lokiec, « La décision médicale », *Revue trimestrielle de droit civil*, 2004, pp. 641–654.

⁷ Dominique Thouvenin, « Le rôle du consentement dans la pratique médicale », *Médecine et Droit*, 1994, n° 6, pp. 57–59.

⁸ Cass. Civ., 1ère ch., 9 octobre 2001, *Bulletin civil*, 2001, I n°249, p. 157.

⁹ Article 16–3 du code civil, article L 1111–4 alinéas 1 et 3 CSPub, articles R 4127–35, 4127–36, 4127–41 et 4127–52 CSPub (code de déontologie médicale). Cass. Civ., 1ère, 11 octobre 1988, *JCP* (*La semaine juridique*), 1989, II, 21358, note Annick Dorsner-Dolivet.

¹⁰ Article L 1111–4 alinéa 2 et R 4127–36 alinéa 2 CSPub.

¹¹ Cass. Civ., 2ème, 19 mars 1997, *Bulletin civil*, II, n° 86, p. 48 ; *Revue trimestrielle de droit civil*, 1997, p. 632, obs. J. Hauser. Stephanie Hennette-Vauchez, « Kant contre Jehovah ? Refus de soins et dignité de la personne humaine », *Recueil Dalloz*, 2004, chron., n° 3154.

une discordance entre la volonté déclarée et la volonté réelle de la personne et, en tout état de cause, cette dernière n'est jamais facile à déterminer. En effet, le contexte (vulnérabilité de la personne liée à sa maladie, charge que le malade peut représenter pour son entourage, incidences économiques de cette maladie...) peut amener le malade à exprimer un consentement qui ne correspondra peut être pas à ce qu'il souhaite au plus profond de lui même. Il est vrai que le système juridique donnant foi à la volonté déclarée permet d'éluder les difficultés.[12] En France, la loi impose simplement un consentement sans donner d'autres précisions mais, en pratique, les juges ont tendance à rechercher la volonté réelle du malade.[13]

Ainsi, on le voit, si la question du consentement est d'une manière générale complexe, elle l'est encore davantage lorsque le malade est hors d'état d'émettre une volonté et que, de surplus, l'intervention médicale doit s'effectuer en fin de vie du patient.[14] En effet, si durant sa vie, la volonté réelle du malade est difficile à déterminer, ce constat s'amplifie du fait des angoisses (liées à la mort mais aussi et surtout à une fin de vie médicalisée peu réjouissante) qui peuvent assaillir le malade. Les directives anticipées concernent cette population de personnes hors d'état d'exprimer sa volonté en fin de vie.

Pour ces individus, pendant longtemps, excepté l'hypothèse d'urgence, le droit français exigeait le consentement des proches. La jurisprudence[15] avait opté pour une théorie dérogatoire au droit commun des contrats[16] en permettant au médecin d'intervenir avec le consentement des « protecteurs naturels ».[17] Cette mesure prétorienne, qui introduisait une sorte d'incapacité de fait,[18] s'insérait dans un contexte où la famille jouait un rôle essentiel dans la vie de l'individu. Néanmoins, pour tenir compte des évolutions de la notion de famille, les juges avaient donné une définition

---

[12] L'Allemagne a opté pour un tel système.

[13] Il faut alors prouver la discordance entre les deux.

[14] Laurence Cimar, « La situation juridique du patient inconscient en fin de vie », *Revue de droit sanitaire et social*, mai 2006, n° 3, pp. 470–484.

[15] Aucun texte ne prévoyait cette règle qui a été admise par la jurisprudence : Lyon 17 novembre 1952, *JCP*, 1953, II, 7541, note René Savatier ; Cass. Civ., 1ère, 8 novembre 1955, *JCP*, 1955, II, 9014, note René Savatier.

[16] En droit commun, seules les techniques de représentation sont envisagées pour suppléer le consentement de la personne incapable majeure ou mineure.

[17] Par exemple, le conjoint, les ascendants ou descendants majeurs.

[18] Savatier, 1955, *supra* note 15. L'intervention des proches peut être analysée comme une gestion d'affaires, voir une stipulation pour autrui (voir Denis Berthiau, *Droit de la santé*, Gualino éditeur, Paris, 2007, p. 159).

large des proches en visant les personnes qui « assurent en fait, avec des marques évidentes d'affection et d'attachement, la garde, l'entretien, la protection du malade »,[19] offrant ainsi la possibilité de consulter des personnes n'appartenant pas à la famille légale.

Avec les réformes récentes successives, la simplicité des règles dégagées par la jurisprudence[20] semble avoir laisser la place à un système confus où, en fin de parcours, le médecin peut, dans certaines hypothèses autres que l'urgence, intervenir sur le patient sans le consentement de celui-ci. En effet, les exceptions légales à la règle du consentement du malade manquent de précisions. L'article 16-3 du code civil prévoit, d'une manière générale, que le consentement doit toujours être requis « hors les cas où son état rend nécessaire une intervention thérapeutique à laquelle il n'est pas à même de consentir ».[21] Ce texte vise l'urgence[22] et l'impossibilité de recueillir le consentement.[23] Mais, au vu de l'article L 1111-4 alinéa 4 du code la santé publique, d'autres hypothèses d'intervention sans le consentement du patient seraient visées. Ce texte distingue effectivement les cas d'urgence ou d'impossibilité où le médecin peut agir seul de situations autres où le praticien doit alors consulter des tiers (personne de confiance, famille ou proches). Or, en rapprochant cette disposition de l'article 16-3 du code civil qui donne pouvoir au médecin d'intervenir sur une personne inapte à donner son consentement en présence d'une nécessité *thérapeutique*,[24] il apparaît qu'un acte *thérapeutique*[25] peut être pratiqué sur un malade sous la seule réserve d'une consultation de certaines personnes. De ce fait, si aujourd'hui l'accent est mis sur la primauté de la volonté du malade lorsque celui-ci est conscient, il n'en n'est pas de même lorsqu'il est hors d'état de donner un consentement.

---

[19] René Savatier, Jean Marie Auby, Jean Savatier et Henri Péquignot, *Traité de droit médical*, Litec, Paris, 1956, p. 226.

[20] Même si elle donnait un pouvoir exorbitant aux protecteurs naturels (création d'une incapacité extra-légale), voir Savatier, Auby, Savatier et Péquignot, précité.

[21] Ce texte énonce les hypothèses d'intervention sur le corps humain.

[22] La notion d'urgence est relativement simple (nécessité évidente, danger immédiat). Cass. Civ., 1ère, 11 octobre 1988, *Bulletin civil*, I, n° 280.

[23] La notion d'impossibilité est, elle, moins facile à appréhender. La jurisprudence y eu recours en matière de psychiatrie (Cass. Civ., 1ère, 23 mai 2000, *Bulletin civil*, I, n° 159, p. 103 ; *JCP*, 2000, 10342, rapport Pierre Sargos). Il peut s'agir d'une impossibilité matérielle du fait de la non compréhension d'une langue mais aussi d'une impossibilité psychologique dans laquelle certains proposent d'inclure *l'exception thérapeutique* (article R 2147–35 CSPub).

[24] L'article 16–3 alinéa 2CCiv se réfère à l'état rendant nécessaire une intervention thérapeutique.

[25] Ce qui semble exclure cette faculté du médecin pour les actes autres que thérapeutiques qu'il serait amené à pratiquer sur le patient.

La jurisprudence antérieure imposant le consentement des proches lorsque le malade ne peut émettre un consentement semble donc écartée et a laissé la place à la simple obligation du médecin d'informer[26] ou de consulter[27] les proches[28] dans certaines hypothèses.

C'est dans ce contexte que le législateur a introduit en 2005 les directives anticipées. L'objectif annoncé pour ces directives étant d'extérioriser par anticipation la volonté du malade sur la manière d'appréhender sa fin de vie, cette réforme pouvait laisser penser à un regain du rôle de la volonté du malade dans un environnement qui, nous l'avons vu, l'a amoindri et allait ainsi rééquilibrer les relations médecin-patient.[29] Or, il n'en est rien. Ces directives ne sont pas un instrument d'extériorisation du consentement du malade mais ne sont qu'un indice de ce consentement (I) dont la portée est extrêmement limitée car le médecin n'est pas obligé de suivre ce souhait du malade pour prendre sa décision d'interrompre des traitements en fin de vie (II).

I. LES DIRECTIVES ANTICIPEES, FAUX MODE D'EXPRESSION DU CONSENTEMENT DU MOURANT

Au vu des dispositions légales, une personne peut donc, par anticipation, indiquer ses souhaits sur des traitements médicaux à venir. Le champ dans lequel cette volonté peut s'exprimer est *a priori* celui de la loi de 2005, à savoir celui énoncé dans l'intitulé de la loi, la fin de vie.[30] Mais le législateur a retenu une conception large de cette notion en visant la fin de vie *stricto sensu* (phase avancée ou terminale d'une maladie grave et incurable) et aussi des hypothèses où l'arrêt des traitements par le

---

[26] Article 4127–36 alinéa 3 CSPub.

[27] Article L 1111–4 alinéa 4 CSPub.

[28] Depuis la loi du 4 mars 2002, la hiérarchie des représentants du malade hors d'état de s'exprimer est inversée ; la personne de confiance semble passer en priorité. Gérard Mémeteau, *Cours de droit médical*, 3 éd., Etudes Hospitalières, Bordeaux, 2006, p. 318.

[29] Frédérique Dreyfuss-Netter, « La santé dans la jurisprudence dans la Cour de cassation », *Rapport annuel de la Cour de Cassation 2007*, La Documentation française, Paris, 2008, p. 66.

[30] Elie Alfandari et Philippe Pedrot, « La fin de vie et la loi du 22 avril 2005 », *Revue de droit sanitaire et social*, septembre 2005, n° 5, pp. 751–765. La loi vise les actes poursuivis par le médecin par une obstination déraisonnable (actes inutiles, disproportionnés ou n'ayant d'autre effet que le seul maintien artificiel de la vie), les soins palliatifs (article L 1110–5 alinéa 2 et 1110–10 CSPub), le soulagement de la douleur, et le refus de soins du malade (article L 1111–4 alinéa 2 et 1111–10 alinéa 1 CSPub : limitation, suspension ou arrêt de traitement).

médecin peut générer la fin de la vie de la personne.[31] Néanmoins, dans ce cadre général, les directives anticipées ont un champ plus restreint. D'abord, elles ne concernent que les situations où, en fin de vie, la personne sera hors d'état d'exprimer un consentement.[32] Ensuite, elles se limitent à indiquer les souhaits de la personne sur « les conditions de la limitation ou l'arrêt de traitement »[33] alors que la loi, elle, a un champ plus important notamment en abordant la question des soins palliatifs.[34] Les directives permettent ainsi au malade de limiter ou refuser (par anticipation[35]), toute intervention médicale,[36] voire tout traitement,[37] qui pourrait être entrepris à l'occasion de sa fin de vie. La loi n'a pas évoqué la possibilité pour le malade de se prononcer sur les actions positives du médecin, notamment sur le fait de soulager la souffrance[38] ou de bénéficier de soins palliatifs. En effet, les directives ne semblent pas avoir été aménagées pour exprimer l'accompagnement médical global dont le patient aimerait pouvoir bénéficier en fin de vie. Il est vrai qu'au vu des textes, le médecin ayant l'obligation de donner les soins les plus appropriés, de garantir les thérapeutiques que l'état de santé du malade requiert[39] et de sauvegarder la dignité du mourant en dispensant des soins palliatifs,[40] le malade n'a pas besoin de se prononcer sur ces actions. Pourtant, face au fossé existant bien souvent entre le droit et la réalité, notamment en matière de soins

---

[31] Article L 1111–4 alinéa 2 et alinéa 5 CSPub. Problème d'application de ces textes au refus de soin des témoins de Jéhovah afin de mettre un terme à la jurisprudence qui limite les effets du refus de soin (CAAdm Paris, 9 juin 1998, *Petites Affiches*, n° 81, 23 avril 1999, obs. Gérard Mémeteau ; CE ord. Référé 16 août 2002, *Recueil CE*, p. 309).

[32] La loi de 2005 est plus générale car aborde la fin de vie lorsque le malade peut émettre un consentement (article L1111–10 CSPub).

[33] Il est vrai que l'essentiel de la loi de 2005 porte sur les limitations ou arrêts de traitement.

[34] Si la loi se consacre essentiellement aux hypothèses où le médecin, confronté à une décision d'investigation, d'intervention ou de traitement du malade, peut décider de limiter ou d'interrompre ces actes, elle envisage aussi la prise en charge de la douleur.

[35] Les directives ne peuvent jouer un rôle que si elles ont été établies moins de trois ans avant l'état d'inconscience (article L 1111–11 alinéa 2 CSPub). Néanmoins, une confirmation de ces directives est possible (article R 1111–18 CSPub).

[36] A *posteriori*, les directives peuvent viser l'arrêt des traitements inutiles, disproportionnée ou n'ayant d'autre effet que le maintien artificiel de la vie même si l'utilité de prévoir de telles dispositions dans les directives est discutable puisque la loi incite le médecin à stopper ces traitements (article L 1110–5 alinéa 2 CSPub).

[37] La loi vise sans nul doute les traitements médicaux mais viserait aussi (à l'article L 1111–4 alinéa 2 CSPub) les traitements non médicaux (ventilation artificielle, hydratation, alimentation).

[38] Même si cela doit conduire à abréger sa vie.

[39] Article L 1110–5 alinéas 1 et 4 CSPub.

[40] Article L 1110–5 CSPub.

palliatifs ou de prise en charge de la douleur, il aurait pu être intéressant que le législateur offre aux personnes la possibilité d'exprimer leurs souhaits de bénéficier de ces prérogatives. L'idée de « droits des malades » inscrite dans l'intitulé de la loi de 2005 aurait d'ailleurs permis de justifier une telle possibilité.

La question essentielle est alors de savoir si ces directives anticipées traduisent (extériorisent) le consentement du malade (en l'occurrence son refus de soins)? Un certain nombre d'éléments pouvait le laisser penser.

En premier lieu, l'esprit de la loi de 2005 allait en ce sens. En effet, cette loi avait vocation à rassurer les personnes angoissées par la perspective de vieillir dans des conditions difficiles en subissant une douloureuse agonie ou une dégénérescence physique et mentale en leur permettant d'exprimer leur volonté sur la cessation de ces situations.[41]

En second lieu, la lecture de l'article 1111-11 CSPub instituant les directives anticipées mais surtout la place de ce texte dans une *Section du Code de la Santé Publique* relative à l' « *Expression de la volonté des malades en fin de vie* » incitaient à considérer que ces directives puissent constituer un mode d'expression du consentement du malade comme l'y invite l'article 9 de la Convention européenne de biomédecine du 4 avril 1997.[42]

En troisième lieu, face à la volonté affichée du législateur en 2005 de renforcer l'autonomie du patient (le médecin a l'obligation de respecter la volonté du malade de refuser ou d'interrompre « tout traitement » au risque de mettre sa vie en danger), les directives anticipées étaient l'occasion d'offrir, par anticipation, cette possibilité à toute personne.

En quatrième et dernier lieu, dans le contexte actuel qui tend à appréhender le formalisme comme modalité de protection du consentement,[43] le fait que le législateur ait prévu que les directives anticipées fassent l'objet d'un écrit[44] pouvait corroborer l'idée de l'expression d'un consentement du malade.

---

[41] Raoul-Cormeil, *supra* note 1.

[42] Ce texte invite les Etats à tenir compte de ces directives.

[43] Jacques Flour, « Quelques remarques sur l'évolution du formalisme », in *Le droit privé français au milieu du XXe siècle – Études offertes à Georges Ripert*, LGDJ, Paris, 1950, t. 1, pp. 93–114.

[44] L'article R 1111–17 CSPub indique les formalités : écrit daté et signé par leur auteur identifié par ses nom, prénoms, date et lieu de naissance. Néanmoins, la rédaction d'un écrit n'est pas obligatoire. Les directives peuvent être énoncées par tout autre moyen d'expression attesté par des témoins (article R 1111–17 alinéa 2 CSPub).

Pourtant, la portée conférée par la loi aux directives anticipées infirme cette théorie. En utilisant le terme de « souhaits » de la personne, le législateur a entendu exclure l'expression d'une volonté génératrice de conséquences juridiques, c'est-à-dire toute référence à un acte juridique. L'anticipation est certainement un des facteurs essentiels ayant conduit à limiter la portée des directives. Ce qu'une personne peut souhaiter un jour ne correspondra pas nécessairement à ce qu'elle souhaitera effectivement le moment venu.[45] La distinction entre un consentement émis au moment de la fin de vie (au présent) et celui émis dans une période antérieure[46] est effectivement importante et peut expliquer le choix législatif. Le caractère anticipé constitue la faiblesse des directives. Pourtant, le législateur a admis dans d'autres situations la possibilité d'exprimer par anticipation une volonté génératrice d'effets juridiques. Le testament en est une des meilleures illustrations.[47] Néanmoins, en prévoyant dans la loi de 2005 que le médecin a pour seule obligation, dans un certain nombre d'hypothèses,[48] de consulter ces directives et en ne lui imposant pas de les suivre, le législateur a voulu écarter un certain nombre de qualifications juridiques.

Les directives ne constituent pas un mode d'extériorisation du consentement du malade à l'acte de soins (ici, son refus de soins). En effet, si le consentement est une condition de validité du contrat médical,[49] le refus d'un tel consentement empêche la formation de ce contrat et, de ce fait, interdit au médecin d'agir. Or, les directives anticipées ne peuvent être conçus comme un élément d'extériorisation de la volonté du malade de refuser des soins (à travers un écrit) puisque qu'elles ne s'imposent pas au médecin.[50] De même, l'objet d'un contrat s'imposant aux parties à la

---

[45] Ce qui est particulièrement vrai pour la question de l'arrêt ou de la limitation des soins en fin de vie, voir infra. Dreifuss-Netter, *supra* note 1.

[46] Antériorité pouvant aller jusqu'à trois ans (voir davantage si les directives ont été confirmées). Article R 1111–18 CSPub.

[47] Sur la possibilité de prévoir même des dispositions extra-patrimoniales dans le testament, voir Michel Grimaldi, « Les dernières volontés », in J. Beauchard et P. Couvrat (dir.), *Ecrits en hommage à Gérard Cornu*, PUF, Paris, 1994, p. 177 ss., p. 185.

[48] Lorsque le patient est hors d'état de consentir, la loi autorise le médecin à arrêter des traitements après recours à une procédure collégiale et consultation de la personne de confiance ou de la famille ou, à défaut, d'un de ses proches « et, le cas échéant, des directives anticipées » (article L 1111–4 alinéa 5 et L 1111–13 CSPub).

[49] Dans le cadre de la relation médicale, le médecin ne peut accomplir ses obligations (faire un diagnostic en procédant notamment à des examens, traiter le patient) que si les conditions de validité du contrat médical sont respectées et principalement celle relative au consentement du malade.

[50] La référence à une simple consultation et le fait que cette consultation soit au même niveau que celle des proches excluent l'idée d'expression du consentement du malade qui, elle, exigerait la soumission du médecin.

convention, les directives anticipées ne peuvent être considérées comme définissant l'objet de la prestation[51] du médecin[52] puisqu'elles ne sont pas obligatoires.

Ces directives ne peuvent également être qualifiées d'offre de contracter (offre de « ne pas faire » faite au médecin) car la rencontre de cette offre avec l'acceptation du praticien lierait ce dernier. D'une manière générale, les directives ne peuvent être considérées comme un acte juridique unilatéral,[53] comme l'est le testament,[54] car aucune conséquence juridique ne s'attache à elles ou comme un acte abdictif par lequel son auteur renoncerait à quelque chose.[55]

En conclusion, ces directives ne constituent qu'un indice de consentement c'est-à-dire un élément de fait indiquant avec probabilité la vision que la personne pourrait avoir, au moment de sa fin de vie, d'un éventuel arrêt de traitement. Elles ne sont qu'un moyen de porter à la connaissance du médecin ce que le malade pensait à un moment donné (date des directives) sur l'arrêt de traitements en fin de vie. A travers les directives anticipées, le malade peut simplement *tester*, au sens de témoigner,[56] de sa perception d'une fin de vie médicalisée au moment où il s'exprime. Cet indice de consentement ne prouve pas la volonté que la personne aurait en fin de vie mais ne constitue qu'un adminicule. La portée de ces directives est faible car se limite à une influence éventuelle sur la décision médicale.

II. Les directives anticipees, aide facultative a la decision medicale d'arret de traitement

Les directives anticipées portent sur les arrêts de traitement en fin de vie. Elles concernent donc concrètement les hypothèses qualifiées antérieurement à la loi de 2005 *d'euthanasie passive*.[57] En effet, cette appellation

---

[51] L'objet du contrat est de soigner, l'objet de la prestation du médecin est ce à quoi il s'engage pour réaliser son obligation de soin.

[52] En l'occurrence, l'obligation du médecin de ne pas faire (limiter ou arrêter les traitements).

[53] Emmanuel Putman, « Le testament de vie est désormais réglementé », *Revue juridique personnes et famille*, mai 2006, n° 5, pp. 10–11.

[54] Ibid.

[55] Yvaine Buffelan-Lanore et Virginie Larribeau-Terneyre, *Droit civil. Les obligations*, 11 éd., Sirey, Paris, 2008, p. 231.

[56] Voir dictionnaire Larousse.

[57] Sur le passage à une *euthanasie active*, voir José Coelho, « Droits des malades et fin de vie : une passerelle législative vers l'euthanasie indirecte à la morphine », *Gazette du Palais*, 23 mars 2006, n° 82, p. 13.

recouvrait les cas où le médecin n'entreprenait pas ou arrêtait des traitements en fin de vie. Or, avant 2005, le médecin qui agissait ainsi tombait
sous le coup de la loi pénale de *non assistance à personne en danger*[58] car
son obligation de soigner ne cessait pas en fin de vie. La loi *Léonetti* a
entendu légaliser ces hypothèses *d'euthanasie passive* en introduisant la
permission pour le médecin de limiter ou d'arrêter des traitements et en
écartant, par voie de conséquence, une éventuelle condamnation pour
ces omissions. Dans le cadre de la législation actuelle, le praticien qui respecte les conditions légales pour arrêter un traitement[59] se retrouve désormais couvert par le fait justificatif de la *permission de la loi* prévue à l'article
122-4 du code pénal.[60] C'est là un apport majeur de la loi de 2005, apport
qui permet de s'interroger sur l'intitulé de la loi qui se réfère aux droits du
malade alors que ce texte aménage les pouvoirs du médecin en fin de vie
du patient.[61]

Cette idée de permission légale du médecin d'interrompre des traitements accentue le caractère limité de la portée des directives anticipées.
La loi autorise le médecin à décider sous la seule réserve du respect d'une
procédure collégiale, de la consultation de tiers[62] et « le cas échéant » des
directives anticipées.[63] La consultation est obligatoire mais il ne s'agit que
d'une simple action de prendre avis qui ne lie pas le médecin. Ainsi, les
directives ne jouent aucun rôle dans la permission donnée au médecin
qui résulte de la seule loi. Elles n'apportent rien à cette autorisation
mais peuvent simplement la conforter en pratique. Ainsi, les directives
anticipées ne peuvent constituer, comme cela est le cas dans de nombreux

---

[58] Poursuites pénales pour défaut d'assistance à personne en péril (article 223–6 alinéa
2 CPen), voir pour homicide volontaire : Cass. Crim., 23 mars 1953, *Recueil Dalloz*, 1953,
p. 371 ; Cass. Crim., 14 novembre 1989, *Gazette du Palais*, 1990, II, p. 571.

[59] La décision motivée du médecin est inscrite dans le dossier médical du patient.

[60] Le fait justificatif neutralise l'élément légal de l'infraction pénale. Jean Pradel, « La
Parque assistée par le droit. Apport de la loi du 22 avril 2005 relative aux droits des malades
et à la fin de vie », *Recueil Dalloz*, 2005, pp. 2106–2113 ; Annick Batteur, Agnès Cerf et Gilles
Raoul-Cormeil, « La mort, le malade et le médecin », *Revue Lamy Droit Civil*, 2005/19, n°
804, pp. 53–64.

[61] L'intitulé de la loi de 2005 (relative aux droits des malades et à la fin de vie) met en
avant les droits du patient alors que ce texte est principalement favorable aux médecins
qui ne pourront plus être condamnés pour non assistance à personne en péril. Sophie
Hocquet-Berg, « Le texte sur la fin de vie : un loi pour les malades ou...pour les médecins ? », *Responsabilité civile et assurances*, mai 2005, n° 5, alerte 47.

[62] La personne de confiance ou la famille et les proches, selon les hypothèses.

[63] Si, dans l'hypothèse de la fin de vie, les directives sont placées au premier rang aux
côtés de l'opinion de la personne de confiance (article L 1111–12 CSPub), dans l'hypothèse
où l'arrêt du traitement est susceptible de mettre la vie du malade en danger, les directives
sont mises au même niveau que l'avis de la personne de confiance mais aussi de la famille
ou des proches (article L 1111–4 alinéa 5 CSPub).

pays et depuis leur origine,[64] un mode de preuve de l'autorisation du patient à l'arrêt de traitement.[65] Même si les débats parlementaires de la loi de 2005 ont montré que le législateur souhaitait autant assurer la sécurité juridique du médecin[66] que l'intérêt du patient, la faible portée donnée aux directives contredit cette tendance.

En fait, ces directives ne constituent qu'un élément qui pourra être consulté par le médecin s'il envisage un arrêt de traitement. A ce titre, ces directives ne portent pas atteinte au principe d'indisponibilité du corps humain car elles ne donnent pas pouvoir à une personne de disposer de sa vie.[67]

Seule la consultation de ces directives est imposée au médecin. Le praticien amené à intervenir en fin de vie a l'obligation de s'enquérir de l'existence de ces directives.[68] Pour faciliter cette connaissance, les textes envisagent une conservation de ces documents par le médecin,[69] laissant néanmoins la possibilité au malade de recourir à une conservation hors du champ médical.[70]

Mais alors quel est l'intérêt de telles directives ? Juridiquement, parce qu'elles ne constituent pas une condition de la permission d'agir donnée au médecin, elles n'ont aucune autorité sur la décision d'arrêt de traitement prise par le médecin et ceci malgré la référence *aux droits du malade* dans l'intitulé de la loi de 2005 qui pouvait pourtant laisser croire

---

[64] A l'origine, les directives anticipées ont été créées pour servir de preuve au médecin. Véronica San Julian Puig, « Les directives anticipées en France et en Espagne », *Revue de droit sanitaire et social*, 2007, pp. 86–96.

[65] L'origine des directives anticipées se trouve aux Etats-Unis ou, si le malade était libre de refuser certains traitements s'il se trouvait en phase terminale, les médecins avaient besoin d'une garantie pour ne pas être accusés d'omission au cas où ils ne mettaient pas en œuvre tous les moyens à leur disposition. Voir San Julian Puig, précité. Etude de législation comparée du Sénat sur l'euthanasie, n° 109, 17 juillet 2002. Hugues Letellier et Christine Lichtenberger, « Testament de fin de vie et droit international », *Gazette du Palais*, 23 septembre 2005, n° 266, pp. 7–8.

[66] Rapport *Léonetti*, t. II, précité, *Journal Officiel Assemblée Nationale*, 30 juin 2004, n° 19–29, p. 5.

[67] Sur l'introduction récente en droit français du droit d'une personne d'en mandater une autre, voir la loi du 5 mars 2007 portant réforme de la protection juridique des majeurs qui introduit le mandat de protection future.

[68] Article R 1111–20 CSPub.

[69] L'article R 1111–19 alinéa 1 CSPub prévoit la conservation de ces directives par « le médecin appelé à prendre une décision de limitation ou d'arrêt de traitement » ou par tout médecin dont le médecin traitant qui joue, en pratique, un rôle important avec le malade.

[70] Par le patient lui-même, la personne de confiance, la famille ou les proches (article R 1111–19 alinéa 3 CSPub). Dans ces hypothèses, les textes prévoient le placement des coordonnées de la personne détentrice dans le dossier du médecin de ville ou dans le dossier médical. Sur la signalisation de l'existence de ces directives en cas d'hospitalisation, voir article R 1111–19 alinéa 4 CSPub, article R 1111–2 CSPub.

à l'existence d'une certaine portée juridique. Reste alors la portée réelle, celle inscrite dans la réalité de la pratique médicale ? Les directives ne sont que des *souhaits* dont la portée sera celle que le médecin voudra lui conférer. Le praticien peut ne pas en tenir compte car les directives sont laissées à son entière discrétion et ne le lient pas. La loi de 2005 n'a donc pas prévu le règlement des conflits entre le médecin et le patient ou son représentant au cas où le praticien ne suivrait pas ces directives.[71]

Mais ces directives ont une portée identique aux avis de la personne de confiance, de la famille, des proches lorsque cette consultation est prévue par les textes ou à la décision motivée de l'équipe de soin à la suite de la procédure collégiale imposée au médecin.[72] Ainsi, lorsque la personne est hors d'état d'exprimer son consentement, le médecin peut donc être le seul à décider de l'arrêt de traitement. Le malade a son mot à dire, mais ce n'est qu'un mot[73]... Face à la difficulté pour de nombreux médecins de se détacher encore aujourd'hui d'un certain paternalisme médical et surtout face à la méconnaissance de la loi de 2005,[74] il y a lieu de penser que l'importance donnée aux directives restera infime en pratique.

Il est vrai que la valeur à accorder aux souhaits exprimés par anticipation par un malade est discutable. En effet, que représente la volonté exprimée par un *bien portant* sur une situation future méconnue (sa fin de vie) ? Elle ne peut être assimilée avec certitude à la volonté de cette même personne au moment de la réalisation de cette situation. En effet, la fluctuation de la volonté du malade en fin de vie au gré des jours, voire des heures, montre la difficulté de tenir compte d'un consentement donné des mois, voir des années, avant la situation de fin de vie. Ceci d'autant plus que cette volonté aura été exprimée, en général, sans qu'une information complète sur les possibilités d'accompagnement des fins de vie (par la médecine, par les centres de soins palliatifs...)[75] ait été donnée. L'anticipation[76] et surtout le contexte dans lequel les directives auront été adoptées (par une personne *bien portante* incapable de pouvoir réellement se projeter dans une situation de fin de vie ou par une personne déjà malade qui, du fait de son état, risque d'être sous l'emprise de contraintes

---

[71] L'hypothèse sera rare en pratique car elle visera celle où le médecin décide de ne pas interrompre un traitement alors que le malade se serait prononcé en ce sens.
[72] Article R 4127–37 CSPub.
[73] Putman, *supra* note 53.
[74] Néanmoins, le défaut de consultation pourrait être sanctionnée juridiquement.
[75] Le décret a introduit la possibilité pour le malade de solliciter son médecin pour qu'il joigne « une attestation constatant qu'il est libre d'exprimer sa volonté et qu'il a délivré toutes informations appropriées » (article R 1111–17 alinéa 2 CSPub).
[76] Voir *supra*.

économiques ou psychologiques viciant son consentement) militent en faveur d'une portée limitée reconnue à ces directives.

Néanmoins, malgré ces considérations, les directives ne constituent-elles pas une trace importante de l'avis de la personne ? Qui peut mieux que cette personne savoir ce qui sera le mieux pour elle ? Les directives anticipées constituent une trace de la volonté sur le *sort de soi*. De plus, le législateur français en consacrant le mandat de protection future, permettant à tout individu pour le cas où il se trouverait dans l'impossibilité d'exprimer un consentement, de désigner un mandataire pouvant le représenter pour les actes de sa vie personnelle,[77] semble favorable à ce qu'une personne puisse, par anticipation, organiser sa vulnérabilité future.[78] Si malgré ces considérations, la société considère que les risques liées aux directives supplantent les aspects positifs, la voie à emprunter ne semble pas être celle adoptée par le législateur en 2005. En effet, sauf à retomber dans le paternalisme médical et à nier l'évolution favorable à la représentation du malade par un tiers désigné,[79] il paraît difficile de reconnaître au seul médecin le pouvoir de décider de l'arrêt des traitements. De même, face aux dangers de confier à une seule personne, même choisie par le malade, cette prérogative, la voie la plus satisfaisante n'est-elle pas celle d'une décision médicale collégiale[80] ? Le législateur français l'a perçu en imposant au médecin le respect d'une procédure collégiale mais il s'est arrêté en chemin en n'imposant pas l'avis motivé adopté à l'occasion de cette procédure et en n'associant pas la personne de confiance à cette décision. Néanmoins, reste à espérer que l'esprit de la loi, qui est bien d'aller vers ce type de décision collégiale d'arrêt de traitement (puisque le texte vise une pluralité d'acteurs : le médecin, une équipe de soin, la personne de confiance et le malade dont un signe de volonté est inscrit dans les directives anticipées), l'emportera à terme sur la lettre de cette loi qui, elle, reste très empreinte du principe de bienfaisance des médecins à l'égard des personnes hors d'état d'exprimer leur consentement...

---

[77] Christilla Glasson, « Le mandat de protection future : des dispositions conventionnelles pour la fin de vie », *Revue de droit sanitaire et social*, septembre 2009, n° 5, pp. 890–902.

[78] Clémentine Lequillerier, « Le mandat de protection future et la personne de confiance : vers une consécration d'un consentement substitué en matière médicale ? », *Gazette du Palais*, 7 juin 2007, n° 158, p. 32.

[79] En instituant le mandat de protection future (article 477 CCiv), la loi de 2007 sur la protection des majeurs va en ce sens. Elle prévoit même que la personne désignée dans ce mandat peut assumer le rôle de personne de confiance (article 479 CCiv).

[80] Alliant, par exemple, la personne de confiance (si une telle personne a été désignée) et un collège pluridisciplinaire.

THE LEGAL AND ETHICAL DIMENSIONS OF END-OF-LIFE DECISION-MAKING IN CONTEMPORARY IRELAND

*Patrick Hanafin**

La mort, ou la mort choisie, est la forme ultime de l'insoumission.[1]

I. Introduction

In Ireland there currently exists no legislation governing advance directives despite a decision of the Supreme Court in 1995 which upheld the constitutionality of the right to refuse life sustaining treatment (artificial nutrition and hydration). Since then successive Governments have failed to introduce a detailed legislative framework to govern this area of medical practice. This has occurred despite recent recommendations for such legislation by both the Irish Law Reform Commission in its Report on *Bioethics: Advance Care Directives*[2] and the Irish Council for Bioethics.[3] Such a reluctance on the part of the legislature to introduce a statutory framework for advance directives reflects the tension which continues to exist in Ireland between a traditionalist Roman Catholic model of bioethics, informed by Thomist Natural Law principles and a more secular model of bioethics which is informed by a more pluralist model of bioethics.

II. Death, Bioethics and Medicine in Irish Society

In the discourse of medicine in postcolonial Ireland which was influenced by the dominant discourse of the Roman Catholic Church, the body was a site to be regulated.[4] Moreover, the imbrication of Roman Catholic

---

* Professor of Law, Birkbeck Law School, University of London, UK; email: p.hanafin@bbk.ac.uk.

[1] Etienne Balibar, "Blanchot l'insoumis", in M. Antelme *et al.* (eds.), *Blanchot dans son siècle* (Paris, 2009), pp. 289–314, p. 306.

[2] Law Reform Commission, *Report: Bioethics: Advance Care Directives* (LRC 94–2009), (Dublin, 2009).

[3] Irish Council for Bioethics, *Is It Time For Healthcare Directives?* (Dublin, 2007).

[4] See further, Tom Inglis, "Foucault, Bourdieu and the Field of Irish Sexuality", 7 *Irish Journal of Sociology* (1997), pp. 5–28, pp. 19–20, where he notes that the language of

S. Negri (ed.), *Self-Determination, Dignity and End-of-Life Care*
2011 Koninklijke Brill NV. Printed in The Netherlands. ISBN 978 90 04 22357 8. pp. 209–220

natural law theory into the legal discourse of postcolonial Ireland marked
law as a means of purifying the threatening otherness of those who did not
conform to the social code. The Constitution, the so-called arbiter of individual rights was in the early postcolonial period a document which
upheld this conservative Roman Catholic social code.[5] Until recently the
medical profession did not support the introduction of a liberal model of
treatment withdrawal. Such a conservative approach was not challenged
by governments which did not want to subvert the presumed traditionalist majority attitude to treatment withdrawal. Instead of attempting to
gain community consensus on this issue (as well as many other bioethical
issues), and working towards a solution which expresses the values of all
sectors of society, governments have tended to see such matters in very
simplistic terms, either they are morally supportable or morally suspect.
In all this the so-called secular Irish State's ethical guide has been until
recently the Roman Catholic Church. However, in recent years one has
begun to see the emergence of a more deliberative model on bioethics
with the establishment of the Irish Council for Bioethics, liberal interventions on the part of the courts, and active calls for balanced regulation by
the Law Reform Commission, as well as a more liberal approach by the
Irish Medical Council (the professional regulatory body for medical professionals). These developments signal the beginnings of a different thinking on bioethical issues in contemporary Ireland.

III. THE EVOLVING JURISPRUDENCE ON END-OF-LIFE DECISION-MAKING

In the case of *Re A Ward of Court*,[6] the Irish Supreme Court encountered,
for the first time, a case involving the right of a chronically ill patient
to die. The person behind the appellation, Ward of Court, was a forty-five
year old woman who at the age of twenty-two suffered irreversible brain
damage during a minor surgical procedure under general anaesthetic.
This left her in a near persistent vegetative state. She was kept alive since
this incident by means of artificial hydration and nutrition. The patient
was unable to communicate. She had minimal capacity to recognise

---

medicine in the opening decades of the newly independent Irish state was not very
different from that of the Roman Catholic Church and in most cases supported and reproduced it.
    [5] See further Patrick Hanafin, *Constituting Identity: Political Identity Formation and the
Constitution in Post-Independence Ireland* (Basingstoke, 2001).
    [6] [1995] 2 ILRM 401.

nursing staff and to react to strangers by showing signs of distress. She was able to follow people with her eyes in a reflex manner. Her family was of the opinion that it was in her 'best interests' that she be allowed to die naturally. However, the institution in which the Ward was resident was under the control of a Roman Catholic nursing order which objected to the withdrawal of artificial nutrition and hydration, claiming that it was contrary to its ethical code. In the High Court the invisibility of this particular patient was encapsulated in the judge's conclusion that the courts in such cases should 'approach the matter from the standpoint of a prudent, good and loving parent in deciding what course should be adopted'.[7] This model would lead in this case to the patient being allowed to have their treatment withdrawn and to be allowed to die. Yet despite this outcome, the model was an overtly paternalistic one which did not allow true autonomy for the patient but merely allowed the family's wishes to be respected in this case. There still remained a lacuna in such cases which could only be filled by the introduction of legislation which would allow individuals to make anticipatory decisions in relation to healthcare including in relation to treatment withdrawal should they ever be in a situation like that of the individual in the *Ward of Court* case.

The High Court decision in this case was appealed to the Supreme Court by the Attorney General, the institution, and the guardian *ad litem* on behalf of the ward. In the Supreme Court the order of Justice Lynch in the High Court was upheld. While favouring Justice Lynch's order, the Supreme Court tended more to applying a discrete 'best interests' test rather than the hybrid 'prudent parent' test favoured by Justice Lynch. However, one must ask the question to what extent are the 'best interests' of the 'best interests' test those of the patient in such cases? The law, no matter how patient-centred its approach appears, can never divine the patient's desires. The patient in this process becomes a mere problem to be solved using the extant tools of the common law. The application of the 'best interests' test in such cases demonstrates the absurd nature of law's attempt to maintain some semblance of control over the dying process. These tests, developed in an age where the interests of the individual were far from paramount, gave the impression of justice where in fact what was being decided was the redistribution of an 'incompetent' person's wealth.[8] Today we use the term 'best interests' to cover a multitude of gaps in the

---

[7] [1995] 2 ILRM 401, p. 419.
[8] Louise Harmon, "Falling off the Vine: Legal Fictions and the Doctrine of Substituted Judgement", 110 *Yale Law Journal* (1990), pp. 1–71.

common law. Louise Harmon has expressed eloquently the difficulties in applying extant common law tests to the patient in a persistent vegetative state:

> common law would not have a name for the [PVS patient]. Certainly she was not an idiot. While her condition was now static, she had not come into the world with a deficient mental apparatus... neither was she a lunatic. Although she had once been competent, there was no waxing and waning of her intellect. Indeed there was no longer any intellect at all. [Her] deficit was more profound than the lunatic's. His was a failure of reason alone; hers was a failure of consciousness... the persistence of her lower brain function and the presence of her warm body made her not dead, not alive, not an idiot, not a lunatic. There was a lacuna in the language of the law, so she was thrown into a general class of incompetents. There was no fine-tuning as to who was in that class—just individuals who were presently incompetent, regardless of how they came to be that way.[9]

The Irish Supreme Court like numerous other courts in the common law world was complicit in the 'best interests' fiction by stating the principle that treatment could be discontinued in such a case if it was in the 'best interests' of the patient so to do.

The best interests test assumes that the interests of the patient necessarily coincide with those of the medical and legal professions. However, as Martha Minow has observed:

> To speak of 'best interests' also veils the very present risk that the decision will fall short of its name. For this reason, some scholars have advocated replacing the term... with the phrase 'least detrimental alternative'. This phrase may at least humble the decision-maker with the recognition that any [patient] in need of such a determination is already far from his or her best interests.[10]

The fact that the court acknowledges that it is in the best interests of the patient to have treatment withdrawn in such cases is not necessarily determinative of a happy ending to the story. The reality of death from treatment withdrawal falls more readily into Minow's notion of the 'least detrimental alternative' or as Margaret Pabst Battin terms it 'the least worst death'.[11] These objections notwithstanding, in Ireland decision-making in such cases is still not in the hands of the patient as the

---

⁹ Ibid., pp. 37–38.
¹⁰ Martha Minow, *Making All the Difference: Inclusion, Exclusion and American Law* (Ithaca, 1990), p. 325.
¹¹ Margaret Pabst Battin, *The Least Worst Death: Essays in Bioethics on the End of Life* (New York, 1994), p. 35.

legislature has not yet introduced the legislative framework necessary for the legal recognition of end-of-life advance directives. As such decision-making in the case of a conflict between a medical institution and a comatose patient's next-of-kin would need to be referred to the courts for decision.

IV. Recommendations for Legislative Change

In the light of this lacuna in the law on advance directives, the Irish Law Reform Commission initiated a process of consultation on the issue in 2008 and produced a Report in 2009. The Commission has recommended that an "appropriate legislative framework should be enacted for advance care directives"[12] and that this should form part of the anticipated reform of Irish mental capacity law.[13] In its 2009 Report the Law Reform Commission recommended that what it termed an "advance care directive"[14] be given formal legislative recognition. The term "advance care directive" rather than the term "advance directive" was preferred by the Law Reform Commission because: "the term 'advance directive' might not fully express the health care context within which the expression of wishes arises".[15] As such the Commission concluded that: "having regard to the wider care setting within which the expression of wishes may arise, such as a hospice care context, the term 'advance care directive' appears to be the most suitable term to use".[16] The Commission recommended that an "advance care directive" be defined for the purposes of such legislation as:

> the expression of instructions or wishes by a person of 18 years with capacity to do so that if... at a later time and in such circumstances as he or she may specify, a specified treatment is proposed to be carried out or continued by a person providing health care for him or her, and... at that time he or she lacks capacity to consent to the carrying out or continuation of the treatment, the specified treatment is not to be carried out or continued.[17]

---

[12] Law Reform Commission, *Report: Bioethics: Advance Care Directives, supra* note 2, p. 101.

[13] In 2008 the Irish Government published a draft legislative model on the law on Mental Capacity in the form of the *Scheme of Mental Capacity Bill 2008*, available at www.justice.ie.

[14] Law Reform Commission, *Report: Bioethics: Advance Care Directives, supra* note 2, p. 3.

[15] Ibid., p. 3.

[16] Id.

[17] Ibid., paragraph 1.82.

The Commission also recommended that a health care proxy could be appointed under the terms of an advance care directive.[18] In the Report the Law Reform Commission noted that "basic care", defined as including but not limited to "warmth, shelter, oral nutrition and hydration and hygiene measures" cannot be refused.[19] This provision could, without more, effectively block a patient's wish to have artificial nutrition and hydration removed in a situation like that in the *Ward of Court* case. However, the Report also recommended that an advance care directive could include a refusal of life-sustaining treatment, defined as "treatment which is intended to sustain or prolong life and that supplants or maintains the operation of vital bodily functions that are incapable of independent operation".[20] This might on first appearance prove to contradict the prohibition on refusal of basic care recommended by the Law Reform Commission. However, the Report provides for the elaboration of a detailed Code of Practice on Advance Care Directives which would, *inter alia*, "provide guidance on the circumstances in which artificial nutrition and hydration (ANH) may be considered to be basic care and, as the case may be, artificial life-sustaining treatment. In deciding whether ANH is basic care or artificial life-sustaining treatment, the decision should be based on the health care professional's judgment only".[21] The Commission did consider that such a distinction could not be the subject of a general legislative definition but would need to be determined in the context of the specific context of each individual case. Thus, it noted that:

> Where there is no possibility of recovery or where the administration of ANH would be considered invasive and providing no real improvement to the patient ANH would be considered artificial life-sustaining treatment. In such a case, ANH is not about improving a person's condition, but merely sustaining their life artificially.[22]

The proposed legislation would thus, *prima facie*, allow for a patient in a condition similar to that of the patient in the *Ward of Court* case to legitimately refuse the continuation of artificial nutrition and hydration, while competent, in an advance care directive, and to have that wish honoured. Such an outcome would of course be contingent on whether the professional bodies governing the health care profession did not object on the

---

[18] Ibid., paragraph 2.31.
[19] Ibid., paragraph 3.09.
[20] Ibid., paragraph 3.18.
[21] Ibid., paragraph 3.27.
[22] Ibid., paragraph 3.24.

grounds of conscience to such an intervention. There has existed in the past in Ireland an antipathy on the part of professional bodies in the health care context towards intervening in such situations. In the next section I examine the extent to which such opposition may still constitute an obstacle to the functioning of such proposed legislation.

V. The Medical Profession and Advance Directives

In the aftermath of the Supreme Court's decision in *Re A Ward of Court* pro-life interest groups reacted by stating that this was an unacceptable erosion of the principle of the sanctity of life. In the rhetoric of those who opposed the decision, treatment withdrawal, even in cases where the patient is in a persistent vegetative state, was seen as a species of unjustifiable killing which threatened the notion of the sanctity of life in the religious and medical contexts. The patient who has expressed a wish to have treatment withdrawn represents a threat to those groups vision of national identity steeped as it is in notions of a pure, Roman Catholic self. This highlights Chris Shilling's assertion that 'the body is ... a metaphor of society as a whole ... when national ... identities are threatened, there is likely to be a concern with the maintenance of existing bodily boundaries and the purity of bodies'.[23] Such a conservative view was also proffered by the professional bodies representing health care professions in the State in response to the Supreme Court's decision in *Re A Ward of Court*. In statements issued in the wake of the Supreme Court's decision both the Irish Medical Council and the Irish Nursing Board were of the view that it was not ethical for a doctor or a nurse to withdraw artificial hydration or nutrition from a patient who is not dying. The Medical Council issued the following statement in the wake of the Supreme Court decision:

> It is the view of the Council that access to nutrition and hydration is one of the basic needs of human beings. This remains so even when, from time to time, this need can only be fulfilled by means of long established methods such as naso-gastric and gastronomy tube feeding.[24]

In the statement issued by the Medical Council in response to the Supreme Court's decision on treatment withdrawal, the Council, by quoting selectively from the then latest version of its *Guide to Ethical Conduct and*

---

[23] Chris Shilling, *The Body and Social Theory* (London, 1993), p. 73.
[24] Irish Medical Council, Statement of the Council after their Statutory Meeting on 4th August, 1995 (Dublin, 1995).

Behaviour and to Fitness to Practise criticised implicitly the stance taken
by the Supreme Court. Thus, the inclusion in the statement of the following paragraph from the ethical guidelines can only be seen as a veiled
attack on the Supreme Court's decision:

> Medical care must not be used as a tool of the State to be granted or with-
> held or altered in character under political pressure.[25]

This position was reiterated by the Medical Council when it updated its
ethical guidelines in 1998. In its revised guidelines on treatment withdrawal it observed:

> For the seriously ill patient who is unable to communicate or understand, it
> is desirable that the doctor discusses management with the next of kin or
> the legal guardians prior to reaching a decision about the use or non-use of
> treatments which will not contribute to recovery from the primary illness.
> The Council reiterates its view that access to nutrition and hydration remain
> one of the basic needs of human beings, and all reasonable and practical
> efforts should be made to maintain both of them.[26]

This ethical injunction was sufficiently widely drawn in the first sentence
to allow for the respecting a patient's previously made decisions about
healthcare, yet in the second sentence the Council adds a dogmatic statement about the need to maintain nutrition and hydration which is a direct
reference to its 1995 reaction to the *Ward of Court* decision. This would
appear to oppose an individual's previously expressed wishes being
respected. This statement of principle falls short of the detailed practical
guidance required in such cases. Such signalling of ethical disapproval is
not acceptable when faced with the complex issues of fact and law raised
by this aspect of medical treatment.

However, the hardline stance of the Medical Council has begun to
change since 1998. It has now begun to move towards a more liberal attitude to the question of treatment withdrawal. Following an increased
critical self-reflection on the question of advance care directives together
with the calls for legislation on the issue from the Irish Law Reform
Commission and the Irish Council for Bioethics, the Medical Council has
moved to a less dogmatic position. In the latest edition of its ethical guidelines produced in 2009 the Council makes explicit reference to advance
healthcare planning and states at paragraph 41.1 that:

---

[25] Ibid., citing Irish Medical Council, *A Guide to Ethical Conduct and to Fitness to Practise*
(Dublin, 1994), para. 12.05.
[26] Irish Medical Council, *A Guide to Ethical Conduct and Behaviour* (Dublin, 1998), p. 38.

Sometimes patients might want to plan for their medical treatment in the event that they become incapacitated in the future. This might include an advance refusal of medical treatment and/or a request for a specific procedure. However, you are not obliged to provide treatment that is not clinically indicated for a particular patient.[27]

Moreover in paragraph 41.2 the Council states:

An advance treatment plan has the same ethical status as a decision by a patient at the actual time of an illness and should be respected on condition that:
- the decision was an informed choice...
- the decision covers the situation that has arisen, and
- the patient has not changed their mind.[28]

This reflects a transformation in thinking on this issue and would appear to see the Medical Council expressing approval for legislation in relation to advance care directives. In this regard we can see how the initial antipathy towards this particular development has been dispelled either through a change in the culture of thinking of the medical elite or a gradual acceptance that a dogmatic religious stance on bioethical issues is no longer acceptable in an increasingly pluralist and ethically diverse society.

VI. Conclusion: Societal Change and the Right to Die

The recent move in Ireland towards an acceptance of a more liberal regulatory framework in the area of anticipatory decision-making in the health-care context could be explained in terms of political theorist William Connolly's discussion of the gradual transformation of societal attitudes and policies on contentious social issues such as, for example, the right to die.[29] Connolly argues that such new rights cannot be created by a top-down 'molarpolitics of public officials',[30] but comes instead from a mobilisation of self-styling selves, 'the molecular movements of micropolitics'.[31] Speaking of the particular case of assisted suicide, Connolly demonstrates the agonistic relationship between what he terms the "micropolitics" of movements of individuals who are attempting to lobby for

---

[27] Irish Medical Council, *Guide To Professional Conduct And Ethics For Registered Medical Practitioners*, (7th ed., Dublin, 2009), p. 39.
[28] Ibid.
[29] William Connolly, *Why I Am Not A Secularist* (Minneapolis, 1999), p. 147.
[30] Ibid., p. 149.
[31] Id.

change on the right to die and public officials, in the form of judges, who attempt to maintain the *status quo* and prevent the creation of this new right. In this agonistic exchange lies the beginning of an elaboration of a new way of thinking on this issue.

Connolly compares this wider collective conflict with the internal conflict faced by individuals who try to work out a position on a contentious social issue in the form of self-artistry or working on the self. An individual in working out their position on controversial ethical issues such as the right to die is confronted with differing sympathies and values. In coming to decide, one is confronted with differing views both outside and within oneself. Connolly gives the example of an individual who believes that death must only come when either God or nature brings it. This person is shocked by movements which call for a right to doctor-assisted death for those in severe pain as the result of a terminal illness. However, once the initial shock of this claim dissipates the person begins to think of the suffering of terminally ill individuals in a world of high-tech medical care. In such a case Connolly claims, *'one part of your subjectivity now begins to work on other parts.* In this case your concern for those who writhe in agony as they approach death may work on contestable assumptions about divinity or nature already burnt into your being'.[32] Connolly highlights the uncertainties and tension within the self on the issue after such an individual starts to weigh up the many competing interests involved. Indeed, having worked on the self:

> You continue to affirm... a teleological conception of nature in which the meaning of death is set, but now you acknowledge how this judgment may be more contestable than you had previously appreciated ... What was heretofore nonnegotiable may now gradually become rethinkable. You now register more actively the importance of giving presumptive respect to the judgment of the sufferer in this domain, even when the cultivation of critical responsiveness to them disturbs your own conception of nature, death, or divinity.[33]

The micropolitical movements of individuals who challenge the prohibition to die in their own way and in their own time, counters the molar ordering of the subject by the medico-legal gaze. They call for another politics, a politics of becoming beyond the time of the political. This micropolitics points the way to a rethinking of bioethics, focusing instead on the actual desires and interests of the individual who claims a right to die

---

[32] Ibid., p. 146.
[33] Ibid., p. 147.

with dignity. This is what Connolly calls an ethos of engagement with existing moral and social givens, which may bring about unexpected consequences or transformations in the societal default thinking on issues like the right to die. This process Connolly terms 'an ambiguous *politics of becoming* by which a new entity is propelled into being out of injury, energy and difference'.[34] Micropolitical movements such as the right to die movement "expose modes of suffering and injury heretofore located below the radar of public discourse. Sometimes the politics of becoming exposes how a list of basic rights that recently seemed complete harboured obscure and inadvertent exclusions inside the sweep of its formulations".[35] Such a process has been evident in Irish societal debate and discussion on the question of advance care directives over the past decade. This has led to a move on the part of professional healthcare bodies from a dogmatic resistance to the introduction of legislation on advance health care directives in cases of refusal of prolonged life-sustaining treatment to a less conservative approach. The final test of such an emerging micropolitics in this area of medical care will come once the "molar politics of public official" in the form of the Government decides to engage with these developments by introducing such legislation.

---

[34] Ibid., p. 160.
[35] Id.

THE LIMITS OF AUTONOMY: LAW AT THE END OF LIFE IN ENGLAND AND WALES

*Penney Lewis**

This chapter describes the law governing end-of-life decision-making in England and Wales.[1] The situation in Scotland is governed by a separate legal regime which will not be covered here. In relation to competent adults, the law seeks to protect their autonomy to make their own medical decisions, although this protection of autonomy is limited by the act/omission distinction and thus does not permit patients to request acts which cause death. The autonomy of those who do not fall into the category of competent adults, including adolescents, children and incompetent adults is not considered by the law to be as important as other values, including protecting life and health.

I. Competent Patients

A. *Competent Adults*

English law protects patient autonomy in decision-making. A competent adult[2] patient has an absolute right to refuse to consent to medical

---

* Professor of Law, Centre of Medical Law and Ethics, School of Law, King's College London, UK; email: penney.lewis@kcl.ac.uk.

[1] Parts of this chapter are derived from Penney Lewis, "England and Wales", in J. Griffiths, H. Weyers and M. Adams (eds.), *Euthanasia and the Law in Europe* (Oxford, 2008), pp. 349–370 and Penney Lewis, "Informal Legal Change on Assisted Suicide: The Policy for Prosecutors", 31(1) *Legal Studies* (2011), pp. 119–134 with the kind permission of Hart Publishing and Wiley-Blackwell. The writing of this chapter was supported by the Fondation Brocher where I was fortunate to be a visiting researcher in the summer of 2010.

[2] Aged 18 or over. Capacity for those aged 16 and over is assessed under the Mental Capacity Act 2005. The assessment starts from a presumption of capacity (s. 1(2)). A threshold test is applied: "a person lacks capacity in relation to a matter if at the material time he is unable to make a decision for himself in relation to the matter because of *an impairment of, or a disturbance in the functioning of, the mind or brain*" (s. 2(1), emphasis added). A functional test is used to determine whether the person is able to make a decision: "a person is unable to make a decision for himself if he is unable (a) to understand the information relevant to the decision, (b) to retain that information, [or] (c) to use or weigh that information as part of the process of making the decision" (s. 3(1)).

S. Negri (ed.), *Self-Determination, Dignity and End-of-Life Care*
2011 Koninklijke Brill NV. Printed in The Netherlands. ISBN 978 90 04 22357 8. pp. 221–248

treatment, even where that refusal may lead to the patient's death.[3] This right extends to pregnant women, even if the refusal may cause the death of the woman or her fetus.[4] To act without the competent patient's consent will constitute a criminal and civil assault.[5] However, the patient has no right to demand treatment against the doctor's clinical judgement.[6]

B. Competent Children

The autonomy of children is not similarly protected. Although competent children[7] may consent to medical treatment regardless of a parental refusal,[8] a competent child's refusal of medical treatment can be overridden by a consent given by a person with parental responsibility who acts within the limits of her power, that is, in the best interests of the child.[9] The child's refusal is a very important factor to be weighed but is not conclusive.[10] A court can also overrule a competent child's refusal to consent to treatment, for example if the person with parental responsibility is unwilling or unable to do so.[11] The power to overrule a competent child

---

   [3] *Re T (An Adult) (Consent to Medical Treatment)* [1992] 3 WLR 782 (CA); *Re MB (Medical Treatment)* [1997] 8 Med LR 217 (CA); *Re B (Adult: Refusal of Medical Treatment)* [2002] EWHC 429. See generally, Elizabeth Wicks, "The Right to Refuse Medical Treatment under the European Convention on Human Rights", 9 *Medical Law Review* (2001), pp. 17–40.
   [4] *Re MB* [1997] 8 Med LR 217; *St George's Healthcare NHS Trust v S* [1999] Fam 26 (CA).
   [5] *St George's Healthcare NHS Trust v S* [1999] Fam 26 (CA).
   [6] *R (on the application of Burke) v General Medical Council* [2005] EWCA Civ 1003, [50].
   [7] There is a rebuttable presumption of lack of capacity to consent to medical treatment for children under 16. Family Law Reform Act 1969, s. 8. The standard by which one can establish that a child under 16 has the capacity to consent is governed by the House of Lords decision in *Gillick* [1986] AC 112, 186. The child must have "sufficient understanding and intelligence to be capable of making up his own mind on the matter requiring decision". There is some evidence that a higher standard of competence is applied to children refusing life-saving or life-sustaining treatment than to adults. See Penney Lewis, "Medical Treatment of Children", in J. Fionda (ed.), *Legal Concepts of Childhood* (Oxford, 2001), pp. 151–163, pp. 152–154.
   [8] See Lord Scarman in *Gillick* [1986] AC 112, 186 ("as a matter of law the parental right to determine whether or not their minor child below the age of 16 will have medical treatment terminates if and when the child achieves a sufficient understanding and intelligence to enable him or her to understand fully what is proposed").
   [9] *Re R (A Minor) (Wardship: Medical Treatment)* [1992] Fam 11, 26; *Re W (A Minor) (Medical Treatment: Court's Jurisdiction)* [1993] Fam 64, 84 (Lord Donaldson), 86 (Balcombe LJ), 94 (Nolan LJ, *dubitante*) (CA).
   [10] *Re W* [1993] Fam 64, 84. See, for example, *Re M (Medical Treatment: Consent)* [1999] 2 FLR 1097 (HC) (refusal of heart transplant by 15½ year old girl overruled).
   [11] *Re R* [1992] Fam 11; *Re W* [1993] Fam 64, 81 (Lord Donaldson), 88 (Balcombe LJ), 91 (Nolan LJ); *Re K, W and H (Minors) (Medical Treatment)* [1993] 1 FLR 854 (HC); *Re C (Detention: Medical Treatment)* [1997] 2 FLR 180 (HC); *Re L (Medical Treatment: Gillick Competency)* [1998] 2 FLR 810 (HC) (in *obiter*). These decisions are discussed critically in

should only be used if the child's welfare is seriously threatened by the refusal.[12]

C. *Advance Decisions*

Advance decisions are made while a person is competent regarding the treatment and care of that person once he or she becomes incompetent.[13] They have been described as expressions of 'prospective'[14] or 'precedent'[15] autonomy as they contain projections of a person's autonomy interests into a future in which the person will no longer be able to make her own autonomous decisions.

In addition to promoting autonomy, advance directives are usually seen as protecting the interests of their creators, by preventing futile and burdensome treatment.[16] Advance directives can also be a mechanism of doing good to others, such as family members, by preventing emotional suffering and financial hardship.[17]

In England and Wales, advance *refusals* of treatment including life-sustaining treatment are legally valid under the Mental Capacity Act 2005 (MCA), ss. 24–26.[18] Prior to the enactment of this statute, the common law allowed persons to refuse unwanted treatment in advance of incapacity.[19] Only adults are covered by the statutory provisions,[20] and while in theory the pre-existing common law position could be applied to a competent child, this appears unlikely as competent children contemporaneously

---

Lewis, "Medical Treatment of Children", *supra* note 7, pp. 154–159. Jane Fortin, "Accommodating children's rights in a post Human Rights Act era', 69 *Modern Law Review* (2006), pp. 299–326 discusses the slim prospects of success for competent minors seeking to challenge this case law under the European Convention on Human Rights.

[12] *Re W* [1993] Fam 64, 88, 94.

[13] Lord Chancellor's Department, *Making Decisions*, Cm 4465 (London, 1999), [13].

[14] Norman Cantor, "Prospective Autonomy: On the Limits of shaping one's post-competence medical fate", 8 *Journal of Contemporary Health Law & Policy* (1992), pp. 13–48.

[15] Rebecca Dresser, "Dworkin on Dementia: elegant theory, questionable policy", 25 *Hastings Center Report* (1995), n° 6, pp. 32–38, p. 34.

[16] Allen E. Buchanan and Dan W. Brock, *Deciding for Others: The Ethics of Surrogate Decision-Making* (Cambridge, 1990), p. 99.

[17] Ibid.

[18] If the advance refusal is to apply to life-sustaining treatment, this must be specifically mentioned in the document. MCA, s. 25(5).

[19] *Re T* [1992] 3 WLR 782; *Bland* [1993] AC 789; *Re C (Adult Refusal of Treatment)* [1994] 1 WLR 290 (HC); *Re AK (Medical Treatment: Consent)* [2001] 1 FLR 129 (HC); *HE v A Hospital NHS Trust* [2003] EWHC 1017. For a discussion of the common law requirements, see Derek Morgan, "Odysseus and the Binding Directive: Only a Cautionary Tale?", 14 *Legal Studies* (1994), pp. 411–442; Kristina Stern, "Advance Directives", 2 *Medical Law Review* (1994), pp. 57–76; Sabine Michalowski, "Advance refusals of life-sustaining medical treatment: the relativity of an absolute right", 68 *Modern Law Review* (2005), pp. 958–982.

[20] MCA, s. 24(1).

refusing life-saving treatment are always overruled,[21] so advance refusals are similarly likely to be overruled once a court is involved.

The MCA provides that when still competent, a person may decide that if

(a) at a later time and in such circumstances as he may specify, a specified treatment is proposed to be carried out or continued by a person providing health care for him, and

(b) at that time he lacks capacity to consent to the carrying out or continuation of the treatment,

the specified treatment is not to be carried out or continued.[22]

The advance decision may be withdrawn or altered at any time while the individual remains competent.[23] The advance decision will not be applicable if "there are reasonable grounds for believing that circumstances exist which [the individual] did not anticipate at the time of the advance decision and which would have affected his decision had he anticipated them."[24] If the advance decision refuses life-sustaining treatment, it must be in writing and signed by the patient or by another person in the presence of the patient and at the patient's direction.[25] The patient must sign or acknowledge the document in the presence of a witness who must sign it (or acknowledge his signature) in the patient's presence.[26]

An advance decision is legally binding on those providing treatment and failure to comply with the advance directive will result in civil liability for battery.[27] However, "[a] person does not incur liability for carrying out or continuing the treatment unless, at the time, he is satisfied that an advance decision exists which is valid and applicable to the treatment."[28] If the doctor is unsure of the validity or applicability of the advance decision, an application can be made to the Court of Protection and treatment can be given while the court's decision is awaited.[29] The doctor will not be liable for failing to provide treatment when following an advance decision reasonably believed to be valid and applicable.[30]

---

[21] See above, text accompanying notes 8–12.
[22] MCA, ss. 24(1)(a),(b).
[23] MCA, s. 24(3).
[24] MCA, s. 25(4)(c).
[25] MCA, s. 25(5), (6).
[26] MCA, s. 25(6).
[27] MCA, s. 26(1). See, e.g., *Malette v Shulman* (1990) 72 OR (2d) 417 (Ontario CA).
[28] MCA, s. 26(2).
[29] MCA, ss. 26(4), (5).
[30] MCA, s. 26(3).

Advance consents are legally effective (for example, a consent to a surgical procedure in advance of anaesthesia), but advance requests are not, although they will be taken into account in assessing the patient's best interests.[31]

II. Incompetent Patients

A. *Incompetent Adults*

Treatment decisions can be made on behalf of an incompetent adult by a proxy or surrogate, whether the proxy was appointed by the person when still competent or judicially appointed.[32] Prior to the MCA, the decision-maker for an incompetent person who had not made an advance refusal was the patient's physician.[33] If no proxy has been appointed, or the proxy does not have the authority to make the particular decision,[34] the patient's doctor will be the decision-maker unless the jurisdiction of the Court of Protection is invoked.[35]

Regardless of the identity of the decision-maker, decisions on medical treatment for incompetent individuals are made using the 'best interests' test, which involves weighing the benefit and detriment that will flow from the proposed procedure.[36] The best interests test is based on the protection of the incompetent individual's welfare interests, and can be used regardless of whether the individual was previously competent. The courts have rejected[37] the alternative 'substituted judgment' test[38] as "simply a fiction".[39] The test was also rejected by the law reform body, the Law

---

[31] *Burke* [2005] EWCA Civ 1003, [50]; MCA, s. 4(6)(a).

[32] See MCA, ss. 9–14, 22–23 (allowing a competent person to appoint a donee of a lasting power of attorney to make medical decisions on her behalf after the onset of incompetence), 16–20 (allowing a court to appoint a deputy to make medical decisions on behalf of an incompetent person who has not made a lasting power of attorney).

[33] Unless the court's intervention was sought. *Re F* [1990] 2 AC 1 (HL).

[34] For example, a court-appointed proxy may not refuse consent to the carrying out or continuation of life-sustaining treatment. MCA, s. 20(5).

[35] MCA, ss. 5, 15. The Court of Protection is a new superior court to deal with matters relating to adults lacking capacity. See MCA, Part II.

[36] *Re F* [1990] 2 AC 1; MCA, s. 4.

[37] *Bland* [1993] AC 789, 895 (Lord Mustill), 872 (Lord Goff). Although see *contra, Re J* [1991] Fam 33, 55, in which Taylor LJ adopts a test which appears to be a form of substituted judgment.

[38] This test requires decisions to conform with those which the incompetent individual would have made were she competent, and is based on respect for the individual's autonomy interests. See Buchanan and Brock, *supra* note 16, pp. 112–114.

[39] This rejection was based on an apparent failure to distinguish between the substituted judgment test and the concept of proxy decision-making. Ian M. Kennedy and Andrew Grubb, *Medical Law*, 3rd ed. (London, 2000), p. 838. Nevertheless, the rejection of

Commission,[40] although it did recommend that the incompetent's views, wishes and feelings should be considered as a part of the best interests test.[41] Section 4(6) of the MCA now provides that the person making the determination of what is in the incompetent person's best interests

... must consider, so far as is reasonably ascertainable—

a. the person's past and present wishes and feelings,
b. the beliefs and values that would be likely to influence his decision if he had capacity, and
c. the other factors that he would be likely to consider if he were able to do so.

The decision-maker must take into account the views as to the patient's best interests of anyone named by the patient as a consultee, anyone engaged in caring for the patient or interested in his welfare, and any proxy decision-maker.[42]

The decision of the House of Lords in *Bland* remains the leading authority on withdrawal of life-sustaining treatment. Anthony Bland was in a persistent vegetative state (PVS) and his family and medical team agreed that it was in his best interests to withdraw artificial nutrition and hydration (ANH). A declaration that such withdrawal would be lawful was sought from the courts. The House of Lords decided that although the intention of the doctor would be to bring about Bland's death, the proposed withdrawal would be lawful as it constituted an omission rather than an act.[43] The doctor's duty did not require the provision of treatment that was not in the patient's best interests.[44] When assessing an incompetent adult's best interests, medical evidence is preferred over evidence of the patient's and their family's religious beliefs.[45]

---

substituted judgment has been confirmed. *W Healthcare NHS Trust v H and others* [2005] 1 WLR 834, [12], [23] (CA).

[40] See Law Commission, *Mentally Incapacitated Adults and Decision-Making: An Overview*, Consultation Paper No. 119 (London, 1991), [4.22]-[4.23].

[41] Law Commission, *Mental Incapacity*, Report No. 231 (London, 1995), [3.25]-[3.31].

[42] MCA, s. 4(7). See also, British Medical Association, *Withholding and withdrawing life-prolonging medical treatment: guidance for decision making*, 3rd ed. (London, 2007); General Medical Council (GMC), *Treatment and care towards the end of life: good practice in decision making* (London, 2010). The predecessor to the new GMC Guidance withstood a challenge to its legality. See *Burke* [2005] EWCA Civ 1003, [64]-[66], [83].

[43] *Bland* [1993] AC 789, 876 (Lord Lowry), 881 (Lord Browne-Wilkinson), 887 (Lord Mustill).

[44] *Bland* [1993] AC 789, 867–869 (Lord Goff), 883–884 (Lord Browne-Wilkinson), 897 (Lord Mustill, holding that "the proposed conduct is not in the best interests of Anthony Bland, for he has no best interests of any kind").

[45] *A NHS Trust v A, SA* [2005] EWCA Civ 1145.

It appears unlikely that the withdrawal of ANH will be found to be in the patient's best interests if the patient is not in a PVS or in the dying phase.[46] This was recently confirmed in a case in which a mother's request for authorisation of the withdrawal of artificial nutrition and hydration from her adult daughter who is in a minimally conscious state was rejected by the Court of Protection.[47]

In *Bland*, Lord Goff held that as a matter of practice,[48] judicial approval should be sought in all PVS cases in which the patient's medical team believe it is in her best interests for ANH to be withdrawn.[49] This practice is reflected in a series of subsequent cases[50] and was included in the Code of Practice issued under the MCA. It will therefore continue to be the case that even when a patient- or court-appointed proxy consents to the withdrawal of ANH from a PVS patient, the approval of the Court of Protection will be sought prior to the implementation of the decision.[51]

This practice of seeking judicial approval in PVS cases has not been extended to other cases in which a decision is made to withdraw life-sustaining treatment, including ANH and ventilation. Although some such cases have come to court,[52] it is clear that most do not. Decision-making in such cases is governed by the general rules discussed above.

---

[46] See *W Healthcare NHS Trust v H and others* [2005] 1 WLR 834, [20], [27]-[32] (CA). See also Clare Dyer, "Withdrawal of food supplement judged as misconduct", 318 *British Medical Journal* (1999), p. 895 (describing a case in which a doctor was found guilty of serious professional misconduct and suspended from practice for 6 months for authorising the withdrawal of artificial nutrition from an incompetent stroke patient who subsequently died).

[47] *W v M* [2011] EWHC 2443 (Fam).

[48] That is, judicial approval is desirable but not essential. Failure to obtain judicial approval will not, in and of itself, render the subsequent decision or action unlawful. Judicial approval is in fact always sought in such cases.

[49] *Bland* [1993] AC 789, 873–874.

[50] See, e.g., *NHS Trust A v M; NHS Trust B v H* [2001] 2 WLR 942 (HC); *Swindon & Marlborough NHS Trust v S* (1995) 3 Med L Rev 84 (HC); *Frenchay Healthcare NHS Trust v S* [1994] 1 WLR 601 (HC); *Re D (Medical Treatment)* [1998] FLR 411 (HC); *NHS Trust A v H* [2001] 2 FLR 501 (HC); *An NHS Trust v J* [2006] EWHC 3152 (Fam). See also, Office of the Public Guardian, *Practice Direction E – Applications Relating To Serious Medical Treatment* (London, 2007), http://webarchive.nationalarchives.gov.uk/20110218200720/http://www .hmcourts-service.gov.uk/cms/files/09E_-_Serious_Medical_Treatment_PD.pdf (accessed 21 July 2011).

[51] Mental Capacity Act 2005 Code of Practice (London, 2007), [6.18], [8.18], [8.19]. For a critical view, see Penney Lewis, "Withdrawal of Treatment from a Patient in a Permanent Vegetative State: Judicial Involvement and Innovative 'Treatment'", 15 *Medical Law Review* (2007), pp. 392–399.

[52] See, e.g., *Re R (Adult: Medical Treatment)* (1996) 31 BMLR 127 (HC); *W Healthcare NHS Trust v H and others* [2005] 1 WLR 834 (CA).

B. *Incompetent Children*[53]

If a child does not meet the test of competence,[54] then he or she can be treated in her best interests with the consent of a person with parental responsibility or the court.[55] If those with parental responsibility refuse the recommended treatment, then the medical team must take steps to bring the issue before a court if the consequences of the refusal are thought serious enough to warrant such a step.[56] The consent of one person with parental responsibility is sufficient even if another person with parental responsibility disagrees, unless the decision falls into a "small group of important decisions" which should only be made if there is agreement between all those having parental responsibility for the child.[57] Although courts have not yet ruled that withdrawals of life-sustaining treatment fall into this category, their seriousness suggests that in any such case in which there is serious disagreement between someone with parental responsibility and the medical team treating the child, the matter should be brought to court for an assessment of the child's best interests:

> There can be no doubt that the best course is for a parent of a child to agree on the course which the doctors are proposing to take, having fully consulted the parent and for the parent to fully understand what is involved. That is the course which should always be adopted in a case of this nature. If that is not possible and there is a conflict, and if the conflict is of a grave nature, the matter must then be brought before the court so the court can decide what is in the best interests of the child concerned. Faced with a particular problem, the courts will answer that problem.[58]

---

[53] Those below the age of 18.
[54] See *supra* note 7.
[55] Children Act 1989; *Gillick* [1986] AC 112 (HL). For a more detailed discussion, see Lewis, "Medical Treatment of Children", *supra* note 7, pp. 159–163.
[56] Unless it is an emergency, to proceed without the consent of either those with parental responsibility or the court would be a battery. If in an emergency situation it is impossible or impracticable to seek parental consent, then treatment reasonably necessary to avoid serious harm or death may be given. However, if an emergency is foreseeable, there is an onus on the Hospital Trust to seek a judicial declaration before the situation becomes urgent. *Glass v UK* [2004] 1 FLR 1019, [70]-[83] (Eur Ct HR). There may also be disciplinary consequences for a doctor who proceeds without parental consent. See Clare Dyer, "Consultant suspended for not getting consent for cardiac procedure", 316 *British Medical Journal* (1998), p. 955 (describing a case of a consultant who was suspended for serious professional misconduct by the General Medical Council for failing to obtain parental consent to a balloon catherisation on a six year old girl).
[57] *Re J (A Minor) (Prohibited Steps Order: Circumcision)* [2000] 1 FLR 571 (HC); *Re C (A Child) (Immunisation: Parental Rights)* [2003] EWCA Civ 1148.
[58] *R v Portsmouth Hospitals NHS Trust (ex parte Glass)* [1999] EWCA Civ 1914.

This would seem to apply whether, as in most cases which come to court, both parents disagree with the medical recommendation, or whether one parent agrees and the other disagrees.[59] In other words, decisions about the withdrawal of life-sustaining treatment for an incompetent child do fall into the special category of important decisions for which parental agreement is needed.

In a series of such cases, courts have considered the appropriate ambit of the autonomous decision-making of those with parental responsibility. In the earlier cases, the test adopted was that treatment should be provided unless the child's life post-treatment would be "intolerable".[60] The courts accepted that this meant that continued life would not always be in the child's best interests: "There is without doubt a very strong presumption in favour of a course of action which will prolong life, but ... it is not irrebuttable."[61] The test of intolerability has since been abandoned.[62] Instead, a balancing approach is used, looking at the child's quality of life:[63] "account has to be taken of the pain and suffering and quality of life which the child will experience if life is prolonged. Account has also to be taken of the pain and suffering involved in the proposed treatment itself."[64]

Courts have also been faced with refusals by those with parental responsibility based on religious convictions. In a series of cases, the courts have consistently overruled the refusals of parents who are Jehovah's Witnesses who refuse life-saving blood transfusions for their children based on their religious convictions.[65] Unconventional medical beliefs have also been treated unsympathetically.[66]

---

[59] See, e.g., *Re RB (A Child)* [2009] EWHC 3269 (Fam).

[60] *Re B (A Minor) (Wardship: Medical Treatment)* [1981] 1 WLR 1421, 1424 (Dunn LJ, CA); *Re J* [1991] Fam 33, 55 (Taylor LJ).

[61] *Re J* [1991] Fam 33, 46.

[62] *Bland* [1993] AC 789, 819–20 (Butler-Sloss LJ, CA); *Burke* [2005] EWCA Civ 1003, [62]-[63]; *Portsmouth Hospitals NHS Trust v Wyatt and another* [2005] EWCA Civ 1181, [76].

[63] *Re J* [1991] Fam 33, 46–7 (Lord Donaldson), 52 (Balcombe LJ), 55 (Taylor LJ); *Re T (A Minor) (Wardship: Medical Treatment)* [1997] 1 WLR 242 (CA). See Penney Lewis, "Proxy Refusals of Medical Treatment", 8 *King's College Law Journal* (1997–98), pp. 101–103; Marie Fox and Jean McHale, "In Whose Best Interests?", 60 *Modern Law Review* (1997), pp. 700–709.

[64] *Re J* [1991] Fam 33, 46.

[65] See, e.g., *Re E (A Minor)* (1990) 9 BMLR 1 (HC); *Re S (A Minor) (Medical Treatment)* [1993] 1 FLR 376 (HC); *Re O (A Minor) (Medical Treatment)* (1993) 19 BMLR 148 (HC); *Re R (A Minor)* (1993) 15 BMLR 72 (HC). See also, *NHS Trust v A (A Child)* [2007] EWHC 1696 (bone marrow transplant ordered when parents refused to consent as they had faith that God would cure their daughter).

[66] *Re C (HIV Test)* [1999] 2 FLR 1004 (HC) (order that a baby be tested for HIV despite her HIV-positive mother's refusal on the basis of her doubts about the validity of the generally accepted theories on HIV and AIDS).

The cases involving quality-of-life determinations and the religious objection cases reflect the fact that judges in England and Wales see themselves as the ultimate arbiters of a child's best interests.[67] The views of the parents are considered, but they do not have determinative weight.[68]

Although those with parental responsibility can consent to treatment on behalf of the child patient, they cannot *demand* treatment which the medical team considers not to be in the child's best interests.[69] Where the medical team and the parents do not agree about the child's best interests, an order of the court can be sought. In almost all such cases, the courts have found that continued treatment would not be in the seriously ill child's best interests.[70]

III. Palliative Care

A. *Pain Relief, 'Double Effect' and the Role of 'Purpose'*

The 'doctrine of double effect' has been embraced by English judges in a number of prosecutions of doctors accused of terminating the life of a patient.[71] Thus a doctor who prescribes pain relief that she knows may or will hasten the patient's death, will not be guilty of murder unless her *purpose* was to cause the patient's death.[72] Such purpose can be inferred when

---

[67] See, e.g., *Wyatt v Portsmouth NHS Trust* [2005] EWHC 693; *Portsmouth NHS Trust v Wyatt* [2004] EWHC 2247; *Re L (A Child) (Medical Treatment: Benefit)* [2004] EWHC 2713; *Wyatt* [2005] EWCA Civ 1181; *An NHS Trust v MB* [2006] EWHC 507.

[68] *Re T* [1997] 1 WLR 242. See Lewis, *supra* note 63; Fox and McHale, *supra* note 63.

[69] See *Re J (A Minor) (Child in Care: Medical Treatment)* [1993] Fam 15, 27, 29 (CA); *Re J* [1991] Fam 33, 41 (CA); *Re R* [1992] Fam 11, 22, 26 (CA); *Re C (Medical Treatment)* [1998] 1 FLR 384, 390–391 (HC). See Jane Fortin, "A Baby's Right to Die", 10 *Child & Family Law Quarterly* (1998), pp. 411–416.

[70] See, e.g., *Portsmouth NHS Trust v Wyatt* [2004] EWHC 2247; *Re L (A Child) (Medical Treatment: Benefit)* [2004] EWHC 2713; *Re K (a child)* [2006] EWHC 1007; *Re RB* [2009] EWHC 3269 (Fam); *Re OT* [2009] EWCA Civ 409, confirming [2009] EWHC 633 (Fam). For an exception, see *MB* [2006] EWHC 507.

[71] "The principle of double effect is a doctrine that distinguishes between the consequences a person intends and those that are unintended but foreseen and may be applicable in various situations where an action has two effects, one good and one bad. In the medical context it is usually relied on when a doctor increases pain-killing medication to a patient; the doctor foresees that the patient may die, although that is not his intention." Glenys Williams, "The Principle of Double Effect and Terminal Sedation", 9 *Medical Law Review* (2001), pp. 41–53, p. 41.

[72] See *Re J* [1991] Fam 33, 46 ("the use of drugs to reduce pain will often be fully justified, notwithstanding that this will hasten the moment of death. What can never be justified is the use of drugs or surgical procedures with the primary purpose of doing so."); *Bland* [1993] AC 789, 867–8 (Lord Goff); *Re A (Children) (Conjoined Twins: Surgical Separation)*

the doctor uses a drug whose only medical function is to cause death. In such a case the doctor has gone beyond accepting a risk to her patient's life and intended her death in the sense of purpose or desire: the only possible effect of the drug was to kill her patient.[73]

This is in stark contrast to the law of intention as generally accepted in English criminal law, under which a consequence is intended if the consequence either is the actor's purpose or desire, or is foreseen by the actor as morally certain to occur.[74] The general criminal law concept of intention therefore includes an undesired but known consequence, as in the case where a doctor knows that death will be hastened by the administration of pain-relieving medication. Nevertheless, this is not the approach used when the defendant is a doctor.[75] The approach taken in the medical cases is therefore "less stringent" than the position in the criminal law more generally: a narrow definition of intention is used which results in the exclusion of many pain relief cases from the ambit of the criminal law.[76]

[2001] Fam 147, 199 (CA); *Adams (Bodkin)* [1957] Crim. L.R. 365 (Central Crim. Ct.) ("the doctor is entitled to relieve pain and suffering even if the measures he takes may incidentally shorten life."). For a more recent example, see Anthony Arlidge, "The Trial of Dr David Moor", *Criminal Law Review* (2000), pp. 31–40; J.C. Smith, "A Comment on Moor's case", *Criminal Law Review* (2000), pp. 41–44. See also, House of Lords Select Committee on Medical Ethics, *Report*, HL Paper 21-I (1993–1994), [242]-[244]; House of Lords Select Committee on the Assisted Dying for the Terminally Ill Bill, *Report*, HL Paper 86-I (London, 2005), [15] (quoting the Attorney General that it is not murder "where a doctor acts to do all that is proper and necessary to relieve pain with the incidental effect that this will shorten a patient's life.").

[73] *Cox* (1992) 12 BMLR 38 (Winchester Crown Ct.). See also, Kennedy and Grubb, *supra* note 39, 1963; David Price, "Euthanasia, Pain Relief and Double Effect", 17 *Legal Studies* (1997), pp. 323–342.

[74] *Woollin* [1999] AC 92 (HL).

[75] Although not a case dealing with pain relief, the conjoined twins case (described below, text accompanying nn. 105–110) confirmed that this narrow view of intention in medical cases survives the enactment of the Human Rights Act 1998 which incorporated the European Convention on Human Rights (ECHR) into English law. Lord Justice Robert Walker commented on the meaning of "intentionally" in article 2(1) of the ECHR, which reads in part: "No one shall be deprived of his life intentionally save in the execution of a sentence of a court following his conviction of a crime for which this penalty is provided by law." Robert Walker LJ held: "The Convention is to be construed as an autonomous text, without regard to any special rules of English law, and the word "intentionally" in article 2(1) must be given its natural and ordinary meaning. In my judgment the word, construed in that way, applies only to cases where the purpose of the prohibited action is to cause death." *Re A* [2001] Fam 147, 256 (Brooke LJ agreed at 238). The passage was also cited with approval in *NHS Trust A v M; NHS Trust B v H* [2001] 2 WLR 942, [22].

[76] Andrew Ashworth, "Criminal Liability in a Medical Context: The Treatment of Good Intentions", in A. Simester and A. Smith (eds.), *Harm and Culpability* (Oxford, 1996), pp. 173–193.

This must reflect "a judgment that some acts (although intended) ought as a matter of moral judgment and public policy to be regarded as attracting no blame because of their social worth."[77]

It is worth noting, however, that this stretching of the criminal law to accommodate the doctrine of double effect may, although well-intentioned, have unintended side effects. In a review of the medical literature worldwide, Sykes and Thorns conclude that:

> there is no evidence that the use of opioids or sedatives in palliative care requires the doctrine of double effect as a defence.... Thus, although the doctrine is a valid ethical device, it is, for the most part, irrelevant to symptom control at the end of life. To exaggerate its involvement perpetuates a myth that satisfactory symptom control at the end of life is inevitably associated with hastening death. The result can be a reluctance to use medication to secure comfort and a failure to provide adequate relief to a very vulnerable group of patients.[78]

B. *Palliative and Terminal Sedation*

As is the case with pain relief, palliative sedation (in the sense of deep and continuous sedation until death) will be lawful provided that the doctor's purpose was not to cause the patient's death. As the sedation is aimed at relieving suffering, it is unlikely that a doctor providing palliative sedation will be criminally prosecuted, even if it were possible to prove that death was hastened.[79] Indeed, there have been no such criminal prosecutions thus far, nor have any objections been raised to the use of palliative sedation where clinically appropriate.

When continuous, deep sedation is coupled with the withdrawal of artificial nutrition and hydration ('terminal sedation'), the principle of double effect is inapplicable to the latter decision.[80] The withdrawal will only be lawful if it meets the test set out in *Bland* and the MCA: it must be in the patient's best interests.[81]

---

[77] Kennedy and Grubb, *supra* note 39, pp. 2113–2114.
[78] Nigel Sykes and Andrew Thorns, "The use of opioids and sedatives at the end of life", 4 *Lancet Oncology* (2003), pp. 312–318, p. 317. See also, Tatsuya Morita *et al.*, "Effects of high dose opioids and sedatives on survival in terminally ill cancer patients", 21 *Journal of Pain and Symptom Management* (2001), pp. 282–289.
[79] There is no evidence that death is hastened by palliative sedation. For a review, see Sykes and Thorns, ibid., 314, 317.
[80] Williams, *supra* note 71, pp. 51–52.
[81] This test is likely to be met if, for example, the patient is dying of cancer. See R.J. Dunlop *et al.*, "On withholding nutrition and hydration in the terminally ill: has palliative medicine gone too far? a reply", 21 *Journal of Medical Ethics* (1995), pp. 141–143, and the

IV. EUTHANASIA AND ASSISTED SUICIDE

Euthanasia constitutes murder under English law.[82] An individual convicted of murder faces a mandatory life sentence, although it is for the trial judge to set the minimum period which the defendant must serve before becoming eligible for parole.[83] Neither the consent of the victim[84] nor the defendant's motives[85] are relevant in relation to her guilt or innocence, although a "belief by [the] offender that the murder was an act of mercy" is a relevant factor counting towards reduction of the minimum period.[86] Proposals have been made to adopt a separate offence of mercy-killing, but they have not been successful.[87] The possibility of a partial defence to murder for mercy-killing (which would result in a conviction for a lesser offence) has also been discussed without any progress in this regard.[88]

---

cancer and dementia cases described by Professor Irene Higginson in *R (on the application of Burke) v General Medical Council* [2004] EWHC 1879 (Admin), [19]. See also, GMC, *supra* note 42, [113]-[115].

[82] *The Queen on the Application of Mrs Dianne Pretty v Director of Public Prosecutions* [2002] 1 AC 800, [5] (HL); *Bland* [1993] AC 789, 865–866 (Lord Goff), 882, 885 (Lord Browne-Wilkinson), 892–893 (Lord Mustill); *Cox* (1992) 12 BMLR 38 (instructing the jury that if the "primary purpose" of the administration of potassium chloride was to hasten death then it was murder).

[83] The recommendation by the House of Lords Select Committee on Medical Ethics, *supra* note 72, [261] to abolish the mandatory life sentence was rejected. Government, *Response to the House of Lords Select Committee on Medical Ethics*, Cm 2553 (London, 1994), 5.

[84] *Bland* [1993] AC 789, 890 (Lord Mustill).

[85] *Bland* [1993] AC 789, 867 (Lord Goff), 890 (Lord Mustill).

[86] Criminal Justice Act 2003, s. 269, Schedule 21, [11(f)]. See *Inglis* [2010] EWCA Crim 2637, [47]-[61].

[87] See Criminal Law Revision Committee, *Working Paper on Offences Against the Person* (London, 1976), [82]. The lesser offence of mercy-killing would have applied in cases where the victim was "(1) permanently subject to great bodily pain or suffering, or (2) permanently helpless from bodily or mental incapacity, or (3) subject to rapid and incurable bodily or mental degeneration". No request requirement was proposed in order to allow the offence to encompass cases where the victim was incompetent. The proposal was dropped due to lack of support from consultees. See Criminal Law Revision Committee, *Offences Against the Person*, Report No. 14 (1980), [115]. See also, Government, *Response to the House of Lords Select Committee on Medical Ethics*, *supra* note 83, pp. 1, 5.

[88] Law Commission, *A New Homicide Act for England and Wales*, Consultation Paper No. 177 (London, 2005), [8.3]-[8.5], (declining to consider a partial defence in mercy-killing cases), confirmed in Law Commission, *Murder, Manslaughter and Infanticide*, Report No. 304 (London, 2006), [7.26]-[7.33]. For a critical view, see Jonathan Rogers, "The Law Commission's Proposed Restructuring of the Law of Homicide", 70 *Journal of Criminal Law* (2006), pp. 223–245, 236–237.

Over the years, there has been recurrent debate on whether euthanasia and physician-assisted suicide should be legalised.[89] Numerous private member's bills have failed to gain Parliamentary support.[90] The most recent of these was the Assisted Dying for the Terminally Ill Bill, which was defeated in the House of Lords in 2006.[91] The reaction of the medical profession to the Bill was mixed. "The Royal Colleges of Physicians and of General Practitioners adopted a neutral stance on the principles underlying the Bill".[92] The General Medical Council has issued no guidance on assisted dying given its legal status, but in evidence to the House of Lords Select Committee it expressed concerns about the prospect of legalisation.[93] Although the British Medical Association briefly adopted a neutral stance, in 2006 it reaffirmed its opposition to "all forms of assisted dying".[94]

One important consequence of this ultimately unsuccessful Bill was the enquiry by the Select Committee set up to examine its provisions. This was the first such Parliamentary enquiry since the publication of the influential report by the House of Lords Select Committee on Medical Ethics in 1994. That report had recommended that voluntary euthanasia should not be legalised, raising the familiar concerns of the risk of abuses and the slippery slope.[95] The report of the House of Lords Select Committee on the Assisted Dying for the Terminally Ill Bill took no clear stand either for or against legalisation. Instead, the report recommended a number of considerations which should be taken into account by the drafters of any future bill to legalise assisted dying. These include: drawing a clear

---

[89] For a flavour of the legalisation debate, see Andrew Grubb, "Euthanasia in England – A Law Lacking Compassion?", 8 *European Journal of Health Law* (2001), pp. 89–95; John Keown, *Euthanasia, Ethics, and Public Policy* (Cambridge, 2002) and the debate between Harris and Finnis in John Keown, *Euthanasia Examined: Ethical, Clinical and Legal Perspectives* (Cambridge, 1995).

[90] See Hazel Biggs, *Euthanasia, Death with Dignity and the Law* (Oxford, 2001), p. 13; N.D.A. Kemp, *'Merciful Release': The History of the British Euthanasia Movement* (Manchester, 2002); Margaret Otlowski, *Voluntary Euthanasia and the Common Law* (Oxford, 1997), pp. 334–336.

[91] Assisted Dying for the Terminally Ill Bill, House of Lords, HL Bill 36, 9 Nov. 2005; *Hansard*, House of Lords, 12 May 2006, cols. 1184–1295. See also, Hazel Biggs, "The Assisted Dying for the Terminally Ill Bill 2004: Will English law soon allow patients the choice to die?", 12 *European Journal of Health Law* (2005), pp. 43–56.

[92] House of Lords Select Committee on the Assisted Dying for the Terminally Ill Bill, *supra* note 72, [108].

[93] Ibid.

[94] British Medical Association, *End-of-Life Decisions: Views of the BMA* (London, 2006), pp. 3–4.

[95] House of Lords Select Committee on Medical Ethics, *supra* note 72. The committee's enquiry and report are discussed extensively in Otlowski, *supra* note 90, pp. 336–339.

distinction between assisted suicide and voluntary euthanasia; providing clear guidance on the actions which a doctor may take in providing assistance in dying; providing a definition of terminal illness which reflects the realities of clinical practice; requiring a psychiatric assessment so that those suffering from psychological or psychiatric disorder can be screened out; using 'unrelievable' or 'intractable' suffering or distress as a criterion rather than 'unbearable' suffering; ensuring real access to palliative care; providing a waiting period which ensures time for reflection without causing increased suffering; not imposing any duty on a doctor with conscientious objections to euthanasia to refer a patient to another doctor; and providing adequate protection for all health care professionals.[96]

A. *Defences*

1. *Diminished Responsibility*

Diminished responsibility is a partial defence, so that if a person who performs euthanasia is suffering from diminished responsibility at the time, she will be convicted of manslaughter instead of murder. The defendant 'D' must have suffered from an "an abnormality of mental functioning" which "(a) arose from a recognised medical condition, (b) substantially impaired D's ability to [understand the nature of D's conduct; ... form a rational judgment; [or] exercise self-control], and (c) provides an explanation for D's acts and omissions in doing or being a party to the killing."[97] Manslaughter does not carry a mandatory life sentence; indeed, a noncustodial sentence may be imposed.

This defence has been used successfully in cases of euthanasia involving family members;[98] such use is likely to continue as one of the scenarios envisaged by the Law Commission in the report which provided the basis for the recent amendment of this defence was that of

---

[96] House of Lords Select Committee on the Assisted Dying for the Terminally Ill Bill, *supra* note 72, [269].

[97] Homicide Act 1957, s. 2, as amended by the Coroners and Justice Act 2009, s. 52 (in force from 4 Oct. 2010).

[98] See House of Lords Select Committee on Medical Ethics, *supra* note 72, [128]. The recent amendment of the defence was in response to the Law Commission, *Murder, Manslaughter and Infanticide*, *supra* note 88, [5.112], although the Law Commission's proposal was that the partial defence would result in a conviction for second degree rather than first degree murder. The Government chose not to adopt the proposals for degrees of murder. *Murder, Manslaughter and Infanticide: proposals for reform of the law*, CP19/08 (London, 2008), [8]-[9]; *Murder, manslaughter and infanticide: proposals for reform of the law: Summary of responses and Government position*, CP(R)19/08 (London, 2009), [117], [120].

a depressed man who has been caring for many years for a terminally ill spouse, [who then] kills her, at her request. He says that he had found it progressively more difficult to stop her repeated requests dominating his thoughts to the exclusion of all else, so that 'I felt I would never think straight again until I had given her what she wanted.'[99]

However, the defence is unlikely to be available to doctors.[100] As the Law Commission explained, the defence would not "assist rational 'mercy' killers and those who understand the nature of what they are doing even if they kill [the victim] with the latter's consent.... the defence of diminished responsibility should not be stretched so far that it becomes a backdoor route to partial excuse for caring but rational 'mercy' killers."[101]

2. *Necessity*

Another possible defence to a charge of murder in a case of euthanasia has received significant academic and judicial attention: the defence of necessity.[102] The defence has developed at common law with no statutory intervention. The common law has held steadfastly to the position that necessity is not available as a defence to murder.[103] The Law Commission has been reluctant to intervene.[104]

A carefully limited exception was made in *Re A* (*Children*) (*Conjoined Twins: Surgical Separation*), which involved a choice between the lives of

---

[99] Law Commission, *Murder, Manslaughter and Infanticide*, ibid. [5.121(2)(c)].

[100] Grubb, *supra* note 89, pp. 89–90.

[101] Law Commission, *Murder, Manslaughter and Infanticide*, *supra* note 88, [7.37]. For a contrary view, see *Hansard*, House of Lords, 18 May 2009, vol. 710, col. 1233.

[102] This is the defence which was used in the Dutch euthanasia jurisprudence. See Griffiths, Weyers and Adams, *supra* note 1, pp. 29–32; Lewis, *Assisted Dying and Legal Change*, *supra* note 1, pp. 76–81.

[103] *Dudley and Stephens* (1884) 14 QBD 273 (two shipwrecked sailors who killed and ate a cabin boy were convicted of murder as necessity was unavailable as a defence to murder); *Howe* [1987] AC 417 (HL) (necessity not available as defence to murder where defendants had been threatened with death if they did not kill the victims); *Pommell* [1995] Cr App R 607 (CA); *Rodger* [1998] 1 Cr App R 143 (CA). For more on the common law's rejection of the defence of necessity in murder cases, see Lewis, *Assisted Dying and Legal Change*, *supra* note 1, pp. 83–94.

[104] Law Commission, *Defences of General Application*, Report No. 83 (London, 1977), pp. 25–32, rejecting the recommendations contained in Law Commission, *Defences of General Application*, Working Paper No. 55 (London, 1974), pp. 20–42. For criticism, see Glanville Williams, "Necessity", *Criminal Law Review* (1978), pp. 128–136; P.H.J. Huxley, "Proposals and Counter Proposals on the Defence of Necessity", *Criminal Law Review* (1978), pp. 141–150. See also, Law Commission, *A New Homicide Act for England and Wales*, *supra* note 88, [1.1(3)], [1.3(1)], [8.3] (exempting issues surrounding necessity and euthanasia from the most recent proposals on homicide), confirmed in Law Commission, *Murder, Manslaughter and Infanticide*, *supra* note 88, [7.26]-[7.33].

two conjoined twins.[105] Without the operation to separate them, both infant twins would die within a few months. If the operation were performed, the weaker twin would die immediately, but it was hoped that the stronger twin would survive to lead a "relatively normal life".[106] In allowing the operation, Brooke LJ adopted Sir James Stephen's formulation of the doctrine of necessity:

> there are three necessary requirements for the application of the doctrine of necessity: (i) the act is needed to avoid inevitable and irreparable evil; (ii) no more should be done than is reasonably necessary for the purpose to be achieved; (iii) the evil inflicted must not be disproportionate to the evil avoided.[107]

The Court of Appeal sought to limit its holding, and Lord Justice Ward specifically excluded the possibility that the defence of necessity could be used to justify or excuse euthanasia.[108] Lord Justice Brooke described the availability of the defence of necessity as "unique" to the circumstances of the present case. He also observed that "[s]uccessive governments, and Parliaments, have set their face against euthanasia."[109] Nevertheless, if the "inevitable and irreparable evil" is the unbearable suffering of the patient which cannot be assuaged by other means than euthanasia, then Stephen's formulation could in theory allow for euthanasia provided it is seen as proportionate to the avoidance of unbearable suffering.

Some commentators on the decision in *Re A* have been concerned about such an implication.[110] Their fears are unconvincing as they fail to acknowledge the reality of the choice facing the judges in *Re A*: either both twins would die in a few months, or the stronger twin might be saved if the

---

[105] [2001] Fam 147. The case can be distinguished from the earlier jurisprudence (*supra* note 103) as the choice would not be one made by the person responsible for the killing but rather determined by the poor prognosis of one of the twins, nor would it be one between the life of the actor and that of the victim. For further discussion of this case, see Elizabeth Wicks, "The Greater Good? Issues of Proportionality and Democracy in the Doctrine of Necessity as Applied in *Re A*", 32 *Common Law World Review* (2003), pp. 115–134; Richard Huxtable, "Separation of Conjoined Twins: Where Next for English Law", *Criminal Law Review* (2001), pp. 459–70; Lewis, *Assisted Dying and Legal Change, supra* note 1, pp. 86–88.

[106] *Re A* [2001] Fam 147, 197. See Sandra Laville, "Surviving Siamese twin Gracie goes home to Gozo", *Daily Telegraph*, 16 June 2001.

[107] *Re A* [2001] Fam 147, 240, derived from Sir James Fitzjames Stephen, *A Digest of the Criminal Law (Crimes and Punishments)*, 4th ed. (London, 1887), p. 24.

[108] *Re A* [2001] Fam. 147, 204–5.

[109] *Re A* [2001] Fam. 147, 239, 211.

[110] See, e.g., Wicks, *supra* note 105, 22; Huxtable, *supra* note 105, 468; Jenny McEwan, "Murder by Design: the 'Feel-Good Factor' and the Criminal Law", 9 *Medical Law Review* (2001), pp. 246–258, 248.

weaker twin were sacrificed by the operation to separate them. In other words, the choice was between saving one twin and saving neither. This is not the choice faced by the doctor in a euthanasia case. That choice is between the duty to preserve life and the duty to relieve suffering.

B. Covert Tools

In practice, while rejecting the defence of necessity to a charge of murder, judges have tended to use covert tools to reach much the same result, holding or suggesting that a doctor performing euthanasia did not *intend* the death of her patient,[111] or did not *cause* the death.[112] Such escape routes are only available when the medication used can be used to relieve pain as well as to cause death. When a euthanaticum, such as potassium chloride, is used these covert tools are usually unavailable[113] and convictions have ensued.[114]

   Another covert tool which may play a role in this context is jury nullification, that is, "the jury's power to acquit on compassionate grounds, even if instructed that the accused has no defence in law".[115] Perhaps because of the risk of jury nullification, prosecutors have been willing to accept guilty pleas to lesser offences, thus avoiding the prospect of a jury trial.[116] Selective charging decisions may also make convictions unlikely.[117] In some cases

---

[111] See above, text accompanying notes 71–78.

[112] See Otlowski, *supra* note 90, pp. 170–184.

[113] Although Robert Walker LJ did make some attempt to bend the concept of intention in *Re A*, a case when the outcome was certain death for the weaker twin. *Re A* [2001] Fam 147, 251, 259.

[114] See, e.g., *Cox* (1992) 12 BMLR 38. This is not invariably the case. For example, in 1990, the prosecution discontinued its case against Dr. Lodwig, an English doctor who had reportedly injected his patient, who was suffering from terminal cancer, with potassium chloride. See Diana Brahams, "The reluctant survivor: Part 1", 140 *New Law Journal* (1990), pp. 586–587 (both causation and intention were apparently doubted).

[115] Barney Sneiderman *et al.*, *Canadian Medical Law: An Introduction for Physicians, Nurses and other Health Care Professionals*, 3rd ed. (Scarborough, Ontario, 2003) 637. See, e.g., *Arthur* (1981) 12 BMLR 1 (defendant who had administered dihydrocodeine to infant with Down's Syndrome following decision not to feed the child acquitted of attempted murder); *Carr*, *Sunday Times*, 30 Nov. 1986 (defendant who had administered massive dose of phenobarbitone to cancer patient acquitted of murder).

[116] See House of Lords Select Committee on Medical Ethics, *supra* note 72, [128] (in 22 'mercy-killing' cases between 1982 and 1991, only one defendant was convicted of murder, charges were downgraded to lesser offences in the other cases, resulting in probation or suspended sentences; all of the defendants were family members or acquaintances).

[117] See House of Lords Select Committee on Medical Ethics, ibid. For example, charging the defendant with an offence which will be difficult for the prosecution to prove beyond a reasonable doubt (e.g. murder) rather than one which would be easier to prove (e.g. attempted murder).

prosecutors may decide not to go forward with a prosecution,[118] or the prosecution may be willing to accept "a sympathetic report from a pliant psychiatrist" which "dress[es] up [a] rational 'mercy' killing ... as ... diminished responsibility".[119]

C. Assisted Suicide

Assistance with suicide, whether or not by a doctor, is specifically prohibited by the Suicide Act 1961:

> s.2(1) A person ("D") commits an offence if—
> (a) D does an act capable of encouraging or assisting the suicide or attempted suicide of another person, and
> (b) D's act was intended to encourage or assist suicide or an attempt at suicide. ...
>
> s.2(1C) An offence under this section is triable on indictment and a person convicted of such an offence is liable to imprisonment for a term not exceeding 14 years.[120]

Under s. 2(4) of the Suicide Act, any prosecution requires the consent of the Director of Public Prosecutions (DPP). Very few prosecutions have been brought under this section. However, in *Attorney-General v Able*, the Attorney General sought a declaration that making available a booklet entitled *A Guide to Self-Deliverance*, which contained guidance on suicide techniques, to members of the Voluntary Euthanasia Society constituted an offence under the Suicide Act. Woolf J held that an offence would only be committed if (a) the defendant intended that the booklet would be used by someone contemplating suicide who would be assisted by its contents; and (b) he distributed the booklet to such a person who used it; and (c) that person was assisted or encouraged by reading the booklet to attempt suicide, whether or not that attempt was successful.[121]

---

[118] Interestingly, the presence of prosecutorial and judicial 'flexibility' in assisted suicide and euthanasia cases was considered favourably by the European Court of Human Rights in support of the proportionality of a blanket ban on assisted suicide under Article 8(2) of the European Convention. *Pretty v UK* (2002) 35 EHRR 1, [76] (Eur Ct HR).

[119] Law Commission, *Murder, Manslaughter and Infanticide*, supra note 88, [7.48].

[120] This offence was recently amended by the Coroners and Justice Act 2009, s. 59(2). The amended version came into force on 1 February 2010.

[121] *Attorney-General v Able* [1984] QB 795, 812. For some other rare examples of such cases see *R v UK* (1983) 6 EHRR 140 (Eur Comm HR) (affirming a conviction of conspiring to aid and abet suicide where the defendant had facilitated contact between individuals desiring assistance in suicide and an individual willing to provide such assistance); *Chard, The Times*, 23 Sept. 1993 (Central Crim Ct) (defendant acquitted on judge's direction of assisting suicide of terminally ill friend whom he had provided with paracetamol).

1. A Rights-Based Challenge

In *Pretty*, the courts were confronted with the question whether the criminal prohibition on assisted suicide complies with the European Convention on Human Rights. Dianne Pretty was suffering from terminal motor neurone disease when she requested an assurance in advance from the DPP that her husband would not be prosecuted if he assisted her suicide. Mrs. Pretty relied on her rights to life, freedom from torture and inhuman or degrading treatment, respect for her private and family life, freedom of thought, conscience and religion and freedom from discrimination under the European Convention.[122] She appealed the DPP's refusal to provide such assurance through the English courts and then to the European Court of Human Rights but was unsuccessful at every level.[123]

2. Prosecutorial Policy and Assisted Suicide Travel

Recent years have seen an increase in the number of Britons travelling to Switzerland for assisted suicide.[124] In 2005, the High Court discharged an injunction preventing the husband of a competent woman suffering from cerebellar ataxia from making arrangements to take her to Switzerland where she wished to receive assistance in suicide. The judge pointed out that "[a]lthough not unique, the provision [requiring the consent of the DPP] is rare and is usually found where Parliament recognises that although an act may be criminal, it is not always in the public interest to prosecute in respect of it."[125] Recent attempts to amend the Suicide Act 1961 to exempt assistance with travel to a permissive jurisdiction for assisted suicide have failed.[126]

---

[122] European Convention on Human Rights, Arts. 2, 3, 8, 9, 14.
[123] *The Queen on the Application of Dianne Pretty v Director of Public Prosecutions* [2001] EWHC Admin 788 (QB); *The Queen on the Application of Mrs Dianne Pretty v Director of Public Prosecutions* [2002] 1 AC 800 (HL); *Pretty v UK* (2002) 35 EHRR 1. The constitutionality of the English prohibition on assisting a suicide had been previously considered by the European Commission on Human Rights in *R v UK* (1983) 6 EHRR 140, 144 (see *supra* note 121). The European Commission upheld the prohibition as necessary in a democratic society to prevent abuses and protect health.
[124] S. Fischer *et al.*, "Suicide assisted by two Swiss right-to-die organisations", 34 *Journal of Medical Ethics* (2008), pp. 810–814, Table 1.
[125] *In re Z (Local Authority: Duty)* [2005] 1 WLR 959, [14].
[126] Acts not capable of encouraging or assisting suicide (exception for travel abroad), proposed amendment to Coroners and Justice Bill, 19 Mar. 2009, www.publications.parliament.uk/pa/cm200809/cmbills/072/amend/pbc0720319a.456-460.html (accessed 22 July 2011); Acts not capable of encouraging or assisting suicide, proposed amendment to Coroners and Justice Bill, 1 June 2009, www.publications.parliament.uk/pa/ld200809/ldbills/033/amend/am033-g.htm (accessed 22 July 2011).

In 2009 in *Purdy*, the House of Lords held, as the DPP conceded, that end-of-life decisions including decisions to seek assistance with suicide *are* covered by the right to respect for private and family life in Article 8(1) of the European Convention on Human Rights. This was consistent with the decision of the European Court of Human Rights in *Pretty v UK*, in which the Strasbourg Court had found that Dianne Pretty's Article 8(1) right was engaged.[127] In addition, the House of Lords held that the refusal of the DPP to issue a published policy on such prosecutions was in conflict with the requirement in Article 8(2) that any limits on the right be "in accordance with the law".[128] The House of Lords asked the DPP to produce guidance for Debbie Purdy and others in a similar position contemplating ending their lives with assistance. Less than two months after the House of Lords' decision, the DPP issued an interim policy for prosecutors setting out the factors to be considered when deciding whether a prosecution in an assisted suicide case is in the public interest.[129] A 12 week public consultation period followed, and a final amended policy was published 10 weeks later.

As in all Crown Prosecution Service (CPS) decisions on prosecution, two consecutive stages of decision-making are involved: the first 'evidential' stage (requiring 'a realistic prospect of conviction')[130] and, where this stage is satisfied, the second 'public interest' stage to determine whether "the offence or the circumstances of its commission is or are of such a character that a prosecution in respect thereof is required in the public interest".[131] The policy sets out two lists of factors to be taken into account by prosecutors when deciding whether a prosecution is in the public interest: factors in favour of and against prosecution.[132] The DPP decided[133] to include all offences which could be prosecuted under s. 2(1) (which could include providing medication, writing a prescription, or other technical or practical assistance with the act of suicide itself), rather than covering only those providing assistance with travel to a country where

---

[127] *Pretty v UK* (2002) 35 EHRR 1.

[128] *R (on the application of Purdy) v DPP* [2009] UKHL 45, [54]-[56].

[129] DPP, *Interim Policy for Prosecutors in respect of Cases of Assisted Suicide* (London, 2009).

[130] Ibid., [9]-[13]. See also, DPP, *Code for Crown Prosecutors* (London, 2010), [4.5]-[4.9].

[131] Sir Hartley Shawcross, Attorney General, *Hansard*, House of Commons, 29 January 1951, vol. 483, cited in *Code for Crown Prosecutors*, ibid., [4.10]. See also, *Purdy* [2009] UKHL 45, [44].

[132] DPP, *Policy for Prosecutors in respect of Cases of Assisted Suicide* (London, 2010), [4.7].

[133] DPP, *Interim Policy*, supra note 129, [5]. No explanation for the decision was provided.

assisted suicide is lawful, as Lord Hope envisaged,[134] and as would be consistent with the facts of the *Purdy* case. While the DPP's broad interpretation could be inferred from some of the other speeches,[135] the DPP's decision to depart from the leading speech of Lord Hope and to issue a policy which will have significantly greater impact than mandated by the decision of the House of Lords is an interesting one, which has accelerated informal legal change on assisted suicide.

The first group of factors in favour of prosecution relate to the victim's request.[136] Capacity is assessed according to the MCA,[137] and the request must be 'voluntary' as well as clear, settled and informed.[138] There is no requirement that the request be in writing, as the DPP is concerned to avoid the charge that he is creating a regulatory regime for assisted suicide.[139] This may explain to some extent the lack of specificity regarding the level of information required for the victim's decision to be considered sufficiently informed,[140] and the choice not to include a waiting period.[141]

Perhaps for the same reason, it is not a factor in favour of prosecution that the victim and/or the suspect were not resident in England and Wales. It remains to be seen whether individuals will travel to England and Wales in order to undertake an assisted suicide with significantly less chance of prosecution than there might be in their home jurisdiction,[142] just as individuals travel to Switzerland for assisted suicides,[143] and to Mexico to obtain veterinary euthanasia medications.[144]

---

[134] *Purdy* [2009] UKHL 45, [54].

[135] Ibid., [63]-[69] (Baroness Hale), [82]-[87] (Lord Brown), [100]-[106] (Lord Neuberger).

[136] For a critique of the use of the word 'victim' to describe the person who has committed or attempted suicide, see Penney Lewis, *The Director of Public Prosecutions' Interim Policy for Prosecutors in Respect of Cases of Assisted Suicide: A Response to the Consultation* (London, 2009), [1.1], http://ssrn.com/abstract=1583439 (accessed 22 July 2011). As the term is used throughout the policy documentation, I have used it here.

[137] See *supra* note 2.

[138] DPP, *Policy for Prosecutors, supra* note 132, factors 2-4 in favour of prosecution, factor 1 against prosecution.

[139] CPS, *Public Consultation Exercise on the Interim Policy for Prosecutors in respect of Cases of Assisted Suicide Issued by The Director of Public Prosecutions: Summary of responses* (London, 2010), [7.6].

[140] Lewis, *supra* note 136, [9.1].

[141] Ibid., [5.5].

[142] See Paulette Kurzer, *Markets and Moral Regulation: Cultural Change in the European Union* (Cambridge, 2001), pp. 175–180.

[143] Fischer, *supra* note 124.

[144] Luis De Uriarte, "La opción Mexicana" *Reforma*, 19 May 2008, 1, 4; 'Tijuana: parada al paraíso' *Reforma*, 19 May 2008, 4; 'Lecciones para "bien morir"' *Reforma*, 20 May 2008, 4; 'Sólo les queda México' *Reforma*, 21 May 2008, 4.

Although the factor-based approach looks quite different to the regulatory regimes found in other permissive jurisdictions, nonetheless certain characteristics of the category of permissible assisted suicides can be discerned. In addition to the validity of the victim's request, the central issues addressed by the policy focus on the condition of the victim, and the identity and mental state of the suspect.

In the interim policy, it was a factor against prosecution if the victim had "a terminal illness; or a severe and incurable physical disability; or a severe degenerative physical condition from which there was no possibility of recovery".[145] The final policy abandoned this requirement or any refinement of it:

> A large number of respondents questioned the inclusion of these factors, arguing that it may be discriminatory to include factors relating to the health and disability status of the victim (over 1,500 respondents argued this in their general comments) ... As a result of these views expressed during the consultation exercise, and upon further consideration, the CPS has removed [these factors] from the Final Policy.[146]

The need to avoid discrimination is undoubtedly important,[147] but the decision to remove any reference to the victim's condition raises two crucial questions. First, is there a non-discriminatory way of delineating relevant public interest factors related to the victim's experience? Second, what will be the effect of excluding consideration of the victim's condition or experience from the public interest analysis?

In relation to the first question, the Dutch approach—requiring that the attending physician be satisfied that the patient's suffering was 'unbearable and hopeless'—may have been helpful here, as it explicitly refers only to the victim's experience of suffering rather than his or her condition, or the cause of such suffering.[148]

As for the second question, by failing to include any reference to the victim's condition or experience, the policy fails to distinguish between, for example, a victim with a terminal illness who is experiencing unbearable suffering, and a victim suffering from depression. (While capacity may be doubted in depression patients, a majority of depressed patients

---

[145] DPP, *Interim policy*, *supra* note 129, factor 4 against prosecution. Factor 6 in favour of prosecution was the converse of this factor.

[146] CPS, *Summary of responses*, *supra* note 139, [2.10], [6.14]-[6.17].

[147] I examine this issue in *Assisted Dying and Legal Change*, *supra* note 1, pp. 37–40.

[148] Termination of Life on Request and Assisted Suicide (Review Procedures) Act 2001, s. 2(1)(b), 8 *European Journal of Health Law* (2001), pp. 183–191.

have capacity.)[149] Factor 10 in favour of prosecution might be relevant
here: "The victim was physically able to undertake the act that constituted
the assistance him or herself."[150] However, this factor does not necessarily
distinguish between a terminally ill victim and one with depression. If the
suspect's assistance is the provision of an opioid (left over from an earlier
illness of a family member, for example, or validly prescribed for the suspect) and the victim had no medical need for the opioid and therefore
would not have been able to procure it him or herself, then factor 10 will
not bite in favour of prosecution, even if the victim could have committed
suicide without assistance using an alternative method.

Another group of factors in favour of prosecution is designed to ensure
that assistance in suicide remains an activity carried out by inexperienced
individuals without the open assistance of professionals or amateur
organisations:

> (11) the suspect was unknown to the victim and encouraged or assisted the
> victim to commit or attempt to commit suicide by providing specific infor-
> mation via, for example, a website or publication;
> (12) the suspect gave encouragement or assistance to more than one victim
> who were not known to each other;
> (13) the suspect was paid by the victim or those close to the victim for his or
> her encouragement or assistance;
> (14) the suspect was acting in his or her capacity as a medical doctor, nurse,
> other healthcare professional, a professional carer [whether for payment or
> not], or as a person in authority, such as a prison officer, and the victim was
> in his or her care;
> (16) the suspect was acting in his or her capacity as a person involved in the
> management or as an employee (whether for payment or not) of an organi-
> sation or group, a purpose of which is to provide a physical environment
> (whether for payment or not) in which to allow another to commit
> suicide.[151]

Unlike all of the other jurisdictions which permit assisted suicide (and in
the Netherlands and Belgium, euthanasia as well), where the activity is

---

[149] Thomas Grisso and Paul S. Appelbaum, "The MacArthur Treatment Competence
Study, III: abilities of patients to consent to psychiatric and medical treatments", 19
Law and Human Behavior (1995), pp. 149–174; Jochen Vollmann *et al.*, "Competence of
mentally ill patients: a comparative empirical study", 33 *Psychological Medicine* (2003),
pp. 1463–1471.

[150] This factor was briefly mentioned in the first case decided under the policy, although
it does not appear to have weighed heavily in favour of prosecution. DPP, "Statement
regarding the deaths of Sir Edward and Lady Downes", 19 Mar. 2010.

[151] Factor 10 in favour of prosecution could also be grouped with these factors. See
above, text accompanying note 150.

carried out in whole or in part by physicians, the inclusion of these factors will discourage the involvement of healthcare professionals, unless the victim is fortunate enough to have someone with medical expertise amongst his or her family or close friends who is willing to provide expert advice or assistance. The advantages of open medical involvement are manifold, and include a lower risk of botched suicides and suffering during the suicide or attempted suicide[152] and the possibility of screening for possibly hitherto unknown mental disorders including depression.[153] By strongly discouraging medical involvement, the policy places a heavy burden on supportive friends and family. Although not being in this group no longer counts as a factor in favour of prosecution,[154] nonetheless, most assisted suicides will involve such assistance, particularly given the risks of involvement for those acting in a professional capacity or as members of an organisation.

Whether intentionally or not, these factors may keep the number of assisted suicides which take place entirely within the UK relatively low. Travel to a jurisdiction which does permit medical involvement will remain attractive to some, and this may have to be done earlier than the victim would otherwise wish. If travelling to a permissive jurisdiction is not possible, for financial or health reasons, then the burden of assisting the suicide will fall on someone with no experience (factor 12) and no access to relevant information (factor 11). "Medical condition, body build, drug history and narcotic tolerance are all variables that must be factored in when developing a specific strategy to achieve death."[155] Without this knowledge, and without access to appropriate medications, the policy is

---

[152] Roger S. Magnusson, *Angels of Death – Exploring the Euthanasia Underground* (New Haven, CT, 2002), pp. 202–210; Stephen Jamison, "When Drugs Fail: Assisted Deaths and Not-So-Lethal Drugs", in M.P. Battin and A.G. Lipman (eds.), *Drug Use in Assisted Suicide and Euthanasia* (Binghamton, NY, 1996), pp. 223–244, p. 241; Stephen Jamison, *Final Acts of Love: Families, Friends, and Assisted Dying* (New York, 1995). This risk was illustrated in the recent *Gilderdale* case. BBC Panorama 'I Helped My Daughter Die', 1 Feb. 2010.

[153] See Oregon Death With Dignity Act, § 3.03; Washington Death with Dignity Act, RCW 70.245.060.

[154] In the *Interim policy*, being "the spouse, partner or a close relative or a close personal friend of the victim" counted against prosecution, and the converse counted in favour (*supra* note 129, factor 6 against prosecution, factor 10 in favour of prosecution). Concerns about voluntariness, undue influence and the risk of abuse from this group led the DPP to drop these factors in the final policy (*Summary of responses, supra* note 139, [6.18]-[6.20]), although it is likely that cases which do not involve such a 'special relationship' will receive additional scrutiny. See, e.g., DPP, "The suicide of Mr Raymond Cutkelvin – Decision on Prosecution", 25 June 2010; DPP, "No charges following death of Caroline Loder", 16 Aug. 2010.

[155] Magnusson, *supra* note 152, p. 203.

likely to result in assisted suicides which are more difficult, less successful and more stressful for the victim and his or her friends and family (including the suspect) than would be the case if medical expertise were permitted in some form. Those without supportive friends and family may commit suicide earlier than they would have wished, or travel to a permissive jurisdiction when they are still able to do so on their own.

A group of factors in favour of prosecution are concerned with the suspect's motives and the possible exercise of undue influence (which might cast doubt on the validity of the victim's decision). Prosecution is more likely if "the suspect was not wholly motivated by compassion"[156] or if there is a history of violence or abuse by the suspect against the victim.[157] Two factors against prosecution encapsulate an idealised scenario that involves an unwilling suspect and a determined victim:

> (4) the suspect had sought to dissuade the victim from taking the course of action which resulted in his or her suicide;
> (5) the actions of the suspect may be characterised as reluctant encouragement or assistance in the face of a determined wish on the part of the victim to commit suicide;

What if the suspect is fully supportive of the victim's decision, recognising that the victim has reached his or her own decision and agreeing that it is the right course of action for him or her in the circumstances? This prosecution will be more likely to be found to be in the public interest than one where the suspect is 'reluctant' and seeks to 'dissuade' the victim. Factor 4 against prosecution envisages the decision to seek assisted suicide as an unwise or irrational one from which the victim should be dissuaded, or at least suggests that this is how the ideal suspect should react to the decision. The inclusion of these two factors seems to prescribe a certain kind of emotional reaction on the part of a family member or friend, for example, not accepting the victim's terminal diagnosis, or wanting the victim to remain alive as long as possible.

The dangers sought to be addressed by the policy focus on the unscrupulous or even abusive family member or friend, and the healthcare professional or activist. The policy opens the door to assisted suicide in cases which would not be permitted by most of the existing regulatory regimes, while exposing to the risk of prosecution those with much-needed expertise and those who agree with the victim's decision.

---

[156] DPP, *Policy for Prosecutors*, *supra* note 132, factor 6 in favour of prosecution, factor 2 against prosecution.
[157] Ibid., factor 9 in favour of prosecution.

V. Conclusion

Both the House of Lords in its last judicial ruling,[158] and the DPP[159] have recently reaffirmed that formal legal change on assisted dying is the exclusive province of the legislature. While Parliament has been unwilling to undertake such formal legal change, informal legal change has been accelerated by the House of Lords' surprising decision in *Purdy*, coupled with a DPP willing to create an expansive policy covering all assisted suicides rather than just those which take place in another more permissive jurisdiction. The DPP has done so by implicitly describing (albeit imperfectly through the use of factors for and against prosecution) a class of assisted suicides which are permissible. We are now in uncharted territory, with a reluctant legislature, little guidance from the courts and an opaque process of informal legal change by prosecutors.

Although competent adults may refuse treatment, children and incompetent adults are treated according to their best interests, with the judiciary as the ultimate arbiters of what these are. It remains to be seen what effect the provisions of the MCA will have on this position. Will a donee of a lasting power of attorney appointed by a patient while still competent be overruled by a judge who disputes the donee's assessment of the patient's best interests, as parents who disagree with the medical team treating their child almost always are?

---

[158] "It must be emphasised at the outset that it is no part of our function to change the law in order to decriminalise assisted suicide. If changes are to be made, as to which I express no opinion, this must be a matter for Parliament." *Purdy* [2009] UKHL 45, [26] (Lord Hope). See also [106] (Lord Neuberger).

[159] The policy begins with the reassurance that "only Parliament can change the law on encouraging or assisting suicide." DPP, *Policy for Prosecutors*, *supra* note 132, [5]. See also, CPS, *Summary of responses*, *supra* note 139, [10.9]-[10.17].

EUTHANASIA IN CHINA:
SOME ISSUES IN HARMONIZATION

*Alessia Magliacane**

Mencius explique très bien, après avoir tenu ces propos que vous auriez tort de croire optimistes sur la bonté de l'homme, comment il se fait que ce sur quoi on est le plus ignorant, c'est sur les lois en tant qu'elles viennent du ciel, les mêmes lois qu'Antigone. Il en donne une démonstration absolument rigoureuse. Il est trop tard pour que je vous la dise ici. Les lois du ciel en question, ce sont bien les lois du désir.

Lacan, L'éthique de la Psychanalyse (1960)

So, in a way, there is a kind of poetic justice in the fact that the final result of Mao's Cultural Revolution is today's unprecedented explosion of capitalist dynamism in China.

Zizek, Mao on practice and contradiction (2007)

Perhaps in a more Western kind of psychoanalytic language... we might think of the new onset of the Utopian process as a kind of desiring to desire, a learning to desire, the invention of the desire called Utopia in the first place, along with new rules for the fantasizing or daydreaming of such a thing - a set of narrative protocols with no precedent in our previous literary institution.

Jameson, The Seeds of Time (1994)

Discussing end-of-life choices in modern Chinese society for a Western scholar is to have the chance of looking at this consolidated area of knowledge and expertise covered by bioethics with renewed experience, although in continuous evolution. Chinese medical ethics, which directly stems from the principles and the values of a world's vision whose medical practice is firstly the application of virtue, is still present both in medical profession and in popular common sense, from small villages to large cities of the country. At the same time, Marxist alternative is clearly a data for the emancipation of Chinese society, despite of a definition of the Chinese system that continues to evade foreign observer.

Through ancient Chinese medical ethics, Chinese humanitarianism has nurtured thousands of noble-minded medical workers and has

---

* Researcher in Comparative Law; email: alessiamagliacane1@gmail.com.

S. Negri (ed.), *Self-Determination, Dignity and End-of-Life Care*
2011 Koninklijke Brill NV. Printed in The Netherlands. ISBN 978 90 04 22357 8. pp. 249–270

contributed to health and human well-being. Contemporary Chinese medical ethics provides an example of a Marxist socialist alternative of society, different from that of Hippocratic and liberal Western medical ethics.[1] However, in the contemporary era, when science and society are developing at a rapid pace, traditional philosophy seems to be no longer able to provide current and scientific guidelines for a physician's actions.[2]

For Chinese practitioners, the long history and the moral depth of their traditional medical ethics carry an influence that, obviously, might conflict with modern government-endorsed ethical programs. Euthanasia and modern bioethics have been extensively debated. The issues are significant representations of man and society registered in national traditions, while offering a remarkable illustration of scientific, technological, economic, even legal interdependencies that characterize the current Chinese society.

We intend to show that the tension between traditional Chinese medical ethics and political and economic Marxist principles is beneficial in a full economic developed society, while addressing these issues in the extent required.

Euthanasia, like other bioethical problems, is quite a new ethical dilemma in China. This makes clear for the reader our choice to select also surveys from the papers and the media world, in a country where free circulation through the web and the governmental control through the same web coexist.

These paradoxes or dilemmas show the possibilities in Chinese society to achieve a diverse sense of bioethics, and suggest strong understandings which permit to reconstruct the values starting from a different perception of the *praxis*. Otherwise, the contemporary approach to the elements of this conflict, rather attentive to the advances in biotechnology and to the problems of medical ethics, classifies the forms of discourse in a way that removes any object of debate or conflict, forbidding a real discussion of these issues.[3]

---

[1] Ralph Crawshaw, "Medical deontology in the Soviet Union", in Robert M. Veatch (ed.), *Cross Cultural Perspectives in Medical Ethics: Readings* (Boston, 1989).

[2] Hubei Z. Wu, "Conflict between Chinese traditional ethics and bioethics", 3 *Cambridge Quarterly of Healthcare Ethics* (1994), pp. 367–371, p. 369.

[3] It is essential to remember that their philosophical and scientific discussion has often been anticipated, and exceeded, by judicial practice (as in the famous case of *Baby M.* in the United States, subject to grant of maternity), concerning the birth of a *bio-law*.

I. A Bioethics of Self-Understanding: Between Eastern
and Western Traditions

Le xìng 性*, c'était justement un des éléments qui nous préoccuperont cette année pour autant que le terme qui en approche le plus, c'est celui de la nature.*

Lacan, *D'un discours qui ne serait pas du semblant* (1971)

Oggi le comuni popolari sono state smantellate, la terra restituita ai contadini, l'idea del "nostro" rimpiazzata da quella molto più naturale, ma anche più disastrosa, del "mio", ed ecco che le dighe cedono. Le alluvioni che colpiscono vaste zone e minacciano di sommergere grandi città come Wuhan, con milioni di abitanti, sono soltanto la punta di uno spaventoso iceberg rappresentato dall'incuria con cui ormai viene gestito tutto ciò che prima era comune e non privato.

Terzani, *La porta proibita* (2010)

Pas de doute: nous sommes en présence de la tentative la plus convaincante de faire durer un régime communiste en le réconciliant avec les règles des sociétés les plus modernes.

Domenach, *La Chine m'inquiète* (2009)

It could be strange to see a substantial lack of debate into euthanasia in traditional Chinese medical ethics as laid down by Sun Si-Mao[4] during Tang Dynasty (in contrast to the moral Hellenic and later Roman). Thus, we have to face a sort of lack of an explicit formulation of the principle of autonomy.

Nevertheless, traditional Chinese medical ethics drew upon China's major tradition. Confucianism, Daoism and Buddhism focused their moral doctrine of beneficence on humaneness and compassion in attempting to save *every* living creature (as the contemporary philosopher of law Martha C. Nussbaum, from Chicago, often outlines in the terms of the greatest difference in Western and Eastern cultures).[5] In this context, it is not surprising that any premature or unnatural death was considered to be an aberration. Compassion (*tz'u*) and humaneness (*ren*) are the basic values of medical practice whose purpose is to help, save life and not to kill any living creature (Sun also advised against using living creatures,

---

[4] Sun Szu-Miao (AD581-682) was a famous physician, Taoist and alchemist, who wrote a monograph entitled *On the absolute sincerity of great physicians*. Tao Lee, "Medical ethics in ancient China", in *Cross Cultural Perspectives in Medical Ethics*, supra note 1, pp. 134–136.

[5] Martha C. Nussbaum, *Frontiers of Justice* (Harvard, 2007).

even a hen's egg, as medication). There is, comprehensively understood, a principle of responsibility to care.[6]

Highlighting righteousness (*yi*) as an inner core of morality beside humaneness (*ren*), that motivates and guides man to pursue the *dao*,[7] the individual responsibility to the group may lead to the interpretation of the four Western principles of bioethics (dignity, integrity, autonomy, vulnerability) in a social oriented way. This is contrary to the mainstream of contemporary Western bioethics which, in general, tends to grant the uppermost position to the "value-complex of individualism which underscores individual right, privacy, autonomy and self-determination".[8] Thus, "ancient Chinese medical ethics calls to mind a precious element that exists in the ancient healing art, the contemporary acceptance of which would stop the alienation between persons caused by overextended autonomy-oriented individualism and would make the doctor-patient relationship meaningful again, namely, the art of humaneness".[9]

The pedagogical attitude to the living is connected with the best tradition of Western philosophy, which recognizes, from the common condition of vulnerability as a (bio)fundamental of ethics,[10] each living

---

[6] Sun Szu-miao's medical ethics professed that: "The object is to help, not to gain material goods" and "a great physician" should "commit himself with great compassion to save every living creature". Kung Hsin in AD1556 wrote: "The good physician of the present day cherishes *humaneness* and *righteousness*... He cares not for vain glory, but is intent upon relieving suffering among all classes". Moreover, Chen Shin-kung (AD1605) said: "Medicine should be given free to the poor. Extra financial help should be extended to the destitute patients; if possible. Whitout food, medicine alone cannot relieve the distress patient". Tao Lee, *supra* note 4.

[7] Daniel Fu-Chang Tsai, "The bioethical principles and Confucius' moral philosophy", 31 *Journal of Medical Ethics* (2005), pp. 159–163.

[8] Daniel Fu-Chang Tsai, "Ancient Chinese medical ethics and the four principles of biomedical ethics", 25 *Journal of Medical Ethics* (1999), pp. 315–321, p. 320. According to Tsai, in Ancient Chinese medical ethics, the idea of justice refers to the equally access to care rather than to distributive justice, which is "very likely to suppress the concept of individual rights or autonomy".

[9] Ibid., p. 321. So, ancient Chinese medical ethics shares the same principles as contemporary Western bioethics, but "the outcome of the "specification", "balancing and overriding" could be totally dissimilar since ACME chooses a different principle as the "predominant" or "overriding" one".

[10] First, one can refer to vulnerability in terms of ethics, as a prescriptive requirement of finiteness, then the whole humanity and all other living species are united by this general state of vulnerability. On the another level, considering the environment no longer as an ecosystem, but as a set of fundamental and indispensable resources, it is clear that there is a universal condition of vulnerability in the sense of lack of control over the conditions that enable a better quality of life. Francesco Rubino, *Etiche incerte: dal corpo alla guerra* (Trento, 2010).

being as irreplaceable,[11] between the "already-given" and the "not-yet-made" of creation, entrusted it to man's responsibility.[12]

From this perspective of an "archeology of the law", there exists a "transcendental grammar" of basic principles to the origins of the cultures, therefore trans-cultural, which is a veritable heritage of humanity.[13]

In this context, in the relationship between nature and the individual, finds a place what we can now draw as the anthropology of the human body, as a general discourse on the meaning of the constitution of the human body. The body is the only practical option available to the individual to communicate with the world: even the most intimate feelings pass through the body. Fragility depends on our uniqueness. "Fragile" is the ability of the subject to argue. "Fragile" is the discourse of the subject's body which wants to make a project. By quoting Kemp: "ontologically speaking, human existence is ultimately of an ethical character".[14]

Universal equality of the extension of body proposes also a revelation of meaning, of value. One can talk of solidarity. In this light, even the sanctity of human life, reflected in the principle of inviolability of the body, can be a value that may have less sense than others. There is an imperative of responsibility even toward those dying. To take charge of one's life implies to take charge of one's dying. In short, bioethics breaks the absolute singularity and contrasts with the same microphysics of power, the domination over other men and over inter-specific and environmental relations, by putting the language and establishing the social ties. In Chinese ancient ethics there is no unconditional duty to preserve and continue life, but there is an unconditional duty to uphold *ren* and *yi*: the biological life there is not of the highest value. The fundamental concept of humanity (*ren*), which not only refers to an inner spiritual condition/virtue, or an aspect of outward action/conduct, but also a dynamic process of *person making*, involves mutual incorporation between the self and the other.

---

[11] Peter Kemp, *L'irremplaçable. Une éthique de la technologie* (Paris, 1997).

[12] Hans Jonas, *The Imperative of Responsibility* (Chicago and London, 1984); Ernst Bloch, *The Principle of Hope* (US, 1995). The imperative of responsibility and the principle of hope, far from being opposed, are the indispensable element of the anti-utopian Marxist conscience for an Ethics of Liberation. Enrique Dussel, *Philosophy of Liberation* (New York, 1990).

[13] Otfried Höffe, *Democracy in an Age of Globalization* (Dordrecht, 2007).

[14] Kemp points toward the "ethical" as a narrative mould. Ethics has its narrative language. It may be in the narrative of historical events, as they are related in the public sphere; it may be in writing critical history of literature. Kemp, *supra* note 11, p. 63.

"To begin with, *ren* is a relational term and is used to describe the relational/social nature of man".[15]

For Mencius, the moral is inherent in human nature *xìng* 性, present in the reaction of everyone to the sight of a child who falls into a well. It is not an emotion linked to an identification with the child or his parents, but it reflects the close interdependence between all existing.

In other words, *ren* and *yi* has been conceived of manifesting in particular human relationships. From this perspective it follows that different views will be taken on bioethical issues such as the beginning of life, death and dying, informed consent. The shape of a new "Asian bioethics" should stand on the new philosophy concerning the relation between Nature and human being, which challenges the universality of human rights. This is a new humanism without human-centrism.[16]

Confucianism would tolerate euthanasia, but the decision-making process would be of the utmost importance. As humanity is the most important life-guiding principle, it also regulates the process of dying as well as the significance of death. The death pales in significance only in such an ethics relational and social determinations. Determinations about the beginning or end of our lives must be made in social settings, individual preference would not be sufficient grounds for such an action. The afflicted individual would not be recognized as fully autonomous and independent to decide whether to live or die. Such a decision would have to include those people closest to the person wanting to die. Siblings, spouses, children and perhaps other close acquaintances might also have a certain moral standing in the decision-making process. Such a behavior is not perceived as an insult to the patient's dignity—which is maybe an intrinsic difference between West and East. The liberal autonomy-heteronomy dichotomization is inapplicable, because self-determination is always a co-determination. "From the patient's point of view, the imperative to respect an individual's right to self-determination, considered to be sacrosanct in the West, is simply not required by the Chinese ethics of personhood. In fact, the Chinese concept of a more holistic and social personhood challenges the assumption that the patient is the one to be told of the diagnosis and prognosis and to make medical decisions".[17]

---

[15] Edwin C. Hui, "Personhood and bioethics: a Chinese perspective", in Ren-Zong Qiou (eds.), *Bioethics: Asian Perspectives. A Quest for Moral Diversity* (Dordrecht, 2004), p. 32.

[16] See *Bioethics: Asian Perspectives*, *supra* note 15.

[17] Edwin C. Hui, "Personhood and bioethics: a Chinese perspective", in *Bioethics: Asian Perspectives*, *supra* note 15, p. 40.

One can talk of dynamic dignity, which includes solidarity and ethics integration of body to maintain the precondition of protection of fundamental rights in a democratic context, namely discursive, communicable, participatory, collective and in potentially general.[18]

As a Chinese philosopher Zhang Chunmei wrote, stressing the importance of the social dimension in the Chinese conception of the human being, *shehui ren*, which involves the social being, "without an overall vision, the call for respect for human dignity seems weak and unconvincing". She proposes to combine the dignity in social relations, because "man is not a mere physical and spiritual individual. When he retreats into introspection and ignores the relations with the outside, or when it improperly uses natural resources and destroys the harmony with nature, he breaks ties with society, with nature, with the community and with reason".[19]

Bioethics is the ethics in the strong sense. Strengthened by membership in the living, that is, the species, society, language. And it is much stronger, this ethic, as the living is not only the species, but its same configuration in the biological environment: bio-ethics as an eco-ethics.

II. END-OF-LIFE CHINESE OPEN DEBATE

Au moment où est proclamée la République Populaire de Chine, en 1949, le parti communiste chinois a derrière lui plus de vingt ans non seulement d'existence et d'organisation, mais plus de vingt ans de direction de lutte de masse, plus de vingt ans de lutte militaire et plus de vingt ans d'expérience de direction politique et de gestion économique sur des régions plus ou moins vastes du territoire chinois libérées à différentes époques.

Bettelheim - Charrière - Marchisio, *La construction du socialisme en Chine*
(1968)

On sent bien l'application de plus en plus étendue de ce concept de contrat dans toutes les espaces publics chinois. Notamment avec l'arrivée massive des compagnies étrangères sur le territoire. Dans une petite entreprise privée de taille familiale, il n'est pas nécessaire, mais on voit bien que les immenses

---

[18] By overcoming the paternalism of the ancient Chinese society, while configuring a principle of autonomy of post-metaphysical type. See Jürgen Habermas, "The Debate on Ethical Self-Understanding of the Species", in *The Future of Human Nature* (Oxford, 2003).

[19] Zhang Chunmei, "La perplexité éthique du début de la vie: une relecture du statut de l'embryon", in Mireille Delmas-Marty and Zhang Naigen (eds.), *Clonage humain, droit et société, étude franco-chinoise*, vol. 3, *Conclusion* (Paris, 2005), pp. 36–37.

usines qui emploient des milliers d'employés adoptent un système de gestion de type occidental. A mon avis, ce système n'est pas totalement adapté à la réalité culturelle chinoise. Nous arriverons certainement dans les années à venir à une synthèse entre la relation de contrat entre deux individus et un lien plus confucianiste père/fils/frère. Cette génération de l'enfant unique va devoir inventer un nouvel ordre public et familial.

Datong, *La Chine sur le divan. Entretiens* (2008)

The town centre is so crowed we can hardly move. An ear cleaner waves his twig and shouts, 'One mao an ear'!' A blind masseur in dark glasses rubs his hands, waiting for his next customer. A spit-patrol officer grabs a middle-aged man and charges him a one-yuan fine. A beggar plays a three-stringed lute on the street corner and sings with his eyes shut: 'Chairman Mao's kindness is deeper than the sea. He comes like thunder in spring to rescue the Communist Party...'

Ma Jian, *Red Dust. A Path through China*

Historically, Chinese people would give up treatment for terminally ill patients. The first official documented case of euthanasia took place in Han Zhong City, Shannxi in June 1986 when a boy and his daughters pleaded that their mother Xia (age 59, diagnosed with hepatocirrhotic ascites, no hope of saving her) be euthanized "in order to bring an end to her suffering".[20]

Since this case—that soon after opposed son and daughters before the court, on the allegations of the only signature of Xia's son at the end of the prescription of euthanasia addressed to the chief physician[21]—the Chinese Dialectical Institute and Beijing Medical Ethics Academy took to hold that euthanasia can be used on a patient who has no hope of being saved (this was obviously in contrast to traditional medical conduct, even if Zhuang Shibin, in the *Peoples' press for military medicine* clearly stated that "when dying is very painful, it is permissible to request euthanasia").

When such a patient was beyond cure, doctors and family members, through a process of consultation, would always agree to withdraw all passive treatment, trying to satisfy the patient's will in order to appease the patient and let him die a good death. As professor Zhang, director of the Beijing Program in Medical Ethics says, even now this practice is considered to be a kind of natural death with great harmony.[22]

---

[20] Shi Da Pu, "Euthanasia in China: a report", 16 *Journal of Medicine and Philosophy* (1991), pp. 131–138.

[21] Anyway, the son and the two doctors who effectuated the terminal treatment passed a short period of detention by the police.

[22] Zhang Ju, "Chinese Controversies on Euthanasia", 4 *Bioethics Research Notes* (1992). A questionnaire survey carried out among 290 students and 111 workers to find out their

However, Zhang continues, socio-economic development—including medical progress and the shortage of medical resources which followed that progress—has resulted in great changes in Chinese mind at this historical juncture.

Since 1979, when a conference of the philosophy of medicine, held in Guangzhou, first discussed euthanasia in China, there has been much attention on the subject, both in public debates and among medical ethics academics in China.[23] Proposals to draft a law of euthanasia were brought to Chinese National People's Congress.[24]

It should be noted that the first legal case of euthanasia—above mentioned—in China happened in 1986, in the middle of Deng Xiaoping's political and economical reforms.[25] "By taking its own peculiar path towards 'socialism with Chinese characteristics' or, as some now prefer to call it, 'privatization with Chinese characteristics', it managed to construct a form of state-manipulated market economy that delivered spectacular economic growth (averaging close to 10 per cent a year) and rising standards of living for a significant proportion of the population for more than twenty years. But the reforms also led to environmental degradation, social inequality, and eventually something that looks uncomfortably like the reconstitution of capitalist class power".[26]

Also worthy to be mentioned is the fact that, all over the last 80s, euthanasia was still not considered as a medical problem: in terms of medicine,

---

opinion of euthanasia showed that most people were receptive to euthanasia (90 77%). They considered that euthanasia is humanistic and can help patients and their family members end of suffering (03% people chose active euthanasia as best way, only 13% people chose passive euthanasia and 84% people chose both). More than half people felt that there was contradictory between intellect and emotion. Sujian Xia and al., "Investigation on the Opinion Poll of Euthanasia among the Medical Students and Workers", 2 *Medicine and Society* (1999).

[23] Ying Zhang, Yi-ting Li, Shuang Li, Fang Liu, Bin-zheng Ke, "The History, Status Quo and Developing Trend of Euthanasia", 4 *Chinese Medical Ethics* (2008); Nong He, Buying Zheng and He Weimei, "University Students' Investigation for Euthanasia and Its Legislation", 6 *Chinese Medical Ethics* (2005).

[24] Although there is no improvement in the legislation of euthanasia. Chinese health care is governed by the legal document formulated by the National People's Congress and its Standing Committee. Health care legislation is divided into two parts, one instituted by the National People's Congress, the other by the Standing Committee of the National People's Congress. The first, called the Fundamental Health Law, has not yet been completed. The other part is the hygienic common law. Tonggan Zhao, *Health Legislation* (Beijing, 2001).

[25] From 1989 to 1995, about one thousand cases were published in the Journal of Chinese Medical Ethics, among which there were 253 cases of active and passive euthanasia. Dapu Shi and Lin Yu, "The Situation of Euthanasia in China Judged from Typical Cases and the Public Opinion", 6 *Chinese Medical Ethics* (1995).

[26] David Harvey, "Neoliberalism 'with Chinese characteristics'", in *A Brief History of Neoliberalism* (Oxford, 2009), p. 122.

it is an ideal terminus to the process of dying, it is not itself the cause of death.[27]

The weakness of health care provisions for the terminally ill in Mainland China has become increasingly poignant since the collapse of collective health care institutions in the countryside under the reforms of the late-1980s. As in most cases where health care facilities are wanting, it is difficult to apply the criteria of gentleness and dignity at reaching death. "The solution lies not in a faster relief from suffering by euthanasia, but in extending the quality of life through distributive justice within Chinese healthcare policy-making".[28]

In the revolutionary period the State-owned enterprises (SOEs) provided job security and social protections for their workforces. The security and the benefits they conferred on their workers, though whittled away over time, kept a social safety net under a significant sector of the population for many years. A more open market economy was created around them by dissolving the agricultural communes in favour of an individualized 'personal responsibility system'. Township and village enterprises (TVEs) were created out of the assets held by the communes, and "these became centres of entrepreneurialism, flexible labour practices, and open market competition".[29]

Since the 1980s, in the absence of a full development of rural people's organizations, the reforms concerning the economic system of integrated urban-rural development—its guideline being the distribution according to the law of the market of forces of production, capital and natural resources of the countryside—led to widespread corruption of the local bureaucracy. This happened firstly because families no longer had the means of production and, secondly, as a partial consequence, because the labor force could no longer be renewed.[30]

"Market pricing was introduced, but this was probably far less significant that the rapid devolution of political-economic power to the regions and to the localities. This last move proved particularly astute. Confrontation with traditional power centres in Beijing was avoided and local initiatives could pioneer the way to a new social order. Innovations that failed could simply be ignored".[31]

---

[27] Shi Da Pu, *supra* note 20, p. 133.
[28] Margaret Sleeboom-Faulkner, "Chinese concepts of euthanasia and health care", 4 *Bioethics* (2006), pp.203–212, p. 210.
[29] Harvey, *supra* note 26, pp. 125–126.
[30] Changping Li, "Point de salut sans organisation autonome paysanne", 5 *Réforme chinoise* (2003).
[31] Harvey, *supra* note 26, p. 121.

Liberated from central state control, local administrations typically took an entrepreneurial stance. This context progressively induced a change even into people's attitudes toward death and their general conceptions about life-and-death issues.

The transition from body to solidarity should lead to identify within our society areas of relations disconnected from the logic of the exchange contract, which is also the sociological and legal form of our being mutually indifferent. The complexity of this scenario—in which some radical issues, as related to the ethical, social and legal dimension of euthanasia, arise—is well illustrated by neonatal euthanasia for families who would have the responsibility of caring for several compromised newborns. Active euthanasia is not yet legal but that practiced in the case of seriously defective newborns and low-birth-weight infants seems to be receiving increased support from professionals as well as the general public in China.[32]

As the child is disabled there are huge costs involved in its ongoing care, and the Chinese governments protocol of 'one family-one child' does not support the reviving of a second child. In the same time, where couples are allowed only one child, the impending death of the only one child may mean an end to their future as parents.

The practitioner faces a complex dilemma: he must balance the will of the government, the parents' will, as well as what is best for the child and his own autonomy as a physician. The practitioner has "interests that may incline away from fulfillment of their obligations to patients".[33] At the heart of this issue lies the practitioner's ideas of life and suffering.[34]

According to Zhang Naigen, the notion of *liangxin* (moral consciousness) is often invoked in connection to euthanasia, whereas the strongest argument is still family ethics. Filial piety was the core of ethics: one could not talk about relationships without talking about the paternal filiation.[35]

---

[32] Pi Hu, "The Acceptability of active euthanasia in China", 12 *Medicine and Law* (1993), pp. 47–52. An investigation concerning the attitudes of nurses to euthanasia in a hospital showed that 98.5% nurses knew euthanasia, 71.7% approved of euthanasia, and 74.7% opposed the law punishment to doctors having performed euthanasia. Simultaneously, 53.3% nurses proposed that euthanasia should be performed by law-officers, and 85.8% thought it more important to alleviate sufferings than prolong lives of patients with cancer. Gaohua Wang, et al., "An Investigation of Euthanasia Conception in Hospital Nurses, 3 *Heath Psychology Journal* (2000).

[33] Christian Meyers, "Cross-cultural medicine - A decade later - Ethical dilemmas in a cross-cultural context - A Chinese example", 157 *The Western Journal of Medicine* (1999), pp. 323–327.

[34] Eun Kyung Kim, "Neonatal euthanasia in modern China", 3 *The Lantern: A Journal of Traditional Chinese Medicine* (2006), p. 25.

[35] Zhang Naigen, *Chapitre introductif*, in *Clonage humain, droit et société, supra* note 19, vol. 1 *Introduction* (Paris, 2002), p. 23.

In modern Chinese society, extended families are replaced by nuclear families, but the emphasis on family is the same. The rejection of the principle of individual self-determination is the same, but the parent-determination is replaced by family co-determination. Although contemporary ethics is no longer what it was, the responsibility to support parents until they die still plays a relevant role, especially in life and death issues. Liu Xiuwen, who works in the ICU, one of the first teaching hospital of Beijing Medical University, commented that it is unfair that the doctor cannot suggest to the family members to stop treatment when the situation is hopeless and it is a waste of expensive medical treatment.

Standing on a brief survey of the questions, it seems still premature to pass a law on euthanasia in China, since moral principles, ethics and the quality of citizens in China are still considered "premature" at this time. One could just remark the fact that some researchers argue that euthanasia could be against the Constitution which states that the country should "provide the facilities for the citizens to survive". Health care reforms in China is at a crossroad: social policies will lose all their meaning without them.[36]

If one examines more critically the discussion on euthanasia in China, there should be less worry about the possibility of legalizing voluntary or

---

[36] Julia Tao (eds.), *Bioethics, Trust and Challenge of the Market* (Hong Kong, 2008). The Chinese government has increasingly recognized the importance of investing in health, and improving health care services has become a key element in economic development plans. The concrete goals includes: enhancing public health by improving the quality and efficiency of health services; providing basic medical insurance for all workers in urban areas; using existing resources efficiently; developing community health services; developing and perfecting rural cooperative medical care; strengthening the development of rural health organizations; strengthening areas such as the prevention of disease and promoting public health. Tongan Zhao, *Health Legislation* (Beijing, 2001). The Chinese health care system includes health service and medical insurance. Health care includes medical service, the Centre for Disease Prevention and Control (CDC), and maternal and pediatric health care. The medical insurance system includes social medical insurance, private medical insurance and medical assistance. However, a recent publication describes a change of the system into four parts: basic medical insurance scheme, urban-resident scheme, rural cooperative medical system, and medical assistance program. Shanlian Hu, Shenglan Tang, Yuanli Liu, Yuxin Zhao, Maria-Luisa Escobar and David de Ferranti, "Health System Reform in China 6. Reform of how health care is paid for in China: challenges and opportunities", 371 *The Lancet* (2008), pp. 1846–1852. The Chinese medical assistance system is a social security system for those who cannot obtain basic medical services, and its main form is low-level free medical care. At the end of June, 2003, only 10 million urban workers in China had medical insurance, accounting for roughly 20% of the urban population. Only 10% of workers in rural areas had access to the new rural cooperative medical care, and only 3% of the population had commercial private medical insurance. The medical assistance system guarantees an individual fundamental medical aid, and it is "the final defense line" of social medical security.

involuntary euthanasia there. The discussion arose mainly because of the concern for suffering during the dying process in modern medical practice. Such suffering should be alleviated by good palliative care[37] and also by establishing guidelines for forgoing futile life-sustaining treatment.[38] Effort should be made to promote palliative care in China, among the public, professionals health-care workers and government officials.[39] Academics and media are encouraged to discuss the forgoing of futile life-sustaining treatment and resource allocation to better debate and decide whether to legalize euthanasia or not.[40]

And the Chinese medicine is a dynamic and systemic perspective of understanding the functioning of the person, treating with any subjective complaint of the terminal patient, including complaints whose cause is unclear and those that cannot be neatly categorized according to a disease classification system.[41]

---

[37] Sun Man NG, "The Role of Chinese Medicine in Cancer Palliative Care", in Cecilia Lai Wan Chan and Ami Yin Man Chow (eds.), *Death, Dying and Bereavement. A Hong Kong Chinese Experience* (Hong Kong, 2006), p. 203; Michael Mau Kong Sham, Kin Sang Chan, Doris Man Wah Tse and Raymond See Kit Lo, "Impact of Palliative Care on the Quality Life of Dying", ibid., pp. 139–150.

[38] Chun Yan Tse and Samantha Mei Cheng Pan, "Euthanasia and Forgoing Life-sustaining Treatment in the Chinese Context", in *Death, Dying and Bereavement, supra* note 37, p. 173.

[39] Professors Shan and Zhang, from the Center for Social Studies of Science, Peking University, argue that Mass media have taken great importance on communication of euthanasia from authors to the public. Public evaluative attitude to euthanasia has turned from acceptance to action, which reflects the acceptable history of euthanasia as a bioethical notion. "It is much help to us for good understanding the public acceptance of new bioethical notion by analysis the function of mass media in forming the public notion". Yan-hua Shan and Da-qing Zhang, "On Attitude Change of Public to Euthanasia in Perspective of Mass Media", 4 *Medicine and Philosophy* (2005), pp. 60–61.

[40] As Chen Fan, a doctor of Beijing Tumor Hospital, says: "I don't think it is the patients' real will to choose euthanasia. It is the real will of the patients to ask for euthanasia only when they are clear-headed, not suffering any pain and master medical knowledge as a whole. None of my patients ask for euthanasia when they have received proper medical treatment and psychological treatment. As a doctor, I suggest cancer patients be given pain killing prescriptions to alleviate their suffering. We should try our best to help terminally ill patients spend the rest of their lives with less pain and more happiness". Interview appeared in the *Beijing Youth Daily* to address questions on whether legalization of euthanasia would be unconstitutional or if China should consider the legalization of euthanasia at this stage on July 30, 2003. See also Hong-zhen Zhang, Jin-di Hu, Lin Bian, "The Reflection of the Advanced Terminally Cancer and Euthanasia", 3 *Medicine & Philosophy* (2006). There were 136 patients with advanced terminally cancer together with their relatives were selected and tested by answering the questionnaires in order to understand the attitudes and acceptance towards euthanasia. The rates of permission towards euthanasia, hospice care and palliative treatment were 2.2%, 95.6% and 97.8% respectively.

[41] Beyond the ethics of Chinese ancient medicine, the concept of "bio-psycho-social medical model" was first introduced into China in the National Medical Dialectic

A recent study on euthanasia and the hospice care outlines that the speeding up of aging in Chinese society—which is the effect of the birth control policy adopted from the beginning of year 1970—enables euthanasia and hospice care to become the focus of increasing social concern. Both euthanasia and hospice care are extraordinary as the core content of death control. "According to the ethic review of the status of euthanasia and hospice care, we put forward the viewpoints of actively carrying on the multi-disciplinary research on euthanasia in our country, profoundly valuing and actively improving hospice care, and promoting harmony and unity between euthanasia and hospice care as an effective move to promote the harmonious development of the aging society in our country".[42]

The first euthanasia case was so much a test case before the public, and debatable, that it took five years to make the final judgment. On 17 May, 1991, the first judgment was declared: "Even though the wintermin

---

Conference in 1981. The focus was to switch from therapy to prevention, from physical care to psychological care, from inpatient to outpatient care, and from ethical service to more social service, to enhance the level of prevention, health care and rehabilitation. The Chinese Ministry of Health issued several regulations in 2004 to promote the establishment of a disease prevention and control system. The aim is to improve measures to prevent and control disease and the ability to deal with public health problems, to safeguard the health and safety of the population, and to promote social stability and economic development. This disease prevention and control system is divided into four levels: national, provincial, city, and county level. The disease prevention and control agencies are organized according to the administrative districts in every city. Each centre is responsible for preventing and controlling disease, health education and promotion, the application of research results and guidelines, technical management and the services within its district. See Yu Jun and Lu-lu Zhang, "Functional problems of Chinese disease control and prevention institutions", 11 *Academic Journal of Second Military Medicine University* (2005), pp. 1230–1232. Besides these organizational levels, there are two other important structures in health care, the Centre for Disease Prevention and Control and the Maternal and Children's Health Service. The Maternal and Children's Health Service offers technical guidance for maternal and children's health care in local areas. They have the same status as medical service organizations and the centers for disease prevention and control, and form an important part of the Chinese health service. There is a relatively complete service network for maternal and children's health care, and in 2006 there were 3,021 maternal and children's health service organizations in the country. Chinese maternal and children's health service organizations have been established in provinces, autonomous regions, cities, and municipalities. Maternal and children's health care clinics have been established in urban regions and counties. Lian-Sheng Zhang, Yan-Xia Zhao and Cui Dan, "Development actuality and suggestion of maternal and child health service of communities in China", 12 *Maternal and Child Health Care of China* (2006), pp. 13–15.

    [42] Fengquan Song, "An Ethical Review of the Status of Euthanasia and Hospice Care in China", 10 *Medicine and Society* (2009). The increasing number of elderly people will put pressure on health care systems in many countries. WHO, *World Health Organization. Health systems: improving performance*, Report (Geneva, 2000).

compound hastened Xia's death the dose was not excessive, and circumstances were not severe enough to constitute criminality".[43]

This judgment shows a kind of reasoning which is, in Chinese judicial practice, for the hard cases, those where "the knowledge of experts was to break the legal syllogism" (instead dominated in the ordinary routine the courts).[44]

Far from being an expression of the arbitrary, the "quintessence of legal knowledge was to overcome the letter of law" to resolve the hard cases according to a principle of "superior essence" that privileges the "government by men" (*renzhi*) as opposed to the "government by law" (*fazhi*).

The fact remains that all authoritarian deviation implicated by this notion of "government by men", during the Chinese Empire, could (and can) be eliminated by the Maoist emancipation of the society from all forms of power's subordination (religious, patriarchal, etc.) in the modern China.[45] And it is interesting to note that Chinese researchers are convinced that the belief in God dominates the Western vision, so they have more freedom in addressing new issues posed by technology and scientific discoveries.

Judged by the literature, the pro-euthanasia side seems to have a larger voice. It is a mind opening arguments when we compare Chinese pro-euthanasia arguments with Western ones.[46]

Chinese cultural resource is important in the debate concerning new bioethical issues and the ethical controversies, which may be a Chinese

---

[43] For the expert conclusion from the Malpractice Appraisal Committee of Sha Xoi Province, of July 1989, "Wintermin compound was not the direct cause of Xia's death, but it did deepen the coma of Xia which promoted death". Yali Cong, "The first euthanasia court case in China", 6 *Eubios Journal of Asian and International Bioethics* (1996), pp. 61–62. The judgment shows a particular sensibility to the pain of the patient, consequently, an attention related to the euthanasia in its literal meaning, that is, in according to ancient Chinese, not "mercy killing", but "peaceful and happy dying" (*anlesi*).

[44] According to Bourgon, this kind of reasoning produced in the Western view on the Chinese science of law so many misunderstandings on the non-permeability of the Chinese thought to the concept of law. Jérôme Bourgon, "Principe de légalité et règle de droit dans la tradition juridique chinoise", in Mireille Delmas-Marty and Pierre-Etienne Will (eds.), *La Chine et la démocratie* (Paris, 2007), pp. 157–176; also Léon Vandermeersch, "Droit et rites in Chine", in Yves Michaud (eds.), *La Chine aujourd'hui* (Paris, 2003), pp. 109–124.

[45] Contrary to a dominant Western legal thought, for whom "the difficulty is increased in China, where the lack of independence of the legal tradition inherited from the imperial policy and where the primacy of moral values has been taken over by Maoist designs". Mireille Delmas-Marty, *Le laboratoire chinois*, in *La Chine et la démocratie, supra* note 44, pp. 803–837.

[46] To an overview, Lo Ping-cheung, "Euthanasia and Assisted suicide from Confucian moral perspective", 9 *Dao* (2010), pp. 53–77.

specificity. However, as traditional Chinese culture can be invoked to defend euthanasia—in the interest of the whole society and community, but also to exclude it, because it breaks family relations—, Shen Mingxian criticizes the claim to change the Confucianism in creative ways, while each has his own ideas on the subject. To be relevant and persuasive on the subject, he believes that assimilate the "quintessence" traditional culture, but also "borrow some concepts of Western culture (e.g. the notions of human rights, justice, etc.) and the modern scientific and technological concepts that serve the human being".[47]

That is a synthesis of transculturalisme and transdisciplinary, integrating the scientific concepts, which proves an extreme complexity of Chinese legal system, characterizing the "*laboratoire chinois*" not just as a simple metaphor of postmodern law.[48]

III. LIFE LAW

It is only when there is class struggle that there can be philosophy. It is a waste time to discuss epistemology apart from practice.
Mao Tsé-toung, *Talk on questions of philosophy* (1964)

L'image di Christ mort sur la croix est inimaginable en Chine. Un Chinois aura toujours beaucoup de mal à comprendre le sacrifice du "Fils de Dieu" venu sur Terre pour sauver les hommes. Cette contradiction est incompréhensible. Pour nous, Jésus meurt. Il a raté. C'est un échec. Dans les temples bouddhistes, les divinités sont assises, sereines ou sans expression, mais ne souffrent pas. Elles ne sont pas mortes.
Datong, *La Chine sur le divan. Entretiens* (2008)

A creative Chinese legal conception is that of *life law*, and then of *life jurisprudence* as the theoretical outline of the life legal problems, advanced by some Chinese jurists during their investigations into bioethics as linked with the development of biotechnology.[49] Nowadays, "life jurisprudence

---

[47] Shen Mingxian, "La culture traditionnelle chinoise et le clonage humain", in *Clonage humain, droit et société, supra* note 19, vol. 2, *Comparaison* (Paris, 2004), p. 109.

[48] See Mireille Delmas-Marty, *Le laboratoire chinois*, in *La Chine et la démocratie, supra* note 44, pp. 803–837.

[49] The word of life law was firstly advanced in the book of jurisprudence of Medicine health care edited by Pinggong Deng in 1989. In June 1997, the Life Law Research Center (LLRC) was established by the Law Instituted of SASS during the first life-jurisprudence conference in Shanghai. After the foundation of LLRC, several conference have been held with the hotspot topic of genetic engineering, the assisted reproductive technology, organ transplantation, brain death, euthanasia and so.

has become a new dominant jurisprudence amongst all jurisprudence in the 21st century China".[50]

Jiang Po holds that *life jurisprudence* is a group of legislation regulating all kinds of relations between human and other creatures in ecology as well as human beings themselves from their survival to their death.[51] It is a comprehensive law system consisting of a group of legislation sets which are "based on traditional health law, making modern biotechnology law as their forward, and stretching their antenna excessively into traditional department law such as civil law, criminal law, administrative law, environmental law, intellectual property law, international law and so on".[52]

This concept of "life law" implies a sort of emphasis as related to the construction of a Chinese life-protection system such as for the brain death law, the organ transplantation law, the assisted reproductive technology law and so forth.[53]

Brain death is a very suitable case that highlights the conflict between modern biomedical technology and traditional culture. Although many experts have suggested that the brain oriented concept of death should be adopted, in mainland China the concept of brain death is still not accepted in the law, the Chinese definition of death remains oriented toward cardio-respiratory function.[54] In circumstances where a number of the functions of an individual's body is being artificially maintained in the

---

[50] Lu Qi, "Issues on Human genetic monopoly", 6 *Journal of Shanghai Institute of Politics & law* (2002).

[51] Jiang Po, "The scientific of modern life law", in Xiaorong Gu and Zhengmao Ni (eds.), *Discussion on Life Law* (Shanghai, 1998), p. 9.

[52] Liu Changqiu, "Definition of Life Law and the Situation with Problems of China's Life Jurisprudence", 19 *Journal International de Bioéthique* (2008), pp. 33–42, p. 38.

[53] During the period 1998–2007, several books on life law were published, including Changqiu Liu, *Organ Transplantation Law* (Shanghai, 2005); Changqiu Liu, Qingsheng Lu and Jianjun Han, *Brain Death Law* (Shanghai, 2005), Zhengmao Ni, *On the Law of Euthanasia* (Shanghai, 2005); Shanguo Li, *Assisted Reproductive Technology Law* (Beijing, 2007); Yanling Zhang, *Legal Problems on Artificial Insemination* (Honk Kong, 2006); Changqiu Liu, *Legal Problem on Biotechnology* (Shanghai, 2007).

[54] After a long debate the Japanese eventually reached a compromise: the Japanese Parliament passed a law in 1998 to accept the definition of brain death in coexistence with the traditional cardiopulmonary paradigm of death, and left the room to choose to the people. As outlined, these laws are subjectivist interesting, because can highlight the conventional dimension, the arbitrary concept of brain death. Death is no longer, in effect, understood as a moment, but as a threshold (arbitrarily set necessarily) in a degradation of vital functions. Stephanie Hennette-Vauchez, *Le droit de la bioéthique* (Paris, 2009). As Henry Beecher said, after chairing the Ad Hoc Committee of Harvard: "Whatever the time that we choose to call death is an arbitrary decision. The death of heart? The hair continues to grow. Brain death? The heart may still continue to fight. You must choose an irreversible stage where the brain no longer functions. It is best to choose a level where, although the brain is dead, the usefulness of other organs is preserved". See Peter Singer, *Rethinking Life and Death. The Collapse of Our Traditional Ethics* (New York, 1996).

presence of severe brain damage, Chinese doctors have to decide whether a brain death patient should be medically "killed" under the name of euthanasia.

Moreover, the Chinese term *anlesi* is used to describe the state of the dying process or even palliative or hospice care, beside euthanasia in the standard sense or forgoing life-sustaining treatment. Public opinion supporting euthanasia may actually include also support for forgoing futile life-sustaining treatment and support for palliative care.

IV. GUIDELINES ON PASSIVE EUTHANASIA IN HONG KONG AND THE ROLE OF PATIENT'S FAMILY

> *Suppose a man were, all of a sudden, to see a young child on the verge of falling into a well. He would certainly be moved to compassion, not because he wanted to get in the good graces of the parents, nor because he wished to win the praise of his fellow villagers or friends, nor yet because he disliked the cry of the child.*
> Mencius, II. A. 6 (1970, 82)

Recently, in Hong Kong, both the Medical Council and the Hospital Authority have issued local guidelines concerning forgoing life-sustaining treatment. It was argued that terminating futile medical treatment is not the same as passive euthanasia, and equating the two is mistaken and misleading.[55] In fact, there was a heated debate among care providers, patients and politicians in the year 2000, when the Hong Kong Medical Council planned to include guidelines on 'passive euthanasia' in its code of conduct for doctors, and the final guidelines did not include euthanasia. Currently in Hong Kong euthanasia is illegal.

As outlined, passive euthanasia and forgoing life-sustaining treatment are substantially the same, any distinction between the two cannot be based on the action or the outcome. But the two different uses of language represent different frames of mind that are not inconsequential, involving different practical implication. Basically, the talk of futile treatment is a doctor-oriented language. To decide whether the treatment is really futile, one state is regarded as necessarily worse than another. The talk of passive euthanasia is a patient-oriented language, focused on what is good for the

---

[55] Hospital Authority Clinical Ethics Committee, *HA Guidelines on Life-sustaining treatment in the terminally ill* (Hong Kong, 2002); see also Chun Yan Tse and Ho Mun Chan, *End-of-life Choices: Euthanasia and Others*, Fact Sheets presented in a seminar on euthanasia organized by the Education Bureau (EDB) and the Hong Kong Bioethics Association on 28th November 2009.

patient and what the patient wants or would want. Thus, "the use of the concept of terminating futile treatment tend to obscure the issues instead of solving it, and it runs the risk of substituting the patient's autonomy with the doctor's paternalism".[56]

More generally, one stresses the tendency to reduce the human person to the one dimensional existence of the biological-physical, while in Chinese culture degradation is entirely conceived with reference to one's moral-social life rather than to one's biological life. According to Lo Ping-cheung, there is a dissonance between the contemporary Western discourse concerning the criterion of unacceptable degradation, which constitutes an indignity so serious and so grave that it is worse than death, and Confucian "death to prevent indignity" as an act of moral construction because it prevents one from moral degradation. An act of voluntary euthanasia as well as physician-assisted suicide on the grounds of deteriorating biological condition cannot be interpreted as an act of moral construction.

Voluntary euthanasia and physician-assisted suicide are not only an issue of individual *vs.* state, nor an issue of law *vs.* morality. It is also an issue in a medical setting which involves a therapeutic relationship. "To divorce bioethics from a comprehensive vision of life is to condemn bioethics to a poverty of vision".[57]

Taking into account the local legal and cultural context, the guidelines of the public hospital in Hong Kong emphasizes the importance of a proper consensus-building process. One could say that, even in this case, family co-determination, rather than individual patient self-determination, is the norm of medical ethics in mainland China and Hong Kong public hospitals today.

The role of patient's family can be involved into three levels in the case of a mentally competent patient.[58]

a) Firstly, the family decides together with the patient.
b) Secondly, the patient asks the family to decide on his or her behalf.
c) Thirdly, the family decides without involving the patient.

---

[56] Yu Kam Por, "Terminating Futile Medical Treatment and Passive Euthanasia: Is There a Difference?", 12 *Eubios Journal of Asian and International Bioethics* (2002), pp. 137–138.

[57] Lo Ping-cheung, "Euthanasia and Assisted Suicide from Confucian Moral Perspective", 9 *Dao* (2010), p. 66.

[58] Chun Yan Tse and Samantha Mei Cheng Pan, "Euthanasia and Forgoing Life-sustaining Treatment in the Chinese Context", in *Death, Dying and Bereavement, supra* note 37.

It is only the third level of family determination that excludes the patient involuntarily. Such a strong paternalistic approach overriding the patient's autonomy needs further justification by showing that "the disclosure of the information brings much harm to the patient".[59]

When a patient has lost the capacity to make a decision, a valid advance directive refusing life sustaining treatment should be respected.

As Hong Kong has not yet had specific legislation on advance directive, the Hospital Authority will operate under common laws principles.[60] The term "advance directive" is usually used in the narrow sense to mean an instructional directive for the refusal of life-sustaining treatment: a valid instructional directive is legally binding in Hong Kong, and should be followed if the directive is applicable to the clinical situation faced, while a proxy directive is not legally binding even if it is valid, and event that is not the case in some other jurisdictions, including US (and UK that also recently changed the law to allow is).

For a mentally incapacitated patient with neither an advance directive nor a guardian, the final decision to withhold or withdraw life-sustaining treatment is a medical decision *tout-court*, theoretically based on the best interests of the patient. Here lies the dilemma of what model to follow.

According to the Medical Council, as far as the substituted judgment is concerned, the common practice for the Chinese to consider the benefits to other family members would make the US model difficult, "as a decision to benefit other family members may be at expense of the benefits to the patient".[61]

However, the health care team should work toward a possible consensus with the family, unless the view of the family is clearly contrary to the patient's best interests.

As emerged in a comparative study focusing on the ethical attitudes of intensive care doctors, in Hong Kong, 83% of intensive care unit doctors (ICU) involve the patient or the family in decisions on the limitation of therapy, and about 90% involve the family in do-not-resuscitate orders

---

[59] Ibid., p. 174.
[60] Reference could be taken from the British practice which contains the relevant section from the British Medical Association Guidance for Decision making on Withholding and Withdrawing Life-prolonging Medical Treatment. The Law Reform Commission of Hong Kong has recommended in 2006 that the concept of advance directive should be promoted by non-legislative means.
[61] Chun Yan Tse and Samantha Mei Cheng Pan, "Euthanasia and Forgoing Life-sustaining Treatment in the Chinese Context", in *Death, Dying and Bereavement, supra* note 37, p. 176.

(DNR). In contrast, in Europe, only half of ICU doctors involve the patient or family in decisions on limitation of therapy and 77% involve the family in DNR orders.[62] And it should be also noted that an advance directive is only a legal tool in order to document the decision of the patient to refuse certain life-sustaining treatment. The case of a patient faced with an incurable disease, this should be part of "advance care planning", which is the process of communication among the patient, the family members and the healthcare team in order to allow improved understanding reflection and decision-making regarding end-of-life care.

---

[62] Hy Yap, GM Joynt and CD Goersall, "Ethical attitudes of intensive care physicians in Hong Kong: questionnaire survey", 10 *Hong Kong Medical Journal* (2004), pp. 244–250.

LES DIRECTIVES ANTICIPÉES EN DROIT SUISSE

Dominique Manaï[*]

I. Introduction

Les directives anticipées ont commencé à être utilisées en Suisse dès le début des années 80. Filles du déclin du paternalisme médical qui a dominé la relation thérapeutique jusque dans les années 70, elles expriment l'autonomie de chacun en matière de décisions de soins et s'inscrivent dans une relation de partenariat entre médecin et patient. Très vite, elles sont apparues comme l'instrument juridique adéquat pour maîtriser les avancées technologiques et scientifiques qui permettent certes de maintenir le patient en vie pendant des années, mais ne lui offrent pas toujours de bénéfice. En droit suisse, toute intervention médicale est considérée comme une atteinte à l'intégrité corporelle. Elle est illégale si elle ne s'accompagne pas d'un motif justificatif. La justification d'une atteinte à la personnalité peut être le consentement de la personne, un intérêt prépondérant privé ou public, ou la loi.[1] Dans le domaine médical, le consentement est la justification la plus importante. Mais pour ce faire, le patient doit être capable de discernement. Qu'advient-il du patient qui ne peut plus exprimer sa volonté en raison d'une incapacité psychique ? Pour le patient incapable de discernement, le consentement est donné par son représentant s'il en a un. Et s'il n'en a pas, comme c'est très souvent le cas, qui décide d'un acte médical ? Le médecin ? La famille ? Et si les proches ne sont pas d'accord entre eux, qui décide ? Et si les proches et le médecin ont des appréciations divergentes quant au geste médical le plus adéquat ? C'est dans ce cadre-là que les directives anticipées sont précieuses pour l'autodétermination du patient qui n'est plus capable d'exprimer sa volonté.

Depuis leur contexte d'émergence, leur champ d'application s'est étendu. De nos jours, il ne se limite plus à la fin de vie. Sur le plan juridique, la plupart des lois sur la santé cantonales les prennent en

---

[*] Professeure à la Faculté de droit, Université de Genève, Suisse ; email : Dominique. Manaï@unige.ch.
[1] Article 28 alinéa 2 Code civil suisse du 10 décembre 1907 (CC), RS 210.

S. Negri (ed.), *Self-Determination, Dignity and End-of-Life Care*
2011 Koninklijke Brill NV. Printed in The Netherlands. ISBN 978 90 04 22357 8. pp. 271–286

considération, certains cantons les considérant comme obligatoires, sauf lorsqu'elles ne correspondent plus à la volonté du patient[2] ; mais d'autres cantons ne les mentionnent même pas dans leur réglementation. Il faut attendre la récente révision du code civil pour voir naître une réglementa-tion fédérale uniforme.[3] Cette loi entrera en vigueur au début 2013. Cette nouvelle loi prévoit quatre dispositions consacrées aux directives antici-pées que nous allons analyser dans cette contribution. Quant aux normes médico-éthiques, elles mettent l'accent sur l'importance des directives anticipées et se soucient de leur mise en oeuvre. L'Académie suisse des sciences médicales a adopté le 19 mai 2009 des directives et recommanda-tions concernant les directives anticipées ; il s'agit d'un texte très étoffé.[4] Il n'est pas superflu de souligner que la pratique des directives anticipées dans les institutions de soins s'est considérablement développée ces der-nières années et les professionnels de la santé encouragent les patients à établir leur volonté qui permettra, en temps opportun, de respecter leurs souhaits dans l'hypothèse où ils deviennent incapables.

Dans notre contribution, nous nous proposons d'examiner d'abord le contexte visé par les directives anticipées (II). Nous analyserons ensuite le contenu possible des directives anticipées (III), puis le lieu où elles sont conservées (IV). Nous terminerons par l'étude de leurs effets (V).

II. LE CONTEXTE VISÉ PAR LES DIRECTIVES ANTICIPÉES

Les directives anticipées ont pour vocation de consigner la volonté de leur auteur pour le cas où il ne serait plus à même d'exprimer ses attentes.[5] Le contexte d'une déclaration anticipée est jalonné par trois moments : le

---

[2] Ainsi, notamment Fribourg, Loi sur la santé du 16 novembre 1999 (LS ; Recueil systé-matique (RS)/FR 821.0.1), art. 49–51 LS ; Genève, Loi sur la santé du 7 avril 2006 (LS ; RS/GE K 1 03), art. 47–49 LS ; Jura, Loi sanitaire du 14 décembre 1990 (Loi sanitaire ; RS/JU 810.01), art. 26b-26d Loi sanitaire ; Neuchâtel, Loi sur la santé du 6 février 1995 (LS ; RS/NE 800.1), art. 25a LS ; Valais, Loi sur la santé du 14 février 2008 (LS ; RS/VS 800.1), art. 24–25 LS ; Vaud, Loi sur la santé publique du 29 mai 1985 (LSP ; RS/VD 800.01), art. 23a-23c LSP.

[3] Code civil suisse (Protection de l'adulte, droit des personnes et droit de la filiation) Modification du 19 décembre 2008 (cité CC).

[4] ASSM, Directives et recommandations médico-éthiques « Directives anticipées » du 19 mai 2009 (cité : ASSM).

[5] Dominique Manaï, « Soins et respect de la volonté de la personne en fin de vie : droit suisse », in O. Guillod et P. Wessner (éd.), *Le droit de la santé : aspects nouveaux, Rapport des contributeurs suisses aux Journées internationales Henri Capitant* 2009, IDS, Université de Neuchâtel, 2010, pp. 49–82.

moment où le patient capable de discernement formule ses directives (A), le moment où le patient n'est plus apte à exercer ses droits (B) et l'éventuel moment où le patient, ayant recouvré sa capacité de discernement, révoque les directives qu'il avait prises (C).

A. *La volonté du patient encore capable de discernement*

L'existence de directives anticipées est soumise à l'exigence de sa *rédaction*.[6] La rédaction est la condition *sine qua non* de la prise en considération de la volonté préalablement exprimée. Le législateur a opté pour la forme écrite, car elle permet de mieux établir la volonté du patient en cas de divergences au sein de l'équipe soignante quant aux souhaits de ce dernier. De surcroît, en cas de litige, ce document peut être utilisé comme moyen de preuve attestant les instructions préalables. Il n'est pas nécessaire que les directives anticipées soient rédigées en entier par le patient. Elles doivent être datées et signées de la main de leur auteur. Les directives anticipées peuvent très bien se présenter sous la forme d'un formulaire proposé dans certaines situations de soins ou par des associations telles que Caritas, la Fédération des médecins suisses ou Pro Senectute. Pourvu que le formulaire soit daté et signé à la main. Sur le formulaire, les patients peuvent aussi faire état de leur volonté concernant des interventions médicales qu'ils seraient susceptibles de subir.

Au moment de leur rédaction, le patient doit être *capable de discernement*.[7] La capacité de discernement est définie, selon la nouvelle formulation, de la manière suivante : « *Toute personne qui n'est pas privée de la faculté d'agir raisonnablement en raison de son jeune âge, de déficience mentale, de troubles psychiques, d'ivresse ou d'autres causes semblables est capable de discernement au sens de la présente loi* ».[8] La faculté d'agir raisonnablement est une notion juridique, qui diffère de la notion médicale et qui n'est pas réductible au caractère raisonnable de la décision. La faculté d'agir raisonnablement est constituée de 2 éléments cumulatifs : 1) la personne doit avoir la faculté d'apprécier le sens, l'opportunité et les conséquences de son acte (élément dit intellectuel) ; 2) elle doit avoir la faculté d'agir librement, sur la base de l'appréciation intellectuelle qu'elle s'est préalablement faite de la situation (élément dit volontaire). Par ailleurs, le niveau de discernement varie selon la nature et l'importance de la

---

[6] Article 371 alinéa 1 CC.
[7] Article 370 alinéa 1 CC.
[8] Article 16 CC.

décision (notion relative du discernement). Le discernement doit être présent au moment où la personne manifeste sa volonté. De plus, la capacité de discernement est présumée, de sorte que celui qui allègue que l'auteur des directives en est dépourvu doit le prouver.

Pour rédiger des directives anticipées, il suffit d'être capable de discernement. Ainsi un mineur peut établir sa volonté de manière anticipée, alors même qu'il ne dispose pas de l'exercice des droits civils.[9] Le grand âge n'influence pas la présomption. Toutefois lorsque l'état de santé psychique et les facultés intellectuelles de la personne sont durablement atteintes, une incapacité de discernement est présumée. C'est pourquoi, il est recommandé de faire confirmer la capacité de discernement par un professionnel au cas où elle pourrait faire l'objet d'un doute ultérieurement.[10]

La déclaration anticipée doit exprimer la *libre* volonté du patient. Il convient de veiller à ce qu'elle soit rédigée sans pression aucune ni contrainte quelconque, tant de la part de ses proches que des professionnels de la santé. Il importe que l'existence des directives anticipées ne soit pas une condition d'admission dans une institution de soins de longue durée ou à l'accès à un traitement médical ou à une prise en charge.[11] Le droit suisse ne prévoit pas de délai de réflexion entre le moment où la personne rédige des directives anticipées et le moment où elle signe le document.

La rédaction anticipée de sa volonté présuppose que l'auteur ait été *informé*. Ceci n'est pas une exigence explicite de la loi, mais découle des normes non juridiques. Dans ses recommandations, l'Académie suisse des sciences médicales conseille au patient de prendre contact avec un professionnel de la santé, par exemple son médecin traitant, afin de pouvoir prendre sa décision de manière éclairée. Mais ceci n'est ni une obligation ni une condition de validité des directives anticipées. De plus, il n'est pas prévu d'attestation que le patient a été bien informé. L'accompagnement médical dans la rédaction de directives anticipées est facultatif. Il est ainsi tout à fait possible pour le patient de rédiger des directives anticipées en dehors de la présence d'un professionnel de la santé. Si le patient le souhaite, les proches peuvent participer à l'entretien de conseil.

Lors de cette activité de conseil, les valeurs du conseiller doivent être passées sous silence. Il s'agit d'un conseil non directif. L'entretien doit

---

[9] Article 18 CC.
[10] ASSM 3.2.
[11] ASSM 3.3.

allier l'empathie et la critique. Son contenu dépend de la situation du patient. Son but est de cerner la volonté de ce dernier, d'identifier les incertitudes, de l'encourager à nommer un représentant thérapeutique et de nommer les éventuelles tensions entre le souhait du patient et la pratique médicale, ou de mettre en évidence les conflits d'intérêts entre les proches. Le patient doit pouvoir exprimer « ses angoisses par rapport à certaines maladies ou mesures de soins, ses expériences négatives avec certains traitements ou encore ses craintes (...). L'auteur doit disposer de suffisamment de temps pour aborder sans contrainte les questions importantes. (...) Les points essentiels de l'entretien incluent la réflexion et la documentation relatives à l'échelle personnelle des valeurs, l'information concernant les situations possibles d'incapacité de discernement ainsi que celle relative aux mesures médicales habituelles dans ces situations. Information sur les conséquences qui découlent de la mise en œuvre, de l'interruption ou du renoncement à des mesures ».[12]

B. *Le patient devenu incapable de discernement*

L'incapacité de discernement est la condition de l'application des directives anticipées. La loi indique, en effet, « *Toute personne capable de discernement peut déterminer, dans des directives anticipées, les traitements médicaux auxquels elle consent ou non au cas où elle deviendrait incapable de discernement* ».[13] Si la personne est incapable de fait d'exprimer sa volonté ou si elle ne dispose plus de la faculté d'agir raisonnablement en raison de l'une des causes légales énumérées à l'article 16 CC, elle sera considérée comme incapable de discernement et il conviendra de rechercher les déclarations anticipées.[14] A cet effet, le médecin doit consulter la carte d'assuré du patient ou se renseigner auprès des proches.

En cas d'*urgence*, la loi confère une portée limitée aux directives anticipées. Selon la loi,[15] « *le médecin administre les soins médicaux conformément à la volonté présumée et aux intérêts de la personne incapable de discernement* ». L'Académie suisse des sciences médicales préconise, lorsque le pronostic vital est engagé, d'administrer des soins même si leur

---

[12] ASSM 5.1.
[13] Article 370 alinéa 1 CC.
[14] Dominique Manaï, « Chapitre VIII : La protection du patient privé de discernement », in Dominique Manaï, *Les droits du patient face à la biomédecine*, Berne, Stämpfli, 2006, pp. 187–204.
[15] Article 379 CC.

succès est incertain.[16] Au moment de la rédaction des directives anticipées, le patient devrait être informé qu'en cas d'urgence, des mesures
médicales doivent être prises sans attendre et qu'il ne sera pas possible de
respecter les directives anticipées dans ce contexte. Mais il sera précisé
que ces mesures prises en urgence pourront être interrompues, si le
patient a formulé des directives anticipées.

C. *La révocation des directives par le patient capable de discernement*

Les directives anticipées ne sont pas limitées dans le temps. C'est pourquoi il est important que leur auteur les réactualise régulièrement tant
qu'il est capable de le faire. Si le patient incapable de discernement rede-
vient capable de discernement, il peut révoquer les directives qu'il a établies antérieurement.[17] Il peut les révoquer, en tout temps, par écrit ou
oralement. Il n'est pas nécessaire de recourir à la forme écrite. Les directives anticipées perdent leur validité. Afin d'éviter tout risque de confusion, il devrait les détruire. S'il ne le fait pas, ce sont les plus récentes qui
primeront.

S'il n'a pas révoqué les directives alors que son incapacité a cessé, les
directives perdent *de facto* leur validité. Celles-ci constitueront tout au
plus un élément dans le cadre du dialogue que le médecin engagera avec
lui à cet effet.

III. LE CONTENU DES DIRECTIVES ANTICIPÉES

La liberté personnelle implique un large droit d'autodétermination,
y compris lorsqu'il s'agit d'exprimer par écrit la volonté pour une situation
future dans laquelle la personne ne serait plus capable d'exercer ses droits.
Mais les directives anticipées présentent la particularité d'être destinées à
autrui et de devoir être appliquées par autrui. Se pose alors la question de
savoir quel genre de décisions le patient peut inscrire dans ses directives
anticipées pour s'assurer que sa volonté soit respectée ?

Le contenu des directives anticipées est très souple. Le droit suisse
accorde une grande liberté de choix.[18] Il n'établit pas de distinction entre

---

[16] ASSM 4.4.1.
[17] Moritz W. Kuhn et Tomas Poledna (éd.), *Arztrecht in der Praxis*, Zurich, Bâle, Genève, Schulthess, 2007, pp. 210–213.
[18] Roberto Andorno, Rapport du Comité directeur pour la Bioéthique au Conseil de l'Europe, 2–5 décembre 2008, *Les souhaits précédemment exprimés au sujet des soins de*

les déclarations anticipées concernant la fin de vie et celles qui s'appliquent à des traitements médicaux durant la vie. Afin de cerner le contenu possible des directives anticipées, nous distinguons quatre genres d'options qui ne s'excluent pas et peuvent au contraire être complémentaires (B – E). Mais au préalable, il importe de préciser que les directives anticipées ne doivent pas avoir un contenu illicite (A).

A. *Leur contenu doit être licite*

Une demande anticipée *d'euthanasie active* n'est pas admissible. En effet, il s'agit d'un acte réprimé pénalement. Le terme « euthanasie » n'est pas utilisé par la loi pénale suisse. Le droit à la vie est un droit fondamental.[19] Il est garanti par les dispositions pénales qui punissent les atteintes à la vie. La protection pénale est très forte : les infractions sont déjà commises lorsqu'il y a mise en danger[20] et aussi bien l'intention que la négligence sont punissables.[21] Par euthanasie active, la doctrine désigne un « acte dont le but immédiat est de mettre fin à la vie d'une personne, à la demande expresse de celle-ci, ou avec son consentement présumé ».[22] L'acte de donner la mort est frappé d'une interdiction absolue. Il est considéré comme un homicide et est qualifié soit de meurtre,[23] soit de meurtre sur la demande de la victime,[24] soit de meurtre passionnel.[25] Une demande anticipée *d'assistance au suicide* est illicite. En effet, pour que l'assistance au suicide ne soit pas punissable au sens de la loi,[26] il est nécessaire que la personne qui la demande ait la maîtrise physique et intellectuelle du geste qui conduit à la mort ; en d'autres termes, il faut que le demandeur ait lui-même le contrôle de l'action provoquant sa mort, ce qui implique qu'il ait encore sa capacité de discernement.[27] Ainsi une demande anticipée

---

santé, Principes communs et différentes règles applicables dans les systèmes juridiques nationaux, Strasbourg, 2008.

[19] Article 10 alinéa 1 Constitution fédérale de la Confédération suisse du 18 avril 1999 (Cst), RS 101.

[20] Articles 127–136 Code pénal suisse du 21 décembre 1937 (CP), RS 311.

[21] Article 117 CP. Ursula Cassani et Marianne Cherbuliez, « L'assistance au décès : questions de droit pénal et d'éthique, remarques de droit pénal suisse et comparé », in A. Bondolfi, F. Haldemann, N. Maillard (éd.), *La mort assistée en arguments*, Genève, Georg, 2007, p. 228.

[22] Ibid., p. 233.

[23] Article 111 CP.

[24] Article 114 CP.

[25] Article 113 CP.

[26] Article 115 CP.

[27] Dominique Manaï, « Assistance au suicide et droit à la vie en Suisse », *Responsabilité*, revue de formation sur le risque médical, juin 2010, vol. 10, n° 38, pp. 38–41.

d'assistance au suicide ne répond pas aux conditions d'impunissabilité, car l'auteur « aide » une personne à se suicider qui n'a plus le discernement suffisant.[28]

Par contre, un consentement à l'administration d'antalgiques même s'ils ont pour effet indirect d'abréger la durée de la vie de la personne (*euthanasie active indirecte*) n'est pas illicite.[29]

B. *Le consentement ou le refus d'une intervention*

Toute manifestation de volonté entre en ligne de compte et peut faire l'objet d'une directive anticipée. L'auteur de directives anticipées peut exprimer aussi bien le refus d'une intervention particulière que le consentement à un acte positif. La loi mentionne que « *toute personne capable de discernement peut déterminer, dans des directives anticipées, les traitements médicaux auxquels elle consent ou non* ».[30] Par traitement médical, il convient de n'exclure aucun acte *a priori*. A l'origine, le testament biologique est né pour refuser l'acharnement thérapeutique. Le droit suisse étend la déclaration anticipée à toutes les manifestations de volonté. Peu importe que l'acte désigné par le patient comporte une visée curative, diagnostique ou préventive. Cet acte peut aussi présenter un caractère vital. Concrètement, les directives anticipées ne se contentent plus d'exprimer un refus d'une réanimation cardio-pulmonaire. Elles visent aussi bien le refus d'interventions, comme le transfert dans un service de soins intensifs, le recours à la respiration artificielle, le recours à l'alimentation artificielle, l'administration de certains médicaments ou une transfusion de sang. L'Académie suisse des sciences médicales recommande « de différencier si l'alimentation artificielle est intervention thérapeutique temporaire (par exemple après une attaque cérébrale au pronostic incertain) ou une intervention à long terme (par exemple chez les patients souffrant d'atteintes cérébrales extrêmes de longue durée). Il est pertinent d'aborder ces situations très différentes durant le conseil à la rédaction ».[31]

---

[28] Ursula Cassani, « L'assistance au décès : quelques repères en droit pénal », in D. Bertrand, JF. Dumoulin, R. La Harpe, M. Ummel (éd.), *Médecin et droit médical. Présentation et résolution de situations médico-légales*, Genève, Médecine & Hygiène, 2009, pp. 399–408 ; Jean Claude Chevrolet et Carlo Foppa, « Quelques réflexions d'un clinicien et d'un éthicien sur l'assistance au décès », ibid., pp. 409–422.

[29] Pour un sondage auprès de la population suisse sur ces questions cf. Christian Schwarzenegger, Patrik Manzoni, David Studer, Catia Leanza, « Was die Schweizer Bervölkerung von Sterbehilfe und Suizidbeihilfe hält. Erste Resultate einer repräsentativen nationale Befragung », *Jusletter*, 6 septembre 2010.

[30] Article 370 alinéa 1 CC.

[31] ASSM 4.4.2.

Les déclarations préalables ne se limitent pas à une opposition mais concernent aussi les *actes médicaux positifs*. Par exemple, il est possible qu'un patient faisant l'objet d'un traitement manifeste sa volonté que celui-ci ne soit pas interrompu s'il perd conscience. Les recommandations de l'Académie suisse des sciences médicales rappellent que le patient souffrant d'une maladie psychique « peut se prononcer sur la question de soins en phase aigüe (isolement, neuroleptiques, etc.). Dans une telle situation, les directives anticipées devraient comprendre une description aussi précise que possible de la maladie, qui inclut aussi bien les symptômes que se présentent en phase aigüe que ceux qui annoncent une telle phase ».[32]

Aucune condition n'est exigée pour l'intensité de la volonté ; même si la volonté n'est pas catégorique, un souhait sera pris en considération.

C. *La désignation d'un représentant thérapeutique*

Contrairement à la Convention pour les droits de l'homme et la biomédecine[33] qui ne prévoit pas la possibilité de formuler une procuration anticipée pour des soins, le droit suisse offre cette opportunité. Par le biais des directives anticipées, le patient peut désigner une personne physique qui le représentera dans les décisions de soins s'il devient incapable de discernement.[34] Ce représentant choisi par le patient dispose d'un pouvoir de décision en matière médicale.[35] Il peut être un proche, une personne de référence ou le médecin de famille.[36] L'auteur des directives anticipées a la possibilité de désigner un ou plusieurs remplaçants au cas où le représentant thérapeutique ne serait pas disponible.[37]

---

[32] ASSM 5.2.5.

[33] Convention du 4 avril 1997 pour la protection des Droits de l'Homme et de la dignité de l'être humain à l'égard des applications de la biologie et de la médecine (Convention sur les Droits de l'Homme et la biomédecine), RS 0.810.2.

[34] Article 370 alinéa 2 CC.

[35] Audrey Leuba, Dominique Bertrand, Marina Mandofia Berney, « Personnes âgées et mesures de protection de l'adulte », in *Médecin et droit médical, supra* note 28, pp. 346–353 ; pour une présentation plus détaillée cf. Henri Deschenaux, Paul Henri Steinauer, *Personnes physiques et tutelle*, Berne, Stämpfli, 2001 ; Martin Stettler, *Représentation et protection de l'adulte*, Fribourg, éd. Universitaires, 1997.

[36] Dominique Manaï, « Le droit des proches du patient dans la prise de décision médicale », in *Médecin et droit médical, supra* note 28, pp. 131–140 ; Martin Stettler, « La référence aux proches dans le droit actuel et futur de la protection des adultes », in *Pour un droit pluriel. Etudes offertes au professeur J.F. Perrin*, Genève-Bâle, Helbing & Lichtenhahn, 2002, pp. 109–121.

[37] Article 370 alinéa 3 CC.

Le patient est libre de désigner un représentant thérapeutique, et le cas échéant un remplaçant, sans formuler d'instructions : il le laisse ainsi décider dans la situation concrète. Il peut aussi plus largement lui fixer l'étendue de son mandat, en lui donnant des instructions concrètes dans l'accomplissement de sa tâche.[38]

Aussi bien les normes juridiques[39] que non juridiques[40] ainsi que la pratique médicale encouragent la désignation d'un représentant thérapeutique.[41]

D. *La description de l'échelle de valeurs du patient*

Il est possible d'inclure dans les directives anticipées non seulement le refus ou le consentement à un traitement médical, mais aussi la description de l'échelle des valeurs du patient. Cette possibilité n'est pas prévue explicitement dans la loi, mais est mentionnée dans les normes non juridiques qui guident la pratique de la rédaction des directives anticipées.

Expliciter l'échelle des valeurs permet de connaître les conceptions de vie, les souhaits, les peurs, les attentes et espoirs qui sont déterminants pour le patient, dans le contexte de la santé et de la maladie. De plus elle fournit des indications sur ce que l'auteur entend par « qualité de vie » et une existence ou une fin de vie « digne », ce qui permet de contribuer à établir des repères concrets dans des cas précis.[42]

L'Académie suisse des sciences médicales a établi une liste de questions types concernant l'échelle des valeurs.[43] Cinq groupes de questions sont posées au patient au moment de la rédaction des directives anticipées : 1) concernant la *motivation*, pour quelle raison souhaitez-vous rédiger des directives anticipées ? Est-ce suite à un événement concret ? Quelle est la finalité de ces directives anticipées, et que voulez-vous

---

[38] Article 370 alinéa 2 *in fine* CC.

[39] Ainsi, en plus du droit fédéral, les lois cantonales : Fribourg, art. 49 al. 2 LS ; Genève, art. 47 al. 2 LS ; Jura, art. 26b al. 2 Loi sanitaire ; Neuchâtel, art. 25a al. 2 LS ; Valais, art. 24 al. 2 LS ; Vaud, art. 23a al. 2 LSP.

[40] ASSM 5.1.

[41] Marinette Ummel, « Testament et directives anticipées », in *Médecin et droit médical, supra* note 28, pp. 141–148 ; Olivier Babaïantz, « Les directives anticipées en matière de soins médicaux et la représentation thérapeutique privée », *Cahier Institut de droit de la santé*, 6, 1988 ; Olivier Guillod et Philippe Meier, « Représentation privée, mesures tutélaires et soins médicaux », in *Mélanges Schnyder*, Fribourg, Ed. Universitaires, 1995, pp. 325–363.

[42] ASSM 4.1.

[43] ASSM, Directives concernant les « directives anticipées » : version abrégée et questions types relatives à l'échelle des valeurs, *Bulletin des Médecins Suisses*, 2010, p. 21.

éviter ? En avez-vous discuté avec vos proches ? Avec votre médecin de famille ? 2) Concernant la *conception de la vie*, où vous voyez-vous dans votre vie ?, Est-il important pour vous de vivre encore longtemps ?, Seriez-vous prêt, pour gagner des années de vie, à accepter certains limitations (un état de dépendance par exemple) ? Ou bien préférez-vous renoncer à vivre quelques années de plus pour rester aussi indépendant que possible ? Que signifie pour vous personnellement et concrètement « mourir dans la dignité » ? Quel est le rôle de vos proches/de votre famille : quelles tâches peuvent-ils assumer, que peut-on leur demander ? 3) Concernant la *qualité de vie*, qu'est-ce qui donne sens à votre vie ? Quelles activités, contenus et valeurs déterminent actuellement votre vie ? Pensez-vous que la maladie ou un âge avancé puisse changer votre conception de la qualité de vie (par exemple en termes de capacité de communication, de mobilité, d'état d'esprit) ? A quel point est-il important pour vous de vivre sans douleur ? Seriez-vous prêt à accepter pour cela un état de conscience diminué voire même, dans le cas extrême, une perte de conscience ? 4) Concernant l'*expérience de la maladie, de la fin de vie et de la mort*, avez-vous personnellement déjà vécu l'expérience de la maladie ? Ou l'avez-vous vécue à travers un tiers (par exemple, parents, conjoint, ami) ? Voyez-vous un sens à la vie, si vous deviez subir des limitations sévères ou si votre personnalité devait changer (comme par exemple dans des cas de comas ou de démences sévères) ? Quels dommages ou préjudices considérez-vous comme assez graves pour ne plus vouloir continuer à vivre ? 5) Concernant les *convictions personnelles et religieuses*, avez-vous des convictions religieuses, spirituelles ou philosophiques ? Faites-vous partie d'une église ou d'une association ? Ces convictions ont-elles une influence sur votre vie dans des « situations limites », c'est-à-dire quand votre vie est en danger (maintenir la vie ou laisser mourir) ? Seriez-vous d'accord de donner vos organes ou tissus après votre mort ?

E. *Autres indications*

Les directives anticipées sont susceptibles de contenir des déclarations concernant d'autres sujets, par exemples transplantation, autopsie, utilisation du cadavre ou de ses parties pour la recherche ou des indications relatives à l'organisation du quotidien, garde des enfants, information de l'employeur.[44]

---

[44] ASSM 4.

Des déclarations relatives au don d'organes dans les directives anticipées sont encouragées. Elles peuvent indiquer le consentement ou le refus
d'un don d'organes, de tissus ou de cellules en vue d'une transplantation.
Selon la loi,[45] toute personne âgée de 16 ans est habilitée à faire une déclaration de don. Le consentement du donneur est nécessaire pour prélever
des organes, des tissus ou des cellules. En l'absence de consentement
documenté ou de refus de la personne défunte et lorsque celle-ci n'a pas
exprimé ses souhaits concernant un éventuel don d'organes, le consentement des personnes les plus proches est nécessaire.

IV. LE LIEU DE CONSERVATION DES DIRECTIVES ANTICIPÉES

La détermination du lieu de conservation des directives anticipées est très
importante. Du lieu de leur conservation découle en partie leurs effets,
dans la mesure où elles doivent être accessibles en temps opportun par les
professionnels de la santé. N'oublions pas que ce qui caractérise une
déclaration anticipée est le décalage temporel entre le moment de sa
rédaction et le moment où elle devra être appliquée.

La loi suisse ne prévoit pas un système d'enregistrement des volontés
du patient sur un document standard, ni ne désigne un lieu précis centra-
lisé pour ce genre de déclarations. Elle laisse à l'auteur des directives toute
la latitude de déterminer lui-même le lieu de dépôt de ce document. En
revanche, il lui appartient de veiller à ce que l'existence des directives
anticipées soit connue. Le médecin consultera la carte d'assuré du
patient[46] ou questionnera les proches, voire le médecin traitant, sur l'existence d'une telle déclaration,[47] mais on ne saurait exiger de lui qu'il fasse
des démarches plus étendues. Dans les travaux préparatoires, il est précisé
que le médecin traitant a l'obligation de contrôler la carte d'assuré du
patient, au cas où celui-ci y aurait fait inscrire la constitution de directives
anticipées et le lieu où il les a déposées.[48] L'Académie suisse des sciences
médicales recommande à une institution médicale, qui accueille un
patient incapable de discernement, de clarifier si le patient a rédigé des

---

[45] Article 8 Loi fédérale du 8 octobre 2004 sur la transplantation d'organes, de tissus et de cellules (Loi sur la transplantation), RS 810.21.
[46] Article 372 alinéa 2 CC.
[47] C'est ce qui a été décidé lors des débats parlementaires : *Bulletin Officiel de l'Assemblée fédérale*, 2008, N 1518 ss ; proposition de la minorité de la Commission, acceptée par 87 voix contre 69.
[48] Conseil fédéral, Message, *Feuille fédérale* (2006), pp. 6635 ss, ad. 372 CC.

directives anticipées ou désigné un représentant thérapeutique, en interrogeant les proches et le médecin traitant. Mais cette démarche n'est pas possible en situation d'urgence.[49]

Cette grande liberté du patient nous permet d'envisager différents lieux de conservation : le patient peut confier à quelqu'un - ses proches, son représentant thérapeutique ou son médecin de famille - sa déclaration avant qu'il ne tombe dans l'inconscience ; il peut aussi la porter sur lui au moment de sa prise en charge par les praticiens ; il peut aussi conserver sur lui une carte indiquant le lieu où se trouvent ses directives anticipées ; enfin, une dernière possibilité : il peut noter le lieu de dépôt sur sa carte d'assuré.[50]

V. LES EFFETS DES DIRECTIVES ANTICIPÉES

Le droit suisse va plus loin que la Convention européenne sur les droits de l'homme et la biomédecine qui préconise qu'il sera tenu compte des souhaits précédemment exprimés.[51] En droit suisse, les directives anticipées déploient des effets obligatoires pour les professionnels de la santé.

Tant que le patient est capable de discernement, sa volonté actuelle prime et ses déclarations préalables demeurent sans effet. L'application des directives anticipées n'entre en considération qu'à partir du moment où leur auteur devient incapable de discernement. Le principe posé par le législateur est que le médecin respecte les directives anticipées.[52] Ce principe avait déjà été admis par les tribunaux, dans un arrêt du 7 mars 1995[53] avant même sa mention en droit fédéral.

Ainsi, la volonté précédemment exprimée a un caractère contraignant pour le praticien,[54] que la déclaration anticipée soit pré-formulée mais signée par le patient ou qu'elle soit entièrement rédigée par le patient importe peu. Il suffit que la volonté soit claire et s'applique à la situation thérapeutique envisagée par son auteur. Il est important pour la valeur

---

[49] ASSM 8.

[50] Article 371 alinéa 2 CC. L'étendue des données enregistrées sur la carte ainsi que l'accès à ces données sont réglées par l'Ordonnance sur la carte d'assuré pour l'assurance obligatoire des soins du 14 février 2007, OCA, art. 6.

[51] Article 9 Convention européenne sur les droits de l'homme et la biomédecine.

[52] Article 372 alinéa 1 CC.

[53] Arrêt du tribunal administratif genevois, 7 mars 1995, Revue de droit administratif et fiscal 1996, 64–74.

[54] Conseil fédéral, Message, *Feuille fédérale* (2006), pp. 6635 ss, ad art. 372 CC.

des directives anticipées que le patient précise les circonstances dans lesquelles elles s'appliqueront et ne se limite pas à formuler une hypothèse générale. Si bien que le caractère obligatoire des déclarations anticipées est prescrit par la loi mais en pratique dépend de la précision de la formulation. Un contenu vague et imprécis *de facto* laissera une grande marge d'appréciation à la personne appelée à décider du traitement médical. L'Académie suisse des sciences médicales déconseille l'exclusion générale de certains mesures, indépendamment de la situation d'application.[55] Les directives anticipées seront respectées même si elles ne correspondent pas au choix que le praticien aurait fait.

Les directives anticipées ne sont pas soumises à un délai et leur force obligatoire ne connaît, *ex lege*, aucune limite dans le temps. Il est néanmoins important pour la validité de la volonté préalablement exprimée de les actualiser régulièrement, en particulier lorsque les conditions de vie ou la santé de son auteur ont subi des changements, dans la mesure où *de facto* plus elles sont anciennes moins elles expriment la volonté que le patient aurait exprimée s'il était encore capable de discernement.[56]

A titre *exceptionnel*, le professionnel de la santé est autorisé à s'écarter de la volonté manifestée préalablement par le patient. Le législateur fait appel au sens critique du praticien vis-à-vis des directives anticipées. Au moment de leur application, il doit s'interroger sur leur fiabilité. Si le médecin ne respecte pas les directives anticipées, il doit consigner dans le dossier médical les raisons qui l'incitent à se distancer d'elles[57]. La loi[58] prévoit que le médecin peut s'écarter des directives anticipées dans trois hypothèses : « *si elles violent des dispositions légales, ou si des doutes sérieux laissent supposer qu'elles ne sont pas l'expression de sa libre volonté ou qu'elles ne correspondent pas à sa volonté présumée dans la situation donnée* ». La première hypothèse concerne le contenu de la volonté préalablement exprimée. La loi vise ainsi la situation où le patient demande de manière anticipée que l'on mette un terme à sa vie, ce qui, comme nous l'avons vu, est une euthanasie active directe prohibée par la loi pénale. Les deux autres hypothèses ont pour objet d'éviter de risquer d'imposer au patient les conséquences d'une volonté qui ne serait plus la sienne. En effet, la deuxième hypothèse vise les doutes fondés quant au caractère libre de sa volonté. Ce sera notamment le cas lorsque les avis des proches,

---

[55] ASSM 4.4.
[56] ASSM 3.4.
[57] Article 372 alinéa 3 CC.
[58] Article 372 alinéa 2 CC.

du représentant thérapeutique, de l'équipe soignante et du médecin responsable sont divergents dans une situation concrète. Dans la mesure du possible, il convient de parvenir à une solution consensuelle, en recourant à une consultation éthique.[59] En cas d'échec d'un consensus, l'autorité de protection de l'adulte sera saisie.[60] Et si le temps est compté, un traitement dans l'intérêt du patient, à savoir dans le but de le guérir et de le soulager, sera entrepris. La troisième hypothèse envisagée par la loi vise la situation où la volonté du patient ne semble plus correspondre à celle exprimée dans les directives anticipées.[61] Pour prouver que les conditions de cette situation sont remplies, des éléments concrets seront invoqués : soit le patient, encore capable de discernement, avait exprimé un autre choix qu'il n'a pas eu le temps de consigner dans les directives anticipées, soit la déclaration anticipée est ancienne et les circonstances ont changé, soit des progrès médicaux ont été faits depuis la rédaction des directives anticipées et tout laisse à supposer que le patient opterait pour ces nouvelles possibilités thérapeutiques. Dans ces trois hypothèses, les directives anticipées ne déploieront pas leurs effets. Le médecin consignera, dans le dossier du patient, les motifs qui l'ont amené à ne pas tenir compte de la volonté anticipée du patient. La décision qui résultera de ces indices devrait faire l'objet d'un consensus entre l'équipe soignante, les proches et, le cas échéant, le représentant thérapeutique.[62]

Il n'est pas superflu de rappeler qu'en cas d'urgence, il est difficile de suivre les directives anticipées. La solution préconisée par la pratique médicale semble être la suivante : les mesures visant à préserver la vie ou empêcher une grave complication doivent être mises en œuvre, puis dès que possible, les directives anticipées seront intégrées dans le traitement.

VI. Conclusion

La question des directives anticipées est sans conteste à l'ordre du jour en Suisse. Elle est d'une grande actualité tant sur le plan législatif que médico-éthique ou dans les pratiques des professionnels de la santé. Les directives anticipées expriment l'autodétermination du patient pour une situation

---

[59] ASSM 10.

[60] Article 373 CC.

[61] Audrey Leuba et Celine Tritten, « Les directives anticipées en Suisse : quelques aspects juridiques », in *Les cahiers de l'action sociale et de la santé*, numéro spécial sur Les directives anticipées, 2005, pp. 27–34.

[62] ASSM 9.

éventuelle et future où il ne serait plus capable de manifester sa volonté. Elles sont perçues comme un « outil d'humanisation des soins ».[63] Le droit suisse est marqué par la grande marge de liberté accordée à l'auteur des directives anticipées : elles ne se limitent pas aux situations de fin de vie ni ne se réduisent à un droit de *veto*. Elles couvrent, au contraire, toutes les situations raisonnablement envisageables et conformes au droit, pourvu que les instructions soient formulées de manière claire et précise. Elles peuvent viser un refus de certains traitements, mais aussi des actes positifs ; elles peuvent désigner un représentant thérapeutique.

Les directives anticipées apparaissent comme un instrument aux mains du patient qui lui permet d'apprivoiser ses appréhensions de subir un traitement non souhaité, d'éviter les désaccords entre les proches au sujet du choix thérapeutique le plus opportun et de guider les professionnels de la santé dans la détermination d'un acte médical respectueux des valeurs du patient.

---

[63] Maya Olmari-Ebbing, Claire-Nicole Zumbach, Martyne-Isabel Forest, Charles Henri Rapin, « Les directives anticipées, un outil d'humanisation des soins », *Revue médicale de la Suisse romande*, 2000, n° 120, pp. 581–584.

TREATMENT DIRECTIVES IN THE NETHERLANDS: THE GAP BETWEEN LEGAL REGULATION AND MEDICAL PRACTICE

Sofia Moratti* and Cristiano Vezzoni**

This chapter describes the regulation of advance treatment directives under Dutch law, within the framework of the law governing end-of-life decision-making in the Netherlands.

I. End-of-Life Decision-Making in the Netherlands

The concept of 'end-of-life decisions' encompasses various sorts of medical behavior, as shown in Dutch[1] and international research.[2] The sort of end-of-life decision that takes place with the highest frequency in medical practice is withholding or withdrawal of life-prolonging medical treatment, when (further) treatment is thought not to benefit the patient. "Terminal sedation", that is, maintaining the patient in a state of unconsciousness until death, and administration of palliative drugs "in doses that may shorten life" take place with a much lower frequency.[3] As a

---

* Max Weber Fellow, European University Institute, Florence, Italy, and Ethics Committee, SISSA Neuroscience, Trieste, Italy; email: info@sofiamoratti.eu.

** Researcher, Faculty of Sociology, University of Trento, Italy, and Department of Health Sciences, Metamedica, University Medical Center Groningen, University of Groningen, The Netherlands; email: cristiano.vezzoni@unitn.it. Both authors hold a PhD in Regulation of Medical Behavior that Potentially Shortens Life from the Department of Legal Theory, University of Groningen, The Netherlands.

[1] Bregje D. Onwuteaka-Philipsen, Agnes van der Heide, Dirk Koper, Ingeborg Keij-Deerenberg, Judith A.C. Rietjens, Mette L. Rurup, Astrid M. Vrakking, Jean Jacques Georges, Martien T. Muller, Gerrit van der Wal, Paul J. van der Maas, "Euthanasia and Other End-of-Life Decisions in the Netherlands in 1990, 1995, and 2001", 362 *The Lancet* (2003), pp. 395–399.

[2] Agnes van der Heide, Luc Deliens, Karin Faisst, Tore Nilstun, Michael Norup, Eugenio Paci, Gerrit van der Wal, Paul J. van der Maas, "End-of-Life Decision-Making in Six European Countries: Descriptive Study", 361 *The Lancet* (2003), pp. 345–350.

[3] Mette L. Rurup, Sander D. Borgsteede, Agnes van der Heide, Paul van der Maas, Bregje D. Onwuteaka-Philipsen, "Trends in the Use of Opioids at the End of Life and the Expected Effects on Hastening Death", 37 *Journal of Pain and Symptom Management* (2009), pp. 144–155 and Judith Rietjens, Johan J.M. van Delden, Bregje D. Onwutheaka-Philipsen, Hilde Buiting, Paul van der Maas, Agnes van der Heide, "Continuous Deep Sedation for Patients Nearing Death in the Netherlands: Descriptive Study", 336 *British Medical Journal* (2008), pp. 810–813 and A.A. Eduard Verhagen, Jo HHM Dorscheidt, Bernadette Engels,

S. Negri (ed.), *Self-Determination, Dignity and End-of-Life Care*
2011 Koninklijke Brill NV. Printed in The Netherlands. ISBN 978 90 04 22357 8. pp. 287–298

matter of fact, recent medical research shows that sedatives and opioids probably do not shorten the life of the patient, even if administered in large doses[4] and the issue is currently disputed in the scientific literature.[5] The last two sorts of end-of-life decisions, euthanasia and assisted suicide, take place very rarely. In clinical practice, euthanasia consists of receiving a lethal injection and assisted suicide of swallowing lethal pills.[6] However, in the Netherlands, the term "euthanasia" encompasses both, as they are subject to essentially the same regulation. Euthanasia in the Dutch sense refers to the behavior of the doctor who ends the life of a severely suffering and incurably ill patient on the competent patient's express, well-considered and voluntary request. In clinical practice, euthanasia is performed on patients who are not dependent on life-prolonging treatment. In principle, euthanasia is not considered, when it is possible to let nature take its course by withholding or withdrawing life-prolonging treatment that is not beneficial or not acceptable to the patient.[7]

The current Dutch regulation of end-of-life decisions is based on the dichotomy between "natural" and "non-natural death". Withholding and withdrawal of treatment and administration of very large doses of palliative drugs are held to be natural causes of death.[8] More precisely, the actual cause of death is taken to be the patient's underlying disease and

---

Joep H. Hubben, Pieter J. Sauer, "Analgesics, Sedatives and Neuromuscular Blockers as Part of End-of-Life Decisions in Dutch NICUs", 94 *Archives of Disease in Childhood – Fetal and Neonatal Edition* (2009), pp. F434–F438.

[4] Andrew Thorns and Nigel Sykes, "Opioid Use in Last Week of Life and Implications for End-of-Life Decision-Making", 356 *The Lancet* (2000), pp. 398–399; Nigel Sykes and Andrew Thorns, "Sedative Use in the Last Week of Life and the Implications for End-of-Life Decision Making", 163 *Archives of Internal Medicine* (2003), pp. 341–344.

[5] Susan A. Fohr, "The Double Effect of Pain Medication: Separating Myth from Reality", 1 *Palliative Medicine* (1998), pp. 315–28; Piet Admiraal and John Griffiths, "Sterven aan pijnbestrijding" [Death from pain relief], 56 *Medisch Contact* (2001), pp. 463–464; Miles J. Edwards, "Opioids and Benzodiazepines Appear Paradoxically to Delay Inevitable Death After Ventilator Withdrawal", 21 *Journal of Palliative Care* (2005), pp. 299–302; Karen Forbes and Richard Huxtable, "Clarifying the Data on Double Effect", 20 *Palliative Medicine* (2006), p. 395; Rob George and Claud Regnard, "Lethal Opioids or Dangerous Prescribers?", 21 *Palliative Medicine* (2007), pp. 77–80; Jan Bakker, Tim C. Jansen, Alex Lima, Erwin J.O. Kompanije, "Why Opioids and Sedatives May Prolong Life Rather Than Hasten Death After Ventilator Withdrawal in Critically Ill Patients", 25 *American Journal of Hospice and Palliative Medicine* (2008), pp. 152–154; Mette L. Rurup, Bregje D. Onwuteaka-Philipsen, "Relieving Pain and Suffering Does not Hasten Death", 36 *Critical Care Medicine* (2008), pp. 2486–2487,

[6] John Griffiths, Alex Bood and Heleen Weyers (eds.), *Euthanasia & Law in the Netherlands* (Amsterdam, 1998).

[7] John Griffiths & Heleen Weyers, and Maurice Adams (eds.), *Euthanasia and Law in Europe* (Oxford, 2008).

[8] The latter is subject to doubt when the drugs used are neuromuscular blockers. Sofia Moratti, "Ethical and Legal Acceptability of the Use of Neuromuscular Blockers (NMBs) in

not the doctor's action or omission. On the other hand, the euthanized patient dies a non-natural death. The doctor must report his action to regional review Committees, consisting of an ethicist, a doctor, and a legal expert who chairs the Committee. If the (majority of the) Committee finds that the behavior of the doctor was consistent with a number of "requirements of careful practice", the case is closed.[9] If the Committee finds that the doctor has departed from the requirements, the case is handled over to the local Prosecutor, for further investigation and possibly prosecution.[10] In the Netherlands, the criminal justice system allows for prosecutorial discretion. Dutch prosecutors are not under an obligation to prosecute every case that comes to their attention.[11]

The current regulation of end-of-life decisions is the result of a process of *de facto* legalization of euthanasia that started in the 1980s.[12] A few doctors who had ended the lives of a patient (and had subsequently reported the fact) were acquitted by Dutch criminal courts in the 1980s and 1990s. The courts held that the defendants had acted in a "state of necessity".[13] The doctors were caught between the two fundamental

Connection with Abstention Decisions in Dutch NICUs: Interviews with Neonatologists", *Journal of Medical Ethics*, online first 28 October 2010, forthcoming and Hilde M. Buiting, Agnes van der Heide, Bregje D. Onwuteaka-Philipsen, Mette L. Rurup, Judith A.C. Rietjens, Gerard Borsboom, Paul J. van der Maas, Johan J.M. van Delden, "Physicians' Labelling of End-of-Life Practices: a Hypothetical Case Study", 36 *Journal of Medical Ethics* (2010), pp. 24–29 and Judith A.C. Rietjens, Paul J. van der Maas, Bregje D. Onwuteaka-Philipsen, Johan J.M. van Delden, Agnes van der Heide, "Two Decades of Research on Euthanasia from the Netherlands. What Have We Learnt and What Questions Remain?", 6 *Journal of Bioethical Inquiry* (2009), pp. 271–283.

[9] Hilde M. Buiting, Johan J.M. van Delden, Bregje D. Onwuteaka-Philpsen, Judith A.C. Rietjens, Mette L. Rurup, Donald van Tol, Joseph K.M. Gevers, Paul van der Maas, Agnes van der Heide, "Reporting of Euthanasia and Physician-Assisted Suicide in the Netherlands: Descriptive Study", 10 *BMC Medical Ethics* (2009), pp. 1–11. Most cases reported to the Committees involve oncological patients.

[10] Tinne Smets, Johan Bilsen, Joachim Cohen, Mette L. Rurup, Els de Keyser, Luc Deliens, "The Medical Practice of Euthanasia in Belgium and The Netherlands: Legal Notification, Control and Evaluation Procedures", 90 *Health Policy* (2009), pp. 181–187 and Agnes van der Heide, Bregje D. Onwuteaka-Philipsen, Mette L. Rurup, Hilde M. Buiting, Johan J.M. van Delden, Johanna E. Hanssen-de Wolf, Anke G.J.M. Janssen, H. Roeline W. Pasman, Judith A.C. Rietjens, Cornelis J.M. Prins, Ingeborg M. Deerenberg, Joseph K.M. Gevers, Paul J. van der Maas, Gerrit van der Wal, "End-of-Life Practices in the Netherlands under the Euthanasia Act", 356 *The New England Journal of Medicine* (2007), pp. 1957–1965.

[11] Peter J.P. Tak, *The Dutch Criminal Justice System: Organization and Operation* (2nd rev. ed., The Hague, 2008).

[12] Heleen Weyers, "Explaining the Emergence of Euthanasia Law in the Netherlands: How the Sociology of Law Can Help the Sociology of Bioethics", 28 *Sociology of Health & Illness* (2006), pp. 802–816 and Griffiths, Weyers & Adams, *supra* note 7.

[13] Barney Sneiderman and Marja Verhoef, "Patient Autonomy and the Defence of Medical Necessity: Five Dutch Euthanasia Cases", 34 *Alberta Law Review* (1996), pp. 374–415.

ethical imperatives of the medical profession: prolonging life and relieving suffering, the courts argued. The medical profession played a crucial
role in the process of regulation of euthanasia. The Dutch Medical
Association defined the conditions of permissibility of euthanasia in a
number of professional reports and position statements, that were taken
very seriously by the courts.[14] The courts decided for or against acquittal
in individual cases, depending on whether the doctor had followed the
requirements laid down in the professional reports by the Medical
Association. There are two sets of "requirements of careful practice" for
legal euthanasia.[15] "Substantive" requirements refer to the condition of the
patient and his (or her) request for euthanasia. The patient must be suffering unbearably and his or her condition must be hopeless, which means,
without prospects for improvement. The patient must be competent and
his or her request for euthanasia must be voluntary and well-considered.
"Procedural" requirements concern the decision-making process and the
mechanisms of control over the doctor's behavior. The doctor responsible
for treatment must consult with at least one independent colleague before
the euthanasia is carried out.[16] The consultant must see the patient and
speak with the patient, and advise on whether the "requirements of careful practice" have been met. Finally, as we have seen, the doctor who carried out the euthanasia must report his action to the regional review
committee, by means of standard forms that cover every aspect of the
decision-making process and of the patient's condition and request.

During the late 1980s and 1990s, decisions not to prosecute became
standard prosecutorial practice in cases of euthanasia, on condition that
the doctor concerned had followed the requirements of careful practice.[17]

---

[14] See Griffiths, *supra* note 6 and Griffiths, Weyers & Adams, *supra* note 7.

[15] The "requirements of careful practice" are also known as "due care criteria". Hilde
M. Buiting, Joseph K.M. Gevers, Judith A.C. Rietjens, Bregje D. Onwuteaka-Philipsen, Paul
van der Maas, Agnes van der Heide, Johan J.M. van Delden, "Dutch Criteria of Due Care for
Physician-Assisted Dying in Medical Practice: A Physician Perspective", 34 *Journal of
Medical Ethics* (2008), e12 and Griffiths, Weyers & Adams, *supra* note 7.

[16] There is a nationwide organization that provides this service. SCEN (Support and
Consultation on Euthanasia in the Netherlands) is a network of doctors who are specially
trained consultants in individual cases, when euthanasia is considered. The SCEN project
was implemented gradually throughout the Netherlands between 1999 and 2002. Compare
Marijke C. Jansen-van der Weide, Bregje D. Onwutheaka-Philipsen, Gerrit van der Wal,
"Quality of Consultation and the Project 'Support and Consultation on Euthanasia in the
Netherlands' (SCEN)", 80 *Health Policy* (2007), pp. 97–106 and Griffiths, Weyers & Adams,
supra note 7.

[17] Henk J.J. Leenen, "The Development of Euthanasia in the Netherlands", 8 *European
Journal of Health Law* (2001), pp. 125–133.

The Dutch prosecutorial system is presided over by a Committee,[18] consisting of the five chief prosecutors attached to the five Dutch Courts of Appeals. The Committee periodically dictates guidelines of prosecutorial policy, that must be followed by all prosecutors in the Netherlands.

In 2002, the Dutch Parliament enacted a statute, known as the "Euthanasia law". The articles in the Criminal Code prohibiting killing on request and assistance with suicide were amended. A new provision was included in the Code, exempting from liability doctors who perform euthanasia, follow the "requirements of careful practice" and properly report their action.[19] As we will see, the Euthanasia law marked an important step in the process of regulation of advance treatment directives. It became possible to request euthanasia in a written advance directive.

II. Regulation of Treatment Directives in the Netherlands

In the Netherlands, there are three sorts of treatment directives. In a treatment directive, the person can either refuse medical treatment ("negative" directive), appoint a representative for healthcare decisions, or make a request for euthanasia.[20] The three sorts of directives have different legal statuses. However, it is not easy to distinguish among the three in practice. The patient often gives different sorts of instructions in one document.[21]

---

[18] *College van Procureurs-Generaal*, literally: Committee of Procurators-General.

[19] Jurriaan De Haan, "The New Dutch Law on Euthanasia" 10 *Medical Law Review* (2002), pp. 57–75.

[20] In Dutch, the three sorts of documents are referred to as *behandelverbod, volmacht*, and *euthanasieverklaring*, respectively.

[21] Cristiano Vezzoni, *Advance Treatment Directives and Autonomy for Incompetent Patients: An International Comparative Survey of Law and Practice, with Special Attention to the Netherlands* (Lewiston, N.Y., 2008), p. 92. By supplying standard forms clearly divided into three sections (refusal of treatment, appointment of a representative and written advance request for euthanasia), the Dutch Association for Voluntary Euthanasia has taken into account the distinction among different sorts of treatment directives. However, the standard forms are subject to a number of limitations. People opposed to euthanasia are not likely to trust the Association as a source. Secondly, distribution is only to members of the Association. And thirdly, a standardized form is no substitute for concrete, expert advice from someone who knows exactly what the medical condition of the patient is and can discuss with him or her in detail precisely what sort of treatment he or she does not want under precisely which circumstances. Compare Vezzoni, p. viii.

A. *Negative Treatment Directives*

Negative treatment directives received statutory recognition in 1995, in the framework of the "Law on Contracts for Medical Treatment".[22] One of the grounds on which the Law rests is article 11 of the Constitution, which states the right to bodily integrity. To implement this right, the Law provides that all medical treatment requires the informed consent of the patient. The doctor must comply with the informed refusal of treatment, no matter the reasons underlying the refusal and however dire its consequences. The Law also provides that medical intervention can be refused in advance. If a patient is no longer competent, refusal of treatment can take the form of a written directive, drafted while competent. The relevant passage reads:

> In case a patient sixteen years of age or older cannot be considered capable of a reasonable assessment of his relevant interests, the healthcare provider and [the personal representative] shall follow the patient's apparent views laid down in writing when he was still capable of such reasonable assessment and containing a refusal of consent [...]. The healthcare provider may depart herefrom if he considers that there are well-founded reasons for doing so.[23]

In order to be valid, the directive must be written[24] and the identity of the author must be certain. Furthermore, there should be no doubt about the authenticity of the document. Finally, the author should be older than sixteen and competent at the time of the drafting, but no longer competent when the directive is implemented. Healthcare providers are in principle bound by the refusal of treatment expressed in a valid negative directive, unless there are "well-founded reasons" to disregard it. This formula has been criticized for its vagueness.[25] It is generally accepted that the doctor's personal views, medical professional standards, and the possible life-shortening effect of foregoing treatment, are not "well-founded reasons" for giving treatment against the patient's express wishes. According to

---

[22] *Wet op de Geneeskundige Behandelingsovereenkomst* (WGBO).

[23] Article 450, para. 3. Translation partly based on Ewoud Hondius and Annet van Hooft, "The New Dutch Law on Medical Services" 43 *Netherlands International Law Review* (2006), pp. 1–17.

[24] A number of considerations may suggest that an oral refusal would also be binding. Moreover, in everyday medical practice, oral instructions (e.g. of a person about to undergo total anesthesia) are surely binding within the context of the implied contract for medical treatment. See Vezzoni, *supra* note 22, p. 84.

[25] Ernst C. de Jong, "Schriftelijke wilsverklaringen en vertegenwoordiging" [Advance directives and representation], in R.J.M. Dillman, J. Legemaate, E.C. de Jong, *Medisch handelen rond het levenseinde bij wilsonbekwame patiënten* [Medical treatment at the end of life for incompetent patients] (Houten, 1997), p. 206.

Van Veen,[26] the phrase "well-founded reasons" refers to situations of uncertainty with regard to:

- the identity of the patient,
- the patient's competence at the time of the drafting,
- the actual correspondence between the content of the directive and the wishes of the person at the time of the drafting,
- the actual correspondence between the conditions of applicability in the directive and the current situation of the (formerly competent) author.[27]

The occurrence of situations of uncertainty can be prevented by taking a number of precautions,[28] that are, however, not required by the Law on contracts for medical treatment.

The *presence of witnesses* to the drafting can prevent controversy over the identity and the competence of the author. It is in general difficult to assess the person's competence,[29] and it often happens that, between the drafting and the implementation, there has been a change of treating doctor, following, for example, the patient's admission to a nursing home. The notarial authentication of the document would be another way to prevent controversy over the identity and the competence of the author.

Although the law does not set a time requirement for the validity of a treatment directive, a *recently drafted or renewed document* can minimize the uncertainty concerning the consistency between the instructions in the directive and the current wishes of their author.

The *involvement of a medical expert* (for example, the patient's general practitioner) in the drafting, may help towards more effective implementation, making the content of the document more adherent to medical practice.

Finally, perhaps the most important thing that can be done to facilitate the interpretation of a directive is to include in it the *appointment of a representative*, to interpret and supervise the implementation of the

---

[26] Evert-Ben van Veen, "De meerderjarige wilsonbekwame patiënt" [The incompetent patient of age], in J. Legemaate (ed.), *De WGBO: van tekst naar toepassing* [The Law on contracts for medical treatment: from legal text to implementation] (Houten, 1998), p. 48.

[27] The last two points can be partly traced back to the category of 'interpretation problems'. See de Jong, *supra* note 26, pp. 214–216.

[28] Vezzoni, *supra* note 22, pp. 85–86.

[29] For a more general discussion of the assessment of competence under the Law on contracts for medical treatment, see van Veen, *supra* note 27, pp. 43–46.

author's instructions.[30] As we will see, this possibility is provided for under the Law on contracts for medical treatment.

There are sanctions for disregarding the patient's refusal of treatment in an advance directive, in the absence of a "well-founded reason". The legislator chose to include the regulation of patient's rights in the Civil Code and gave a contractual character to the relationship between doctor and patients. Therefore, a treatment directive is in effect part of the contract between the two parties. It follows that sanctions for infringement are primarily civil. However, a major violation of the requirement of informed consent could in principle give rise to tort liability and to penal sanctions, because the patient's denial of informed consent removes the legal justification for an invasion of bodily integrity. All of this remains largely speculative: only two cases involving disregard of a treatment directive have been brought to court and both of them involved persons found after having attempted suicide. The decisions did not significantly contribute to legal clarification, for different reasons. The first case was decided prior to the enactment of the Law on contracts for medical treatment, and the authenticity of the refusal was unclear because the document was neither signed nor dated.[31] In the second case, the treatment directive was not available at the beginning of the treatment, and changes in the document made the identity of the appointed representative unclear.[32]

B. *Appointment of a Representative*

The Law on contracts for medical treatment provides for the appointment in writing of a representative for healthcare decision-making, should the author of the directive become incompetent. The relevant passage states:

---

[30] "The mentor is a natural person, appointed by a judge, who represents a person who has reached the age of majority but cannot be considered capable of evaluating his non-material interests because of mental or physical deficiency." Hondius and van Hooft, *supra* note 24, p. 15, note 24.

[31] TvGR 1990/63 and 1993/66. Charges were brought against a doctor who had performed resuscitation on a woman after she had attempted suicide. The woman had left a note, stating that she did not want attempts made to resuscitate her, under any circumstance. The doctor was acquitted because there was insufficient ground to determine whether the request of the woman was authentic, giving that the note was unsigned and undated.

[32] See Mensje Melchior, "Als de patiënt het opgeeft: niet elk behandelverbod wordt gerespecteerd" [Not every negative treatment directive is followed], 62 *Medisch Contact* (2007), pp. 324–327.

> If an adult patient cannot be considered capable of a reasonable assessment of his relevant interests and he has not been placed under guardianship or had a mentor appointed for his benefit, then the obligations on the part of the healthcare provider towards the patient arising from the Law on contracts for medical treatment, shall be fulfilled towards the person authorized in writing by the patient to act on his behalf.[33]

Except where a guardian or a mentor has been appointed by a court, in the decision-making process over administration of life-prolonging treatment, the proxy appointed by the patient in a written directive *takes precedence* over the patient's family members. The healthcare proxy must behave as a "conscientious representative", he must try to involve the patient as much as possible in the decision-making process, and the proxy's decisions should reflect the patient's wishes. If the behavior of the healthcare proxy is "not compatible with the level of care expected from a conscientious care provider", doctors and nurses can refuse to comply with the representative's instructions. The autonomy of the incompetent patient is further protected by the provision that, even when consented to by the healthcare proxy, medical treatment cannot be performed when the patient strongly resists it, with the exception of medical treatment that "is clearly necessary to avoid serious harm to the patient's health".[34]

C. *Written Advance Request for Euthanasia*

The Euthanasia Law, enacted in 2002, provides for the possibility of a directive requesting euthanasia under specific conditions, should the author become incompetent. The relevant article reads:

> If a patient aged sixteen years or older is no longer capable of expressing his will, but prior to being in this condition was considered capable of a reasonable assessment of his relevant interests, and has made a written statement containing a request for termination of life, then the physician may carry out this request. The requirements of due care [referred in the preceding paragraph of the law] are applicable in such a case.[35]

There is a major difference between implementing a written request for euthanasia while the patient is still competent or after the patient has become incompetent. In the former case, the written request only serves as evidence that the patient actually requested euthanasia. The request is

---

[33] Article 465, para. 3. Translation partly based on Hondius and van Hooft, *supra* note 24.

[34] Article 465, paras. 4, 5 and 6.

[35] Article 2, para. 2. Translation based on Vezzoni, *supra* note 22, p. 90.

included in the dossier that accompanies the doctor's formal report of the case to the regional review Committee. The competent patient can at any time (orally or otherwise) withdraw the request for euthanasia. If the patient has become incompetent, the written directive itself is the basis on which the euthanasia is performed. Written advance requests for euthanasia are unambiguously recognized in the Euthanasia Law. However, doubts persist about the actual permissibility of performing euthanasia on an incompetent patient based on a previously written request. A prominent Dutch ethicist, Hans van Delden, has argued that euthanasia performed after the patient has become incompetent and pursuant to a written request cannot be consistent with the "requirements of careful practice" and would therefore constitute a criminal offence.[36] In medical practice, a request for euthanasia is often included in the advance directive together with a negative treatment directive.

Between the enactment of the Euthanasia law and 2009, no cases of euthanasia involving demented patients with an advance written request for euthanasia were reported, "despite the fact that the only real innovation of the Euthanasia law [with respect to the previous regulation of end-of-life decisions] consisted precisely in allowing physicians to act upon such directives".[37]

III. CONCLUSIONS

The Dutch have much experience with regulating end-of-life decision-making and advance directives. However, the implementation of advance directives in the Netherlands is not unproblematic, especially in the case of patients who suffer from a condition that causes cognitive impairments that worsen over time, such as Alzheimer's disease. In a written directive drafted while still competent, the patient may choose to set a specific boundary that he or she would never like to cross (for example, not being able to recognize one's own children). After that boundary has been

---

[36] Johan J.M. van Delden, "The Unfeasibility of Request for Euthanasia in Advance Directives", 40 *Journal of Medical Ethics* (2004), pp. 447–451.

[37] Mette L. Rurup, H. Roeline Pasman, Bregje D. Onwuteaka-Philipsen, *Euthanasieverklaringen bij dementie. Kwalitatief onderzoek onder artsen en patiënten* [Advance euthanasia directives in dementia rarely carried out. Qualitative study in physicians and patients], 154 *Nederlandse Tijdschriften voor Geneeskunde* (2010), A1273 and Cees M.P.M. Hertogh, "The Role of Advance Euthanasia Directives as an Aid to Communication and Shared Decision-Making in Dementia", 35 *Journal of Medical Ethics* (2009), pp. 100–103.

crossed, the alert but incompetent patient may appear altogether serene and smiling, notwithstanding his or her condition and severe cognitive impairment. In that situation, the caregivers may be unsure whether (and when) to carry out the end-of-life decision requested by the patient in his or her treatment directive.

The strongest resistance to implementation is found with regard to written advance requests for euthanasia.[38] The literature offers two explanations.[39] Firstly, almost all severely demented patients are institutionalized in a nursing home, and institutional policies are often more restrictive than Dutch law with regard to euthanasia; in addition, most Dutch elderly care doctors subscribe to these policies. Secondly, if the demented patient is alert but no longer competent, it is difficult to determine whether he or she is suffering "unbearably and hopelessly" (one of the "requirements of careful practice" for lawful euthanasia). Very recent research explored both issues in depth.

A. Institutional Policies and Doctors' Views

De Boer and colleagues[40] administered a questionnaire to all elderly care doctors in the Netherlands.[41] Almost all respondents (94%) report that the institution where they work has a policy regarding euthanasia in cases of dementia.[42] Roughly three-quarters of respondents say that it is the policy of their institution *not* to comply with advance written request for euthanasia in cases of dementia. The remaining doctors report that in their

---

[38] Mette L. Rurup, Bregje D. Onwuteaka-Philipsen, Agnes van der Heide, Gerrit van der Wal, Paul J. van der Maas, "Physicians' Experiences with Demented Patients with Advance Euthanasia Directives in the Netherlands", 53 *Journal of the American Geriatrics Society* (2005), pp. 1138–1144 and Cees M.P.M. Hertogh, Marike E. de Boer, Rose-Marie Droes, Jan A. Eefsting, "Would We Rather Lose Our Life Than Lose Our Self? Lessons From the Dutch Debate on Euthanasia for Patients With Dementia", 7 *American Journal of Bioethics* (2007), pp. 48–56.

[39] These explanations did not change after the enactment of the Euthanasia law. See Bregje D. Onwutheaka-Philipsen, Joseph K.M. Gevers, Agnes van der Heide, *Evaluatie Wet toetsing levensbeëindigend handelen op verzoek en hulp bij zelfdoding* [Evaluation of the implementation of the Euthanasia Law] (Den Haag, 2007).

[40] Marike E. de Boer, Rose-Marie Droes, Cees Jonker, Jan A. Eefsting, Cees M.P.M. Hertogh, "Advance Directives for Euthanasia in Dementia: Do Law-Based Opportunities Lead to More Euthanasia?", *Health Policy*, online 27 July 2010, forthcoming (doi: 10.1016/j.healthpol.2010.06.024).

[41] Because 92% of all patients with dementia are admitted to a nursing home in an advanced stage of their disease and die there, nursing home doctors are the medical professionals most likely to be confronted with a request to carry out euthanasia pursuant to an advance directive.

[42] The policy is almost always (92%) laid down in writing.

institution compliance is an option only when the "criteria of careful practice" are met in the individual case. About 88% of all doctors whose institution has a policy regarding euthanasia for demented patients, approve
of the policy. Over 80% of respondents claim that the enactment of the
Euthanasia law has not lead them to change their views with regard to
euthanasia in cases of dementia, and another 7% say their views have
actually become more restrictive. One of the possible explanations of doctor's skepticism towards written advance requests for euthanasia may be
the low technical-medical quality of these documents, partly a consequence of the low involvement of doctors in the drafting phase.[43]

B. *Understanding Suffering in Alert but Incompetent Demented Patients, and the Importance of Meaningful Communication*

Almost three-quarters of respondents in the study by De Boer and colleagues do *not* believe that dementia and a written advance request for
euthanasia are "valid reasons" for performing euthanasia on a patient.
Roughly the same percentage of respondents think that it is "impossible"
to determine when the written advance request for euthanasia should be
carried out, if the patient has dementia. Over half of respondents say it is
"impossible" to determine whether the incompetent patient with late
stage dementia experiences his own condition as "unbearable and hopeless suffering". Hertogh[44] argues that the demented patient may not experience the suffering he or she feared, due to progressive psychological
adaptation to his (or her) condition and progressive loss of awareness, and
contends that meaningful communication with the patient is a *conditio
sine qua non* for lawful euthanasia. Therefore, he argues, patients with
dementia can lawfully obtain euthanasia only in the early stages of their
disease, when they can still be considered competent, having preserved
"intact recognition" and "executive functioning". The study by De Boer
and colleagues shows that most Dutch elderly care doctors share Hertogh's
views.[45]

---

[43] Vezzoni, *supra* note 22, p. 77.
[44] Hertogh, *supra* note 38, p. 100. A similar position is argued for in Marike E. de Boer,
Cees M.P.M. Hertogh, Rose-Marie Droes, Ingrid I. Riphagen, Cees Jonker, Jan A. Eefsting,
"Suffering from Dementia – The Patient's Perspective: A Review of the Literature", 19
International Psychogeriatrics (2007), pp. 1021–1039.
[45] De Boer et al., *supra* note 42, p. 4. The argument is discussed also in Marike E. de Boer,
Cees M.P.M. Hertogh, Rose-Marie Droes, Cees Jonker, Jan A. Eefsting, "Advance Directives
in Dementia: Issues of Validity and Effectiveness", 22 *International Psychogeriatrics* (2010),
pp. 201–208.

ADVANCE DIRECTIVES IN SPAIN

*José Antonio Seoane**

I. Introduction

The recognition and protection of patient autonomy as a right in Spain began with the Spanish Constitution of 1978 (CE). This has neither a right to autonomy nor a general right of liberty. This does not have a right to informed consent either, but informed consent is an expression of and based on the basic right to physical and moral integrity (article 15 CE). Furthermore, the Spanish Constitution includes a catalogue of fundamental rights and liberties which support and develop patient autonomy: human dignity and free development of personality (article 10.1 CE), the right to life (article 15 CE), the freedom of conscience (ideological and religious freedom) (article 16 CE) and other fundamental rights and liberties, such as the right to health protection (article 43 CE).

Its first significant legislative development was the General Health Act (Act 14/1986, of 25 April: LGS), recognising the patient's right to autonomous decision-making—to be informed and to choose among different treatments—as consent (article 10 LGS), but only for the present, without regulating advance directives.[1]

A second step consolidating and enhancing patient autonomy came from the European Council's Convention on Human Rights and Biomedicine (CHRB),[2] a kind of bioethics Constitution whose most eminent legislative development is Act 41/2002, of 14 November, regulating patient autonomy, and rights and obligations regarding clinical information and documentation (LBAP). For the first time in Spanish Law,

* Associate Professor of Philosophy of Law, University of A Coruña, Spain; email: jaseoane@udc.es.

[1] See Juan María Pemán Gavín, *Asistencia sanitaria y Sistema Nacional de Salud. Estudios jurídicos* (Granada, 2005); José Antonio Seoane, "Las autonomías del paciente", 3 *Dilemata* (2010), pp. 61–75.

[2] Convention of 4th April 1997 (ratified by Document of 23rd July 1999), for the protection of human rights and dignity of the human with regard to the applications of biology and medicine (Convention on human rights and biomedicine).

S. Negri (ed.), *Self-Determination, Dignity and End-of-Life Care*
2011 Koninklijke Brill NV. Printed in The Netherlands. ISBN 978 90 04 22357 8. pp. 299–330

the CHRB introduces the institution of advance directives (article 9 CHRB: "previously expressed wishes"). Following the example of the CHRB and some Autonomous Communities' laws which preceded it,[3] the LBAP regulates advance directives (article 11 LBAP) for the entire State.

In a third stage of increasing patient autonomy, the creation and regulation of the national Registry of advance directives[4] and other options of advance care planning[5] deserve a special mention in national area. In Autonomous Communities the legislative development of advance directives ensued, setting out legal concepts and clinical situations in order to specify the scope of patient autonomy and advance directives.

II. Legal Framework

A. *Legislation*

The legislative scene of advance directives in Spanish Law is difficult to summarise. Besides the State regulation, applicable on the entire Spanish territory, all Autonomous Communities possess their own regulation of advance directives,[6] resulting in a huge normative body which contains diverse institutions of advance care planning.[7]

This normative heterogeneity is both quantitative and qualitative. On one hand, neither the State nor the Autonomous Communities have regulated the question with similar extension and detail. On the other hand, the quality is unequal: there are laws that appropriately guide the clinical decision-making, as well as imprecise, confused and also contradictory laws.[8] Moreover, the legal accuracy and the terminology are varied.

---

[3] The first was Catalonia: Act 21/2000, 29 December, on information rights concerning health, patient's autonomy and clinical documentation (article 8).

[4] See Royal Decree 124/2007, 2 February, regulating the national Registry of advance directives and the corresponding personal data file.

[5] See *infra* Section X.

[6] The Spanish State is made up of seventeen Autonomous Communities and two Autonomous Cities (articles 137 ff. CE). Each Autonomous Community has authority to legislate in health matters, including advance directives (article 149 CE).

[7] See Appendix. *Legal norms on advance directives in Spain.*

[8] And maybe unconstitutional, because some regional legislation on advance directives deals with Civil Law matters, and not every Autonomous Community has authority to legislate in these matters.

Finally, some contents of a suitable legal development are still pending, because of a defective previous regulation.

1. *State legislation*

Advance directives are a recent legislative phenomenon in Spanish Law. The first legal regulation which was directly applicable was article 9 CHRB, signed 4 April 1997 and in force in Spain since 1 January 2000:

> Article 9. *Previously expressed wishes*
> The previously expressed wishes relating to a medical intervention by a patient who is not, at the time of the intervention, in a state to express his or her wishes shall be taken into account.

The need to establish and clarify this regulation and guarantee the autonomy and rights of the patient, amongst other reasons, led to the enactment of the LBAP, whose article 11 is the basic and common regulation of advance directives for the entire Spanish territory:

> Article 11 LBAP. *Advance directives*
> 1. For the advance directives document, a person who is of age, competent and free states in advance his will regarding healthcare and treatments or, after his death, the destination of his body or his organs, with the aim that his will will be complied when he is no longer competent to express them personally. The person who issues the document can appoint a proxy who, in the event, acts as an interlocutor with the doctor or medical team to ensure that advance directives are complied with.
> 2. Each health service will regulate the correct procedure so that, if the case arises, compliance with everyone's advance directives is guaranteed. Advance directives must always set down in writing.
> 3. Advance directives which are contrary to the norms of the legal order or to the *lex artis* shall not be applied, nor those which do not correspond with the previous statement of the interested party at the time of issuing them. The patient's clinical history shall include a reasoned record of the notes related to these considerations.
> 4. Advance directives can be freely revoked at any time recording it with a written statement.
> 5. In order to ensure in the entire national territory the efficacy of advance directives expressed by patients and formalised in accordance with the legislation of the respective Autonomous Communities, the national Registry of advance directives will be created within the Ministry of Health and Consumer Affairs, which will be governed by the norms determined by regulation, with prior agreement of the Inter-territorial Council of National Health System.

Later, according to article 11.5 LBAP, and again after Autonomous Communities' legal norms, the national Registry of advance directives was created.[9]

Finally, two special laws have regulated the use of advance directives in their respective areas, widening its content and allowing the patient to decide on the use of his reproductive material[10] and on obtaining or analysing his biological samples after he has died.[11]

2. *Autonomous Communities' Legislation*

Regional legislation on advance directives preceded national legislation (LBAP). From the end of the year 2000 many legal norms have been enacted, leading to the current complicated and huge normative body. Such variety complicates the knowledge of legal regulation even though at the time it contributes to complete the national legislation and define the characteristics of advance directives.

B. *Case Law*

There are just five rulings on advance directives. Three of them referring to Jehovah's witnesses. An early ruling (*Auto*) of Ciudad Real Provincial Court of 31 December 2001[12] examines article 9 CHRB, and concludes that its invocation would require legislative development (at that time, there was no LBAP nor Autonomous Community legal norm applicable to the case), and that art. 9 CHRB does not establish a link with the previously expressed wishes but simply requires "taking into account". Therefore, the Court rejects the appeal to the previous judicial decision authorising blood transfusion to the patient. The two remaining cases, the rulings (*Autos*) of Guipúzcoa Provincial Court (section 2) of 22 September 2004[13] and of 18 March 2005,[14] adopt a different way of reasoning. They recognise the validity and priority of a Jehovah's witness' opposition to a blood transfusion included in his advance directives document, in the first case in opposition to the medical doctors request of judicial authorisation to

---

[9] See Royal Decree 124/2007, 2 February. Also see Order SCO/2823/2007, 14 September.
[10] Act 14/2006, 26 May, on techniques of assisted human reproduction (Article 9.2 LTRHA).
[11] Act 14/2007, 3 July, on biomedical research (Article 48.2 LIB).
[12] [Tirant TOL 142.031].
[13] Appeal N. 2086/2004 [JUR 2004308812].
[14] Appeal N. 2006/2005 [JUR 2005196739].

carry out a blood transfusion, and in the second case after the judge *a quo's* decision authorising the blood transfusion.

The fourth case, the ruling (*Auto*) 160/2010 of 2 June 2010 of Tenerife Provincial Court (section 3), regarding the use of reproductive material of a deceased husband to inseminate his wife, correctly states that a typed letter signed by the deceased husband can not be deemed an advance directive.[15]

Finally, the judgement (*Sentencia*) 353/2010 of 8 October of A Coruña Provincial Court (Section 5) deals with the designated proxy in an advance directive, and concludes that this designation provides a strong argument for choosing him/her for the guardianship.[16]

III. CONCEPT

Advance directives are the most important legal instrument of *advance care planning*, but only a part of it.[17] Advance care planning is a wider and overall continuous process which includes a host of dimensions (clinical, cultural, familiar, social, psychological, emotional) to improve the quality of care and decisions at the end of life, enhancing communication among the patient, the healthcare professionals (doctors, nursing, psychologists, ...), relatives and other close people, and guaranteeing the respect of patient's autonomy, values and rights.

Advance directives develop the general theory of informed consent and enhance autonomy. They are a singular specification because consent and the faculty of autonomous decision-making are protected like prospective or *ad futurum* autonomy. Unlike current informed consent, which is granted for an immediate or almost immediate action or intervention, advance directives consist of two moments: the moment of issue, which coincides with the patient's competence to take autonomous decisions, and the moment of application, which occurs later when the patient lacks the competence to decide autonomously.

---

[15] Appeal N. 296/2010 [AC20101755].

[16] Appeal N. 139/2010 [JUR2010411796].

[17] See Inés M. Barrio, Pablo Simón, Javier Júdez, "De las voluntades anticipadas o instrucciones previas a la planificación anticipada de la atención", 5 *Nure Investigación* (2004), pp. 1–9; Pablo Simón, Inés M. Barrio, *Quién decidirá por mí? Ética de las decisiones clínicas en pacientes incapaces* (Madrid, 2004); Diego Gracia, Juan José Rodríguez Sendín (dir.) et al., *Guía de ética de la planificación anticipada de la asistencia médica: historia de valores, instrucciones previas, decisiones de representación* (Madrid, 2011).

Article 11.1 LBAP states a legal definition, also referring to its content:

> For the advance directives document, a person who is of age, competent and free states in advance his will regarding healthcare and treatments or, after his death, the destination of his body or his organs, with the aim that his will will be complied when he is no longer competent to express them personally. The person who issues the document can appoint a proxy who, in the event, acts as an interlocutor with the doctor or medical team to ensure that advance directives are complied with.

Taking into account the national and regional legal norms, a more precise and comprehensive legal concept of advance directives can be proposed:

> Advance directives are the free, voluntary and informed expression of a competent person (who is of age) on his preferences of healthcare and treatments; and/or the designation of a proxy who acts as an interlocutor with the healthcare professionals and contributes to the interpretation, respect and compliance of his instructions and wishes; and/or the expression of his personal values, preferences and objectives; and/or, after death, the destiny of his body and/or organs and/or tissues, and/or the use of his reproductive material, and/or the prohibition to obtain and analyse his biological samples. The advance directives are issued with the aim of being respected and complied in the event that the patient cannot not longer express his will autonomously, and must be set down in writing and issued in compliance with the legal procedure.

Two issues need a further commentary. Firstly, the host of legal denominations of advance directives, especially in Autonomous Communities' legislation, generates legal uncertainty and insecurity. Is this a simple variety of terminology or, on the contrary, is it a semantic or conceptual variety? For the variety of terminology does not imply conceptual or semantic variety, the different denominations must be understood as different ways to formulate the same reality or concept. Therefore, the national and regional norms must be interpreted in the same way and referred to a single institution.[18]

---

[18] Spanish legal norms on advance directives comprehend the following denominations: deseos expresados anteriormente (CDHB); instrucciones previas (LBAP, Asturias, Canaries, Castile and Leon, Galicia, La Rioja, Madrid, Murcia); voluntades anticipadas (Aragon, Balearics, Cantabria, Castile-La Mancha, Cataluña, Navarre, Basque Country, Valencia); expresión anticipada de voluntades (Extremadura); manifestación anticipada de voluntad (Canaries); voluntad expresada con carácter previo (Cantabria); voluntades previas (Cantabria); voluntad vital anticipada (Andalusia, Balearics); testamento vital (Andalusia, Valencia).

Secondly, a more relevant matter comes from conceptual imprecision: the confusion between advance directives and the advance directives document, which can potentially lead to a misinterpretation and to an unsuitable application, with harm to patient's rights and autonomy and lack of protection to healthcare professionals. Even when it is necessary a formal and documentary expression of advance directives, which actually matters is not the document but the decisions expressed within it. The advance directives document supports and expresses patient's will, resulting from a process of reflection and dialogue with healthcare professionals on how the patient wants to be treated when he can no longer make autonomous decisions. And furthermore, advance directives must be understood as a part of the broader advance care planning process.

IV. JUSTIFICATION AND PURPOSE

From an ethical point of view, the justification of advance directives is the principle of respect for autonomy, which has led to a new model of doctor-patient relationship, decision-making and definition of health[19]. In Spain, a patient's right to take autonomous decisions on his own life and health and on the treatments he wishes to receive belongs to the basic right to physical and moral integrity (article 15 CE)[20] and is legally recognised.[21] This patient's right co-exists with a duty of healthcare professionals to know, respect and apply advance directives (articles 2.6 and 11 LBAP).[22]

As an instrument of advance care planning, advance directives have different aims and purposes. An immediate purpose is to strengthen the patient's right to express his will in advance, widening the scope of informed consent. Moreover, they are a relevant assistance in interpreting the patient's directives and guiding clinical decision-making when the patient can no longer express his will in an autonomous way. They allow forecasting future situations and planning healthcare in an integral

---

[19] See Diego Gracia, *Como arqueros al blanco. Estudios de bioética* (Madrid, 2004), p. 84.
[20] See Judgement (*Sentencia*) of Spanish Constitutional Court 37/2011, of 28 March.
[21] See Mónica Navarro-Michel, "Advance directives: the Spanish perspective", 13 *Medical Law Review* (2005), pp. 137–169, at 140–146; Federico de Montalvo Jääskeläinen, *Muerte digna y Constitución. Los límites del testamento vital* (Madrid, 2009).
[22] Art. 2.6 LBAP: "Every professional involved in the healthcare activity is required to perform not only the correct techniques, but to comply with the duties of clinical information and documentation and to respect the decisions freely and voluntarily adopted by the patient".

and continuous way. Finally, advance directives contribute to improve patient's well-being and also that of the professionals and relatives involved in healthcare.

V. Who Can Issue the Document?

"A person who is of age, competent and free…" is the answer of article 11.1 LBAP to the question on who can issue a document of advance directives. Here, there are two elements of the theory of informed consent and also of advance directives: competence and voluntariness. To these a third basic element must be added: information.

Article 11.1 LBAP requires that the person who issues the advance directives is competent and legally of age. He must be at least 18 (article 12 CE), the age from when he is considered (*iuris tantum* presumption) competent (articles 315 and 322 Civil Code: CC). Some regional legal norms set exceptions to being of age and allow certain minors to issue advance directive documents: a mature minor, an aged 16 and above individual who has intellectual and emotional competence to understand the purpose and consequences of the intervention (article 9.3.c) LBAP), and the under 16 year old minor who is emancipated by his legal parents or a judicial decision (articles 314–321 ff. CC) or the minor from the age of 14 when emancipated through marriage (articles 46 and 48 CC).[23]

The reference to the patient's liberty or free character (article 11.1 LBAP) means voluntariness and refers to guaranteeing that the decision-making process takes place without coercion, intimidation or any other unlawful influence.

Thirdly, and even when it is not included as a legal requirement in article 11.1 LBAP, information must be considered a further requirement for the valid issue of advance directives, in order to avoid other defect of consent: error about the object (articles 1265 and 1266 CC), and to control own decisions. Despite this, the patient has the right that his wish not to be informed will be respected (articles 4.1 and 9.1 LBAP). Information must be truthful and be communicated to the patient in a comprehensible way and suited to his needs, and it shall help him to express in advance his wishes regarding his care (article 5 CHRB; articles 2.3, 4.2 LBAP).

---

[23] See Andalusia, Aragon, Navarre, Valencia.

Issuing an advance directive is so personal that can only be exercised by the right-holder, i.e. the patient. This is not a right which can be exercised by a proxy or third party. When a patient is incompetent to make his own decisions it cannot be used an advance directive (whereby a competent patient takes an autonomous decision which will be applied when he is no longer able to do so: article 11 LBAP) but rather a substitute or surrogate decision-making (whereby a surrogate takes a decision on behalf and for the benefit of the incompetent patient: article 9 LBAP).

VI. Content

What can the patient decide in his advance directives? Article 11.1 LBAP highlights three distinct statements, which must be completed with the regional and health legislation to arrive at the six statements which constitute the current legal contents of advance directives. In any case, those legal references to the content of advance directives might not be understood as a *numerus clausus* but as an open set, in accordance with the broad scope of autonomy.

1. *Medical interventions, care and health treatments*

Due to the increasing chances of extending life, advance directives (living will) were originally issued to limit healthcare professionals' interventions. Nevertheless, the patient can decide both on the interventions he does not wish to receive and on the interventions and care which he wishes to receive in concrete clinical situations, including the withholding and the withdrawal of life-sustaining treatments as well as decisions on palliative treatment, sedation, comfort and other measures.

2. *Designation of a proxy*

Advance directives can include the designation of a proxy. He plays an important role in the advance care planning process, and should be a trustworthy person, aware of patient's wishes and values. The proxy cannot take decisions on behalf of the patient on situations previously issued in the advance directives document. Otherwise it would imply misunderstanding advance directives and confusing them with surrogate decisions. The function of the appointed proxy is to act as an interlocutor with healthcare professionals helping them to interpret patient's wishes and guaranteeing the respect of values and the compliance of instructions included in the advance directives document.[24]

3. *Personal values, preferences and objectives*

Another important support for interpreting advance directives is the patient's expression of his values, preferences, objectives and life prospects.[25] The so-called *values history* provides information on the patient's general stance to life and health, illness, pain and death; his family relationships; his relationships with healthcare professionals; his thoughts on autonomy, independence and self control; his religious beliefs or personal values; or his preferences on healthcare. Despite the incompetence of the patient at the moment of clinical assistance, his values history can guide decision-making process, eliminate conflicts and reduce the uncertainty and anxiety of those who undertake this task.

It is recommended to communicate the values history to the doctors, to the appointed proxy and to relatives or close friends who will probably accompany the patient during the healthcare process. It should be updated in cases of relevant changes (e.g. death of a close friend or relative, previous experiences of illness, etc.) so that it contains the patient's real and current values. Likewise, in order to being known, implemented and documented, the values history must be included in the clinical history as a part of the advance care planning process.

4. *Destiny of the body, organs or tissue*

The patient can donate his body for research or for training future healthcare professionals, or simply indicates what he desires for his body after death. Likewise, when death has been confirmed, the patient can donate all or some of his organs and tissues. Despite the fact that Spanish legislation adopts the model of presumed consent in the case of a deceased donor (we are all potential organ donors unless we have an expressed

---

[24] Some Autonomous Communities norms admit the appointment of a proxy as a substitute or surrogate in decision-making. Most of them (e.g. Andalusia, Basque Country, Cantabria, La Rioja) require the acceptance of the appointment, and some also regulate the designation procedure and establish incompatibility criteria for the appointment (e.g. Castile-La Mancha).

[25] This content is not included in LBAP, but it is included in some Autonomous Communities' norms (e.g. Andalusia, Aragon, Balearics, Basque Country, Canaries, Extremadura, La Rioja, Navarre).

opposition),[26] in practice the family of the deceased are asked for authorisation and their opposition to donation would prevail. Therefore every decision on donation (acceptance or refusal, total or partial) included in the advance directives document states doubtlessly patient's will about it and promotes the respect of his autonomy.

5. *Use of reproductive material*

Health legislation offers a new content to be included in an advance directives document. Concerning the assisted human reproduction, the husband of a woman receiving fertility treatment can decide about the use of his reproductive material within the year following his death.[27]

6. *Obtaining and analysing biological samples*

Health legislation provides a sixth content, that refers to the possibility of using the advance directives document to prevent the deceased patient's biological samples from being obtained and analysed after his death.[28]

VII. Limits

Article 11.3 LBAP expressly establishes three limits for applying advance directives, enforcing the healthcare professional to include a reasoned record of the notes relating to it in the patient's clinical history.

---

[26] Act 30/1979, 27 October, on organ extraction and transplantation (article 5); Royal Decree 2070/1999, 30 December, regulating the activity of clinical obtaining and use of human organs and the territorial co-ordination of organs and tissues donation and transplantation (article 10); Royal Decree 1301/2006, 10 November, establishing the quality and safety norms for donation, obtaining, evaluation, process, preservation, storage and distribution of human cells and tissues and the co-ordination norms and functioning for their use in humans (article 8).

[27] Article 9.2 LTRHA: "Despite what is stated in the previous section, the husband can give his consent for his reproductive material being used to inseminate his wife in the 12 months following his death, in the document which is referred to in article 6.3, in a public document, in a testament or in an advance directives document. [...]".

[28] Article 48.2, first paragraph LIB: "Samples of deceased people can be obtained and analysed in health area, providing it is always for health protection, unless the deceased has expressly forbidden this when alive and thus this is proved. With this aim the advance directives documents and, when not available, the opinions of the closest relatives to the deceased will be consulted".

Moreover, the Autonomous Communities' norms qualify the second of these limits and add, in a questionable manner, another two.[29]

1. *The legal order*

This limit aims to reaffirm not taking into account any request for assisted suicide or euthanasia included in a document of advance directives. Both behaviours are criminal offences in Spanish Criminal Code (article 143 CP).[30] On the other hand, a request to refuse treatment, both withdrawing or withholding life-supporting treatment (incorrectly labelled "passive euthanasia"), is lawful and protected by Spanish legislation (articles 2.4 and 8.5 LBAP).

2. *The* lex artis

The legal criteria to determine the correction and diligence of medical practice is *lex artis*. It is an undetermined and imprecise limit whose meaning changes over time and from one action to another. Moreover, it is difficult to set as it demands positive determination by law. Interpreting *lex artis* solely from medical or technical criteria, without taking into account patient's wishes and values stated in advance directives, could lead to paternalism and unjustified restrictions of patient's rights.[31] Because of this, instead of *lex artis* or, similarly, good or sound medical practice,[32] it has been suggested a new limit instead: contra-indication, i.e. an intervention that the healthcare professional must neither indicate nor carry out even under patient request.[33]

---

[29] See Azucena Couceiro Vidal, "Las directivas anticipadas en España: contenido, límites y aplicaciones clínicas", 22/4 *Revista de Calidad Asistencial* (2007), pp. 213–222, at 217–221.

[30] Article 143 CP. 1. Anyone who induces another to commit suicide shall be punished by imprisonment from four to eight years. 2. The punishment of imprisonment from two to five years shall be imposed for cooperating with necessary acts to the suicide of a person. 3. When cooperation amounts to implementing the person's death shall be punished by imprisonment from six to ten years. 4. Anyone who causes or actively cooperates through necessary and direct acts to the death of another, when there is an express, serious and unequivocal request, in the case where the victim suffers a serious illness which will necessarily lead to his death or which causes serious and permanent suffering which is difficult to withstand, shall be punished to imprisonment in one or two degrees lower than those mentioned in numbers 2 and 3 of this article.

[31] See Judgements (*Sentencias*) of Supreme Court (Civil Section) 830/1997, of 2 October; 1132/2006, of 15 November; 1267/2006, of 5 December. See also Judgement (*Sentencia*) of Constitutional Court 37/2011, of 28 March.

[32] See e.g. Aragon, Cantabria, Catalonia, La Rioja, Valencia.

[33] See Basque Country, La Rioja.

3. *The lack of correspondence with advance directives statement*

Advance directives can be drawn up in a generic way or in a more specific one. The professional must establish the correspondence between the statements of the advance directives document and the actual situation in which it has to be implemented. This limit to implementing advance directives is at stake when the statement of the document does not match the current situation. Correspondence between previous and current situation must not be understood as an exact match or identity but rather as an analogy, established by the healthcare professional after interpreting patient's will. For this, two contents of advance directives have special significance: the designation of a proxy and the expression of patient's values and objectives.

4. *Professional ethics or medical ethics*

Some Autonomous Communities have unfortunately and unjustifiably introduced two additional limits to the application of advance directives. Firstly, *professional ethics* or *medical ethics*,[34] a confusing limit which wrongly assumes that ethical criteria of healthcare activity are fixed unilaterally by medical profession and neglects the norms and criteria shared by all, especially those included in the legal regulation on advance directives and patients' rights.

5. *Conscientious Objection*

Even more objectable, secondly, is the consideration of the *conscientious objection* as a generic limit to applying advance directives, as it introduces more confusion amongst professionals on the meaning of advance directives and the conscientious objection.[35] On one hand, because the recognition of the conscientious objection does not vary because of the form or time of the patient's expression of his wishes (informed consent or advance directive), but depends on the activity to which the professional claims to object. On the other hand, one cannot recognise the conscientious objection in a generic form but one must specify to what concrete activity one wants to oppose such an objection.[36]

---

[34] Aragon (medical ethics), Madrid (professional ethics).
[35] See Balearics, Cantabria, Extremadura, La Rioja, Madrid, Murcia, Valencia.
[36] See Azucena Couceiro, José Antonio Seoane, Pablo Hernando, "La objeción de conciencia en el ámbito clínico. Propuesta para un uso apropiado (I)", 26/3 *Revista de Calidad Asistencial* (2011), pp. 188–193.

VIII. FORMAL AND PROCEDURAL REQUIREMENTS

Advance directives must be set down in a written form (articles 11.1 and 11.2 LBAP).[37] The Autonomous Communities' norms have regulated in great detail the formal and procedural requirements, establishing two general procedures to issue advance directives (before a notary and before three witnesses) and, in the case of some Autonomous Communities, adding a third procedure (before the person in charge of the Registry of advance directives or corresponding public Administration).[38]

Compliance with formal requirements is a condition of validity and efficacy in advance directives. This *ad solemnitatem* requirement is sound, in order to protect patient's autonomy and rights in such a delicate and relevant matter. Consequently, oral or unsuitably documented expressions are not advance directives but, at the most, relevant indications in surrogate or substituted decision-making.

A. *Issuing Procedures*

1. *Before a notary*

The first way to issue an advance directives document is before a notary, a legal practitioner who confers authenticity, veracity and legal force to the acts and declarations made before him. The notary states the authenticity of the advance directives document and the patient's true identity, competence and will as well as the correspondence of the document's content with the patient's wishes. In this case, witnesses are not needed.

2. *Before three witnesses*

Secondly, the document of advance directives can be issued before three witnesses. Legislation establishes the requirements and causes of incompatibility of witnesses. They must be over 18 and full competent; and at least two of them cannot be in the second level of lineal consanguinity or affinity nor be linked by patrimonial relations.[39] Like the notary, the witnesses' function is to guarantee compliance of the validity of authorisation, that the patient is competent, acts freely without being subject to

---

[37] The patient can draw up and document his advance directives in the way that he wants. He can follow one of the existing guideline models or forms. Some Autonomous Communities (e.g. Andalusia) requires that an official form or model is completed.

[38] See Andalusia, Basque Country, Castile and Leon, La Rioja.

[39] In some cases (e.g. Cantabria, La Rioja) the incompatibility is stricter.

unlawful influence and that the expression contained in the document corresponds to his wishes with no errors in the declaration.

3. *Before the person in charge of the Registry of advance directives or the corresponding Administration*

Finally, some Autonomous Communities establish a third procedure before the civil servant or member of the Registry of advance directives or the corresponding Administration, and the latter will check compliance with the minimum legal requirements and contents of the advance directives document presented.

B. *The Registry of Advance Directives*

The National Registry and Autonomous Communities' Registries of advance directives were created to ensure the efficacy of advance directives.[40] Their main objectives are to collect information of advance directives (the existence of the document, the place and date of inscription, the contents) and facilitate healthcare professionals in knowing about the advance directives document and its consultation in the event that it must be applied. In order to guarantee the efficient compliance of its purposes, the Registry acts in accordance with certain basic functioning principles: coordination, interconnection, security and confidentiality.

Registration of advance directives documents must be voluntary and with a merely declarative effect of the document's existence and content, rejecting thus its mandatory and constitutive nature, according to which advance directives would only achieve validity after registration.[41] Registration is not a requirement of validity although it influences the efficacy of advance directives. In this sense, it is highly advisable to register advance directives documents to ensure and to permit the access, knowledge and application of its updated version on the entire national territory.

IX. VALIDITY AND EFFICACY

Once the advance directives have been issued in the aforementioned manner, and having met the remaining requirements, they are valid with

---

[40] Art. 11.5 LBAP and Royal Decree 124/2007, 2 February. See Appendix.
[41] In some Autonomous Communities (e.g. Andalusia, Cantabria) the registration of advance directives is constitutive and mandatory.

no further requests. For their validity and efficacy Spanish legislation does not demand renewal or ratification. Providing there is no evidence or proof of the contrary, the instructions and wishes included in the advance directives document remain. Nevertheless, a lack of ratification could impact the efficacy of advance directives in some cases (e.g. a considerable length of time has passed and a notable change in conditions or values stated in the advance directives document, contravening the patient's initial purpose). To guarantee its applicability and efficacy, temporal ratification is advised. This will facilitate the interpretation and application of advance directives; it will avoid legal uncertainty to professionals and will strengthen the protection of patient's autonomy and rights. In short, ratification or renewal of advance directives is not nor should be a requirement for its validity. Although this could impact its efficacy, the lack of ratification or renewal must not cause the invalidity or inapplicability of advance directives, for the continuance and respect of the patient's autonomy and will.[42]

What is relevant is revocation, which can be exercise freely and at any time by the patient, just doing so in writing (article 11.4 LBAP). Revocation *stricto sensu* means the cancellation of the previously issued document and the inexistence of a new one. The faculty of revocation also encompasses the modification, or partial alteration of the document maintaining its validity and effects, and the substitution, or total revocation followed by a new issue of advance directives.[43]

With regards to its nature, advance directives become effective and applicable once the patient becomes incompetent to express autonomously his own wishes. Until then, the patient's current will and decision prevail over the wishes and decisions stated in the advance directives document.

Healthcare professionals must respect and take into account advance directives because of their ethical and professional obligation to respect patient's autonomy and rights. They have a categorical duty to know the existence and the content of the advance directives and also the duty to comply with the content, even though this is a *prima facie* duty and not an automatic or *all things considered* duty of application.

---

[42] There is a legal solution in cases of uncertainty: the limit of application due to the mismatch of the current clinical situation and the circumstance expressed in the document (art. 11.3 LBAP).

[43] See Appendix of Royal Decree 124/2007, 2 February.

Like legal field, medical field requires prudential reasoning which leads to the respect of the patient's autonomy but not to blind or unconditional obedience of every autonomous decision. The patient's advance directives are not an exclusionary reason for the healthcare professional which obliges him to comply with them without balancing and harmonizing the principles, values, duties and rights at stake.[44] Advance directives, often imprecise as it is humanly impossible to accurately and completely forecast future situations, need to be interpreted and contextualised by the healthcare professionals, using the values history and the appointed proxy as support. This interpretative task must go beyond literal and subjective criteria in favour of a teleological interpretation. Only in this way the patient's real will and wishes can be understood and respected, determining their meaning in each concrete case and complying with them or, if necessary, not applying them, where the healthcare professional must record the reasons of non application of advance directives in clinical history (article 11.3 LBAP).

In this sense, it is important to distinguish two types of normative content in advance directives, with a different form of fulfilment and application. The first one adopts the form of rules, i.e. dilemmatic or all-or-nothing norms (they are either fulfilled or not) which indicate in a direct and definitive manner what one "ought to do": e.g. the decision on organ or tissue donation, or the designation of a certain person as a proxy. In these cases, one must comply with the clearly expressed instruction as it cannot be questioned. Conversely, the second type adopts the form of principles, i.e. norms which aim to obtain or realise in the greatest possible degree a state of affairs, how they "ought to be": e.g. instructions on healthcare and treatments ("not to withhold or withdraw any life-sustaining measures to prolong my life"; "no extraordinary measures to be adopted"). The lack of precision of these decisions does not eliminate their normativity nor the obligation of the healthcare professionals to respect them, but it demands that the situation and wishes stated by the patient are defined and match real conditions in context and in the moment in which they are to be implemented, which excludes their automatic application and demands interpretation and deliberation for compliance.[45]

---

[44] See José Antonio Seoane, "El significado de la Ley básica de autonomía del paciente (Act 41/2002, 14 November) en el sistema jurídico-sanitario español. Una propuesta de interpretación", 12 *Derecho y Salud* (2004), pp. 41–60.

[45] See Recommendation CM/Rec(2009)11 of the Committee of Ministers to member states on principles concerning continuing powers of attorney and advance directives for incapacity (adopted by the Committee of Ministers on 9 December 2009).

X. OTHER LEGAL ANSWERS ON ADVANCE CARE PLANNING

Advance directives are not the only legal institution for advance care planning in Spanish Law. Almost simultaneously, self-guardianship (*auto-tutela*) was introduced into the state legal system.[46] Both institutions share the same purpose: to respect the individual's autonomy to manage his life and health and participate in advance care planning; to widen the scope of autonomous decisions forecasting future incompetence; to improve the decision-making process in the case of incompetent patients, helping them to interpret and apply their instructions and wishes. However, its significance and scope are not identical. Self-guardianship acts on a wider personal area, not limited to health matters, and also on the patrimonial area, banned from advance directives. It allows some decisions of the competent person to forecast future incapacitation and not mere incompetence, which is the case of advance directives. Amongst such decisions is the designation of a guardian, whilst advance directives refer to the possible designation of a proxy. Moreover, the only valid procedure for issuing self-guardianship is a notarial public document unlike the three procedures in advance directives.[47]

Another option of advance care planning is preventive powers of attorney, whose aim is the appointment of someone who voluntarily acts when a person's incompetence occurs or worsens. Two types of powers must be highlighted: the *ad cautelam* power of attorney, in the event of future incompetence, which takes effect when this occurs (both incompetence and incapacitation, depending on what has been established), and the power of attorney granted for immediate effect, even in a situation of competence, with continuity and subsistence of effects once incompetence occurs.[48] The granter of power must be in full competence. The proxy can be any individual or legal person and can be designed as guardian or not (separate protection of personal and patrimonial matters: art. 236 CC). Its content can be very varied: patrimonial matters (e.g. management and disposal of assets) and some personal matters, amongst which decisions on care and medical treatments or the designation of a proxy, are common. This power does not require a special form but, for the sake

---

[46] See article 223 CC, reformed by Act 41/2003, 18 November.

[47] With a similar purpose but less detail, article 4.2.f) Act 39/2006, 14 December, to promote personal autonomy and care of people in situation of dependence, recognises the right to decide, when he is competent, on the protection of his person and property for the case of becoming incompetent.

[48] See article 1732 CC, reformed by the aforementioned Act 41/2003, 18 November.

of its efficacy, knowledge and publicity, it is recommended being granted in public document, as the registral publicity of these appointments is limited.

XI. Conclusions

Spanish legislation on advance directives represents a step forward in the consolidation of autonomy as a core of doctor-patient relationship and in the guarantee of patients, healthcare professionals and health institutions' rights and duties. Moreover, it guides professionals and eases decision-making process in healthcare. Finally, it improves the quality, humanisation and justice of our health system.

Nevertheless, despite the comprehensive legal regulation of advance directives in Spain, there are unresolved challenges for advance care planning. Some challenges, linked to the legal system, must be resolved by jurists, in particular by the legislator, completing the normative development. Apart from the necessary homogenisation of national and regional legal norms, normative errors need to be corrected, ambiguities in terminology need to be clarified and the vagueness of some concepts needs to be dealt with.[49] Other challenges, linked to healthcare, must be dealt by healthcare professionals and institutions, trusting in Law as an instrument which improves healthcare relationships and favour its reception and suitable use by means of appropriate knowledge, respect and application,[50] moving beyond advance directives and promoting the more comprehensive advance care planning.

---

[49] Some *lege ferenda* proposals in José Antonio Seoane, "Derecho y planificación anticipada de la atención. Panorama jurídico en España", 14 *Derecho y Salud* (2006), pp. 285–295.

[50] See Pablo Simón-Lorda, María-Isabel Tamayo-Velázquez, Inés-María Barrio-Cantalejo, "Advance Directives in Spain. Perspectives from a Medical Bioethicist Approach", 22/6 *Bioethics* (2008), pp. 346–354; Cristina Nebot, Blas Ortega, José Loaquín Mira, Lydia Ortiz, "Morir con dignidad. Estudio sobre voluntades anticipadas", 24/6 *Gaceta Sanitaria* (2010), pp. 437–445. Also see http://www.voluntadesanticipadas.com.

APPENDIX:
LEGAL NORMS ON ADVANCE DIRECTIVES IN SPAIN

Legal norm	Advance directives	Registry of advance directives
SPAIN		
Convenio de 4 de abril de 1997 (ratificado por Instrumento de 23 de julio de 1999), para la protección de los derechos humanos y la dignidad del ser humano con respecto a las aplicaciones de la biología y la Medicina (Convenio relativo a los derechos humanos y la biomedicina)	9	
Ley 41/2002, de 14 de noviembre, básica reguladora de la autonomía del paciente y de derechos y obligaciones en materia de información y documentación clínica	11	11.5
Ley 14/2006, de 26 de mayo, sobre técnicas de reproducción humana asistida	9.2	
Real Decreto 124/2007, de 2 de febrero, por el que se regula el Registro nacional de instrucciones previas y el correspondiente fichero automatizado de datos de carácter personal	All	All
Ley 14/2007, de 3 de julio, de investigación biomédica	48.2	
Orden SCO/2823/2007, de 14 de septiembre, por la que se amplía la Orden de 21 de julio de 1994, por la que se regulan los ficheros con datos de carácter personal gestionados	All	All

Legal norm	Advance directives	Registry of advance directives
por el Ministerio de Sanidad y Consumo y se crea el fichero automatizado de datos de carácter personal denominado Registro nacional de instrucciones previas		
ANDALUSIA		
Ley 2/1998, de salud (modificado por DA única de la Ley 5/2003, de 9 de octubre)	6.1.ñ)	
Ley 5/2003, de 9 de octubre, de declaración de voluntad vital anticipada (*ex* DF segunda de la Ley 2/2010, de 8 de abril, de derechos y garantías de la dignidad de la persona en el proceso de la muerte)	All	9; 2, 5, 6, 7, 8
Decreto 238/2004, de 18 de mayo, regulador del Registro de voluntades vitales anticipadas de Andalucía	All	All
Orden 17 de enero de 2005, que regula y suprime los ficheros automatizados que contienen datos de carácter personal gestionados por la Consejería de Salud		All; Appendix I, 11
Ley Orgánica 2/2007, de 19 de marzo, de reforma del Estatuto de Autonomía para Andalucía	20.1	
Ley 2/2010, de 8 de abril, de derechos y garantías de la dignidad de la persona en el proceso de la muerte	5.d), k), p) y q); 9; 10.1 y 4; 19; sole transitory provision; final provision two	9.2 y 3; sole transitory provision; final provision two

(*Continued*)

Legal norm	Advance directives	Registry of advance directives
ARAGON		
Ley 6/2002, de 15 de abril, de salud (*ex* Ley 8/2009, de 22 de diciembre, por la que se modifica la Ley 6/2002, de 15 de abril, de salud de Aragón, en lo relativo a voluntades anticipadas)	15	15.5
Decreto 100/2003, de 6 de mayo, que aprueba el Reglamento de organización y funcionamiento del Registro de voluntades anticipadas	All	All
Ley Orgánica 5/2007, de 20 de abril, de reforma del Estatuto de Autonomía de Aragón	14.4	
Ley 10/2011, de 24 de marzo, de derechos y garantías de la dignidad de la persona en el proceso de morir y de la muerte	2.), 5.e), f), l), m), 9, 11.3, 14, 19, final provision one	5.e), 9.2, 19.2, final provision one
ASTURIAS		
Decreto 4/2008, de 23 de enero, de organización y funcionamiento del Registro del Principado de Asturias de instrucciones previas en el ámbito sanitario	All	All
Resolución de 29 de abril de 2008, de la Consejería de salud y servicios sanitarios, sobre desarrollo y ejecución del Decreto 4/2008, de 23 de enero de 2008, de organización y funcionamiento del Registro del Principado de Asturias de instrucciones previas en el ámbito sanitario	All	All
BALEARICS		
Ley 1/2006, de 3 de marzo, de voluntades anticipadas	All	8; 3.2.b), 3.4

Legal norm	Advance directives	Registry of advance directives
Ley Orgánica 1/2007, de 28 de febrero, de reforma del Estatuto de Autonomía de las Illes Balears	25.4	
Decreto 58/2007, de 27 de abril, por el que se desarrolla la Ley de voluntades anticipadas y del registro de voluntades anticipadas de las Illes Baleares	All	1, 2, 5–11; additional provisions one and two
CANARIES		
Orden de 28 de febrero de 2005, por la que se aprueba la Carta de los derechos y de los deberes de los pacientes y usuarios sanitarios y se regula su difusión	Appendix. Rights. 25	
Decreto 13/2006, de 8 de febrero, por el que se regulan las manifestaciones anticipadas de voluntad en el ámbito sanitario y la creación de su correspondiente Registro	All	9–24; 1, 6.b), additional provision, transitory provision
Orden de 30 de marzo de 2009, por la que se aprueba la creación del fichero de datos de carácter personal de Manifestaciones anticipadas de voluntad en el ámbito sanitario	All	All
CANTABRIA		
Ley 7/2002, de 10 de diciembre, de ordenación sanitaria de Cantabria	29.2.b), 34	34.5
Decreto 139/2004, de 5 de diciembre, que crea y regula el Registro de voluntades previas de Cantabria	All	All
Orden SAN/27/2005, de 16 de septiembre, por la que se establece el documento tipo	All	

(*Continued*)

Legal norm	Advance directives	Registry of advance directives
de voluntades expresadas con carácter previo de Cantabria		
Orden SAN/28/2005, de 16 de septiembre, por la que se creas el fichero automatizado de datos de carácter personal del Registro de voluntades previas de Cantabria	All	All
CASTILE-LA MANCHA		
Ley 6/2005, de 7 de julio, sobre la declaración de voluntades anticipadas en materia de la propia salud	All	9; 4.3, 5, 8.3, 10, final provision one
Decreto 15/2006, de 21 de febrero, del Registro de voluntades anticipadas de Castilla-La Mancha	All	All
Orden de 31 de agosto de 2006, de la Consejería de Sanidad, de creación del fichero automatizado de datos del Registro de voluntades anticipadas de Castilla-La Mancha	All	All
Resolución de 8 de enero de 2008, de la Consejería de Sanidad, de creación de nuevos puntos del Registro de voluntades anticipadas de Castilla-La Mancha	All	All
Ley 5/2010, de 24 de junio, sobre derechos y deberes en materia de salud de Castilla-La Mancha	24; 26.2.q)	
CASTILE AND LEON		
Ley 8/2003, de 8 de abril, sobre derechos y deberes de las personas en relación con la salud	30	30.2

Legal norm	Advance directives	Registry of advance directives
Orden SBS/1325/2003, de 3 de septiembre, de publicación de las Cartas de derechos y deberes de las Guías de información al usuario	Appendix	
Orden SAN/279/2005, de 5 de abril, que desarrolla el procedimiento de tramitación de las reclamaciones y sugerencias en el ámbito sanitario y regula la gestión y el análisis de la información derivada de las mismas	Appendix I	
Decreto 101/2005, de 22 de diciembre, por el que se regula la historia clínica	Additional provision two	Additional provision two
Decreto 30/2007, de 22 de marzo, por el que se regula el documento de instrucciones previas en el ámbito sanitario y se crea el Registro de Instrucciones Previas de Castilla y León	All	1, 10–22
Ley Orgánica 14/2007, de 30 de noviembre, de reforma del Estatuto de Autonomía de Castilla y León	13.2.e)	
CATALONIA		
Ley 21/2000, de 29 de diciembre, sobre derechos de información concernientes a la salud, a la autonomía del paciente y a la documentación clínica (*ex* Ley 16/2010, de 3 de junio, de modificación de la Ley 21/2000, de 29 de diciembre, sobre los derechos de	8; 12.7	

(*Continued*)

Legal norm	Advance directives	Registry of advance directives
información concerniente a la salud y la autonomía del paciente, y la documentación clínica)		
Decreto 175/2002, de 25 de junio, que regula el Registro de voluntades anticipadas (artículo 5 y Anexo II derogados por la Orden SLT/519/2006, de 3 de noviembre)	All	All
Resolución BEF/3622/2003, de 4 de noviembre, que da publicidad al Acuerdo del Gobierno de 8 de octubre de 2003, que establece la Carta de derechos y deberes de la gente mayor de Cataluña	Appendix 3.3	
Ley Orgánica 6/2006, de 19 de julio, de reforma del Estatuto de Autonomía de Cataluña	20.2	
Orden SLT/519/2006, de 3 de noviembre, por la que se regulan ficheros que contienen datos de carácter personal en el ámbito del Departamento de Salud	2, Appendix II; repealing provision	2, Appendix II; repealing provision
Ley 25/2010, de 29 de julio, del libro segundo del Código civil de Cataluña, relativo a la persona y la familia	212-3; 212-1.4, 226-2.2	
EXTREMADURA		
Ley 10/2001, de 28 de junio, de salud	11.5	
Ley 3/2005, de 8 de julio, de información sanitaria y autonomía del paciente	15.4.a, 17–22	22; 17.5, 18.2, 20.1.2), 20.1.4)
Decreto 311/2007, de 15 de octubre, por el que se regula el contenido, organización y	All	All

Legal norm	Advance directives	Registry of advance directives
funcionamiento del Registro de expresión anticipada de voluntades de la Comunidad Autónoma de Extremadura y se crea el Fichero automatizado de datos de carácter personal del citado Registro		
GALICIA		
Ley 3/2001, de 28 de mayo, reguladora del consentimiento informado y de la historia clínica de los pacientes (*ex* Ley 3/2005, de 7 de marzo, de modificación de la Ley 3/2001, de 28 de mayo...)	4; 5	5.6
Ley 7/2003, de 9 de diciembre, de ordenación sanitaria de Galicia	133.1.n)	
Decreto 259/2007, de 13 de diciembre, por el que se crea el Registro gallego de instrucciones previas sobre cuidados y tratamientos de la salud	All	All
Ley 8/2008, de 10 de julio, de salud de Galicia	8.3	
LA RIOJA		
Ley 2/2002, de 17 de abril, de salud (*ex* Disposición Final primera de la Ley 9/2005, de 30 de septiembre)	6.5	6.5.c) and d)
Decreto 37/2203, de 15 de julio, de atribución de funciones administrativas en desarrollo de la Ley 3/2003, de organización del sector público de la Comunidad Autónoma de La Rioja (*ex* Decreto 21/2005, de 4 de marzo)	4.7.11.c)	4.7.11.c)

(*Continued*)

Legal norm	Advance directives	Registry of advance directives
Ley 9/2005, de 30 de septiembre, reguladora del documento de instrucciones previas en el ámbito de la sanidad	All	10; final provision two
Decreto 30/2006, de 19 de mayo, por el que se regula el Registro de instrucciones previas de La Rioja	All	All
Orden 8/2006, de 26 de julio, sobre la forma de otorgar documento de instrucciones previas ante personal de la Administración	All	All
MADRID Ley 3/2005, de 23 de mayo, que regula el ejercicio del derecho a formular instrucciones previas en el ámbito sanitario y crea el registro correspondiente	All	12
Decreto 101/2006, de 16 de noviembre, del Consejo de Gobierno, por el que se regula el Registro de instrucciones previas de la Comunidad de Madrid	All	All
Orden 2191/2006, de 18 de diciembre, por la que se desarrolla el Decreto 101/2006, de 28 de noviembre, por el que se regula el registro de instrucciones previas de la Comunidad de Madrid y se establecen los modelos oficiales de los documentos de solicitud de inscripción de las instrucciones previas y de su revocación, modificación o sustitución	All	All

Legal norm	Advance directives	Registry of advance directives
Orden 228/2007, de 26 de febrero, del Consejero de Sanidad y Consumo, por la que se crean dos ficheros de datos de carácter personal para el desarrollo del Registro de Instrucciones Previas de la Comunidad de Madrid	All	All
Orden 645/2007, de 19 de abril, que regula el otorgamiento de las instrucciones previas, su modificación, sustitución y revocación ante el personal al servicio de la Administración	All	All
MURCIA		
Decreto 80/2005, de 8 de julio, por el que se aprueba el reglamento de instrucciones previas y su registro	All	8–13; 2.2.b), 7; additional provisions one and two
Orden de 22 de febrero de 2006 de la Consejería de Economía y Hacienda por la que se crean ficheros con datos de carácter personal gestionados por la Consejería de Sanidad	All, Appendix	All, Appendix
NAVARRE		
Decreto foral 140/2003, de 16 de junio, que regula el Registro de voluntades anticipadas	All	All
Ley foral 17/2010, de 8 de noviembre, de derechos y deberes de las personas en materia de salud en la Comunidad Foral de Navarra	5.8, 26.3, 54, 55, 59.1.b)	55.3
Ley foral 8/2011, de 24 de marzo, de derechos y garantías de la dignidad de la persona en el proceso de la muerte	2.b); 5.d), k), q), r); 9; 10; 11; 18; additional provisions	additional provision five; sole transitory provision

(*Continued*)

Legal norm	Advance directives	Registry of advance directives
	four and five; sole transitory provision	
BASQUE COUNTRY		
Ley 7/2002, de 12 de diciembre, de voluntades anticipadas en el ámbito de la sanidad	All	6; 2.3.a), 3.2.b), 4.2, 7, final provision one
Decreto 270/2003, de 4 de noviembre, que crea y regula el Registro vasco de voluntades anticipadas	All	All
Orden de 22 de noviembre de 2004, que establece normas sobre el uso de la firma electrónica en las relaciones por medios electrónicos, informáticos y telemáticos con el Sistema Sanitario de Euskadi	11	11
Orden de 1 de junio de 2005, del Consejero de Sanidad, por la que se regulan los ficheros de datos de carácter personal del Departamento de Sanidad	Appendix I	Appendix I
VALENCIA		
Ley 1/2003, de 28 de enero, de derechos e información al paciente de la Comunidad valenciana	17; 3.16, 22.1.c)	17.7
Decreto 168/2004, de 10 de septiembre, por el que regula el documento de voluntades anticipadas y crea el Registro centralizado de voluntades anticipadas de la Comunidad valenciana	All	6–9; 2.2, 3.2, 5.2, final provision one

Legal norm	Advance directives	Registry of advance directives
Orden de 25 de febrero de 2005, de desarrollo del Decreto 168/2004, de 10 de septiembre	All	All
Orden de 20 de julio de 2005, del Conseller de Sanidad, por la que se crea el fichero automatizado Volant Registros		

ADVANCE DIRECTIVES AND LEGALITY OF
EUTHANASIA UNDER GERMAN LAW

Jochen Taupitz* and Amina Salkić**

I. Introduction

A. *Introductory Remarks*

During the last few decades the prior paternalistic decision making approach in health care issues has significantly shifted toward a more patient-centred decision making process giving primacy to the principle of autonomy, holding that the patient, if mentally competent, has the right to forego or withdraw any treatment.[1] This shift to less paternalism and more patient autonomy simultaneously raised the question of medical decision making on behalf of patients who lack decision making capacity. As a result of this debate various options have been developed during the last two decades to enable competent persons to influence, in advance, the decision making process concerning their medical treatment in case they become incompetent. At the same time this raised the question about the legal status of such statements, asking if they are fundamentally different from actual consents or refusals to consent regarding medical treatment. It's an issue that has been passionately debated in Germany for several years[2] and that has come to an end for the time being with the new

---

* Professor Dr. Jochen Taupitz, member of the German Ethics Council, holder of the Chair of Civil Law, Civil Procedure Law, Private International Law and Comparative Law at the University of Mannheim and Managing Director of the Institute for German, European and International Medical Law, Public Health Law and Bioethics (IMGB) of the Universities Heidelberg and Mannheim, Germany; email: taupitz@jura.uni-mannheim.de.

** Amina Salkić, LL.M., research assistant at the Institute for German, European and International Medical Law, Public Health Law and Bioethics (IMGB) of the Universities Heidelberg and Mannheim, Germany; email: amina.salkic@imgb.de.

1 Compare: Preamble and principle no. 3 of the *WMA Declaration on the Rights of the Patient*, last revised in 2005, available at http://www.wma.net/en/30publications/10policies/l4/index.html (last accessed 30 September 2010); Sec. 7 and 8 of the *Model Professional Code for Physicians in Germany*, last changed in 2006, available at http://www.bundesaerztekammer.de/downloads/MBOStand20061124.pdf (last accessed 30 September 2010).

2 The parliamentary debate started back in 1985, after a publicity campaign of assisted suicide proponents. Accordingly, the public hearing held by the Committee on Legal

act, that has come into force on September, the 1st 2009.[3] The German Parliament voted in favour of the law, which regulates living wills and the role of surrogate decision-makers in the scope of civil law.[4] The legislator intentionally missed the opportunity to regulate the associated criminal law issues that have dominated the end-of-life debate for years.[5]

B. *Terminology*

Under strong influence of the debate on patient autonomy and anticipatory decision making, a number of instruments have been developed to enable competent persons to express their wishes in advance, thus striving to ground all medical decisions in autonomy, even when the patient is no longer able to express his real-time volition. All these instruments that provide guidance or rules for medical decisions to be made after the person becomes incapacitated are called advance directives (*Vorausverfügungen*). European comparative studies usually differ between two main types of advance directives,[6] instructional and proxy directives. An *instructional directive* provides particular details about wishes and preferences for treatment decisions that might be anticipated (for example living wills, but also the more specific physician orders to limit care[7] and even organ donation instructions), while a *proxy directive*

Affairs of the German Bundestag focused mainly on criminal law provisions. For more information on this initial debate, see: *Stenographisches Protokoll über die 51. Sitzung des Rechtsausschusses des Deutschen Bundestages* (1985), protocol no. 51.

[3] "3rd Act Changing the Custodianship Law" (*3. Gesetz zur Änderung des Betreuungsrechts - 3. BtÄndG*") of 29 July 2009 (entered into force on 1 September 2009), in *Federal Law Gazette*, part I, no. 48.

[4] This law was supported by different members of all parties, even though mainly by members of the Social Democrats, the Greens and the Liberals. In this case, the usual practice to vote in line with the own party was skipped, since this issue was considered to be a matter of conscience.

[5] Nevertheless, an indirect impact on the criminal law occurred due to recognizing primacy of the patient's will over the physician's position as the guarantor of life (sec. 323c of the Criminal Code). See also: BGH decision of 25 June 2010 no. 2 StR 454/09 = NJW 2010, 2963 (2966).

[6] Roberto Andorno, Nikola Biller-Andorno and Susanne Brauer, "Advance Health Care Directives: Towards a Coordinated European Policy?" 16 *European Journal of Health Law* (2009), pp. 207–227; John M. Clements, "Patient Perceptions on the Use of Advance Directives and Life Prolonging Technology", 26 *American Journal of Hospice & Palliative Medicine* (2009), pp. 270–276; Linda L. Emanuel, "Advance Directives", 59 *Annual Review of Medicine* (2008), pp. 87–98; Erich H. Loewy, "Advance directives: Good, bad or indifferent", 116 *Wiener Klinische Wochenschrift* (2004), pp. 411–416; Muriel R. Gillick, "Advance Care Planning", 350 *The New England Journal of Medicine* (2004), pp. 7–8.

[7] There are different such orders or requests, such as *DNR* (*"do not resuscitate"*), *CPR* (*"cardiopulmonary resuscitation"*), *DNAR* (*"do not attempt resuscitation"*), *AND* (*"allow*

designates one or more individuals—health care agent, attorney or proxy—to make surrogate medical decisions for the patient, if he becomes incapable of making them on his own. Nevertheless, the German literature traditionally differs between three main types of advance directives, thus this paper will maintain this tripartite division differing between a living will (*Patientenverfügung*), a power of attorney (*Vorsorgevollmacht*) and a custodianship directive (*Betreuungsverfügung*), which may also be combined. Powers of attorney and custodianship directives might be described as "proxy directives" in the above-mentioned sense, but the term "proxy" might be misleading in the case of custodianship directives that are strongly influenced by custodianship (former guardianship) courts and are specific legal instruments. However, just like proxy directives, powers of attorney and custodianship directives focus on who will make the decision, rather than on what those decisions should be, although all advance directives might overlap. In this sense, this paper uses the umbrella term "surrogate", therewith meaning any person who has been, according to German law, properly designated to make health care decisions on behalf of another adult person unable to give consent to or refuse medical treatment.

II. Informed Consent as the Basis

A. *No Treatment without Consent*

Any health care measure that intervenes into the physical integrity of a person (article 2 II 1 of the German Constitution – GG[8]) is legally

---

natural death"), "*comfort measures only*", "*no tube feeding*" or "*no IV-fluids*" etc. For further information: Muriel R. Gillick, "The Use of Advance Care Planning to Guide Decisions About Artificial Nutrition and Hydration", 21 *Nutrition in Clinical Practice* (2006), pp. 126–133; Jeffrey P. Burns, Jeffrey Edwards, Judith Johnson, Ned H. Cassem and Robert D. Truog, "Do-not-resuscitate order after 25 years", 31 *Critical Care Medicine* (2003), pp. 1543–1549; Ferdinando L. Mirachi, "Does a Living Will Equal a DNR? Are Living Wills Compromising Patient Safety?", 33 *The Journal of Emergency Medicine* (2007), pp. 299–305; Frank P. Schmidt, "DNR-Anordnungen. Das fehlende Bindeglied", 106 *Deutsches Ärzteblatt* (2009), pp. A-1511/B-1292/C-1260; Sonja Rinofner-Kreidl, "'Natürlicher Tod' – Do Not Resuscitate (DNR) oder Allow Natural Death (AND)?: Zur Rolle der Sprache im Aufbau einer ethischen Kultur in medizinischen Kontexten", 21 *Psychologische Medizin* (2010), pp. 24–32; Schweizerische Akademie der Medizinischen Wissenschaften (SAMW), *Reanimationsentscheidungen* (2008), etc.

[8] "Basic Law for the Federal Republic of Germany" (*Grundgesetz für die Bundesrepublik Deutschland -GG*) of 23 May 1949 (Federal Law Gazette p. 1), in the revised version published in the *Federal Law Gazette*, part III, class. no. 100-1, as last amended by the Law

considered to contain elements of the legal offense of bodily harm as defined by sections 223 et seq. of the German Criminal Code (*Strafgesetzbunch* – StGB)[9] and section 823 I of the German Civil Code (*Bürgerliches Gesetzbuch* – BGB).[10] The Federal Court of Justice (*Bundesgerichtshof* – BGH) consistently maintained this position, already developed in 1894 by the Imperial Court of Justice (*Reichsgericht* – RG).[11] Therefore, every medical professional must obtain a valid consent from the patient through a personal dialogue before starting medical treatment, informing him[12] of the nature, significance, implications and risks of the measure or treatment (informed consent).[13] This means that it is not enough just to take account of a "formal" consent, but much more to enable the patient to make a free and self-responsible decision, based on the necessary information for or against a specific medical measure (*"materialisation of the consent"*[14]). Patients who refuse this measure must be informed about the consequences of their refusal.[15] This dialogue may be condensed or even skipped only in exceptional cases, for example when an immediate treatment is necessary and any delay would pose a serious threat to the patient's life.[16] These exceptions must be well justified and

---

of 29 July 2009 (*Federal Law Gazette* I p. 2248)", English unofficial translation available at http://www.gesetze-im-internet.de/englisch_gg/index.html (last accessed 30 September 2010).

[9] "Criminal Code" (*Strafgesetzbuch* – StGB) of 15 May 1871, in the version promulgated on 13 November 1998 (*Federal Law Gazette*, part I, p. 3322), last amended by Article 3 of the Law of 2 October 2009 (*Federal Law Gazette*, part I, p. 3214). Unofficial English translation available at http://www.gesetze-im-internet.de/englisch_stgb/index.html (last accessed 30 September 2010).

[10] "Civil Code" (*Bürgerliches Gesetzbuch* – BGB) of 18 August 1896, in the version promulgated on 2 January 2002, last amended by law of 24 July 2010 (*Federal Law Gazette* I p. 977), in force since 30 July 2010. Unofficial English translation available at http://www.gesetze-im-internet.de/englisch_bgb/index.html (last accessed 30 September 2010).

[11] Repeated judicial decisions of the German Federal Court of Justice (BGHSt 11, 111; 16, 309; 35, 246; BGHZ 29, 33; 106, 153) based on judicial decisions of the Imperial Court of Justice dating back to 1894 (RGSt 25, 375; 38, 34).

[12] In order to improve readability, only the male form is used in the text, nevertheless all data apply to members of both genders.

[13] For further information on informed consent see: Markus Parzeller, Maren Wenk, Barbara Zedler and Markus Rothschild, "cme: Patient Information and Informed Consent before and after Medical Intervention", 104 *Deutsches Ärzteblatt* (2007), pp. A 576–586.

[14] Jochen Taupitz, *Empfehlen sich zivilrechtliche Regelungen zur Absicherung der Patientenautonomie am Ende des Lebens?, Gutachten A für den 63. Deutschen Juristentag* (2000), pp. A 28–35.

[15] Taupitz, *supra* note 14, p. A 28.

[16] For an overview of exceptions to the physician's duty of informing the patient see Markus Parzeller *et al.*, *supra* note 13, p. A 581.

documented. Any medical measure carried out against the patient's will is prohibited and would therefore lead to prosecution.[17]

The right of a competent patient to give informed consent to medical treatment is also guaranteed by the German Constitution (*Grundgesetz* – GG) dated 1949. According to the right to self-determination in regard to one's body, constitutionally enshrined in the guarantee of human dignity (art. 1 I GG), the general right of personality (art. 2 I in conj. with art. 1 I GG) and the right to physical integrity (art. 2 II 1 GG), every person, if mentally competent, has the right either to permit or refuse any medical treatment. In this sense, decisional capacity in the context of health care is not the same as contractual capacity in the terms of civil law. There is no legally binding chronological moment (such as the age of majority) constituting the patient's capacity to decide about health care issues by giving, refusing or withdrawing consent to medical treatment. A person, who can understand the nature, relevance, impact and risks of a certain medical measure and create a will of his own on this basis, is considered to be capable of consenting.[18] Minors (at least from the age of 14[19]) and even patients, who are under custodianship due to health matters, are potentially capable of consenting in all areas, provided that they possess the "*mental and moral maturity*" to assess the "*significance and extent of the intervention and its development*".[20] It is an individual issue that the medical professional should prove in every single case.[21]

B. *Patients Who Are Unable to Give Consent*

The right to self-determination equally applies to all persons, regardless of their medical condition.[22] However, in several cases, such as when patients are suffering from conditions influencing their mental capacity, thus making them unable to make own decisions, it can be very difficult or even impossible to assess a person's will. During the 1990's and early 2000's, criminal panels of the German Federal Court of Justice (*Bundesgerichtshof* – BGH) and the German Constitutional Court (*Bundesverfassungsgericht* – BVerfG) established a general hierarchy of

---

[17] Compare: BVerfG decision of 25 July 1979 no. 2 BvR 878/74 = BVerfGE 52, 131; BGH decision of 5 July 2007 no. 4 StR 549/06 = MedR 2008, 158.

[18] BGH decision of 5 December 1958 no. VI ZR 266/57 = BGHZ 29, 33.

[19] Taupitz, *supra* note 14, pp. A 60 et seq.

[20] BGH, decision of 10 February 1959 no. 5 StR 533/58 = BGHSt 12, 379.

[21] More information: *supra* note 14, pp. A 58 et seq.

[22] BVerfG decision of 25 July 1979 no. 2 BvR 878/74 = BVerfGE 52, 131.

decision-making criteria for cases in which a patient is unable to give or refuse consent to medical treatment, acknowledging the primacy of patient's autonomy and legal validity of advance directives and in particular living wills, which could have been in oral or written form.[23] If the described situation actually happened, the living will had to be followed, unless there was evidence that the patient changed or revoked his will. However, in a controversial decision from 2003,[24] a civil panel of the BGH considerably differed from those prior judgements by holding the contradictory position that relevant living wills indeed must be followed, but at the same time giving the power to refuse life-sustaining treatment only for situations in which the patient is suffering from a terminal disease that is *"irreversibly leading to death"*. Hereby, the BGH considerably restricted the right to self-determination. This new requirement of a *"terminal"* and *"irreversible"* disease led to several contrary and disturbing court decisions of lower courts overruling advance directives and triggered a lively debate on the legal requirements of advance directives, particularly living wills.[25] In the following years the debate was intensified and produced several reports and recommendations on this issue, holding contrary positions, especially on the mentioned requirement of a terminal, irreversible disease, which was of special importance for cases of persistent vegetative state and dementia. Finally, the discussion diminished in 2009 when the German Parliament passed the already mentioned act,[26] now explicitly regulating living wills and the decision-making process for the case that the patient becomes incapable of giving or refusing consent to medical

---

[23] BVerfG decision of 02 August 2001 no. 1 BvR 618/93 = NJW 2002, 206; BGH decision of 13 September 1994 no. 1 StR 357/94 = BGHSt 40, 257; compare also: BGH decision of 4 July 1984 no. 3 StR 96/84 - BGHSt 32, 367 (379); BGH decision of 25 March 1988 no. 2 StR 93/88 = BGHSt 35, 246 (249); BGH decision of 8 May 1991 no. 3 StR 467/90 = BGHSt 37, 376 (378).

[24] The Federal Court of Justice ruled that a living will can't require physicians and custodians to provide something that is forbidden by criminal law. The decision-making power of the custodian is not more far-reaching than the legal forms of "help-to-die". Though in the sense of criminal law, withdrawal or withholding of life-sustaining measures would only be permissible if the physician would determine that the underlying disease had become irreversible and would immanently lead to death. The court considered these requirements to be fulfilled in the respective case of a persistent vegetative state patient [BGH decision of 17 March 2003 no. XII ZB 2/03 = BGHZ 154, 205 (205)], which is not correct, since those patients never die due to this underlying disease.

[25] For example: AG Siegen decision of 28 September 2007 - 33 XVII B 710 = NJW-Spezial 2008, 103; LG Essen - decision from 29 November 2007 no. 7 T 385/07 = NJW 2008, 1170; LG Fulda decision of 30 April 2009 no. 16 Js 1/08 - 1 Ks = BeckRS 2010, 6420.

[26] See *supra* note 3.

treatment. According to sec. 1901a III the decision of the patient that fulfils certain requirements is binding regardless of the nature and stage of any illness of the patient, may it irreversibly lead to death or the patient having the possibility to fully recover.

III. Surrogate Decision-Makers under German Law

According to the German custodianship law, if a person of full age, by reason of a mental illness or a physical, mental or psychological handicap, cannot in whole or in part take care of his affairs, the custodianship court, following his application or of its own accord, appoints a custodian for him (sec. 1896 I BGB), unless the patient has issued a power of attorney to a trusted person, while being mentally competent to still do so (sec. 1896 III 2 BGB). Despite the widespread misbelief among the German population, in Germany there are no default legal representatives or health care proxies for adults, like for example in England,[27] which would automatically empower next of kin to make any decisions on behalf of an adult who lacks decisional capacity. Even though in practice they often act as legal representatives, especially in emergency situations, next of kin must be authorized as legal representatives first—either as custodians by the custodianship court or as proxies / attorneys by the person, on whose behalf they are supposed to act, thus becoming legally valid surrogate decision-makers.[28]

---

[27] Ralf J. Jox, Sabine Michalowski, Jorn Lorenz and Jan Schildmann, "Substitute decision making in medicine: comparative analysis of the ethico-legal discourse in England and Germany", 11 *Medicine, Health Care and Philosophy* (2008), pp. 153–163.

[28] A bill presented to the German parliament regarding this issue and suggesting that relatives should be considered as standard surrogate decision-makers for incompetent patients was rejected in this point (Bundestag printed paper no. 15/4874 p. 26, in conj. with Bundestag printed paper no. 15/2494). For further information: Bundesrat printed paper no. 865/03; *Abschlussbericht der Bund-Länder-Arbeitsgruppe "Betreuungsrecht": zur 74. Konferenz der Justizministerinnen und -minister* (2003), pp. 78–97, available at http:// www.dnoti.de/DOC/2005/abschlussbericht.pdf (last accessed 30 September 2010); crit. Meinolfus Strätling, Helga Strätling-Tölle, Volker E. Scharf and Peter Schmucker, "'Automatische' gesetzliche Stellvertretung nicht entscheidungsfähiger Patienten durch 'nahe Angehörige'?: Kritische Anmerkungen zu einem Reformvorschlag der Bund-Länder-Arbeitsgruppe 'Betreuungsrecht' aus sozialwissenschaftlicher, rechtstatsächlicher, medizinrechtlicher und ärztlich-praktischer Sicht", 21 *Medizinrecht* (2003), pp. 372–379; in favour of a default system Stephan Sahm and Regina Will, "Angehörige als 'natürliche' Stellvertreter: Eine empirische Untersuchung zur Präferenz von Personen als Bevollmächtigte für die Gesundheitssorge bei Patienten, Gesunden und medizinischem Personal", 17 *Ethik in der Medizin* (2005), pp. 7–20.

A. *Custodianship Directive* (Betreuungsverfügung)

The most common representatives are the court appointed custodians[29] (sec. 1896 I 1 BGB) who may be appointed only for specific groups of tasks in which the custodianship is necessary (sec. 1896 II 1 BGB). These groups are not explicitly listed in the law. Therefore, the judge of the respective custodianship court is free to decide how to name them in a concrete case.[30] The scope of tasks should be phrased as precise as possible and relate to the current life situation of the person concerned. Exceptionally, it is also possible to appoint one custodian for all groups of tasks,[31] but this is an extremely rare exception.[32] If the custodian is supposed to meet decisions in health care issues, he must be explicitly appointed to do so.[33]

When deciding about the person of the custodian, the court has to take into account the currently or previously expressed wishes of the person who is supposed to be put under custodianship (sec. 1897 IV BGB). The expressed wishes can be positive or negative, proposing or even rejecting one or more persons to be appointed as custodians. Positive suggestions have to be accepted, unless the person does not meet the legal requirements or such an appointment would run contrary to the best interests of the person to be under custodianship.[34] Negative suggestions aren't obligatory, but only proposing.[35] In order to make any suggestions, the person who is nominating or rejecting potential candidates does not necessarily have to be legally competent.

If a (still) capable individual wanted to propose or reject somebody as his custodian in advance, he would need to create a custodianship

---

[29] Bundesamt für Justiz: *Verfahren nach dem Betreuungsgesetz. Zusammenstellung der Bundesergebnisse für die Jahre 1992 bis 2010* (latest version from 30 May 2011), available at http://www.bundesjustizamt.de/nn_2103244/DE/Themen/Buergerdienste/Justizstatistik/Betreuung/Betreuungsgesetz__ab1992,templateId=raw,property=publicationFile.pdf/Betreuungsgesetz_ab1992.pdf (last accessed: 24 November 2011).

[30] Usually they cover property and financial or personal welfare matters, but they can also be more detailed like e.g. "*apartment clearing out*" (BayObLG decision of 19 June 2001 no. 3Z BR 125/01 = NJW 2002, 381) etc.

[31] Compare: sec. 276 I no. 2 of the Law on the Proceedings regarding Family Matters and Voluntary Jurisdiction (*Gesetz über das Verfahren in Familiensachen und in den Angelegenheiten der freiwilligen Gerichtsbarkeit* = FamFG).

[32] Bundestag printed paper no. 11/4528, p. 122; BayObLG decision of 3 June 2002 no. 3Z BR 94/02 = FamRZ 2002, 1225 et seq.; BGH decision of 4 August 2010 no. XII ZB 167/10.

[33] Compare: BayObLG decision of 3 August 1995 no. 3 Z BR 190/95 = BtPrax 1995, 218; BayObLG decision of 24 August 2001 no. 3 Z BR 274/01 = FPR 2002, 203.

[34] Otto Palandt and Uwe Diederichsen, *Kommentar zum BGB* (69. ed., 2010), sec. 1897 BGB, recital 16.

[35] Bundestag printed paper no. 11/4528, pp. 127–128.

directive (*Betreuungsverfügung*),[36] which is not subject to any formal requirements. For provability reasons though it is advisable to put it into writing or even get it verified by a notary. If the person suggests no one, who may be appointed as a custodian, the court has to consider his family and other personal ties, in particular the ties to parents, to children, to the spouse and to the civil partner and the danger of conflict of interests (sec. 1897 V BGB). Only if no other suitable person is available, who is prepared to perform the task of a custodian on a voluntary basis, the court can appoint a person who conducts custodianships on a professional basis (sec. 1897 VI BGB). In practice, most custodians—either suggested by the person itself, or appointed by the court according to sec. 1897 V BGB—are usually close family members. Despite this fact the German legislator deliberately did not introduce a system of default legal representatives for adults and retained the obligatory court appointment procedure in 2005.[37]

The content of a custodianship directive is not limited to nominations or rejections of potential custodians. It can also contain wishes on how to manage the affairs of the person under custodianship, which the custodian must comply with to the extent that this, firstly, is not inconsistent with the best interests of the grantor and secondly, can be expected of the custodian (sec. 1901 III BGB). In this regard, the content of a custodianship directive might overlap with the content of a living will.

B. *Power of Attorney* (Vorsorgevollmacht)

The entire German custodianship law is dominated by the principles of necessity and subsidiarity (1896 II BGB). In the interaction of these principles they are deemed to protect individual's privacy against state interferences or minimize their impact as much as possible. In accordance with these principles, private precautions explicitly override any state ordered or provided support.[38] For this reason or in order to avoid the above mentioned very formal and costly court procedure,[39] it is possible to grant a

---

[36] For more information see: Volker Lipp, "Presentation and evaluation of the German legislation on enduring powers of attorney – a model other countries should consider adopting?", in Justis- og politidepartementet (ed.), *Rapport "Nordisk seminar om framtidsfullmakter"* (Oslo, 2007), pp. 29–48.

[37] See *supra* note 28.

[38] Andreas Roth, "sec. 1896 II BGB", in Dodegge/Roth, *Systematischer Praxiskommentar Betreuungsrecht* (Köln, 2010), part C recital 2 et seq.

[39] Powers of attorney "*are also in the public interest as they avoid costly guardianship proceedings as well as the appointment of guardians who, if the ward is poor, have to be paid for by the general public.*" (Lipp, *supra* note 36, p. 30). See also: Bundestag printed paper no. 11/4528, p. 122.

trusted person power of attorney (*Vorsorgevollmacht* – sec. 1896 II 2 alt. 1 BGB). This is a legal instrument that gives this person the legal authority to act on behalf of the grantor, and to make legally binding decisions for him.[40] Since it is a legal act, the grantor must be legally competent at the time of the issuance.[41] Similar to custodianship directives, it can be granted for specific groups of tasks, dealing for example with property and financial or personal welfare matters. According to the principle of subsidiarity if there is an existing power of attorney for personal welfare matters, there is no need to appoint a custodian for this group of tasks and the authorized attorney is entitled to make legally binding health care decisions on behalf of the grantor. The grantor is free to establish restrictions or conditions on the power of the donee. However, if an individual limits the power of attorney to specific groups of tasks, there is a high risk that a custodianship would become necessary for other groups. If possible, a coexistence of a custodianship and a power of attorney should therefore be avoided.[42]

Unlike the custodians, authorized attorneys aren't under direct control of public courts, thus evading direct state interference and control of the private sphere of the person who's granting the power of attorney. Therefore, it is advisable to grant a trusted person a "general" power of attorney (*Generalvollmacht*), enabling this person to act on one's own behalf in all matters (*Vertretung in allen Angelegenheiten*) where a custodianship might become necessary. Generally, a power of attorney is not required to be in writing. It can also be granted orally or even implicitly.[43] Since there are some very important exceptions from this general rule,

---

[40] More information: Lipp, *supra* note 36.

[41] A legally incompetent person may apply to the custodianship court to appoint a trusted person as his custodian. For more information see: Taupitz, *supra* note 14, p. A 102; Roth, *supra* note 38, part C, recital 125; Partial legal capacity sufficient according to e.g. Petra Baltz, *Lebenserhaltung als Haftungsgrund* (Regensburg, 2009), p. 77 with further reference; capacity to give informed consent sufficient according to e.g. Palandt and Diederichsen, *supra* note 34, sec. 1904, recital 26.

[42] Information brochure on the custodianship law of the German Federal Ministry of Justice (2009), p. 28, available at http://www.bmj.de/SharedDocs/Downloads/DE/broschueren_fuer_warenkorb/DE/Das_Betreuungsrecht.pdf?__blob=publicationFile (last accessed 30 September 2010).

[43] Peter Winterstein, in Andreas Jürgens, *Betreuungsrecht Kommentar* (München, 2005), sec. 167 BGB, recital 3; the content of such instruments is hardly provable, and therefore can't be verified, compare: OLG Hamm decision of 12 May 2009 no. I-15 Wx 1-4/09 = FGPrax 2009, 217 (219). For this reason, some authors argue that a power of attorney for health care has to be in writing in any case; for example: Georg Dodegge, "Die Entwicklung des Betreuungsrechts bis Anfang Juni 2010", 63 *Neue Juristische Wochenschrift* (2010), pp. 2628–2633, p. 2630.

inter alia considering health care issues, it is absolutely recommendable for reasons of legal certainty to set it up in writing, preferably with a notary. According to the new law, if there is a justified risk that the represented person would die or suffer serious and long-lasting detriment to health due to a medical measure, an attorney may consent to this measure only if the power of attorney expressly includes these measures and is given in writing (sec. 1904 V 2 in conj. with sec. 1904 I BGB). This also refers to non-consent or revocation of the consent if the suggested measure is medically indicated and there is justified reason to fear that the represented person will die or suffer serious and long-lasting detriment to health if the measure is not carried out or is discontinued. (sec. 1904 V 2 in conj. with sec. 1904 II BGB). The same applies to putting the represented person in accommodation that is associated with deprivation of liberty (sec. 1906 BGB).

With the new act regulating the custodianship law, the German legislator also intended for equality between the court-appointed custodians and the patient-designated attorney (sec. 1901a III, 1904 V 1 BGB), with the already mentioned exception that an attorney can only consent or refuse consent to life-sustaining or -prolonging treatment when explicitly and in writing authorized by the grantor to do so (§ 1904 V 2 BGB).

IV. New Legal Regulation on Living Wills

A. *Sec. 1901a BGB as the Key-Provision*

Within the context of the new regulation, sec. 1901a BGB is the key provision, stipulating legal requirements and the scope of living wills and regulating the duties and the role of a surrogate decision-maker. The law differentiates between immediately binding "*living wills*" (sec. 1901a I BGB) and indirectly binding "*wishes with regard to treatment or the presumed will*" (sec. 1901a II BGB). In this sense, a "*living will*" is defined as a written determination of a competent adult, for the event of his becoming unable to consent, as to whether he consents to or prohibits specific examinations of his state of health, treatment or medical interventions not yet directly immanent at the time of determination. Accordingly, to be binding a living will must meet all formal and content-related requirements specified by law. According to the explicit wording of the law, it is not the physician but the custodian or the person given power of attorney, who must examine whether the determinations written in the living will correspond to the current life and treatment situation. If it does, such a living will must be followed and the surrogate decision-maker (custodian or the person given power of attorney) must see to it that the will of the patient is attended to (sec. 1901a I BGB). The other constellation—if there is no living will, or if the determinations of a living will do not correspond to the current life and treatment situation—stipulates that the custodian or attorney must determine the wishes with regard to treatment or the presumed will of the represented person, and decide accordingly whether he, meaning the surrogate decision-maker, consents to or prohibits a medical measure (sec. 1901a II BGB).[44]

B. *Living Will* (Patientenverfügung)

1. *Legal Requirements*

a. *Written Form*

According to the new sec. 1901a I 1 BGB, a living will must be set up in writing (sec. 126 BGB), thus changing the previous prevailing opinion that binding living wills can be in written or oral form.[45] This new formal requirement is aimed to warn the individual, who is making the will, of potential "*hasty and injudicious determinations*".[46] In contrast to a last will that must be hand-written (holographic) (sec. 2247 I BGB), a living will does not. It just must be signed personally. The signature or the living will does not necessarily have to be authorized or certified by a notary, or witnessed by someone else. Only when the individual can not sign personally or has lost the ability to sign, the attendance of a notary and a witness, who has to sign the notary report, is compulsory.[47] Many organizations provide various standardized forms for different kinds of advance directives and living wills,[48] but there are no official statutory forms, like, for example, in Israel.[49] Such standardized forms should be

---

[44] Bundestag printed paper no. 16/13314, p. 4.

[45] LG Fulda decision of 30 April 2009 no. 16 Js 1/08 - 1 Ks = BeckRS 2010, 06420; LG Waldshut-Tiengen decision of 20 February 2006 no. 1 T 161/05 = NJW 2006, 2270.

[46] Bundestag printed paper no. 16/8442, p. 13.

[47] Sec. 25 of the Certification Act (*Beurkundungsgesetz*) of 28 August 1969 (*Federal Law Gazette*, part I, p. 1513), as last changed by art. 7 of the Law of 15 July 2009 (*Federal Law Gazette*, part I, p. 1798).

[48] Arnd T. May, *Verfügungsliste. Liste Vorsorglicher Verfügungen wie Patientenverfügung, Vorsorgevollmacht und Betreuungsverfügung* (15 July 2010), available at http://www.ethikzentrum.de/verfuegungen.htm (last accessed 12 July 2010).

[49] Silke Schicktanz, Aviad Raz and Carmel Shalev, "The cultural context of patient's autonomy and doctor's duty: passive euthanasia and advance directives in Germany and Israel", 13 *Medicine, Health Care and Philosophy* (2010), pp. 363–369, p. 365; Carmel Shalev,

treated with high caution, especially when a medical professional was not consulted prior to filling out the form. In situations where a patient might die, due to compliance to his own written living will, it would be preferable and in accordance with the idea of sec. 1904 V BGB, to acknowledge this living will as immediately binding, only if preceded by a professional medical consultation.[50] In contrast to the execution, the revocation of a living will implies no formalities and may be withdrawn at any time without any specific formal requirements (sec. 1901a I 3 BGB).

b. *Age of Majority and Decisional Capacity*
Contrary to the previous legal position and the commonly held opinion in the German legal literature,[51] an individual who wants to set up a valid living will, now must be of legal age, beginning at the age of eighteen (sec. 2 BGB). Unfortunately, the parliamentary documents give no answers concerning the reasons or the purpose of this formal requirement. Before the reform, the basic tenet of the German law was that a minor may be able to give fully binding consent independently, provided that he is deemed to have the necessary *"mental and moral maturity"* to assess the *"significance and extent of the intervention and its development"*.[52] Decisional capacity was unanimously considered to be the basic requirement to give, refuse or withdraw consent considering health care issues. In this sense, the new rigid age limit for living wills caused reasonable doubts that this formal requirement infringes the constitutionally guaranteed right to self-determination (art. 2 I in conj. with art. 1 I GG) and the principle of equality (art. 3 GG). Moreover, the German Federal Court of Justice (BGH) also modified the mentioned tenet in 2006, denying the competent minor patient exclusive authority to decide on his own health care issues, but acknowledging him the right to *"veto"* the consent given by

---

"Reclaiming the Patient's Voice and Spirit in Dying; an Insight from Israel", 24 *Bioethics* (2010), pp. 134–144, p. 141.

[50] Taupitz, *supra* note 14, p. A 111 et seq.; compare also: Decision III 2.3. of the Civil Law Section of the 63. German Jurists Forums (2000) = FamRZ 2000, 1484 (1485); Nationaler Ethikrat, *Patientenverfügung* (Berlin, 2005), p. 33, available at http://www.ethikrat.org/dateien/pdf/Stellungnahme_Patientenverfuegung.pdf (last accessed 30 September 2010), different in cases of dementia, p. 34.

[51] Wolfgang Lange, "Das Patientenverfügungsgesetz - Überblick und kritische Würdigung", 16 *Zeitschrift für Erbrecht und Vermögensnachfolge* (2009), pp. 537–544, p. 539; Andreas Spickhoff, "Rechtssicherheit kraft Gesetzes durch sog. Patientenverfügungen?: zum Dritten Gesetz zur Änderung des Betreuungsrechts", 56 *Zeitschrift für das gesamte Familienrecht* (2009), pp. 1949–1958, p. 1951, each with further references.

[52] BGH decision of 9 December 1958 no. VI ZR 203/57 = BGHZ 29, 46.

his legal representatives.[53] Nevertheless, a living will usually, but according to German law not necessarily, contains a refusal of consent to certain medical measures or treatments, which in the end means that even according to the mentioned BGH ruling, minors can refuse unwanted medical measures, though only by vetoing. On this account, decisional capacity remains to be a mandatory requirement for all health care decisions, including living wills. Admittedly, this prerequisite is not undisputed. On the one hand, it is already questionable where to draw the line between decisional capacity and incapacity,[54] especially in cases when it is progressively diminishing, like it is the case with dementia. In addition to this, it remains questionable if the person concerned had (still) been capable of consenting when signing the living will. In order to avoid such concerns, it should be ensured that witnesses are able to confirm decisional capacity afterwards. This problem has certainly been reduced with the legal age requirement, since adults are presumed competent to consent.[55]

c. *Content-Related Requirements*

Besides the very few formal prerequisites, a valid living will is required to contain "*determinations*" showing if its signer consents to or prohibits "*specific*" examinations concerning his state of health, treatments or medical interventions "*not yet directly immanent*" at the time of determination. Since the legislator did not define how specific these determinations must be in order to be directly binding, this requirement has been highly discussed shortly after the reform.[56] Nevertheless, the regional court of Kleve rightly notices that it "*is not decisive to anticipate one's own biography as a patient*", but to loosely *determine* one's own wishes regarding specific life

---

[53] BGH decision of 10 October 2006 no. VI ZR 74/05 = MedR 2008, 289 with a comment by Volker Lipp. Providing parents with information required also by OLG Karlsruhe, decision of 7 April 2010 no. 7 U 114/09 = BeckRS 2010, 08386. Further crit. comments: Bernd-Rüdiger Kern, "Einwilligung und Aufklärung Minderjähriger", 8 *Kommentierte BGH-Rechtsprechung Lindenmaier-Möhring* (2007), n° 4, p. 220412. One part of the literature had already demanded a similar system of "co-consent" of the minor capable of consenting and his parents, see: Taupitz, *supra* note 14, pp. A 63 et seq.

[54] More detailed: Taupitz, *supra* note 14, pp. A 58 et seq.

[55] Volker Lipp, *Handbuch der Vorsorgeverfügungen* (München, 2009), sec. 17, recital 127.

[56] Julia Roglmeier and Nina Lenz, "Live and let die - die gesetzlichen Neuregelungen zur Patientenverfügung", 11 *Zeitschrift für die Steuer- und Erbrechtspraxis* (2009), n° 8, pp.236–239, p. 239, Benedikt Schmitz, "Voraussetzungen und Umsetzung der Patientenverfügung nach neuem Recht: Ein dialogischer Prozess", *Familienrecht und Familienverfahrensrecht* (3/2009), p. 64; Palandt and Diedrichsen, *supra* note 34; Damian W. Najdecki, "Generalvollmacht mit Betreuungs- und Patientenverfügung", 33 *Neue Wirtschaftsbriefe* (2009), pp. 2594–2603, p. 2602.

or treatment situations. The living will, therefore, must merely contain determinations that make it possible to conclude a decision for or against a treatment in question.[57] In this sense, accepting depictions of *"the main treatment situations and symptoms"*[58] or completely renouncing *"concrete detailed listings"*[59] entails the risk of creating a too vague living will, giving space for misinterpretations, or even a written document that does not meet the legal requirements for a directly binding living will. There is, however, unanimous agreement that general wishes and guidelines do not meet the legal requirements for a valid living will.[60] Notwithstanding, the surrogate decision-maker must take them into consideration when deciding on the basis of the patient's wishes or presumed will pursuant to sec. 1901a II BGB. In practice, it will certainly prove difficult to assess if a determination is precise enough or not.

Living wills that have been set up before the new law entered into force on 1 September 2009 remain valid provided that they meet the above-mentioned legal requirements.[61] Many of them probably do not fulfil the required level of accuracy stipulated in sec. 1901a I BGB[62] and are likely to be implemented according to sec. 1901a II BGB.

2. *Optional Elements*

In order to prevent unnecessary barriers of the right to self-determination, there are no other formal requirements for living wills apart from the written form. A medical or legal *consultation* is not necessary,[63] even though the legislator has emphasised the valuable consulting role of a medical

---

[57] LG Kleve decision of 31 May 2010 no. 4 T 77/10 = NJW 2010, 2666 (2668). Accordingly, Palandt and Diederichsen, *supra* note 34, § 1901a, recital 18 with further references.

[58] Najdecki, *supra* note 56.

[59] Benedikt Schmitz, "Voraussetzungen und Umsetzung der Patientenverfügung nach neuem Recht: Ein dialogischer Prozess", *Familienrecht und Familienverfahrensrecht* (2009), n° 3, p. 64.

[60] Bundestag printed paper no. 16/8442, p. 13.

[61] During the parliamentarian debate, the German legislator relied on the number of 8.6 million living wills (ca. 10% of the total population), that has been estimated by the German Hospice Foundation; compare Bundestag printed paper 16/8442, p. 8.

[62] The legislator explicitly recognised this risk in Bundestag printed paper no. 16/8442, p. 14. See also: Elisabeth Albrecht and Andreas Albrecht, "Die Patientenverfügung – jetzt gesetzlich geregelt", *Mitteilungen des Bayerischen Notarvereins, der Notarkasse und der Landesnotarkammer Bayern* (2009), n° 6, p. 428.

[63] Critical on this: Wolfgang Lange, "Das Patientenverfügungsgesetz - Überblick und kritische Würdigung", 16 *Zeitschrift für Erbrecht und Vermögensnachfolge* (2009), pp. 537–544; Wolfram Höfling, "Das neue Patientenverfügungsgesetz", 62 *Neue Juristische Wochenschrift* (2009), pp. 2849–2852; Dirk Olzen, "Die gesetzliche Neuregelung der Patientenverfügung", *Juristische Rundschau* (2009), n° 9, pp. 354–362.

professional prior to the execution of a living will.[64] According to general principles, a physician is obliged to inform the patient in a personal conversation about the nature, benefits and risks associated with the treatment. The concept of informed consent aims at protecting patients from acting under pressure or as a result of misleading information. Within this concept it is incumbent upon physicians to ascertain whether the person is able to make own health care decisions. In spite of these general rules the legislator has refrained from making a medical consultation a mandatory requirement for advance directives. It suffices that the patient is legally competent at the moment of his decision (sec. 1901a BGB).

A valid living will may be revoked at any time without a specific form and it does not have to be renewed periodically, which by implication means that it has no *expiry date* like in Austria. Nevertheless, it is absolutely advisable to add a date, since the individual life situation or treatment options might essentially change between the moment of execution of a living will and the moment of its potential application.

C. *Treatment Wishes and Presumed Will (sec. 1901a II BGB)*

The right to self-determination is certainly the key-element considering legal aspects of health care issues. As long as the anticipated situation actually happened, the living will is binding, unless there is evidence or a reason to assume that a patient has changed or revoked his will (sec. 1901a I BGB). If there is no living will or if the living will does not meet the legal requirements, it is the duty of the surrogate decision-maker to determine the treatment wishes or the presumed will of the patient, and decide respectively (sec. 1901a II BGB). The presumed will must be ascertained "*on the basis of concrete indications*", considering "*in particular patient's prior oral or written statements, ethical or religious convictions and other personal values of the patient*".[65] In order to fulfil this task, the surrogate decision-maker should communicate with the patient's close relatives and other persons enjoying patient's confidence, as far as this is possible without any considerable delay. If none of this is possible, the decision is to be made upon values deemed to be universally shared, acting in the patient's best interest, thus taking the risk to act in accordance with one's own values. However, if there are any doubts about what is in the patient's best

---

[64] Bundestag printed paper no. 16/13314, pp. 19–20. Compare also: Jochen Taupitz, "Grenzen der Patientenautonomie", *ARSP-Beiheft* (2000), n° 84, pp. 83, 116 et seq.

[65] Bundestag printed paper 16/13314, p. 5.

interest, the principle *in dubio pro vita* must prevail.[66] This is to prevent that surrogate decision-makers meet any decisions based on *"mere speculations about the will".*[67] The criterion of the treatment wishes or presumed will is justifiably being criticized as a *"gateway for heteronomy",*[68] since it certainly bears a risk of misinterpretation.[69] But there is no other solution if one takes the principle of human autonomy seriously. For the sake of patient safety, the custodianship court has to prove the decision of the surrogate decision-maker in cases when the treating physician and surrogate decision-maker disagree if the met decision to conduct or omit a specific measure is in accordance with the wishes or presumed will of the patient (sec. 1904 IV BGB).

D. *Implementation of a Living Will and its Addressee*

According to the wording and systematization of the new law within the provisions of custodianship law, the role of surrogate decision-makers has substantially increased. If a person makes any health care determinations for the case of becoming unable to give consent, it is the surrogate decision-maker who—first of all—must prove if there's a valid living will at all. The following step is to *"examine whether these determinations correspond to the current living and treatment situation"* (sec. 1901a I 1 BGB). If this is the case, he must see to it that the will of the respective person is attended to (sec. 1901a I 2 BGB). Legally, the contained determinations are being treated as equals to real-time decisions. However, if the determinations differ only slightly, the surrogate decision-maker faces a great challenge. Especially the question, where to draw the line between an immediately binding living will and an indirectly binding wish or presumed will, bears a huge responsibility, but this is the basic problem when interpreting "anticipative" declarations. In this context, the content-related requirement of *"specific determinations"* plays a major role.[70] Where there's no immediately binding living will, it is the surrogate decision-maker who

---

[66] Ibid. at p. 4.

[67] Jürgen Seichter, *Einführung in das Betreuungsrecht* (Heidelberg, 2010), p. 162.

[68] Höfling *supra* note 63, p. 2851; same position: Palandt and Diederichsen, *supra* note 34, sec. 1901a, recital 6.

[69] See LG Oldenburg decision of 16 March 2010 no. AZ 8 T 180/10; crit. remark on the decision from Oliver Tolmein, "Sterbehilfe: Wie mutmaßlich kann ein Wille sein?", in FAZ Blog on Biopolitics of 27 April 2010.

[70] See also: Jochen Taupitz and Kristiane Weber-Hassemer, "Zur Verbindlichkeit von Patientenverfügungen", in *Festschrift für Adolf Laufs* (2006), pp. 1117 et seq.

plays the central role, since he's supposed to determine the patient's treatment wishes or his presumed will.

However, the new wording should not belie the fact that the role of the physician is still absolutely essential and inevitable. The patient's representatives can not make any decisions until the physician examines *"which medical measure is indicated with regard to the patient's overall condition and prognosis"* (sec. 1901b I 1 BGB). If a medical measure or its continuation is not medically indicated (anymore), the physician has to withhold or withdraw it. Neither the patient, nor his representative or next-of-kin can require that the doctor performs a non-indicated measure.[71] The reality, however, is often quite different. A typical case where patients are systematically provided with non-indicated life-sustaining measures is that of artificial nutrition or hydration in the care of patients with advanced dementia. *"Recent studies demonstrate that there is no proof of any benefit, that tube-feeding often results in further harm to the dementia patient and that the patient's will is not sufficiently taken into consideration."*[72] Nevertheless it is performed over 100.000 times a year in Germany.

Once the physician decides that a measure is medically indicated, he must discuss it with the patient's representative in order to ascertain the patient's will. Any decision met pursuant to the aforementioned rules, must be approved by the custodianship court *"if the justified danger exists that the person under custodianship will die or will suffer serious and long-lasting detriment to his health due to the measure"*, unless the then caused delay would entail this danger (sec. 1904 I BGB). The same counts for *"non-consent to or revocation of the consent"* to a measure that is medically indicated (sec. 1904 II BGB).[73] According to sec. 1904 IV BGB, approval is not required if the surrogate decision-maker and the physician agree that the granting, non-granting or revocation of consent corresponds to the will of the patient established pursuant to section 1901a BGB. In accordance with general principles, any person may turn to the custodianship court in cases of suspected abuse.

---

[71] "Empfehlungen der Bundesärztekammer und der Zentralen Ethikkommission bei der Bundesärztekammer zum Umgang mit Vorsorgevollmacht und Patientenverfügung in der ärztlichen Praxis", 107 *Deutsches Ärzteblatt* (2010), n° 18, p. A882.

[72] Matthis Synofzik, "PEG-Ernährung bei fortgeschrittener Demenz: eine evidenzgestützte ethische Analyse", 78 *Nervenarzt* (2007), pp. 418–428 with further references. See also Public experts hearing of the Judicial Committee of the German Bundestag on living wills from 4 March 2009: expert opinion of Gian Domenico Borasio, pp. 3, 8.

[73] Procedural rules contained in sec. 287 and 298 FamFG (*supra* note 31); see also: Jochen Taupitz, "Das Patientenverfügungsgesetz: Mehr Rechtssicherheit?", 15 *Jahrbuch für Wissenschaft und Ethik* (2010), pp. 176 et seq.

The new law gives no specific answer concerning the question whether a physician is allowed to decide on his own when there is no surrogate decision-maker yet. This loophole in the law already caused a new debate about which person is the addressee of a living will—if it is the surrogate decision-maker, the physician or even other medical staff. Having in mind that the German custodianship law is dominated by the principles of necessity and subsidiarity, giving primacy to patient's volition, it would be reasonable to state that concrete determinations stated in a living will should be immediately binding, even when there is no valid surrogate decision-maker. In this sense, the physician and other medical staff could be considered to be addressees of a living will,[74] despite the explicit wording of the law.[75] However, the opposing opinion[76] is more convincing for several reasons.[77] In the explanation of the law draft, the physician and other persons involved in the medical treatment process were mentioned as addressees,[78] but this statement is contrary to the unequivocal wording of the law. Besides that, it is contrary to the new very formal procedure aiming to protect the incompetent patient. The first step is the duty of the physician to examine if a measure is medically indicated with regard to the patient's overall condition and prognosis. If it's not, all other steps are dispensable. If it is indicated, then *"he and the custodian must discuss this measure, considering the patient's will as a basis for the decision to be taken pursuant to section 1901a"* (sec. 1901b I BGB). This dialogue between the physician and the surrogate decision-maker cannot be waived. If this dialogue is required in cases when there is a court- or patient-appointed representative, then it would be a mistake to assume that the physician can forego this dialogue. Only exceptionally, in cases of emergency, physicians and other medical staff should be allowed to act independently. In these cases, it is of utmost importance to decide if a measure is medically indicated or not. Like it was the case before the reform, such a measure should be conducted relying on the criminal law of *"principle of necessity"* (sec. 34 StGB), the *"presumed consent"* and the civil law instrument of

---

[74] Accordingly Bundestag printed paper 16/8442, p. 11.

[75] Palandt and Diederichsen, *supra* note 34, sec. 1901a BGB, recital 20; Rolf Coeppicus, "Der Patientenwille gilt auch ohne Betreuer", in *Frankfurter Allgemeine Zeitung* (2010), n° 31 of 6 February 2010, p. 9.

[76] For example: Thomas Diehn and Ralf Rebhahn, "Vorsorgevollmacht und Patientenverfügung", 63 *Neue Juristische Wochenschrift* (2010), pp. 326–331.

[77] More information: Lipp, *supra* note 55, sec. 17 recital 198 in conj. with sec. 16, recital 116; Taupitz, *supra* note 73, pp. 166–169.

[78] Drucksache 16/8442, pp. 11, 15.

"*acting without mandate*" (sec. 677 BGB). In such a case, a representative of the patient must be included as soon as possible.[79] If there is no indication, there is no need to ascertain the patient's will and therefore there is no need for a representative.

V. Living Wills and Euthanasia

With the new law, the German legislator dismissed the restricting requirement of a terminal and irreversible disease and thus explicitly regulated the scope of applicability of living wills to any situation requiring a medical decision of the incompetent person.[80] The above-mentioned criteria for determining the actual or presumed will or wishes of a patient, who is no longer able to give informed consent, are applicable regardless of the nature and stage of any illness of this person (sec. 1901a III BGB),[81] thus solving the controversial debate on applicability of living wills in cases of vegetative state or dementia, but simultaneously raising a new question on the applicability in—for example—psychiatry, since there are already some efforts to tailor the living will into a "*psychiatric living will*" as an alternative to involuntary treatment.[82] Just like before the reform, the determined will does not have to be reasonable. For example, if a Jehovah's Witness rejects a blood transfusion for religious reasons, this decision would be binding, even though the transfusion could save the patient's life.[83] However, a living will must comply with state law, meaning that living wills, which refer to the legally forbidden termination of life (sec. 212 et seq. StGB), even on request of the patient (sec. 216 StGB), remain void. Criminal and professional law prohibit deliberately hastening a patient's death and there had been no attempts this far to change the current legal situation and legalise active euthanasia, in Germany usually called "active

---

[79] Empfehlungen der Bundesärztekammer, *supra* note 71.

[80] The German Federal Court of Justice confirmed this position in his recent decision: BGH *supra* note 5, p. 2965.

[81] Reasons for this decision stated in Bundestag printed paper no. 16/8442, p. 16 and 16/13314, pp. 20–21.

[82] Compare: http://www.patverfue.de/; http://www.antipsychiatrieverlag.de/info/voraus.htm (last accessed 30 September 2010).

[83] For more information on the legal situation concerning Jehovah's Witnesses: Philip Schelling and C. Lippstreu, "Der Glaube der Zeugen Jehovas und der ärztliche Heilauftrag", 43 *Gynäkologe* (2010), pp. 47–52; Thomas Standl, "Glaube oder Leben?", 59 *Der Anaesthesist* (2010), pp. 289–292; BVerfG decision of 2 August 2001 no. 1 BvR 618/93 = NJW 2002, 206; OLG München decision of 31 January 2002 no. 1 U 4705/98 = NJW-RR 2002, 811.

help to die" (*aktive Sterbehilfe*).[84] The traditional terminology concerning end-of-life decisions, which usually differs between active, passive and indirect euthanasia, had been dismissed in the international debate as ambiguous and of little use.[85] The German National Ethics Council described it as "misleading" and "open to misunderstanding". It therefore suggested a new terminology instead. According to the Council's opinion, *"decisions and actions at the end of life which directly or indirectly affect the dying process and the onset of death can be appropriately described and distinguished by the use of the following terms: "end-of-life care", "therapy at the end of life", "letting die", "assisted suicide", and "killing on request".*"[86] Nevertheless, the German jurisprudence still makes a distinction between the illegal "active" and the legal "passive" and "indirect" euthanasia.[87] Besides that, the Federal Court of Justice recently modified its own case law and terminology acquitting a renowned lawyer, who had advised the daughter (and simultaneously custodian) of a comatose woman to cut off her feeding tube, for the purpose of preventing an unwanted resumption of artificial nutrition. In order to be a case of legal euthanasia, it's no longer important if the withdrawal or withholding of a medical measure or treatment occurs as a result of an action or omission, as long as it is in accordance with the patient's determined will or wishes. It's only important that the specific act is necessary to implement the patient's will in connection with a concrete medical treatment. The court explained that the expressed wishes of the patient justified not only the end of treatment via the withholding of further nourishment but also the active step of ending or preventing the treatment that the comatose patient no longer wanted. Simultaneously, the new term: *"help to die by omitting, limiting or forgoing treatment"* was introduced. Deliberate induction or hastening of death remains illegal, even if the patient asks for it.

---

[84] Outside Germany, such actions are usually referred to as active (voluntary) "euthanasia", but in Germany this term has been discredited due to the Nazi practices during the World War II. For the sake of better international comparability this paper uses the international term of *"euthanasia"*. Further information on this terminological debate: Nationaler Ethikrat, *Self-determination and care at the end of life* (Berlin, 2006), pp. 45–48, available at http://www.ethikrat.org/_english/publications/Opinion_end-of-life_care.pdf (last accessed 30 September 2010).

[85] Fuat S. Oduncu and Stephan Sahm, "Doctor-cared dying instead of physician-assisted suicide: a perspective from Germany", 13 *Medicine Health Care and Philosophy* (2010), pp. 371–381, p. 373; Schicktanz et al., *supra* note 49, pp. 366–367, each with further information and references.

[86] Nationaler Ethikrat, *supra* note 84, pp. 48–51.

[87] BGH, *supra* note 5.

Even prior to this ruling and the new law, there was a strong consensus that withholding or withdrawing medical treatment is not necessarily a form of active euthanasia in cases where the following applied: if either there is no medical indication, or the withholding or withdrawal is in accordance with the patient's explicit or presumed will or wishes. Unfortunately, in practice withholding or withdrawing life-sustaining measures or treatments are often falsely considered to be an act of active euthanasia, thus implying cases of severe medical overtreatment. Due to the distinctive anthropological significance of eating and drinking, withholding or withdrawing artificial nutrition or hydration was one of the most controversial issues in the run-up of the reform, like it is still the case in Italy. Even though one of the three draft bills aimed at a prohibition on secession of artificial nutrition and hydration,[88] the German Bundestag followed the opinion of a renowned medical expert that artificial nutrition via an oral or percutaneous feeding tube can also be more harmful than beneficence at the end of life,[89] thus giving primacy to the patient's autonomy and medical argumentation rather than the duty to protect life.

Refusing medically indicated life-sustaining or life-prolonging measures is not considered to be an act of suicide. If someone dies because he merely does not want to influence the natural process of the own illness, the physician's duty to rescue this person (sec. 323 c StGB) has to stand down for the benefit of the patient's autonomy.[90] Moreover, medical professionals are not forced to preserve life under all circumstances, since there are situations in which "*appropriate diagnostic and therapeutic measures are no longer indicated and limitation of treatment and intervention can be necessary or even compulsory*".[91] Regardless of the medical indication, the physician and medical staff are always obliged to provide the so-called "*basic care*",[92] including "*dignified accommodation, personal attention, personal hygiene, the alleviation of pain, of respiratory distress and of nausea, and the alleviation of hunger and thirst*"[93] in a natural way. In this sense artificial nutrition and hydration are not considered to be basic care measures.

---

[88] Bundestag printed paper no. 16/11360.
[89] Borasio, *supra* note 72.
[90] Ulsenheimer in Laufs/Kern, *Handbuch des Arztrechts* (4. ed., 2010), § 132 Die ärztliche Sterbehilfe, rec. 42.
[91] Oduncu and Sahm, *supra* note 85, p. 373.
[92] OLG München decision from 31 July 1987 no. 1 Ws 23/87 = NJW 1987, 2940 (2943).
[93] Oduncu and Sahm, *supra* note 85, pp. 372–373.

VI. Conclusion

Facing cases like that of Eluana Englaro and Piergiorgio Welby, the Italian Senate has chosen to follow a different approach to the German parliament in dealing with living wills. While Germany very much strengthened patient's autonomy, the Italian Senate aspires to introduce a more paternalistic regulation than it is the case in practice today. The main goal of the German legislator was to provide more legal security and to increase the level of respect for the principle of patient's autonomy, which was partially achieved. Many former controversial issues have indeed been resolved. This is particularly true for the question concerning the level of bindingness of living wills and their formal prerequisites. At the same time the new law raised new issues that require further clarification: the question concerning the addressee of a living will is now being highly debated. Further, the debate has arisen if a surrogate decision-maker is always mandatory or not, even if the living will is precise enough. Moreover, clear instructions and rules on a valid revocation of a living will are missing, making it perhaps more difficult for stakeholders interacting with these patients to ensure that they act lawfully. It is also unclear where to draw the line between persons who are capable of giving consent and thus decide about their own health care issues, and persons who are not (anymore). Furthermore, the legislator renounced the often required professional consultation before setting up a living will, thus certainly diminishing the number of valid and immediately binding living wills. Altogether, the implementation of living wills remains quite precarious, but this is an immanent problem of end-of-life issues.

In the end, according to the new German law, the central question concerns what the particular patient would want, if he knew of his current situation. In this sense, the newly spreading concept of the so called *advance care planning* (ACP), suggesting to focus less on forms and documents, but instead put some more emphasis on communicative processes between patients, their next-of-kin, medical professionals and surrogate decision makers, might gain more attention and acceptance. At least on the international level, advance care planning is a concept that might be suitable to every European country, regardless of its religious, philosophical, legal or whichever other background.

THE RIGHT TO DIE WITH DIGNITY: SOCIO-LEGAL IMPLICATIONS OF THE RIGHT TO A DIGNIFIED LIFE AND DEATH IN THE BRAZILIAN EXPERIENCE

*Sandra Regina Martini Vial**

I. INTRODUCTION

Humanity is more essential to the people than water and fire. I saw men lose their lives by submitting themselves to water and fire; never saw someone lose life by surrendering to humanity. (Art. 15.36, Confucius)

The subject of death and dying with dignity is treated in this article as a matter of Sanitary Law, for health rules the way we live and die. The approach of dying with dignity means living under the same conditions. Today's society surrenders with ease to the various *fires and waters*, but it surrenders little to humanity. Paradoxically a process of universal inclusion like the one we live in nowadays has never happened before. It is not difficult to identify that, in this society, we all have more rights than we can effectively enjoy. In this era of universal fundamental rights, we notice that the possibility of access to the right for life and death does not often occur through the health system, but through the legal system. The realization of the right to have rights is still far from being achieved, although it is crucial to recognize that progress is already being carried on. In this sense we note that the health system cannot provide answers, thus it constantly requests the legal system to decide on issues that it is not always prepared to face; law and health are not always willing to *surrender to humanity*.

In this article we will present some reflections and concerns on the subject of dying with dignity. We have come across many difficulties due to the lack of permission to choose a dignified death. There is a limited understanding of the possibility of *dying with dignity* as a right of every individual, or of his family in its inability to decide how and when he wants to

* Professor of Sociology of Law, University of Vale do Rio dos Sinos, São Leopoldo, Brazil; email: srmvial@terra.com.br. For the relevant legislative and legal aspects this survey has benefited from the collaboration of Bel. Silvia Regina dos Santos Martini.

S. Negri (ed.), *Self-Determination, Dignity and End-of-Life Care*
2011 Koninklijke Brill NV. Printed in The Netherlands. ISBN 978 90 04 22357 8. pp. 355–378

die—considering life as sovereign to all other goods, makes this subject vulnerable to interferences of all orders, from religious aspects to criminalization. Due to the complexity of the subject we initially ponder the possibility to live and die with dignity; at this point we will present data that will help us consider the question: to whom does the body belong? Next we will discuss the relationship between the legal and the health systems, showing that *dying with dignity* requires contributions from both systems, and we will highlight the need to speak with healthcare teams and not only with the physician as the one in charge. Then while considering the legal system we will highlight the role of the judge, but also acknowledge that all systems of law are involved in this issue. We will cover the *social right* debate, where we will see the importance of the public prosecutor. In addition to the role of the law we will address the issue of social politics, showing how many draft bills have already been submitted and the difficulty of approval of these projects, to such an extent that Brazil remains in a limbo. Within the text we will focus on the difficulties of defining the terms: dignified death, dying with dignity, right to die. To substantiate our position we met with a group of families that faced the difficulties that arise in letting a family member legally die with dignity.

II. LIVING WORTHILY TO DIE WITH DIGNITY: IS IT POSSIBLE?

A. *The Possibility of Living a Life Worthy of a Dignified Death*

Whoever I am, sadness is expected from me, but not this state of absence. Seeing me so lonely doesn't tranquilize them, so away from me. In Africa, the deads do not die ever except those who die bad, those so-called abortions. Yes, the same name that is given to the born dead. After all, death is another birth. (Mia Couto)[1]

It is necessary to characterize the current society to illustrate the size of the inequalities that currently exist, as presented by Niklas Luhmann:[2] *the world society* [...] *hard to deny the entangles in the environment of all the functional systems*. It is this society of approximately 7 billion people, where at least 1.2 million suffer from severe malnutrition (FAO), 2.5 million do not have basic sanitation (UN), 18 million die annually due to poverty (WHO), 2 billion have no access to medication (WHO), and 218 million children and young people work under a regime of slavery (ILO).

---

[1] Mia Couto, *Um rio chamado tempo, uma casa chamada terra* (São Paulo, 2003), p. 30.
[2] Niklas Luhmann, *El derecho de la sociedad* (México, 2002), pp. 648–649.

We also noted that the concentration of wealth has increased, in the past two decades the richest 10% of the world have significantly increased their wealth: in 1988 the same group of people had 64% of the wealth, and today it comprises a total of 71%.

In this global society, the processes of inclusion and exclusion accentuate themselves. The need for a global democracy is even more evident, because democracy means reduction of major inequalities that marked the previous century and continue to mark this new century. As Avelãs Neto writes, we observe the civilization of inequalities, which may be transformed only by a world society that respects the basic assumptions of democracy. Despite the criticisms presented by that author, he concludes the text saying:

> [...] But, despite the profound contradictions of this time of ours (time of high hopes and despair), we have reason to believe that we can live in a world of cooperation and solidarity, in a world that is able to respond satisfactorily to the fundamental needs of all inhabitants of the planet.[3]

The complexity of the current society can be seen everywhere, social inequalities are at the centre and at the peripheries of modernity. In Latin America, for example, it is possible to find some of the richest people in the world alongside with millions of people in situations of extreme poverty. We have at the same time, vast possibilities and severe limitations imposed by poverty, non-distribution of income and wealth, enormous energy richness and low use of ecological and friendly energy. As the result of a perverse development process, all around the world rates of urbanization are significantly growing. In other words: we live in a continent with a great potential for sustainable development, but our practices point to economic models of social exclusion, or a partial inclusion. This is often accomplished through assistencialist policies, even though some of them are essential to continue reducing the local/regional inequalities.

Inequalities are continuously studied by CEPAL – (Economic Commission for Latin America and Caribbean –) which states that although GDP is growing, there are many disparities both among countries and within each country: in Brazil, Brasilia is nine times richer than Piauí. Another alarming data, according to UNESCO, is access to education among poorer young people: only 1 out of every 5 finishes junior high

---

[3] António José Avelãs Nunes, *Neoliberalismo, Capitalismo e Democracia* (Coimbra, 2003), pp. 53–55.

school. The greatest inequalities can be observed in the following three regions:

1. the Nations with the greatest inequalities are Bolivia, Ecuador, El Salvador, Guatemala, Honduras, Nicaragua, Paraguay, Peru and Dominican Republic, that, in the biennium 2007/8, invested only $ 181 on average per person in social policies;
2. Brazil, Argentina, Chile, Costa Rica, Panama and Uruguay have invested, on average, $ 1,029 in that same period. This block boasts the largest GDP per person in Latin America;
3. midway are Colombia, Mexico and Venezuela, with an average investment of $ 619.

These data raise questions regarding living and dying. So before speaking of the right to die worthily it is necessary to discuss the right to live, though only briefly, as this is not the subject of this article. We need to discuss *to whom we belong and how we belong*. Our body not only has an individual dimension, but also a social one.[4] Thus, the new health policies cannot ignore the questions concerning this body and its dimensions. It is necessary to try to find a way to answer the following questions: whose body is it and who is responsible for taking care of it? Or we must revel in the deeply discussed hypothesis by A. Puni in the Machine Man.[5] When we look at the report from CNDSS[6] held in Brazil in 2008, we have:

> The Northeast region, as expected, presents the highest rates of childhood mortality in all fifths of income, particularly in the first fifth, although historic trend is also of falling over the years. If, in 1990, the rate was 95.7%, it declines to 64% in 2000 and 56.4% in 2005. It is important to highlight that, when this stratum is compared with other regions of Central-Southern, it appears a decrease in differentials, over the years.

That said, we can return with the questions raised by Rodotà, namely: who owns *the body* of the children born *in the northeast of the world*? How will we consider these children from the perspective of the assumption of brotherhood, of solidarity? Which minimum rules of acquaintanceship

---

[4] Eligio Resta, *Diritto vivente* (Roma-Bari, 2008), p. 47.
[5] On this issue, see Antonio Punzi, *L'ordine giuridico delle macchine* (Torino, 2003).
[6] Brasil, Relatório da Comissão Nacional de Determinantes Sociais em Saúde. Brasília, Comissão Nacional de Determinantes Sociais em Saúde, 2008. Available at http://www.determinantes.fiocruz.br (last accessed on 10 November 2010).

are we establishing? Which set of oaths do we adhere to? These responses certainly can and should be given by social policies, which somehow must take into account populations—*as expected*—traditionally more vulnerable. Still following the reflections of Rodotà, we can think about the issues of death,[7] ownership of the body and *healing* of diseases. When we see such significant differences regarding infant mortality, we see that the social determinants, allied to the ineffectiveness of public policies, aggravate the situation. "The dignity of dying addresses some always more intricate social dynamics and reveals an inalienable technological root". Who dies? This is a reflection about the world we live in, which can produce death even where it could be avoidable.

III. Legal System and Health System: A Complex Relationship

A. *The Legal and Health Systems: A Complex Relationship*

Il pensiero attorno alla salute, sia esso un pensiero rivolto alla concettualizzazione del tema oppure ad una riflessione attorno a quale idea di salute si condivida, non può quindi essere posto come pensiero statico e a-storico, ma deve essere legato a realtà fisiche, ambientali, culturali, sociali in continua trasformazione: soggetti vivono immersi in situazioni che influenzano direttamente gli stati psicofisici, e i comportamenti sono il risultato complesso della espressivitá che scaturisce da una somma di più variabili: valori, modelli culturali, motivazioni. (Tullia Saccheri)[8]

Saccheri carries on stating that health, more than a state, is an ability to deal with, because the possibility of having health is based on adaptability, equilibrium in constant correlation with the knowledge of one's own body.

The relationship between life and death and how one lives and dies, has been the subject of many discussions, but still lacks an adequate response. Neither the legal system nor the health system is capable of an acceptable response; both prove powerless against many implications. In Brazil, as well as in many other countries, the right to a dignified death is far from

---

[7] Stefano Rodotà, *La vita e le regole – Tra diritto e non diritto* (Milano, 2006): "La dignità del morire rimanda così a dinamiche sociali sempre più intricate, e rivela una ormai ineliminabile radice tecnologica" (p. 249); "Chi muore? Questa è una domanda che impone una riflessione sul mondo e sul modo in cui viviamo, che può produrre morte anche là dove sarebbe evitabile" (p. 266).

[8] Tullia Saccheri, Giuseppe Masullo, and Emiliana Mangone, *Sociologia della Salute. Fondamenti e Prospettive* (Mercato San Severino, 2008), p. 33.

being effected, but it is on the agenda of various disciplines. What was initially considered to be a medical, religious or deontological concern, is now being studied by other areas, getting legal and health systems a good portion of this concern, as the systems are the ones that should come up with the answers: even though they may seem inappropriate, they must respond. Often we observe health professionals[9] questioning what they should do with a terminal patient without any chance of survival. Not only patients but the family too asks for healthcare professionals *to terminate life*. These professionals in turn do not know what is more worthy, but only consider the punishments they may face for doing so. In other words: the operators of the health system may conclude that it would be better *to turn off life-sustaining equipments*, but fear the reaction of the legal system.

In October 2009—at the School of Public Health of Rio Grande do Sul, we held a meeting with relatives of patients who remained hospitalized for a long time and wanted to end their life. We observed that many relatives made the decision and did it illegally, in respect for the dignity of their beloved one. The meeting was not intended to focus on this topic, it was just a discussion during one of the courses of specialization of the School, but as it took a bigger proportion than expected, some people—autonomously, i.e. without official authorization—gathered to talk of dilemmas they faced for their actions. In this specific case they were all people with high educational and financial level, and are either currently or were at the time of the disease attending therapy or psychoanalysis. We will highlight four testimonials that synthesize the others:

Testimonial 1

> Ever since my father got ill I attend psychoanalysis, I can't think of the final moments and in the constant requests for us to let him die with dignity. He was a doctor and have always said that we should shut down the equipment if we ever faced that situation. Often I felt like doing it ... in fact I don't recall what happened anymore. All my family used to say that I should do it because he had begged for me to take the decision, because he knew that my

---

[9] We use the expression "health professionals" because we live in a time when medical hegemony loses its place, to share space with other professionals. In the case of the right to a dignified death, it is extremely important the performance of the transdisciplinary team, where even the operators of law are professionals who must be part of the team.

mother wouldn't get to do it and my brother could not afford to jeopardize his career for he is from the health system too.

Testimonial 2

Strange things happened ... I turned the devices off and they got on again. The health team began to watch me, and then one day I arrived and everything was resolved, but I did not do it! Today I treat myself and am very afraid of death.

Testimonial 3

I just feel like crying, but it is not sadness is joy, because I followed my relative till the end and I was responsible for the beautiful death he had. The health team realized it and supported me even though in a very discreet way for they were afraid of the consequences. Today I feel tranquil.

Testimonial 4

What a confusion, we didn't find support from anyone to accomplish what my mother wanted, consulted with priests, lawyers, psychologists and everyone said what we didn't want to hear, but in the end we decided. Today we all have the peace of mind of having done the best, we couldn't stand anymore, those were 4 years of despair, after that my family just got even more united.[10]

As it can be noted the difficulties to deal with this situation go beyond the structures given. It was exactly for this reason that the right was far from the theme, because it was not considered as a theme, but as a matter of medical ethics, currently law is also studying this question. We have several problems in this field, starting with the formation, not always appropriate of the operators, of law on the subject, because little is discussed; law in its traditional role has to respond.

According to Chieffi:

il diritto non può non intervenire quando é possibile che nelle scelte (bio) etiche individuali siano coinvolti interessi dei terzi e tanto più l'intervento dovrà essere irrinunciabile quanto più grandi possono essere immaginabili le lesioni a terzi.[11]

---

[10] Testimonials from the Meeting of discussion about psychoanalysis, held at the Public School of Public Health of Rio Grande do Sul, 2010.

[11] See Paolo Becchi, "Bioetica e implicazioni giuridiche. Una mappa dei problemi", in Lorenzo Chieffi and Pasquale Giustiniani (eds.), *Percorsi tra bioetica e diritto. Alla ricerca di un bilanciamento* (Torino, 2010), p. 36.

Thus we can observe that the law[12] cannot be apart and away from this subject, especially with the major transformations in science and in particular when the human body becomes, in many situations, a commercial object. The legal system, particularly in situations of illegality, must give an answer, because the right to live of a wealthy citizen cannot mean the avoidable death of another citizen. This has been the situation in Brazil for a long time, but it has become much more apparent towards the end of the 1990s. In Rio Grande do Sul one case drew major media attention, after a patient found internet advertisements for the sale of organs (case can be seen on the Internet[13]), where the donor states: "I offered my kidney because I saw that there are other ads on the Internet. I'm in need of money. With this, I arrange my life."

This situation brings out some major humanitarian questions. In this and similar situations the magistrates must sift through previous case law, agreements and treaties to find an answer. On the other hand, these responses always present disputes from religious groups, scholars of bioethics, human rights defendants, amongst others. One can identify this through the observations of Mauro Fusco:[14]

> [...] se da un lato l'intervento giurisprudenziale si è rivelato in molte occasione un provvido rimedio all'inerzia del legislatore, non occorre certamente la preparazione del giurista per rendersi conto che tal funzione, *latu* – ma non troppo – *sensu* "creatrice di diritto", sia chiaramente estranea alle funzioni che nell'ordinamento italiano sono attribuite al giudice, che dovrebbe limitarsi ad interpretare l'ordinamento normativo vigente ed applicarlo al caso di specie. Ma quando la norma non esiste? ...lo sforzo del giudice di sopperire alle lacune ordinamentali con l'applicazione di principi costituzionali o giurisprudenziali in assenza di un riferimento legislativo, anche solo 'di principio', ha preso le vie più disparate a seconda delle convinzioni etiche del singolo magistrato.

The limitations and possibilities of magistrates have been discussed in recent years. People talk about a "Government of the Judges", but we don't

---

[12] "The great challenge of the 21st century will be that of developing a bioethics and as biolaw to fix exaggerations caused by scientific researches and the imbalance of the environment, rescuing and enhancing human dignity, considering him as a new biomedical humanist paradigm, giving him a truly alternative vision which can enrich the multicultural dialogue among peoples." Maria Helena Diniz, *O Estado Atual do Biodireito* (7 ed., São Paulo, 2010), p. 894.

[13] See http://itacarenews.blogspot.com/2009/09/comercio-criminoso-venda-de-orgaos.html.

[14] Mauro Fusco, "La bioetica italiana tra l'incudine della politica ed il martello della magistratura", in *Percorsi tra bioetica e diritto, supra* note 11, p. 43.

agree with this statement, we prefer to see the judges as actors who can contribute to the process of social transformation, even though it is clear that this is not always the case.[15]

At the moment we see a major breakthrough in the relationship between the health system and the legal system, where the most diverse groups manage to discuss and agree on the routing of demands that arrive in the judiciary. Moreover, both sides acknowledge the future implications of each decision taken. But on matters concerning the right to die with dignity the courts are still far from the real needs of the citizens. It is not difficult to understand the reasons, for they vary from religious issues, ethical ones and even issues of lack of information.

B. *Dying with Dignity*

Discussing the right to die with dignity involves a series of preliminary concepts. This implies stipulating criteria, which will lead us to justify a definition over another, so we take into account the comments of Caprio:

> Al físico non interessa sapere cos'è la lunghezza, come al medico non importa sapere cos'è la vita o cos'è la morte. Entrambi legittimano le loro definizioni attraverso i criteri, i modi, le procedure. Il concetto di Morte s'identifica nella definizione di morte cerebrale, ed è sinonimo delle operazioni cliniche che la verificano; allo stesso modo quello di vita è sinonimo delle misurabili reazioni chimiche corrispondenti e quello di persona nella verificabile organizzazione dell'embrione.[16]

Not to mention that we are facing one of the issues that leads us to profound reflections, because life and death are two poles of the same "line". This subject, perhaps one of the most sensitive for Bioethics, faces issues that generate endless discussions about the human right to have one's own life (in case an unbearable life), especially when man expresses, while still lucid, the desire to die, avoiding suffering and causing suffering, the so-called "living will". There are situations, however, when the patient has

---

[15] "Here is the leading case for judges: operational reasons and doctrinal opinions lay in charge of them very complex tasks and a wide quota of creative capacity, of constitutive interpretation. It should materialize, trying to make effective, become operative, the substantial promises of democratic order. Promises that, at the same time, constitute the control and the limit of its hermeneutical development". Carlos María Cárcova, *Direito, política e magistratura*, transl. by Rogério Viola Coelho and Marcelo Ludwig, (São Paulo, 1996), p. 178.
[16] Lorenzo de Caprio, "Sotto una luce scialba corre, danza, si torce senza ragione la Vita, chiassosa e impudente", in *Percorsi tra bioetica e diritto, supra* note 11, p. 104.

a terminal illness, fully awake, in pain, and therefore asks to terminate his/ her own "life".

Hospitals are full of situations that bring about a big question mark on the subject: what to do when the maintenance of vital signs just becomes the unbearable prolongation of the dying process? Life extends in an inhumane way, because beyond confrontation of the person against all the apparatus and tubes into every orifice of his body, there is suffering without hope for the family. That is exactly what we observed in the meetings with relatives of terminal patients, where families claim the right of their relative to have the right to die with dignity. As the poet Carlos Drummond de Andrade[17] says: "Pain is inevitable, suffering is optional". The pain is even greater when we know the patient's wish not to feel pain, and to have his final moments with dignity.

We still have to consider the issue of modern technology that increasingly allows an extension of the body and palliative care, with ever more refined drugs that can extend the long suffering of the terminally ill.

Thus, we witness a paradox, because these advances, used to save lives, can compromise the quality of life that they are intended to keep. So, Resta is right in saying that the same technique that saves is the technique that kills, it is the ambivalence of the *phármakon*, which is at the same time remedy and poison. In this context emerges the task of law:

> Compito del diritto non è quello di stabilire ambivalenti interdizioni: si sa che si interdice quello che si prescrive e si prescrive quello che si interdice. È al contrario quello di non escludere, regolando; ad esempio, non penalizzare l'eutanasia significa garantire che la volontà del soggetto sia quella, ma non significa anche che non sarebbe consentito darsi fuoco nella pubblica piazza in nome del diritto a morire.[18]

Considering the timely comments of Resta, we note that the subject deserves reflecting upon some basic concepts like orthothanasia and euthanasia, that is, when one faces every one of these situations. Knowing that the definition of any concept is not unanimous, but finds many differences in academic literature.

According to André Stefan,[19] there are two forms of euthanasia, the active one, which is divided into direct and indirect, and passive euthanasia (so-called orthothanasia). Thus, there is direct active euthanasia in the

---

[17] Carlos Drumond de Andrade, *Definitivo*, available at http://pensador.uol.com.br/ autor/Carlos_Drummond_de_Andrade/biografia/ (last accessed on 22 October 2010).

[18] Resta, *Diritto vivente, supra* note 4, p. 79.

[19] André Stefan, *Direito Penal* (São Paulo, 2010), vol. 2.

case, for example, of the introduction of a lethal injection in a person in a state of irreversible coma, or when the patient was "disillusioned" by doctors, for not finding enough curative care; on the other hand, the author asserts that in the case of indirect active euthanasia, also called palliative euthanasia, death is not desired, but predictable, because the patient is administered drugs that relieve pain but do not shorten life considerably; and finally, passive euthanasia or orthothanasia, which occurs with the "interruption of medical treatment", such as turning off life-sustaining equipments of a terminally ill patient.

From the analysis of these concepts emerges a slight difference between euthanasia and orthothanasia, since the former implies a medical action, while the latter implies inertia in the face of a disease without chances of being cured.

The episode occurred in Italy in 2009 well illustrates the present issue.[20] It is the case of Eluana Englaro, a young girl who suffered a serious car accident at the age of 21 and was maintained alive with the aid of equipments for 17 years. Her father applied to the Italian courts in order to gradually discontinue nutrition and hydration which would culminate in her death, because Eluana would have expressed the willingness to die in case of a coma or vegetative state.

The Court of Appeal of Milan denied the request on the grounds that it was murder. However in July 2008—taking also into account the will of Eluana to die, had she found herself in such a situation—a new trial allowed the suspension of artificial nutrition and hydration on the grounds that a person may refuse medical treatment as long as he/she does not endanger public health.

The decision highlighted the issue of "informed consent" with the possibility of the patient to reject the treatment and let the illness run its natural course, as well as the expression of will whilst in full mental capacity, which brings us to a range of questions about whether or not to suspend, as in this case, the nutrition and hydration and not the drugs and the treatment itself.

Looking at the matter from another perspective, in cases like the one of the Italian Eluana there is no life, much less dignity, in the prolongation of a vegetative body, because the artificial prolongation of life through medical devices and medicines is a solution only in the ethical field. However, we are far from an agreed solution, since there is a conflict of fundamental

---

[20] See *Percorsi tra bioetica e diritto, supra* note 11.

rights, namely: on one side the right to life, in its broadest sense, and on the other side the right to human dignity. But how can speak of dignity in a body kept alive by equipments and medicine?[21]

In criminal law euthanasia is compared to murder. Professor Lia Felberg[22] states that Uruguay has been perhaps the first country to legislate on the possibility of euthanasia being performed worldwide. Under Uruguayan law, the judge is granted exemption from punishment to those who carried out this type of procedure, provided that the *subject has honorable antecedents and death has been carried out by pious reason after repeated pleas from the victim.*[23]

Lia Felberg affirms that Colombia, in 1997, authorized euthanasia in cases of terminally ill and with the previous consent of the patient. However, the practice is considered as privileged manslaughter in most Latin American countries.

Under Brazilian law, the state treats life as an unavailable good, for this reason the Brazilian criminal law considers euthanasia a typical criminal fact, culpable and anti-juridical, characterizing it as a pious murder under Article 121, paragraph 1, of the Penal Code, which reads:

> Article 121. Killing somebody
> Penalty - imprisonment from 6 (six) to 20 (twenty) years.

The interest in preserving human life derives from the defense of human dignity, in two ways, both material and moral. In this sense Nelson Hungria:[24]

> [...] The human person, under the double point of view material and moral, is one of the most relevant objects of penal protection. The State does not protect it only by deference to the individual, but mainly by the requirement of undeniable public interest or regarding the basic conditions of life in society.

Pious murder, that is the one practiced by relevant moral or social value, is still considered "killing somebody" by our criminal justice system, which provides for a mitigation of sentence to the agent. It means that the doctor who practices active euthanasia can be punished for the crime of murder with a decrease of one-sixth to one third of the penalty.

---

[21] Ibid.
[22] Lia Felberg, *A Ortotanásia no projeto do Código Penal,* available at http://www.mackenzie.br (last accessed on 5 October 2010).
[23] Resta, *Diritto vivente, supra* note 4.
[24] Nelson Hungria, *Comentários ao Código Penal de 1942* (Rio de Janeiro, 1942) p. 23.

In addition to the concepts mentioned before, this discussion brings up the question, also stormy, of the concept of death, when there is irreversible vegetative life or any inhuman situation artificially prolonged. The Brazilian doctor, surgeon and oncologist, Ademar Lopes said:

> It is extremely difficult to determine the onset of irreversible end. Often it is appropriate to use experimental procedures when conventional ones fail.[25]

Still, Zuben says that

> the very acceptance of the concept of brain death, defined as the loss of the integrative function of the organism as a whole by the central nervous system, has not prevented that many doubts were raised about the legitimacy of this diagnosis.[26]

Besides all the complexities and paradoxes that this issue raises, we also have to deal with complex situations, where the death diagnosis is preliminary to any decision about shortening life or not, since this concept goes beyond the limits of medicine itself, as stated by Zuben:

> The concept of death was until recently a medical concept. Today it is required to be contextualized, transporting the whole issue that concerns the conditions of life and death to the whole society.[27]

C. *The Socio-Legal Debate in Brazil*

> [...] *Da strumento di difesa il diritto si trasformava in mezzo d'aggressione. Lacerato il velo protettivo della astratta soggettività giuridica, tutti, e non solo le vittime, si ritrovano nudi nella loro condizione esistenziale, ed è su questa nuda vita che va sempre misurato il ricorso al diritto. (Stefano Rodotà)*[28]

As it was briefly mentioned before, Brazil is a country of profound contradictions and the debate is quite confusing. Criminalization of the issue raises some odd discussions. At this point we will take a look at the diverse ways that the issue is currently being approached. We realized that both law enforcement and the political system are making efforts to address the new emerging demands. Nowadays all topics relative to the issue can be discussed freely, including its *illegality*.

---

[25] Veja Revista, *Ética na vida e na morte*, ed. 2126 of 28 April 2010, p. 103.
[26] Newton Aquiles Von Zuben, *Questões de Bioética: Morte e Direito de Morrer*, "Diálogos" mesa redonda pela UNISO – PUCSP, Sorocaba, June 1998.
[27] Ibid.
[28] Rodotà, *La vita e le regole, supra* note 7, p. 19.

Either passive or active euthanasia is viewed as simple homicide by article 121 of the Brazilian Penal Code, Decree-Law 2.849/1940, with a penalty of 6 (six) to 20 (twenty) years imprisonment, however, that legislation does not even mention the word euthanasia or orthothanasia. Although sentence might be reduced, in both cases, based on the first paragraph of that article, from one sixth to one third, if the judge finds out that murder was committed due to relevant social value (compassion due to suffering of patient) or moral. These cases are what the law refers to as pious or compassionate homicide. However it will be treated as a reduction to manslaughter, that is, it is decreased the penalty of the agent whom, theoretically wanted death as a result of his act. Let's see:

> Art. 121. Killing somebody
> Penalty – imprisonment from 6 (six) to 20 (twenty) years.
> Paragraph 1 – If the agent commits the crime impelled by reason of relevant social value [...] the judge can reduce his penalty from one sixth to one third.[29]

It is, however, an attenuation of the murder, i.e., decreases the penalty of the agent that wanted the victim's death. Thus, the pious murder occurs when the agent commits murder by relevant moral reasons (compassion for the suffering of the patient).

It is observed that there are specific and objective predictions applying in the case of euthanasia, the penalty of privileged manslaughter. However, it is important to mention that depending on the circumstances the crime can be typified as participation in suicide, with a penalty of 2 (two) to 6 (six) years of imprisonment, as disposed in article 122 of the Brazilian Penal Code.

The ruling of the Trial Court of Minas Gerais highlighted the closing, by our legal system, of that framework as euthanasia, arguing that if the agent caused the death by pious killing, it will be considered to be a murder, as it can be seen here:

> The condition of being the accused the victim's wife is not a logical reason of aggravation, when it comes to euthanasia. There is no one closer to the suffering person than the spouse. If euthanasia, although prohibited by law, does not sound as criminal as the true homicide, the fact of having been

---

[29] Antonio Luiz de Toledo Pinto, Márcia Cristina Vaz dos Santos Windt, and Lívia Céspedes (Orgs), *Código penal, Código de processo penal, Constituição Federal* (3 ed., São Paulo, 2007).

committed against a spouse cannot logically be an aggravating factor. The crime of pity is so less serious as more connected is the accused to the victim. Euthanasia is a crime motivated by feelings of compassion and such feeling is so much more pure, the closer to the agent the person who is suffering. (Criminal Appeal n° 19.701/2 – 1st Criminal Chamber – Judge Rapporteur Gudesteu Biber – Judgment 22.3.1994).[30]

The introduction of the institution of euthanasia into the legal system has been a topic of discussion in Brazil for the past 20 years (usually the indirect one, also called orthothanasia). In 1983, however, Deputy Inocencio Oliveira presented the Project of Law No. 732/1983 also addressing direct euthanasia. The bill provided the possibility for a doctor to pull the plug of terminally ill patient off or to cease administering medication aimed to prolong vegetative life, considering that this was in agreement with the family.[31]

Deputy Gilvan Borges (PMDB Amapá) also presented bills dealing with laws attempting to legalize euthanasia. In 1991, Project of Law No. 1989/1991 stated that euthanasia would be allowed in cases of terminal patients with no chance of recovering neurocerebral functions, thus configuring clinical death. The application of the procedure could be done either by the spouse or partner, natural and adoptive sons, ascendants or the patients themselves. The bill also stated that a patient who had been given less than six months of life by two or more doctors could request the administration of drugs to shorten his life.[32]

In 1993, the Legislative Decree No. 244/1993, also authored by Deputy Gilvan Borges, called for a referendum qualifying those who could vote to decide on the merits or otherwise for the institution of euthanasia in the case of terminal patients.[33]

Project of Law No. 125/96 by Senator Gilvan Borges was prepared in 1995, and has been in Congress since 1996, yet it has never been put to a vote. This project proposes to legalize euthanasia, establishing criteria so as to require the materialization of the procedure, the authorization given

---

[30] Brasil, Tribunal de Justiça do Estado de Minas Gerais, Apelação criminal no. 19.701/2, 1994. available at http://www.tjmg.jus.br/ (last accessed on 30 October 2010).

[31] Gabriel Gualano Godoy and Rebeca Fernandes Dias, "Os paradoxos do direito de morrer e de viver", in *Anais do CONPEDI – Conselho Nacional de Pesquisa e Pos-graduação em Direito de 2006* (Manaus, 2006), pp. 1–19. Available at http://www.conpedi.org.br/manaus/arquivos/anais/manaus/teoria_do_direito_gabriel_gdoy_e_rebeca_dias.pdf (last accessed on 17 November 2010).

[32] Ibid.

[33] Ibid.

by a board of five (5) physicians, 2 (two) of them experts on the problem of the applicant. It also foresees the possibility of a relative or friend applying to court, if the patient is unable to express himself. In an attempt to finally legalize euthanasia, the Deputy tried to establish in this Project criteria for completion, as well as previous procedures and execution manner.[34]

It is pertinent to mention that it went through the Congress an anti project of Bill of the Brazilian Penal Code,[35] which regulated euthanasia and orthothanasia, in paragraphs 3 and 4, respectively, of art. 121, as follows:

> Paragraph 3. If the perpetrator acted out as of compassion or mercy, by request of the victim, attributable, in order to abbreviate his or her unbearable physical suffering due to serious illness. Penalty: imprisonment from three to six years.
> Paragraph 4. It is not a crime to fail to keep someone's life by artificial means, if previously certified by two doctors death as imminent and inevitable, as long as there is consent from the patient, or in his/her impossibility, the ascendant, descendant, spouse, partner or brother.

The referred project has gone through some changes in the commissions that analyzed the issue of euthanasia, however, in essence, it still aims to regulate euthanasia and orthothanasia respectively in paragraphs 3 and 4 of article 121. It can be observed that euthanasia is still treated as being a commissive crime (murder of compassion), but with comparatively lower sentence than crimes against life. The treatment provided the Penal Code currently in force, i.e., manslaughter against life, is maintained, but with a specially reduced sentence, which means that the reduced penalty is not on the one who judges the case.

Moreover, the draft bill devotes an entire paragraph exclusively to orthothanasia excluding the wrongfulness of the agent's conduct. In other words there is no crime in failing to maintain the patient's life, provided that the requirements of diagnosis are fulfilled and prior consent is maintained. Therefore, indirect euthanasia, also called orthothanasia would be legalized with the approval of the reform of the Penal Code.

---

[34] Ibid.
[35] Brasil, Congresso Nacional. *Anteprojeto de lei do Código Penal*, available at http://www.senado.gov.br/ (last accessed on 19 October 2010.

However, it is noteworthy that our country has a minority doctrine which supports the right to die with dignity. In this sense the criminal law scholar Andre Stefan[36] sustains that indirect active euthanasia (for which he gives the example of lethal injection) may be treated under the light of the state of necessity under Article 24 of the Penal Code.

In this case, we'll be facing a lawful conduct. Stefan asserts:

> It is taken care of the ponderation of goods (or jury duty), for it comes into conflict the maintenance of life and human dignity, assuming there is a slight anticipation of death in order to provide relief or comfort to the hopeless patient.

Therefore, facing this position, a physician who perpetrates the will of a patient—who has an advanced state of Kaposi's Sarcoma, a common cancer amongst AIDS patients, and whose body is covered by ulcers that do not heal and there is no medication to decrease the pain—could act in state of necessity and we would be facing a totally lawful conduct.

Claus Roxin[37] states, in a broad sense, the possibility of lawful euthanasia:

> the aid provided to a critically ill person, by his/her will or at least on behalf of his/her presumed will, to allow him/her a humanely dignified death in correspondence with their own convictions.

One cannot fail to mention, a more recent attempt by Senator Gerson Camata to try to introduce the legalization of orthothanasia in Brazilian law, through Senate Bill No. 116, of April 25, 2000. This Project of Law excludes the wrongfulness of orthothanasia introducing a significant amendment to Article 136 of the current Penal Code, which would be worded as follows:

> Art. 136-A. It is not a crime, under the palliative care applied to terminally ill patients, failing to make use of disproportionate and extraordinary means, in a situation of imminent and inevitable death, provided that there is consent from the patient or, in his/her impossibility, the spouse, ascendant, descendant or brother/sister.
> § 1° The situation of imminent and inevitable death must first be attested by 2 (two) physicians.

---

[36] Stefan, *supra* note 19.
[37] "Tratamento Jurídico-penal de la eutanásia", *El Criminalista Digital. Revista Eletrônica de Ciência Penal y Criminologia* (1999); Edgardo Alberto Donna, *Derecho Penal: parte especial* (2 ed., Buenos Aires, 2003), t. I.

§ 2° The exclusion of unlawfulness provided under this article shall not apply in case of omission in the use of ordinary and proportionate means of treatment due to a terminal patient.[38]

Like many previous dispositions having established requisites to authorize orthothanasia, the Project mentioned before also requires a certificate of two physicians and the consent of the patient or close relatives. However, it requires that the means to sustain life are "disproportionate and extraordinary", expressions that require precise and technical interpretation, since one faces an irreversible procedure. Still, in the second paragraph, there is the need for an accurate evaluation of the term "ordinary and proportionate means of treatment" because they are very technical requirements for non-application of the exclusion of unlawfulness announced in the chapeau of the Article.

As is the case in any argument, it is vital to acknowledge the opposite argument. In 2005 Deputy Osmânio Pereira presented the Project of Law No. 5058, that regulates paragraph 7 of Article 226 of the Constitution of 1988 *"providing for the inviolability of the right to life, defining euthanasia and abortion as hideous crimes in any case."*

Therefore, contrary to recent attempts to alleviate the pain of terminally ill patients, we still find statements similar to the one above for the illegitimacy of euthanasia, in the clear attempt to preserve the constitutional right to life, as a total and absolute unavailable good.

It is also convenient to take a closer look at the so-called "living will" issue that occurs when an individual expresses what he/she wants to be done with his/her health in the event of finding himself/herself in danger of life and unable to express his/her will.

From this theory arises a multitude of questions, such as: are there any limits to the moral and ethical duty to maintain life at any cost? What about the fundamental right to life versus the fundamental right to human dignity? Can doctors be so sure to enforce categorically incurable?

In this sense we can say that the Brazilian legislature took a step forward compared to the criminal provision, as the status of the elderly in its Article 17 reads as follows:

> Art. 17. An elderly person who is in command of his mental faculties is entitled to opt for the health care that is reputed by him to be more favorable.

---

[38] Brasil, Senado, *Projeto de Lei do Senado n° 116* of 25 April 2000, by Senador Gerson Camata, available at http://www.senado.gov.br/atividade/materia/detalhes.asp?p_cod _mate=43807 (last accessed on 17 November 2010).

Unique paragraph. Not being the elder in a position to make an option, this will be done:

I – By the curator, when the elderly person has been interdicted;

II – By family members, when the elderly has no curator or if this one cannot be reached in time;

III – By the physician, when there is imminent risk to life and there is no time to contact the curator or family;

IV – By the physician himself, whenever there is no curator or known relative, in this case the Public Attorney must be informed.[39]

So, according to this Brazilian legal procedure, is it possible to conclude in favor of the possibility to practice orthothanasia to the elderly?

The Code of Medical Ethics, in Article 41, prohibits the doctor to "shorten a patient's life even under the request of him/her or his/her legal representative." However, this discussion has become a bit stormy for these professionals, because the Federal Council of Medicine (CFM) has approved Resolution 1805/06 authorizing the practice of orthothanasia with permission of the patient's family.

According to Eduardo Luiz Santos Cabette[40] the referred Resolution meant "an important step for the increment of the discussion of such a relevant problem, occasioning some legitimate pressure in order to push Brazilian society to take a position inclusively and specially in the legal sphere, so lacking of a safe approach over this matter."

Though it is necessary to take into account that we are facing a rule of administrative nature towards a professional category, in this case the physicians, this solution is acceptable on an ethical level, but has no force against the criminal deplorableness of orthothanasia. However, although the resolution cannot solve by itself the issue of legalization of orthothanasia, there is a new flame to heat up the discussion in Brazil.

In practice the solution was not as simple as it sounds, since that resolution is not law, and the physician in an extremely difficult position, in cases where orthothanasia could be a less painful solution for the patient and his family, the physician might face legal problems and might have to answer to a charge of privileged (pious) murder, under the Brazilian Penal Code.

---

[39] *Código penal, Código de processo penal, Constituição Federal, supra* note 29.

[40] Eduardo Luiz Santos Cabette, *Eutanásia e ortotanásia: comentários à Resolução 1.805/06 CFM. Aspectos éticos e jurídicos* (Curitiba, 2009), p. 14.

Despite the conflict of legal rules under Brazilian law, Cabette[41] defends the need for a balance whilst searching a solution to this relevant discussion:

> The balance, the mean term resides in fighting for life anytime there is 'how' and 'why' to fight for it and in accepting death, bolstering the dying humanely when the end imposes itself inexorably and any effort to deflect it involves merely an imposition of unnecessary suffering. The option can never be too kill nor cause senseless suffering.

After the publication of this resolution in the Official Gazette of CFM on November 28, 2006, Section I, pg. 169, the Federal Public Attorney filed in Administrative Procedure No. 01/2006 1.16.000.002480/2006-21 with recommendation number 01/2006 for immediate withdrawal. In defending the constitutional right to life, the representative of the Federal Public Attorney Wellington Divino Marques De Oliveira cited Asúa's questions:

> 1) Is pain so intolerable that it is necessary to shut it up with death and so appalling the agony that imposes its acceleration? 2) Can anyone decide in such an irrevocable way the incurability of a patient? and 3) Does the criterion of uselessness allow termination? Answers: 1) We cannot rely on pain as the decisive influence to determine euthanasia. Modern medicine is not demarcated before the most acute pains. The risk due to the bearing or not of the patients is great. 2) Incurability concept is one of the most doubtful. Prolonging life is living it. For these situations, when death is not immediate, euthanasia should not be practiced, even though the disease continues to destroy the body and ultimately ends with existence. 3) Motivating termination by the uselessness is the extreme of moral insensitivity. It is necessary to organize in life an ethical conception in which positivism and idealism find themselves in agreement. Orthothanasia is nothing but a murderous stratagem.

The Public Attorney therefore considers all questions surrounding the issue and does not allow at a peaceful solution to the issue of euthanasia and orthothanasia. And with such arguments he recommends to the Federal Medical Council to "immediately repeal the Resolution on the termination of life".[42]

The procedures mentioned above led to a public civil action in which the referred Federal Attorney sustained that this decision is impractical to be left exclusively in the hands of the physician, and rules:

---

[41] Ibid.

[42] Brasil, Resolution of MPF n° 01/2006. Available at http://www.pgr.mpf.gov.br/ (last accessed on 25 October 2010).

[...] only a multidisciplinary team (psychologists, psychiatrists, social assistants, etc.) would have full conditions to evaluate a possibility to bring to an end the life of terminally ill patients, everything, ALWAYS, with the effective participation of the Constitutionally legitimate organs to ensure effectively for the rights and individual guarantees, the judiciary and Public Attorneys.[43]

That is, before such an approach further criteria should be created for authorization of orthothanasia, surrounding the physician's decision with much more care, involving professionals that can provide a broader picture of the situation in order to take a final decision.

The public civil suit also claims that "In the case of a terminally ill, *aware*, without a multidisciplinary team to support the patient, it is impossible to properly self-determine according to his will—the resolution of the CFM (Federal Council of Medicine) speaks only of patient consent and physician's diagnosis. *Impossible*, because patients in this state fit in the general concept of hiposufficiency, or better, the *absolute incapacity*, even if temporary, to self-determine in any business, especially if you dispose of life. *Indispensable* the presence and prior hearsay of the Public Attorney and consent of the competent Judge."

Therefore the Prosecutor argued the need for more detailed criteria for the authorization of orthothanasia along the lines proposed by the resolution of the Federal Council of Medicine and at the end questions whether Brazil is prepared for the legalization of such institution.

Thus, it is to analyze the conflict of fundamental rights (life X dignity) and taking into consideration all the ethical and moral debate surrounding the legalization of orthothanasia and even euthanasia. However, the arguments presented against the recent Resolution of the CFM which demand wider criteria (multidisciplinary) for the final decision of aborting the suffering and terminating life, must be undoubtedly considered.

IV. FINAL CONSIDERATIONS

[...] *o conhecimento desvenda mistérios, mostrando que nada é, no fundo, misterioso* [...] (*Pedro Demo*)[44]

The issue of dignified death, not prolonging life at any cost, is a subject of endless discussions, complexities and paradoxes. It deserves not to

---

[43] Brasil, Ministério Público Federal, *Procedimento Administrativo de n° 1.16.000.002480/2006-21*. Available at http://www.pgr.mpf.gov.br/ (last accessed on 25 October 2010).

[44] Pedro Demo, *Metodologia do conhecimento científico* (São Paulo, 2000), p. 88.

trivialize one of the most precious belongings of human beings: life. Therefore, the need to unveil mysteries in order to conclude that *deep inside nothing is mysterious.*

However, the prolongation of life at any cost should receive special attention, because although we are facing the conflict of two fundamental rights (life vs. dignity), there is a preponderance of the right before dignity, because practically no one is standing before "life". By this principle the doctor must feel totally safe for the completion of orthothanasia or euthanasia, stopping treatment that no longer guarantees the dignity of his patient. Saying that the doctor must feel safe means that he will not be held liable for having relieved the pain of a patient. That is, he will act in the best interest of the patient and be supported by a law that guarantees the legality and legitimacy of the act committed.

On the one hand we question how to balance the protection of life by the State as opposed to the unbearable sufferings of the citizen. On the other hand, we ask if man can dispose of life, in case of an irreversible diagnosis with 100% certainty. Is it possible that we are using technology to transform this suffering into something more dramatic and even lasting longer? And what about ethical and religious questions that have not allowed this discussion to end? Should a person have the right to conduct his life and his personality as his own conscience and choose to die rather than suffer with no chance of being cured?

Perhaps the solutions to all these questions are far from being pacific. However, we are facing an old subject whose discussion is on the "agenda" in various parts of the world as well as in the domestic system. Every time we discuss of an individual right to euthanasia in some part of the world, it comes to discussion the diverse positions about this issue, as it happened recently with the death of the Italian Eluana Englaro.

The suffering of a terminally ill person or in a vegetative state is a time of enormous physical and emotional stress for all involved that can make the decision to take or not to keep the patient's life. But this emotional vulnerability of those involved cannot mean unworthy life at any cost!

As it was well observed by the Federal Public Prosecution in the ADIN, in its above-mentioned Recommendation 01/2006 concerning orthothanasia, the path is perhaps the establishment of deeper and wider criteria for the legal permission of euthanasia. These criteria must supply a *safe* sensation for the patient, as well as for the health professional and society, among which we can mention transdisciplinary analysis of the situation, analyzing the concrete problem by other professionals such as psychologists, psychiatrists and social workers, among others.

Thus we would have not only medical structure but also social and emotional situation, so society would have more confidence that the pious death occurs only after a broad and deep analysis of the whole context.

Thus it is concluded that the dignified death and the permission of euthanasia is a reality, because there is no reason to prolong the suffering of a person who actually has no "life" and therefore one does not really protect "life". Legislation should provide a possibility of choice but to establish the most diverse criteria for its legal authorization. So the problem does not remain in an individual plan, it is resolved by all of the specialists, not only clinically, which may give a response and conclude that the solution is to end suffering.

In this society, where we have access to all goods and services, in which all are universally included, we still have to think about, following the suggestions of Rodotà: Who dies? Because this question requires new-old ideas about how we live in this artificial inclusion, which can promote death (in its various meanings) but also where and how it could be avoided.

PART III

THE ONGOING DEBATE ON ADVANCE DIRECTIVES REGULATION
IN ITALY

EXPLORING SELF-DETERMINATION AND INFORMED CONSENT IN ADVANCE DIRECTIVES IN LIGHT OF THE ITALIAN LEGAL SYSTEM

*Vitulia Ivone**

I. Introduction:
"Do End-of-Life Issues Expose the Limits of Italian Law?"

Any Civil Law scholar should consider each and every sector of life in order to identify the existence of a *corpus* of fundamental individual rights pertaining to each person in our society.

End-of-life issues are an integral part of this consideration and as such must be explored in light of the Italian legal system considered as a whole.

The Living Will and its relationship with philosophical and ethical issues must lead the lawyer to put the value of human dignity at the foundation of law. On March 26, 2009 the Draft Law No. 10 titled "Provisions on therapeutic alliance, informed consent and advance treatment directives" was approved: the call for that law was the result of both a highly emotional journalistic wave as well as the result of a long period of reflections carried out at the ethical and legal levels. This situation has given strength to a renewed debate among multiple voices and multiple interests, all aimed to outline a new legal category, less assertive than the "living will" of Anglo-Saxon origin, but interested to qualify the "advance will" (i.e. the will at the time of its crystallization) or the "living will" (i.e. the instrument through which decision-making on post-mortem issues is anticipated to a vital moment) or "advance directives of treatment" (i.e. the consent that can be freely expressed and also the consent deduced from facts and determinations of the competent person).

First of all, the methodological approach of civil law requires an initial assessment: the distinction between the moment when the person is perfectly able to make his own decisions and the time when that capacity is annulled by the presence of a crippling disease. In both cases—inevitably approached with a different method—the problem is what value (absolute or relative?) is given to every individual's autonomous capacity to

---

* Associate Professor of Private Law at the Faculty of Law of the University of Salerno, Italy; email: vituliaivone@unisa.it.

S. Negri (ed.), *Self-Determination, Dignity and End-of-Life Care*
2011 Koninklijke Brill NV. Printed in The Netherlands. ISBN 978 90 04 22357 8. pp. 381–410

express his will in order to make choices regarding his future. Therefore, the different importance acknowledged to the person's capacity of self-determination affects the evaluation of the Draft Law No. 10, considering it either over-restrictive or responding to the needs expressed by the society. In order to provide a reader of the draft bill consistent with the whole legal system, this paper aims to propose two separate and parallel interpretations: the first being independent of the introduction of the legal measure in question and looking into the legal system for the "instruments of aggression" and their "antibodies"; the other exploring the scope of the draft law without making reference to the vast trail of controversy that has been accompanying this parliamentary process.[1]

To move in this direction, my paper will first provide an analysis of the concept of the Living Will, and its relationship with the Italian law and the ability of self-determination of the person, the role of consent, as provided in Italian law in relation to fundamental choices of a person and, last but not least, the impact of the capacity of supervision entrusted with the Italian Constitution when the protection of the human person and its fundamental rights are at risk.

The second part of this paper details the elements of the "Calabrò" draft bill and its incompatibility and disharmony with the Italian legal system. My contribution aims to highlight that the Italian legal system already holds adequate means, structures and precedents to treat cases when a patient's consent or refusal to medical treatments are upheld. In addition, the lack of consideration for the respect of the human dignity of a terminally-ill patient—even ignoring legal precedents—exposes the Italian legislator to the risk of being indifferent and narrow-sighted with regard to the "*diritto vivente*" ("living law").

II. AUTONOMY IN CHOICES OF HEALTH CARE TREATMENT: THE RIGHT TO SELF-DETERMINATION OF THE PERSON AS SUBJECT OF LAW

The Italian legal system lacks a rule that identifies the kind of declaration or conduct that might properly and effectively represent the expression of

---

[1] See Demetrio Neri, "Autonomia e dignità della persona alla fine della vita: chi decide?", *Bioetica* (2010), 1A, pp. 45–47, who says "The philosophy behind this law is an expression of that creeping sectarianism that unfortunately chronically afflicts our country and that from time to time, has its moments of acute worsening. It is disheartening to have to realize it but we are a country with limited sovereignty in ethically sensitive matters". The author denounces the dependence of politicians and government bodies "on the wishes of the Roman Catholic Church".

the wish to avoid medical care, once the interested person has totally lost consciousness. This determines the need to identify the boundaries of informed consent. Article 5 of the legislative decree no. 211/2003 or Article 6 of the Oviedo Convention rely on a legal representative as the one to decide in the place of the incapacitated person and in his best interest.

These provisions exist solely to ensure "therapeutic alliance" as the ideal model of a doctor-patient relationship. Therefore, the basis of informed consent as an act of exercising the constitutional right to consent to or to refuse medical treatment must be sought elsewhere.

That means especially when the choice is oriented to refuse medical treatment when the person will be no longer capable of understanding. This hypothesis must be framed in accordance with personal beliefs and interests, together with the understanding of all the information concerning the possible consequences of that act.

As correctly observed by the National Bioethics Committee,[2] the fact that a person who has been duly informed and reflected on the implications of his choice, provides a strong argument against one of the objections that are typically addressed to the acceptability of this legal instrument: reference is to the reliability of the directives due to the impossibility that the interested person, if still conscious, may change his mind.

Underlining the free and voluntary character of health care, the Code of Medical Ethics (CDM)[3] states that physicians are bound by the free and conscious will expressed by the person to receive medical care. When a

---

[2] This refers to the opinion of the National Bioethics Committee on advance treatment directives of 18 December 2003.

[3] The Code of Medical Ethics was approved by FNOM-CeO on December 16, 2006. A study of the medical ethics Codes which followed one another over time shows the progressive evolution undergone by this subject. The first Code of ethics of 1954—known as Frugoni Code and never made official—discussed the issue of consent stating that "consent may be validly given only by those who know exactly the scope and consequences of consent itself, which can occur only exceptionally in the doctor-patient relationship". It is thus established that consent may be requested only by the physician. In the Code of ethics of 1978 this topic is dealt with in articles 30 and 39: the latter rule states that the patient's consent is required when in the proposed treatment there is an inherent risk and that consent must be valid. In article 30 the problem of disease with poor prognosis is dealt with: it could be hidden from the patient, but had to be disclosed to the family. A new Code of ethics was published in 1989, first replaced in 1995 and again in 1998: in this new text it is shown that consent is now well-established in the medical culture. In particular, article 30 refers clearly and simply to the kind of information which is required for consent to treatment, stating that it must be appropriate and consistent with reality, taking into account the capacity of understanding of the patient in order to promote maximum adhesion to the proposed diagnosis and therapy.

patient refuses this care, the doctor "must desist" from acts of diagnosis or treatment. If the patient is incompetent, he is invited to "take account" of his earlier will, in the absence of a law on advance directives.

Article 13 of the CDM recognizes the autonomy of the physician in planning decisions and implementations of diagnostic and therapeutic methods, "except when the patient's will is to reject or refuse taking responsibility for himself". In the observance of the fundamental rights of the person, the Code sought to avoid any exhaustive manner of using coercion against a patient able to decide for himself. The difficult balance is highlighted between the right of the patient to be treated effectively and the right to be respected as a person in his physical and mental integrity: this right is enshrined in Article 32, paragraph 2 of the Italian Constitution as the insurmountable limit also in medical treatment that may be imposed as required by law to protect public health.[4] It is necessary to emphasize the role of doctors within the constitutional framework of the right to health care. Paragraph 2 provides that "nobody can be forced to accept a specific medical treatment unless required by law" and shows the insurmountable limit of the respect of the human person: in this way, it highlighted the issue of configurability, under Italian law, of the right to refuse health care. This issue falls within the broader context of the liberty rights granted to the individual, especially when the pathology only affects the sick person, without any involvement of other members of the community.[5]

Medical treatments referred to in Article 2 have been interpreted in legal literature as "any therapeutic or diagnostic activities, to prevent or treat diseases".[6] These activities have been divided into several categories:

---

[4] Ferrando Mantovani, "Eutanasia", *Digesto Discipline Penalistiche* (Torino, 1990), pp. 424–434, who states that "collective health cannot be conceived as a good in contrast to that of individual health". In the event of a clash between those two interests, "the collective interest of health cannot prevail over that of the individuals and therefore the imposition of the sacrifice of those goods would be in breach of the principle of protection of the human personality in its intangible rights".

[5] Massimo Luciani, "Il diritto costituzionale alla salute", *Diritto e società* (1980), pp. 769–779; Franco Modugno, "Trattamenti sanitari non obbligatori e Costituzione", *Diritto e società* (1982), pp. 303–320. In particular, in cases where the need to protect the health of the individual joins the equal need to protect the entire community, the right of the individual must be balanced with that of the community to the extent available, regarding health treatment, mandatory or coercive (paragraph 2 of article 2 of the Constitution).

[6] Diana V. Amato, "Rapporti etico-sociali", in A. Scialoja and G. Branca (eds.), *Commentario alla Costituzione*, sub Art. 32, (Bologna-Roma, 1976), pp. 176–472; Aldo M. Sandulli, "La sperimentazione clinica sull'uomo", *Diritto e società* (1978), pp. 507–518; Adele Anzon, "Trattamenti sanitari obbligatori e competenza regionale", *Giurisprudenza costituzionale* (1980), p. 1449; Pietro Perlingieri and Paola Pisacane, "Commento sub art. 32 Cost.", in P. Perlingieri (a cura di), *Commento alla Costituzione italiana* (Napoli, 2001), pp. 202–208.

compulsory treatment, coercive and non-binding. The first are those characterized by a compulsory treatment provided by law, punished and referred to actually work with the use of a variety of mechanisms (such as the inability to travel to countries where certain vaccinations are not practiced); coercive treatment imposed by force; compulsory treatments are not provided by any provision, for which there is the other problem with the role and limits of consent in relation to Article 5 c.c.[7] Determining the legitimacy of health treatment poses a problem of coordination between Article 32, para. 2 of the Constitution and Article 13 of the Constitution. Legal literature is not unanimous: according to some authors,[8] the medical treatment applies only to Article 32, para. 2; according to others,[9] bearing in mind the distinction between compulsory and coercive medical treatment, Article 13 is deemed to apply to the latter. Thus, this rule would arise as a general framework for all forms of limitation of personal freedom and, therefore, for any coercive measures affecting the freedom of the individual to decide for his own.

In the reference to the Italian Constitution there is the assurance that it is not possible to read Article 32 as a rule that expresses primarily the duty to preserve the health in the exclusive interest of the community, legitimating a power of public intervention; nor can it be thought to accentuate only during the individual moment, transforming the personal inviolability. Non-systematic readings of Constitutional rules would allow the temptation to recognize as inherent to the individual right an unlimited power that would include the lawfulness of the "dissolution" of the person. Therefore, leaving aside the problem of qualifying the consent in terms of contract or, conversely, in terms of simple act,[10] it is necessary

---

[7] On the specific issue of vaccination, see Sergio P. Panunzio, "Trattamenti sanitari obbligatori e Costituzione", *Diritto e società* (1979), pp. 890–902.

[8] Vezio Crisafulli, "In tema di emotrasfusioni obbligatorie", *Diritto e società* (1982), pp. 557–566.

[9] Alessandro Pace, *Libertà individuali e qualità della vita* (Napoli, 2008), p. 87.

[10] Pasquale Stanzione, "Rapporto giuridico", in *Enciclopedia Giuridica Treccani* (Roma, 1991), vol. XXV, pp. 1–32. The author does not share this position, judging it of little practical significance, since "even postulating the negotiation of consent, one would be forced to admit that this implies the automatic application of the regulation of agreement in the classic sense". The reference is to the contrast between two opposing doctrinal positions. According to some scholars, the person "who seeks treatment, does not allow his freedom to be violated, but rather makes use of his discretion to decide himself what concerns his body, and the doctor who treats a person does not breach his freedom, but he implements his patient's own free will": this position contends that the patient's act of consent is equivalent to a non-negotiating statement of intention (Giovanni Cattaneo, "Il consenso del paziente al trattamento medico-chirurgico", *Rivista trimestrale di diritto e procedura civile* (1957), pp. 450–471). Another theory is inclined, on the contrary, to admit the negotiating

that its analysis be connected with the issue of information. In other
words, it is necessary to analyze informed consent as the legitimacy and
foundation of health care. Without informed consent, a medical treatment may be illegal, even if it is in the interest of the patient. The practice
of free and informed consent[11] is a form of respect for individual freedom
and a means to attain the person's best interest. The principle of informed
consent expresses a choice of value in the way of understanding the relationship between doctor and patient, which appears to be based first and
foremost on the rights of patients. Consent pertains to the moral freedom
of the subject, his self-determination and his physical ability, understood
as the right to respect for the individual's bodily integrity: that said, then
the right to be cured by the doctor is being taken away but the general
"right to cure" against the will of the sick person remains. The patient cannot be considered a person in a position of awe: it is more appropriate to
recognize the doctor's right or the power to heal and also the patient's
right to choose or refuse or terminate therapy at all stages of life, even the
terminal one. It honors the personal principle enunciated in the Italian
Constitution that interprets the human person as a value in itself, prohibits any manipulation of it and notices the intervention of solidarity only
on the basis of the person and its harmonious development.[12]

---

nature of consent by reason of its being the expression of the patient's self-determination:
in fact, the patient's expression of will confers on the doctor the ability to act with regard
to a right which is in his full availability (Gilda Ferrando, "Consenso informato del paziente
e responsabilità del medico. Principii, problemi e linee di tendenza", *Rivista critica di
diritto privato* (1998), pp. 37–87.

[11] The issue of informed consent has been fully covered in literature. See, in particular
Ugo G. Nannini, *Il consenso al trattamento medico* (Milano, 1989), p. 74; Amedeo
Santosuosso, *Il consenso informato. Tra giustificazione del medico e diritto del paziente*
(Milano, 1996); Ferrando, *supra* note 10; Andrea Pinna, "Autodeterminazione e consenso:
da regola per i trattamenti sanitari a principio generale", *Contratto e impresa* (2006),
pp. 580–594; Vito Calderai, "Il problema del consenso nella bioetica", *Rivista critica di
diritto civile* (2005), pp. 325–330; Giuliano Guerra, "Consenso informato: tutela del diritto
alla salute o della libertà di scelta?", *Danno e responsabilità* (2005), pp. 868–875; Giovanni
Facci, "Il consenso informato all'atto medico: esercizio di un diritto costituzionalmente
garantito per il paziente o una 'trappola' per il sanitario?", *Responsabilità civile* (2006),
pp. 137–145; Simona Cacace, "Il consenso informato del paziente al trattamento sanitario",
Danno e responsabilità (2007), pp. 283–290; Luciano Moccia, "Il rapporto medico-paziente
tra autodeterminazione, consenso informato e direttive anticipate di trattamento", in
Nessuno deve scegliere per noi (Milano, 2007), p. 87.

[12] The function of Article 2 Constitution, considered in the totality of its systematic
articulations, is that of a general "open" clause aimed to protect the person. Through the
statement of the unique value of the human person, the rule "requires that the person is
protected in all its manifestations essential to its development, even when they have not
been made explicit through a type of regulatory legislation". In this way, "the protection of
personality can be considered unitary, undefined, unlimited, flexible and adaptable as far

III. ADVANCE TREATMENT DIRECTIVES AS A LOGICAL EXTENSION OF THE
PRINCIPLE OF INFORMED CONSENT

Advance directives can be defined as the instrument that creates the right
to "make their voices heard" when patients are in a state of incapacity
determined by the irreversibility of their state. In this sense, the directives
can be the starting point to reconstruct the will of the patient: this assertion does not diminish the scope, but allows the interested parties to recognize that the will of the patient in a permanent vegetative state could be
well reconstructed in the absence of directives. They are an important
means of exaltation of the will of the patient while not the only one to be
considered in extremely dramatic cases as those that affect people in a
permanent vegetative state.[13] It follows that no "living will" can be applied
bureaucratically and in the abstract without being lowered into the reality
of the patient: indeed, the fundamental purpose of advance directives is
to provide a means to recover "at best"[14]—in situations of incapacity to
decide—the role that is ordinarily played by informed dialogue of the
patient and the doctor: the patient, through the process of consent or dissent, must warn the doctor of any item deemed to be significant in order
to assert the rights related to health protection and more generally to the
integral good of the person. This is as if the dialogue between doctor and
patient, with the advance directives continued "ideally" even when the
patient can no longer consciously take part to it. In fact, one of the most
critical aspects is the vagueness of the content of an advance directive: as
it always happens in the clinical course of diseases of a different nature
and even within the same disease, the stage considered "terminal" of the
clinical course can have very different duration. In addition, the guidelines may not foresee all possible treatments. To overcome such problems,
it was suggested that guidelines should be prepared with detailed descrip-
tions of the conditions that will trigger their application. This device is not
optimal, because it is impossible to predict all the circumstances that will
terminate life, and because when a patient is hospitalized in an intensive
care unit, the circumstances described in advance directives "in life" are

---

as possible to the concrete situations and to the cultural and environmental problems in
which it occurs": Pietro Perlingieri, *La personalità umana nell'ordinamento giuridico*
(Napoli, 2000), p. 75.
    [13] Maurizio De Tilla, "Introduzione", in *Il testamento biologico. Riflessioni di dieci giuristi*
(Milano-Roma, 2006), p. XI.
    [14] Luigi Balestra, "Efficacia del testamento biologico e ruolo del medico", in *Il testamento
biologico, supra* note 13, pp. 89–105, p. 96.

not necessarily those that the doctor records. Therefore, the most likely hypothesis is that health workers draft a template form for advance directives, containing declarations of intent against the application of medical treatment in terminal conditions of life that can be configured as aggressive medical treatment, provided that they do not constitute active or passive euthanasia. Compared to the "living will"[15]—intended as a declaration by which it is determined how doctors should behave in the terminal phase of the illness of a patient, when he is in possession of mental faculties or is unable to take such decisions—advance treatment directives widen the scope of the principle of informed consent in relation to medical treatment of persons who, for whatever reason, have lost their ability to express themselves and are in a medical condition that precludes the possibility of providing for their own interests.

IV. The Welby Case and the Freedom of Self-Determination

On 16 December 2006, the Court of Rome deposited the order which declared inadmissible the appeal of Piergiorgio Welby,[16] who had asked the separation from the respirator that kept him alive. Indeed, after asserting the constitutional nature of the rights and freedoms of the person in relation to his body and the right to self-determination, the Court of Rome stated conclusively that they cannot get practical implementation because

---

[15] Roberta Bailo and Paolo Cecchi, "Direttive anticipate e diritto di rifiutare le cure: aspetti etici e giuridici", *Rassegna di diritto civile* (1998), pp. 490–501; Francesco Campione, *L'etica del morire e l'attualità. Il caso Englaro, il caso Welby, il testamento biologico e l'eutanasia* (Milano, 2009), p. 11; Carlo Casonato, "Consenso e rifiuto delle cure in una recente sentenza della Cassazione", *Quaderni del dipartimento di scienze giuridiche dell'Università degli studi di Trento* (2008), pp. 545–576; Id., "Bioetica e pluralismo nello Stato costituzionale", in C. Casonato and C. Piciocchi (a cura di), *Biodiritto in dialogo* (Padova, 2006), pp. 7–34; Paolo Cendon, "Prima della morte. I diritti civili dei malati terminali", *Politica del diritto* (2002), pp. 198–212; Giorgio Cosmacini, *Testamento biologico. Idee ed esperienze per una morte giusta* (Bologna, 2010), p. 45; Beppino Englaro and Adriana Pannitteri, *La vita senza limiti. La morte di Eluana in uno Stato di diritto* (Milano, 2009), p. 63; Paolo Girolami, *La salute e le regole* (Milano, 2010), p. 78; Demetrio Neri, "L'eutanasia in Olanda: una difesa (con qualche riserva)", in C. Viafora (a cura di), *Quando morire? Bioetica e diritto nel dibattito sull'eutanasia* (Padova, 1996), pp. 157–168; Giannino Piana, *Testamento biologico* (Torino, 2010), p. 81; Amedeo Santosuosso, "A proposito di 'living will' e di 'advance directives': note per il dibattito", *Politica del diritto* (1990), pp. 457–478.

[16] The reference is to Piergiorgio Welby, who had suffered from a serious degenerative pathological state, inhibiting any movement of the body, for which there was no medical treatment that could halt the development of the disease. Despite this condition, Welby had retained all his mental faculties intact and had interested himself on the evolution of his illness and had expressed the conscious desire on the treatments themselves.

"the underlying principle inspiring the legal system is the inviolability of life". The reference is to Article 5 c.c., prohibiting acts of treatment on a person that can cause permanent damage,[17] and to Articles 575, 576, 577, § 3, 579 and 580 of the penal code punishing murder by consent and assistance to suicide.[18] The decision upholds two principles: first, the rights and freedoms of the person in relation to their body are affirmed, up to the refusal of life-saving treatment; second, these rights and freedoms, while having constitutional status, succumb in the balancing with the right to life, which is prevalent as the basis and precondition of all other rights. Finally, the greater weight of the right to life is inferred by the placement of Article 2 of the Constitution, which comes before Arts. 13 and 32 of the Constitution, as well as the position of the guarantee of the doctor and the prohibition of acts of treatment on a person. This legal route is identical to that made in the case of Eluana Englaro: the Court of Appeal of Milan—as will be seen—in its decision of 16 December 2006 first recognized that "under the right to health and self-determination in health, the able subject can refuse also the treatment necessary to keep him alive", and that in case of incapable person, there must be a balance between the right to self-determination and right to life and that it "can be resolved in favor of the right to life". This fundamental analogy made by the courts leads to the conclusion that, although we have two totally different situations—Eluana Englaro in a permanent vegetative state for 15 years, and Piergiorgio Welby perfectly lucid and able—it clearly appears the idea of life as a "super-right" that does not allow any distinction on a case by case basis and cancels the important distinction between conscious and competent patients and incompetent patients. In particular, Welby's request was to detach the ventilator under terminal sedation to avoid suffering. The hospital and the doctor had given a negative answer: the right of freedom and to conscious determination on the completion or the denial of the completion of any medical therapy was recognized, but with a limit: the protection of life, not disposable even to the person

---

[17] The wording of Article 5 c.c. also refers to therapeutic treatments. In particular, when they involve or could involve a permanent reduction of bodily integrity, the patient's consent is effective only when there is the risk, also possible, of considerable danger to human health. In this sense, the judgment delivered by the Constitutional Court in 1985. If the patient is unable to express his consent to treatment, the permissibility of the latter is dependent on the existence of a state of necessity.

[18] Also suicide and self-inflicted acts that permanently injure physical integrity are contrary to the principle of non-availability of the right to life and health. The refusal of consent, by those who have the power on the incompetent person, is illegal.

concerned.[19] Welby's motivations were based on the principle of informed consent as the basis of any therapy, on the consequential configuration of a full and informed right of self-determination in rejecting the accomplishment of any intrusive activities of a medical nature, including the right to discontinue therapy for which consent is revoked. In addition, a whole new level of medical research has emerged, due to the new possibilities of treatment and to the evolution of science that necessarily affects the natural events such as life and death. Welby's request for urgent action by the court to ensure the right to validly express the refusal of continuation of unwanted medical treatment, was in part accepted by the judge[20] who stated that he could not command the doctor not to reinstate the therapy because that choice fell within the physician's discretion to assess the usefulness of a therapy, as enshrined in Article 37 of the Code of Conduct. This rule states that "in case of diseases with confirmed unfavorable prognosis, or at least in the terminal stage, the doctor should guide his actions for the purposes of moral support and of administration of any pain therapy by providing those in need, as far as possible, with treatments appropriate to preserve the quality of life". By order of 23 July 2007, the Magistrate Court of Rome recognized Welby's "right" to refuse treatment and the "duty" of the physician to respond to the request of the patient. So, a very important role in the Welby case was played by his doctor, Dr. Riccio, who was finally acquitted on the criminal charge at the end of a very difficult judicial proceeding,[21] which showed that the heart of the problem was the relationship between doctor and patient, thus freeing this situation of all instrumental exploitations.[22] The importance of informed consent is great not only from a legal viewpoint, but also under the ethical and deontological profiles. The power to heal is limited by the patients' will of self-determination in relation to their health needs, except in cases of compulsory treatment provided by law or emergency situations that pose a serious hazard to health and life. Therefore, informed consent to

---

[19] Specifically, if the patient has been sedated and is therefore no longer able to decide, the doctor and the hospital are required to re-attach the ventilator to restore breathing and avoid the risk of life.

[20] Procura di Roma, parere 11 dicembre 2006, *Bioetica* (2010), p. 34.

[21] Having noted that his request to the President of the Republic "to obtain euthanasia" could not be upheld, Welby had spoken to two doctors so that they could satisfy his request. While Dr. Casale had preferred to wait for the intervention of the judiciary, Dr. Riccio considered it to be his duty to grant the request of the patient and to accompany him in the short period of time between the plugging off of the ventilator and death.

[22] Mario Riccio, "Riflessioni ad un anno dalla morte di Piergiorgio Welby", *Bioetica* (2008), pp. 11A–17A.

medical acts not only has ethical, or contractual, relevance in the provision of medical assistance, but it is a precondition for the legitimacy of medical and surgical treatments.

V. THE ENGLARO CASE AND THE PERMANENT VEGETATIVE STATE

A reflection on living wills and advance directives cannot prescind from a reference to the Englaro case,[23] which raised the issue of the scope and limits of patient autonomy and the problem of what is the status of the legal guardian of the incapacitated person and the sense of the expression "personal care". The story concerns the young Eluana, who remained in a vegetative state following a car accident occurred in January 1992 and since then nourished and hydrated through a naso-gastric tube. Eluana's father, her legal guardian, asked the court for permission to stop "treatment allowing her body to prolong the vegetative state":[24] in particular, in his submissions to the Court of Appeal of Milan of 8 October 1999, Eluana's father stated how difficult it was "in such conditions to bring back the subject to the concept of the human person and even to that of a living person". This was because Eluana had stated many times, when she was healthy, that she did not want "to be held in such undignified conditions". Therefore, the refusal of treatment expressed by the guardian was the expression of a wish expressed by the girl when she was in "a state of total capacity". In 1999 the Court of Lecco stated that "any form of euthanasia" is an unacceptable attempt to justify the tendency of the community—unable to provide adequate support for individuals forced to extreme dedication toward the sick in the hope of recovery—to neglect the rights of its weakest members and particularly of those who are no longer in a position to lead a conscious, active and productive life. In rejecting the appeal, the Court of Appeal of Milan in 2003 emphasized the role of the legislator to identify and develop the correct tools for the effective protection of the person and the respect of his right to self-determination. By decision of October 16, 2007, no. 21748, the case was referred to the Court of Appeal of Milan to determine whether the statements made by Eluana before falling into unconsciousness were able "to draw [...] her personality and her way of conceiving [...] the very idea of personal dignity, in light of

---

[23] The case of Eluana has a difficult qualification: this is due to its strong symbolic power and the fact that, for the first time, the issue of the interruption of artificial hydration is addressed.

[24] Tribunale di Lecco, 18 gennaio 1999, *Foro italiano* (1999), p. 1306.

her values and the ethical, religious, cultural and philosophical beliefs which guided her will".[25] The reasoning of the Court led it to extend the scope of its final determination, expanding on other major issues concerning the limits within which a patient in full possession of his capacity may refuse treatment and the effectiveness of advance directives. The key part of the decision is its reference to the principle of informed consent as a direct result of Articles 2, 13 and 32 of the Italian Constitution: such a principle, which is accepted in many rules of national[26] and international law,[27] has to be construed as "inclusive of the possibility for the patient to request cessation of treatment even when that involves his death". Before the ruling of 2007, the courts had always rejected the applicant's request, although for different reasons. The decree of July 9, 2008 endorsed the option to turn off the artificial feeding via nasogastric tube enunciating the following principle: "When the patient has been for many years in a permanent vegetative state, resulting in a radical inability to relate himself to the outside world, and when he is kept artificially alive by a tube that provides him nutrition and hydration, at the request of the guardian representing him, and after hearing the 'tutor ad litem', the court may authorize the withdrawal of such medical practice only on the following conditions: a) when the condition of vegetative state is, according to a rigorous clinical appreciation, irreversible and there is no medical fundament, according to internationally accepted scientific standards, which suggest even the slightest possibility of some, although weak, recovery of consciousness and return to a perception of the world, b) provided that such application is truly expressive, on the basis of clear, unequivocal and convincing evidence, of the voice of the patient himself, as drawn from his earlier statements or from his personality, his lifestyle and his beliefs, thus corresponding to his way of conceiving, before falling into unconsciousness, the very idea of human dignity". This principle forms the basis of the rescissory judgment delivered by the Court of Appeal of Milan on July 9, 2008, by which it authorized the discontinuation of life support through an artificial feeding tube after having verified consistency with the parameters set by the Court of Cassation. On November 11, 2008 the Supreme Court declared the action brought by the public prosecutor of Milan

---

[25] Luca Nivarrra, "Autonomia (bio)giuridica e tutela della persona: istruzioni per l'uso", *Bioetica* (2010), pp. 61–96.

[26] The reference is to Articles 1 and 33 of Law No. 833/1978, which established the National Health Service.

[27] The reference is to Article 5 of the Council of Europe Convention on Human Rights and Medicine (Oviedo Convention) and to Article 3 of the Charter of Nice.

against the order of July 9, 2008 of the Court of Appeal of Milan inadmissible, considering that the classification of the case put in place in that judgment was correct. On February 9, 2009 Eluana died. The close relationship between the Englaro case and the issues related to the subject of human dignity is reinforced by the decision of the TAR (the Regional Administrative Court) of Lazio, on September 17, 2009, no. 8560, according to which "Patients in a permanent vegetative state, who are not able to express their will about the health care being practiced, or to be practiced on them, should not in any case be discriminated in comparison to other patients who are able to give their consent, and they may, where their will has been reconstructed, avoid that certain medical treatments be practiced on their body". And also, the patient "has a constitutionally qualified right to be healed according to his desires, since it is entirely up to him to decide which treatment to undergo". In the same direction also moves the decision issued on appeal by the Movement in Defense of the Citizen "against the directive by the Secretary Mr. Sacconi ordering all facilities of the national health service to prevent always the interruption of artificial feeding and hydration in patients in permanent vegetative state, and thus even to prohibit it when the reconstruction of the patient's will points to the rejection of such practice". The TAR, after stressing that the issues at stake involved the "constitutional right to personal freedom that Article 13 (the Constitution) qualifies as inviolable"—enhanced by the entry into force of the International Convention on the Rights of Persons with disabilities,[28] which requires for the same situations the guarantee of informed consent—stressed that "the importance of the constitutional rights involved prevents that they be limited by the exercise of power of the public authority. As a consequence, they are excluded from the jurisdiction of the administrative judge and in case of violation of the principles set out by the TAR, it is up to ordinary courts to ensure full respect of dignity and personal freedom". The importance of this decision lies in that the TAR has established the jurisdiction of ordinary courts just after stating the constitutional nature of the individual right to choose which medical treatment or intervention should be practiced on one's body.

---

[28] The Convention on the Rights of Persons with Disabilities was adopted on December 13, 2006 during the sixty-first session of the General Assembly of the United Nations by resolution A/RES/61/106. The Convention and its Optional Protocol were opened for signature March 30, 2007. Until May 14, 2007 there were 92 signatures to the Convention, 50 signatures to the Optional Protocol and one ratification to the Convention. This is the first major human rights treaty of the twenty-first century.

With reference to persons who are unable to express their will, such as patients in persistent vegetative state, the TAR has made it clear that they cannot be discriminated against. Therefore, it is very important to grasp the scientific and legal aspects related to the qualification of a permanent vegetative state (PVS),[29] regardless of the different positions expressed over time.[30] In the case of Eluana, by decree of July 9, 2008, the Court of Appeal of Milan reconstructed her will, highlighted that the continuation of nutrition and hydration had to be qualified as an (unlawful) aggressive medical treatment, hence consenting to its suspension. However, contrary to the view that hydration and nutrition are nutritional therapies subject to the principle of informed consent and subject to the prohibition of aggressive treatment, Article 3 of the Calabrò bill, concerning the content of advance treatment directives, expressly bans the withdrawal of hydration and nutrition, which cannot be the object of advance treatment directives.[31]

VI. Aggressive Treatments and Human Dignity: The "Best Interest" of the Patient and the Role of the Physician

The recent scientific and technological progress has made available powerful pharmacological and surgical means by which patients derive enormous benefits such as increased survival rates and the improved quality of life. The negative outcome of this progress is the aggressive treatment in the advanced or terminal stage of a disease. The term "aggressive

---

[29] The official definition of permanent vegetative state was coined in 1972 (Bryan Jenette, *The Vegetative State. Medical Facts, Ethical and Legal Dilemmas* (Cambridge, 2002), pp. 12–31). Unlike the coma, PVS is a state or condition in which there is not a real disease: the subjects may not have precise pathologies, but still in situations characterized by the loss of upper and sensory functions. The PVS is distinguished from brain death: this requires, instead, a complete and irreversible injury throughout the brain that is equivalent to the death of the body. A study group of the Italian Society of Neurology proposed to consider lawful the suspension of any life-sustaining treatment, including artificial nutrition and hydration, giving reasons for this opinion in the substantially identification between the essential condition of PVS and the death of the person. This conclusion was criticized by the National Bioethics Committee which noted that the legal system does not foresee any "cortical" criterion for ascertaining death.

[30] Gilda Ferrando, "Stato vegetativo permanente e sospensione dei trattamenti medici", in *Il testamento biologico, supra* note 13, pp. 141–161, p. 149.

[31] Also in compliance with the UN Convention on the Rights of Persons with Disabilities, "nutrition and hydration, in the various forms in which science and technology provide them to the patient, are forms of life support and physiologically designed to relieve suffering until the end of life. They may not be the subject of an advance treatment directive".

treatment" (AT)[32] refers to the administration of disproportionate treatments,[33] or "useless" and excessive on both sides of the medical objective and subjective assessment.

The premise of aggressive therapy is that the person is terminal: however, the suspension or non-administration of life-prolonging treatment should be considered as a normal exercise of medical profession and not as (assisted) legalized euthanasia. The concept of aggressive therapy does not include treatments that appear unnecessary or excessive for the patient and discontinuing therapies which have disappointed the hopes placed in them.[34] The doctor, before beginning treatment, should establish if the chosen therapy is palliative or therapeutic. Consider for a moment the use of assisted breathing which helps patients breathe: the respirator is not a disproportionate treatment, because it doesn't "extend" life, rather it preserves life, preventing dyspnea and subsequent death from suffocation.

---

[32] Amedeo Santosuosso, "Situazioni critiche: eccessi terapeutici ed eutanasia", in *Guida per i medici-chirurghi e odontoiatri* (Torino, 1996), pp. 165–177. The author states that "the expression of aggressive treatment, imprecise and allusive to negative moral judgments, negative relative to the work of doctors in certain situations, may incorrectly be replaced by that of excessive therapy and/or treatments, which have the dual advantage of removing any emotional reflex linked to the term 'aggressive' and to permit them to refer directly to apply a criteria of evaluation. The key criteria are those of the will of the patient and of the appropriate treatment".

[33] In two papers of outstanding reference for the Catholic Church (Pontifical Council for Pastoral Assistance to Health Care Workers, Charter for Health, 1995 and the document on euthanasia of the Congregation for the Doctrine of the Faith, dated May 5, 1980) is stated the principle of proportionate care: "The health professional must provide all proportionate cares. There is no obligation instead to use those disproportionate ones ... i.e. where there is due proportion between the means employed and the aim pursued" and then this principle is stated in its possible applications, stating the legality of the interruption of operations: "It is permissible to interrupt the resources made available by the most advanced medicine, when the results disappoint the hopes placed in them ... because the techniques bring to the patient suffering greater than the benefits that can be drawn". The criterion of proportionate care has found ample space in the bioethics literature of Catholic inspiration, satisfying the instance of delimiting the scope of life-prolonging and defining also the concept of "futility" of a given treatment, i.e. of a treatment that does not meet the purposes of medicine: to prevent, cure, heal, rehabilitate, relieve pain. Although the principle so widely shared that there is no difference between, from the ethical point of view, to take and suspend therapy if you configure an aggressive treatment, it is agreed that there is a psychological difference between the two behaviors. It is in fact different to decide not to initiate artificial nutrition, order not to prolong the dying process, and decide to suspend it once started.

[34] Please note the position taken by the National Bioethics Committee in 1996 regarding the definition of the life-prolonging therapy as "treatment of documented ineffectiveness in relation to the objective, which is added, in the presence of high risk and/or of a particular gravity for the patient with a further suffering, in which the exceptionality of the means used is clearly disproportionate to the objectives of the specific condition".

In assessing treatment effectiveness, we not only have to consider the "technical success" of the treatment, but also the improvement of the clinical (therapeutic) and general conditions (palliative) of the patient. As for the criterion of excessive treatment for the patient, the likely negative outcome is a necessary and unique consideration when deciding to follow an aggressive medical treatment regime: what must be also taken into account are the practical and emotional needs of terminal patients, who could be ready to die[35] or who could "want some more time", for personal and unquestionable reasons such as their desire to receive the last rights, to reach a reconciliation with someone, to settle their business affairs, to make a will, or say goodbye to loved ones etc.

When the level of suffering becomes unbearable and there is no way of knowing what the patient wants, we could follow two guidelines: one could choose for the relief of physical suffering through appropriate palliative care, because only an expressed consent would justify the heroic endurance of pain; or, one could choose life, that is to consider that every person desires to maintain their quality of life, even when the same is severely compromised. In all cases, pain control is certainly useful: the means to alleviate suffering already exist, for example through the increased doses of sedation and analgesics, and are lawful even when the same drugs may indirectly cause death (increasingly less likely considering the advances in pharmacology).

Practical experience has shown that health treatments during the final stage of a terminal patient's life are very expensive for the patient, his family and our society. At times, economic reasons as the concept of "medical futility"[36] are over-emphasized, thus losing sight the best interests of those involved. Moreover, the idea that the life-sustaining treatments consume limited health funds and in doing so detract resources and personnel from

---

[35] Maria De Hennezel, *La morte amica* (Milano, 1998), p. 55; Id., *Morire ad occhi aperti* (Torino, 2006), p. 48, where she speaks of the hypothesis in which "we surrender to the death".

[36] The concept of "medical futility" refers to those acts "deemed inappropriate and ineffective to achieve the desired goal". The concept of "futility" and the same Latin word "futilis" from which takes origin the Greek myth of the daughters of Argos, condemned for eternity to collect water with sieves. Contrary to what may seem, futile treatment "in the strict sense" are almost never practiced (i.e. Cardiopulmonary resuscitation in the event of rupture of the myocardium, mechanical ventilation in case of bilateral pulmonary neoplasia, NA in the terminal unconscious patient, etc.). while there are frequent clinical situations in which you may consider treatments of efficacy highly unlikely, of marginal benefit in terms of quality of life, burdened by high costs. They cannot be defined as futile in the strict sense, can be regarded as inappropriate in a clinical setting, and its use can be avoided.

other more needy patients, is on the whole theoretical. For example, assisted breathing is correctly considered as "standard treatment" which every health care facility is able to provide without excessive costs or risks. Certainly, in the absence of other remedies, one can use, with the consent of the patient, the most advanced medical resources available, even those which are still in the experimental stage and may present some risk to the patient.

Thus, the principal motivation of any doctor must be to consider his patient's best interest, with respect to the ethical base of consent, in other words, the choice of appropriate therapeutic program which would protect the best interests of their patient. In general, one can assume that the patient intends to maintain their independence and their dignity, to be capable of interacting with others, to have quality of life and to avoid pain and suffering. Certainly one can configure the conditions in which patient preferences are difficult to identify because the said preferences may be based on personal moral convictions rather than clinical choices.

One of the most obvious risks is when the quality of life of the patient is determined by a person other than the patient himself: it seems obvious that this concept is very personal and includes physical, mental, social and existential dimensions. Some degree of disability or a particular condition of life should not be the determining factor in the quality of life of an individual, but rather their specific personal experience of life.[37] Basically, in one sector of bioethics there is a growing awareness that the patient's autonomy should be expressed via a previously expressed living will as to the level of treatment that the person wants to receive in specific circumstances,[38] whereas another sector holds that it is more important that the treating doctor honors his Hippocratic oath. This oath creates a situation in which the doctor is not "competent" in considering other elements which do not enter in the logic of safeguarding and extending their patient's life. For this reason, the doctor is unable to place any value on any previously expressed legal wishes of the patient or the views expressed by their relatives on his behalf.

---

[37] Consider, for example, a prolonged support of artificial nutrition, that extending the process of dying of a terminal cancer patient who could be seen as undesirable or, on the contrary, required for different moral or religious reasons; or the condition of PVS, according to someone, a condition worse than death and according to others to be preserved even in its biological essence, devoid of personality.

[38] The reference is, for example, to diseases such as cardiopulmonary arrest, condition of PVS, need for tracheotomy and permanent dependence from the ventilator, need for NA Standing, etc.

The Italian legal system has failed to recognize and correct the ongoing abovementioned dilemma faced by medical professionals and their patients. This situation has arisen only now because, when the Italian Civil code was stipulated in 1942, this dilemma did not exist and has only become an issue with the advances of medical research and therefore the subsequent increased life expectancy. An important recognition of the right to self-determination is expressed in the Convention on Human Rights and Biomedicine, adopted November 19, 1996 by the Council of Europe, which states in Article 9 that the previously expressed wishes of a person regarding future medical intervention must be taken into consideration in any given future medical situation if the said person is unable to communicate.[39]

An increasingly popular operational tool is the appointment of the trustee by the Consulta Nazionale di Bioetica of Milano[40] which considers the "declaration of intent" as a valuable tool "for the time following the loss of natural ability". This instrument also enables a person the opportunity to nominate his executor who would be responsible for providing binding decisions as to the approval, rejection and/or proposal of medical treatment "in the case of the patient being in a state of natural ability judged irreversible on the basis of medical opinion". Certainly we can say that living wills cannot resolve the complex ethical dilemmas posed by the condition of a doctor's "incompetency".[41] However, living wills can provide a great resource for the health professionals involved in the decision making process affecting the patient.

VII. ARTIFICIAL NUTRITION AND HYDRATION IN TERMINALLY ILL PATIENTS

A crucial and much debated issue is whether artificial hydration and nutrition of a terminal patient falls under the term "aggressive treatment". These medical practices, which are performed intravenously or, better still, internally via a feeding tube or PEG (percutaneous endoscopic

---

[39] The new text of the Code of Medical Ethics opens a window of sensitivity for the advance directives made by the patient: indeed, in Art. 34 "The doctor, if the patient is unable to express his will in case of serious life-threat, cannot do without taking account of what has been previously expressed by the patient".

[40] The reference is to Consulta of Bioetica, Proposta di legge sul consenso informato e sulle direttive anticipate, *Bioetica* (1998), pp. 308–314.

[41] Antonio Magliona, "Nuovo Codice di Deontologia Medica e Direttive Anticipate: una timida apertura", *Sanità Pubblica e Medicina Pratica* (1999), pp. 14–21.

gastrotomy[42]), satisfies the nutritional needs of patients who are unable to eat unassisted. There procedures are simple and manageable even at home and improve the quality of life of the patient. These represent a form of basic care, defined by some "nutrition-hydration by other means", because it is not feasible via normal means. In fact, these methods of technical nutrition are means of life support, without any active participation on the part of the patient.

During the late '70s, scientific and technical progress provided doctors with a variety of procedures for administering the entire supply of nutrients either intravenously or intra-gastrically: for this reason, we can define assisted nutrition as an alternative therapy in cases where the patient could not be fed orally. At that time, it was not possible to define assisted nutrition as a "standard"[43] treatment and therefore obligatory from a moral point of view, because the means of administration were not physiological and because artificially-administered nutrition was entirely devoid of any individual and social gratification related to the natural method of nutrition by mouth.

Only recently a consensus in bioethics has emerged in the United States, which was then confirmed by an important judgment reached by the Supreme Court[44] in the case of *Cruzan v Director of the Missouri*

---

[42] It is defined as total parenteral nutrition, a type of artificial nutrition implemented with artificial liquid nutrients that are administered through a probe to ensure the nutritional needs people who can not take food by mouth, for example, in pathological conditions such as stroke, cancer, etc. dysphagia. The enteral nutrition (EN) is today the method most chosen by all the subjects that need to be fed artificially and have a proper gastric function. To allow nutrition, various types of tubes are employed, as naso-gastric tube (a tube that goes from the nasal cavity to the back of the pharynx and, therefore, hypopharynx, esophagus and stomach). If, however, it is necessary to place a tube, recourse is had to gastrostomy (PEG) or jejunostomy (PEJ), that is minor surgery is performed to place it through the skin of the abdomen, drilling the layers of the abdominal wall to reach the gastric or jejunal lumen.

[43] This terminology is no longer in use for the awareness that procedures "extraordinary" over time can become "ordinary" and that each clinical situation is unique and original.

[44] In 1990, in the United States the judgment in the case *Cruzan v. Director Missouri Department of Health and others* was delivered on the following problem: a young woman, Nancy Cruzan was in a permanent vegetative state since 1983, following a car accident. She could breath spontaneously, without artificial respirator, but was fed artificially, through "tube feeding". Her cognitive skills were hopelessly compromised. According to standard medical and legal definitions, the individual in such a state is "living". The person cannot be said to be close to death or terminal conditions. Therefore, the parents of Nancy Cruzan asked the health facility, where she was admitted—at the expenses of the State of Missouri—to discontinue artificial feeding on the basis of the alleged will of the patient who "in a rather serious conversation" had expressed the determination not to go

Department of Health and others[45] in which the nutrition and hydration of a patient via intra-gastric, intravenous or intra-intestinal means are in the end considered medical treatments and as such are considered the same as any other life-support therapy, i.e. following the evaluation of the balance between the benefits of treatment and the intensity of the care to the patient.

In the light of this bioethical approach, nutrition and hydration are now considered a form of basic life support, but it is crucial to distinguish between the intake of fluids and nutrients by natural means and that administered via artificial methods. In this sense, the prevention of oral feeding is morally unjustifiable and comparable to interfering with the patient's ability to breathe; while the suspension or refusal of artificial feeding can be ethically justified and should be evaluated using the same ethical standards applicable to other vital support methods. Although complete approval of this bioethical position is not reflected in official documents prevalent in the U.S. and Northern Europe, even the Catholic Church seems to be willing to open discussion about its traditional position on nutrition and hydration as "standard care". In fact, the Pontificio Consiglio della Pastorale per gli Operatori Sanitari states that "the provision of food and hydration, even when administered artificially, falls within the normal treatments available to a patient in cases where such treatment does not worsen the patient's condition: and when the suspension of said treatment would represent assisted euthanasia".[46]

---

on living if she were in similar conditions. Following the refusal of the hospital, the first decision of the Trial Court of Missouri in 1988 considered the evidence produced by the parents sufficient, invoking the general principle of privacy. In November 1988 the Court of Missouri rejected the policy of privacy and reversed that decision, framing the problem within the doctrine of informed consent, which requires that evidence consistent shows that a person would not have wanted to be treated in certain conditions. Therefore, the Supreme Court considered "insufficient" the simple statement made to a person of her family that she did not want to survive as a vegetable. The Federal Court had the task of analyzing and deciding the case: while the parents of Nancy had asked a decision regarding medical treatments on the body, the fact that she could no longer express her opinion conferred on the physician the competence to take the right decision. The Court held that the State of Missouri could not be denied the right to require that clear and convincing evidence prove the wishes of a patient who was incapable concerning the possible interruption of life-sustaining treatments.

[45] Giulio Ponzanelli, "Nancy Cruzan, la Corte Suprema degli Stati Uniti e il «right to die»", *Foro italiano* (1991), col. 72–75.

[46] Pontificio Consiglio della Pastorale per gli Operatori Sanitari, Carta degli Operatori sanitari, *CdV* (1995).

VIII. Euthanasia and the Principle of Inviolability of Life

The theme of the rejection of the right to practice euthanasia was the premise of all draft laws presented to the Italian Parliament.[47] This is because aiding and abetting suicide (Art. 580 penal code) and murder by consent (Article 579 penal code) are considered crimes under the Italian legal system. In the first case, suicide is carried out by the victim. In the second case the reason of those who practice euthanasia—that is the desire to alleviate the suffering of a terminal patient—is not sufficient to justify the act, even though it would be considered as a possible mitigating factor. Even the Italian Civil Code provides an important provision that enunciates the inviolability of a person's body (Article 5 c.c.). These three norms, though different, have as a common element, the protection and the inviolability of human life, better known as humane or "ethical minimum" that the courts are called upon to protect in a civil society. This approach has its limits in cases where euthanasia is the only way to enable a terminal patient to die with dignity, in peace and without any prolonged suffering. Preliminarily, it is necessary to distinguish between "passive euthanasia" which consists of stopping medical treatments, the discontinuance of which allows a terminal patient to die more quickly, thus putting an end to his suffering; and "active euthanasia" which involves using drugs thereby inducing the deliberate death of the patient. In addition, there also exists a form of "voluntary euthanasia", which is not performed on the initiative of a doctor, but at the request of the terminal patient:[48] this is called "voluntary" because the law allows the patient, on one hand,

---

[47] The draft laws that have followed one another over time are several: Draft Law Marino, no. 10: Provisions relating to informed consent and statements of advance will in medical treatment in order to avoid aggressive treatment, and in the field of palliative care and pain therapy; Draft Law Tomassini, no. 51: Provisions on informed consent and advance directives for health care; Draft Law Perduca Poretti, no. 136: Rules on informed consent and statements of advance will in medical treatment; Draft Law Carloni-Chiaromonte, no. 281: Provisions on informed consent and statements of advance intention in medical treatment; Draft Law Baio and others, no. 285: Provisions relating to informed consent; Draft Law Massidda, no. 483: Rules to protect the dignity and the will of the dying; Draft Law Musi and others, no. 800: Advance directives for end of life; Draft Law Veronesi, no. 972: Provisions relating to informed consent and advance directives; Draft Law Baio and others, no. 994: Provisions on advance treatment directives; Draft Law Rizzi, no. 1095: Provisions for the protection of life in the terminal phase.

[48] This form of euthanasia was first codified in the "Natural Death Act", issued in 1976 in California: the parameters that allow the doctor to apply voluntary euthanasia are: pain unbearable by any means, the fatality of the disease, the terminal condition, the lack of hope that the means of resuscitation that at the time of decision will lead to the restoration of a condition of life more bearable.

and the doctor, on the other, to draw up a contract in which the patient waives any exceptional treatment approved by law and, by doing so, authorizes the doctor not to practice the said treatment to prolong the patient's life.

At this point in the discussion, leaving aside the consideration that there is probably no real difference between "active euthanasia" and "passive euthanasia",[49] the problem is how to define "consent" in a patient's choice to end his life. The danger in considering "letting the patient die" as lawful is what some writers have described as "slippery slope":[50] once one accepts the legitimacy of voluntary euthanasia in the name of the principle of autonomy (the right to decide) then it becomes easily to accept a situation whereby others, in the name of compassion and/or the presumed consent of the patient, assist them to die. The only advantage of this position, although widely criticized,[51] is that the legal prohibition of "active euthanasia" is the only way to prevent any possible administration of therapies which would be dangerous to the patient not choosing to die.

The Italian legal system already prohibits euthanasia according to the principle of the inviolability of human life as expressed in the Constitution, together with the Charter of Human Rights. Beyond these legal motivations, there is also a clear ethical reason enshrined in the obligation of a health system to care for its patients rather than in the justification for their patients' elimination.

IX. PALLIATIVE CARE: PAIN, THE DIGNITY OF THE PATIENT AND THE
QUALITY OF LIFE

Modern medicine is based on the concept that the care of a patient should be viewed holistically and not only physically. As such, it is correct to distinguish the two different phases of a patient's assistance program: the therapeutic phase and the palliative phase.

---

[49] This is because the "don'ts", the abstention, is always a way to act and therefore, recourse to the suspension of life care—when they do not fall into the category of aggressive treatment—denounce a deliberate will to actively terminate the life of the patient.

[50] Francesco D'Agostino, "L'autodeterminazione ideologica. Pendio scivoloso senza stop", in *Avvenire*, 15 aprile 2009.

[51] Jean Y. Goffi, *Pensare l'eutanasia* (Torino, 2006), p. 166, who, in the debate on euthanasia, "meet often sharp and irreconcilable points of views as to arise the legitimate belief that people do not use the common words in the same way. The term euthanasia in fact covers a multitude of meanings: those who see it as a death sentence on a large scale, inevitably judge it as a barbaric killing; instead, others who consider it as letting die or hastening the death of a hopelessly ill at his request, see it as an action that respects human dignity.

The therapeutic phase tends to heal the patient or to retard the progression of a disease. When this attempt becomes ineffective, the patient enters the palliative phase in which the control of pathological symptoms is useful in relieving any kind of pain and/or suffering, using treatments which permit the patient to continue their existence without the added burden of suffering and disability. In addition to this type of intervention, the dignity of a terminal patient can be further respected by providing an appropriate level of psychological support to them and their family.[52] Therefore in addiction, an adequate treatment of pain relief—as is a doctor's duty—already exists in all professional Code of Ethics according to the logic of protecting the dignity of sedated patients, while excluding any consideration of disproportionate treatment.

This is expressly confirmed by Article 37 which states that "in case of diseases with ascertained unfavorable prognosis, or in the terminal stage, the physician should direct their actions for the purpose of providing moral support and for the administering of effective pain control therapy. The doctor and the health system should ensure that those in need receive, for as long as necessary, treatments that are appropriate to preserve their quality of life".

The "quality of life" refers not only to the subjective dimension of health of what represents an acceptable and good quality of life in a broader sense but the perception of an individual's idea of what is for them an acceptable quality of life and corresponds to their individual degree of mental and physical autonomy, to their ability to continue working, to their ability to participate within their family and society. In other words, the concept of "quality of life" has become increasingly considered as a concept of humanity and as a deciding factor in establishing the rights which protect the patient and the need for society to respect these rights.[53] Therefore, in addition to it being a physician's duty, an adequate pain control therapy should also be considered the patient's right to expect a dignified end of life, thanks to multidisciplinary support.

---

[52] This requires the involvement of several professionals. The duty extends even to accompanying the patient in the "process of dying" speaking not only on survival but also on the quality of his remaining life in order to improve it. Così Salvatore Patti, "L'autonomia decisionale della persona alla fine della vita", in *Il testamento biologico, supra* note 13, pp. 87–102.

[53] Maurizio Faggioni, "Conferenza stampa di presentazione dell'assemblea generale della pontificia accademia per la vita", 21–23 febbraio 2005 (Roma), available at http://www.vatican.va.

In Italy, the pursuit of this objective has been a path fraught with difficulties. In 1986, the World Health Organization established a protocol for
opioid drugs, or "analgesic scale" and their administration as the principle
pain-control treatment for cancer patients. It was not until February 8,
2001, that the Italian law (No. 12) established "laws and standards to facilitate the use of opioid analgesics for the treatment of pain", paving the way
for a change in the type of pain medication in Italy. In particular, this legislative intervention recognized 'LEA', which means Essential Level of
Assistance, considered as the "basic health care and social welfare for the
terminal patient". This ruling enforces the State and the regions to provide
a model of health care networks to guarantee the quality of life and human
dignity, even in the terminal stages of an incurable disease, at the expenses
of the state.

The regulations referred to in the Decree 22 February 2007, no. 43, on
"Defining the standard of palliative treatment care for a terminal patient,
according to Article 1 para. 169 of Law December 30, 2004 no. 311". In this
decree, eight objectives were set which the regions need to achieve to
demonstrate that they have ensured the activation of LEA throughout the
Italian territory.

However, the absence of a real national plan for standardizing palliative care has led to the increase of differences from region to region, without any concrete realization of an effective system which would assist
terminally-ill patients. Despite the development of health facilities to provide such care, it is clear that a program of palliative care which provides
a standard criteria for a patient's access to these facilities, is totally absent.
Also missing in this plan are the minimum requirements for accreditation
of providers, as well as a common evaluation criteria and economic assistance to access services, facilities and pharmaceuticals which the state
system is unable to provide.

X. THE CALABRO DRAFT LAW

In the prologue to the Italian Draft Law no. 10, there is the recognition of
the inviolability of human life. This principle considers protecting the
sanctity of life at all costs. Article 1 recognizes and protects human life as
an inviolable right, to be guaranteed even in the terminal phase of life and
until death as assessed according to the law, and in cases where the patient
is no longer capable of deciding for himself. It is clear that this article
excludes euthanasia, as well as the suspension of artificial nutrition and

hydration of the terminal patient. This is in strong contrast to certain guidelines to be found in case law, as previously illustrated in paragraphs IV and V.[54] Following the application of Article 1, an important consequence is that advance treatment directives cannot be used to legitimately request and/or obtain the means to practice euthanasia. Dealing with "the contents and limits of advance treatment directives", Article 3 of the Calabrò draft law states that they should be used only to provide guidelines on care, on starting and ending medical treatment and/or dispensing with special therapeutic treatments if such treatments are disproportionate or of experimental nature. The fact that the title of the article contains the word "limits" clearly indicates the intention of the legislator to restrict the content of advance directives. Therefore, this draft law does not allow the expression of a plurality of personal choices,[55] but rather sets objective limitations to these declarations.

The Calabrò draft law, unlike the text from which it originates, does not speak explicitly of aggressive treatment. Indeed, Article 3 of the original text stated that "especially in case of a patient's imminent death the physician must refrain from extraordinary medical treatment, which are disproportionate, ineffective and/or not technically appropriate with regard to the clinical condition of the patient or the goals of healing and life support". In contrast, the amended paragraph states "the prohibition of aggressive medical treatment cannot justify activities which directly or indirectly constitute euthanasia or absence of treatment".

The absence of a disposition devoted solely to futile treatments could be justified by the need to link such a prohibition to the issue of consent to medical treatment. In this way, every medical intervention is considered "aggressive" if it is administered without the patient's consent, except as provided by the law in cases where such consent is not required.

As far as the patient's "legal substitute" is concerned, Article 6 of the Calabrò bill provides for the appointment of a trustee who, in the case he accepts, must sign a declaration attesting that he is the sole legitimate interlocutor between the attending physician and the patient in case of the latter's incompetency. In this sense, the trustee has a key role in promoting

---

[54] See the Englaro case.

[55] In the advance directives the person may give guidance on several sensitive issues: religious assistance, the intention to donate his organs for research, the method of use of palliative care, the suspension of treatments, refusal of aggressive treatment, the identification of a person acting as trustee in the dialogue with his doctor in case of impaired decision-making capacity.

the "best interests" of the patient: he carries out the wishes and preferences of the patient in any given situation where the patient is no longer
capable of discernment, and as such, the trustee protects the patient
against any situation of aggressive therapeutic treatment or treatment
abandonment. It is possible to waive treatment either orally or in writing.
Therefore, this situations begs the question: if the person referred to in
Article 6 is seen as an 'executor', he would only perform the role of following the previously expressed wishes of the patient, while he is fulfilling the
role of a 'trustee' to whom the patient has entrusted the difficult task of
expressing his will in the absence of advance directives.[56] In Article 6 of
the said draft law, the possibility to reconstruct the desires and will of the
patient, according to previously expressed convictions and/or statements,
is not mentioned: namely "the trustee, if appointed, is the only person
legally authorized to communicate with the treating doctor and undertakes to act in the best interest of the patient, always and exclusively bas-
ing his actions on the patient's intentions recorded in the advance
directives". In this sense, the task of the trustee is reduced to a mere executor of the advance directives: by doing so, the said draft law will not result
in the correct realization of the patient's wishes and preferences. The *ratio*
of this rule is apparent in the results of the recent Italian *Englaro* case:
when the Court of Appeal of Milano approved the request of the patient's
guardian (Eluana Englaro's father) for the suspension of nutrition and
hydration, the court in fact highlighted her father's role as legal guardian
and his function in protecting the best interest of Eluana.

Notwithstanding this precedent, the role of the trustee as described in
the Calabrò bill has been diminished as compared to the one previously
recognized in the relevant case-law. Another more recent precedent was
established in the decision of the Civil Court of Varese whereby, in the
Decree of 25 August 2010, it affirmed that "the stated wishes of a competent person concerning the medical treatments he would accept or reject,
when during an illness or at the moment of an emergency recovery the
said person is not able to communicate his informed consent", are to be
considered valid and applicable. In addition, in the presence of advance
directives, the court stated and affirmed "the validity of the appointment

---

[56] The rule is very clear on this point because it highlights the need for a substitute will
in case of lack of advance directives requiring the trustee or in the absence of this figure,
that oblige the trustee, or guardian or "the spouse unless legally separated or de facto, the
unmarried, the children, the relatives within the fourth degree". The Supreme Court in
2007 has extended the powers of the legal representative, subjecting them to two constraints: the exclusive interest of the patient's and the best interests for him.

of a trustee whose role is to fulfill and realize the expressed wishes of a patient, *at any time present or future, based on the past"*. The judge admitted that the trustee could also fulfill the function of Power of Attorney (with the Italian Law 9 January 2004, No. 6, the Power of Attorney was established as the person who would be able to intervene in situations where another person is unable to protect his own interests). The Civil Court of Florence affirmed the same position by confirming that the holder of a Power of Attorney could be the trustee (not executor) of another person's wishes.

It is clear that the importance of the role of the trustee—if interpreted as a trustee and not as a simple executor—is strategic in the therapeutic alliance and in the respect for the principles of inviolability of human life and of health protection. Despite the awareness of the problems that this figure brings,[57] the appointment of a trustee leaves the question open as to the exact legal and ethical importance of his functions. As with any ethical assessment, the figure of the trustee must be authoritative and his tasks are summarized in the identification of the patient's best interest. To those who contend that the trustee is also intended to convey the patient's preferences,[58] it is replied that this power would devoid the doctors of their freedom of choice of the appropriate therapy, which characterizes his professionalism.

An important question is related to the form of advance directives. In civil law, the will is essentially a formal act, which is meant to honor two positions: the guarantee of a reflective and thoughtful wording of the last will and testament and a pre-established proof of the will of the testator, crystallized in a document and therefore enforceable *"erga omnes"*. The involvement of economic interests is one of the reasons for this formalism. In the case of advance directives, it is a different matter. One could imagine any form—even oral—to express free consent, since in the Italian legal system there is freedom of form. However, the importance of the "vital" character leads us to prefer the written form by persons of full age, competent, informed, independent and not subject to any family, social or environmental pressure. This option, which does not privilege the use of preprinted forms prepared in generic form but suggests provisions in

---

[57] The figure of the trustee is modeled on the paradigm that governs the protection of legal rights and interests of the capable adult. This reference is unsatisfactory because the protection provided by the law for incompetent adults to care for the assets and interests of family members or third parties.

[58] Laura Palazzani, "L'autonomia nelle fasi finali della vita: legittimità o illegittimità della carta dell'autodeterminazione?", in *Quali regole per la bioetica?* (Milano, 2003), p. 98.

writing and addressed to the physician, is also present in the Calabrò draft law, which in Article 4 summarizes the rules for proper preparation of a directive. The function of the form is certainly inspired by reasons of security and promotion of interests and values of protection of individual interests. And in this sense it should be noted that Article 8 provides for the creation of a registry of advance directives for treatment at the national level. Besides having found inspiration in the American register of living wills,[59] this register is under the ownership of the Ministry of Labor. The Council of Notaries gave a favorable opinion and showed its willingness to arrange for its creation and preservation, but in practice there are many municipalities that have set computerized records of advance treatment directives. Through Directive 19 November 2010, the Ministry of Labor gave an indication on the Registers for the collection of advance directives in response to some requests for opinions expressed by the municipalities, concerning the possibility to set up special registers for the collection of the advance treatment directives that each citizen wishes to receive or refuse in situations where he has lost the ability to express his own will. First it is claimed that, in general, we must consider that the matter of the end of life falls within the exclusive competence of national legislation and is not regulated by it. The intervention of municipalities in these areas is seen as excessive in comparison to their own powers as local government, which means that their acts are devoid of legal effect. It was observed that the task of regulating the issue of legal certainty—implying significant effects that can also influence the exercise of fundamental rights—has always been reserved to the State, which is responsible for determining what are the effects of acts kept by public officials. The Directive makes it clear that in this sector the municipality, in accordance with Article 14 of Legislative Decree of 18 August 2000, no. 267 manages, on behalf of the State and by the Mayor in his official capacity of the government, only the electoral services, civil status and the registry office. Therefore, no rule of law enables the Municipality to manage the service regarding advance treatment directives. In these matters, a law of the state is also particularly necessary because there are other themes involved, such as health, family and privacy, under which the Municipality cannot certainly act in the

---

[59] Umberto Veronesi, *Il diritto di morire. La libertà del laico di fronte alla sofferenza* (Milano, 2006), p. 36: "In countries where this possibility exists and has its own legislation, public support is strong. In the U.S., the first to regulate the living will, it seems to concern 15 per cent of the population. In Germany, where legislation is more recent, we are already between 10 and 18 per cent".

absence of state legislation that sets the principles and defines the respon-sibilities of the various public entities involved. The Directive concludes that it is clear that the administrative functions related to advance treat-ment directives, which pertain to the personal sphere of the individual, are matters reserved for the national legislature. Therefore, in light of the above considerations, the Directive does not find evidence to suggest ini-tiatives aimed at the introduction of a registry for advance directives. This intervention by the Ministry of Labor puts an end to this question, so that the ongoing initiatives of this kind are seen as a misuse of human and financial resources, with possible responsibility of the supporter.

XI. Perspectives

The analysis carried out so far highlights some pressing questions, includ-ing the preliminary question whether informed consent, as expressed in the draft law Calabrò, respects the principle of self-determination that originally inspired it. In other words, was the practice of informed consent already present in the Italian legal system or are we trying, through legal instruments, to define its borders? Could it be questioned whether the bill is not too unbalanced in favor of the reaffirmation of medical paternal-ism? Can a document, albeit circumstantial, grasp the deep meaning of a directive that looks at a highly pathological stage of the life of a human being? When the civil lawyer comes to informed consent and correlates it with a contract of an economic character, it is easy to find in the legal sys-tem the rules for its implementation and the sanctions for any violations. The displacement of such a framework in the personal field demands a reflection on alternative ways in which bureaucracy certainly is not the answer. Reducing information to its minimal contents lessens the main objective, namely the protection of human dignity as a general assump-tion, which can never be derogated from, even by laws of circumstance. It is dignity—not survival at all costs—that defines human life and repre-sents the imperative limit for the legislator itself according to the wording of Article 32 of the Constitution. It is the ultimate value to be served by advance treatment directives. Although there are academic positions and conflict of interests, we cannot allow bioethics to become a field of politi-cal struggle and of intervention of religious authorities. The increased awareness of physicians of the need to analyze the moral problems raised by technological progress has been, over the years, a great enrichment to the debate. The aid of anesthesiologists and neurologists has provided opportunities for closer examination and comparison. For patients in PVS, the physician cannot avoid taking into account the previously expressed wishes of the patient when the patient is no longer able to express his will. About the lawfulness of the denial of a life support measures such as artificial feeding, a new study by two research teams from Cambridge and Liège has highlighted the possibility that some individuals held in a vegetative state are not entirely without conscience.[60] In other words, the use of modern methods have shown metabolic responses and possible emergence of conscience. From this we can deduce the overcoming of the schematic pattern of vegetative state, understood as a medical condition in which the cortex is completely devoid of functions. The possibility of any residual mental activity calls into play the principle of self-determination of the patient. In view of these scientific breakthroughs the debate has stopped in Italy, both in the progress of the analysis of the bill, and in the debate within civil society. This situation of intellectual stagnation is likely to miss the opportunities offered by the biomedical revolution and is likely to confer only to the legislator the task of making law an instrument that does not meet the expectations of those who suffer. The contingent circumstances of the low degree of authority that research enjoys in Italy does not help the debate: all this does not open up the door to a serene view of the near future.

---

[60] The group of Liège directed by Steven Laureys, and the Cambridge group led by Adrian Owen have made use of diagnostic imaging of the nervous system and neurophysiological methods. They studied a series of 51 cases, of which 23 were in SV and 28 in SMC (minimally conscious state): in two cases of PSV and in three of SMC were found viable responses to external stimuli. They showed that it was not intended as phenomena of automatic responses, but of real communication with the outside world. The work is contained in Martin M. Monti, "Willful modulation of brain activity in disorders of consciousness", 362 *New England Journal of Medicine* (2010), pp. 570–589.

NON-NEGOTIABILITY OF ETHICAL VALUES
AND CONSTITUTIONAL DEMOCRACY

Francesco Mancuso*

Reference to the theme of "non negotiable ethical values" might seem to be inappropriate in a book on the living will legislations. Nevertheless, even the most technically correct analysis (whether of a legal or medico-scientific nature) cannot ignore the political and cultural context which affects the substance of certain laws or intended legislation, especially if these concern the area of ethical and legal implications of biomedical treatment.[1]

A glaring example is the Italian draft law on the living will: it is well known that the political drive to speed up the parliamentary proceedings sprang from the great impact the "Englaro" case had on public opinion, on political discussions and even on the balance of constitutional powers.[2]

The whole affair was hampered by constant appeals to so-called "non-negotiable values": meaning values that can neither be negotiated nor weighted because they are felt to be universal and deeply-rooted in human 'nature'; claims to truth that serve both as an acid test of the law (the presumption of legitimacy of those values is so strong that it can even be an element that delegitimises legal norms thought to be incompatible with them), and as an objectively just content, something unquestionably 'good' that cannot be ignored by any legal regulation of bioethical questions.

Even though not explicitly mentioned (perhaps because even its champions regard it as a "blunt weapon"),[3] the *éminence grise* is natural law, which, after its 'constitutionalist' compromise, is returning to the attack as

---

* Associate Professor of Philosophy of Law at the Faculty of Law of the University of Salerno; email: fmancuso@unisa.it.
   [1] I refer to political and cultural context, rather than social context: it is particularly significant to highlight how perceptions, judgments and the actual social behaviours with regard to specific "ethically sensitive" themes such as bioethics display a more secular nature.
   [2] See Federico G. Pizzetti, "In margine ai profili costituzionali degli ultimi sviluppi del caso Englaro: limiti della legge e progetto di vita", 40 *Politica del diritto* (2009), pp. 445–482.
   [3] A phrase used by Pope Benedict XVI.

S. Negri (ed.), *Self-Determination, Dignity and End-of-Life Care*
2011 Koninklijke Brill NV. Printed in The Netherlands. ISBN 978 90 04 22357 8. pp. 411–418

an attempt to anchor law to moral values that are 'objective', and therefore 'universal'.

The question is whether these moral values (which are not law but
aim at becoming *jus condendum*) can constitute elements of that overlapping consensus of contemporary pluralistic societies, or whether they
represent a factor of further conflictive disintegration or even, as has been
written, a call for "civil war".

Recent political news tells us that the biomedical 'corpus' and biomedical techniques have become factors in an active type of biopolitics
that, in the form of biolaw, takes on the traditional appearance of *jus naturalism* (not rationalistic but religious). The resurfacing of natural law
comes as a surprise to people who thought that, with the continental constitutions of the second post-war period and the European constitution-
building process, the theoretical-ideological clash between positivism and
jus naturalism was now 'water under the bridge', and there are two reasons for this: first and foremost, many elements of natural law, whether
rationalist or of a religious origin, have been included and positivised,
in different ways and with different degrees of intensity, in today's constitutional charters; at the same time, as a reaction to the failure of the
experience of the nineteenth-twentieth century 'State under law' and
the experience with totalitarianism, legal systems have become gradually 'constitutionalised' by making the law subject to constitutionally
mandatory precepts and principles (the main one being the personalist
principle).

I shall not go into these matters here, because they are far too broad to
be fully described in a short article, neither shall I analyse the contents of
the "Calabrò draft" (disegno di legge "Calabrò"),[4] even though they display
an extremely ideological approach and, in particular, a concept of the law
as a "rule of preponderance",[5] in other words, as a system of monolithic
unitary values. Moreover, it's common knowledge that 'hard cases make
bad law'.

---

[4] On the DDL Calabrò (http://www.lucacoscioni.it/senatoreperdueore), see Guido Alpa,
"Il disegno di legge sul testamento biologico: note lessicali" (http://www.astrid-online.it/
rassegna/Rassegna-27/12-03-2009/ALPA_Testamento-biologico_23_02_09.pdf) and Francesco Mancuso, "Valori, democrazia, princìpi. A partire dal testamento biologico", in
Francesco Lucrezi and Francesco Mancuso (eds.), *Diritto e vita. Biodiritto, bioetica, biopolitica* (Soveria Mannelli, 2010), pp. 213–221.

[5] An expression used by Stefano Rodotà, "Per un nuovo statuto del corpo umano", in
Antonio Di Meo and Claudia Mancina (eds.), *Bioetica* (Roma-Bari, 1989), p. 45. See also
Francesco Rimoli, "Laicità e pluralismo bioetico" (http://archivio.rivistaaic.it/materiali/
convegni/aic200710/index.html).

I shall, instead, concentrate on a more or less intermediate level of values. For a person interested in the evolutions (or involutions) of constitutionalism (which, in my opinion, is the juridical translation of humanism), it is impossible to underestimate the effects produced on it when the 'polytheism' of values results in a conflict between values that cannot be negotiated, that is to say, when the constitution no longer represents an ethical-juridical and political minimum common denominator and is not capable of producing what has been called 'solidarity between strangers'.

Therefore the questions that I shall try to answer are basically two.

The first one is: how does constitutionalism, taken to be an official and even strategic regulative strategy for defending rights and political plans, relate to the subject of values?

This question can be answered (leaving aside all the difficult philosophical and theoretical-general implications of the law-morality relationship) by recognising the separate but assimilable constitutional strategies for inclusion-integration by means of values that have developed through the interaction (not the merging) between the axiological elements and regulative elements of the constitution: this is a norm (not an ethical value) or, rather, a supernorm because it incorporates substantive and universal ethical elements in the form of legal principles.

As we shall see later, the translation of ethical values into legal principles is, together with other solutions, such as jurisdictional control over the constitutionality of laws and the rigidity of constitutional norms, a key factor in this strategy which, generally speaking, has moved forward on "two tracks": legitimising constitutional super-law by incorporating ethical principles; and an attempt to reconcile, juridify and universalise differing ethical-political traditions.

On the one hand, substantialisation of law and an attempt to free it from the classical legal positivist theory that it can be "filled up" with any content; on the other, 'juridical' constitutionalisation of ethical-political trends (obviously, moral values are not suspended in a vacuum but, as Bobbio has already mentioned, take concrete shape in history).

Naturally, opinions can differ about the degree of effectiveness of what we might call, adopting a realistic approach, this 'narration' of constitutionalism, and also on its possible 'perverse effects': erosion of the certainty of law, increased weight of the jurisprudential sphere, crisis of the canons of classical constitutionalism. I shall not go into this really vast class of problems, nor even into the equally serious question of the material constitution, as this expression is understood by Costantino Mortati, that is to say, the relation between social and political forces and the "living" constitution: it would be of no help to 'loyalty' to the constitution to maintain that it can sustain itself without perhaps having a daily effect on political culture, in other words on the motivation and convictions of the citizens.

What, in my opinion, is unquestionable is the existence of the performative force of an attempt, precisely constitutionalism, to reconcile law, ethics and politics.

Now the fact that 'non-negotiable values' are resurfacing in the increasingly pluralistic societies of today does not merely mean that people are retreating behind their identities and fears but it also highlights the tricky problem that the inclusion of values in the constitution leaves many hazy areas.

Now we come to the second question: are 'non-negotiable' values compatible with today's constitutionalist plan and, if so, in what terms? The subject of values is a vast and philosophically challenging one. In my opinion, the intellectual contribution of two great legal and political thinkers of the 20th century, like Carl Schmitt and Hans Kelsen, can give us some useful ideas.

Both authors, influenced in different ways by Max Weber's intellectual legacy, dealt in a very special way with the Weberian theory of the 'polytheism' of historically determined values: the inclination toward values cannot be eliminated from social behaviour; the basic feature of values is that they are inflexible and controversial; rationalisation is powerless against the controversial 'power' of values, which can neither be broken down into hierarchies nor, due to their intimate structure, enter into negotiation with other 'values'.

It is true, and Weber's political writings confirm it several times, that totally non-valuation political action is a kind of contradiction in terms: politics means adopting values, it means responsibility, it means dealing with the 'powers' represented by values.

Therefore, there are very fine margins by which to hold politics back from, or to delay, the fate of the clash of values, the friend/enemy mentality, the conflict that taken to extremes is simply the annihilation of politics and even of the legal system.

Kelsen's theories deal precisely with this fine and hazardous line: on the one hand Kelsen adopts Weber's theory of the 'subjectivity', relativity and basic irrationality of values (in the sense of their essential 'ambiguity': an analysis of the concept of 'justice' is also an analysis of the impossibility of universalising 'values'); on the other, he offers a political strategy for deflating values by procedural democracy (which, in turn, is based on a fairly relativistic vision of the world).

The rule of majority is the key to the relativisation of conflicts in what Kelsen calls a "dialectic process of the democratic formation of the will of the State", based on discussion, and presupposing a certain, basically relativistic, philosophical attitude: thus the opposite of democracy is autocracy, the opposite of relativism (taken as being inaccessibility to human knowledge of any form of 'absolute') is philosophical absolutism.

The latter is the essential prerequisite of any kind of autocracy and proves to be a source of 'absolute values' (in a nexus linking them to "absolute authority" and the "absolute being").

Certainly, the democratic procedure cannot guarantee any of the content of a political decision: Kelsen makes frequent reference to the example of the trial of Jesus as a "tragic" symbol of the lack of guarantee of 'justness' as a result of decisions by the democratic procedure. But the example of the democratic 'choice' in favour of Barabbas is inherent, according to Kelsen, in the rejection of any mystification about the sovereignty of the people and the rule of the majority, which is not an ordeal.

Kelsen's 'political' outlook, which originates from an exercise of anti-metaphysical disenchantment, hinges on a kind of ideal self-surpassing of the conflict of values and the neutralisation of the latter is the product of both an exercise in the relativisation of 'self', which becomes a non-cognitive attitude to the world, and of the democratic procedural medium, looked on as a meta-value: a value in itself, insofar as it ensures tolerance, equilibrium and a dialogue between plural values.

The formulation of "arguments" that are competing (not conflicting, because of the necessary "fallibilistic awareness that we may always be wrong") is the 'spirit' of liberal democracy: from this point of view, Kelsen is an important (and often overlooked) precursor of contemporary deliberative political theories. On the other hand, it is also true that Kelsen can be credited with having been the first to imagine a full picture of one the pillars of contemporary constitutionalism, in other words, jurisdictional control of the constitutionality of the laws.

These *political* (procedural democracy) and *juridical* neutralisation strategies (jurisdictional 'guardianship' of the constitution) show how aware Kelsen was of the inflexible controversiality of values. On this basis a surprising closeness to an author like Carl Schmitt emerges. The absolutism of values is at the centre of a famous (and late) work by Schmitt entitled *Die Tyrannei der Werte*.

Where Kelsen thought it necessary to demystify the concept of democracy productively, freeing it from the traditional metaphysical hypostases and from any conceptual absolution (Kelsen's deconstruction of the concept of general will is famous) and hypervaluation of the demos (in this way, unlike Schmitt, Kelsen is radically anti-Jacobin); Schmitt thought the problem was one of the clash of values, of the nihilistic results of what Weber called their "fight to the death", and of the risk of the "terror of the direct and automatic [constitutional] application of a value".

Schmitt's work is as short as it is complex but the controversial objectives and the theoretical lines are clear (less so are the solutions, which seem to be nostalgia, we do not know how sincere, for liberal constitutionalism and positivistic faith in the "negotiation" of values by means of "implementable and calculable rules").

The theoretical-juridical context of Schmitt's idea of the tyranny of values consists, on the one hand, of the criticism expressed by them of the criminalising 'moralisation' of international law and, on the other, of Ernst Forsthoff's criticism of the value interpretation of *Grundgesetz* and the theories known today as 'neoconstitutionalist'.[6]

The 'troubling' element of values is their subjectivity, which of necessity leads to an "everlasting *bellum omnium contra omnes*"; however, the reaction to subjectivity as an attempt to construct an "objective and material philosophy of values" not only conceals the ineradicability of the 'subjective' aspect but makes the 'point of attack', the conflictuality of the values themselves, even more conflictive: there is no valuation without devaluation, and a value of necessity involves a non-value against which to drive (and the conflict involves no negotiation). This is the tyranny of values (an expression taken up by Nicolai Hartmann): "the theory of value must always hold fast to the principle that for the supreme value the highest price is never too high, and must be paid". This is also the violent and irresponsible approach of *fiat justitia, pereat mundus* since it foresees potential annihilators and annihilated, supreme values opposed to absolute non-values.

While Kelsen sees 'relativisation' and opening up to pluralism of values as producing tolerance and coexistence, for Schmitt the 'thetic' theory of values (values "arise and prevail") automatically excludes any form of negotiation and sublimation of the conflict, which can never happen with

---

[6] Schmitt and his followers do not believe that the pluralistic State can survive its own contradictions. For Kelsen instead these contradictions are the strength of parliamentary democracy.

inclusion of values in the constitution. On the contrary, according to Schmitt, constitutional 'valuations' simply mean the incubation of a dangerous controversial risk for the juridical system.

In the opinion of both authors, the solution of the problem of conflicting values is not their incorporation into constitutions.

Neither Schmitt nor Kelsen can guide us in this matter, one being conservatively tied to a traditional idea of the constitution; the other restrained by the methodological assumption of his 'pure doctrine' from making a connection between philosophical-political thought and juridical theory (in the broad sense) and therefore of thinking of 'constitutional' democracy.

But it is on the disastrousness of the clash of values that the teachings of Schmitt and Kelsen are still topical: the former because essential for understanding the extremely close link between politics and law; the latter because they foresee the relevance of contemporary pluralism, to which the response is relativistic but not indifferentist.

Both warn us about the perils of extreme valuations within the 'juridical' system, without however being in conflict with all those interpretations, from Smend to Mortati, of the constitution as a 'table of values'. However, what saves us from the controversiality and the inevitable value reductionism is precisely 1) the ineradicable plurality of values; 2) the fact that the constitution is a kind of meta-value that makes sense because it is a composite, plural but nevertheless homogeneous set of values 'translated' into legal principles, so as to lose the 'closed' and non-negotiable nature of a 'value'.

The real challenge to the lay approach to the contents of 'value' in law lies in discussing (and deciding) by principles and in not reducing the principles (open and plural) to values (closed and single).[7]

If we think of the recent and numerous appeals to the principle of human dignity, which, reduced to the mere right to life, ends up by becoming a 'non-negotiable' value impervious to the very many cases that call for legal intervention and challenge the (kantian?) ethical-value monolithism.[8]

---

[7] Here I am using the conceptual values/principles distinction clearly explained by Gustavo Zagrebelsky, *La legge e la sua giustizia* (Bologna, 2008).

[8] See for example the criticizable essay of Ernst-Wolfgang Böckenförde, "Menschenwürde als normatives Prinzip. Die Grundrechte in der bioetischen Debatte", 17 *Juristen Zeitung* (2003).

The pluralist and secular public sphere, damaged by the conflict of values impervious to negotiation and intrinsically polemogenic and 'all-encompassing', would be greatly enriched by debate based on plural principles, especially constitutional ones, by the shifting of one's own point of view to understand the point of view of the 'other', and especially by a permanent tendency toward concrete cases.

In that way it is possible to make *positive* use of the porosity of principles (like that of 'dignity') imagining a mobile *but never separable* relationship between the various ideas (the different values) that make up their 'plural' aspect: autonomy, respect, recognition, integrity of the body, right to life, equality of treatment, *et caetera*. Not so much a relativistic concept of dignity, suited for all purposes and abandoned to decisions lacking justification, *ita lex*, as the idea of its necessary flexibility in order to be a 'continuous'—'constitutional'—stimulus to the normative centrality of rights, and a permanent reminder of their possible conflictuality, of the 'tragedy' of certain situations and choices and of the fact that revisability (we might say: humanity often errs) of decisions is coessential with the ideal and political substance of constitutional States.

Therefore, a dual structure of constitutional principles invocable in the case of decisions on ethically sensitive hard cases and, in particular, the principle of 'dignity', which is both *thick* and *thin*: on the one hand dignity as a fundamental limit; on the other dignity as a complex and mobile structure of plural principles for guidance, evaluation, decision-making. Overall, the categorical imperative of integrating the *ethic of responsibility* and the *politics of responsibility* with a necessary idea of the *law (and jurisprudence) of responsibility*. Only in this way, seeking a difficult middle course between technicised law, insensitive to ethical *stimuli*, and substantial non-negotiable values, insensitive to concrete cases, can we achieve a positive reconciliation between ethics and law that defends human beings, their freedom and their centrality.

EUTHANASIA AND ASSISTED SUICIDE IN THE ITALIAN CRIMINAL CODE AND IN THE DRAFT LAW ON "ADVANCE TREATMENT DIRECTIVES"

*Maria Elena Castaldo**

I. THE REASONS FOR A *DE IURE CONDENDO* ANALYSIS ON "ADVANCE TREATMENT DIRECTIVES": THE SEARCH FOR SENSE AMONG LEGAL CONSIDERATIONS

The Chamber of Deputies of the Italian Parliament has recently amended the Draft law on "*Provisions on therapeutic alliance, informed consent and advance treatment directives*" and transmitted it to the Senate.[1]

The legislative debate on end-life directives is expected to be difficult and lengthy. This is due to various reasons, some tied to the specific characteristics of this subject matter, and others that are exogenous and contingent.

It should be noted above all that the Italian political climate is currently the primary contingent and external factor clouding the Parliament's work in this sector.

Italian politics are currently undergoing a difficult historical moment, not only externally but also, and above all, within Parliament, where "partisan stadium cheering" grows increasingly louder, along with "the idea of having to win against an adversary at all cost".[2]

In essence, the "day of reckoning" to which the various political parties of the majority and opposition each refer risks damaging for mere political purposes a serious debate, not only of the different issues that are on the agendas of the Parliamentary assemblies, but, above all, of the draft law on

---

* Researcher of Criminal Law at the Faculty of Law of the University of Salerno, Italy; email: m.castaldo@libero.it.

[1] Draft law A.C. 2350 also known as the "Calabrò proposal" based on the name of the rapporteur, originates from the approval of draft law A.S. 10, which unifies the different bills on advance treatment directives presented to the Senate of the Republic during the current legislature. The uniform text was passed by the Senate on 26 March 2009 and later approved with amendments by the Chamber of Deputies on 12 July 2011. Parliamentary works are available at the websites http://www.camera.it and http://www.senato.it.

[2] Ignazio Marino, *Sul fine vita fermiamo il tifo da stadio*, Corriere della Sera, 12 January 2011.

S. Negri (ed.), *Self-Determination, Dignity and End-of-Life Care*
2011 Koninklijke Brill NV. Printed in The Netherlands. ISBN 978 90 04 22357 8. pp. 419–436

"advance treatment directives", which, to the contrary, requires a responsible, calm confrontation, which is not conditioned by the suspicion of
ideological prejudices deriving from political expediency.

The undoubted complexity tied to the specific characteristics of this
subject matter must be added to this.

On the one hand, any consideration of "end-life issues" must inevitably
face the difficulties linked to the role of "segment" issues within the
broader "system" of protection of life and physical integrity in a specific
legal system. As the playing field at the "crossroads" between law, ethics,
religion and philosophy, such sector does not leave space for the illusion
of an aesthetic and technical treatment of the issue, free of any influence
of "moral reasons".[3]

On the other hand, there is an inability to craft satisfactory legislation,
characterized by appropriate terms and concepts. The confusion is, above
all, "semantic." Various problems and contradictory phenomenology have
been attributed to euthanasia, reducing it to a simple "word used as a
clothes rack",[4] functional to changing its significance but misleading when
it is to be the object of an efficient and effective legal regime.

Therefore, the political climate, the difficult intersection of all of the
"philosophies" involved in the debate, the ambiguity of the language used
and which can be used, all appear to be indications of the complexity of a
subject matter for which it might be opportune to "abandon the attempt
to legislate", with the inevitable consequent "abandonment" of the doctor,
patient and family members in the current limbo, consisting of "final decisions" burdened by the yoke of reason (experiences of pain, deontological
rules, religious creeds) of each of these figures.

In essence, the endogenous and exogenous characteristics of the subject matter would justify an apparently liberal type of option, i.e. a "space
unrestricted by the law",[5] leaving issues regarding the "right to die", or the
"right to live one's death" and the "manner of dying" reserved only to science and the conscience, as well as to the mercy of the parties involved,

---

[3] On the difficulty of legal reasoning *see* Fausto Giunta, "Diritto di morire e diritto
penale. I termini di una relazione problematica", 40 *Rivista italiana di diritto e procedura
penale* (1997), pp. 74–125.

[4] *See* Patrick Verspieren, *Face à celui qui meurt. Euthanasie. Acharnement thérapeutique.
Accompagnement* (Paris, 1984), p. 65.

[5] On the concept of *"rechtsfreier Raum" see* the enlightening contributions of Albin Eser
(Hg), *Suizid und Euthanasie als human- und sozial wissenschaftliches Problem*, (Stuttgart,
1976), p. 392; Karl Engisch, "Suizid und Euthanasie nach deutschem Recht", ibid., pp. 312–
321; generally Arthur Kaufmann, "Euthanasie – Selbsttötung – Tötung auf Verlangen",
1 *Medizinrecht* (1983), pp. 121–125.

and behaviour that is neither prohibited nor lawful, but simply "not legally regulated".[6]

One solution, that of the *"rechtsfreier Raum"*, is to be avoided because although it formally respects "ethical pluralism", which is the enemy of forced choices and which is necessarily subjective, it leaves the field open to a kind of "self-regulatory" societal code, in whose existence and effectiveness no-one, political parties included, believes.[7]

Sharing the comments of the most authoritative legal scholars, a positive regulation of the subject matter is necessary, above all due to respect for the principle of legal reservation[8] in the discussion on the fundamental rights of life and health, sectors which, even though ontologically related to a pre-legal dimension, cannot permit the law to be excluded according to a logic of legislative "neutrality" understood as the absence of the State.

A legal regime should, in fact, be agreed upon due to the appropriateness, if not precisely the need, that in a modern State of law there are no categories of parties who are "outside" of the legal system, for whom choices of life or death are entrusted to the exclusive variables of faith and science, aimed at a sort of "self-regulation" according to the discretion of the players involved.[9]

The legal system, in essence, does not have to choose in an authoritative or "paternalistic" manner[10] one "morality" instead of another, but it

---

[6] Massimo Donini, *Il volto attuale dell'illecito penale. La democrazia penale tra differenziazione e sussidiarietà* (Milano, 2004); Id., "Il caso Welby e le tentazioni pericolose di uno 'spazio libero dal diritto'", 47 *Cassazione penale* (2007), pp. 902–918, p. 906.

[7] With reference to the historical experience of the failure of self-discipline in sectors left to the unrestricted self-determination of the parties involved *see* Federico Stella, "Il problema giuridico dell'eutanasia: l'interruzione e l'abbandono delle cure mediche", 6 *Rivista italiana di medicina legale* (1984), pp. 1007–1025; Ferrando Mantovani, *Eutanasia*, in *Digesto delle discipline penalistiche* (Torino, 1990), vol. IV, pp. 422–430, p. 425.

[8] Stella, *supra* note 7, p. 1007.

[9] Mantovani, *supra* note 7, p. 425; Stella, *supra* note 7, p. 1007.

[10] In the "paternalistic" vision inspired by Hippocrates, the doctor has to "treat" the patient and make the necessary therapeutic choices, which can only be judged with respect to whether or not they correspond to the dictates of science. The *patiens*, instead, is considered to be a mere "passive subject" of the medical activity and does not have to express consent to the activity itself, but simple approval, which serves the purpose of avoiding the danger, in effect not really realistic, of forced therapies imposed by the doctor. With respect to the debate on the paternalistic concept in international scholarship *see* Joel Feinberg, *The Moral Limits of the Criminal Law - Vol. III: Harm to Self* (Oxford, 1989) and Ronald Dworkin, *Il dominio della vita. Aborto, euthanasia, e libertà individuale* (Milano, 1994). In Italian scholarship *see*, among others, Alberto Cadoppi, "Liberalismo, paternalismo e diritto penale", in G. Fiandaca and G. Francolini (ed.), *Sulla legittimazione del diritto penale. Culture europeo-continentale e anglo-americana a confronto* (Torino, 2008); Mario Romano, "Danno a se stessi, paternalismo legale e limiti del diritto penale", 51 *Rivista italiana di diritto e procedura penale* (2008), pp. 1088–1119.

must raise the issue of "how to prepare a legal ethic that can include with rational authority the most diverse moral concepts, whose content can only be defined negatively, i.e. a morality that does not consist of the oppression of others".[11]

The legal system must not make "a choice" on its own, suffocating the typical antinomy of the subject matter, which sees "science" opposed to "morality", applying constitutional principles according to their more or less historic versions, or proposing the adoption of models of other legal systems such as, for example, the Anglo-American common law systems.

The solution must come from allowing options that are as ethically dramatic as possible, when they are the result of a procedure that has previously been established by the legislator as a vehicle for recognition of the last and prevalent will of the individual.

There must be, in essence, an objective legal source that regulates the process of the creation of the final will regarding the patient's fate. The road is thus cleared for "procedural exoneration", i.e. "a procedure capable of authorizing the behaviour and results of such conduct, even if injurious to fundamental rights".[12] This solution is therefore "atypical and beyond the causes of justification".[13]

In this context, the criminal lawyer is responsible for repeating the punishment function and subsidiarity of criminal law with respect to the violation of "extra-criminal law regimes", supervising, at the time the laws are drafted, that the legislator determines the outline of the legal framework with respect to the fundamental principles of the obligatory nature and certainty of the case, using precise terms and concepts, and reserving the function of *extrema ratio* to criminal law.

II. Euthanasia, Consensual Murder and Instigation to or Assistance with Suicide in the Italian Criminal Code: The "Terms" of the Problem and the Limits of the Criminal Law Debate

Once the conceptual *aporia* has been overcome of a "space unrestricted by the law", it is necessary to establish the limits of the argument and

---

[11] Maria Beatrice Magro, "Etica laica e tutela della vita umana: riflessioni sul principio di laicità in diritto penale", 37 *Rivista italiana di diritto e procedura penale* (1994), pp. 1382–1448, Id., *Euthanasia e diritto penale*, (Torino, 2001).
[12] Donini, *supra* note 6, p. 907.
[13] Mario Romano and Federico Stella, *Aborto e legge penale* (Milano, 1975), p. 18.

organize the "terms" that can be used in legal language and their meanings.

The scarce ability of the words used in the context of end-life issues to provide guidelines has been clearly acknowledged. Any "legal qualification" in this sector is subject to language that is full of emotional resonance or ethical implication, as well as the difficulty of establishing the requisites of the typical nature of the act to which the review refers, i.e. the conditions in the presence of which the expression can be properly used.[14]

This is even more evident when one considers the term "euthanasia".[15]

The etymological value of the word, the "good" or "sweet" death, expresses the "idea" of a tranquil death, but states nothing with respect to the "manner and characteristics" of realizing this "good passing", i.e. the "actions" that render it concrete.[16]

The epistemological effort and determination of a conceptual status of words that is functional to outlining the issue is opportune in order to limit the "playing field", i.e. the range of action of the regime *in fieri* being reviewed by the legislator.

Draft law A.C. 2350 does not aim at creating a "framework regime", intended to cover the entire phenomenological range of euthanasia, already the object of debate in legal scholarship and in case law, but aims at "organizing" the choices of the players according to a specific and pre-determined procedure in the context of euthanasia that is linked to the category of "passive euthanasia", i.e. the possible legal legitimacy, and on what conditions, of the "refusal of treatment".

In effect, solicited by the paradigmatic cases of Piergiorgio Welby and Eluana Englaro, which were heavily debated on the social level and the object of clear and innovative positions taken by case law,[17] the Italian Legislator, by means of the bill being discussed at Parliament, is concentrating its attention, on the basis of the norms already contained in the Criminal Code, which is a framework, on the level of values, that is still considered to be valid, in those extreme and painful situations in which

---

[14] Magro, *Eutanasia, supra* note 11, p. 98.

[15] There is a large body of scholarship on the issue of euthanasia. For a precise reconstruction of the meanings historically attributed to the term *see* Magro, *Eutanasia, supra* note 11, p. 93.

[16] Mario Porzio, *Eutanasia*, in *Enciclopedia del diritto* (Milano 1967), vol. XVI, p. 103.

[17] The debate in public opinion, and consequently in the political and legal context, was activated by the personal histories but above all by the legal proceedings involving Piergiorgio Welby and Eluana Englaro. See GUP – Court of Rome 23 July 2007, no. 2049 (*Welby* case) and Court of Cassation, United Section, 13 November 2007, no. 27145 (*Englaro* case).

the "right to die" must find space, without activating repression in the
form of criminal liability as provided in the laws of reference.

Regardless of the numerous classifications of the *genus* euthanasia,[18] for
our purposes it is sufficient to clarify the term's semantic space, and,
therefore, to which "euthanasia" phenomenology the analysis refers to.

The term "euthanasia" currently refers to the conclusive moment of the
therapeutic relationship, linking the phenomenology of the "suppression
of someone else's life *pietatis causa*". Euthanasia is therefore characterized by a "beneficial and altruistic motivation corresponding to the use of
suitable means to render death serene and rapid, and by a generic factual
condition that casts doubt on the postulate of the absolute nature of the
protection of human life, to the extent that death prevails over the natural
instinct for life".[19]

"Active", "passive" and "indirect" euthanasia constitute the three *species*, the three epi-phenomena, of "merciful" euthanasia.

On the basis, therefore, of two common factual conditions, such as the
condition of suffering and the patient's physical and mental pain (due, for
example, to an illness that has reached the terminal stage) and the reasons
for the conduct, i.e. *pietas* with respect to the victim, we can distinguish
"active" euthanasia (*mercy killing*), as the suppression of the life of a person *manu aliena* (relatives, friends, doctor in charge of the case), by means
of active conduct. One speaks of passive euthanasia (*letting die*), as the
suppression of the life of the patient, always *manu aliena*, but when the
conduct consists of an omission, such as, for example, the unplugging of
an artificial respirator. In such cases death is found to be linked to the illness from the viewpoint of a causal connection.

Lastly, there is "indirect" euthanasia, also known as "disguised" or
"pseudo" euthanasia,[20] which occurs when a patient in a terminal state, in
addition to normal therapy, is given analgesic-narcotic substances in
doses that are sufficient to alleviate the pain, but with the inevitable

---

[18] The expression was applied extensively to numerous and various experiences of
"sweet death". For a review of the phenomenology included in the term euthanasia, from
"collective" practice, in terms divided into eugenic, economic, experimental, solidarity,
preventive, and criminal euthanasia, to "individualistic", or merciful, euthanasia *see*
Mantovani, *Eutanasia*, *supra* note 7; Id., *Diritto penale. Delitti contro la persona* (Padova,
1995), p. 118.

[19] With respect to the development of the meanings of the term, also related to the passage of death from an "event" to a "process", until reaching the current concept of euthanasia as a "merciful death" *see* Magro *Eutanasia*, *supra* note 11, p. 99; Pierpaolo Martucci,
Eutanasia (profili criminologici), in *Enciclopedia Giuridica Treccani* (Roma, 2004), p. 2.

[20] Francesco D'Agostino, *Parole di bioetica* (Torino, 2004), p. 81.

"unwanted" side effect of lowering cardio-respiratory functions and thus hastening the time of death.

A. *Euthanasia, Assisted Suicide and the Italian Criminal Code*

The terms "euthanasia" and "assisted suicide", present above all in the political and social debate tied to the draft legislation on "advance treatment directives", do not appear in the Italian Criminal Code due to the already mentioned semantic and phenomenological variance of the words, which generates undoubted difficulties of standardizing them.

The 1930 Criminal Code does not provide a specific regime for euthanasia,[21] but the relative conduct can be considered, certainly with some difficulty, by reference to the paradigmatic cases of "consensual murder" (Article 579 of the Criminal Code)[22] and "instigation or assisted suicide" (Article 580 of the Criminal Code),[23] as well as, obviously, "murder" (Article 575 of the Criminal Code).[24]

1. *Euthanasia*

With respect to indirect euthanasia, i.e. death "hastened" by the administration of analgesics, but in fact linked to the illness as the "cause" of the act, the lack of criminal liability of the doctor's behaviour is currently clear because it conforms to the professional, curative and therapeutic responsibilities for which he/she is responsible. The need to alleviate the patient's

---

[21] With respect to the need for a legislative intervention that specifically regulates euthanasia as a crime *see* Stella, *supra* note 7, p. 1007.

[22] Art. 579 of the Criminal Code. *Consensual murder*: "1. Anyone who causes the death of a person, with his consent, shall be punished by imprisonment ranging from six to fifteen years. 2. The aggravating circumstances indicated in Article 61 do not apply. 3. The provisions related to murder apply if the act is committed: 1) against a person who is under eighteen years of age; 2) against a person who is mentally ill, or who is in a state of mental deficiency due to another illness or the abuse of alcoholic substances or drugs; 3) against a person whose consent was extorted by the guilty party with violence, threats or suggestion, or deceit".

[23] Art. 580 of the Criminal Code. *Instigation or assistance to suicide*: "1. Anyone who causes others to commit suicide or reinforces another's intent to commit suicide, or facilitates it in any way, shall be punished, if the suicide occurs, by imprisonment ranging from five to twelve years. If the suicide does not occur, he shall be punished by imprisonment ranging from one to five years, as long as there is a grave or very grave personal injury resulting from the suicide attempt. 2. The penalties are increased if the person instigated or excited is in one of the conditions indicated in paragraphs 1 and 2 of the previous article. Nevertheless, if the above person is younger than fourteen years old or lacks the ability to provide consent, the provisions related to murder apply".

[24] Art. 575 of the Criminal Code. *Murder*: "Anyone who causes the death of a person shall be punished by imprisonment of at least twenty-one years".

suffering, in fact, is the other face of the "duty to provide treatment", i.e. the doctor's obligation to perform all activities that are useful for alleviating the patient's suffering.[25]

The assessment of active euthanasia is completely different, which the criminal law represses *tout court*.

Focusing on the pre-requisite of the consent of the subject-victim to euthanasia, acts disposing of one's own life *manu aliena*, i.e. death requested and obtained by the patient by means of the commission of an act by a third party, constitute the elements of the crime of consensual murder (Article 579 of the Criminal Code). Common murder (Article 575 of the Criminal Code) is instead committed when there is no "valid"[26] consent. The provision of Article 579(3) of the Criminal Code, in listing the cases in which consent is invalid, aims at greater severity in determining whether there was an ability to provide consent with respect to the liability regime pursuant to Article 85 of the Criminal Code, without any space for reasons involving mercy, and above all, without any distinction between total or partial, permanent or transitory psychological impairment.

At the level of the relative sanction, this approach suffers from excessive rigor and severity. It therefore requires, as a request of artful legal scholarship,[27] in view of the rather severe and intransigent case law,[28] legislative revision so that space is given to "reasons of mercy" in weighing the penalty, allowing the application of the extenuating circumstances

---

[25] With respect to "pain therapy" by means of the various positions of legal scholarship and case law *see* Stefano Canestrari, "Le diverse tipologie di eutanasia: una legislazione possibile", in S. Canestrari (ed.), *Reati contro la vita e l'incolumità individuale* (Torino, 2006), pp. 117–143.

[26] The requisites for the validity of consent are expressly indicated by case law, which requires consent that is not only serious, explicit and unequivocal, but which also continues through the time in which the guilty party commits the crime (Court of Cassation, I section, 27.06.1991, Vernetti, CP 1992, 3047).

[27] Giunta, *supra* nota 3.

[28] Ass. Catania 24.10.1977, *Fabiano*, in *Giurisprudenza di Merito*, 1978, II, p. 1211, who argues that euthanasia, breaking the connection of proportion and adequacy with the primary need of respect for human life, with respect to which it is in alternative relationship, cannot constitute even the elements of the extenuating circumstances of particular moral and social value. *See* further, Court of Cassation, 17.04.1989, *Billo*, in *Giustizia Penale*, 1993, II, page 201, with the critical note of M. Bellotto, where the Supreme Court held that the abstract compatibility of the extenuating circumstances pursuant to Article 62(1) of the Criminal Code with the crime pursuant to Article 579 of the Criminal Code, cannot also be accepted with respect to euthanasia, as this practice still lacks "that general positive appreciation from an ethical-moral viewpoint by current society, necessary for the qualification of the reason as of particular moral and social value".

pursuant to Article 62(1) and 62 *bis* of the Criminal Code, i.e. reasons of particular moral and social value.[29]

The criminal law assessment of "passive" euthanasia is in different terms, used in all cases in which a "merciful" death is granted to a party by means of conduct constituting an "omission", i.e. passive behaviour that consists of the lack of administration by the doctor or health care professional of treatment that would prolong life as well as prolong the time of death.

In such cases, the lack of criminal liability for consensual passive euthanasia is clear, i.e. the refusal and interruption of the care requested by the patient who refuses therapeutic intervention, by means of a valid and current consent. This is due to the fact that it is precisely the patient's consent that is the mandatory pre-requisite of any medical-surgical treatment.

The lawfulness of non-consensual passive euthanasia remains controversial, which is a situation in which there would appear to be the need for the doctor, pursuant to Article 40(2) of the Criminal Code, as the holder of a position of guarantee connected to the legal obligation to impede death, to provide the "care" necessary to avoid death. In practice, the problem is linked to the limit or limits of the "treatment obligation" with respect to the patient's right to refuse treatment and the prohibition against aggressive medical treatment.

In addition to issues related to the concept of action and omission, and the relative issues, in the case of passive euthanasia, of the possibility of constituting the elements of an "act due to omission", the principal issue regards the possibility and limits of the entry into the Italian legal system of a "refusal of treatment" expressed at a time prior to the moment in which it must be enforced, and the conditions on which such refusal can be accepted. In other words, the possibility to find that no criminal liability derives from the doctor's abstaining from an attempt to save the patient's life or provide treatment, on the basis of instructions issued by the patient when he/she was still capable of providing consent.

2. *Suicide*

When the conduct that suppresses life falls within the sphere of sovereignty of the individual who wishes to die, and therefore the "final

---

[29] With reference to whomever deems the reference to reasons of particular moral or social value to be inadequate because in any event unable to mitigate the rigor of the regime of sanctions *see* Canestrari, *supra* note 25, p. 216.

decision" of life or death refers to such individual, the Criminal Code only applies to the third party who acts to instigate or facilitate the suicide (Article 580 of the Criminal Code). As in the case of consensual murder, in the specific cases of a minor who is less than fourteen years old or anyone who is incapable of providing consent, the crime is instead common murder pursuant to Article 575 of the Criminal Code, as in these cases the reasons of mercy underlying the final gesture are not extenuating circumstances.

In effect, suicide and attempted suicide are lawful acts.

Independently from the political-criminal reasons that such choice is based on, such as the impossibility of punishing the person who commits suicide and the inappropriateness, in the case of an unsuccessful suicide attempt, of criminal repression against a person who is already psychologically weakened to the extent that they tried, without success, to kill themselves, the lawfulness of suicide demonstrates the existence and the recognition of a right to die in the Italian legal system. Such right, however, is only granted to the person who attempts to commit suicide on their own. If this person, for any reason, is physically incapacitated and is therefore unable to take care of him or herself alone, the intervention of a third party who assists at the time of the final act results in a charge of consensual murder being brought against such party (Article 579 of the Criminal Code).

III. A *REDUCTIO AD UNITATEM* OF VARIOUS CONSIDERATIONS: THE CRUX
OF THE ITALIAN DEBATE ON THE RIGHT TO DIE AND ADVANCE
TREATMENT DIRECTIVES

This organization of the phenomenon and norms in a system of "end-of-life" protection still suffers from numerous "complications".

The formulation of the 1930's Code is considered by many not only to be obsolete, because it is based on a State idea of the legal system and is not "person-centric", as is instead the case of the Italian Constitution, but above all, is inadequate in view of scientific progress in the medical field and is deaf to the needs of a civil society that has been transformed with respect to the perception of matters of "life" and "death". In particular, it attempts to deal legally with a new phenomenon, i.e. the possibility of controlling the time and manner of one's death, caused by the progress of medical technologies and requested by the spread of new mortal diseases or by the ability of illnesses to "last" over time due to scientific progress, at the cost, however, of grave suffering and the impossibility, in some cases, to "kill oneself without assistance".

The complex problems of suicide, a lawful act for the person who commits suicide but which results in criminal liability, in Italy, for anyone who has instead "assisted" the suicide, both in the sense of facilitation or instigation, as well as in the sense of the substitution of an incapacitated party to implement his/her suicidal will alone, introduces a broader theme linked to whether or not there is a "right to die", a "right to the dignity of one's own death" and a "right to live one's own death according to a principle of self-determination", and what guarantees the legal system gives or should give to such right.[30]

Without prejudice to the distinction between suicide and euthanasia with the criteria of the sphere of sovereignty of an enforceable act, the final act which in itself is the irrevocable implementation of the decision and which supports its weight when it cannot be distinguished from consensual murder,[31] it currently appears to be the time to reflect on whether it is opportune to continue to keep the case set forth in Article 579 of the Criminal Code alive and the unlawfulness of assisted suicide.

In essence, the issue is raised as to whether by now the lawfulness of the suppression of life *manu propria* (suicide) or *manu aliena* (in the version of consensual passive euthanasia) unites not only the existence of a right to die, but also the legal system's recognition of such right and, therefore, its guarantee.

Italian scholarship[32] recognizes the right to die as an inalienable right of the person pursuant to Article 2 of the Italian Constitution, which must be adequately guaranteed by the norms of the Codes, i.e. the possibility that punishment be graduated by means of special extenuating circumstances based on altruistic objectives, through the exclusion from punishment in the most significant cases (impossibility of recovery and intolerance of suffering).

Without changing the aspect of the unlawfulness of the act, but acting on the level of its punishment, the legal system needs to find uniformity and the lack of contradiction of its legislative provisions, in addition to

---

[30] Lucia Risicato, *Dal diritto di vivere al diritto di morire* (Torino, 2008).

[31] Luigi Stortoni, "Riflessioni in tema di eutanasia", 3 *Indice Penale* (2000), pp. 477–486, p. 479; Id., "Riflessioni in tema di eutanasia", in S. Canestrari, G. Cimbalo and G. Pappalardo (eds.), *Eutanasia e diritto. Confronto tra discipline* (Torino, 2003).

[32] About the different opinion of the italian jurists see Luigi Stortoni (ed.), *Vivere: diritto o dovere* (Trento, 1992).

proceeding along the road of the full recognition of the value of the patient's self-determination with respect to end-life choices.[33]

Other authors instead claim that the lawful nature of the act of suicide can be traced back to the mere exercise of a freedom that is negatively authorized by the legal system, which must maintain a neutral outlook with respect to all of those activities which, whether or not morally disapproved of, do not threaten third party rights.[34]

Still others think that the right to die is an aspect of respect of the dignity of man, and therefore even of the dignity of his death, and find the legitimacy of the refusal of invasive practices on one's body by granting the individual the same rights of defence, with the right to refuse treatment, including life-saving treatment, that is deemed, however, to be intolerable, recognized by the State with respect to intrusions into its territory.[35]

Beyond the pre-chosen interpretative option, the problem remains of evaluating the cases in which the person must express his or her final decision but who is no longer capable of manifesting his or her will due to different cases of mental infirmity which, from the temporary loss of consciousness resulting from an acute and unexpected event can range to a permanent vegetative state.

The situation has been shown to be complex if one considers the need in these circumstances to validate an express consent given at a time prior to the loss of consciousness, including from the viewpoint of whether it is "current", and, even more so, the difficulty of reconstructing the will of the patient when no express indications have been left.

It is, in effect, the equivalence of these cases to those in which an actual will exists and is manifested that creates confusion and generates regulatory problems.

Beyond the possibility of "standardizing" the circumstances that affect the punishment or that determine whether an act is punishable, discussed prevalently at the time of reform projects of the Italian Criminal Code, and in the lack of true unanimity or even only cultural homogeneity in order to proceed with a Copernican revolution (360 degrees) of the system

---

[33] See Sergio Seminara, "Riflessioni in tema di suicidio e eutanasia", in 38 *Rivista italiana di diritto e procedura penale* (1995), page 670; Giunta, *supra* note 3; Mantovani, *supra* note 7, p. 425.

[34] See Canestrari, *supra* note 25, p. 233.

[35] See Giovanni Fiandaca, *Il diritto di morire tra paternalismo e liberalismo penale*, report to the Congress on "*Il rifiuto di cure: libertà, diritto o delitto*", organized by Specialization School for Legal Profession, University of Foggia, 12 December 2008.

of end-life protection, the legislator is currently debating advance treatment directives as a short-mid term solution.

By enhancing the patient's responsibility for decision making by means of a living will, or the patient's charter of self-determination, the legislator chooses an instrument that is compatible with the Italian constitutional legal system to the extent that it exalts compliance with personal convictions by applying the criteria of the lowest possible differences from the will of the individual.

It is clear that in view of the proper use of the instrument of advance directives, an adequate solution must be found for the issues related to the content of the directives, their authenticity and spontaneity, their renewal and the manner in which they can be revoked, as well as the very thorny problem of a representative for persons who are incapable of providing consent.

IV. The Draft Law on "Advance Treatment Directives" and "Procedural Exoneration"

The choice that the current draft legislation is aimed at with respect to advance directives consists of putting the technique of "procedural exoneration"[36] into practice, from the viewpoint of a criminal law intervention.

The draft law, in the version approved by the Senate and amended by the Chamber of Deputies, does not innovate the level of the reference values of the code system. Confirming the prohibition against "any form of euthanasia and every form of assistance or help with suicide", without the provision of any mitigation of liability in cases in which there are ethical reasons of mercy towards the patient, a system is constructed for the recognition of the patient's final decision according to the formula of "procedural standing".

As authoritatively noted in legal scholarship, "the State does not prohibit nor liberalise, but simply regulates in a balanced manner that leaves an autonomous choice to individual decision-making", by means of the "guarantee of an adequate social control" using a "procedure aimed at ensuring compliance with certain ethical or technical conditions of acceptability that have been pre-determined by the law".

---

[36] About the procedural exoneration in this matter see Donini, *supra* note 6, p. 906.

In brief, the procedure allows acts to be legitimised that would otherwise be prohibited and the procedure is not declarative but "constitutes" lawfulness, limiting itself, however, to verifying the consent of the party or that such consent is current.

The Italian experiment crystallized in the bill, which constitutes a procedural justification for the construction of a system based on advance directives, refers to Dutch and Belgian legislation, which paved the way for the decriminalization of medical activity deliberately aimed at causing or facilitating the death of a person who wishes to end their life.

An example of a "consociationalism approach"[37] to developing criminal law, prior to the 2001 law Holland was already characterized as being a legal system in which there was a "factual" tolerance for euthanasia, even while there were outstanding laws against assisted suicide or consensual murder. The law formalized pre-existing guidelines in order to have the "underground number" of cases of euthanasia emerge, in order to control it. The legitimacy of medical action aimed at provoking death is based on the "voluntary and well thought out" request of the patient together with a grave condition and intolerable physical suffering, which must be verified by the doctor assisted by another colleague, who intervenes to guarantee recognition of a voluntary will to die, which is connected to the conviction that there is no other reasonable solution. The solution adopted renders euthanasia and assisted suicide not punishable in the cases indicated.

In 2002, Belgium also approved a law on euthanasia, which uses the Dutch format and legalizes consensual euthanasia and assisted suicide.[38]

In 2009 also Luxembourg enacted legislation to legalise euthanasia, thereby becoming the third European country, after the Netherlands and

---

[37] See *Eutanasia e diritto. Confronto tra discipline, supra* note 31; Martucci, *supra* note 19, p. 7.

[38] About the Belgian experience see Kenneth Chambaere, Johan Bilsen, Joachim Cohen, Bregje D. Onwuteaka-Philipsen, Freddy Mortier, Luc Deliens, "Physician-assisted deaths under the euthanasia law in Belgium: a population-based survey", 182 *Canadian Medical Association Journal* (2010), p. 873. The interpretation of the results by the authors is that "Physician-assisted deaths with an explicit patient request (euthanasia and assisted suicide) and without an explicit request occurred in different patient groups and under different circumstances. Cases without an explicit request often involved patients whose diseases had unpredictable end-of-life trajectories. Although opioids were used in most of these cases, misconceptions seem to persist about their actual life-shortening effects". See also Els Inghelbrecht, Johan Bilsen, Freddy Mortier, Luc Deliens, "The role of nurses in physician-assisted deaths in Belgium", 182 *Canadian Medical Association Journal* (2010), pp. 905–910: "By administering the life-ending drugs in some of the cases of euthanasia, and in almost half of the cases without an explicit request from the patient, the nurses in our study operated beyond the legal margins of their profession".

Belgium, to permit the intentional killing of dying or otherwise vulnerable people. The Palliative Care bill provides that doctors who carry out euthanasia and assisted suicides will not face "penal sanctions" or civil lawsuits.

Aside from some comments on the format used, a serious projection of what will be the final form of the law on living wills does not currently appear to be possible, crushed in the bud by the inclination to be a counter-move to the *Englaro* case, and hostage, in the discussion and approval of the law, to the already mentioned tensions among government and opposition forces. At the end of the day, the choices are still precarious and go in different directions, and the legislator is being rigid in balancing the constitutional rights at play, also demonstrating all of its concern for issues of a *slippery slope*, i.e. for any drifting of the legislation if excessively open to euthanasia.

On a general level, the possibility for the doctor to ignore the will expressed by the patient, thus resulting in the prevalence of the decision of the health care professional over that of the patient, alienates and distorts the underlying reason for advance directives.

By replacing the figure of the doctor at the centre, according to the current formulation, the legislator would be clearly turning backwards with respect to the difficulty of overcoming a paternalistic concept of medicine, denying value to the therapeutic alliance and debasing the role of informed consent, with consequences even from a criminal law standpoint in relation to the inevitable distortion of the doctor's position as guarantor.

The appointment of the fiduciary, according to a criminal law perspective, is heavily discouraged, affected by the risk of criminal liability when there is an omission pursuant to Article 7, that would result in an indictment for assisted suicide or consensual murder, without any provision of special extenuating circumstances or impact on liability based on underlying reasons of mercy.

Even on the level of sufficient certainty, the draft legislation for criminal law purposes is unconvincing to the extent in which the use of the term euthanasia appears to be excessively casual without further specifications, a word which refers to different behaviour and phenomenon, with the relative implications of whether or not they are lawful.

Further, there are the restrictions provided in relation to the refusal of treatment in the draft legislation, which risk being in net contrast with the approaches that case law has developed over the past years, by means of the coherent application of constitutional principles, and according to a tendency by now in substitution of case law with respect to the path of legislative reform.

As in similar cases,[39] in fact, even in the sector of end-life directives, the legislator is undoubtedly subject to the difficulty of safeguarding ethical-religious precepts, an option that conflicts with the fundamental principle of the secular nature of the State, according to the orientation of the Constitutional Court, and by the principle of equality and the reasonableness of the laws pursuant to Article 3 of the Italian Constitution.

Beyond what the Parliament is about to discuss and approve with respect to advance directives, the decisions of Italian case law[40] must be acknowledged which, "pre"- regulatory intervention, take a position on this issue and appear to be moving from a perspective according to which, in the sectors tied to the inalienable rights of the person, the choices of the legislator would have already risked, or are risking, unjustly repressing areas of the fundamental rights of the individual, which as such are not alienable by the Parliamentary majority in office. Such arguments obviously solicit, more or less explicitly, the stigmatization of excessive creativity for those who should instead be performing their function of interpreting and implementing outstanding law.

If this corresponds to what can be understood from the judgments of the courts in the *Welby* and *Englaro* cases, it appears even more so from the *Santoni* case, decided by a judgment of the Court of Florence on 13 December 2010, whose grounds were filed on 12 January 2011, just a few days from the resumption of the discussion on the draft legislation.

The Guardianship Judge of the Court of Florence accepted the request of a petitioner to appoint a guardian, in the person of his wife, to ensure compliance with the advance treatment directives for which he had given his consent and those for which he withheld his consent, and therefore he expressed a clear anticipated refusal of treatment should he become

---

[39] Reference is made to the law of medically assisted procreation (Law 40/2004), which was strongly desired by the current Parliamentary majority according to a scheme that has confined the practice of assisted procreation to exceptionally reduced limits, and which at present appears to be increasingly controversial due to court decisions at every level (ordinary courts, administrative courts, Constitutional Court, European Court of Human Rights). *See* Emilio Dolcini, *Fecondazione eterologa: ancora un'ordinanza di rimessione alla Corte Costituzionale*, available at http://www.penalecontemporaneo.it (2011).

[40] With respect to the intervention of the courts, in this as in other sectors of the legal system, in aid of a legislator that moves slowly along the path of reform, engulfed by political problems of the Parliamentary discussion, or even to make a collective feeling explicit that is not perceived by the Parliament, and urge legislative options, some have spoken of the need for a "scientific study" of case law, which is currently the true protagonist of change, with decisions that anticipate or conflict with the choices of legislative power.

incapacitated, i.e. unable to manifest his will. This uproots the approach sustained through the present, according to which an obstacle to the effective implementation of the patient's will to die was the legal obligation to safeguard the health or life of a person unable to give their consent, or the assisted person according to the Italian Civil Code.

From a legal standpoint, therefore, it appears that there is a lost occasion to make a living will an instrument not to say "what life is" from the doctor's viewpoint, but to say "what life means" for the patient, according to a perspective of discussion in which it is the guarantee of the individual's choice that is the protagonist, because the ethical-legal problem is not, and should not be, the merits of the choice but only the instruments to guarantee that such choice is freely made and is current.[41]

---

[41] Silvia Bagni, "Dov'è finita la carità? Riflessioni etico-giuridiche sul testamento biologico", in *Forum dei quaderni costituzionali* (2009), pp. 1–5, available at http://www.quadernicostituzionali.it.

THE INTERFACE BETWEEN END-OF-LIFE CARE AND RELIGIOUS RIGHTS: LEGISLATION OF A CHRISTIAN OR A SECULAR STATE?

Giuseppe D'Angelo *

I. The Legal Regulation of "End-of-Life Care" in the Light of the Principle of Secularism

There is no doubt that legal scholars engaged in the study of what the Italian literature currently defines as "ecclesiastical law (of the State)",[1] or—if we prefer to have recourse to an expression which is perhaps broader and, consequently, less conditioning—of the relationship between law and religion, can find in bioethics generally and, more specifically, as in our case, in "end-of-life care" related issues, a (relatively recent but) very interesting field of investigation.

In fact, exploring the deeper meaning of the solutions being outlined with reference to those issues is equivalent, for the same researcher, to take care about the status of one of the most important principles concerning the relationship between law and religion, better known as the "principle of secularism".[2]

---

* Researcher of Ecclesiastical law of the State and Canon Law at the Faculty of Law of the University of Salerno, Italy; email: gdangelo@unisa.it.

[1] In the language of the Italian legal literature, this expression usually indicates the specific branch of the legal system governing the relationships between the State (or, broadly, public institutions) and the Churches or religious groups and organizations; but in a deeper, more recent, interpretation it indicates all the rules involving religious freedom. Instead, the expression "canon law" indicates the body of laws and regulations governing the Catholic Church. See Francesco Finocchiaro, *Diritto ecclesiastico* (Bologna, 1986) and, more recently, Maria Cristina Folliero, *Diritto ecclesiastico. Elementi. Principi non scritti. Principi scritti. Regole. Quaderno I. I principi non scritti* (Torino, 2007).

[2] In this paper, we will have recourse to the attribution of secular (and the correspondent substantive of secularism) to translate the attribution of "laico" (and the correspondent substantive of "laicità"), used by Italian scholarship as well as Italian Courts and Tribunals, as it will result clearly afterwards. It is not easy to establish if the expression secularism and "laicità" can be really considered perfectly equivalent but we would probably muddle things up if we acted differently. However, it is worth pointing out that, according to its origin and to its literal meaning, the term "laity" seems to be more usefully used as a way to distinguish, in the ecclesiastical perspective, what is not directly regarding clerical life: see, Antonio Vitale, *Corso di diritto ecclesiastico. Ordinamento civile e fenomeno religioso* (Milano, 2005).

S. Negri (ed.), *Self-Determination, Dignity and End-of-Life Care*
2011 Koninklijke Brill NV. Printed in The Netherlands. ISBN 978 90 04 22357 8. pp. 437–454

But there is still more.

Inverting that observation, we can also consider that this topic can help us understand what is the real sense of secularism as a legal principle; to understand, what it should be before considering which is the current level of respect in which it is held in our legal system.

Indeed, the question is not secondary.

Because, if we want to deal with it from a legal viewpoint, we must first take note of the fact that the current (or, if we prefer, the abstract) idea of secularism may not be entirely coincident with its legal sense. In fact, we already know that, assuming a comparative perspective, we are forced to realize that we cannot find an unanimously recognised definition of secularism and of its real meaning.[3]

It is probably true that a definition of secularism according to the representation that common sense would be inclined to assume should be interpreted as involving a condition of complete independence of political powers from religious (or ideological and institutional but not public) powers,[4] although it must be also considered that this aspiration has to confront itself with the actual, renewed and widespread tendency of religious groups and institutions to assume an increasingly pervasive public role.[5] In social and legal contexts like the Italian one, this trend appears to be more relevant and this is not surprising in the light of Italian legal history and the widespread presence of the Catholic Church in the Italian society.

On a specific legal ground, the same trend is somehow reinforced by the (more or less, depending on the specific circumstances to be considered) explicit formalization of a constitutional process of (necessary) negotiation between the Church and the State in legislation involving their reciprocal relationships (better known in the Italian literature as the

---

[3] «Non esiste una definizione assoluta di laicità. Una sua formula applicabile al di là e al di qua del meridiano zero»: Folliero, *supra* note 1, p. 135. As the Author further explains (p. 107), "Tra l'essenza della laicità e il relativo principio giuridico – l'ultimo è il modo in cui la *laicità* entra concretamente a fare parte degli ordinamenti costituzionali occidentali, esercitando una concreta funzione di indirizzo dell'esperienza giuridica – vi è sempre una frattura. Mantenerla aperta o tendere a riassorbirla, e i modi per farlo, sono tutte scelte che, nel nostro Paese, come negli altri d'altronde, portano l'impronta dei soggetti che vi hanno messo mano nella filiera di produzione e monitoraggio del diritto".

[4] See, for a closer examination and other bibliographical references, Folliero, *supra* note 1, pp. 107 ff.

[5] See, W. Cole Durham Jr. and Javier Martinez Torrón (eds.), *Religion and the Secular State / La Religion et l'État laïque: Interim Reports*, prepared for and issued upon the occasion of *The XVIIIth International Congress of Comparative Law*, held on 25 July - 1 August 2010 in Washington, D.C.

"principle of bilateralism");[6] as it will be better explained below, that mechanism is now substantially bent, under a broad interpretation, to cover areas wider than those for which it was originally designed.[7]

Thus, actually, the same consideration of secularism as one of the supreme principles of the Italian constitutional system—first enunciated by the Italian Constitutional Court in the very important decision no. 203 of 1989 (which, significantly, had the effect of recognizing the constitutional legitimacy of the system of Catholic education in public schools[8])— can be said to constitute, in substance, a far more prosaic (but very hard) attempt to strike a reasonable balance between seemingly contradictory constitutional provisions. In this perspective, we can surely talk about a fundamental compromise between the recognition of a specific channel of collaboration between the State and the Churches[9] and the relocation of its rightful outcomes within the broader framework of constitutional legitimacy, with reference to both specific[10] and general rules.[11]

In short—although by way of simplification—the legal principle of secularism shows, particularly in the Italian context, a two-fold objective: on the one hand, it facilitates the entry (by selection) of confessional and religious inputs in the democratic circuit and, on the other, it confirms the

---

[6] We must consider art. 7, para. 2, and 8, para. 3 of Italian Constitution, providing, the first, *inter alia*, that the mutual (between the State and the Catholic Church) relations are regulated by the Lateran Pacts, and, the second, that the relations between the State itself and the non-Catholic denominations are regulated by law in accordance to a prior agreement. On these basis, Italian scholarship has just deduced the existence of the so-called "principle of bilateralism". According to this principle, the State is obliged to find a preventive agreement (or in the case of Catholic Church, to subscribe a Concordat) when it intended to regulate its relations with religious denominations or the Catholic Church itself; consequently it could not unilaterally abrogate those regulations. We should also consider that the existence of this principle is almost pacific, although there are some discussions regarding its real extension: See, for example, Vitale, *Corso di diritto ecclesiastico, supra* note 2.

[7] As it was authoritatively pointed out in the Italian literature, the principle of bilateralism should be acted—as a constitutional necessity—only in presence of "reciprocal relations" to be regulated; in this perspective, the same Authors have explained that the formula "reciprocal relations" should be intended as the field involving the religious freedom of the individuals as a consequence of their being, at the same time, citizens and believers. See Salvatore. Berlingò, "Fonti del diritto (diritto ecclesiastico)", *Digesto delle discipline pubblicistiche*, vol. VI, (Torino, 1991),pp. 454–484; Giuseppe Casuscelli and Sara Domianello, "Intese con le confessioni diverse dalla cattolica", *Digesto delle discipline pubblicistiche*, vol. VIII, (Torino, 1993), pp. 518–543.

[8] See, for further references, Folliero, *supra* note 1, p. 115 ff.

[9] See arts. 7, para. 2, and 8, para. 3, of the Constitution.

[10] First of all art. 19 and, accordingly, art. 20 of Constitution.

[11] First of all arts. 2 and 3 of the Constitution, in their substantive role as the essence of the democratic principle enshrined in art. 1.

need to verify the consistency of the outcomes of those processes with constitutional legality.

As a consequence, our aim is necessarily to analyze the Italian draft law on advance directives (hereinafter Draft Bill) in the light of this dual characterization.

II. The Italian Draft Law on Advance Directives in the Perspective of the Relationships Between the State and the Churches or Religious Institutions

A. *The Intervention of the Catholic Church in the Bioethical Debate as a Way to Reaffirm Its Political Role in the Italian System*

It is really difficult not to realize that the subject of advance directives regulation constitutes for the Religion of more established presence in Italy, the Catholic Church, a very important field to reaffirm its right to intervene in the dynamics of the relationships between law and politics.

We could think that it represents a really intolerable interference, while some Authors consider it a significant example of an instrumental use of the appeal to "natural law".[12]

But, above all, it appears to be in a substantially continuous line with the sharp turn impressed by the ecclesiastical hierarchy in the direction of taking a direct political role in the Italian context. We could place this event in the first half of the 2010's; it is worth underlining at the same time, that one of the occasions of such restatement was provided by an "ethically significant" subject such as the law on medically assisted fertilization (Law No. 40 of 2004), whose referendum failed miserably—under

---

[12] See Luciano Zannotti, "Questioni di vita o di morte", in V. Tozzi, G. Macrì and M. Parisi (eds.), *Proposta di riflessione per l'emanazione di una legge generale sulle libertà religiose* (Torino, 2010), pp. 289–382, at p. 292, who points out that the reference to natural law "(in seconda battuta, perché del diritto divino la Chiesa può chiedere il rispetto solo al suo interno) sia un passaggio decisivo della dottrina tradizionale e della concezione cattolica del mondo, uno stratagemma, un espediente per alludere a qualcosa che vale in generale e che però generale non è, che indica arbitrariamente un dover essere in nome dell'essere, che serve ad abilitare la Chiesa a intervenire non solo a proposito di bioetica, rappresentando in effetti la ragione più profonda della sua vocazione politica". The Author sees in this position "ciò che Aldo Schiavone ha chiamato naturalizzazione ideologica della morale, dell'economia, del diritto, ma, si potrebbe aggiungere, di qualsiasi argomento riferibile alla convivenza umana. La gerarchia ecclesiastica"—he continues significantly—"diventa così l'unica fonte etica autorizzata. Di qui l'inevitabile attrazione al magistero della Chiesa di ogni materia che riguardi la società civile".

the auspices of the Church, in fact—for not reaching the required quorum for validity.[13]

However, such a consideration is corroborated, in my view, by several elements.

In the first place, we must consider the role of the decisive polarization of the relationship between the unavailability/inviolability of life and its sacredness as a key to the solution of bioethical questions.[14] This is a trend that could be considered, in many respects, improper and reprehensible, but at the same time it is clearly useful to allow assessments of a religious nature, and, in this way, legitimize the official position taken by the ecclesiastical institutions within the relevant political debate. As some Authors duly note, in art. 1 of the Draft Bill life is indeed defined as yet unavailable and inviolable, but we should perhaps note that the real object of legal protection is the sacredness of life itself[15] or, in other words, a conceptual reference that is well suited for practical implementation of the absolute opposition of the Church to every solution regarding a positive evaluation of advance directives.[16]

In the second place, we should point out the public position taken by leading members of the Catholic Church on the occasion of the tragic events that have brought the matter under the spotlight and, therefore, have affected the legislator; those positions have certainly not contributed to a serene and objective assessment of the problems that are connected

---

[13] Folliero, *supra* note 1, p. 146.

[14] I would like to refer to my review of the book by Enrico Maestri, *La vita umana «presa sul serio». Uno studio sul perfezionismo bioetico di John M. Finnis e sul liberalismo bioetico di Ronald Dworkin* (Napoli, 2009), in *Diritto e Religioni* (2010), no. 1, p. 513.

[15] See Lucia Risicato, *Indisponibilità o sacralità della vita? Dubbi sulla ricerca (o sulla scomparsa) di una disciplina laica in materia di testamento biologico*, available at http://www.statoechiese.it (March 2009), p. 22, who states that "solo in questo senso può spiegarsi la distinzione concettuale e giuridica, adottata sino ad ora dalla legge, tra terapie mediche, terapie di sostegno vitale ed accanimento terapeutico" ed ancora "solo in questo senso, d'altro canto, può spiegarsi la sovrapposizione concettuale tra indisponibilità ed inviolabilità della vita. I due aggettivi, si riferiscono notoriamente a caratteristiche molto diverse tra loro: l'inviolabilità della vita è un dato strettamente connesso al rispetto della persona umana in materia terapeutica, e ben può essere ricollegato al diritto fondamentale di non subire trattamenti sanitari indesiderati. A rigore, pertanto, l'inviolabilità delle scelte di fine vita potrebbe persino essere antinomica rispetto al dato dell'assoluta intangibilità del *bios*".

[16] Or, more broadly, "l'assoluta contrarietà della Chiesa a cercare un compromesso sulle questioni attinenti la morale di cui si attribuisce la piena ed unica competenza". In this sense Zannotti, *supra* note 12, at p. 292, who lingers over the reference—in Pope Benedict XVI's argumentations—to "non-negotiable values", as a formula to be used to "indicare una soglia al di sotto della quale nessuno deve scendere, un nucleo etico di cui gli uomini e gli ordinamenti civili non possono disporre".

to those topics, so that they have brought new life to the rather short circuit occurring between law and politics, politics and justice. This has contributed to a strong distortion of the institutional environment, namely
the balance between the powers of the State, resulting in a condition of
potential neutralization of the founding principles of the pact of civil
coexistence formalized in the Constitution.

We could think, as an example, to the public opinions expressed by
cardinal Javier Lozano Barragan after the conclusion of the terrestrial history of Eluana Englaro: for many Authors they raise perplexities, although
we can consider them substantially coherent with the stance taken by
part of the ecclesiastical hierarchy.[17] Even television programmes and
especially their conductors have not been spared, being instead submitted to a shut criticism because of their failure to act with due impartiality
in the choice of their guests.[18]

On the contrary, the Italian Ministers of Health (Ferruccio Fazio), of the
Interior (Roberto Maroni), of the Labour and Social Policy/Welfare
(Maurizio Sacconi) have more recently received the approval of Cardinal
Elio Sgreccia, for the special circular with which they have criticized the
initiative of some municipalities to create special registers to collect the
advance directives of their citizens.[19]

It seriously risks to be—according to the case—frankly naive or, to be
generous, a useless exercise of hypocrisy to deny the real following of such
"indications" in the high spheres of politics. Otherwise, there have been
reconstructions aimed to highlight a suspected coincidence of timing
with regard to the scan of each stage of the process concerning the Draft
Bill and the positions, more or less official, of the Holy See, trying to point
out the dangers of legalization of euthanasia dangerously placed in proper
motion by the judicial solution of the Englaro case.[20]

---

[17] Lucia Risicato, *Indisponibilità o sacralità della vita? Dubbi sulla ricerca (o sulla scomparsa) di una disciplina laica in materia di testamento biologico*, available at http://www.statoechiese.it (March 2009), p. 21.

[18] See, *Avvenire*, 16 November 2010.

[19] See http://www.repubblica.it (20 November 2010).

[20] See the interview of Cardinal Camillo Ruini in *Avvenire* of 25 September 2008, quoted by Emilio Carnevali, "Storia politica del testamento biologico in Italia", *Micromega* (2009), no. 2, pp. 122–134, at p. 133. In the opinion of this Author, the statement that: "soltanto attraverso una norma di legge è possibile impedire che quel pronunciamento apra a una deriva eutanasica, fino a consentire l'interruzione della nutrizione e dell'idratazione", indi-cates a change in the attitude of the Catholic Church (or, in other words, a real "turning point"). In his perspective, the Catholic Church is now interested, differently than in the past, to the approval of a specific law which formally regulates advance directives while substantially preventing actual recourse to them.

But, in my opinion, there is an element in particular that highlights, more than any other, the singularity of the Italian case and witnesses some propensity by the ecclesiastical hierarchy to develop a purely political role.

Even a brief review of the European situation shows in fact an interesting distinction with regard to the official position of the Episcopal Conferences which operate as representative bodies of the bishops in the individual States and representing, at once, one of the most significant reference in the relationship with public institutions and the expression of the most important official positions of the Church of Rome.

As it is highlighted in Italian literature,[21] in countries like Germany and Spain, in contrast to what happens in Italy, the Episcopal Conferences have shown an attitude far more open with regard to advance directives.[22] It seems to me that this significant difference is not easily explainable, if not through the use of the pattern (indeed inappropriate, considering that we are talking about a religious Institution, but probably corresponding to reality) of politic mediation (or opportunism?).

This also seems to testify that the unconditional opposition otherwise shown by the Italian integral special component of the universal Church is not to be regarded—as one would be led to believe—as a necessary consequence of the assumption of faith on the protection of life or, if you prefer, of the Christian view of life. Particularly sensitive and careful Authors have not failed to observe, in fact, that the Papal Magisterium itself has previously highlighted the need to consider in a proper way the decision of those who refuse to be subjected to more invasive treatments that science makes available to lengthen (sometimes, just artificially) a vegetative life.[23]

At the same time, even those Authors who—with respect to individual freedom of conscience—are engaged in stressing that the Christian concept of life conflicts with any regulation of advance directives, are first willing to point out that, in reality, there are no official documents and position statements on this matter and, second, they are, more or less directly, forced to assume a notion of advance directives which is not fully congruent with the legal regulation in progress, leaving on the background

---

[21] Stefano Rodotà, *Perché laico* (Roma-Bari, 2009), p. 83.
[22] See also Erminia Camassa, "Le questioni bioetiche: direttive anticipate di trattamento e libertà religiosa", in *Proposta di riflessione, supra* note 12, pp. 303–315, p. 314, sub footnote 19.
[23] Rodotà, *supra* note 21, p. 88.

the real *punctum dolens* of the matter, that is—as we will see below—the classification of artificial nutrition and hydration.[24]

B. *Right to Intervene or Prohibition of Interference?*

It is therefore not unreasonable to hypothesize that, as we pointed out in the introduction, bioethical issues and, in this case, advance directives regulation represent, in essence, a significant test of the tendency of the Catholic Church to assume a more direct role in Italian politics[25] or, if you prefer, clear evidence of the real importance (indeed remarkable) that the dictates of the Church's hierarchy have in the institutional practice of political decision-making, first of all in Parliament.[26]

As a result, the evidence gathered so far might lead to conclude that we are dealing with a law emanating from a Christian State rather than a

---

[24] See Marco Canonico, *Eutanasia e testamento biologico nel magistero della Chiesa cattolica*, available at http://www.statoechiese.it (May 2009): "Sulla base delle esposte indicazioni del magistero ecclesiastico in tema di concezione della vita, sacralità ed indisponibilità della stessa, con conseguente divieto di ogni forma di eutanasia, si può prudentemente ritenere, pur in assenza di formali documenti ed ufficiali prese di posizione al riguardo, che la Chiesa non possa accettare la prospettiva del cosiddetto testamento biologico, inteso come dichiarazione preventiva del soggetto che, ricorrendo determinate circostanze, valga ad autorizzare l'interruzione di terapie o trattamenti necessari al mantenimento della vita, provocando pertanto in maniera volontaria la morte dell'interessato in virtù del consenso dal medesimo preventivamente rilasciato. Si parla in proposito anche di dichiarazioni anticipate di trattamento, trattandosi di espressioni di volontà da valere per il futuro in presenza di certe condizioni (per esempio il versare del soggetto in stato vegetativo). Risulta evidente"—the Author continues—"che attraverso simili dichiarazioni l'individuo mira in sostanza a disporre della propria vita, sebbene al realizzarsi di specifiche condizioni e dunque in linea eventuale. Se nella visione cristiana la vita costituisce un bene indisponibile per l'uomo, in tale ottica sarà per forza di cose inaccettabile ogni determinazione comunque tendente ad incidere sul naturale corso dell'umana esistenza ed a consentire una forma di eutanasia".

[25] As Professor Folliero points out (*supra* note 1, p. 150), this phenomenon could even be considered as a specific consequence of the disregard of the famous Italian party, named "Democrazia Cristiana".

[26] See the conclusions of the paper of Geminello Preterossi, "Fede e sapere (secondo Papa Ratzinger)", in F. Lucrezi and F. Mancuso (eds.), *Diritto e Vita. Biodiritto, bioetica, biopolitica* (Soveria Mannelli, 2010), pp. 635–640, at 640, with regard to the speech that the Pope had to give at the University "La Sapienza" in Rome, which he did not give as a consequence of the protests of part of the academy: "La forza di tale impostazione, caratterizzata da una notevole compattezza della struttura interpretativa generale – pur intrisa di assunti concettuali, dimenticanze e relativizzazioni storiche, corto-circuiti teorici assai discutibili – sta tutta nella difficoltà degli attuali soggetti politici e culturali laici, mondani di governare le trasformazioni complesse in cui siamo immersi e di generare nuovi discorsi egemonici secolarizzati. Oltre che, in Italia, in una patologica e grottesca tendenza generale della classe dirigente alla subalternità verso poteri indiretti e non pubblici, al fine di ottenere vantaggi di piccolo cabotaggio in termini di consenso e potere".

Secular State (even if this is basically an attribute that, as said before, has a relative meaning). But, considering the question more carefully, one could think that those considerations cannot be really decisive in this respect; rather, they are merely circumstantial evidence, although very serious.

Indeed, it is not easy to prove that the contents of the Draft Bill are the result of external interference and not an inherent ambiguity of the (only Italian?) political class, which is naturally inclined to seek consensus on the basis of easy slogans, just as easy and simplistic is the recall to the unconditional protection of life; in the second place, it is not possible to limit the analysis to the consideration of the particular weakness of the Italian political system and, correspondingly, of the (untenable) interference by inherent pervasiveness of the Holy Roman Church with regard to matters which do not fall within its competence, because this would risk to constitute a mere rhetorical exercise or even to be counterproductive.[27]

Outstanding Authors have argued that the Catholic Church shows some problems with constitutional loyalty and with regard to its relationships with Eastern democracies and, especially, with the Italian Republic,[28] while other authorities have noted that the Church in Italy is increasingly struggling for cultural hegemony.[29] It is probably true, moving from these assumptions, that these dynamics obviously require similar strength and determination on the part of the institutions and the civil society.

However, at the same time, public institutions themselves are bound not to overcome those limits that they have self-imposed through the Constitution. In other words, the interference of which the Church can be accused and the real suffering of the principle of secularism may well contribute to an interpretation of this principle in a very defensive, and then

---

[27] It should be also considered that in the history of humanity the relationships between political powers and religious powers have been more complex: see, *ex multis*, Ivana Vecchio Cairone, *Forme di Stato e forme del sacro*, (Roma, 2009) and, by the same Author, *Introduzione allo studio della storia e sistemi dei rapporti tra Stato e Chiesa. I sistemi unionisti* (Roma, 2009).

[28] Gustavo Zagrebelsky, "Stato e Chiesa. Cittadini e cattolici", *Diritto pubblico* (2007), no. 3, pp. 697–720, at p. 704.

[29] Rodotà, *supra* note 21, p. 97. The Author points out that "Non si tratta di misurare il grado di «ingerenza» accettabile, di discutere intorno al ruolo della religione nella sfera pubblica, valutando così la legittimità di quello che, con cadenze ormai quotidiane, dicono il Pontefice e i cardinali. Bisogna riprendere una discussione costituzionale, perché ai principi e ai diritti sanciti nella prima parte della Costituzione si contrappongono valori cristiani di cui si afferma in modo perentorio l'essenzialità e l'irrinunciabilità".

anti-clerical and anti-religious way,[30] but we should probably also consider that such an interpretation would not be fully consistent with the
Italian constitutional context.

In fact, any countermeasures regarding the breach of the duty of non-
interference emerging from art. 7, para. 1, of the Italian Constitution[31]—
consider, for example, the unilateral abrogation of Law No. 121 of 1985 (i.e.
the law ratifying the "New Agreement" between the Italian Republic and
The Catholic Church of 18 February 1984), or at the international level, the
termination of this Agreement—remain difficult to be practised. At this
level, the real problem is perhaps made up of the "dual" characterization
of the ecclesiastical institution—being considered at the same time as an
original order (just like a State!) and as a social group—which could actually be considered the real vice of origin in the civil setting of the relationship between the state and the religious phenomenon that inspired the
Italian model.

But, above all, such a claim to (preventive) neutralization of any intervention of the Church is deeply problematic: it would be easily overcome
in relation to the deemed denial of general rights, formalized in the
Constitution, and powers expressly recognized in that Concordat (or,
more exactly, the "New Agreement" between the Italian Republic and The
Catholic Church of 18 February 1984) or, respectively, freedom of thought
and expression of propaganda in the field of belief and religion and freedom of exercise of the pastoral and educational activities.[32]

---

[30] The words of Sergio Romano, *Prefazione* to Voltaire, *Sulla tolleranza*, italian translation by Piero Bianconi (Milano, 2010), p. 8, are really significant: as the Author points out,
"Se tornasse sulla terra Voltaire scoprirebbe di non essere laico, ma laicista".

[31] Art. 7, para. 1, of the Italian Constitution provides, in fact, that the State and the
Church are independent and sovereign each within its own order of competence.

[32] In this perspective, see Canonico, *supra* note 24, p. 19 ff. In the Author's opinion, "Dal
punto di vista dell'ordinamento civile l'istituzione ecclesiastica, al pari di ogni individuo e
di qualsiasi collettività presente all'interno di un sistema pluralista, ha il diritto di esprimere
liberamente il proprio pensiero. Per giunta, in quanto confessione religiosa ha facoltà
di propagandare il proprio credo e le proprie ideologie. Né, trattandosi di entità sovrana
(art. 7, primo comma, Cost.), può esserle impedito di perseguire le proprie finalità, e
dunque l'esercizio dell'attività pastorale ed educativa, come del resto espressamente
riconosciuto e garantitole dall'Italia in sede pattizia (art. 2 Accordo di Villa Madama) ... Il
richiamo alla laicità,"—the Author continues—"se vale dunque legittimamente ad esclu-
dere una dipendenza ideologica ed un difetto di autonomia decisionale da parte dello
Stato e dei suoi organi, non può certo, senza sfociare in un bieco laicismo ovvero negazione
della stessa libertà ideologica, precludere ai cattolici ed alle istituzioni ecclesiastiche,
al pari di ogni altro soggetto, il diritto di esprimere e propagandare le proprie idee, come
un ordinamento democratico deve permettere e garantire a pena di negare la sua stessa
natura .... In temi implicanti scelte morali, come quello dell'eutanasia, ciascuno deve

On the other hand, it is to be considered that the Catholic Church should refer, in substance, to a specific matter of positive law, exploiting the full potential inherent in art. 1 of the same 1984 Agreement (which substantially provides that the Catholic Church contributes, as well as the State itself (!), to the goal of the promotion of humanity and the good of the Country) whose substantial incoherence (or, if you prefer, difficult coherence) has been pointed out by a very sensitive and forward-looking doctrine.[33]

Of course, this argument could be reversed, stressing that the recent "encroachments" of the Church can be seen as confirmative of the inadequacy of the same art. 1 or of its heterogeneity, at least, with regard to the principle of the separation of orders between the Church and the State.[34]

To take the intervention of the Church in the debate on these issues as an expression of democracy could probably seem to be inconsistent and unconvincing (just considering the disproportion of the forces present in the political arena); but, at the same time, you could consider that this is a risk that is worth to be taken.

The reinterpretation of secularism in the sense of the exclusion of religious views from the political debate might, in fact, lead to a significant retreat from the (already far from happy) rate of the Italian political system of democracy. That's the risk, in other words, of the so-called "protected democracy", that is the recent, paradoxical attitude of democracy, that is forced to deny itself, in trying to defend itself.[35]

In this sense, you should perhaps courageously confirm that diversity of opinion is the spice of democracy and constitutes an element for its decisive implementation. So the contribution of the Catholic Church too, even with regard to bioethical issues, might be useful to better understand the problems and to provide the most satisfactory answers. At the same time, you also should observe that there are other positions, even religiously oriented but otherwise much more willing to consider adequately the individual right to self-determination.[36] These conceptions are really

---

essere libero di scegliere la posizione che ritiene condivisibile...Laddove si cerchi di soffocare il dialogo fra le parti interessate si esce dall'ambito del pluralismo e della democrazia, facendo anzi sorgere il sospetto della mancanza, in quanti auspicano il silenzio dell'avversario, di valide argomentazioni per confutare la tesi di segno contrario".

[33] Vitale, *Corso di diritto ecclesiastico, supra* note 2, p. 208.

[34] As enshrined in art. 7, para. 1, of the Italian Constitution.

[35] On today's tensions of democracy, in a legal perspective, see Antonio Vitale, *La forma di Stato democratica* (Roma, 2005).

[36] See Ermina Camassa and Carlo Casonato (eds.), *Bioetica e confessioni religiose* (Trento, 2008).

interesting, because they have already passed through on a more properly operating plan.[37]

To conclude on this point, it is surely not easy to consider the political debate as a confrontation between equals and this is a very negative aspect of the Italian democratic system, but it does not seem to be a good solution, at present, to prevent religious groups and institutions—firstly the Catholic Church—to fulfill their public role of pressure and rivalry with regard to public institutions.

III. The Draft Bill in the Perspective of Religious Freedom

A. *The Individual Profile*

From a legal perspective it is not possible to assess the legislations relating to "ethically significant" topics only seeing them in the light of the alleged contamination resulting from the dissolution of the alternative between the right of intervention and the prohibition of interference (in the sense of the prevalence of the former).

You should also consider, in this perspective, that respect for minority opinions in the context of the political debate or, in other words, the balance between the principle of majority and the constitutional protection of minorities, is not a matter concerning the relationship between law and religion alone, as the Italian case shows very well. This is a question involving, more widely, the very meaning of democracy in its latest variation of "constitutional democracy" and invoking the deepest meaning of the Constitution itself as a defense appeal for the guarantee of minority rights: a legal precept, just based on the strength of numbers and in total disregard of minorities (but we can say of individuals) cannot be considered compatible with the concept of democracy as envisaged by the Constitution itself.

As a priority, we could say *ex ante*, political decision-making should be the result of a compromise, the largest and most respectful of the different positions in the field, even if we should remember too that minorities should be able to find in the whole legal system additional forms of guarantee and protection (even, we could say, *ex post*).

---

[37] We can see, as an interesting example, the initiative of the Waldesian Church in Milan that instituted a public office and set up a special register to collect the advance directives of citizens: see, for details, http://www.olir.it, news, altre notizie (2 December 2009).

We could therefore legitimately think that the Draft Bill is the result of the specific inputs of the Catholic Church but it should be now clear that the real problem is represented by the concrete contents of the Bill: we have now to consider them just moving from their relationship with the constitutional right to self-determination of individuals.

This is a very interesting subject for scholars studying the "Ecclesiastical law of the State", because it brings to our attention the other profile of the legal principle of secularism, which concerns the constitutional guarantee of the right to religious freedom.

Moving in this direction, the question can be approached according to a double perspective.

The first is "general" and "principled": it concerns the value of individual conscience.

The second is to be considered, instead, in a more specific way, having technical consequences. It affects, in fact, one of the most critical steps of the Draft Bill, because it could neutralize the distinction—that we can consider really artificial—between medical treatments (for which, in principle, a refusal would seem to be possible) and "merely support" treatments (specifically, artificial nutrition and hydration, for which no prior declaration of refusal would be allowed).

From the first viewpoint, it seems particularly significant that in the context of art. 1 of the Draft Bill there is no reference to art. 19 of the Constitution, which guarantees freedom of religion.

In my opinion, this is a real important circumstance, because, firstly, it is a clear sign of the marginal consideration of art. 19 Const. and of its potential. But, above all, it constitutes a (mediate) confirmation that, in reality, the Draft Bill does not intend to consider adequately the right to self-determination of the individual as a direct manifestation of his freedom of conscience.[38]

It is worth remembering, in this perspective, that the Italian Constitution does not expressly and independently protect the individual conscience; as the Italian scholarship observes, it seems to take its own special significance due to a systematic and evolutionary reading of the above-mentioned art. 19, in its interaction with art. 2 of the same Constitution.

---

[38] In fact, in this case, we should consider that "E' la coscienza individuale, con i suoi tormenti, a dover essere rispettata da un legislatore al quale si addice la sobrietà e, nei casi limite, il silenzio": Rodotà, *supra* note 21, p. 97.

In particular, the assertion of a specific protection of the individual consciousness is a logical necessity of the same religious freedom: in its constitutional significance, freedom of religion is above all freedom to choose or not to choose a religion, so that there can be no religious freedom without recognizing the protection of individual conscience and, more profoundly, of the path leading to that choice.[39]

It is probably hard to talk about freedom of conscience as a right just operating like every other right (for example, like the right of property) but we should consider, however, that every violation of the freedom of conscience leads inevitably to the violation of religious freedom, which is certainly protected by the Constitution.

At the same time, the broadest view of the guarantees underlying the recognition of conscience as the original projection and indispensable element of the human person strengthens and substantiates the duty of neutrality of the State or, if you prefer, its secularism.

It is thus confirmed that secularism cannot be regarded as an abstract value, but in its projection as an instrument for ensuring better protection of the conscience of every individual. As you can see, the infringement of the principle of secularism perpetrated with the Draft Bill becomes, along this line of argument, much more clear and, above all, more intolerable, because it conflicts, in essence, with specific and constitutionally relevant individual rights.

Moreover, as anticipated, there is another important, but specific, element we have to consider too, because it could otherwise lead to significant technical-legal consequences on the Draft Bill.

We know that, according to art. 3, para. 4, of the Draft Bill, nutrition and hydration, in the various forms which science and technology can provide to the patient, are considered as forms of life support and physiologically designed to relieve suffering until the end of life, so that they may not be the object of advance directives.

In this way, the legislator intends to resume the line of argument made by the advocates of the living will, acting on its potential weakness: the disposition of the draft bill is so principally focused on the meaning

---

[39] I would like to refer (also for further references) to my "I simboli c.d. passivi nello spazio pubblico tra tutela delle libertà (di coscienza, di espressione, religiosa) e principi di non identificazione e separazione degli ordini: spunti di comparazione (ed in una prospettiva de iure) dalla più recente giurisprudenza statunitense", in N. Fiorita and D. Loprieno (eds.), *La libertà di manifestazione del pensiero e la libertà religiosa nelle società multiculturali* (Firenze, 2009), pp. 151–173.

of art. 32 Const. which, as we know, includes a ban on compulsory treatment only if they represent a "medical treatment".[40]

We also have to consider that art. 32, in conjunction with arts. 2 and 13 Const., constitute the regulatory axis along which Italian judges and scholars unfold the solution of the case that kicked off the need for normative regulation of advance directives (i.e. the Englaro case[41]).

In my opinion, this is like saying that the stance taken by the legislator on the meaning of art. 32 is basically a need imposed by judicial events, but it may prove not to be decisive with regard to the protection of the individual freedom of self-determination.

In this context, I also believe that this is an unproductive line of argumentation for both supporters and opponents of advance directives, because it relies on a concept, that of medical treatment, which is only apparently characterized by an aura of objectivity.

On this basis, we can point to the expansive potential of the real meaning of religious freedom, as it is considered by the above mentioned art. 19 Const., to derive very important consequences for this subject.

In particular we first have to consider, that, at this moment, freedom of religion cannot be defined yet as a mere freedom to profess a faith but it should manifest itself, in a qualitatively significant and innovative way, as the right to act consistently with the dictates of one's faith.

This is a very crucial point.[42]

A broader interpretation of the possibilities which are inherent in the constitutional recognition of the right of religious freedom may allow the principle of individual self-determination to be anchored on more solid foundations, passing reference to the narrow nature of the treatment (medical/non medical) that the individual himself intends to refuse.

---

[40] On the interpretation of art. 32 of the Italian Constitution see, *ex multis*, Giuseppe Ugo Rescigno, "Dal diritto di rifiutare un determinato trattamento sanitario secondo l'art. 32, co. 2, Cost., al principio di autodeterminazione intorno alla propria vita", *Diritto pubblico* (2008), no. 1, pp. 85–112.

[41] See *ex multis*, Roberto Romboli, "Il caso Englaro: la Costituzione come fonte immediatamente applicabile dal giudice"; Annalisa Stefani, "Il caso Englaro: le due Corti a confronto"; Carlo Casonato, "Il caso Englaro: fine vita, il diritto che c'è", all published in *Quaderni costituzionali* (2009), no. 1, respectively at pp. 91–94; 95–98; 99–102.

[42] I have just pointed out, even in a different field, the potential of such an interpretation in my "Diritti fondamentali e condizione dello straniero alla luce dell'ampia declinazione assunta dal diritto di libertà religiosa nell'odierno quadro di legalità costituzionale: spunti problematici dalla più recente giurisprudenza in tema di ricongiungimento familiare e rilascio del permesso di soggiorno per «motivi religiosi»", in V. Tozzi e M. Parisi (eds.), *Immigrazione e soluzioni legislative in Italia e Spagna. Istanze autonomistiche, società multiculturali, diritti civili e di cittadinanza* (Ripalimosani, 2007), pp. 159–181.

Naturally, this applies, first of all, where the choice of the individual of not using artificial nutrition and hydration practices is made on grounds of a religious nature.

It is worth considering, in this perspective, that the issues currently at stake were somewhat anticipated by legal proceedings that have more clearly highlighted a problematic relationship between the right to health and the right to religious freedom.

The Courts that have intervened at that time substantially rejected the legitimacy of the (religiously motivated) refusal of blood transfusions[43] (the facts of the case involved Jehovah's witnesses[44]); however[45], it is to point out that it was the health of a person under age to be discussed and we certainly cannot consider that freedom of religion of the parents and their right to education can prevail over the health of a child.[46]

In my opinion, by this way, the limitation placed by art. 3, para. 4, of the draft bill could hardly be warranted if there is a declaration of refusal based on religious grounds.

The same reference to "human dignity" requires to move in the direction we have pointed out: the believer who rejects a particular (medical or non medical) treatment would probably conclude not to be able to live a worthy life if he discovered to have been kept alive as a result of a violation of his faith.[47] That's the same, in my opinion, to say that he has suffered an intolerable violence.

---

[43] We really should consider that this was a very complex question but we cannot analyze it now. See, however, the bibliographical references considered by Francesco Finocchiaro, *Diritto ecclesiastico* (Bologna, 2010), p. 198, particularly sub footnotes 3 and 4.

[44] A useful overview of the question, from an internal perspective, has been recently provided by Paolo Piccioli, *Il prezzo della diversità. Una minoranza a confronto con la storia religiosa in Italia negli scorsi cento anni* (Napoli, 2010), p. 371 ff.

[45] And considering that we can finally say that, at the moment, the Italian legal system is substantially inclined to recognize, under certain conditions, the right of individuals to refuse blood transfusions.

[46] "[L]'ordinamento, infatti, non può legittimamente tutelare scelte genitoriali che, se pur motivate da convincimenti religiosi, pongano in pericolo l'integrità fisica del minore": Raffaele Botta, *Tutela del sentimento religioso ed appartenenza confessionale nella società globale. Lezioni di diritto ecclesiastico per il triennio* (Torino, 2002), p. 220.

[47] See ibid., p. 221, where the Author observes, with specific regard to these cases, that "il riconoscimento dell'obiezione per motivi di coscienza al trattamento medico non significa riconoscimento di un *diritto di ammalarsi* o di un *diritto di morire*: l'obiettore, che rifiuta l'emotrasfusione, l'intervento chirurgico o chemioterapico non pensa che morirà (o che il suo stato patologico peggiorerà), egli pensa di guarire, che la preghiera, Dio basterà a sanarlo. E, soprattutto, egli pensa a salvarsi l'anima. L'obiettore, quindi, rivendica non il «diritto ad essere (e a restare) ammalato» – in quanto, nella sua prospettiva, il *male* è proprio la cura che gli si vuole imporre –, bensì, ancora una volta, il diritto alla propria *identità*, a vivere, cioè, anche la propria patologia coerentemente ai dettami della propria

But looking more carefully at the question, a very similar argument could be proposed with respect to declarations of refusal not necessarily justified on religious grounds.

In this case—and considering the legal principle of equality—freedom of religion can serve as a driving force for each instance of protection of social and cultural identities.

B. *The Collective Profile*

But there is still another aspect to be considered: the need for respect of the options based on religious reasons is yet problematic from several points of view.

This perspective draws another *leitmotiv* of the analysis of the researcher of Ecclesiastical law of the State, which is the complexity of the relationships between the two facets of religious freedom, between its individual and its collective profile.

On this ground, this question is really delicate.

It should be prevented that the will and the decisions of individuals be coerced by religious groups or their hierarchies.

Individual freedom absolutely prevails on the freedom of the group, so that individual freedom must be protected against any possible intrusion of the group, considering that the latter is naturally led to demand an absolute devotion and consistency of behavior.

If one really believes that the matter must somehow be regulated by law, one should, at the same time and according to the appropriate "fee of precaution", avoid recognizing a specific role to private organizations and religious institutions.

In my opinion, advance directives should probably be filed only with public institutions or agents or, otherwise, remain in a strictly private sphere.

IV. BRIEF CONCLUSIONS

I would like to conclude reverting to the basic question considered in the title of this paper: does the draft bill represent the legislation of a Christian or a Secular State?

Well, we had to consider, firstly, that this question does not intend to point out the unfairness of the interventions of the Catholic Church into the debate on this issue; in fact, this cannot be the very real problem, if we consider the general subject which has been here analyzed in the light of civil legal system.

As we have seen above, the positions of the Catholic Church as well as the positions of other religious groups and institutions may even be useful to the debate and, however, we had to consider that political decision-making processes fall within the province of public institutions.

In this perspective, the real need is the consistency of the contents of the Draft Bill, or its consequences, with our constitutional basis.

Particularly from this point of view, we have to consider that the Draft Bill basically follows a line which is fundamentally incompatible with the protection of the individual right to self-determination,[48] since it imposes its interpretation of what life is.

It does not matter if this particular view of life and its meaning is of a religious or not of a religious nature; it is rather important that, in the Draft Bill, there is no space for freedom and especially for religious freedom.

But on this common ground (the guarantee of individual rights and liberties) we have really to be severe, particularly in demanding that the State does not renounce to its sovereignty.[49]

coscienza e della propria fede. Del resto, per un credente dannarsi l'anima è un prezzo troppo alto da pagare, persino per salvarsi la vita".

[48] "[I]l principio di autodeterminazione non riguarda solo la materia delle prestazioni sanitarie ma l'intero ordinamento": Rescigno, *supra* note 40, p. 109.

[49] I wish to refer to my book *Crisi dello Stato, riforme costituzionali, principio di sussidiarietà* (Roma, 2005), particularly at pp. 110 ff.

ANNEX: ITALIAN DRAFT BILL ON
"DISPOSITIONS IN MATTER OF THERAPEUTIC ALLIANCE,
INFORMED CONSENT AND ADVANCE TREATMENT DIRECTIVES"*

ARTICLE 1
(Protection of Life and Health)

1. In consideration of the principles enshrined in articles 2 [protection of inviolable rights], 3 [principle of equality], 13 [protection of personal freedom], and 32 [protection of the right to health] of the Italian Constitution, the present law:
a) recognizes and protects human life as an inviolable and indisposable right, guaranteed also in the terminal phase of life and in case the person is no longer competent, until death is verified according to the law;
b) recognizes and protects the dignity of every person as a priority over the interest of society and of the applications of technology and science;
c) prohibits under articles 575 [murder], 579 [murder by consent] and 580 [aiding and abetting suicide] of the Italian criminal code every form of euthanasia, assistance and aid to suicide, considering that medical activities and assistance to patients are exclusively aimed to protect life and health and to relieve suffering;
d) mandates doctors to inform patients of the most appropriate medical treatments – except for what is provided in article 2, paragraph 4 – and of the prohibition on every form of euthanasia, recognizing as a priority the therapeutic alliance between the doctor and the patient, which is of particular significance at the end of life;
e) recognizes that no medical treatment can be performed without informed consent as provided in article 2, considering that health must be protected as an individual fundamental right and as a collective interest, and that nobody can be compelled to receive a specific medical treatment except under a mandatory provision of law and with the limits imposed by the respect for the human person;
f) guarantees that in case of patients at the end of life or for whom death is imminent, doctors shall abstain from medical treatments that are extraordinary and disproportionate with respect to the patient's clinical conditions or to healing objectives.
2. The present law guarantees, within the framework of those interventions already provided by the legislation in force, social and economic policies aimed at

---

* Draft Bill passed by the Senate of the Italian Republic on 26 March 2009 and approved with amendments by the Chamber of Deputies on 12 July 2011, currently under examination by the Senate 12th Standing Committee. Unofficial English translation by Stefania Negri.

S. Negri (ed.), *Self-Determination, Dignity and End-of-Life Care*
2011 Koninklijke Brill NV. Printed in The Netherlands. ISBN 978 90 04 22357 8. pp. 455–460

taking care of patients, in particular of those who are mentally incompetent – be they citizens, foreigners or stateless persons – and of their families.

3. Patients mentioned in subparagraph 1.*f*) are entitled to receive appropriate pain therapies in accordance with the relevant law in force and in conformity with palliative care protocols.

ARTICLE 2

(*Informed Consent*)

1. Except for cases provided by law, every medical treatment must be performed after informed consent is expressly, freely and consciously given by the patient.

2. The expression of informed consent shall be preceded by correct and comprehensible information provided by the attending physician to the patient as to the diagnosis, prognosis, scope and nature of the proposed medical treatment, foreseeable benefits and risks, possible side effects, as well as possible treatment alternatives and the consequences of refusal of treatment.

3. The therapeutic alliance built within the doctor-patient relationship according to paragraph 2, can be expressed, whenever the doctor deems it necessary and the patient so requests, in a document on informed consent, signed by the patient and the doctor. This document is included in the medical record upon request of the doctor or of the patient.

4. The patient retains the right to refuse in whole or in part the information he is entitled to receive. Such refusal may occur at any time and must be expressed in a document, signed by the interested subject, which becomes an integral part of the medical record.

5. Informed consent to medical treatment shall always be fully or partially revocable. The revocation shall be recorded in the medical record.

6. In the case of a disqualified person, informed consent is given by the legal custodian, who signs the document. In the case of an incapacitated person or emancipated minor, informed consent is given jointly by the guardian and the interested person. Whenever an administrator has been appointed by court, and the court's decree statues that assistance and representation shall also be provided in health-related situations, informed consent is given also by the administrator, or by the administrator alone. The decision of these subjects also encompasses the provisions of article 3 and it is taken with the sole aim of protecting the health and life of the incapacitated person.

7. Informed consent to medical treatment of children is given or refused by those who exercise parental or guardian authority after having heard the wishes and requests of the child. The decision of these subjects is taken with the sole aim of protecting the life and the psycho-physical health of the child.

8. With respect to all disqualified or incapacitated persons, lacking any declaration of advance treatment directives, the health personnel shall always act with the sole aim of protecting the life and health of the patient.

9. Informed consent to medical treatment is not required where, in case of emergency, there is a real and immediate risk to the patient's life.

ARTICLE 3
(*Contents and Limits of the Advance Treatment Directive*)

1. In an advance treatment directive, the declarant, who is fully mentally competent and has received complete medical information, with regard to a possible future permanent loss of mental capacity, expresses his directions and useful information as to the medical treatments he wishes to receive, in conformity with the provisions of the present law.

2. The advance treatment directive may contain an express renunciation of any or of some specific therapeutic treatment of disproportionate or experimental nature.

3. The advance treatment directive shall not contain instructions corresponding to the crimes proscribed by articles 575, 579, and 580 of the Criminal Code.

4. Also in compliance to the United Nations Convention on the Rights of Persons with Disabilities, signed in New York on 13 December 2006, artificial nutrition and hydration, in the various forms that science and technology can provide, must be maintained until the end of life, except in cases where they are no longer efficacious in providing the patient with the nutritional elements necessary for the essential physiological functions of the body. They shall not be the object of an advance treatment directive.

5. The advance treatment directive is activated when the subject is in a state of permanent incompetence – due to an assessed absence of integrative cortical-subcortical brain activity – and cannot understand information on medical treatment and its consequences, so that he cannot make decisions about himself. Such assessment is certified by a medical board composed, without additional or new costs for the public finances, of an anaesthetist-intensivist, a neurologist, the attending physician and the specialist in the disease affecting the patient. With the exclusion of the attending physician, these doctors are appointed by the directive board of the medical facility where the patient is hospitalised or by the relevant local health authority.

ARTICLE 4
(*Form and Duration of the Declaration of Advance Treatment Directives*)

1. Advance treatment directives are not binding, they are redacted in writing, dated and signed by the interested fully competent adult after the provision of appropriate and exhaustive medical information, and they are collected only by the general practitioner, who simultaneously signs them.

2. Advance treatment directives shall be made in full freedom and consciousness, and signed with an autograph signature. Any declaration of intent or direction expressed in ways different from the forms and modalities provided by the present law have no value and shall not be used to reconstruct the patient's will.

3. Unless the subject has become mentally incompetent, the advance treatment directive is valid for 5 years starting from the date of the drafting of the act

according to paragraph 1, after which term it is no longer valid. The advance treatment directive can be renewed several times in the same form and modalities as
provided in paragraphs 1 and 2.

4. The advance treatment directive can be revoked or modified at any time by the
interested person. Revocation of the advance treatment directive, even partially,
must be signed by the interested person.

5. The advance treatment directive must be included in the medical record from
the moment it is activated from a clinical point of view.

6. In case of emergency or when the subject is in immediate peril of life, the
advance treatment directive does not apply.

ARTICLE 5
(*Assistance to Subjects in a Vegetative State*)

1. In order to grant and guarantee equitable access to assistance and quality of
care, the assistance to subjects in a vegetative state represents an essential level of
health care, in accordance with the modalities provided in the Decree of the
President of Ministers of 29 November 2001, as published in the ordinary supplement of the *Gazzetta Ufficiale* n. 33 of 8 February 2002. Healthcare assistance to
persons in vegetative state or affected by other neurological conditions is provided through hospital, residential and home care, according to the modalities
provided in the above mentioned Decree and the agreement between the
Ministry of Health, the Regions and the Autonomous Provinces of Trento and
Bolzano on the Guidelines for assistance to persons in a vegetative state and
minimally conscious states, as approved on 5 May 2011 by the Unified Conference
provided by article 8 of the legislative decree no. 281 of 28 August 1997 and
following amendments. Home care is as a rule provided by the local health
authority with territorial jurisdiction over the place where the subject in a vegetative state is.

ARTICLE 6
(*Proxies*)

1. In the advance treatment directive, the declarant can appoint an adult mentally
competent proxy, who accepts the appointment by signing the directive.

2. The declarant who has appointed a proxy may substitute him according to the
same modalities followed for his appointment, at any time and without any obligation to give reasons for such a decision.

3. The appointed proxy is the sole subject who is legally authorized to interact
with the doctor with regard to the content of the advance treatment directive and
he undertakes to act exclusively in the best interests of the patient, always and
solely in accordance with the wishes legitimately expressed by the subject in his
advance treatment directive.

4. The proxy is entitled to ask and receive from the doctor every information on
the state of health of the declarant.

5. The appointed proxy undertakes to ensure that the patient is administered the best available palliative treatments, avoiding any situation of therapeutic futility or therapeutic abandonment.

6. The appointed proxy undertakes to verify carefully that no situation amounting to the crimes proscribed by articles 575, 579, and 580 of the Criminal Code affects the patient.

7. The proxy can renounce the appointment in writing, communicating his renunciation to the declarant or, if he is mentally incompetent, to the doctor who is responsible for the medical treatment.

8. In case no proxy has been appointed, the tasks provided in paragraphs 2, 3 and 4 above are undertaken by the relatives indicated by the Civil Code in Book II, title II, headings I and II.

ARTICLE 7
(*The Role of the Doctor*)

1. The directions expressed by the declarant in the advance treatment directive are taken into consideration by the attending physician, who, after having heard the proxy, writes down in the medical record the reasons why he does or does not follow them.

2. In case the attending physician decides not to follow the directions expressed by the patient in the advance treatment directive, he has to consult the proxy or the patient's relatives, as indicated by the Civil Code in Book II, title II, headings I and II, and give detailed reasons for his decision, which has to be written down and signed in the medical record or in a separate document annexed to the advance treatment directive.

3. The doctor cannot take into consideration directions which are meant to cause the death of the patient or are in conflict with the law or medical deontology. After having heard the proxy, the doctor evaluates the instructions according to science and conscience, and applying the principles of the inviolability of human life and the protection of health and life, according to the principles of precaution, proportionality and prudence.

ARTICLE 8
(*Final Provisions*)

1. A Registry of advance treatment directives is created within a single national information archive. The subject entitled to the processing of data inserted in this archive is the Ministry of Health.

2. By regulation to be adopted according to article 17, paragraph 3, of Law No. 400 of 23 August 1988, within 120 days from the date of entry into force of the present law, the Ministry of Health, after having heard the Guarantor for the protection of personal data, shall provide the technical rules and the modalities of access, conservation and consultation of the Registry sub paragraph 1. The decree shall also establish the terms and forms according to which the interested persons will be

able to draft the advance treatment directive at the general practitioner's office, as well as those concerning registration and conservation at the local health authority, and telematics transmission to the Registry mentioned in paragraph 1 above. Every information concerning the possibility to draft an advance treatment directive are made available on the website of the Minister of Health.

3. [...]

4. [...]

NOTES ON CONTRIBUTORS

Roberto Andorno is Senior Research Fellow at the School of Law of the University of Zurich, Switzerland. Originally from Argentina, Dr. Andorno holds doctoral degrees in law from the Universities of Buenos Aires and Paris XII, both on topics related to the ethical and legal aspects of assisted reproductive technologies. Between 1999 and 2005 he conducted various research projects relating to bioethics, human dignity and human rights at the Faculty of Philosophy of the University Laval (Canada), and at the Universities of Göttingen and Tübingen (Germany). From 1998 to 2005 he also served as a member of the International Bioethics Committee of UNESCO as representative of Argentina, and participated in this capacity in the drafting of international declarations and reports relating to bioethics. Dr. Andorno has published extensively on issues at the intersection of bioethics and law, and is member of the editorial boards of "Medicine, Health Care & Philosophy", the "Journal international de bioéthique", and "Bioethica Forum. Swiss Journal of Biomedical Ethics".

Heloisa Helena Barboza is Head Teacher of the Chair of Civil Law at Rio de Janeiro State University (UERJ Law School). PhD in Law (UERJ) and Sciences (ENSP/Fiocruz), Specialist in Applied Ethics and Bioethics (IFF/Fiocruz), Researcher in Civil Law, BioLaw, and Bioethics.

Estelle Brosset, maître de conférences en droit public à l'Université Aix-Marseille III (France), est spécialisée en droit de l'Union européenne, droit de l'environnement et droit de la santé. Elle a dirigé plusieurs ouvrages collectifs en la matière, en particulier un ouvrage sur le droit international et européen du vivant (la Documentation française, 2009) et un ouvrage sur les enjeux de la normalisation technique internationale dans les domaines environnementales et sanitaires (la Documentation française, 2006). Elle est chargée de plusieurs enseignements dans les Masters 2 de droit de la santé et le Master de droit international et européen de l'environnement de la Faculté de droit d'Aix-en-Provence.

Maria Elena Castaldo is Researcher of Criminal Law at the Faculty of Law of the University of Salerno since 2006 and Ph.D. in International law, Law

S. Negri (ed.), *Self-Determination, Dignity and End-of-Life Care*
2011 Koninklijke Brill NV. Printed in The Netherlands. ISBN 978 90 04 22357 8. pp. 461–470

School, University of Salerno, 2005. She is Adjunct Professor of Advanced Criminal Law at M.A. in business and legal affairs, Link Campus University of Malta, Rome. Since 2007 she has been a member of the Academic Board of the Ph.D. Programme in International Law at the Faculty of Law of the University of Salerno. Since 2002, she has been a member of the "Osservatorio Giuridico sulla Criminalità Economica (O.G.C.E)", in collaboration with C.E.R.A.D.I. (Centro di Ricerca per il Diritto d'Impresa) at the Luiss "Guido Carli" University (Rome).

Carl H. Coleman is Professor of Law at Seton Hall Law School, where he also serves as Director of Global Initiates for Seton Hall's Center for Health & Pharmaceutical Law & Policy. Before coming to Seton Hall, he was Executive Director of the New York State Task Force on Life and the Law, a nationally recognized interdisciplinary commission that developed New York State's legislation on health care proxies and surrogate decision-making. From 2006–07, Professor Coleman served as Bioethics and Law Adviser to the World Health Organization (WHO) in Geneva, Switzerland. He received his J.D., magna cum laude, from Harvard Law School, where he was Supervising Editor of the *Harvard Law Review*. Following law school, he served as law clerk to the Hon. James L. Oakes, Chief Judge of the U.S. Court of Appeals for the Second Circuit. He holds an A.M. in East Asian Studies from Harvard University and a B.S.F.S., cum laude, from Georgetown University's School of Foreign Service.

Giuseppe D'Angelo is Researcher in Canon Law and Ecclesiastical Law of the State in the University of Salerno (Faculty of law, Department of International Studies) and Ph.D. in «Theory and history of Italian compared political institutions. The decline of the Nation-State». Some of his most important works are: *Principio di sussidiarietà ed enti confessionali* (Napoli, 2003); *Crisi dello Stato, riforme costituzionali, principio di sussidiarietà* (Roma, 2005); *L'Ordine Mauriziano. Vicenda ed esiti giuridici. Ecclesiasticità genetica e laicizzazione dei fini* (Roma, 2007); *Lineamenti di diritto regionale* (Salerno, 2009); *L'Ente Ordine Mauriziano di Torino tra riordino strutturale e riconversione funzionale. Diritto ecclesiastico, garanzie costituzionali, legislazione di emergenza* (Soveria Mannelli, 2009); *Factor religioso, procesos constituyentes, transiciones constitucionales: la experiencia de Sudán*, in Revista general de Derecho Publico comparado, www.iustel.com, vol. 4 (1/2009); *Sudan (National Report)* in W. Cole Durham Jr. and Javier Martinez Torrón (eds.), Religion and the Secular State/La Religion et l'État laïque: Interim Reports, prepared for and issued upon the occasion of The XVIIIth International Congress of Comparative Law, held 25 July - 1 August 2010 in Washington, D.C.

Angela Di Stasi is Full Professor of European Union Law at the Law Faculty of the University of Salerno and Lecturer in International Relations at the same Faculty. Director of the *post lauream* Specialization Course in "Applied European Union Law" at the University of Salerno (I, II and III ed.). Member of the Director Board of the "Scuola di Specializzazione delle Professioni legali" of the University of Salerno. Dean's delegate for the relations between the University of Salerno and the "Direzione generale della Cooperazione allo sviluppo" of the Italian Ministry of Foreign Affairs. Member of the Scientific Commissions for Research Activities of the University of Salerno. Main publications: *L'Euro-G8. La nuova Unione europea nel Gruppo degli Otto*, Giappichelli Editore, Torino, 2001, I ed.; *L'Euro-G8. Contributo alla teoria dello Stato euro-globale*, Giappichelli, Torino, II ed., 2006; *Il sistema americano di tutela dei diritti umani. Circolazione e mutamento di una international legal tradition*, Giappichelli, Torino, 2004; *Diritti umani e sicurezza regionale. Il «sistema» europeo*, Editorale Scientifica, Napoli, I ed., 2000 - II ed., 2010; *Cooperazione internazionale allo sviluppo e tutela dei diritti umani* (ed.), Pubblicazioni della Collana scientifica dell'Università di Salerno, Edizioni Rubbettino, Catanzaro, 2008.

Thomas A. Faunce, BA/LL.B. (Hons) (ANU), B.Med. (Newcastle), Ph.D. (ANU), is an Australian Research Council Future Fellow and Associate Professor in the Australian National University (ANU) College of Medicine and College of Law. Associate Professor Faunce has extensive practice experience in both professions, as a commercial solicitor in one of Australia's largest law firms and as a senior registrar in Intensive Care Medicine. Associate Professor Faunce's main areas of research involve pharmaceutical and nanotechnology regulation and he has been the lead chief investigator on three Australian Research Council Discovery Grants in these areas. Associate Professor Faunce serves on numerous university and clinical ethics committees and professional bodies related to Bioethics, Health and International Law and has published widely in this field. He has served with UNESCO as an expert in the development of a global ethics and law database.

Brigitte Feuillet est Professeur à la Faculté de droit et de science politique de Rennes, Membre de l'Institut Universitaire de France, Directeur du

CRJO (Institut de l'Ouest : Droit et Europe, UMR CNRS 6262), Faculté de droit et de science politique de Rennes, France.

Patrick Hanafin is Professor of Law at Birkbeck Law School, University of London, where he also directs the Law School's Centre for Law and the Humanities. He has been a Visiting Professor at the School of Law at the University of Porto, Portugal, and at the Law Faculty at the University of Pretoria in South Africa. He has held research fellowships at the European University Institute in Florence and at the Human Rights Program at Harvard Law School. His books include: *Deleuze and Law: Forensic Futures* (with Rosi Braidiotti and Claire Colebrook, 2009); *Conceiving Life: Reproductive Politics and the Law in Contemporary Italy* (2007); *Law and Literature* (with Joseph Brooker and Adam Gearey, 2004); *Constituting Identity: Political Identity Formation and the Constitution in Post-Independence Ireland* (2001); *Identity, Rights and Constitutional Transformation*, (with Melissa Williams, 1999), and *Last Rights: Death, Dying and the Law in Ireland* (1997).

Vitulia Ivone is Associate Professor of Private law, Faculty of Law, University of Salerno; lecturer of Civil law at the Specialization School for Legal Professions; lecturer of Law of industrial enterprises at the Faculty of Engineering; member of the Patent Commission of the University of Salerno; member of the Secretariat for Intellectual Property and Bioethics of the Foundation RedBio International; recipient of a scholarship for the international mobility of researchers granted by the Province and the University of Salerno; visiting researcher at the "Institut fur ausländisches und internationales Privat- und Wirtschaftsrecht", Heidelberg Universitat (April-October 2008). In 2010 she was conference speaker at the Universities of Monte Scopus, Zefat College and Bar-Ilan (Israel), at the Universidade do Vale do Rio dos Sinos and at the Escola de Saúde Pública in Porto Alegre (Brazil).

Penney Lewis studied mathematics, law and philosophy in the United States, Canada and the United Kingdom. She clerked for Mr. Justice Iacobucci at the Supreme Court of Canada and is qualified as a Barrister and Solicitor in Ontario. She is Professor of Law at King's College London where she teaches Medical Law and Law at the End of Life in the Centre of Medical Law and Ethics and the School of Law. In the area of medical law, her research focuses on end of life issues including advance decision-making and refusal of treatment. She is the author of a number of articles on assisted dying and her monograph *Assisted Dying and Legal Change* was published in 2007 by Oxford University Press. She has also published articles and chapters dealing with a wide range of medical law topics, including wrongful life, medical treatment of children and medical procedures which are against the interests of incompetent adults, such as organ donation and non-therapeutic research. She is a member of the UK Donation Ethics Committee, Vice-Chair of the King's College London Research Ethics Committee and a member of the Clinical Ethics Committee of St Christopher's Hospice.

Alessia Magliacane lives and works in Paris, where she is Ph.D. student and she conducts research in comparative law at the University of Paris 1 Sorbonne. Her research interests lie in fundamental rights and children's rights, mediation and conflict, constitutional history and methodology. She has published *Forme e crisi della norma-stato. Contributi per una critica del diritto* (2009, with Francesco Rubino), *El lenguaje entre tiempo y norma* (2009), *Habités par l'absence. La création normative de l'esprit: monstres, fantasmes, dieux, souverains* (in press).

Dominique Manaï est Professeur Ordinaire à la Faculté de droit de l'Université de Genève (Suisse). Elle enseigne le droit médical et le droit de la personnalité. Ses recherches et expertises portent en particulier sur les droits des patients, des médecins et des tiers dans la relation thérapeutique, sur le droit biomédical, la procréation médicalement assistée, les analyses génétiques, la transplantation d'organes et la recherche impliquant des personnes humaines. Elle dirige des recherches interdisciplinaires (droit, sociologie, médecine, éthique), participe à l'enseignement de l'éthique clinique et collabore régulièrement avec la Faculté de médecine de l'Université de Genève. Elle a présidé la Commission d'experts lors de l'élaboration de la loi fédérale sur la recherche avec des êtres humains. Sur le plan international, elle contribue à développer un Réseau universitaire international de bioéthique (RUIB).

Francesco Mancuso is Associate Professor in Philosophy of Law at the Faculty of Law of the University of Salerno. He is co-editor with Francesco Lucrezi of *Diritto e vita. Biodiritto, bioetica, biopolitica* (Rubbettino, 2010) and with Alfonso Catania of *Natura e artificio* (Mimesis, 2011). His books include: *Gaetano Mosca e la tradizione del costituzionalismo* (Esi, 1999); *Diritto, Stato, sovranità. Il pensiero politico-giuridico di Emer de Vattel tra assolutismo e Rivoluzione* (Esi, 2002).

Panos Merkouris, LL.B. (University of Athens), LL.M. (University of Athens & UCL), Ph.D. (Queen Mary, University of London). Dr. Panos Merkouris is currently the Managing Editor of the *International Community Law Review* and General Co-Editor of the *Queen Mary Studies in International Law*. His publication include: Malgosia Fitzmaurice, David Ong & Panos Merkouris (eds.), *Research Handbook on International Environmental Law* (London: Edward Elgar, 2010) and Malgosia Fitzmaurice, Olufemi Elias & Panos Merkouris (eds.), *Treaty Interpretation and The Vienna Convention on the Law of Treaties: 30 Years On* (Leiden: Martinus Nijhoff, 2010).

Sofia Moratti is a Max Weber fellow at the Department of Law of the European University Institute, Florence. She is a member of the Ethics Committee at SISSA Neuroscience, an international school for advanced studies located in Trieste, Italy. She is currently interested in the ethical, legal and social implications ('ELSI') of technical and scientific advancements in the brain sciences. She works on selected issues at the interface between brain science and the law. She was formerly a lecturer in Legal Theory at the University of Trieste. She holds a JD in Comparative Law (University of Pavia, Italy) and a Ph.D. in Sociology of Law (Faculty of Law, University of Groningen, the Netherlands). Her doctoral research is an investigation of the regulation and medical practice of end-of-life decisions in neonatology in the Netherlands. She carried out field research in two Dutch Neonatal Intensive Care Units. In addition, she has been interested in the regulation of end-of-life decisions in Italy. Some of her contributions appeared in the *Journal of Medical Ethics*, the *Medical Law Review*, the *Cambridge Quarterly of Healthcare Ethics, Issues in Law and Medicine* and *Medicine & Law*.

Stefania Negri, Ph.D. in International Law (University of Salerno), is Associate Professor of International Law and Lecturer of International Human Rights Law at the Faculty of Law; Professor of International Law at the School of Specialisation for Legal Professions (University of Salerno). Research fellow at the Graduate Institute for International and Development Studies of Geneva with a research project on *Health and human rights* (May-October 2009). She is the founder and director of the *Observatory on Human Rights: Bioethics, Health, Environment* (Faculty of Law, University of Salerno); co-director with Prof. Dr. Jochen Taupitz of the Vigoni Research Project on *Legal and ethical questions raised by advance care decision-making in Germany and Italy: a comparative, European and international law perspective* (approved and financed by

DAAD and MIUR); director of the international research project on *Bioethics and international law: life, death and human dignity* (financed by the University of Salerno). Professor Negri has published extensively on international human rights law and international procedural law; her current research interests mainly focus on human rights, international biolaw and international health law.

Mario J.A. Oyarzábal, BA, JD, PostGradDip in Law (University of La Plata), Master Studies in Diplomacy (Argentine Foreign Service Institute), LL.M. (Harvard Law School); Adjunct Professor of International Law (University of La Plata); Member of the Foreign Service of Argentina; Former Deputy Consul of Argentina in New York; Former Counselor at the Office of the Legal Adviser of the Argentine Ministry of Foreign Affairs; Delegate to the Hague Conference on Private International Law; currently serving at the Permanent Mission of Argentina to the United Nations.

Amina Salkić, LL.M., graduated from the Law Faculty of the Sarajevo University in 2005. In 2007 she finished her Master of Laws degree in German law (LL.M.) at the University of Heidelberg, where she's currently enrolled as a Ph.D. student, writing her thesis concerning living wills. From 2006 to 2009 she was involved in the project "Human Dignity" of the "Interdisciplinary Forum for Biomedicine and Cultural Sciences (IFBK)" and in 2008/09 she worked as a research assistant at the project "Human Dignity" (subproject "Human Dying") of the "Marsilius Kolleg", both at the University of Heidelberg. Since 2008 she is working as a research assistant at the Institute of German, European and International Medical Law, Public Health Law and Bioethics of the Universities of Mannheim and Heidelberg.

José Antonio Seoane, Ph.D. (Universidade da Coruña, Spain, 1996); Expert in Biomedical Ethics (Universidad Complutense de Madrid, Spain, 2000); Associate Professor of Philosophy of Law (Universidade da Coruña, Spain); Alexander von Humboldt Fellow. Main research areas: Transformation of modern legal systems; Practical and legal reasoning; Human rights; Bioethics; Health Law; Disability and Justice. Member of the Healthcare Ethics Commission, Hospital de A Coruña (Spain).

Jochen Taupitz studied law in Göttingen and Freiburg. Prof. Dr. Taupitz finished his doctoral thesis concerning problems of tort law in 1980. Two years later he passed his Second State Examination. In 1988 he finished the post-doctoral thesis on "Professional Codes of Ethics". He taught as a professor at the University of Göttingen before he took up the Chair of Civil Law, Law of Civil Procedure, Private International Law and Comparative Law at the University of Mannheim (1990). Further appointments to full professorships followed at the universities of Kiel (1993), Bonn (1997), Heidelberg (2003) and to the Swiss Institute for Comparative Law (2003). Since 1998 he is the managing director of the Institute for German, European and International Medical Law, Public Health Law and Bioethics of the Universities of Heidelberg and Mannheim. From 2001 until 2008 he has been a member of the (German) National Ethics Council; since 2008 he is a member of the German Ethics Council and since 2007 a member of the European Academy of Sciences and Arts.

Ruth Townsend is a lecturer in Health Law, bioethics and human rights at the Australian National University jointly in both the College of Law and School of Medicine. Ruth's teaching asks students to consider the normative intersections between the humanities, conscience, bioethics, health law and human rights and the corresponding regulation of the health professions. Ruth is currently involved in a research project examining the legal 'Right to Health' in Australia. Ruth has also taught in the area of Indigenous Mental Health, ethics, law and human rights. Ruth has previously worked as both a health practitioner and as a legal practitioner.

Cristiano Vezzoni is Assistant Professor in Research Methodology at the University of Trento (Italy) and Researcher at the Department of Health Sciences, University Medical Center Groningen (NL). He holds a Ph.D. in Sociology of Law (University of Groningen, NL), obtained with a dissertation on the legal status and social practice of advance directives in the Netherlands. His current research is addressed to the analysis of political behaviour, especially the relation between religiosity and vote, and to the study of medical practice at the end of life. Among his contributions to the topic of medical regulation, the volume "Advance treatment directives and autonomy for incompetent patients in law and practice" (Edwin Mellen Press, 2008).

Sandra Regina Martini Vial is Ph.D. in Law, "Evoluzione dei Sistemi Giuridici e Nuovi Diritti" at the University of Lecce and Postgraduate Doctor in Law at the University of Roma Tre. She is professor at University of Vale do Rio dos Sinos, Foundation of Public Prosecutors, Scuola Dottorale Internazionale Tullio Ascarelli and visiting professor at the University of Salerno. She is the former Director of the School of Public Health of Rio Grande do Sul and Member of the Board of Fundação de Amparo à Pesquisa do Estado do Rio Grande do Sul (FAPERGS).

INDEX